Lecture Notes in Computer Science 14903

Founding Editors

Gerhard Goos

Juris Hartmanis

The series Lecture Notes in Computer Science (LNCS), including its subseries Lecture Notes in Artificial Intelligence (LNAI) and Lecture Notes in Bioinformatics (LNBI), has established itself as a medium for the publication of new developments in computer science and information technology research, teaching, and education.

LNCS enjoys close cooperation with the computer science R & D community, the series counts many renowned academics among its volume editors and paper authors, and collaborates with prestigious societies. Its mission is to serve this international community by providing an invaluable service, mainly focused on the publication of conference and workshop proceedings and postproceedings. LNCS commenced publication in 1973.

Joseph K. Liu · Liqun Chen · Shi-Feng Sun ·
Xiaoning Liu

Editors

Provable and Practical Security

18th International Conference, ProvSec 2024
Gold Coast, QLD, Australia, September 25–27, 2024
Proceedings, Part I

 Springer

Editors
Joseph K. Liu
Monash University
Clayton, VIC, Australia

Liqun Chen 🆔
University of Surrey
Guildford, Surrey, UK

Shi-Feng Sun
Shanghai Jiao Tong University
Shanghai, China

Xiaoning Liu
RMIT University
Melbourne, VIC, Australia

ISSN 0302-9743   ISSN 1611-3349 (electronic)
Lecture Notes in Computer Science
ISBN 978-981-96-0953-6   ISBN 978-981-96-0954-3 (eBook)
https://doi.org/10.1007/978-981-96-0954-3

This Springer imprint is published by the registered company Springer Nature Singapore Pte Ltd.
The registered company address is: 152 Beach Road, #21-01/04 Gateway East, Singapore 189721, Singapore

If disposing of this product, please recycle the paper.

Preface

This volume contains the papers presented at ProvSec 2024: The 18th International Conference on Provable and Practical Security held on September 25–27, 2024 in Gold Coast, Australia.

ProvSec is an international conference on provable security in cryptography and practical security for information systems. ProvSec is designed to be a forum for theoreticians, system and application designers, protocol developers, and practitioners to discuss and express their views on current trends, challenges, and state-of-the-art solutions related to various issues in provable and practical security. Topics of interest include but are not limited to provable security for asymmetric cryptography, provable security for symmetric cryptography, provable security for physical attacks, privacy and anonymity technologies, secure cryptographic protocols and applications, security notions, approaches, and paradigms, leakage resilient cryptography, lattice-based cryptography and post-quantum cryptography, blockchain and cryptocurrency, IoT security, cloud security, and access control.

There were 79 submissions to ProvSec 2024. The committee decided to accept 26 full papers and 8 short papers. There were two keynote speakers: Man Ho Au from Hong Kong Polytechnic University and Kazue Sako from Waseda University.

We thank the Program Committee members and the external reviewers for their hard work reviewing the submissions. We thank the Organizing Committee, in particular, our General Co-Chairs, Leo Zhang, Guangdong Bai, and Xingliang Yuan, and all volunteers for their time and effort dedicated to arranging the conference.

September 2024

Joseph K. Liu
Liqun Chen

Organization

Program Chairs

Joseph K. Liu   Monash University, Australia
Liqun Chen   University of Surrey, UK

General Chairs

Leo Zhang   Griffith University, Australia
Guangdong Bai   University of Queensland, Australia
Xingliang Yuan   University of Melbourne, Australia

Program Committee

Elena Andreeva	TU Wien, Austria
Man Ho Au	Hong Kong Polytechnic University, China
Shi Bai	Florida Atlantic University, USA
Liqun Chen	University of Surrey, UK
Jie Chen	East China Normal University, China
Yu Chen	Shandong University, China
Cheng-Kang Chu	Huawei, Singapore
Hui Cui	Monash University, Australia
Nada El Kassem	University of Surrey, UK
Keita Emura	Kanazawa University, Japan
Junqing Gong	East China Normal University, China
Guang Gong	University of Waterloo, Canada
Jinguang Han	Southeast University, China
Xinyi Huang	Hong Kong University of Science and Technology, China
Sabyasachi Karati	Indian Statistical Institute, India
Shabnam Kasra Kermanshahi	UNSW Canberra, Australia
Yang Li	University of Electro-Communications, Japan
Fagen Li	University of Electronic Science and Technology of China, China
Yannan Li	University of Wollongong, Australia
Joseph K. Liu	Monash University, Australia

Xiaoning Liu	RMIT University, Australia
Dongxi Liu	Data 61, Australia
Zhen Liu	Shanghai Jiao Tong University, China
Xingye Lu	Hong Kong Polytechnic University, China
Xianhui Lu	Chinese Academy of Sciences, China
Kirill Morozov	University of North Texas, USA
Khoa Nguyen	University of Wollongong, Australia
Baodong Qin	Xi'an University of Posts and Telecommunications, China
Olivier Sanders	Orange Labs, France
Daniel Slamanig	Universität der Bundeswehr München, Germany
Shi-Feng Sun	Shanghai Jiao Tong University, China
Willy Susilo	University of Wollongong, Australia
Koutarou Suzuki	Toyohashi University of Technology, Japan
Atsushi Takayasu	University of Tokyo, Japan
Yangguang Tian	University of Surrey, UK
Yuntao Wang	University of Electro-Communications, Japan
Lei Wang	Shanghai Jiao Tong University, China
Zhe Xia	Wuhan University of Technology, China
Peng Xu	Huazhong University of Science and Technology, China
Haiyang Xue	Hong Kong Polytechnic University, China
Guomin Yang	Singapore Management University, Singapore
Zuoxia Yu	University of Wollongong, Australia
Fangguo Zhang	Sun Yat-sen University, China
Mingwu Zhang	Hubei University of Technology, China
Lei Zhang	East China Normal University, China
Liang Zhao	Sichuan University, China

Publication Co-chairs

Shi-Feng Sun	Shanghai Jiao Tong University, China
Xiaoning Liu	RMIT University, Australia

Publicity Co-chairs

Cong Zuo	Beijing Institute of Technology, China
Shujie Cui	Monash University, Australia

Web Chair

Xiangwen Yang   Monash University, Australia

Contents – Part I

Signature

Contents – Part II

Key Exchange and Privacy

Short Papers

Multi-Party Computation

SecFloatPlus: More Accurate Floating-Point Meets Secure Two-Party Computation

Tao Huang[1], Jian Weng[1(✉)], Jiasi Weng[1], Minrong Chen[2], and Ming Li[1]

[1] Jinan University, Guangzhou, China
wengjiasi@gmail.com
[2] South China Normal University, Guangzhou, China

Abstract. Implementing secure two-party computation (2PC) protocols with floating-point numbers, balancing accuracy and efficiency, has been challenging. Despite advancements with SecFloat (in IEEE S&P'22) and Beacon (in USENIX Security'23), there is room for improvement in precision, efficiency and functionality. This paper introduces *SecFloatPlus*, which complements SecFloat with a new spline generation approach for implementing efficient and accurate 2PC-enabled mathematical functions. It significantly enhances accuracy, achieving up to $1000\times$ better performance for the hyperbolic tangent function (*i.e.*, tanh) and $6\times$ better performance for the Gaussian Error Linear Unit (GELU) function, compared to Beacon. It also introduces precise inverse trigonometric functions (*i.e.*, arcsin, arccos and arctan) which are never implemented by previous works. Besides, when integrated into secure transformer inference, SecFloatPlus outperforms SecFloat in runtime efficiency and communication cost for the SoftMax activation function, while maintaining precision.

Keywords: Secure Two-Party Computation · Secret Sharing · Floating-Points · Non-linear Functions

1 Introduction

Floating-point representation is fundamental in computer science, widely used in fields such as scientific computing, financial analysis, computer graphics, and machine learning. It offers significant advantages, including the ability to represent a broad range of values with fewer bits and superior precision compared to fixed-point representation. Many computer processors have specialized units for efficient floating-point arithmetic, following the IEEE 754 standard [1]. Additionally, well-known mathematical computing software like GMP [21], MPFR [22], and Intel-MKL [25] provide easy-to-use interfaces for arbitrary-precision floating-point primitive operations and complex mathematical functions like (inverse) trigonometric functions and hyperbolic functions. These libraries support various precision-sensitive analysis scenarios effectively, but they are not inherently crypto-friendly.

© The Author(s), under exclusive license to Springer Nature Singapore Pte Ltd. 2025
J. K. Liu et al. (Eds.): ProvSec 2024, LNCS 14903, pp. 3–22, 2025.
https://doi.org/10.1007/978-981-96-0954-3_1

Secure two-party computation (2PC) protocols, which have been developed since the 1980s, allow two parties to jointly compute a function over their inputs while keeping those inputs private, theoretically enabling arbitrary programs [20,42]. However, these protocols initially lacked concrete implementations for floating-point arithmetic. Subsequent research [2,3,7–11,13,14,17–19,28,32, 33] has shown that designing secure computation protocols for real numbers, while balancing efficiency and accuracy, has been a challenging issue. One approach in previous secure protocols [10,11,17,18] involves converting floats into integers or fixed-point numbers, but this often leads to either overflow or high overhead. Some arts [2,3,7–9,13,19,26] focus on maintaining floating-point representation but struggles with computational inaccuracy and inefficiency.

One the other hand, accurate floating-point computing is crucial as evidenced by previous several notable incidents. In 1994, an imprecise floating-point division (FDIV) instruction in Intel's Pentium processors necessitated the recall and replacement of defective units [15]. Another significant case was the Ariane 5 rocket explosion, caused by the conversion of a 64-bit floating-point number to a 16-bit signed integer, resulting in an overflow error [29].

The state-of-the-art 2PC works with floating-points, SecFloat [33] and Beacon [32], are notably well-conceived. Firstly, they provide new range reductions and implement them efficiently within a 2PC framework. Secondly, they present crypto-friendly spline generation by leveraging the numerical computation library RLIBM [30]. Furthermore, they introduce a novel general functionality for securely, accurately and efficiently evaluating splines. *However, their work does not readily support inverse trigonometric functions* (i.e., arcsin, arccos and arctan), *which our study achieves.* The main reason is that they construct accurate math functions relying on RLIBM, which inherently limits the functions we mention. Moreover, SecFloat's math functionalities are implemented using its own primitive operations, posing challenges in integrating the RLIBM library. This construction process consumes considerable space and time for execution.

Therefore, we propose SecFloatPlus, independent of RLIBM, to develop efficient and accurate 2PC-enabled mathematical functionalities. We particularly focus on inverse trigonometric functions, crucial for computing angles and distances between locations, and the hyperbolic tangent function serving as the active function in machine learning. Notably, 2PC protocols for inverse trigonometric functions have not been implemented in previous work, including SecFloat [33] and Beacon [32]. In conclusion, our contributions can be summarized as follows:

– We introduce a new *Cubic Spline Interpolation* technology in spline generation, and implement 32-bit single-precision floating-point math functionalities, supporting both trigonometric and inverse trigonometric functions, as well as the hyperbolic tangent function (*i.e.*, tanh). This improves both accuracy and communication efficiency compared to previous studies.
– We assess the precision of our inverse trigonometric functionalities in privacy-preserving proximity testing scenarios, demonstrating superior performance, as shown in Table 1 and Table 3.

- Our experiments reveal that our tanh function implementation achieves *1000 times greater accuracy* than that of Beacon, despite a slight increase in computation and communication overhead.
- We evaluate common non-linear functionalities in a secure transformer inference scenario, involving the Gaussian Error Linear Unit (GELU), the LayerNorm, and the SoftMax functions. Our SoftMax implementation has *lower runtime and communication costs* while maintaining the same level of precision as SecFloat's. Our GELU implementation demonstrates *a nearly sixfold improvement in precision* compared to Beacon's.
- Our source code is available at https://github.com/huangtaojnu/SecFloatPlus.

1.1   Related Work

We primarily review previous work on secure multi-party computation (MPC) protocols involving real numbers, a challenging issue in the field. In particular, Fouque *et al.* [17] designed 2PC protocols for rational number addition and multiplication. Catrina *et al.* [10, 11] developed secure protocols for fixed-point arithmetic operations, restricted to at most 128 bits. Franz *et al.* [18] employed homomorphic encryption to construct secure protocols for quantized real numbers. Additionally, Franz *et al.* [19] proposed secure protocols specifically for IEEE 754 standard floating-point arithmetic operations, without providing a concrete implementation. Subsequently, Aliasgari *et al.* [2] developed secret-sharing based MPC protocols for more complex operations over floating-point numbers, such as exponentiation and logarithmic computation. Other researchers [13, 14] established secure protocols using garbled circuits (GC). Specifically, one [14] focused on arithmetic and sqrt operations, while the other [13] addressed trigonometric functions and introduced a privacy-preserving proximity testing scenario based on these functions. However, their computation precision and efficiency were found to be unsatisfactory, as highlighted by the state-of-the-art works [32,33]. Moreover, as we delve deeper into the realm of secret sharing-based secure protocols for floating-point numbers [3,7–9,28], there remains substantial room for improvement in terms of performance, precision, and functionality.

To fill the improvement space, recently, state-of-the-art works like SecFloat [33] and Beacon [32] have successfully implemented floating-point computations for complex non-linear functions, including trigonometric functions, softmax, and tanh, achieving remarkable accuracy and performance. These secure functions are instrumental in achieving secure machine learning. In parallel, Blanton *et al.* [4] introduced secure and accurate accumulation for floating-point numbers. By leveraging innovative lookup table technology, Flute [5] emerged as an outstanding implementation for numerous non-linear functions, but its implementation code has not yet been made publicly available.

In this work, we introduce secure computation with floating-point numbers for inverse trigonometric functions, which have not been supported in previous research. Our secure inverse trigonometric functions facilitate privacy-preserving proximity testing and enhance secure machine learning, as demonstrated in

Sect. 5. Importantly, SecFloat [33] and Beacon [32] may not be extended to support inverse trigonometric functions, as their underlying RLIBM library does not include these functions. Additionally, our implementation achieves a more efficient SoftMax function and more accurate tanh function.

2   Preliminaries

2.1   Notations

Let λ be the computational security parameter. $[k]$ refers to the set $\{0, 1, 2, \ldots, k-1\}$. $\mathbf{1}\{B\}$ is the indicator function that equals 1 if the boolean expression B is true and 0 otherwise. We use $a \leftarrow b$ to denote the assignment of b to a. The floor function $\lfloor x \rfloor$ represents the largest integer less than or equal to x. We employ a bold lowercase letter $\boldsymbol{x}$ to represent a vector. A d-dimensional vector $\boldsymbol{x}$ is denoted as $(x_0, x_1, \ldots, x_{d-1})$. Additionally, a bold uppercase letter $\mathbf{A}$ is used to denote a matrix. Each element in $\boldsymbol{x}$ or $\mathbf{A}$ is a floating-point number as discussed in this section. We define the inverse trigonometric functions $\arcsin \pi(\alpha) = \arcsin(\alpha)/\pi$, and $\arccos \pi(\alpha), \arctan \pi(\alpha)$ follow similar definitions.

2.2   Floating-Point Representation

A floating-point number α is expressed as a tuple (z, s, e, m), in which $z \in \{0, 1\}$ is the zero-bit and $z = \mathbf{1}\{\alpha = 0\}$, $s \in \{0, 1\}$ is the sign-bit of α and $s = \mathbf{1}\{\alpha < 0\}$, $e \in \{0, 1\}^{p+2}$ is the signed unbiased exponent and takes values within $[-2^{p-1} + 1, 2^{p-1})$, and $m \in [2^q, 2^{q+1}) \cup \{0\}$ is an unsigned unbiased fixed-point integer representing the mantissa. Herein, we note $p, q \in \mathbb{Z}^+$. We can express the real number α as $(1 - z) \cdot (1 - 2s) \cdot 2^{e-(2^{p-1}-1)} \cdot (m \cdot 2^{-q})$. We use $\alpha.s$ to denote α's component s and consistently for other components.

2.3   2PC

2PC [16,23] involves two parties, denoted as P_0 and P_1, each holding private inputs x and y respectively. The parties agree to jointly compute a public function f with these inputs, ensuring that only the result $z = f(x, y)$ is revealed without disclosing any additional information beyond the result. 2PC protocols guarantee the property of *privacy*, ensuring that both parties cannot learn anything beyond the output z. Additionally, these protocols satisfy the property of *correctness*, meaning that the intended function f is computed, as opposed to other functions.

2-out-of-2 Additive Secret Sharing. We use the 2-out-of-2 additive secret sharing schemes [27] over ring $\mathbb{Z}_{2^\ell}$. An ℓ-bits unsigned integer x is represented as $\langle x \rangle^\ell = (\langle x \rangle_0^\ell, \langle x \rangle_1^\ell)$ in secret sharing form, and P_b holds $\langle x \rangle_b^\ell$ for $b \in \{0, 1\}$. The 2-party secret sharing holds $x = (\langle x \rangle_0^\ell + \langle x \rangle_1^\ell) \bmod 2^\ell$.

2PC Building Blocks. We next introduce the underlying building blocks that we use to construct our functionalities in a black-box manner, as previous works [33–35]. The symbols $+, -, *, \leq, >, \mathbf{1}\{B\} ? x : y$, and $\wedge$ are employed to denote addition, subtraction, multiplication, comparison (LE and GT), selection (return x if $\mathbf{1}\{B\}$ is 1, otherwise return y), and bit-wise AND operations when dealing with fixed-point numbers. LS, MSNZB, ZXT, L, mod 2^ℓ and TR are used to represent left shift, most significant non-zero bit, zero extension, lookup-table, the last ℓ bits and truncate-reduce operations with fixed point numbers. $\boxplus, \boxminus, \boxtimes, \boxslash$, Round* and Float are used to represent addition, subtraction, multiplication, division, round mantissa and convert a real number to a floating-point number shares. Coef is used to obtain the polynomial coefficients, which will be described in detail in Sect. 3. FPsinπ, FPcosπ and FPexp represent the floating-point functionalities for evaluating sine, cosine and exponentiation, respectively. FPsum and FPmax are used to represent the summation and maximum operations on a floating-point vector.

3   Our Floating-Point Functionalities

We extend the floating-point functionalities in SecFloat [33] to support more useful math functions, including the inverse trigonometric functions (represented as $\mathcal{F}_{\mathsf{FParcsin}\pi}$, $\mathcal{F}_{\mathsf{FParccos}\pi}$, $\mathcal{F}_{\mathsf{FParctan}\pi}$), the hyperbolic tangent function $\mathcal{F}_{\mathsf{FPtanh}}$, and the square root operation $\mathcal{F}_{\mathsf{FPsqrt}}$. All mathematical functionalities utilize splines for polynomial approximation, drawing inspiration from the methodology outlined in SecFloat. Different from SecFloat relying on the RLIBM library [30], we introduce a novel method for spline generation that demonstrates increased efficiency while preserving accuracy in 2PC.

To enable crypto-friendly computation, we following the parameter settings as SecFloat, and use three generic steps [12] for computing the mathematical functions: *range reduction, polynomial approximations, and output compensation* [33]. We implement mathematical functions, denoted as f, over the floating-point numbers with $p = 8$ and $q = 23$. We use $\mathcal{F}_{\mathsf{Func}}^{\mathsf{Params}}$ to denote our functionality Func with a parameters list Params. We denote $\prod_{\mathsf{Func}}^{\mathsf{Params}}$ as the corresponding secure protocol. If Params contains only $p = 8$ and $q = 23$ (and possibly includes the dimension d), we will omit the constants and use $\mathcal{F}_{\mathsf{Func}}$ to denote the functionality. We focus on the computation of 32-bit single-precision floating-point numbers, as SecFloat. The concatenation operation $a\|b$ of two bit-strings in secret sharing can be expressed as $a\|b = (\mathcal{F}_{\mathsf{ZXT}}^{n+m}(a) *_{n+m} 2^m) + \mathcal{F}_{\mathsf{ZXT}}^{n+m}(b)$, given that $a \in \{0,1\}^n$ and $b \in \{0,1\}^m$.

We next elaborate on the workings of spline evaluation, spline generation, and the precision measurement of the approximation.

Spline Evaluation. An n-piece spline F is determined by two parameters: $\Xi = \{\xi_j\}_{j=1}^{n+1}$ is an *ordered* knot list for F, meaning the jth spline belongs to the interval $[\xi_j, \xi_{j+1})$; $\Theta = \{\theta_i^{(j)}\}_{i=0,j=1}^{d,n}$ represents a $(d+1) \times n$ table, indicating the coefficients of n polynomials for F, with each polynomial being of degree d.

Then for each input α, we have

$$f(\alpha) \approx F(\alpha) = \sum_{i=0}^{d} \theta_i^{(j)} \cdot \alpha^i, \text{if } \exists \ j \text{ s.t. } \alpha \in [\xi_j, \xi_{j+1}). \tag{1}$$

We set each knot in Ξ following two strategies: 1) the knot for this functionality within the current interval is flat; 2) the knot is determined by the lower bits of exponent $\alpha.e$ and the higher bits of the mantissa $\alpha.m$. Using the second strategy, we can map the floating-point number to ℓ bits. That is, the input α is mapped to an idx $\in \{0,1\}^{\ell}$ and the knot ξ_j is mapped to $k_j \in \{0,1\}^{\ell}$, such that idx $\in [k_j, k_{j+1})$ if and only if $\alpha \in [\xi_j, \xi_{j+1})$. The mapping strategy enables us to conveniently use the building blocks in Sect. 2.3. Specifically, we can choose the lower bits of the exponent and the upper bits of the mantissa, and lastly combine them together.

The functionality $\mathcal{F}_{\mathsf{Coef}}^{\ell,n,d,p,q}(\Theta, K, x)$ is employed to choose the spline j_0 to which the ℓ-bit integer x belongs, and $K = \{k_i\}_{i=1}^{n+1}$ is mapped from Ξ. It returns the coefficients $\{\theta_i^{(j_0)}\}_{i=0}^{d}$, which x has been mapped from a floating-point number α. In the corresponding protocol $\prod_{\mathsf{Coef}}^{\ell,n,d,p,q}$, the inputs Θ and K are plaintext, while x is an ℓ-bit secret shares. After we get $\{\theta_i^{(j_0)}\}_{i=0}^{d}$, we can evaluate $F(\alpha)$ using the Horner's method [6] (e.g., evaluating $(\theta_2 \alpha + \theta_1)\alpha + \theta_0$ instead of $\theta_2 \alpha^2 + \theta_1 \alpha + \theta_0$).

Spline Generation. We employ a technique known as *Cubic Spline Interpolation* [31] for achieving the desired approximation. In the context of an interval $[\alpha, \beta)$, all knots are determined by considering the least significant k_1 bits of the exponent and the most significant k_2 bits of the mantissa. This implies that the difference between α and β is at most $k_1 + k_2$ bits. It is important to carefully select values for k_1 and k_2 for the efficiency optimization while preserving accuracy. Subsequently, the interval $[\alpha, \beta)$ is partitioned into at most $2^{k_1+k_2}$ sub-intervals, and the cubic spline interpolation is applied to these segments to derive the coefficients for all corresponding polynomials. Additionally, we heuristically merge neighboring intervals to further enhance efficiency. Following the final merging, a tuple (Ξ, Θ) is obtained for the interval $[\alpha, \beta)$. We take an instance by considering the 9-piece spline F in $\mathcal{F}_{\mathsf{FPtanh}}$ discussed in Sect. 3.5. We observe that $\xi_8 = 2^{-3} \times 1.625$, $\xi_9 = 2^{-3} \times 1.875$, and $\xi_{10} = 2^{-2}$. When attempting to merge the intervals $[\xi_8, \xi_9)$ and $[\xi_9, \xi_{10})$, the resulting spline function exhibits significant errors.

Cubic Spline Interpolation. Cubic spline interpolation [31] is a mathematical technique employed to create a smooth curve through a series of discrete data points. Each segment of the curve, located between pairs of adjacent data points, is represented by a cubic polynomial. These polynomial segments ensure continuity across the entire interpolation interval and possess continuous first and second derivatives at the data points, resulting in a seamless transition along the curve. Cubic spline functions can be defined under various boundary conditions, including natural splines and clamped splines [31]. To closely approximate the original function, we utilize clamped splines. This approach involves setting the first derivatives at the left and right endpoints of the spline function to be equal, ensuring the curve's smoothness and adherence to the desired behavior at the boundaries.

To ensure the functionality $\mathcal{F}_{\mathsf{Func}}$ to be crypto-friendly, the table Θ is generated, consisting of double-precision floating-point elements, while using cubic spline interpolation on plaintext with a precision level of $q = 52$. Subsequently, all entries in Θ are rounded to a reduced precision of $q = 27$. This rounding induces a minimal error magnitude of $\frac{1}{2^q}$. In the context of single-precision floating-point computations, these rounding errors were negligible when y was represented as a double with $q = 52$. However, in single-precision floating-point computations, reducing q from 52 to 27 does not impact accuracy. Ultimately, we opt for $q = 27$ over $q = 52$ during polynomial evaluation, thereby achieving a reduction in cryptographic costs while maintaining an acceptable level of precision.

Precision. To measure the precision of our functionality, we use the ULP (Unit in the Last Place) error that is more suitable for floating-point representations compared to absolute and relative errors. We denoted $\mathrm{ULP}(\sigma, \sigma')$, measuring the discrepancy between the actual output value σ and the floating-point output value σ'. Let σ_+ be the smallest floating-point number that exceeds σ, and let σ_- be the largest floating-point number less than σ. The ULP error can be defined as: $\mathrm{ULP}(\sigma, \sigma') = \frac{|\sigma' - \sigma|}{\sigma_+ - \sigma_-}$.

3.1   Arcsine

Algorithm 1: Floating-point $\mathcal{F}_{\mathsf{FParcsin}\pi}$

Input: a floating-point number α
Output: the floating-point number $\arcsin \pi(\alpha)$

1   $p \leftarrow 8, q \leftarrow 23, Q \leftarrow 27$;

2   $\sigma \leftarrow (\alpha.z, 0, \alpha.e, \alpha.m *_{Q+1} 2^{Q-q})$;   // Range Reduction

3   **if** $1\{\sigma.e < -14\}$ **then**

4      $\beta \leftarrow \sigma \boxtimes_{p,Q} \mathcal{F}^{P;Q}_{\mathsf{Float}}(1/\pi)$;

5   **return** $(\beta.z, \alpha.s, \mathcal{F}^{P,q,Q}_{\mathsf{Round}*}(\beta.e, \beta.m))$;

6   **else if** $1\{\sigma.e = 0 \wedge \sigma.m = 2^Q\}$ **then return** $(0, \alpha.s, -1, 2^q)$;

7   **else if** $1\{\sigma.e < -2\}$ **then**

8      $\mathsf{idx}_1 \leftarrow ((\sigma.e + 14) \bmod 2^4)\|(\mathcal{F}^{Q-2}_{\mathsf{TR}}(\sigma.m) \bmod 2^2)$;   // Polynomial Evaluation

9      $(\theta_0, \theta_1, \theta_2, \theta_3) \leftarrow \mathcal{F}^{6,9,3,p,Q}_{\mathsf{Coef}}(\Theta^1_{\mathsf{arcsin}}, K^1_{\mathsf{arcsin}}, \mathsf{idx}_1)$;

10   **else if** $1\{\sigma.e = -2\}$ **then**

11      $\mathsf{idx}_2 \leftarrow \mathcal{F}^{Q-4}_{\mathsf{TR}}(\sigma.m) \bmod 2^4$; $(\theta_0, \theta_1, \theta_2, \theta_3) \leftarrow \mathcal{F}^{4,10,3,p,Q}_{\mathsf{Coef}}(\Theta^2_{\mathsf{arcsin}}, K^2_{\mathsf{arcsin}}, \mathsf{idx}_2)$;

12   **else**

13      $\mathsf{idx}_3 \leftarrow \mathcal{F}^{Q-7}_{\mathsf{TR}}(\sigma.m) \bmod 2^7$; $(\theta_0, \theta_1, \theta_2, \theta_3) \leftarrow \mathcal{F}^{7,35,3,p,Q}_{\mathsf{Coef}}(\Theta^3_{\mathsf{arcsin}}, K^3_{\mathsf{arcsin}}, \mathsf{idx}_3)$;

14   $\omega \leftarrow ((\theta_3 \boxtimes_{p,Q} \sigma) \boxplus_{p,Q} \theta_2) \boxtimes_{p,Q} \sigma; \omega \leftarrow ((\omega \boxplus_{p,Q} \theta_1) \boxtimes_{p,Q} \sigma) \boxplus \theta_0$;

15   **return** $(\alpha.z, \alpha.s, \mathcal{F}^{P,q,Q}_{\mathsf{Round}*}(\omega.e, \omega.m))$;   // Output Compensation

---

Our implementation for computing the $\arcsin \pi(\alpha)$ function with $\mathcal{F}_{\mathsf{FParcsin}\pi}$ is shown in Algorithm 1. To start with, the domain α of $\mathcal{F}_{\mathsf{FParcsin}\pi}$ spans $[-1, 1]$. However, for our analysis, we focus on the input range $|\alpha| \in [0, 1 - 2^{-4}) \cup \{1\}$. Initially, we handle two straightforward cases in the evaluation process, see Line 3–6. Firstly, if $|\alpha| < 2^{-14}$, i.e. $\alpha.e < -14$, we use α/π to approximate $\arcsin \pi(\alpha)$ with the ULP error less than 0.5 (Line 3–5). Secondly, if $|\alpha| = 1$, we return $1/2 \cdot (1 - 2 \cdot \alpha.s)$ which is a precise output (Line 6).

For other inputs, we evaluate the function by the following steps: range reduction, polynomial evaluation, and output compensation.

Range Reduction (Line 2): Since $\arcsin \pi(\alpha)$ is an odd function, we can reduce the computation $\arcsin \pi(\alpha)$ that $|\alpha| \in [2^{-14}, 1 - 2^{-4})$ to $\arcsin \pi(\sigma)$ that $\sigma \in [2^{-14}, 1 - 2^{-4})$. Let $s = \mathbb{1}\{\alpha < 0\}$, and $\sigma = |\alpha|$. We have $\arcsin \pi(\alpha) = (-1)^s \cdot \arcsin \pi(\sigma)$. Now we have the sign bit s and the reduced input $\sigma \in [2^{-14}, 1 - 2^{-4})$.

Polynomial Evaluation (Line 7–14): We split the reduced input $\sigma \in [2^{-14}, 1 - 2^{-4})$ into 3 parts. For the first part, we consider the inputs $\sigma \in [2^{-14}, 2^{-2})$ and we use a 9-piece 3-degree splines F^1 (i.e. $\{\theta_3^{(j)}\sigma^3 + \theta_2^{(j)}\sigma^2 + \theta_1^{(j)}\sigma + \theta_0^{(j)}\}_{j=1}^9$) to approximate (Line 7–9). Each interval is determined by the lower 4 bits of the exponent and the upper 2 bits of the mantissa. Next, we consider $\sigma \in [2^{-2}, 2^{-1})$, a 10-piece 3-degree spline F^2 whose intervals are determined by the upper 4 bits of the mantissa and the exponent of σ is constant (Line 10-11). For the third part, since $\sigma \in [2^{-1}, 1 - 2^{-4})$, we use a 35-piece 3-degree spline F^3 and each interval is determined by the upper 7 bits of mantissa (Line 12–13).

Output Compensation (Line 15): $\mathcal{F}_{\text{FParcsin}\pi}$ returns $\arcsin \pi(\sigma)$ if s is 0 and $-\arcsin \pi(\sigma)$ otherwise.

The Inputs of $|\alpha| \in [1 - 2^{-4}, 1)$. Let $f(\alpha) = \arcsin \pi(\alpha)$. We know that $f'(\alpha) = \frac{1}{\pi \cdot \sqrt{1 - \alpha^2}}$. We observe the property that $\lim\limits_{\alpha \to 1^-} f'(\alpha) = +\infty$, indicating that as α approaches 1 from the left side, $f(\alpha)$ will rapidly increase with α growing up. Consequently, even a slight change in the *lower* bits of the mantissa of α will result in a noticeable alteration in the output $f(\alpha)$. For instance, consider two inputs: $\alpha_1 = 1 - 2^{-24}$ (0x3f7fffff) and $\alpha_2 = 1 - 2^{-23}$ (0x3f7ffffe), we can get output 0x3efff198 and 0x3effeba1 respectively. With the flip of the last bit of the mantissa of the input, there is a clear change in the mantissa of the output. We thus do not consider $|\alpha| \in [1 - 2^{-4}, 1)$.

3.2   Arccosine

Algorithm 2: Floating-point $\mathcal{F}_{\text{FParccos}\pi}$

Input: a floating-point number α
Output: the floating-point number $\arccos \pi(\alpha)$
1 Perform Line 1–18 from Algorithm 1 and get ω;
2 $\omega \leftarrow \mathcal{F}_{\text{Float}}^{p,Q}(0.5) \boxminus_{p,Q} (\alpha.z, \alpha.s, \omega.e, \omega.m)$;
3 **return** $(\alpha.z, \alpha.s, \mathcal{F}_{\text{Round}*}^{p,q,Q}(\omega.e, \omega.m))$;

We implement $\mathcal{F}_{\text{FParccos}\pi}$ with Algorithm 2. To begin with, we streamline our computation to leverage $\mathcal{F}_{\text{FParcsin}\pi}$, which has already been implemented in Sect. 3.1, for the inputs $|\alpha|$ falling within the rage of $[0, 1 - 2^{-4}) \cup \{1\}$. Due to $\arcsin \pi(\alpha) + \arccos \pi(\alpha) = \frac{1}{2}$, we obtain $\arccos \pi(\alpha) = \frac{1}{2} - \arcsin \pi(\alpha)$ by treating $\mathcal{F}_{\text{FParcsin}\pi}$ as a subordinate operation. Specifically, we begin by computing $\beta = \arcsin \pi(\alpha)$. Next, we negate the sign of β (i.e., $\beta.s$), and add $\frac{1}{2}$. As a result, we obtain the final output.

3.3   Arctangent

Algorithm 3: Floating-point $\mathcal{F}_{\mathsf{FParctan}\pi}$

Input: a floating-point number α
Output: the floating-point number $\arctan \pi(\alpha)$

1 $p \leftarrow 8, q \leftarrow 23, Q \leftarrow 27$;
2 $\gamma \leftarrow (\alpha.z, 0, \alpha.e, \alpha.m *_{Q+1} 2^{Q-q})$;
3 **if** $1\{\gamma.e = 0 \wedge \gamma.m = 2^Q\}$ **then return** $(0, \alpha.s, -2, 2^q)$;
4 $b \leftarrow 1\{\gamma.e \geq 0\}; \sigma \leftarrow b \;?\; \mathcal{F}^{p,Q}_{\mathsf{Float}}(1.0) \boxtimes_{p,Q} \gamma : \gamma$;   // Range Reduction
5 **if** $1\{\sigma.e < -14\}$ **then**
6       $\psi \leftarrow \sigma \boxtimes_{p,Q} \mathcal{F}^{p,Q}_{\mathsf{Float}}(1/\pi)$;   // Polynomial Evaluation
7 **else**
8   **if** $1\{\sigma.e < -2\}$ **then**
9            $\mathsf{idx}_1 \leftarrow ((\sigma.e + 14) \bmod 2^4) \| (\mathcal{F}^{Q-3}_{\mathsf{TR}}(\sigma.m) \bmod 2^3)$;
10            $(\theta_0, \theta_1, \theta_2, \theta_3) \leftarrow \mathcal{F}^{7,14,3,p,Q}_{\mathsf{Coef}}(\Theta^1_{\mathsf{arctan}}, K^1_{\mathsf{arctan}}, \mathsf{idx}_1)$;
11   **else**
12            $\mathsf{idx}_2 \leftarrow ((\sigma.e + 2) \bmod 2^1) \| (\mathcal{F}^{Q-4}_{\mathsf{TR}}(\sigma.m) \bmod 2^4)$;
13            $(\theta_0, \theta_1, \theta_2, \theta_3) \leftarrow \mathcal{F}^{5,23,3,p,Q}_{\mathsf{Coef}}(\Theta^2_{\mathsf{arctan}}, K^2_{\mathsf{arctan}}, \mathsf{idx}_2)$;
14       $\psi \leftarrow ((\theta_3 \boxtimes_{p,Q} \sigma) \boxplus_{p,Q} \theta_2) \boxtimes_{p,Q} \sigma; \psi \leftarrow ((\psi \boxplus_{p,Q} \theta_1) \boxtimes_{p,Q} \sigma) \boxplus \theta_0$;
15 $\omega \leftarrow b \;?\; \mathsf{Float}_{p,Q}(0.5) \boxminus_{p,Q} \psi : \psi$;   // Output Compensation
16 **return** $(\alpha.z, \alpha.s, \mathcal{F}^{p,q,Q}_{\mathsf{Round}*}(\omega.e, \omega.m))$;

The implementation of $\mathcal{F}_{\mathsf{FParctan}\pi}$ is shown in Algorithm 3. We perform the following steps as before:

Range Reduction (Line 2–4): Like $\arcsin \pi(\alpha)$, $\arctan \pi(\alpha)$ is also a odd function. Let $s = 1\{\alpha < 0\}$ and $\beta = |\alpha|$. Now $\arctan \pi(\alpha) = (-1)^s \cdot \arctan \pi(\beta)$. We reduce the computation of $\arctan \pi(\alpha)$ to $\arctan \pi(\beta)$ where $\beta \in (0, +\infty)$. Since $\arctan \pi(\beta)$ satisfies this property: $\arctan \pi(\beta) + \arctan \pi \left(\frac{1}{\beta}\right) = \frac{1}{2}$, we can use this property to reduce the range to $(0, 1]$. Let $b = 1\{\beta \geq 1\}$. Now consider $\sigma \in (0, 1]$, which is defined as β if b is 0 otherwise $\frac{1}{\beta}$ instead. Now we can compute $\arctan \pi(\alpha)$ using this function:

$$\arctan \pi(\alpha) = \begin{cases} (-1)^s \cdot \arctan \pi(\sigma) & \text{if} \quad b = 0; \\ (-1)^s \cdot \left[\dfrac{1}{2} - \arctan \pi(\sigma)\right] & \text{otherwise.} \end{cases} \tag{2}$$

In this function, $\sigma \in (0, 1]$ always holds. We get bits $s, b \in \{0, 1\}$ and a reduced input $\sigma \in (0, 1]$.

Polynomial Evaluation (Line 5–14): For these reduced inputs $\sigma \in (0, 2^{-14})$, we approximate it by σ/π simply (Line 5–6). The result of $\arctan \pi(\sigma)$ on other inputs is as below, which is split into two parts. In the first part, we consider the reduce inputs $\sigma \in [2^{-14}, 2^{-2})$ and use a 14-piece 3-degree separate splines F^1 to approximate, each interval is determined by the lower 4 bits of exponent upper 3 bits of mantissa (Line 8–10). The other part we consider $\sigma \in [2^{-2}, 1)$, we use a 23-piece 3-degree splines which intervals are determined by lower 1 bits of exponent and upper 4 bits of mantissa is enough (Line 11–13).

Output Compensation (Line 15–16): According to the Eq. 2, when we learn the polynomial evaluation output $\omega = \arctan \pi(\sigma)$, if $b = 1$ we set $\omega \leftarrow \frac{1}{2} - \omega$ otherwise do nothing. We return ω if s is 0 and $-\omega$ otherwise.

3.4 Square-Root

Algorithm 4: Floating-point $\mathcal{F}_{\mathsf{FPsqrt}}$

Input: a floating-point number α
Output: the floating-point number sqrt(α)
1 $p \leftarrow 8, q \leftarrow 23, Q \leftarrow 27$;
2 $\sigma \leftarrow (\alpha.z, 0, 0, \alpha.m *_{Q+1} 2^{Q-q})$;   // Range Reduction
3 $t \leftarrow \alpha.e + 1; a \leftarrow \mathcal{F}_{\mathsf{ZXT}}^{p+2}(\mathcal{F}_{\mathsf{TR}}^{1}(t)) + 2^{p-2} - 1; b \leftarrow t \bmod 2^1$;
4 $\mathsf{idx} \leftarrow \mathcal{F}_{\mathsf{TR}}^{Q-4}(\sigma.m) \bmod 2^4$;   // Polynomial Evaluation
5 $(\theta_0, \theta_1, \theta_2, \theta_3) \leftarrow \mathcal{F}_{\mathsf{Coef}}^{4,15,3,p,Q}(\Theta_{\mathsf{sqrt}}, K_{\mathsf{sqrt}}, \mathsf{idx})$;
6 $\psi \leftarrow ((\theta_3 \boxtimes_{p,Q} \sigma) \boxplus_{p,Q} \theta_2) \boxtimes_{p,Q} \sigma; \psi \leftarrow ((\psi \boxplus_{p,Q} \theta_1) \boxtimes_{p,Q} \sigma) \boxplus \theta_0$;
7 $\omega \leftarrow b ? \psi \boxtimes_{p,Q} \mathcal{F}_{\mathsf{Float}}^{p,Q}(\sqrt{2}) : \psi$;   // Output Compensation
8 $e, m \leftarrow \mathcal{F}_{\mathsf{Round}*}^{p,q,Q}(\omega.e, \omega.m)$;
9 **return** $(\alpha.z, \alpha.s, a, m)$;

The implementation of $\mathcal{F}_{\mathsf{FPsqrt}}$ is shown in Algorithm 4. Here, we consider inputs $\alpha \in [0, 2^{128})$. Initially, we evaluate the function in a straightforward case: when $\alpha = 0$, i.e., $\alpha.z = 1$, we return sqrt(α) $= 0$. For other inputs, we process the following steps:

Range Reduction (Line 2–3): Let $\alpha = \sigma \cdot 2^e$, where $\sigma \in [1, 2)$ and $e \in [-126, 128) \cap \mathbb{N}$. Let $e = 2 \cdot a + b$, where $a = \lfloor e/2 \rfloor$ and $b = e \bmod 2$ (i.e. b is the least significant bit of e). We define β is $\sqrt{2}$ if $b = 1$ and 1 otherwise. Then we have sqrt(α) = sqrt(σ) $\cdot 2^a \cdot \beta$. And now we get the bit b and a reduced input $\sigma \in [1, 2)$.

Polynomial Evaluation (Line 4–6): As the reduced input $\sigma \in [1, 2)$, we don't need to care about the exponent of σ. We design a 15-piece 3-degree splines F to approximate. Each interval of the spline is determined by the upper 4 bits of the mantissa.

Output Compensation (Line 7–8): The final output is express as $\omega \cdot 2^a \cdot \beta$, where ω is the polynomial evaluation output. We can simply multiply the output by β. Since $a \in \mathbb{N}$, the multiplication of 2^a is equivalent to adding a to $\omega.e$.

3.5 Hyperbolic Tangent

We denote $\tanh(\alpha) = \frac{e^\alpha - e^{-\alpha}}{e^\alpha + e^{-\alpha}}$, and our implementation for the functionality $\mathcal{F}_{\mathsf{FPtanh}}$ is shown in Algorithm 5. Similar to previous sections, we begin by considering an easy case of the functionality. When the absolute value of the input is greater than or equal to 2^4, i.e., when $\alpha.e \geq 4$, we return 1 with a ULP error of less than 0.5 (Line 3). For other inputs where $|\alpha| < 2^4$, we proceed with the following steps:

Range Reduction (Line 5–10): We also observe that $\tanh(\alpha)$ is an odd function, let $s = \mathbf{1}\{\alpha < 0\}$ and we get $\tanh(\alpha) = (-1)^s \cdot \tanh(\beta)$, where $\beta \in [0, 2^4)$. We

---

Algorithm 5: Floating-point $\mathcal{F}_{\mathsf{FPtanh}}$

Input: a floating-point number α
Output: the floating-point number $\tanh(\alpha)$
1 $p \leftarrow 8, q \leftarrow 23, Q \leftarrow 27, M \leftarrow 4, O \leftarrow -2$;
2 $\gamma \leftarrow (\alpha.z, 0, \alpha.e, \alpha.m *_{Q+1} 2^{Q-q})$;
3 **if** $\mathbf{1}\{\alpha.e \geq 4\}$ **then return** $(0, \alpha.s, 0, 2^q)$;
4 **else**
5   **if** $\mathbf{1}\{\sigma.e < O\}$ **then**
6          $k \leftarrow 0; \sigma \leftarrow \gamma$;   // Range Reduction
7   **else**
8          $m \leftarrow \gamma.m *_{Q+M-O} 2^{\gamma.e-O}; k \leftarrow \mathcal{F}_{\mathsf{TR}}^{Q}(m); m' \leftarrow \mathcal{F}_{\mathsf{ZXT}}^{Q+1}(m \bmod 2^{Q})$;
9          $(i, I) \leftarrow \mathcal{F}_{\mathsf{MSNZB}}^{Q+1}(m'); \sigma \leftarrow (\mathbf{1}\{m' = 0\}, \alpha.s, O - (Q - i), m' *_{Q+1} I)$;
10      $\psi \leftarrow \mathcal{F}_{L}^{p,Q,6}(\mathsf{tanh}\text{-}k, k), k \in [2^6]$;
11   **if** $\mathbf{1}\{\sigma.e < -14\}$ **then**
12          $\omega \leftarrow \sigma$;   // Polynomial Evaluation
13   **else**
14          $\mathsf{idx} \leftarrow ((\sigma.e + 14) \bmod 2^4) \| (\mathcal{F}_{\mathsf{TR}}^{Q-3}(\sigma.m) \bmod 2^3)$;
15          $(\theta_0, \theta_1, \theta_2, \theta_3) \leftarrow \mathcal{F}_{\mathsf{Coef}}^{7,9,3,p,Q}(\Theta_{\mathsf{tanh}}, K_{\mathsf{tanh}}, \mathsf{idx})$;
16          $\omega \leftarrow ((\theta_3 \boxtimes_{p,Q} \sigma) \boxplus_{p,Q} \theta_2) \boxtimes_{p,Q} \sigma; \omega \leftarrow ((\psi \boxplus_{p,Q} \theta_1) \boxtimes_{p,Q} \sigma) \boxplus \theta_0$;
17      $\phi \leftarrow \psi \boxplus_{p,Q} \omega; \chi \leftarrow \mathcal{F}_{\mathsf{Float}}^{p,Q}(1) \boxplus_{p,Q} (\psi \boxtimes_{p,Q} \omega)$;   // Output Compensation
18      $\iota \leftarrow \phi \boxtimes_{p,Q} \chi$;
19   **return** $(\alpha.z, \alpha.s, \mathcal{F}_{\mathsf{Round}^*}^{p,q,Q}(\iota.e, \iota.m))$;

---

can get $\beta = \frac{k}{2^2} + \sigma$, where $k \in [2^6]$ and $\sigma \in [0, 2^{-2})$. Lastly, using the the equality $\tanh(x+y) = \frac{\tanh(x)+\tanh(y)}{1+\tanh(x)\cdot\tanh(y)}$ and we can get:

$$\tanh(\alpha) = (-1)^s \cdot \frac{\tanh(\frac{k}{4}) + \tanh(\sigma)}{1 + \tanh(\frac{k}{4}) \cdot \tanh(\sigma)}. \tag{3}$$

We get a bits $s \in \{0, 1\}$, a flag $k \in [2^6]$ and a reduced input $\sigma \in [0, 2^{-2})$.

Polynomial Evaluation (Line 11–16): If $\sigma \in (0, 2^{-14})$, we can use σ to approximate $\tanh(\sigma)$ similarly to above (Line 11–12). For $\sigma \in [2^{-14}, 2^{-2})$. We design an 9-piece 3-degree splines F to approximate. Each interval of F is determined by the lower 4 bits of exponent and upper 3 bits of mantissa (Line 14–16).

Output Compensation (Line 17–19): When we learn the reduced output $\tanh(\sigma)$ and $\tanh(\frac{k}{4})$ from the lookup table, We use the Eq. 3, set the sign $\alpha.s$ to the value $\frac{\tanh(\sigma)+\tanh(\frac{k}{4})}{1+\tanh(\sigma)\cdot\tanh(\frac{k}{4})}$ and learn the final output.

4 Secure Transformer Inference

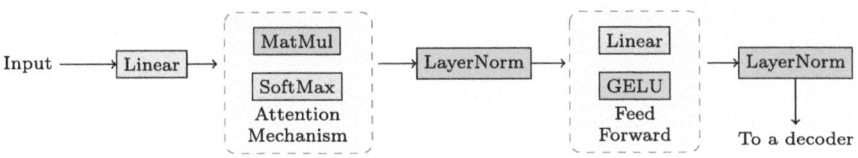

Fig. 1. The overall architecture of an encoder.

We are ready to delve into the evaluation of a specific application that leverages our earlier non-linear mathematical functionalities within a 2PC setting. In particular, we introduce secure transformer inference. Notably, the Transformer is a neural network model that is fundamentally rooted in the attention mechanism [40]. Transformer operates on an encoder-decoder architecture, and the encoder and decoder share a similar structure. We focus on the encoder, which comprises two essential layers: the multi-head attention mechanism and the feed-forward neural network. Following each layer, residual connection and layer normalization are applied. Figure 1 illustrates the specific architecture of an encoder, with detailed descriptions of these two layers provided below.

Attention Mechanism. The attention layer takes the query matrix $\mathbf{Q}$ as input, along with a pair of key-value matrices $(\mathbf{K}, \mathbf{V})$, and produces a word weight matrix as output. This layer can be defined formally as Attention$(\mathbf{Q}, \mathbf{K}, \mathbf{V}) =$ SoftMax$\left(\frac{\mathbf{Q}\mathbf{K}^T}{\sqrt{d}}\right)\mathbf{V}$, where $\mathbf{Q}, \mathbf{K}, \mathbf{V}$ are obtained by applying three different sets of linear transformations to the input $\mathbf{X}$, that is, $\mathbf{Q} = \mathbf{X}\mathbf{W}^{\mathbf{Q}}$, $\mathbf{K} = \mathbf{X}\mathbf{W}^{\mathbf{K}}$, $\mathbf{V} = \mathbf{X}\mathbf{W}^{\mathbf{V}}$, and d is the dimension of each vector in $\mathbf{X}$. Multi-head attention mechanisms combine the outputs of several different attention mechanisms.

Feed Forward. The output of the previous attention mechanism serves as the input for the feedforward neural network. This network executes two linear transformations, interspersed with a GELU activation function for nonlinear transformation, with the GELU function applied between the two linear transformations [24]. The feedforward neural network can be defined formally as Feed-Forward$(\mathbf{X}) = $ GELU$(\mathbf{X} \cdot \mathbf{W_1} + \mathbf{B_1}) \cdot \mathbf{W_2} + \mathbf{B_2}$, where $\mathbf{W_1}, \mathbf{B_1}, \mathbf{W_2}, \mathbf{B_2}$ are the coefficient matrices in the linear layer.

Notably, in Fig. 1, we exclude from consideration the input embedding layer and the position encoding operation. Essentially, these operations convert input tokens into feature vector representations. Besides, the linear layer of transformer has three operations, namely input embedding, attention mechanism and linear transformation, which all rely on matrix multiplication.

Our emphasis is on the non-linear layers, specifically GELU, LayerNorm and SoftMax. In the subsequent sections, we provide detailed descriptions of each operation.

4.1 GELU

The GELU approximation presented by [24] specifically takes the following computation: GELU$(x) \approx 0.5x\{1 + \tanh[\sqrt{2/\pi}(x + 0.044715x^3)]\}$. Our GELU functionality, denoted as $\mathcal{F}_{\mathsf{FPGELU}}$, is outlined in Algorithm 6. $\mathcal{F}_{\mathsf{FPGELU}}$ invokes $\mathcal{F}_{\mathsf{FPtanh}}$ once, as proposed in Sect. 3.5. $\mathcal{F}_{\mathsf{FPGELU}}$ also necessitates additional 2 additions, 4 multiplications. Notably, when multiplied by 0.5, necessitating a subtraction of 1 from the exponent of ω.

4.2 LayerNorm

For a d-dimensional vector $\boldsymbol{a} = (a_0, \ldots, a_{d-1})$, the LayerNorm operation is defined as LayerNorm$(\boldsymbol{a}) = \frac{a-\mu}{\sigma}$, where μ is the mean of $\boldsymbol{a}$, i.e. $\mu = \frac{1}{d}\sum_{i=0}^{d-1} a_i$,

---

Algorithm 6: Floating-point $\mathcal{F}_{\mathsf{FPGELU}}$

Input: a floating-point number α
Output: the floating-point number $\mathrm{GELU}(\alpha)$

1 $p \leftarrow 8, q \leftarrow 23, Q \leftarrow 27, M \leftarrow 4, O \leftarrow -2$
2 $\delta \leftarrow (\alpha.z, 0, \alpha.e, \alpha.m *_{Q+1} 2^{Q-q}); \beta \leftarrow \delta \boxtimes_{p,Q} \delta \boxtimes_{p,Q} \delta$
3 $\gamma \leftarrow \delta \boxplus_{p,Q} (\mathcal{F}_{\mathsf{Float}}^{p,Q}(0.044715) \boxtimes_{p,Q} \beta); \sigma \leftarrow \mathcal{F}_{\mathsf{Float}}^{p,Q}(\sqrt{2/\pi}) \boxtimes_{p,Q} \gamma$
4 **if** $1\{\sigma.e \geq 4\}$ **then** $\iota \leftarrow (0, \alpha.s, 0, 0);$
5 **else** Perform Line 6-19 from Algorithm 5 and get $\iota; \iota.s \leftarrow \alpha.s; \iota.z \leftarrow \iota.z;$
6 $\omega \leftarrow \delta \boxtimes_{p,Q} (\mathcal{F}_{\mathsf{Float}}^{p,Q}(1) \boxplus_{p,Q} \iota);$
7 **return** $(\omega.z, \omega.s, \mathcal{F}_{\mathsf{Round}*}^{p,q,Q}(\omega.e - 1, \omega.m))$

---

and σ is the standard deviation of $\boldsymbol{a}$, i.e. $\sigma = \sqrt{\frac{1}{d}\sum_{i=0}^{d-1}(a_i - \mu)^2}$. The functionality to evaluate $\mathcal{F}_{\mathsf{FPNorm}}$ is shown in Algorithm 7. In order to compute μ and σ, $\mathcal{F}_{\mathsf{FPNorm}}$ will invoke the summation functionality $\mathcal{F}_{\mathsf{FPsum}}$ twice, and call $\mathcal{F}_{\mathsf{FPsqrt}}$ once (see Sect. 3.4). Besides, evaluating $\mathcal{F}_{\mathsf{FPNorm}}$ requires only 1 division operation.

Algorithm 7: Floating-point vector $\mathcal{F}_{\mathsf{FPNorm}}$

Input: a floating-point d-dimension vector $\boldsymbol{a}$
Output: the floating-point d-dimension vector $\mathrm{LayerNorm}(\boldsymbol{a})$

1 $p \leftarrow 8, q \leftarrow 23, Q \leftarrow 27;$
2 **for** $i \leftarrow 0$ **to** $d-1$ **do** $a_i' \leftarrow (a_i.z, a_i.s, a_i.e, a_i.m *_{Q+1} 2^{Q-q});$
3 $\gamma \leftarrow \mathcal{F}_{\mathsf{FPsum}}^{p,Q,d}(\boldsymbol{a}');$
4 $\mu \leftarrow \gamma \boxtimes_{p,Q} \mathcal{F}_{\mathsf{Float}}^{p,Q}(1/d);$ // μ is the mean of a
5 **for** $i \leftarrow 0$ **to** $d-1$ **do**
6      $b_i \leftarrow a_i' \boxminus_{p,Q} \mu;$
7      $c_i \leftarrow b_i \boxtimes_{p,Q} b_i;$
8 $\sigma \leftarrow \mathcal{F}_{\mathsf{FPsum}}^{p,Q,d}(c) \boxtimes_{p,Q} \mathcal{F}_{\mathsf{Float}}^{p,Q}(1/d);$ // the variance of a
9 $\alpha \leftarrow \sigma; \sigma.e \leftarrow 2^{p-1} - 1;$ Perform Line 3-8 from Algorithm 4 and get $m, a;$
10 $\sigma \leftarrow (\sigma.z, \sigma.s, a, m);$ // the actual standard deviation of a
11 $\gamma \leftarrow \mathcal{F}_{\mathsf{Float}}^{p,Q}(1) \boxslash_{p,Q} \sigma;$ // the only instance of floating-point division
12 **for** $i \leftarrow 0$ **to** $d-1$ **do**
13      $d_i \leftarrow b_i \boxtimes_{p,q} \gamma; d_i' \leftarrow (d_i.z, d_i.s, \mathcal{F}_{\mathsf{Round}*}^{p,q,Q}(d_i.e, d_i.m));$
14 **return** $(d_0', d_1', \ldots, d_{d-1}');$

4.3 SoftMax

SoftMax is one type of operations in attention mechanism. The SoftMax operation takes a d-dimensional vector $\boldsymbol{x} = (x_0, \ldots, x_{d-1})$ as input and outputs a d-dimensional vector $\boldsymbol{y}$, where $\boldsymbol{y}$ is defined as $y_i = \frac{e^{x_i}}{\sum_{j=0}^{d-1} e^{x_j}}$ for $i \in [d]$. The functionality to evaluate $\mathcal{F}_{\mathsf{FPSoftMax}}$ is shown in Algorithm 8. However, direct exponentiation here may lead to overflow. One way to do this is to find the maximum value χ of the vector $\boldsymbol{x}$ and get a new vector $\boldsymbol{x}' = \boldsymbol{x} - \chi$. And now we get $x_i' \leq 0$ for all $i \in [d]$ since $\mathrm{SoftMax}(\boldsymbol{x}) = \mathrm{SoftMax}(\boldsymbol{x} - \alpha)$ for any constant α. In order to evaluate χ, $\mathcal{F}_{\mathsf{FPSoftMax}}$ also invokes $\mathcal{F}_{\mathsf{FPmax}}$ once. In addition, $\mathcal{F}_{\mathsf{FPSoftMax}}$ requires d calls to $\mathcal{F}_{\mathsf{FPexp}}$, along with 1 $\mathcal{F}_{\mathsf{FPsum}}$, d multiplications, and 1 division.

Algorithm 8: Floating-point vector $\mathcal{F}_{\mathsf{FPSoftMax}}$

Input: a floating-point d-dimension vector $\boldsymbol{x}$
Output: the floating-point d-dimension vector $\mathrm{SoftMax}(\boldsymbol{x})$

1 $p \leftarrow 8, q \leftarrow 23, Q \leftarrow 27$;
2 $\chi \leftarrow \mathcal{F}_{\mathsf{FPmax}}(\boldsymbol{x})$;   // χ is the maximum value of the vector x
3 **for** $i \leftarrow 0$ **to** $d - 1$ **do**
4        $a_i \leftarrow \mathcal{F}_{\mathsf{FPexp}}(x_i \boxminus_{p,q} \chi)$;
5        $a'_i \leftarrow (a_i.z, a_s, a_i.e, a_i.m *_{Q+1} 2^{Q-q})$;   // compute vector $a = x - \chi$.
6 $\beta \leftarrow \mathcal{F}_{\mathsf{FPsum}}(a')$;
7 $\gamma \leftarrow \mathcal{F}_{\mathsf{Float}}^{p,Q}(1) \boxtimes_{p,Q} \beta$;   // the only instance of floating-point division
8 **for** $i \leftarrow 0$ **to** $d - 1$ **do**
9        $b'_i \leftarrow a'_i \boxtimes_{p,Q} \gamma$;
10       $b_i \leftarrow (b'_i.z, b'_i.s, \mathcal{F}_{\mathsf{Round}*}^{p,q,Q}(b'_i.e, b'_i.m))$;
11 **return** $(b_0, b_1, \ldots, b_{d-1})$;

---

5   Implementation and Evaluation

Experimental Setup. We have implemented all functionalities introduced in Sect. 3 and Sect. 4 with about 700 lines of C++ code, leveraging the EzPC framework [36] and the SecFloat library [33]. Notably, despite SecFloat's existing low-level interfaces, we develop a new interface called `divpow2`. This interface performs the division of a floating-point number by a power of two, thereby reducing the overhead associated with multiply-by-0.5 operations. The primary challenge in our implementation is correctly programming secure computation protocols in line with the functionalities introduced in Sect. 3. Each sub-operation within a functionality essentially functions as a sub-protocol within the corresponding secure computation protocol. This requires precise specification and adherence to the execution order of these sub-protocols to ensure correct implementation.

Similar to [33,34], we configure a Local Area Network (LAN) to simulate the interaction between two parties. The specifications for the two machines are equipped with AMD Ryzen 7 5800H CPUs at 3.2 GHz. Also, the bandwidth of the network is 1000 Mbps, with a round-trip time of 0.8 ms. We provide our source code at https://github.com/huangtaojnu/SecFloatPlus.

Evaluation Methodology. Building upon our implementation, we conduct a three-fold evaluation aimed at showcasing our superior performance in terms of precision. Firstly, we benchmark our newly proposed functionalities in terms of computation cost, communication overhead, and average ULP error. We evaluate the $\mathcal{F}_{\mathsf{FPtanh}}$ and the $\mathcal{F}_{\mathsf{GELU}}$ operations, also implemented in Beacon [32] to enable a fair comparison. Next, we extend the evaluation to encompass scenarios involving privacy-preserving proximity testing which uses our inverse trigonometric functionalities. Finally, we assess the non-linear functionalities outlined in Sect. 4 that are employed in secure transformer inference.

5.1   Microbenchmarks and Comparison

We evaluate the performance of our proposed functionalities, including $\mathcal{F}_{\mathsf{FParcsin\pi}}$, $\mathcal{F}_{\mathsf{FParccos\pi}}$, $\mathcal{F}_{\mathsf{FParctan\pi}}$, $\mathcal{F}_{\mathsf{FPsqrt}}$ and $\mathcal{F}_{\mathsf{FPtanh}}$. We execute various batches of instances

Table 1. Microbenchmarks over different batches of instances.

Functionalities	Time for Batch Size (s)				Communication Cost (KB)	Average ULP Error
	10^2	10^3	10^4	10^5		
$\mathcal{F}_{\text{FParcsin}\pi}$	0.61	0.92	4.88	48.14	36.06	0.62
$\mathcal{F}_{\text{FParccos}\pi}$	0.73	1.09	5.91	56.64	42.94	1.57
$\mathcal{F}_{\text{FParctan}\pi}$	0.81	1.23	6.62	63.76	50.06	<0.5
$\mathcal{F}_{\text{FPsqrt}}$	0.56	0.86	4.48	42.83	33.81	<0.5

for each functionality, with batch sizes ranging from 10^2 to 10^5. We then measure the total runtime and communication overhead for these batches. As Table 1 shown, columns 2–5 display the runtime under different batch sizes, while column 6 indicates the interaction overhead for individual instances. For each instance, we also calculate the ULP error for these functionalities using the MPFR computation results, for precision measurement.

Table 2. Performance comparison between our work and Beacon.

Scenarios		Time for Batch Size (s)				Communication Cost (KB)	Average ULP Error
		10^2	10^3	10^4	10^5		
$\mathcal{F}_{\text{FPtanh}}$	**Ours**	0.94	1.50	8.11	78.41	60.77	< 0.5
	Beacon	0.85	1.22	5.93	57.31	46.43	≈ 500
$\mathcal{F}_{\text{FPGELU}}$	**Ours**	1.44	2.15	10.99	105.52	85.70	5.96
	Beacon	1.36	1.88	9.03	86.49	71.35	30.17

Subsequently, we compare the evaluation performance of the functionality $\mathcal{F}_{\text{FPtanh}}$ with that of Beacon [32], as demonstrated in Table 2. It is noteworthy that our design for $\mathcal{F}_{\text{FPtanh}}$ is based on the mathematical properties of $y = \tanh(x)$. Unlike Beacon, which directly employs $\tanh(x) = 2\sigma(2x) - 1$, where σ is the sigmoid function defined as $\sigma(y) = \frac{1}{1-e^{-y}}$, we achieve at least 1000 times the precision with only increasing 1.33× runtime and 1.30× communication cost.

5.2 Privacy-Preserving Proximity Testing

Table 3. Efficiency across various batches for both scenarios.

Scenarios	Time for Batch Size (s)				Communication Cost (KB)	Average ULP Error
	10^2	10^3	10^4	10^5		
1	3.50	5.19	25.94	238.61	201.29	3.05
2	4.02	5.94	28.61	273.10	231.71	<0.5

We use the scenarios mentioned in [13,33], and further extend the proximity testing on Earth as described in [41]. In particular, given the coordinates of two

Table 4. Performance comparison for SoftMax and LayerNorm functionalities. "-" signifies that this functionality is not provided by SecFloat.

Functionalities	Bach Size × Demension	Time (s)		Communication Cost (KB)		Average ULP Error
		Ours	SecFloat	Ours	SecFloat	
$\mathcal{F}_{\mathsf{FPSoftMax}}$	10×10	1.14	1.16	417.95	453.17	9.62
	400×10	2.78	2.88			
	10×400	3.35	3.47	15310	16805	
	400×400	77.29	84.04			
$\mathcal{F}_{\mathsf{FPNorm}}$	10×10	1.18	-	306.19	-	2.88
	400×10	2.93	-			
	10×400	3.90	-	9950	-	
	400×400	53.09	-			

points $p_0(\varphi_0, \lambda_0)$ and $p_1(\varphi_1, \lambda_1)$ on Earth, where φ_0, φ_1 represent the latitudes, and λ_0, λ_1 represent the longitudes. The information of points p_0 and p_1 should not be disclosed to any party. Our task is to compute some private information about these privacy inputs.

In the first scenario, both parties possess secret shares of p_0 and p_1 and aim to securely compute the distance d between p_0 and p_1. When $d < \tau$, where τ is an upper bound, both parties can precisely compute the value of d using the Haversine formula [38]: $d = 2r \arcsin \pi(\sqrt{\iota})$, where

$$\iota = \sin \pi^2 \left(\frac{\varphi_1 - \varphi_0}{2} \right) + \cos \pi(\varphi_0) \cdot \cos \pi(\varphi_1) \cdot \sin \pi^2 \left(\frac{\lambda_1 - \lambda_0}{2} \right). \tag{4}$$

Herein, r denotes the radius of Earth. We implement the computation process involving 2 $\mathcal{F}_{\mathsf{FPsin}\pi}$, 2 $\mathcal{F}_{\mathsf{FPcos}\pi}$, 3 additions, 4 multiplications, 1 $\mathcal{F}_{\mathsf{FPsqrt}}$, and 1 $\mathcal{F}_{\mathsf{FParcsin}\pi}$.

In the second scenario, both parties also possess secret shares of p_0 and p_1 and aim to securely compute the azimuth θ from p_0 to p_1. This involves determining the direction from p_0 to p_1, with the reference direction typically being true north. Both parties can precisely compute the value of θ using the azimuth formula [39]: $\theta = \arctan \pi(\nu)$, where

$$\nu = \frac{\sin \pi(\lambda_1 - \lambda_0) \cdot \cos \pi(\varphi_1)}{\cos \pi(\varphi_0) \cdot \sin \pi(\varphi_1) - \sin \pi(\varphi_0) \cdot \cos \pi(\varphi_1) \cdot \cos \pi(\lambda_1 - \lambda_0)}. \tag{5}$$

We implement the computation process involving 3 $\mathcal{F}_{\mathsf{FPsin}\pi}$, 3 $\mathcal{F}_{\mathsf{FPcos}\pi}$, 3 additions, 4 multiplications, 1 division and 1 $\mathcal{F}_{\mathsf{FParctan}\pi}$.

In Table 3, we illustrate the computational instances and evaluation results of the above two scenarios. Due to our more precise implementation for $\mathcal{F}_{\mathsf{FParctan}\pi}$, we compute the azimuth θ with less than 0.5 ULP error in the second scenario.

5.3   Non-linear Functions in Machine Learning

We now evaluate the secure non-linear functionalities included in transformer inference, which involve GELU, SoftMax, and LayerNorm. For GELU (see the last two lines in Table 2), we achieve a ULP error of 5.96. The runtime ranges from 1.44 s to 105.52 s, as the batch sizes vary from 10^2 to 10^5, while the communication cost is 85.70 KB. In comparison, using the tanh functionality provided by Beacon results in an evaluation of the GELU function with nearly 30 ULP error with only increasing 1.2× runtime and 1.2× communication cost. This unexpected ULP error is due to the uneven distribution of the input $\sqrt{2/\pi}(\alpha + 0.044715\alpha^3)$ to the $\mathcal{F}_{\mathsf{FPtanh}}$.

For SoftMax and LayerNorm (see Table 4), we conduct a performance evaluation considering different batch sizes and dimensions from that of Table 1. We primarily compare our advanced performance on SoftMax with that of SecFloat, since LayerNorm is not implemented by SecFloat. We demonstrate that for the same-level ULP error, our implementation of $\mathcal{F}_{\mathsf{FPSoftMax}}$ runs faster than SecFloat's, regardless of batch sizes and dimensions, while also saving on communication costs.

6   Conclusion and Future Work

This paper integrates floating-point math functionalities into 2PC protocols, encompassing both trigonometric and inverse trigonometric functions. Notably, our enhancements result in a significant improvement in the accuracy of the tanh function compared to Beacon. Evaluating our functionalities in privacy-preserving proximity testing and machine learning scenarios, our experimental results demonstrate robust performance across common non-linear functionalities. Particularly, the SoftMax implementation stands out for surpassing SecFloat's performance in both runtime and communication cost. In addition, our designed scheme can be extended to secure multi-party computation, provided that the underlying sub-protocols offer the same implementation.

In the future, we aim to delve deeper into research in this field through the following aspects:

(a) Optimizing the efficiency of current protocols, such as reducing splines while maintaining accuracy and constructing 64-bit double-precision floating-point common mathematical functionalities;
(b) Integrating the Core-Math project [37] to further enhance the accuracy of the protocol, in which the Core-Math project offers crypto-friendly, ready-to-use programs designed to evaluate single-precision and double-precision floating-point nonlinear functions on plaintext data;
(c) Developing more precise evaluation protocols to support various privacy-preserving machine learning scenarios beyond transformer inference.

Acknowledgements. The work was supported in part by the National Natural Science Foundation of China (Nos. 62332007, U22B2028, 62302192, U23A20303 and 62032025), the Science and Technology Major Project of Tibetan Autonomous Region of China (No. XZ202201ZD0006G), the Natural Science Foundation of Guangdong Province (No. 2024A1515010086), and the Science and Technology Program of Guangzhou (No. 2024A04J3691), National Joint Engineering Research Center of Network Security Detection and Protection Technology, Guangdong Key Laboratory of Data Security and Privacy Preserving, Guangdong Hong Kong Joint Laboratory for Data Security and Privacy Protection, and Engineering Research Center of Trustworthy AI, Ministry of Education. The authors are very grateful to the anonymous reviewers for their detailed comments and suggestions regarding this paper.

References

1. IEEE standard for floating-point arithmetic: IEEE Std 754–2008, pp. 1–70 (2008). https://doi.org/10.1109/IEEESTD.2008.4610935
2. Aliasgari, M., Blanton, M., Zhang, Y., Steele, A.: Secure computation on floating point numbers. In: 20th Annual Network and Distributed System Security Symposium, NDSS 2013, San Diego, California, USA, 24–27 February 2013. The Internet Society (2013). https://www.ndss-symposium.org/ndss2013/secure-computation-floating-point-numbers
3. Archer, D.W., Atapoor, S., Smart, N.P.: The cost of IEEE arithmetic in secure computation. In: International Conference on Cryptology and Information Security in Latin America, pp. 431–452. Springer (2021)
4. Blanton, M., Goodrich, M.T., Yuan, C.: Secure and accurate summation of many floating-point numbers. Proc. Priv. Enhanc. Technol. **2023**(3), 432–445 (2023). https://doi.org/10.56553/POPETS-2023-0090 https://doi.org/10.56553/POPETS-2023-0090
5. Brüggemann, A., Hundt, R., Schneider, T., Suresh, A., Yalame, H.: Flute: fast and secure lookup table evaluations. In: Proceedings of IEEE S&P, pp. 515–533. IEEE (2023)
6. Burrus, C.S., Fox, J.W., Sitton, G.A., Treitel, S.: Horner's method for evaluating and deflating polynomials. DSP Software Notes, Rice University (2003)
7. Catrina, O.: Evaluation of floating-point arithmetic protocols based on Shamir secret sharing. In: E-Business and Telecommunications: 16th International Conference, ICETE 2019, Prague, Czech Republic, 26–28 July 2019, Revised Selected Papers 16, pp. 108–131. Springer (2020)
8. Catrina, O.: Performance analysis of secure floating-point sums and dot products. In: 2020 13th International Conference on Communications (COMM), pp. 465–470. IEEE (2020)
9. Catrina, O.: Complexity and performance of secure floating-point polynomial evaluation protocols. In: Computer Security–ESORICS 2021: 26th European Symposium on Research in Computer Security, Darmstadt, Germany, 4–8 October 2021, Proceedings, Part II 26, pp. 352–369. Springer (2021)
10. Catrina, O., Dragulin, C.: Multiparty computation of fixed-point multiplication and reciprocal. In: 2009 20th International Workshop on Database and Expert Systems Application, pp. 107–111. IEEE (2009)
11. Catrina, O., Saxena, A.: Secure computation with fixed-point numbers. In: Financial Cryptography and Data Security: 14th International Conference, FC 2010, Tenerife, Canary Islands, 25–28 January 2010, Revised Selected Papers 14, pp. 35–50. Springer (2010)

12. Cody, W.J.: Software Manual for the Elementary Functions. Prentice-Hall Series in Computational Mathematics. Prentice-Hall, Inc. (1980)
13. Demmler, D., Dessouky, G., Koushanfar, F., Sadeghi, A.R., Schneider, T., Zeitouni, S.: Automated synthesis of optimized circuits for secure computation. In: Proceedings of ACM CCS, pp. 1504–1517. Association for Computing Machinery (2015). https://doi.org/10.1145/2810103.2813678
14. Dimitrov, V., Kerik, L., Krips, T., Randmets, J., Willemson, J.: Alternative implementations of secure real numbers. In: Proceedings of the 2016 ACM SIGSAC Conference on Computer and Communications Security, pp. 553–564 (2016)
15. Edelman, A.: The mathematics of the pentium division bug. SIAM Rev. **39**(1), 54–67 (1997)
16. Evans, D., Kolesnikov, V., Rosulek, M., et al.: A pragmatic introduction to secure multi-party computation. Found. Trends® Priv. Secur. **2**(2-3), 70–246 (2018)
17. Fouque, P.A., Stern, J., Wackers, G.J.: Cryptocomputing with rationals. In: International Conference on Financial Cryptography, pp. 136–146. Springer (2002)
18. Franz, M., Deiseroth, B., Hamacher, K., Jha, S., Katzenbeisser, S., Schröder, H.: Secure computations on non-integer values. In: 2010 IEEE International Workshop on Information Forensics and Security, pp. 1–6. IEEE (2010)
19. Franz, M., Katzenbeisser, S.: Processing encrypted floating point signals. In: Proceedings of the Thirteenth ACM Multimedia Workshop on Multimedia and Security, pp. 103–108 (2011)
20. Goldreich, O., Micali, S., Wigderson, A.: How to play any mental game, or a completeness theorem for protocols with honest majority. In: Providing Sound Foundations for Cryptography: On the Work of Shafi Goldwasser and Silvio Micali, pp. 307–328 (2019)
21. Granlund, T., Sjödin, G., Stallman, R., Riesel, H., Beuning, B., et al.: The gnu multiple precision arithmetic library (2020). https://gmplib.org/
22. Hanrot, G., Zimmermann, P., Lefèvre, V., Pélissier, P., Théveny, P., et al.: The gnu MPFR library (2023). https://www.mpfr.org/
23. Hazay, C., Lindell, Y.: Efficient Secure Two-Party Protocols: Techniques and constructions. Springer, Heidelberg (2010)
24. Hendrycks, D., Gimpel, K.: Gaussian error linear units (GELUs). arXiv preprint arXiv:1606.08415 (2016)
25. Intel Corporation: Intel® oneAPI math kernel library (oneMKL) (2024). https://www.intel.com/content/www/us/en/developer/tools/oneapi/onemkl.html
26. Kamm, L., Willemson, J.: Secure floating point arithmetic and private satellite collision analysis. Int. J. Inf. Secur. **14**(6), 531–548 (2015)
27. Karnin, E., Greene, J., Hellman, M.: On secret sharing systems. IEEE Trans. Inf. Theory **29**(1), 35–41 (1983). https://doi.org/10.1109/TIT.1983.1056621
28. Kerik, L., Laud, P., Randmets, J.: Optimizing MPC for robust and scalable integer and floating-point arithmetic. In: Financial Cryptography and Data Security: FC 2016 International Workshops, BITCOIN, VOTING, and WAHC, Christ Church, Barbados, 26 February 2016, Revised Selected Papers 20, pp. 271–287. Springer (2016)
29. Le Lann, G.: An analysis of the Ariane 5 flight 501 failure-a system engineering perspective. In: Proceedings International Conference and Workshop on Engineering of Computer-Based Systems, pp. 339–346. IEEE (1997)
30. Lim, J.P., Nagarakatte, S.: High performance correctly rounded math libraries for 32-bit floating point representations. In: Proceedings of PLDI, pp. 359–374 (2021)
31. McKinley, S., Levine, M.: Cubic spline interpolation. Coll. Redwoods **45**(1), 1049–1060 (1998)

32. Rathee, D., Bhattacharya, A., Gupta, D., Sharma, R., Song, D.: Secure floating-point training. In: 32nd USENIX Security Symposium (USENIX Security 23), pp. 6329–6346 (2023)
33. Rathee, D., Bhattacharya, A., Sharma, R., Gupta, D., Chandran, N., Rastogi, A.: SecFloat: accurate floating-point meets secure 2-party computation. In: Proceedings of IEEE S&P, pp. 576–595 (2022)
34. Rathee, D., et al.: SIRNN: a math library for secure RNN inference. In: Proceedings of IEEE S&P, pp. 1003–1020. IEEE (2021)
35. Rathee, D., et al.: CryptFlow2: practical 2-party secure inference. In: Proceedings of the 2020 ACM SIGSAC Conference on Computer and Communications Security, pp. 325–342 (2020)
36. Rathee, D., Rathee, M., Kumar, N., et al.: Ezpc (2022). https://github.com/mpc-msri/EzPC
37. Sibidanov, A., Zimmermann, P., Glondu, S.: The CORE-MATH project. In: 2022 IEEE 29th Symposium on Computer Arithmetic (ARITH), pp. 26–34. IEEE (2022)
38. Sinnott, R.W.: Virtues of the haversine. Sky Telesc. **68**(2), 158 (1984)
39. Smith, J.R.: Introduction to Geodesy: The History and Concepts of Modern Geodesy, vol. 1. Wiley, Hoboken (1997)
40. Vaswani, A., et al.: Attention is all you need. In: Advances in Neural Information Processing Systems, vol. 30 (2017)
41. Šeděnka, J., Gasti, P.: Privacy-preserving distance computation and proximity testing on earth, done right. In: Proceedings of ACM CCS, ASIA CCS 2014, pp. 99–110. Association for Computing Machinery (2014). https://doi.org/10.1145/2590296.2590307
42. Yao, A.C.C.: How to generate and exchange secrets. In: 27th Annual Symposium on Foundations of Computer Science (SFCS 1986), pp. 162–167 (1986). https://doi.org/10.1109/SFCS.1986.25

Consecutive Adaptor Signature Scheme: From Two-Party to N-Party Settings

Kaisei Kajita[1]([⊠]), Go Ohtake[1], and Tsuyoshi Takagi[2]

[1] Japan Broadcasting Corporation, Setagaya-ku, Japan
kajita.k-bu@nhk.or.jp
[2] The University of Tokyo, Bunkyo-ku, Japan

Abstract. Adaptor signatures have attracted attention as a tool to address scalability and interoperability issues in blockchain applications. Adaptor signatures can be constructed by extending common digital signature schemes that both authenticate a message and disclose a secret witness to a specific party. In Asiacrypt 2021, Aumayr et al. formulated the two-party adaptor signature as an independent cryptographic primitive. In this study, we extend their adaptor signature formulation to N parties, present its generic construction, and define the security to be satisfied. Then, we present a concrete construction based on Schnorr signatures and discuss the security properties.

1 Introduction

1.1 Background

An adaptor signature was first proposed by Andrew Poelstra et al. [30,31] in 2017 as the concept of Scriptless Script and later formulated as an independent cryptographic primitive by Aumayr et al. [2]. Adaptor signatures have recently attracted attention as a tool to address issues such as scalability and interoperability for blockchain applications. An adaptor signature scheme is constituted as an extension of a digital signature scheme through a dialogue between two parties: a signer and a secretary. First, the signer generates a pre-signature based on a certain mathematical condition. The conditions are defined by a computationally hard algebraic relation between the public information and the secret information, such as the discrete logarithm problem or the preimage of a hash function. Next, the secretary, who possesses a secret witness for the above conditions, fits the pre-signature to create a valid adaptor signature. Once the valid adaptor signature is completed, the secret information is disclosed to the signer. A valid adaptor signature is a digital signature that is verifiable in the original signature scheme. Particularly in blockchain applications, a miner will not know that an ordinary signature is the output of an adaptor signature scheme and will simply verify it. At the same time, the two parties involved in generating the adaptor signature can embed conditions that are not restricted to the blockchain's scripting language. Thus, adaptor signatures can be used in off-chain payment instruments such as a payment channel network (PCN) [2,14],

J. K. Liu et al. (Eds.): ProvSec 2024, LNCS 14903, pp. 23–42, 2025.
https://doi.org/10.1007/978-981-96-0954-3_2

which is an off-chain payment method, and an atomic swap [17,30], which is a P2P transaction between different cryptocurrencies. Moreover, they can be used in scriptless blockchain applications. A PCN is a second-layer technology created to accelerate the transaction processing of cryptocurrencies [16].

To date, adaptor signatures have mainly been considered for applications like PCNs and atomic swaps, which are implemented via a dialogue between two parties. Accordingly, all existing studies on adaptor signature schemes have been based on this two-party case.

1.2   Related Works

As the adaptor signature was originally formulated as an independent cryptographic primitive by Aumayr et al., here, we mainly introduce related works that sought to analyze and improve adaptor signatures as cryptographic primitives.

Erwig et al. [12] proposed method for a general conversion method from IDs to adaptor signatures, following the work of Aumayr et al. Indeed, since that work, various adaptor signature schemes have been proposed as cryptographic primitives [14,23,38,44]. The adaptor signature constructed by Aumayr et al. was based on Schnorr signature [33]. Lattice-based [14], isogeny-based [38], and code-based [23] signatures have been proposed as schemes that satisfy quantum security resistance. Along this line, Esgin et al. constructed a lattice-based adaptor signature (LAS) based on the Dilithium signature [11]. Tairi et al. constructed a isogeny-based adaptor signature by applying the Fiat-Shamir transformation [15] from the CSI-FiSh variant to the Schnorr type identification protocol [33,38]. An optimized version (O-IAS) was then proposed by [37]. Klamti et al. proposed a code-based adaptor signature [23]. They used algebraic relations that were defined from the syndrome decoding problem to construct an adaptor signature based on Debris-Alazard et al.'s sign-based signature scheme of hash-and-sign [9].

On the security side, Erwig et al. [13] proposed an adaptor signature with re-randomizable keys to securely store secret information via algebraic relations with respect to the signing key. Dai et al. [8] strengthened the existing security definition, added a new security definition, and improved the security model of adaptor signatures. As for efficiency, Tu et al. [41] constructed an efficient adaptor signature based on ECDSA by generating zero-knowledge proofs in the pre-signature stage in a batch and offline.

As noted above, atomic swaps [10,18,19,41] and payment channel networks (PCNs) [3,4,25–29,36,37,39,42] use adaptor signatures and have been actively studied in terms of various practical aspects. Both applications rely on technology to exchange secret information for signatures, which is precisely the functionality provided by adaptor signatures. Note again that adaptor signatures were originally designed to solve scalability and interoperability issues in blockchain applications, and they have various other applications [7,24,34]. Liu et al. [24] proposed a data sharing protocol on a blockchain, which is based on adaptor signatures and zero-knowledge proofs.

Regarding the functionality of adaptor signatures, Sui et al. [35] proposed a two-party, consecutive linkable ring adaptor signature (2P-CLRAS) to construct a PCN compatible with Monero [1], a privacy-preserving cryptocurrency. They constructed 2P-CLRAS from a sequential adaptor signature (CAS) by using a new cryptographic primitive called a Verifiable Consecutive One-Way Function (VCOF). This led to the proposal of MoNet, a two-way, Monero-compatible PCN. Qin et al. [32] proposed a blind adaptor signature (BAS) based on blind signature schemes to construct a new privacy-preserving payment channel hub (PCH), BlindHub, and a privacy-preserving bidirectional PCN protocol, BlindChannel, in a PCH that supports off-chain payments between senders and receivers via an intermediary (called a tumbler). Hu and Chen [20] also proposed an anonymous, fair transaction scheme for electronic resources by using a new BAS technology. To reduce the PCN's computational complexity, Zhou et al. [43] proposed a new cryptographic primitive called a verifiable timed adaptor signature. Thvagarajan et al. [40] proposed a scheme that is similar to the adaptor signature, called a lockable signature, which does not require computationally difficult algebraic relations. Lockable signatures provide an effective signature scheme for constructing PCNs and can be seen as a special case of adaptor signatures. Finally, Ji et al. [21] proposed multi-adaptor signatures and threshold adaptor signatures based on Schnorr signature and Dilithium schemes, respectively.

1.3   Our Contribution

As explained above, while adaptor signatures are an important key technology for addressing issues such as the scalability of cryptocurrencies, simply repeating the current two-party setting is insufficient for ensuring security when consecutively generalizing adaptor signatures to multiple parties (i.e., an N-party protocol). In this paper, we introduce a novel concept, *the N-party consecutive adaptor signature* (or simply *N-party adaptor signature*), to address this problem. We first propose a formal security model for three-party adaptor signatures and demonstrate a specific construction example using Schnorr signatures. Then, we rigorously establish that the proposed scheme precisely satisfies the defined security model. Following the discussion on three-party scenarios, we delve into the security and concrete constructions for N-party scenarios. The security proofs are demonstrated inductively by leveraging the established security among three parties[1].

Technical Contributions. The paper's technical contributions include the generalization of constructing pre-signatures for pre-signatures. This allows the formation of concatenated adaptor signatures from two- to N-party settings. The mechanism for creating this "pre-signature of a pre-signature" is enabled by the additivity that appears in the syntax of adaptor signatures. We call our algorithm for this "pre-signature of a pre-signature" the PreAdapt algorithm. Furthermore,

---

[1] Due to page limitations, please refer to [22] for the full security proofs.

we provide rigorous security proofs. It is evident that if security holds for three-party adaptor signatures, then it easily extends to N-party settings. However, the security proof for three-party settings cannot be trivially derived from that of two-party settings, because of differences not only in the form of pre-signatures but also the addition of a pre-adaptation oracle.

Distinction from the 2-Party Setting. We explain the difference between our N-party adaptor signature and N iterations of a 2-party adaptor signature. A simple 2-party iteration is not sufficient for the security to be satisfied. For example, consider the scenario of an adaptor signature between Alice, Bob, and Charlie. After Alice and Bob execute the adaptor signature protocol, Bob transforms Alice's pre-signature and then creates another pre-signature for Charlie. If the two-party setup is repeated, then Alice and Bob, and Bob and Charlie, each independently generate adaptor signatures interactively. However, in this case Bob communicates with Charlie using messages from Alice after his interaction with Alice. If an attacker were to eavesdrop on the communication between Bob and Charlie, he would be able to observe Alice's information. Therefore, in order to create consecutive adaptor signatures between multiple parties, it is necessary to satisfy a higher security level than applying 2-party to each hop, i.e., being secure under an attacker who can observe the input and output of all previous users.

1.4   Application

In this section, we will consider an application example of the proposed N-party adaptor signature. As explained above, adaptor signatures are primarily used for applications that improve the efficiency of cryptocurrency transactions such as PCN and Atomic Swap. However, the functionality of adaptor signatures is not limited to a specific field, allowing for applications beyond cryptocurrency. For example, Liu et al. [24] developed a secure data sharing protocol using adaptor signatures. We focus on the pre-signature compatibility of the adaptor signature and consider the application of the proposed N-party adaptor signature to *a content provenance management system.* A content provenance management system is a technology that is attracting attention as a practical countermeasure to the problem of disinformation and misinformation caused by deep fakes, etc., which have become one of the social problems. The system creates a content provenance, including all of the histories in the supply chain of the content (e.g., shooting, editing, publishing), and attaches it to the content or records it on a blockchain. The content provenance can be verified by anyone, so that they can decide whether or not to trust the content they try to watch. C2PA (Coalition for Content Provenance and Authenticity) [5] is an international standardization body that standardizes technical specification [6] for the above system. In the C2PA specification, digital signatures are used to verify the content and its provenance information. However, the current C2PA specification does not take into account the relationship between entities. For instance, in the content creation field, it's common for a major production company (let's call it Company A) to subcontract certain tasks to another company (let's call it Company B), such as shooting or producing specific parts of the content of Company A. In such a case, using a standard digital signature compliant with C2PA, such as ECDSA, may record the provenance of the works as the sign of Company B, even if Company A has an originality and a copyright. Here, it is common for the contract to conceal the name of the subcontractor, Compny B, or not require it to be revealed. This problem can be solved by using adaptor signatures. Once Company B sends pre-signed adaptor signatures along with the content to Company A by employing adaptor signatures, Company A can then adapt Company B's pre-signed adaptor signatures into regular digital signatures. Based on the contract between Company A and B, Company A can maintain the provenance of the content as its own work while still allowing Company B to receive consideration for the work. Moreover, in the content creation field, subcontracting often occurs hierarchically, with secondary and tertiary subcontracting being common. Therefore, by utilizing our proposed N-party adaptor signatures, it's possible to construct a content provenance management system in the supply chain among any number of entities without restrictions, while meeting the requirements mentioned above.

2   Preliminary for Adaptor Signatures

A (two-party) adaptor signature scheme is essentially a two-step signing algorithm that is bound to a secret: a partial signature is first generated such that it can be completed only by a party knowing a certain secret, with the complete signature revealing that secret. More precisely, we define the adaptor signature scheme with respect to a digital signature scheme Σ and a hard relation R. For any statement $Y \in L_R$, a signer holding a secret key can produce a pre-signature w.r.t. Y on any message m. Such a pre-signature can be adapted into a valid signature on m if and only if the adaptor knows a witness for Y. Moreover, it must be possible to extract a witness for Y given the pre-signature and the adapted signature.

The (two-party) adaptor signature scheme AS is constructed using a digital signature scheme $\Sigma = (\mathsf{KGen}, \mathsf{Sign}, \mathsf{Vrfy})$ and a computationally intractable algebraic relation $(Y, y) \subseteq R$. Let $(Y, y) \leftarrow \mathsf{GenR}(\lambda)$ be a PPT algorithm that takes the security parameter λ as input and generates a pair comprising public and secret information related by an algebraic relation. For instance, when using the discrete logarithm problem, let $\mathbb{G} = \langle g \rangle$ be a cyclic group of prime order q, as defined in the previous section. In this case, the computationally intractable algebraic relation R_g is defined as $R_g = \{(Y, y) | Y = g^y\} \subseteq \mathbb{G} \times \mathbb{Z}_q$.

We use a signature scheme that satisfies SUF-CMA (strong existential unforgeability under chosen-message attack). SUF-CMA security guarantees that a PPT attacker with access to the signature oracle by entering his public key pk cannot generate a new valid signature for any message M. The formal definition is in Appendix B. Due to page space limitations, the syntax and security of the two-party adapter signature scheme should be referred to in [2].

3   Three-Party Adaptor Signatures

In this section, we describe a three-party adaptor signature scheme to prepare for our later N-party construction. The original adaptor signature scheme initially involves two entities, the secretary and the signer. However, in the proposed three-party scheme presented here, we consider three entities: U_1 as the secretary, U_2 as the main signer, and U_3 as a sub-signer. In this configuration, the sub-signer U_3 generates a pre-signature; the main signer U_2 generates another pre-signature for the same message, based on the pre-signature generated by U_3; and finally, the secretary U_1 performs adaptation to transform the pre-signature into a (normal) signature. At this point, it is evident that the adapted (normal) signature does not reveal the presence of U_2 or U_3, thus providing anonymity for the signers. We now define two primitives that serve as the foundation for constructing the adaptor signature. The first primitive is a digital signature scheme $\Sigma = (\mathsf{KeyGen}, \mathsf{Sign}, \mathsf{Vrfy})$, where U_2 and U_3 possess pairs of public and private keys, denoted as $(\mathsf{pk}_2, \mathsf{sk}_2)$ and $(\mathsf{pk}_3, \mathsf{sk}_3)$, respectively. The signatures generated using these keys are represented as $\sigma_2 \leftarrow \mathsf{Sign}(\mathsf{pk}_2, \mathsf{sk}_2, M)$ and $\sigma_3 \leftarrow (\mathsf{pk}_3, \mathsf{sk}_3, M)$. Then, the second primitive is a hard relation R with statement/witness pairs (Y, y) (as defined in Appendix B).

Syntax of Three-Party Adaptor Signatures. A three-party adaptor signature scheme w.r.t. a hard relation R and a signature scheme $\Sigma = (\mathsf{Gen}, \mathsf{Sign}, \mathsf{Vrfy})$ comprises six algorithms, $\Xi_{R,\Sigma}=(\mathsf{PreSign}, \mathsf{PreVrfy}, \mathsf{PreAdapt}, \mathsf{Adapt}, \mathsf{PreExt}, \mathsf{Ext})$, with syntax defined as follows. $\hat{\sigma}_3 \leftarrow \mathsf{PreSign}((\mathsf{pk}_3, \mathsf{sk}_3), Y_2, M)$ is a PPT algorithm that takes as input a public key pk_3, a secret key sk_3, a statement $Y_2 \in R$, and a message $M \in \{0,1\}^*$, and outputs a pre-signature $\hat{\sigma}_3$. $b = \mathsf{PreVrfy}(Y_1, (\mathsf{pk}_2, \mathsf{pk}_3), (\hat{\sigma}_2), \hat{\sigma}_3), M)$ is a DPT algorithm that takes as input a statement $Y_1 \in R$, public keys $(\mathsf{pk}_2, \mathsf{pk}_3)$, pre-signatures $(\hat{\sigma}_2, \hat{\sigma}_3)$, and a message M, and outputs a bit b. $\mathsf{PreAdapt}((Y_2, y_2), Y_1, \mathsf{pk}_3, (\mathsf{sk}_2, \mathsf{pk}_2), \hat{\sigma}_3, M)$ is a PPT algorithm[2] that takes as input a pair of hard relations, (Y_2, y_2), a statement Y_1, a public key pk_3, a pair of keys $(\mathsf{sk}_2, \mathsf{pk}_2)$, a pre-signature $\hat{\sigma}_3$, and a message M; then, it outputs a pre-signature $\hat{\sigma}_2$. $\mathsf{Adapt}((Y_1, y_1), \mathsf{pk}_2, \hat{\sigma}_2, M)$ is a DPT algorithm that takes as input a pair of a statement and a witness, (Y_1, y_1), a public key pk_2, a pre-signature $(\hat{\sigma})$, and a message M. $\mathsf{PreExt}(Y_2, \hat{\sigma}_3, \hat{\sigma}_2)$ is a DPT algorithm that takes as input a public statement Y_2 and pre-signatures $(\hat{\sigma}_3, \hat{\sigma}_2)$, and outputs either a witness y_2' such that $(Y_2, y_2') \in R$, or $\bot$. $\mathsf{Ext}(Y_1, \hat{\sigma}_2, \sigma_2)$ is a DPT algorithm that takes as input a public statement Y_1, a pre-signature $\hat{\sigma}_2$, and an (original) signature σ_2, and outputs either a witness y_1' such that $(Y_1, y_1') \in R$, or $\bot$.

---

[2] The $\mathsf{PreAdapt}$ algorithm simultaneously performs internal processing of the Adapt and $\mathsf{PreSign}$ algorithms. While it includes elements of a DPT algorithm because of this simultaneous processing, the overall procedure involves probabilistic steps when generating pre-signatures. Therefore, it is defined as a PPT algorithm.

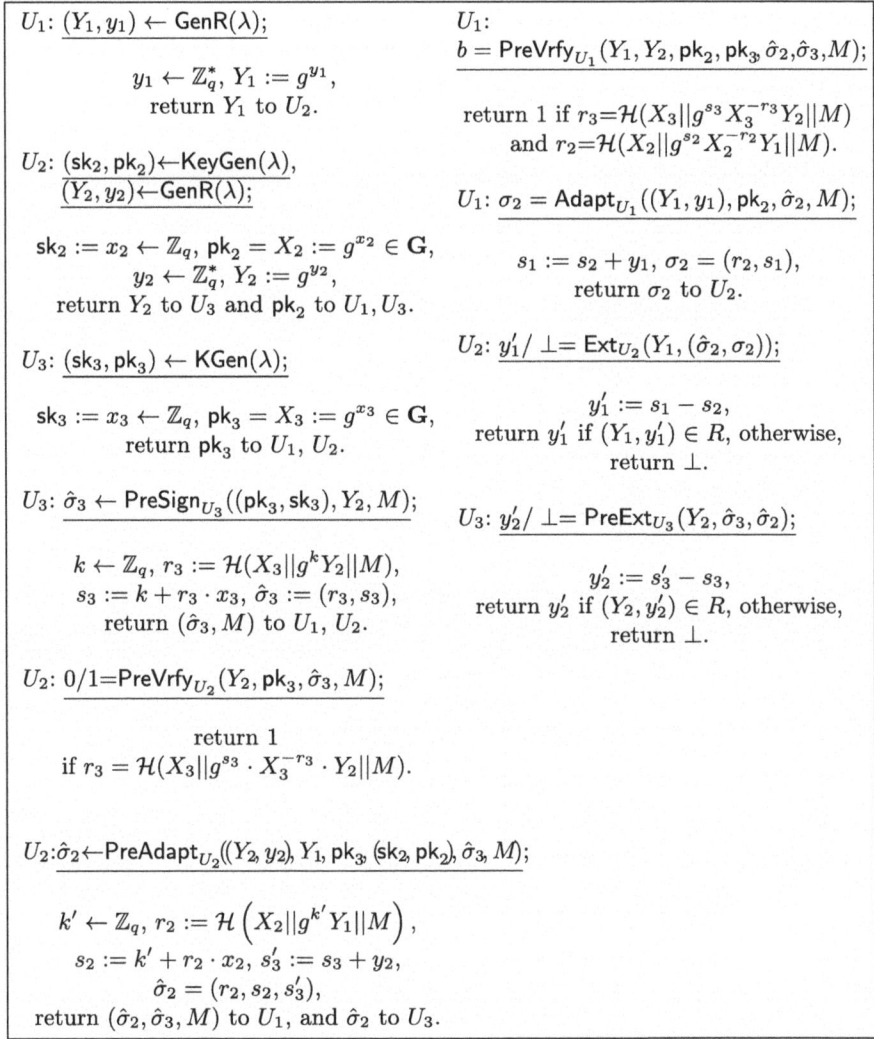

U_1: $(Y_1, y_1) \leftarrow \mathsf{GenR}(\lambda)$;

$$y_1 \leftarrow \mathbb{Z}_q^*, \ Y_1 := g^{y_1},$$
$$\text{return } Y_1 \text{ to } U_2.$$

U_2: $(\mathsf{sk}_2, \mathsf{pk}_2) \leftarrow \mathsf{KeyGen}(\lambda)$,
$(Y_2, y_2) \leftarrow \mathsf{GenR}(\lambda)$;

$$\mathsf{sk}_2 := x_2 \leftarrow \mathbb{Z}_q, \ \mathsf{pk}_2 = X_2 := g^{x_2} \in \mathbf{G},$$
$$y_2 \leftarrow \mathbb{Z}_q^*, \ Y_2 := g^{y_2},$$
$$\text{return } Y_2 \text{ to } U_3 \text{ and } \mathsf{pk}_2 \text{ to } U_1, U_3.$$

U_3: $(\mathsf{sk}_3, \mathsf{pk}_3) \leftarrow \mathsf{KGen}(\lambda)$;

$$\mathsf{sk}_3 := x_3 \leftarrow \mathbb{Z}_q, \ \mathsf{pk}_3 = X_3 := g^{x_3} \in \mathbf{G},$$
$$\text{return } \mathsf{pk}_3 \text{ to } U_1, U_2.$$

U_3: $\hat{\sigma}_3 \leftarrow \mathsf{PreSign}_{U_3}((\mathsf{pk}_3, \mathsf{sk}_3), Y_2, M)$;

$$k \leftarrow \mathbb{Z}_q, \ r_3 := \mathcal{H}(X_3 \| g^k Y_2 \| M),$$
$$s_3 := k + r_3 \cdot x_3, \ \hat{\sigma}_3 := (r_3, s_3),$$
$$\text{return } (\hat{\sigma}_3, M) \text{ to } U_1, U_2.$$

U_2: $0/1 = \mathsf{PreVrfy}_{U_2}(Y_2, \mathsf{pk}_3, \hat{\sigma}_3, M)$;

$$\text{return } 1$$
$$\text{if } r_3 = \mathcal{H}(X_3 \| g^{s_3} \cdot X_3^{-r_3} \cdot Y_2 \| M).$$

U_2: $\hat{\sigma}_2 \leftarrow \mathsf{PreAdapt}_{U_2}((Y_2, y_2), Y_1, \mathsf{pk}_3, (\mathsf{sk}_2, \mathsf{pk}_2), \hat{\sigma}_3, M)$;

$$k' \leftarrow \mathbb{Z}_q, \ r_2 := \mathcal{H}\left(X_2 \| g^{k'} Y_1 \| M\right),$$
$$s_2 := k' + r_2 \cdot x_2, \ s_3' := s_3 + y_2,$$
$$\hat{\sigma}_2 = (r_2, s_2, s_3'),$$
$$\text{return } (\hat{\sigma}_2, \hat{\sigma}_3, M) \text{ to } U_1, \text{ and } \hat{\sigma}_2 \text{ to } U_3.$$

U_1:
$b = \mathsf{PreVrfy}_{U_1}(Y_1, Y_2, \mathsf{pk}_2, \mathsf{pk}_3, \hat{\sigma}_2, \hat{\sigma}_3, M)$;

$$\text{return } 1 \text{ if } r_3 = \mathcal{H}(X_3 \| g^{s_3} X_3^{-r_3} Y_2 \| M)$$
$$\text{and } r_2 = \mathcal{H}(X_2 \| g^{s_2} X_2^{-r_2} Y_1 \| M).$$

U_1: $\sigma_2 = \mathsf{Adapt}_{U_1}((Y_1, y_1), \mathsf{pk}_2, \hat{\sigma}_2, M)$;

$$s_1 := s_2 + y_1, \ \sigma_2 = (r_2, s_1),$$
$$\text{return } \sigma_2 \text{ to } U_2.$$

U_2: $y_1' / \perp = \mathsf{Ext}_{U_2}(Y_1, (\hat{\sigma}_2, \sigma_2))$;

$$y_1' := s_1 - s_2,$$
$$\text{return } y_1' \text{ if } (Y_1, y_1') \in R, \text{ otherwise,}$$
$$\text{return } \perp.$$

U_3: $y_2' / \perp = \mathsf{PreExt}_{U_3}(Y_2, \hat{\sigma}_3, \hat{\sigma}_2)$;

$$y_2' := s_3' - s_3,$$
$$\text{return } y_2' \text{ if } (Y_2, y_2') \in R, \text{ otherwise,}$$
$$\text{return } \perp.$$

Fig. 1. Concrete construction: Schnorr-based three-party adaptor signatures.

3.1 Concrete Construction of Three-Party Adaptor Signatures

In this section, we extend the two-party adaptor signature defined in Sect. 2 to describe a specific instantiation of the Schnorr-based three-party adaptor signature scheme outlined in Fig. 1. For Schnorr signatures Σ_{Sch} and a hard relation $R_g := \{(Y, y) | Y = g^y\}$, we show the concrete construction of an N-party adaptor signature scheme $\mathsf{N\text{-}AS}_{R_g, \Sigma_{\mathsf{Sch}}}$ for the case of $N = 3$. Here, $\mathcal{H}(\cdot)$ denotes any cryptographic hash function, and $\mathbb{Z}_q^*$ denotes the set of all integers from 1 to q, excluding 0. First, we denote the three entities in this scheme as U_1, U_2, and U_3. In the construction of the three-party adaptor signature, an algorithm's subscript (e.g., $\mathsf{PreSign}_{U_3}$) corresponds to the entity executing the algorithm, and a subscript in an argument (e.g., Y_2 in $\mathsf{PreSign}_{U_3}$ or 3 in $\hat{\sigma}_3$) corresponds to the entity that initially owns (or generates) that value.

Table 1. Experiments $\text{3-aSigForge}_{\mathcal{A}_1, \text{3-AS}_{R,\Sigma}}$ and $\text{3-aSigForge}_{\mathcal{A}_2, \text{3-AS}_{R,\Sigma}}$

$\text{3-aSigForge}_{\mathcal{A}_1, \text{3-AS}_{R,\Sigma}}(\lambda)$

$1 : Q := \emptyset$

$2 : (\mathsf{pk}_2, \mathsf{sk}_2)(\mathsf{pk}_3, \mathsf{sk}_3) \leftarrow \mathsf{Gen}(1^\lambda)$

$3 : (Y_1, y_1)(Y_2, y_2) \leftarrow \mathsf{GenR}(1^\lambda)$

$4 : M^* \leftarrow \mathcal{A}_1^{\mathcal{O}_S(\cdot), \mathcal{O}_{pS}(\cdot), \mathcal{O}_{pA}(\cdot)}(\mathsf{pk}_2, \mathsf{pk}_3)$

$5 : \sigma_3^* \leftarrow \mathsf{PreSign}((\mathsf{pk}_3, \mathsf{sk}_3), Y_2, M^*)$

$6 : \sigma_2^* \leftarrow \mathsf{PreAdapt}_{U_2}((Y_2, y_2), Y_1, \mathsf{pk}_3, (\mathsf{sk}_2, \mathsf{pk}_2), \sigma_3, M^*)$

$7 : \sigma_1 \leftarrow \mathcal{A}_1^{\mathcal{O}_S(\cdot), \mathcal{O}_{pS}(\cdot), \mathcal{O}_{pA}(\cdot)}(\sigma_2^*, \sigma_3^*, Y_1, Y_2)$

$8 : \mathbf{return}\ (M^* \notin Q \wedge \mathsf{Vrfy}(\mathsf{pk}_3, \sigma_2^*, M^*))$

$\text{3-aSigForge}_{\mathcal{A}_2, \text{3-AS}_{R,\Sigma}}(\lambda)$

$1 : Q := \emptyset$

$2 : (\mathsf{pk}_3, \mathsf{sk}_3) \leftarrow \mathsf{Gen}(1^\lambda)$

$3 : (Y_2, y_2) \leftarrow \mathsf{GenR}(1^\lambda)$

$4 : M^* \leftarrow \mathcal{A}_2^{\mathcal{O}_S(\cdot), \mathcal{O}_{pS}(\cdot, \cdot)}(\mathsf{pk}_3)$

$5 : \sigma_3^* \leftarrow \mathsf{PreSign}_{U_3}((\mathsf{pk}_3, \mathsf{sk}_3), Y_3, M^*)$

$6 : \sigma_{n-1} \leftarrow \mathcal{A}_2^{\mathcal{O}_S(\cdot), \mathcal{O}_{pS}(\cdot, \cdot)}(\sigma_3^*, Y_2)$

$7 : \mathbf{return}\ (M^* \notin Q \wedge \mathsf{Vrfy}(\mathsf{pk}_3, \sigma_2, M^*))$

$\mathcal{O}_{pA}(M, (Y_1, Y_2), \sigma_3)$

$1 : \sigma_2 \leftarrow \mathsf{PreAdapt}_{U_2}((Y_2, y_2), Y_1, \mathsf{pk}_3, (\mathsf{sk}_2, \mathsf{pk}_2), \sigma_3, M)$

$2 : Q := Q \cup \{M\}$

$3 : \mathbf{return}\ \sigma_2$

$\mathcal{O}_S^{\mathcal{A}_i}(M)$	$\mathcal{O}_{pS}(M, Y_2)$
$1 : \sigma_i \leftarrow \mathsf{Sign}(\mathsf{sk}_i, M)$	$1 : \sigma_3 \leftarrow \mathsf{PreSign}(\mathsf{sk}_3, Y_2, M)$
$2 : Q := Q \cup \{M\}$	$2 : Q := Q \cup \{M\}$
$3 : \mathbf{return}\ \sigma_i$	$3 : \mathbf{return}\ \sigma_3$

3.2   Security Definitions for Three-Party Adaptor Signature Scheme

We now define the security definitions for three-party adaptor signatures. In total, four security requirements must be satisfied, the most important and core of which is unforgeability. Here, we focus on unforgeability and show the lemma for that. Existential unforgeability under chosen message attack in the context of three-party adaptor signatures (3-aEUF-CMA) is an extension of the unforgeability for two-party adaptor signatures to the three-party setting. In the three-party case, we need to consider unforgeability for two separate dialogues involving all three entities. First, for unforgeability between entities U_3 and U_2, U_3 generates pre-signatures via the PreSign algorithm, and the attacker attempts to forge signatures via the signature/pre-signature oracle. Second, for unforgeability between U_1 and U_2, U_2 generates pre-signatures via the PreAdapt algorithm, and the attacker tries to forge signatures via the signature/pre-adaptation oracle. We define 3-aEUF-CMA as follows:

Definition 1 (Existential unforgeability for three parties). *A three-party adaptor signature scheme* 3-AS$_{R,\Sigma}$ *is 3-aEUF-CMA secure if for any PPT adversary* $\mathcal{A} = (\mathcal{A}_1, \mathcal{A}_2)$, *there exists a negligible function* negl(λ) *such that*

$$\Pr[\text{3-aSigForge}_{\mathcal{A}_1, \text{3-AS}_{R,\Sigma}}(\lambda) = 1] + \Pr[\text{3-aSigForge}_{\mathcal{A}_2, \text{3-AS}_{R,\Sigma}}(\lambda) = 1] \leq \text{negl}(\lambda)$$

where the experiments 3-aSigForge$_{\mathcal{A}_1, \text{3-AS}_{R,\Sigma}}$ *and* 3-aSigForge$_{\mathcal{A}_2, \text{3-AS}_{R,\Sigma}}$ *are as defined in the figure Table 1.*

3.3 Proof of Unforgeability for Three-Party Adaptor Signature Scheme

We show the security of three-way adaptor signatures. An adaptor signature is secure if the following four conditions hold: pre-signature correctness, pre-signature adaptability, existential unforgeability, and witness extractability. Hence, the Theorem 1 is proved by lemmas showing these four. Among them, pre-signature correctness and pre-signature adaptability can be verified by computation, and witness extractability can be verified by a small change from existential unforgeability. Therefore, we mainly focus on Lemma 1 for the existential unforgeability, and the other proofs are omitted here due to page limitations. For the full proofs, please refer to [22].

Theorem 1. *If Schnorr signature scheme* Σ_{Sch} *is SUF-CMA-secure, and* R_g *is a computationally hard algebraic relation, then* 3-AS$_{R_g, \Sigma_{Sch}}$ *in Fig. 1 is secure in the ROM.*

Lemma 1 (3-aEUF-CMA security). *Assuming that Schnorr digital signature scheme* Σ_{Sch} *is SUF-CMA secure and* R_g *is a hard relation, the three-party adaptor signature scheme* 3-AS$_{R_g, \Sigma_{Sch}}$, *as defined in Fig. 1, is 3-aEUF-CMA secure.*

Before formally proving this lemma, we discuss the main idea behind the proof intuitively. The goal is to reduce the forgery resistance of the three-party adaptor signature scheme to the strong resistance of the standard Schnorr scheme. In the three-party scheme, we have two cases to consider: an adversary $\mathcal{A}_1$ between U_1 and U_2, or an adversary $\mathcal{A}_2$ between U_2 and U_3, where the adversary wins the 3-aSigForge experiment as a PPT attacker. We design an adversary (or simulator) S for this purpose. First, case (i) can be proved by using almost the same game-hopping steps as in the proof of the two-party adaptor signature scheme [Lemma 4 (aSigForge) in [2]], so we skip the proof here. Next, for case (ii), the proof follows a completely different approach from the two-party case. The technical challenge is that A_1 can access not only the interaction between U_1 and U_2 but also the information exchanged between U_2 and U_3 that A_2 had. Specifically, A_2 has access to previous pre-signatures.

Proof of Lemma 1. We consider two cases, (i) and (ii) as explained above, and we perform several game hops in each case to prove Lemma 1. For case (i), we follow a similar procedure to the proof of unforgeability in the original two-party scenario of Lemma 4 in [2]. Then, for case (i), we demonstrate each game hop and reduction loss via a sketch proof.

For case (i), we have the following game definitions for strongSigForge and G_0 to G_4.

Game G_0: The original 3-aEUF-CMA game, 3-aSigForge$_{A_2, \text{AS}_{R,\Sigma}}$.
Game G_1: An abort game for when the adversary forges a pre-signature for the challenge public statement Y^* without knowing the secret witness s^*.
Game G_2: An abort game for when queries to the oracle overlap.
Game G_3: A game where the pre-signature oracle returns a regular signature.
Game G_4: A game where the pre-signature given to the adversary is turned into a regular signature.
Game strongSigForge: A SUF-CMA game for regular signatures.

The reduction loss for the above is as follows, and it can be directly obtained from the original two-party scenario:

$$\Pr[\text{3-aSigForge}_{A_2, \text{3-AS}}(\lambda) = 1]$$
$$= \Pr[G_0 = 1]$$
$$\leq \Pr[G_1 = 1] + v_1(\lambda)$$
$$\leq \Pr[G_2 = 1] + v_1(\lambda) + v_2(\lambda)$$
$$= \Pr[G_3 = 1] + v_1(\lambda) + v_2(\lambda)$$
$$\leq \Pr[G_4 = 1] + v_1(\lambda) + v_2(\lambda)$$
$$= \Pr[\text{strongSigForge}_{S^{A_2}, \text{3-AS}}(\lambda) = 1] + v_1(\lambda) + v_2(\lambda), \tag{1}$$

where v_1 and v_2 are the negligible functions in λ.

Next, for case (ii), we have 3-aSigForge$_{A_2, \text{AS}_{R,\Sigma}}$.

Game $\mathbf{G_0}$: This game corresponds to the original 3-aSigForge, where the adversary A_1 has to produce a valid forgery for a message m of his choice, while having access to a pre-signature oracle $\mathcal{O}_{\text{pS}}$, a signature oracle $\mathcal{O}_{\text{S}}$, and a pre-adaptation oracle $\mathcal{O}_{\text{pA}}$. Since we are in the ROM, the adversary (as well as all of the scheme's algorithms) also has access to a random oracle $\mathcal{H}$. The simulator S wins if $b = 1$ and $M^* \notin Q$.

$$\Pr[\text{3-aSigForge}_{A_2, \text{AS}_{R,\Sigma}}(\lambda) = 1] = \Pr[\mathbf{G_0} = 1]. \tag{2}$$

Game G_1: This game works exactly like G_0 with the following exception. When the adversary outputs a forgery σ_1^*, the game G_1 checks whether completion of the pre-signature $\hat{\sigma}_2$ by using the secret value y_1 yields σ_1^*. If so, the game aborts.

Claim of Game G_1. Let Bad_1 be the event that G_1 aborts. Then, $\Pr[\mathsf{Bad}_1] \leq v_1(\lambda)$, where v_1 is a negligible function in λ.

Since games G_1 and G_0 are equivalent except if event Bad_1 occurs, it holds that

$$\Pr[G_0 = 1] \leq \Pr[G_1 = 1] + v_1(\lambda), \tag{3}$$

where v_1 means the probability of breaking the hard relation R.

Game G_2: This game behaves similarly to the previous game, with the only difference being in the $\mathcal{O}_{\mathsf{pS}}$ oracle. In this game, the $\mathcal{O}_{\mathsf{pS}}$ oracle first makes a copy of the list H before executing the algorithm PreSign. Then, it extracts the randomness used during the PreSign algorithm, and checks whether, before the signing algorithm's execution, a query of the form $\mathsf{pk}_3||K||M$ or $\mathsf{pk}_3||K \cdot Y_2||M$ was made to $\mathcal{H}$ by checking whether $H'[\mathsf{pk}_3||K||M] \neq \bot$ or $H'[\mathsf{pk}_3||K \cdot Y_2||M] \neq \bot$. If such a query was made, the game aborts.

Claim of Game G_2. Let Bad_2 be the event that G_2 aborts in $\mathcal{O}_{pS}$. Then $\Pr[\mathsf{Bad}_2] \leq v_2(\lambda)$, where v_2 is a negligible function in n.

Game G_3: This game behaves similarly to the previous game, but with several differences in the oracle $\mathcal{O}_{\mathsf{pA}}$. In this game, $\mathcal{O}_{\mathsf{pA}}$ first makes a copy of the list H before executing PreAdapt. Afterward, it extracts the randomness values r_2, s_2, and s_3' that were used in the PreAdapt algorithm. For r_2 and s_2, it checks whether, before the signing algorithm's execution, a query of the form $\mathsf{pk}_2||K_2||M$ or $\mathsf{pk}_2||K_2 \cdot Y_1||M$ was made to $\mathcal{H}$ by checking whether $H'[\mathsf{pk}_2||K_2||M] \neq \bot$ or $H'[\mathsf{pk}_2||K_2 \cdot Y_1||M] \neq \bot$. If such a query was made, the game aborts.

Regarding s_3', it is used when extracting the witness y_2' ($y_2' := s_3' - s_3$). The adversary checks whether its forged witness y_2' corresponds (by chance) to the challenge statement Y_2^* on the oracle side. (The same verification performed by the simulator in G_1 is performed here on the oracle side.) In other words, on the side of the pre-adaptation oracle $\mathcal{O}_{pA}$, if y_2' is computed from $\sigma_3' = (r_3, s_3)$ and $\sigma_2 = (r_2, s_2, s_3')$ as $y_2' = s_3' - s_3$, and if $(Y_2^*, y_2') \in R^*$, then the game aborts. While it aborts if a valid witness y_2' for the challenge statement Y_2^* exists, a separate list S is prepared because of possible overlapping queries.

If A_1 uses a challenge M^* as an oracle query, this can be determined by checking whether $M \notin \mathcal{Q}$; similarly, if A_1 uses $M(\neq M^*)$ and a challenge Y_1^* as oracle queries, this can be determined by the Adapt algorithm. For the case where A_1 uses $M(\neq M^*)$ and a challenge Y_2^*, however, further consideration is needed. Therefore, on the simulator side, S executes the algorithm $y_1' \leftarrow \mathsf{Ext}(Y_1, \hat{\sigma}_2, \sigma_2)$. If the forged σ_2^* output by A_1 corresponds to the legitimate witness y_1^* derived from the challenge Y_1^* when $\sigma_2' \leftarrow$ PreAdapt is computed using $M(\neq M^*)$ and the challenge Y_2^*, then the game aborts. This probability is bounded by the probability of breaking the hard relation, at most.

Claim of Game $\mathbf{G_3}$. Let $\mathsf{Bad_3}$ be the event that $\mathbf{G_3}$ aborts in $\mathcal{O}_{pA}$. Then $\Pr[\mathsf{Bad_3}] \leq v_3(\lambda)$, where v_3 is a negligible function in n.

Game $\mathbf{G_4}$: In this game, upon an $\mathcal{O}_{pS}$ query, the game produces a valid full signature $\tilde{\sigma} = (r, s) = (\mathcal{H}(pk||K||m), k + rs \cdot k)$ and adjusts the global list H as follows. It assigns the value stored at position $pk||K||m$ to $H[pk||K \cdot Y||m]$ and samples a fresh random value for $H[pk||K||m]$. These changes make the full signature $\tilde{\sigma}$ "look like" a pre-signature to the adversary A, because it obtains the value $H[pk||K||m]$ upon querying the random oracle on $pk||K \cdot Y||m$. The adversary can only notice the changes in this game if the random oracle was previously queried on either $pk||K||m$ or $pk||K \cdot Y||m$. This case is captured in the previous game, and it thus holds that $\Pr[G_3 = 1] = \Pr[G_4 = 1]$.

Game $\mathbf{G_5}$: This game aims to appear like a pre-signature to the adversary upon an $\mathcal{O}_{pA}$ query. However, because a pre-signature's structure differs from that of a regular signature, adversaries may notice the changes in this game, unlike with $\mathbf{G_4}$. Therefore, to simulate $\hat{\sigma}_2 = (r_2, s_2, s'_3)$, where the first two components are indistinguishable from a regular signature $\sigma_2 = (r_2, s_1)$ and s'_3 is just random noise, we need to perform a similar procedure to that in $\mathbf{G_4}$, ensuring that $\sigma_2 = (r_2, s_1)$ remains indistinguishable and replacing s'_3 with a random value. When using a randomly chosen s'_3 to extract y'_2, the probability that y'_2 corresponds to the challenge Y_2^* is bounded by the advantage of breaking the hard relation, denoted as v_1. Hence, $\Pr[G_4 = 1] = \Pr[G_5 = 1] + v_1(\lambda)$ holds.

Game $\mathbf{G_6}$: In this game, the pre-signature generated upon A outputting the message M is created by modifying a full signature to a pre-signature.

The simulator S modifies the pre-signatures passed to adversary A_1 to pre-signatures converted from regular signatures. Specifically, from regular signatures σ'_2 and σ'_3, S creates $\sigma_2 = \mathsf{Adapt}(\sigma'_2, -y_1)$ and $\sigma_3 = \mathsf{Adapt}(\sigma'_3, -y_1)$. The difference in this transformation lies in k_2 and k_3 becoming $k'_2 = k_2 - y_1$ and $k'_3 = k_3 - y_2$; however, because k is uniformly random, it is indistinguishable, and A_1 cannot determine whether a signature is a pre-signature or a regular signature. This transformation can be viewed as k being modified to $k' = k - y_2$. Because k is chosen uniformly at random, and because the adversary's view is identical between this game and previous game, it holds that $\Pr[G_5 = 1] = \Pr[G_6 = 1]$.

Game strongSigForge: In analogous fashion, we seek to establish the existence of a simulator that can faithfully reproduce G_6 while harnessing the capabilities of A_1 to achieve success in the **strongSigForge** game. Here, we succinctly delineate how the simulator responds to oracle queries.

Signature Queries: When the adversary A_1 queries oracle $\mathcal{O}_S$ with an input M, the simulator S forwards M to oracle $\mathcal{O}_{\mathsf{Sign}}^{Sch}$ and relays the response to A_1.

Random Oracle Queries: When A_1 queries oracle $\mathcal{H}$ with input x, if $\mathcal{H}[x] = \perp$, then S queries $\mathcal{H}^{Sch}(x)$; otherwise, it returns $\mathcal{H}[x]$.

Pre-signature Queries: 1. When A_1 queries oracle $\mathcal{O}_{pS}$ with input (M, Y_2), S forwards M to oracle $\mathcal{O}_{\mathsf{Sign}}^{Sch}$ and receives a signature $\sigma_3 = (r_3, s_3)$ ($r_3 =$

$\mathcal{H}^{Sch}(pk_3||K_3||M))$. 2. If oracle $\mathcal{H}$ was previously queried on $(pk_3||K_3||M)$ or $(pk_3||K_3 \cdot Y_2||``M")$, $S$ aborts. 3. $S$ programs the random oracle $\mathcal{H}$ such that queries made by $A_1$ on input $(pk_3||K_3 \cdot Y_2||``M")$ are answered with the value $\mathcal{H}^{Sch}(pk_3||K_3||M)$, and queries on input $(pk_3||K_3||M)$ are answered with $\mathcal{H}^{Sch}$ ($pk_3||K_3 \cdot Y_2||M)$. 4. S returns σ_3 to A_1.

Pre-adaptation Queries: 1. When A_1 queries oracle $\mathcal{O}_{pA}$ with input (M, Y_1, Y_2, σ_2), S forwards M to oracle $\mathcal{O}_{Sign}^{Sch}$ and receives a signature $\sigma_2 = (r_2, s_2)$ $(r_2 = \mathcal{H}^{Sch}(pk_2||K_2||M))$. 2. If oracle $\mathcal{H}$ was previously queried on $(pk_2||K_2||M)$ or $(pk_2||K_2 \cdot Y_1||``M")$, $S$ aborts. 3. $S$ programs the random oracle $\mathcal{H}$ such that queries made by $A_1$ on input $(pk_2||K_2 \cdot Y_1||``M")$ are answered with the value $\mathcal{H}^{Sch}(pk_2||K_2||M)$, and queries on input $(pk_2||K_2||M)$ are answered with $\mathcal{H}^{Sch}(pk_2||K_2 \cdot Y_1||M)$. 4. S returns σ_2 to A_2.

Challenge Phase: S selects $(Y_1, y_1)(Y_2, y_2) \leftarrow GenR(1^n)$ and runs A_1 on pk_2, pk_3 and Y_1, Y_2. If A_1 outputs a challenge message M^*, then S queries the Sign^{Sch} oracle with input M^*. If A_1 outputs a forged signature σ^*, then S outputs (M^*, σ^*) as its own forgery.

The main difference between the simulation and G_6 lies in the syntax. Instead of generating public and secret keys and calculating the algorithm Sign_{sk} and random oracle $\mathcal{H}$, the simulator S uses its own oracles Sign^{Sch} and $\mathcal{H}^{Sch}$. Thus, S perfectly simulates G_6. We still need to demonstrate that S can use the forgery output by A_1 to win the **strongSigForge** game.

Claim of Game **strongSigForge**. (M^*, σ^*) is a valid forgery of **strongSigForge**.

As S provides a perfect simulation of G_6, from games $\mathbf{G_0}$ to $\mathbf{G_6}$, we have the following:

$$\Pr[\text{3-aSigForge}_{A_2, AS_{R_g, \Sigma}}(\lambda) = 1] \tag{4}$$
$$= \Pr[\mathbf{G_0} = 1] \le \Pr[G_1 = 1] + v_1(\lambda)$$
$$\le \Pr[G_2 = 1] + v_1(\lambda) + v_2'(\lambda)$$
$$= \Pr[G_3 = 1] + 2v_1(\lambda) + v_2'(\lambda) + v_3'(\lambda)$$
$$= \Pr[G_4 = 1] + 2v_1(\lambda) + v_2'(\lambda) + v_3'(\lambda)$$
$$= \Pr[G_5 = 1] + 3v_1(\lambda) + v_2'(\lambda) + v_3'(\lambda)$$
$$= \Pr[G_6 = 1] + 3v_1(\lambda) + v_2'(\lambda) + v_3'(\lambda)$$
$$= \Pr[\text{strongSigForge}_{S^{A_2}, 3\text{-AS}}(\lambda) = 1] + 3v_1(\lambda) + v_2'(\lambda) + v_3'(\lambda).$$

Then, from Eqs. (1) and (4), the overall reduction loss for three-party unforgeability is as follows:

$$\Pr[\text{3-aSigForge}_{A_1, AS_{R_g, \Sigma}}(\lambda) = 1] + \Pr[\text{3-aSigForge}_{A_2, AS_{R_g, \Sigma}}(\lambda) = 1] \le \mathsf{negl}(\lambda).$$

$\square$

4   N-Party Adaptor Signatures

In this section, we extend the three-party adaptor signatures to construct an N-party adaptor signature scheme $\mathsf{N\text{-}AS}_{R,\Sigma}$. Here, we denote the N entities as $U_1, \cdots, U_i, \cdots, U_n$. Each entity is classified into one of three types: U_n as the entity that generates the initial pre-signature, U_1 as the entity that finally adapts from pre-signatures to a regular signature, and U_i as all the other entities. In constructing N-party adaptor signatures, we assume the same digital signature scheme and computationally hard algebraic relation used in the three-party case. Additionally, the subscripts for each algorithm (e.g., U_n in $\mathsf{PreSign}_{U_n}$) correspond to the entity executing the algorithm, and the subscripts for each argument (e.g., i in Y_i or n in σ_n) correspond to the entity that initially owns (or generates) that value. The specific construction based on the syntax of the n-party adaptor signature is an extension from three-party.

Syntax of N-Party Adaptor Signatures Setup. U_1 executes the algebraic relation generation algorithm $(Y_1, y_1) \leftarrow \mathsf{GenR}(1^n)$; the U_i $(2 \leq i < n)$ execute the key generation algorithm $(\mathsf{sk}_i, \mathsf{pk}_i) \leftarrow \mathsf{KeyGen}(\lambda)$ and the algebraic relation generation algorithm $(Y_i, y_i) \leftarrow \mathsf{GenR}(1^n)$; and U_n executes the key generation algorithm $(sk_n, pk_n) \leftarrow \mathsf{KeyGen}(\lambda)$.

Pre-signing: $\sigma_n \leftarrow \mathsf{PreSign}_{U_n}((\mathsf{pk}_n, \mathsf{sk}_n), Y_{n-1}, M)$. The pre-signing algorithm $\mathsf{PreSign}_{U_n}$ is executed by U_n and takes as input the key pair $(\mathsf{pk}_n, \mathsf{sk}_n)$ of U_n, the public information Y_{n-1} of U_{n-1}, and the message M; then, it outputs the pre-signature σ_n. Note that all entities except U_1 generate pre-signatures, but because entities other than U_1 and U_n generate pre-signatures with the $\mathsf{PreAdapt}$ algorithm, only U_n executes this pre-signing algorithm.

Pre-verification: $0/1 \leftarrow \mathsf{PreVrfy}_{U_i}(\{Y_j\}_{j=i}^{n-1}, \{\mathsf{pk}_j\}_{j=i+1}^{n}, \{\sigma_j\}_{j=i+1}^{n}, M)$. The pre-verification algorithm $\mathsf{PreVrfy}_{U_i}$ is executed by the U_i $(1 \leq i < n)$. It takes as input the public information $(Y_i, \ldots, Y_{n-1})$ from U_i to U_{n-1}, the pre-signatures $(\sigma_{i+1}, \ldots, \sigma_n)$ and public keys $(\mathsf{pk}_{i+1}, \ldots, \mathsf{pk}_n)$ generated by U_{i+1} to U_n, and the message M, and it performs pre-signature verification. It outputs 1 if the signature is accepted, or 0 otherwise.

Pre-adaptation: $\sigma_i \leftarrow \mathsf{PreAdapt}_{U_i}((Y_i, y_i), Y_{i-1}, \mathsf{pk}_{i+1}, (\mathsf{sk}_i, \mathsf{pk}_i), \sigma_{i+1}, M)$. The pre-adaptation algorithm $\mathsf{PreAdapt}_{U_i}$ is executed by the U_i $(2 \leq i < n)$. It takes as input the algebraic relation pair (Y_i, y_i) of U_i, the public information Y_{i-1} of U_{i-1}, the public key pk_{i+1} of U_{i+1}, the key pair $(\mathsf{sk}_i, \mathsf{pk}_i)$ of U_i, the pre-signature σ_{i+1} generated by U_{i+1}, and the message M; then, it outputs the pre-signature σ_i.

Adaptation: $\sigma_1 \leftarrow \mathsf{Adapt}_{U_1}((Y_1, y_1), \mathsf{pk}_2, \sigma_2, M)$: The adaptation algorithm Adapt_{U_1} is executed by U_1. It takes as input the algebraic relation pair (Y_1, y_1) of U_1, the public key pk_2 of U_2, the signature σ_2 generated by U_2, and the message M, and it outputs the signature σ_1.

Extraction: $y_{i-1} \leftarrow \mathsf{Ext}_{U_i}(Y_{i-1}, \sigma_i, \sigma_{i-1})$: The extraction algorithm Ext_{U_i} is executed by the U_i $(2 \leq i \leq n)$. It takes as input the public information Y_{i-1}

of U_{i-1} and the signatures σ_i and σ_{i-1} generated by U_i and U_{i-1}, respectively, and it outputs the secret information y_{i-1}.

4.1   Security of N-Party Adaptor Signature Scheme

We now extend the security definitions of three-party to define the security of N-party adaptor signatures. As with three-party, we describe the unforgeablity in detail here.

First, because the security of adaptor signatures depends on the generating entity, it is necessary to consider unforgeability for n entities with $n-1$ interactions each. Hence, we consider two cases. The first case is unforgeability between U_n and U_{n-1}. In this case, U_n generates a pre-signature via the PreSign algorithm, and the adversary attempts to forge signatures via the signature/pre-signature oracle. The second case is unforgeability between U_i and U_{i+1} for $1 \leq i \leq n-2$. Here, U_{i+1} generates a pre-signature via the PreAdapt algorithm, and the adversary attempts to forge signatures via the signature/pre-adaptation oracle. We define the existential unforgeability against chosen-plaintext attacks for N-party adaptor signatures (N-aEUF-CMA) as follows.

Definition 2 (Existential unforgeability for N parties). *An N-party adaptor signature scheme* N-AS$_{R,\Sigma}$ *is* N-aEUF-CMA *secure if for any PPT adversary* $\mathcal{A} = (\mathcal{A}_1, \ldots, \mathcal{A}_{N-1})$, *there exists a negligible function* negl(λ) *such that*

$$\sum_{i=1}^{N-2} \Pr[\text{N-aSigForge}_{\mathcal{A}_i, \text{N-AS}_{R,\Sigma}}(\lambda) = 1] + \Pr[\text{N-aSigForge}_{\mathcal{A}_{N-1}, \text{N-AS}_{R,\Sigma}}(\lambda) = 1]$$
$$\leq \text{negl}(\lambda)$$

where the experiments N-aSigForge$_{\mathcal{A}_i, \text{N-AS}_{R,\Sigma}}$ *and* N-aSigForge$_{\mathcal{A}_{N-1}, \text{N-AS}_{R,\Sigma}}$ *are as defined in the Table 2.*

Theorem 2. *If the Schnorr signature scheme* Σ_{Sch} *is* SUF-CMA *secure, and* R_g *is a computationally hard algebraic relation, then* N-AS$_{R_g, \Sigma_{Sch}}$ *is secure in the random oracle model.*

Regarding existential unforgeability for N parties, the following lemma holds.

Lemma 2 (N-aEUF-CMA security). *Assuming that Schnorr digital signature scheme* Σ_{Sch} *is* SUF-CMA *secure and* R_g *is a hard relation, the N-party adaptor signature scheme* N-AS$_{R_g, \Sigma_{Sch}}$ *is* N-aEUF-CMA *secure.*

We can apply similar case-by-case reasoning as in the three-party case. In the three-party scenario, we considered an attacker A_2 between U_2 and U_3 as case (i) and an attacker A_1 between U_1 and U_2 as case (ii). The same approach can be used for the N-party scenario: we consider an attacker A_{n-1} between U_{n-1} and U_n as case (i), and an attacker A_i between U_i and U_{i+1} as case (ii), with iteration over $1 \leq i \leq n-2$. This straightforward extension yields the desired results.

Table 2. Experiments N-aSigForge$_{\mathcal{A}_i, \text{N-AS}_{R,\Sigma}}$ and N-aSigForge$_{\mathcal{A}_{N-1}, \text{N-AS}_{R,\Sigma}}$

N-aSigForge$^i_{\mathcal{A}, \text{AS}_{R,\Sigma}}(\lambda)$

$1 : Q := \emptyset, (\text{sk}_{i+1}, \text{pk}_{i+1}) \leftarrow \text{Gen}(1^\lambda)$

$2 : (Y_i, y_i) \leftarrow \text{GenR}(1^\lambda)$

$3 : (M, \text{st}) \leftarrow \mathcal{A}_1^{\mathcal{O}_S(\cdot), \mathcal{O}_{pA}(\cdot, \cdot)}(\{\text{pk}_j\}_{j=i+1}^n, \{Y_j\}_{j=i}^{n-1})$

$4 : \sigma_{i+1} \leftarrow \text{PreAdapt}_{U_{i+1}}((Y_i, y_i), Y_{i-1}, \text{pk}_{i+1}, (\text{sk}_i, \text{pk}_i), \sigma_{i+1}, M)$

$5 : \sigma_i \leftarrow \mathcal{A}_2^{\mathcal{O}_S(\cdot), \mathcal{O}_{pA}(\cdot, \cdot)}(\{\sigma_j\}_{j=i+1}^n, \text{st})$

$6 : \textbf{return } (M \notin Q \wedge \text{Vrfy}(\text{pk}_{i+1}, \sigma_i, M))$

N-aSigForge$^{n-1}_{\mathcal{A}, \text{AS}_{R,\Sigma}}(\lambda)$

$1 : Q := \emptyset, (\text{sk}_n, \text{pk}_n) \leftarrow \text{Gen}(1^\lambda)$

$2 : (Y_{n-1}, y_{n-1}) \leftarrow \text{GenR}(1^\lambda)$

$3 : (M, \text{st}) \leftarrow \mathcal{A}_1^{\mathcal{O}_S(\cdot), \mathcal{O}_{pS}(\cdot, \cdot)}(\text{pk}_n, Y_{n-1})$

$4 : \sigma_n \leftarrow \text{PreSign}_{U_n}((\text{pk}_n, \text{sk}_n), Y_{n-1}, M)$

$5 : \sigma_{n-1} \leftarrow \mathcal{A}_2^{\mathcal{O}_S(\cdot), \mathcal{O}_{pS}(\cdot, \cdot)}(\sigma_n, \text{st})$

$6 : \textbf{return } (M \notin Q \wedge \text{Vrfy}_{U_n}(\text{pk}_n, \sigma_{n-1}, M))$

$\mathcal{O}_{pA}(M, (Y_i, Y_{i+1}), \sigma_{i+2})$

$1 : \sigma_i \leftarrow \text{PreAdapt}_{U_i}((Y_i, y_i), Y_{i-1}, \text{pk}_{i+1}, (\text{sk}_i, \text{pk}_i), \sigma_{i+1}, M)$

$2 : Q := Q \cup \{M\}$

$3 : \textbf{return } \sigma_i$

$\mathcal{O}_S(M)$ $\mathcal{O}_{pS}(M, Y_{n-1})$

$1 : \sigma_i \leftarrow \text{Sign}(\text{sk}_i, M)$ $1 : \sigma_n \leftarrow \text{PreSign}(\text{sk}_n, Y_{n-1}, M)$

$2 : Q := Q \cup \{M\}$ $2 : Q := Q \cup \{M\}$

$3 : \textbf{return } \sigma_i$ $3 : \textbf{return } \sigma_n$

5 Conclusion

In this paper, we explored a general extension of adaptor signature schemes that previously applied for two parties. First, we extended the two-party adaptor signature scheme to three parties and presented the security requirements that the extended scheme should satisfy. We also provided a specific construction example using Schnorr signatures. Then, we demonstrated that the resulting Schnorr-signature-based, three-party adaptor signature scheme satisfies all the defined security properties. Furthermore, by extending the scheme to N parties, we showed a general construction method for N-party adaptor signatures and again provided a specific construction example using Schnorr signatures. This illustrates the ease of extending from three to N parties.

A   Comparison with Existing Multi-party Settings

Our contribution lies in extending adaptor signatures to multi-party settings and investigating the gap with respect to two-party settings. Ji et al. [21] proposed a multi-adaptor signature scheme, but their multi-party setting differs from ours. In their setting, users who are performing pre-signatures exist *simultaneously* and the resulting n pre-signatures are aggregated into one via signature aggregation techniques before being sent to Alice, the secretary. Thus, Ji et al. considered n signers, and this extension could also be of interest in blockchain applications. In real-world applications, however, protocols that end in a single round trip are rare, and scenarios often involve routing or proxies, where someone else intervenes, or where Alice needs to forward messages to someone else. Therefore, our multi-party setting is more generalized. That is, given an initial pre-signer Bob, we consider the scenario of non-simultaneously receiving n users from Bob, who then passes on the pre-signatures sequentially. Eventually, the nth user performs adaptation to obtain a regular signature. At each handover, the execution of an Extract operation to obtain the secret witness enables the fair exchange desired in the two-party setting. Accordingly, we expect our approach to be applicable in data sharing and supply chain management, among other applications.

B   Other Preliminaries

We first introduce the cryptographic primitives and notations used in this paper. We denote by $x \leftarrow X$ the uniform sampling of a variable x from a set X. Throughout this paper, λ denotes the security parameter, and all our algorithms run in polynomial time in λ. By writing $x \leftarrow A(y)$, we mean that, on input y, a probabilistic polynomial time (PPT) algorithm A outputs x. If A is a deterministic polynomial time (DPT) algorithm, then we use the notation $x := A(y)$. A function $\mathsf{negl} : \mathbb{N} \rightarrow \mathbb{R}$ is negligible in n if, for every $k \subset N$, there exists $n_0 \in N$ s.t. for every $n \geq n_0$ it holds that $|\mathsf{negl}(n)| \leq 1/n^k$.

We next recall the definition of a hard relation R with statement/witness pairs (Y, y). Let L_R be the associated language defined as $\{Y | \exists y \text{ s.t.} (Y, y) \in R\}$. We say that R is a hard relation if the following hold: (i) There exists a PPT sampling algorithm GenR that, on input 1^λ, outputs a statement/witness pair $(Y, y) \in R$; (ii) the relation is poly-time decidable; and (iii) for all PPT A on input Y, the probability of A outputting a valid witness y is negligible.

B.1   Digital Signatures

A digital signature scheme Σ comprises the three algorithms KGen, Sign, and Vrfy. The key generation algorithm $(\mathsf{pk}, \mathsf{sk}) \leftarrow \mathsf{KGen}(\lambda)$ takes a security parameter λ as an input and outputs a secret (signing) key sk and a public (verification) key pk. The signing algorithm $\sigma \leftarrow \mathsf{Sign}(m, \mathsf{pk}, \mathsf{sk})$ takes a message m, pk, and sk as inputs and outputs a signature σ. The verification algorithm $1/0 \leftarrow \mathsf{Vrfy}(m, \mathsf{pk}, \sigma)$ takes m, pk, and σ as inputs, and it outputs 1 if the signature is accepted, or 0 otherwise.

B.2   Schnorr Signatures

Schnorr signatures are the most intuitive and most compatible signature scheme with adaptor signatures, because Poelstra [30] used them as a base when he first presented the concrete structure of adaptor signatures. First, let $\mathbb{G} = <g>$ be a cyclic group of prime order q, and let $R_q \subset \mathbb{G} \times \mathbb{Z}_q$ be a relation defined as $R_q := \{(Y, y) | Y = g^y\}$, where $\mathbb{Z}_q$ is the set of integers modulo q.

Next, we briefly introduce Schnorr signature scheme $\Sigma_{Sch} = (\mathsf{Gen}, \mathsf{Sign}, \mathsf{Vrfy})$. The key generation algorithm samples $x \leftarrow \mathbb{Z}_q$ uniformly at random and returns $X := g^x \in \mathbb{G}$ as the public key and x as the secret key. On an input message $m \in \{0,1\}^*$, the signing algorithm computes $r = \mathcal{H}(X||g^k||m) \in \mathbb{Z}_q$ and $s := k + rx \in \mathbb{Z}_q$, for $k \leftarrow \mathbb{Z}_q$ chosen uniformly at random, and it outputs a signature $\sigma := (r, s)$. Finally, on an input message $m \in \{0,1\}^*$ and signature $(r, s) \in \mathbb{Z}_q \times \mathbb{Z}_q$, the verification algorithm verifies that $r = \mathcal{H}(X||g^s \cdot X^{-r}||m)$.

B.3   Security Classes

Definition 3 (SUF-CMA). *A digital signature scheme Σ is considered a strong existentially unforgeable against adaptively chosen-message attack (SUF-CMA) secure if for any PPT adversary $\mathcal{A}$, $\Pr[\mathsf{strongSigForge}_{\mathsf{SIG},\mathcal{A}}(\lambda) = 1] = \mathsf{negl}(\lambda)$, where $\mathsf{strongSigForge}_{\mathsf{SIG},\mathcal{A}}(\lambda)$ and $\mathcal{O}_S(\cdot)$ are defined in Fig. 2.*

$\mathsf{strongSigForge}_{\mathsf{SIG},\mathcal{A}}(\lambda)$:	$\mathcal{O}_S(m)$:
$\mathcal{Q} := \emptyset$	$\sigma \leftarrow \mathsf{Sign}(m, \mathsf{pk}, \mathsf{sk})$
$(\mathsf{pk}, \mathsf{sk}) \leftarrow \mathsf{KGen}(1^\lambda)$	$\mathcal{Q} := \mathcal{Q} \cup \{m, \sigma\}$
$(m^*, \sigma^*) \leftarrow \mathcal{A}^{\mathcal{O}_S(\cdot)}(\mathsf{pk})$	Return σ
If $(m^*, \sigma^*) \in \mathcal{Q}$, then return 0	
Return $\mathsf{Vrfy}(\mathsf{pk}, m^*, \sigma^*)$	

Fig. 2. Experiment with SUF-CMA.

References

1. Monero. https://www.getmonero.org/
2. Aumayr, L., et al.: Generalized channels from limited blockchain scripts and adaptor signatures. In: Asiacrypt (2021)
3. Aumayr, L., Thyagarajan, S.A., Malavolta, G., Moreno-Sanchez, P., Maffei, M.: Sleepy channels: bi-directional payment channels without watchtowers. In: ACM CCS (2022)
4. Bagaria, V., Neu, J., and Tse, D.: Boomerang: Redundancy improves latency and throughput in payment-channel networks. In: FC (2020)
5. Coalition for Content Provenance and Authenticity [n. d.]. https://c2pa.org/
6. C2PA Technical Specification. https://c2pa.org/specifications/specifications/2.0/specs/C2PA_Specification.html

7. Chen, Y., et al.: PACDAM: privacy-preserving and adaptive cross-chain digital asset marketplace. IEEE Internet Things J. (2023)
8. Dai, W., Okamoto, T., Yamamoto, G.: Stronger security and generic constructions for adaptor signatures. In: Indocrypt (2022)
9. Debris-Alazard, T., Sendrier, N., Tillich, J.-P.: Wave: a new code-based signature scheme. Cryptology ePrint Archive, 2018/996 (2018)
10. Deshpande, A., Herlihy, M.: Privacy-preserving cross-chain atomic swaps. In: FC (2020)
11. Ducas, L., Lepoint, T., Lyubashevsky, V., Schwabe, P., Seiler, G., Stehle, D.: CRYSTALS–dilithium: digital signatures from module lattices. In: CHES (2018)
12. Erwig, A., Faust, S., Hostáková, K., Maitra, M., Riahi, S.: Two-party adaptor signatures from identification schemes. In: PKC (2021)
13. Erwig, A., Riahi, S.: Deterministic wallets for adaptor signatures. In: ESORICS (2022)
14. Esgin, M. F., Ersoy, O., Erkin, Z.: Post-quantum adaptor signatures and payment channel networks. In: ESORICS (2020)
15. Fiat, A., Shamir, A.: How to prove yourself: Practical solutions to identification and signature problems. In: Eurocrypt (1986)
16. Gudgeon, L., Moreno-Sanchez, P., Roos, S., McCorry, P., Gervais, A.: Sok: layer-two blockchain protocols. In: FC (2020)
17. Han, R., Lin, H., Yu, J.: On the optionality and fairness of atomic swaps. In: The 1st ACM Conference on Advances in Financial Technologies (2019)
18. Hoenisch, P., del Pino, L.S.: Atomic swaps between bitcoin and monero. arXiv preprint arXiv:2101.12332 (2021)
19. Hoenisch, P., Mazumdar, S., Moreno-Sanchez, P., Ruj, S.: LightSwap: an atomic swap does not require timeouts at both blockchains. In: DPM (2022)
20. Hu, X., Chen, H.: Design and analysis of an anonymous and fair trading scheme for electronic resources with blind adaptor signature. In: The 6th International Congress on Image and Signal Processing, BioMedical Engineering and Informatics (CISP-BMEI), pp. 1–5. IEEE (2023)
21. Ji, Y., Xiao, Y., Gao, B., Zhang, R.: Threshold/multi adaptor signature and their applications in blockchains. Electronics 13(1), 76 (2023)
22. Kajita, K., Ohtake, G., Takagi, T.: Consecutive adaptor signature scheme: from two-party to n-party settings. Cryptology ePrint Archive, 2024/241 (2024)
23. Klamti, J.B., Hasan, M.A.: Post-quantum two-party adaptor signature based on coding theory. In: Cryptography (2022)
24. Liu, Z., Yang, A., Zeng, H., Jiang, C., Ma, L.: A generalized blockchain-based government data sharing protocol. Secur. Commun. Netw. (2023)
25. Madathil, V., Thyagarajan, S.A., Vasilopoulos, D., Fournier, L., Malavolta, G., Moreno-Sanchez, P.: Cryptographic oracle-based conditional payments. In: NDSS (2023)
26. Malavolta, G., Moreno-Sanchez, P., Schneidewind, C., Kate, A., Maffei, M.: Anonymous multi-hop locks for blockchain scalability and interoperability. In: NDSS (2019)
27. Minaei, M., et al.: Unlinkability and interoperability in account-based universal payment channels. In: FC (2023)
28. Mirzaei, A., Sakzad, A., Yu, J., Steinfeld, R.: FPPW: a fair and privacy preserving watchtower for bitcoin. In: FC (2021)
29. Moreno-Sanchez, P., Blue, A., Le, D.V., Noether, S., Goodell, B., Kate, A.: DLSAG: non-interactive refund transactions for interoperable payment channels in Monero. In: FC (2020)

30. Poelstra, A.: Scriptless scripts. Presentation Slides. https://download.wpsoftware.
net/bitcoin/wizardry/mw-slides/2017-05-milan-meetup/slides.pdf. Accessed 17
Aug 2023
31. Poelstra, A., Nick, J.: Adaptor signatures and atomic swaps from scriptless scripts
(2017). https://github.com/ElementsProject/scriptless-scripts/blob/master/md/
atomic-swap.md
32. Qin, X., et al.: BlindHub: bitcoin-compatible privacy-preserving payment channel
hubs supporting variable amounts. In: IEEE S&P (2023)
33. Schnorr, C.-P.: Efficient identification and signatures for smart cards. In: CRYPTO
(1990)
34. Shao, W., Wang, J., Wang, L., Jia, C., Xu, S., Zhang, S.: Auditable blockchain
rewriting in permissioned setting with mandatory revocability for IoT. IEEE Internet Things J. (2023)
35. Sui, Z., Liu, J. K., Yu, J., Qin, X.: MoNet: a fast payment channel network for
scriptless cryptocurrency Monero. In: IEEE DCS (2022)
36. Sui, Z., Liu, J.K., Yu, J., Au, M.H., Liu, J.: AuxChannel: enabling efficient bi-
directional channel for scriptless blockchains. In: ACM AsiaCCS (2022)
37. Tairi, E., Moreno-Sanchez, P., Maffei, M.: A^2L: anonymous atomic locks for scalability in payment channel hubs. In: IEEE S&P (2021)
38. Tairi, E., Moreno-Sanchez, P., Maffei, M.: Post-quantum adaptor signature for
privacy-preserving off-chain payments. In: FC (2021)
39. Thyagarajan, S.A.K., Malavolta, G., Schmidt, F., Schröder, D.: Paymo: payment
channels for Monero. Cryptology ePrint Archive, 2020/1441 (2020)
40. Thyagarajan, S.A.K., Malavolta, G.: Lockable signatures for blockchains: scriptless
scripts for all signatures. In: IEEE S&P (2021)
41. Tu, B., Zhang, M., Yu, C.: Efficient ECDSA-based adaptor signature for batched
atomic swaps. In: ISC (2022)
42. Wang, X., Lin, C., Huang, X., He, D.: Anonymity-enhancing multi-hop locks for
Monero-enabled payment channel networks. IEEE Trans. Inf. Forensics Secur.
(2023)
43. Zhou, X., He, D., Ning, J., Luo, M., Huang, X.: Efficient construction of verifiable timed signatures and its application in scalable payments. IEEE Trans. Inf.
Forensics Secur. (2023)
44. Zhu, X., He, D., Bao, Z., Peng, C., Luo, M.: Two-party adaptor signature scheme
based on IEEE P1363 identity-based signature. IEEE Open J. Commun. Soc.
(2023)

Secure Five-Party Computation with Private Robustness and Minimal Online Communication

Hikaru Tsuchida[1]([✉]) and Takashi Nishide[2]([✉])

[1] Saitama Institute of Technology, Saitama, Japan
h_tsuchida@sit.ac.jp
[2] University of Tsukuba, Ibaraki, Japan
nishide@risk.tsukuba.ac.jp

Abstract. Multi-Party Computation (MPC) is a cryptographic technology that enables multiple parties to compute an arbitrary function represented as a circuit while revealing only the function's output. Secret-Sharing-based MPC (SS-MPC) is the most popular MPC scheme. SS-MPC protocols that achieve high performance and strong security simultaneously are attracting much attention. In particular, both communication efficiency and strong security during the *online phase*, i.e., the computation with actual inputs, are desired for SS-MPC protocols with a small number of parties.

Private Robustness (PR) is one of the strongest security notions, ensuring that honest parties learn the correct outputs without aborting the protocol or revealing the parties' inputs regardless of the adversary's behavior. To the best of our knowledge, the SS-MPC protocol with PR proposed by Dalskov et al. (CCS'22) represents the current state-of-the-art in terms of communication efficiency for protocols with PR.

In this paper, we propose a novel Five-Party Computation (5PC) protocol with a single malicious corruption that achieves PR. Our 5PC protocol is more efficient than the current state-of-the-art SS-MPC protocol with PR in terms of communication efficiency during the online phase.

Keywords: Multi-party computation · Secret sharing · Robustness

1 Introduction

1.1 Background

Multi-Party Computation (MPC) is a cryptographic technology that enables multiple parties to compute an arbitrary function represented as a circuit while revealing only the function's outputs through arithmetic operations and communications between parties [3,13,22]. Popular applications and services based on MPC include machine learning algorithms [4,7,8,15,16,19,20]. These MPC-based applications and services are considered valuable because they enable the secure processing of confidential information.

J. K. Liu et al. (Eds.): ProvSec 2024, LNCS 14903, pp. 43–62, 2025.
https://doi.org/10.1007/978-981-96-0954-3_3

Secret-Sharing-based MPC (SS-MPC) [3,13] is the most popular MPC scheme. SS-MPC enables parties to compute a function securely through communications among parties and arithmetic operations. Consequently, many SS-MPC protocols face a trade-off between the number of communication rounds and the amount of communication. The *offline-online paradigm* is a common methodology to improve this trade-off regarding communication complexities. It divides an SS-MPC protocol into two phases: *offline* and *online*.

In the offline phase, an SS-MPC protocol processes computations that can be performed independently of the parties' inputs. In the online phase, the SS-MPC protocol processes the remaining computations using the parties' inputs. The offline-online paradigm helps to reduce the response time of SS-MPC application queries in the online phase through pre-computations in the offline phase. Our focus is on the efficiency of the online phase.

Most SS-MPC protocols also face a trade-off between their achievable performance and security notions. The security that an SS-MPC protocol can achieve varies depending on the proportion of corruptions and the adversary's behavior.

Let n and t be the number of parties and the number of parties that can be corrupted, respectively. The proportion of corruptions can be roughly divided into two types: *dishonest majority* (i.e., $t \geq n/2$) and *honest majority* (i.e., $t < n/2$).

An adversary's behavior can be roughly divided into two types: *semi-honest* and *malicious*. Parties corrupted by a semi-honest adversary attempt to learn as much information as possible while following the protocol's specifications. Parties corrupted by a malicious adversary may not follow the protocol specifications and can attempt to not only learn as much information as possible but also deviate arbitrarily from the protocol (e.g., by sending incorrect values). The security against the former and latter is called semi-honest security and malicious security, respectively.

SS-MPC protocols with a few parties that aim to achieve both high performance and strong security against malicious adversaries have been actively studied. There are three typical security notions related to the delivery of outputs in the presence of malicious adversaries: *security with abort* (the protocol aborts if it detects malicious behavior), *fairness* (a malicious adversary can obtain the correct output only if the honest parties also obtain it), and *robustness* (also known as guaranteed output delivery).

Robustness ensures that all honest parties always obtain the correct output regardless of the adversary's behavior, without aborting the protocol. Hence, robustness is a stronger security notion than security with abort and fairness.

From a practical viewpoint, real applications or services may be required to use robust SS-MPC protocols because SS-MPC protocols that only achieve abort or fairness may not be secure enough against a malicious adversary who aims to shut down the application or service. If a corrupted party by the malicious adversary sends incorrect values, an SS-MPC protocol that achieves only abort or fairness will detect the cheating and abort. Hence, the adversary can achieve their goal of shutting down the application or service. However, if the underlying SS-

MPC protocol is robust, the malicious adversary will fail because the robust SS-MPC protocol ensures that all honest parties always obtain the correct outputs regardless of the adversary's behavior, without aborting the protocol. Therefore, robust SS-MPC protocols that achieve high performance are more desirable.

For $t < n/2$, a broadcast channel is required to construct an MPC protocol for an arbitrary function with robustness [13, 21]. Constructing a broadcast channel necessitates either a physical broadcast channel or digital signatures with a Public Key Infrastructure (PKI). Hence, a broadcast channel is an expensive assumption. To avoid the theoretical necessity of a broadcast channel, we focus on MPC protocols with $t < n/3$, e.g., $(n, t) = (4, 1)$.

In several Four-Party Computation (4PC) protocols based on replicated secret sharing with a single malicious corruption, two sending parties send the same value they shared to one receiving party. If the two values received by the receiving party do not match, the receiving party broadcasts a message indicating that cheating has occurred. Since there can be no more than one corrupted party, one of the two senders or the receiver must be corrupted. In other words, the remaining party, who is neither a sender nor a receiver, can be identified as an honest party. Robustness can be achieved by using the identified honest party. Therefore, 4PC protocols [4,8,9,16,17] with a single malicious corruption can avoid the theoretical necessity of a broadcast channel and achieve high performance and two types of robustness simultaneously.

Robustness can be divided into two types: *Traditional Robustness* (TR) [16, 17] and *Private Robustness* (PR) [4,8,9]. TR ensures that all honest parties learn the correct outputs, but the parties' inputs may be revealed to certain honest parties. PR ensures that all honest parties learn the correct outputs while keeping information about the parties' inputs secret from all parties. Hence, PR is a stronger security notion than TR.

1.2   Our Contribution

We propose a Five-Party Computation (5PC) protocol based on secret sharing with PR, requiring no broadcast channel. Our 5PC with PR requires only 1 round and 4 ring elements for the share multiplication in the online phase.

To the best of our knowledge, the SS-MPC protocol with PR and $t < n/3$ proposed by Dalskov et al. [9] is the current state-of-the-art SS-MPC protocol with PR. We refer to their protocol [9] as DEN22. DEN22 with $(n, t) = (4, 1)$ has two trade-off variants. We refer to these two variants as DEN22-I and DEN22-II. DEN22-I requires 2 rounds and 4 ring elements for the share multiplication in the online phase. DEN22-II requires 1 round and 4.5 ring elements in the online phase. Therefore, our 5PC with PR has better communication efficiency of the share multiplication in the online phase than previous studies with PR (see Table 1).

We also propose a Dot Product (DP) protocol with PR. As mentioned in [20], the DP protocol is a fundamental building block for most of the machine learning algorithms. Hence, the DP protocol with good communication efficiency is useful for providing the machine learning service based on MPC. Our DP protocol

Table 1. Comparison of maliciously secure MPC requiring no expensive assumptions. n: number of parties, t_m: number of maliciously corrupted parties, t_s: number of semi-honest corrupted parties, Mult.: share multiplication protocol, DP: dot product protocol, M: vector length, Rounds: number of communication rounds in online phase, Comm.: number of transmitted ring elements for all parties in online phase as amortized cost.

Schemes	(n, t_m, t_s)	PR	Mult.		DP	
			Rounds	Comm.	Rounds	Comm.
ABY3 [19]+ [1]	$(3,1,0)$	(abort)	1	9	1	$9M$
BLAZE [20]	$(3,1,0)$	(fairness)	1	3	1	3
Trident [7]	$(4,1,0)$	(fairness)	1	3	1	3
FLASH [4]	$(4,1,0)$	Achievable	5	12	5	12
SWIFT [16]	$(4,1,0)$	(TR)	1	3	1	3
Fantastic four [8]	$(4,1,0)$	Achievable	1	6	1	6
Tetrad [17]	$(4,1,0)$	(TR)	1	3	1	3
PentaGOD [15]	$(5,1,1)$	Achievable	1	8	1	8
DEN22-I [9]	$(4,1,0)$	Achievable	2	4	2	4
DEN22-II [9]	$(4,1,0)$	Achievable	1	4.5	1	$4.5M$
Ours	$(5,1,0)$	Achievable	1	4	1	4

requires only 1 round and 4 ring elements in the online phase, independent of the vector length M. Table 1 shows that our DP protocol with PR has better communication efficiency in the online phase than previous studies with PR.

1.3   Related Work

For $t < n/3$, in particular, for $(n,t) = (4,1)$, Gordon et al. proposed a 4PC with PR requiring a digital signature and public key encryption (committing encryption) [14]. Byali et al. proposed the 4PC called FLASH with PR requiring no broadcast channel, i.e., no digital signature with PKI or physical broadcast channel [4]. However, it requires a commitment scheme. Koti et al. proposed the 4PC called SWIFT that requires no broadcast channel or commitment scheme [16]. Koti et al. proposed the 4PC with TR called Tetrad to improve SWIFT [17]. However, SWIFT and Tetrad are only with TR.

Dolskov et al. proposed a 4PC called Fantastic four with PR requiring no broadcast channel or commitment scheme [8]. Koti et al. proposed a 5PC called PentaGOD that can achieve PR against one malicious corruption and one semi-honest corruption without broadcast channel or commitment scheme [15]. Dolskov et al. proposed an SS-MPC with PR for $t < n/3$ [9]. However, these schemes [8,9,15] require more communications for the share multiplication protocol in the online phase than our 5PC.

2 Preliminaries

2.1 Notations

Let $\mathbb{Z}_L$ be the residue ring modulo L, where L is an integer and $L \geq 2$. We use $\cdot$ as the multiplication operator on $\mathbb{Z}_L$. Let P_j be the j-th party ($j = 0, 1, 2, 3, 4$). We define the set of parties as $\mathcal{P} = \{P_0, P_1, P_2, P_3, P_4\}$. For a set $\mathcal{X}$, $|\mathcal{X}|$ denotes the number of elements in $\mathcal{X}$. For example, $|\mathcal{P}|$ is 5. The security parameter is denoted as κ. The set of κ-bit strings is $\{0,1\}^\kappa$. For example, the unique identifier uid is a κ-bit bit string. The notation uid is the public value as a counter value.

We define a set of pre-shared keys as follows:

- One key shared between every group of four parties, $k_{\{a,b,c,d\}} \in \{0,1\}^\kappa$ for $\{P_a, P_b, P_c, P_d\}$ where $a, b, c, d \in \{0, 1, 2, 3, 4\}$.
- One key shared among all parties, $k \in \{0,1\}^\kappa$.

$\mathcal{F}_{\text{init}}$ - (initialization)

1. Parties in $\mathcal{P}' = \{P_{i_1}, \ldots, P_{i_{|\mathcal{P}'|}}\}$ send the message init to $\mathcal{F}_{\text{init}}$.
2. After receiving the message, $\mathcal{F}_{\text{init}}$ generates the random values $k_{\mathcal{P}'} \in \{0,1\}^\kappa$.
3. $\mathcal{F}_{\text{init}}$ sends $k_{\mathcal{P}'}$ to parties in $\mathcal{P}'$.

Fig. 1. Ideal functionality for initialization (sharing pre-shared keys)

We assume that these pre-shared keys are given to parties by the ideal functionality $\mathcal{F}_{\text{init}}$ (Fig. 1) in the same manner as with Trident [7]. For details on the actual initialization protocol that computes $\mathcal{F}_{\text{init}}$ securely, see Sect. 3.3.

Note that we ignore the differences in the order of the subscripts of $k_{\{a,b,c,d\}}$. For example, it holds that $k_{\{0,1,2,3\}} = k_{\{1,0,3,2\}}$.

We use the cryptographically secure pseudo-random functions $F_L : \{0,1\}^\kappa \times \{0,1\}^\kappa \rightarrow \mathbb{Z}_L$. We also use the collision-resistant hash function H in the same manner as with Trident [7]. That is, we use H for checking the message consistency.

2.2 2-Out-of-5 Replicated Secret Sharing ((2,5)-RSS)

We denote the (2,5)-RSS shares of x on $\mathbb{Z}_L$ as $[x] = ([x]_0, [x]_1, [x]_2, [x]_3, [x]_4)$ where $x \in \mathbb{Z}_L$. Each P_j ($j = 0, \ldots, 4$) obtains each share $[x]_j$ as follows.

$$P_0 : [x]_0 = (\lambda_{x,1}, \lambda_{x,2}, \lambda_{x,3}, \lambda_{x,4})$$
$$P_1 : [x]_1 = (m_x, \lambda_{x,2}, \lambda_{x,3}, \lambda_{x,4})$$
$$P_2 : [x]_2 = (m_x, \lambda_{x,1}, \lambda_{x,3}, \lambda_{x,4})$$
$$P_3 : [x]_3 = (m_x, \lambda_{x,1}, \lambda_{x,2}, \lambda_{x,4})$$
$$P_4 : [x]_4 = (m_x, \lambda_{x,1}, \lambda_{x,2}, \lambda_{x,3})$$

It holds that $\mathsf{m}_x = x + \lambda_x$ and $\lambda_x = \lambda_{x,1} + \lambda_{x,2} + \lambda_{x,3} + \lambda_{x,4}$ where m_x, λ_x, $\lambda_{x,1}$, $\lambda_{x,2}$, $\lambda_{x,3}$, $\lambda_{x,4} \in \mathbb{Z}_L$.

The following visualization shows who holds which value over the $(2,5)$-RSS.

$$
\begin{array}{c}
\mathsf{m}_x = x + \lambda_{x,1} + \lambda_{x,2} + \lambda_{x,3} + \lambda_{x,4} \bmod L \\
\mid \qquad \mid \qquad \mid \qquad \mid \qquad \mid
\end{array}
$$

$$
\begin{array}{ccccc}
 & P_0 & P_0 & P_0 & P_0 \\
P_1 & & P_1 & P_1 & P_1 \\
P_2 & P_2 & & P_2 & P_2 \\
P_3 & P_3 & P_3 & & P_3 \\
P_4 & P_4 & P_4 & P_4 &
\end{array}
\tag{1}
$$

We use the fact that all parties except $P_{j'}$ hold $\lambda_{x,j'}$. In other words, if x and y are shared values by $(2,5)$-RSS, any $\lambda_{x,i'}$ and $\lambda_{y,j'}$ $(i' \neq j')$ are always held by the same three parties in $\mathcal{P} \setminus \{P_{i'}, P_{j'}\}$. Hence, any cross-term $\lambda_{x,i'} \cdot \lambda_{y,j'}$ $(i' \neq j')$ can be computed by the same three parties. Three parties in $\mathcal{P} \setminus \{P_0, P_{j'}\}$ also hold the cross-terms $\mathsf{m}_x \cdot \lambda_{y,j'}$ and $\mathsf{m}_y \cdot \lambda_{x,j'}$ for $j' = 1, \ldots, 4$. We employ these observations about the cross-terms in constructing the share multiplication and DP protocols, i.e., Protocols 7 and 8.

Let's assume that $[x]$ and $[y]$ are the shares of the $(2,5)$-RSS on $\mathbb{Z}_L$. We describe $[x]_j$ and $[y]_j$ as $[x]_j = (x_{j,0}, x_{j,1}, x_{j,2}, x_{j,3})$ and $[y]_j = (y_{j,0}, y_{j,1}, y_{j,2}, y_{j,3})$ in this paragraph, respectively. Then each party P_j (for $j = 0, \ldots, 4$) can perform the share addition, $[x + y] = [x] + [y]$ by setting $[x + y]_j = (x_{j,0} + y_{j,0},\ x_{j,1} + y_{j,1},\ x_{j,2} + y_{j,2},\ x_{j,3} + y_{j,3})$. By performing the share addition of $[x]$ to $[x]$ repeatedly, parties can perform scalar multiplication, $[cx] = c \cdot [x]$ where $c \in \mathbb{Z}_L$ is public. If parties perform scalar addition, $[c + x] = c + [x]$ where $c \in \mathbb{Z}_L$ is public, P_0 sets $[c + x]_0 = [x]_0$ and $P_{j'}$ (for $j' = 1, 2, 3, 4$) sets $[c + x]_{j'} = (x_{j',0} + c,\ x_{j',1},\ x_{j',2},\ x_{j',3})$.

Therefore, the linearity of shares of the $(2,5)$-RSS holds, i.e., $[c_0 \cdot x + c_1 \cdot y] = c_0 \cdot [x] + c_1 \cdot [y]$, where $c_0, c_1 \in \mathbb{Z}_L$.

Remark: The sub-share m_x depends on an actual input x, but $\lambda_{x,j'}$ (for $j' = 1, \ldots, 4$) does not depend on it. In the offline-online strategy, parties reduce the online communication cost by carrying out a process that can be computed using only $\lambda_{x,j'}$ in the offline phase. To make it easier to understand whether the value depends on the actual input, we adopt the same notation as [7].

3   Our Protocol

We assume each party is connected by point-to-point private and authentic channels in a synchronous network, as with Trident [7]. That is, every message each party sends arrives within a known period. Therefore, a party that does not send a message or intentionally delays a message is considered corrupted. We also assume that there is, at most, a single static corruption in the five parties.

Our 5PC, similarly to Trident [7], is composed of four stages, i.e., initialization, input sharing, evaluation, and output reconstruction. Figure 2 shows the

---

$$\mathcal{F}_{5PC} \text{ - (circuit evaluation)}$$

Each party P_i $(i = 0, \ldots, 4)$ and the ideal functionality $\mathcal{F}_{5PC}$ compute the circuit $\mathcal{C} = (\mathcal{W}_{input}, \mathcal{W}_{const}, \mathcal{W}_{intermediate}, \mathcal{W}_{output}, \mathcal{G}_{input}, \mathcal{G}_{shareAdd}, \mathcal{G}_{scalarAdd}, \mathcal{G}_{scalarMult}, \mathcal{G}_{shareMult}, \mathcal{G}_{DP}, \mathcal{G}_{openOne})$ as follows:

- **Initialization** : $\mathcal{F}_{5PC}$ gives the pre-shared keys as follows:
  - One key shared between every group of four parties, $k_{\{a,b,c,d\}} \in \{0,1\}^\kappa$ for (P_a, P_b, P_c, P_d) where $a, b, c, d \in \{0, 1, 2, 3, 4\}$.
  - One key shared among all parties, $k \in \{0,1\}^\kappa$.
- **Input sharing** : For $g_j \in \mathcal{G}_{input}$ $(j = 0, \ldots, |\mathcal{G}_{input}| - 1)$, the parties and $\mathcal{F}_{5PC}$ evaluate input gates for $(2, 5)$-RSS shares, g_j.
- **Evaluation** :
  - (Share addition) For $g_j \in \mathcal{G}_{shareAdd}$ $(j = 0, \ldots, |\mathcal{G}_{shareAdd}| - 1)$, the parties and $\mathcal{F}_{5PC}$ evaluate a share addition gate g_j.
  - (Scalar addition) For $g_j \in \mathcal{G}_{scalarAdd}$ $(j = 0, \ldots, |\mathcal{G}_{scalarAdd}| - 1)$, the parties and $\mathcal{F}_{5PC}$ evaluate a scalar addition gate g_j.
  - (Scalar multiplication) For $g_j \in \mathcal{G}_{scalarMult}$ $(j = 0, \ldots, |\mathcal{G}_{scalarMult}| - 1)$, the parties and $\mathcal{F}_{5PC}$ evaluate a scalar multiplication gate g_j.
  - (Share multiplication) For $g_j \in \mathcal{G}_{shareMult}$ $(j = 0, \ldots, |\mathcal{G}_{shareMult}| - 1)$, the parties and $\mathcal{F}_{5PC}$ evaluate a share multiplication gate g_j.
  - (Dot product) For $g_j \in \mathcal{G}_{DP}$ $(j = 0, \ldots, |\mathcal{G}_{DP}| - 1)$, the parties and $\mathcal{F}_{5PC}$ evaluate a dot product gate g_j.
- **Output reconstruction** : For $g_j \in \mathcal{G}_{openOne}$ $(j = 0, \ldots, |\mathcal{G}_{openOne}| - 1)$, the parties and $\mathcal{F}_{5PC}$ evaluate gates of reconstruction of $(2, 5)$-RSS shares, g_j.

Fig. 2. Ideal functionality for secure 5PC with PR

ideal functionality $\mathcal{F}_{5PC}$ for secure 5PC with PR and its four stages. Our 5PC and $\mathcal{F}_{5PC}$ take the circuit $\mathcal{C}$ as inputs. $\mathcal{C}$ is composed of the wires and gates. $\mathcal{W}_{input}, \mathcal{W}_{const}, \mathcal{W}_{intermediate}$ and $\mathcal{W}_{output}$ are the sets of wires of parties' input values, constant values, intermediate values (output from gates) and output of the calculation results, respectively. $\mathcal{G}_{input}, \mathcal{G}_{shareAdd}, \mathcal{G}_{scalarAdd}, \mathcal{G}_{scalarMult}, \mathcal{G}_{shareMult}, \mathcal{G}_{DP}$ and $\mathcal{G}_{openOne}$ are the sets of gates in input sharing, evaluation and output reconstruction stages.

In the initialization stage, an ideal functionality $\mathcal{F}_{init}$ sends the pre-shared keys to parties, as with [7]. In the input sharing stage, each party inputs its value as shares. In the evaluation stage, parties perform local operations and share multiplication. In the output reconstruction stage, parties reconstruct the computation result.

3.1   Technical Overview

To achieve PR while reducing communication costs for cheating detection and identifying a corrupted party, we employ the strategy of the *joint message passing* (JMP) and propose an extended version of the JMP, Π_{EJMP}. The JMP protocol is widely utilized in recent 4PC [8,17] and 5PC [15] with PR to detect cheating and to narrow down the number of suspicious parties to two.

The JMP protocol is a three-party scheme involving two senders and one receiver. In this protocol, senders P_a and P_b both possess a message v. Sender P_a sends v to the receiver P_c, while sender P_b sends the hashed value of v to P_c. The receiver P_c then verifies the integrity of the received message by comparing the hash of the message from P_a with the hashed value received from P_b. If the hashes match, P_c confirms the correct reception of v. If there is a mismatch, P_c detects a cheating attempt. Subsequently, P_a, P_b, and P_c exchange their sent and received messages. By cross-referencing these messages, the protocol narrows down the potential cheaters to two from P_a, P_b, and P_c.

For example, in Fantastic four [8], after reducing the number of suspected parties by JMP, the two identified honest parties and one suspicious party engage in a maliciously secure Three-Party Computation (3PC) protocol to identify the corrupted party without revealing the parties' inputs. However, since Fantastic four performs this 3PC according to the circuit segment size, the amount of communication required to identify the corrupted party is large according to the circuit size. As another example, DEN22 [9], the current state-of-the-art SS-MPC that achieves PR and has good communication efficiency in the online phase, has a verification cost that depends on the circuit segment size because the verification process with cheating identification is performed for each divided circuit segment.

To reduce the communication costs required to identify the corrupted party, our Π_{EJMP} takes three senders with the message v, unlike the JMP protocol, which takes two senders. In Π_{EJMP}, first, two (not three) senders send v to the receiver in the same manner as with the JMP. If cheating is detected, the one sender, except the two senders who sent v is identified as an honest party because we assume up to one corrupted party in the protocol. The identified honest party sends v to the receiver. Once an honest party is identified, it always plays the sender's role when Π_{EJMP} on the same combination of the three senders and one receiver is called after that. Hence, our 5PC using Π_{EJMP} can efficiently achieve PR without the communication cost for identifying the corrupted party being proportional to the circuit size.

To construct the share multiplication and DP protocols by using Π_{EJMP}, we use an extended variant of the RSS scheme in Trident [7], $(2,5)$-RSS. As shown in Eq. (1), when x is shared via the $(2,5)$-RSS we adopt, e.g., $\lambda_{x,1}$ and $\lambda_{x,2}$ (also known as *sub-share*) are held by the same three parties P_0, P_3, P_4. Therefore, this enables P_0, P_3, P_4 to reshare the cross term $\lambda_{x,1} \cdot \lambda_{y,2}$ (where $\lambda_{y,2}$ is a sub-share from another shared value y) by Π_{EJMP} robustly, and we use this observation to construct our robust share multiplication and DP protocols.

However, since there are five parties, the amount of communication for share multiplication and DP in our 5PC will increase more than that of 4PC if the share multiplication and DP protocols are constructed in a straightforward manner using $(2,5)$-RSS. To reduce the number of ring elements sent by parties in the online phase of our 5PC, we use the offline-online paradigm in the same manner as with Trident [7].

We note that there exists, e.g., a general protocol compiler [10] that can convert a 5PC tolerating 2 semi-honest corruptions into the 5PC tolerating 1 malicious corruption with abort. This compiler can also convert a 7-party protocol tolerating 3 semi-honest corruptions into the 7-party protocol tolerating 1 malicious corruption with robustness. Compared with this type of general protocol compiler, our approach extends the previous 4PC with fairness, i.e., Trident [7] to a 5PC tolerating 1 malicious corruption and achieving PR simultaneously just by adding only one party.

3.2 Basic Operations for 5PC via (2, 5)-RSS

Protocol 1. Extended JMP protocol Π_{EJMP}

Input: Senders $\{P_a,\ P_b,\ P_c\}$ $(a, b, c \in \{0, 1, 2, 3, 4\}, a < b < c)$, senders' value $v \in \mathbb{Z}_L$, receiver P_i (where $i \in \{0, 1, 2, 3, 4\} \setminus \{a, b, c\}$)

Output: P_i receives m as the correct value v (and the senders $\{P_a,\ P_b,\ P_c\}$ get nothing)

1: P_a sets $m_a = v$ and sends m_a to P_i. P_b computes the hash value of v, $h = H(v)$. Then, P_b sets $m_b = h$ and sends m_b to P_i. // 1 round & $(\log_2 L + \log_2 h)$ bits

2: /*** Verification ***/
   P_i checks whether $H(m_a) = m_b$ or not. If it holds, then P_i sets $m = m_a$ as the correct value and does not execute the following steps. If not, P_i broadcasts the 1-bit flag, meaning that cheating occurred. // 1 round & 4 bits

3: /*** Resending the value for robustness ***/
   If P_c receives the 1-bit flag meaning that cheating occurred, then P_c sets $m_c = v$ and sends m_c to P_i. P_i sets $m = m_c$ as the correct value. // 1 round & $\log_2 L$ bits

---

Intuition of Protocol 1. Our Π_{EJMP} is the protocol by which the three senders $\{P_a,\ P_b,\ P_c\}$ $(a, b, c \in \{0, 1, 2, 3, 4\}, a < b < c)$ can send $v \in \mathbb{Z}_L$ to one receiver P_i $(i \in \{0, \ldots, 4\} \setminus \{a, b, c\})$ robustly. If no cheating has occurred, P_a and P_b are senders. If it has occurred, P_c is identified as an honest party and regarded as the sender.

At Step 1, two senders P_a and P_b send messages to P_i in the same manner as with the JMP [8,16]. At Step 2, if the hashed value of the message sent from P_a and the message sent from P_b match, P_i obtains v correctly. If not, P_i broadcasts the 1-bit flag, meaning that cheating occurred. That is, unlike the JMP, the process for reducing the number of suspicious parties is not done. Then, at step 3, P_c acts as the identified honest party and sends $m_c = v$ to P_i.

Our Π_{EJMP} requires 1 round and $\log_2 L$ bits, i.e., 1 ring element as the amortized communication cost. Note that for the communication cost of the hashed value at step 1 in Protocol 1, $\log_2 h$ bits are amortized away over multiple instances. In addition, Steps 2 and 3 are needed only when a cheating occurs during the execution of Π_{EJMP}, not each time Π_{EJMP} is called.

Remark: For each combination of senders P_a, P_b, and P_c and receiver P_i, if Step 3 occurs once when Π_{EJMP} is run, then the identified honest party P_c always sends the value v as the correct value in Step 1 and Steps 2 and 3 are skipped when Π_{EJMP} is run with the same combination.

Protocol 2. Robust resharing protocol over $(2,5)$-RSS (Type I) $\Pi_{\mathsf{RRS-I}}$

Input: Senders $\{P_a, P_b, P_0\}$ $(a, b \in \{1, \ldots, 4\}, a < b)$, value $v \in \mathbb{Z}_L$ which P_a, P_b, and P_0 hold.

Output: $[v]$

1: /*** Offline phase ***/
2: We let $\mathcal{P} \setminus \{P_a, P_b, P_0\} = \{P_d, P_e\}$.
3: Parties in $\mathcal{P} \setminus \{P_d\}$ compute $\lambda_{v,d} = F_L(\mathsf{uid}_d, \mathsf{k}_{\{a,b,0,e\}})$.
4: Parties in $\mathcal{P} \setminus \{P_e\}$ compute $\lambda_{v,e} = F_L(\mathsf{uid}_e, \mathsf{k}_{\{a,b,0,d\}})$.
5: Parties in $\mathcal{P}$ compute $\lambda_{v,a} = F_L(\mathsf{uid}_a, \mathsf{k})$ and $\lambda_{v,b} = F_L(\mathsf{uid}_b, \mathsf{k})$.
6: /*** Online phase ***/
7: P_a, P_b, and P_0 compute $\mathsf{m}_v = v + \sum_{j'=1}^{4} \lambda_{v,j'} \bmod L$.
8: P_a, P_b, and P_0 run $\Pi_{\mathsf{EJMP}}(\{P_a, P_b, P_0\}, \mathsf{m}_v, P_d)$ and $\Pi_{\mathsf{EJMP}}(\{P_a, P_b, P_0\}, \mathsf{m}_v, P_e)$. // 1 round & $2\log_2 L$ bits
9: Each P_j sets $[v]_j$ as follows.

$$P_0 : [v]_0 = (\lambda_{v,1},\ \lambda_{v,2},\ \lambda_{v,3},\ \lambda_{v,4})$$
$$P_1 : [v]_1 = (\mathsf{m}_v,\ \lambda_{v,2},\ \lambda_{v,3},\ \lambda_{v,4})$$
$$P_2 : [v]_2 = (\mathsf{m}_v,\ \lambda_{v,1},\ \lambda_{v,3},\ \lambda_{v,4})$$
$$P_3 : [v]_3 = (\mathsf{m}_v,\ \lambda_{v,1},\ \lambda_{v,2},\ \lambda_{v,4})$$
$$P_4 : [v]_4 = (\mathsf{m}_v,\ \lambda_{v,1},\ \lambda_{v,2},\ \lambda_{v,3})$$

10: $[v] = ([v]_0, [v]_1, [v]_2, [v]_3, [v]_4)$.

Protocol 3. Robust resharing protocol over $(2,5)$-RSS (Type II) $\Pi_{\mathsf{RRS-II}}$

Input: Senders $\{P_a, P_b, P_c\}$ $(a, b, c \in \{1, \ldots, 4\}, a < b < c)$, value $v \in \mathbb{Z}_L$ which P_a, P_b, and P_c hold.

Output: $[v]$

1: /*** Offline phase ***/
2: We let $\mathcal{P} \setminus \{P_a, P_b, P_c\} = \{P_d, P_0\}$.
3: Parties in $\mathcal{P} \setminus \{P_d\}$ compute $\lambda_{v,d} = F_L(\mathsf{uid}_d, \mathsf{k}_{\{a,b,c,0\}})$.
4: Parties in $\mathcal{P}$ compute $\lambda_{v,a} = F_L(\mathsf{uid}_a, \mathsf{k})$, $\lambda_{v,b} = F_L(\mathsf{uid}_b, \mathsf{k})$ and $\lambda_{v,c} = F_L(\mathsf{uid}_c, \mathsf{k})$.
5: /*** Online phase ***/
6: P_a, P_b, and P_c compute $\mathsf{m}_v = v + \sum_{j'=1}^{4} \lambda_{v,j'} \bmod L$.
7: P_a, P_b, and P_c run $\Pi_{\mathsf{EJMP}}(\{P_a, P_b, P_c\}, \mathsf{m}_v, P_d)$. // 1 round & $\log_2 L$ bits
8: Parties perform Steps 9 and 10 of Protocol 2.

Intuition of Protocols 2 and 3. The robust resharing protocols $\Pi_{\mathsf{RRS-I}}$ and $\Pi_{\mathsf{RRS-II}}$ distribute the value v, which is held by three senders as $[v]$ robustly. These protocols are used as subprotocols in the share multiplication protocol. The difference between $\Pi_{\text{RRS-I}}$ and $\Pi_{\text{RRS-II}}$ is whether or not P_0 is among the three senders. First, we explain $\Pi_{\text{RRS-I}}$ (Protocol 2), which takes P_0 as one of senders.

The goal of offline phase of $\Pi_{\text{RRS-I}}$ is to compute $\lambda_{x,j'}$ by using the pseudorandom function F_L, unique identifier $\text{uid}_{j'}$, and pre-shared key without communications for $j' = 1, \ldots, 4$ at Steps 2, 3, and 4. We must compute $\lambda_{v,d}$ and $\lambda_{v,e}$ without revealing them to the parties in $\{P_d, P_e\} = \mathcal{P} \setminus \{P_a, P_b, P_0\}$ because P_d and P_e do not hold $\lambda_{v,d}$ and $\lambda_{v,e}$ in the $(2, 5)$-RSS, respectively[1]. For this reason, at Step 3 in Protocol 2, parties in $\mathcal{P} \setminus \{P_d\}$ compute $\lambda_{v,d} = F_L(\text{uid}_d, \mathsf{k}_{\{a,b,0,e\}})$ where the pre-shared key $\mathsf{k}_{\{a,b,0,e\}}$ is not known to P_d. At Step 4, parties in $\mathcal{P} \setminus \{P_e\}$ compute $\lambda_{v,e} = F_L(\text{uid}_e, \mathsf{k}_{\{a,b,0,d\}})$ where the pre-shared key $\mathsf{k}_{\{a,b,0,d\}}$ is not known to P_e. At Step 5, all parties compute $\lambda_{v,a}$ and $\lambda_{v,b}$ by using F_L, uid_a, uid_b and the pre-shared key k held by all parties because the senders and receivers can know $\lambda_{v,a}$ and $\lambda_{v,b}$.

In the online phase of $\Pi_{\text{RRS-I}}$, i.e., at Step 7 in Protocol 2, P_a, P_b, and P_0 compute $\mathsf{m}_v = v + \sum_{j'=1}^{4} \lambda_{v,j'} \mod L$ by using $\lambda_{v,j'}$ computed in the offline phase. Then, they send it to P_d and P_e by Π_{EJMP}, robustly at Step 8. Finally, each party P_i sets the shares $[v]_i$ by using the values computed in the offline phase and received in the online phase at Steps 9 and 10.

Protocol 3, $\Pi_{\text{RRS-II}}$ is almost the same as $\Pi_{\text{RRS-I}}$, except that P_0 is not included in the senders. The P_0's share of v can be computed without communications in the offline phase because of $[v]_0 = (\lambda_{v,1}, \lambda_{v,2}, \lambda_{v,3}, \lambda_{v,4})$. Hence, the amount of communication of $\Pi_{\text{RRS-II}}$ in the online phase is half of that of $\Pi_{\text{RRS-I}}$.

3.3   Protocol in Initialization Stage

Protocol 4. Initialization protocol Π_{init}

Input: Set of parties $\mathcal{P}' = \{P_{i_1}, \ldots, P_{i_{|\mathcal{P}'|}}\} \subseteq \mathcal{P}$ where $|\mathcal{P}'|(\geq 4)$ is the size of $\mathcal{P}'$

Output: Parties in $\mathcal{P}'$ hold $\mathsf{k}_{\mathcal{P}'}$ without the party in $\mathcal{P} \setminus \mathcal{P}'$ knowing it.

1: **for** $j' = 1, \ldots, |\mathcal{P}'|$ **do in parallel**

2:    Each party $P_{i_{j'}} \in \mathcal{P}'$ generates a random value $\mathsf{k}_{i_{j'}} \in \{0,1\}^\kappa$ and sends it to the parties in $\mathcal{P}' \setminus \{P_{i_{j'}}\}$.

3:    Parties in $\mathcal{P}' \setminus \{P_{i_{j'}}\}$ mutually exchange the received $\mathsf{k}_{i_{j'}}$ and determine if the received values match by majority vote.
    If the majority vote works, then the most frequent value is taken as the correct value and the following steps are continued. If not, parties in $\mathcal{P} \setminus \{P_{i_{j'}}\}$ engage in semi-honest 4PC excluding $P_{i_{j'}}$ and the following steps are ignored.

4: **end for**

5: Each party in $\mathcal{P}'$ sets the pre-shared key among $\mathcal{P}'$ as $\mathsf{k}_{\mathcal{P}'} = \bigoplus_{j'=1}^{|\mathcal{P}'|} \mathsf{k}_{i_{j'}}$ and holds it.

---
[1] We note that $\{a, b, d, e\} = \{1, 2, 3, 4\}$ and a, b, d, and e are different values from each other.

Intuition of Protocol 4. Each party $P_{i_{j'}}$ in $\mathcal{P}'$ generates the κ-bit random value and sends it to the parties in $\mathcal{P}' \setminus \{P_{i_{j'}}\}$ at Step 2. Parties in $\mathcal{P}' \setminus \{P_{i_{j'}}\}$ use the majority vote to verify that the received values match at Step 3. If the majority vote works correctly, the parties in $\mathcal{P}'$ set the pre-shared key among $\mathcal{P}'$ as $\mathsf{k}_{\mathcal{P}'} = \bigoplus_{j'=1}^{|\mathcal{P}'|} \mathsf{k}_{i_{j'}}$ and hold it[2]. If not, parties in $\mathcal{P} \setminus \{P_{i_{j'}}\}$ engage in semi-honest 4PC excluding $P_{i_{j'}}$. Then, Protocol 4 can generate the pre-shared key $\mathsf{k}_{\mathcal{P}'}$ among $\mathcal{P}'$ robustly because we assume that there is at most a single (static) corruption.

We note that parties set $\mathcal{P}' = \mathcal{P}$ and run Π_{init} when they generate the pre-shared key among all parties, k. In the initialization stage of our 5PC, to generate the pre-shared keys robustly, parties run multiple executions of Π_{init} while changing $\mathcal{P}'$.

3.4 Protocols in Input Sharing Stage

Protocol 5. Input protocol (Type-I) $\Pi_{\mathsf{input-I}}$

Input: Modulus L, input dealer P_0, input value $x \in \mathbb{Z}_L$
Output: $[x]$
1: /*** Offline phase ***/
2: **for** $j' = 1, 2, 3, 4$ **do in parallel**
3:     Parties in $\mathcal{P} \setminus \{P_{j'}\}$ compute $\lambda_{v,j'} = F_L(\mathsf{uid}_{j'}, \mathsf{k}_{\{0,1,2,3,4\} \setminus \{j'\}})$.
4: **end for**
5: /*** Online phase ***/
6: P_0 computes $\mathsf{m}_x = x + \lambda_x \bmod L$ where $\lambda_x = \sum_{j'=1}^{4} \lambda_{x,j'} \bmod L$.
7: P_0 sends m_x to parties in $\mathcal{P} \setminus \{P_0\}$. // 1 round & $4 \log_2 L$
8: Parties in $\mathcal{P} \setminus \{P_0\}$ mutually exchange the received m_x and determine if the received values match by majority vote. // 1 round & $12 \log_2 L$ bits
    If the majority vote works, then the most frequent value is taken as the correct value and the following steps are continued. If not, parties in $\mathcal{P} \setminus \{P_0\}$ engage in semi-honest 4PC excluding P_0 with a default input for P_0 and the following steps are ignored.
9: Each P_j sets $[x]_j$ as follows.

$$P_0 : [x]_0 = (\lambda_{x,1}, \ \lambda_{x,2}, \ \lambda_{x,3}, \ \lambda_{x,4})$$
$$P_1 : [x]_1 = (\mathsf{m}_x, \ \lambda_{x,2}, \ \lambda_{x,3}, \ \lambda_{x,4})$$
$$P_2 : [x]_2 = (\mathsf{m}_x, \ \lambda_{x,1}, \ \lambda_{x,3}, \ \lambda_{x,4})$$
$$P_3 : [x]_3 = (\mathsf{m}_x, \ \lambda_{x,1}, \ \lambda_{x,2}, \ \lambda_{x,4})$$
$$P_4 : [x]_4 = (\mathsf{m}_x, \ \lambda_{x,1}, \ \lambda_{x,2}, \ \lambda_{x,3})$$

10: $[x] = ([x]_0, [x]_1, [x]_2, [x]_3, [x]_4)$.

---

[2] We denote $\oplus$ as a binary operator, meaning exclusive OR. That is, $\bigoplus_{j'=1}^{|\mathcal{P}'|} \mathsf{k}_{i_{j'}}$ means $\mathsf{k}_{i_1} \oplus \cdots \oplus \mathsf{k}_{i_{|\mathcal{P}'|}}$.

Protocol 6. Input protocol (Type-II) $\Pi_{\text{input−II}}$

Input: Modulus L, input dealer $P_i \in \mathcal{P} \setminus \{P_0\}$, input value $x \in \mathbb{Z}_L$
Output: $[x]$
1: /*** Offline phase ***/
2: **for** $j' = 1, 2, 3, 4$ **do in parallel**
3:     **if** $i = j'$ **then**
4:        All parties compute $\lambda_{x,i} = F_L(\text{uid}_i, \text{k})$.
5:     **else**
6:        Parties in $\mathcal{P} \setminus \{P_{j'}\}$ compute $\lambda_{x,j'} = F_L(\text{uid}_{j'}, \text{k}_{\{0,1,2,3,4\}\setminus\{j'\}})$.
7:     **end if**
8: **end for**
9: /*** Online phase ***/
10: P_i computes $\text{m}_x = x + \lambda_x \bmod L$ where $\lambda_x = \sum_{j'=1}^{4} \lambda_{x,j'} \bmod L$.
11: P_i sends m_x to parties in $\mathcal{P} \setminus \{P_0, P_i\}$. // 1 round & $3\log_2 L$
12: Parties in $\mathcal{P} \setminus \{P_0, P_i\}$ mutually exchange the received m_x and determine if the received values match by majority vote. // 1 round & $6\log_2 L$ bits
     If the majority vote works, then the most frequent value is taken as the correct value and the following steps are continued. If not, parties in $\mathcal{P} \setminus \{P_i\}$ engage in semi-honest 4PC excluding P_i with a default input for P_i and the following steps are ignored.
13: Parties perform Steps 9 and 10 of Protocol 5.

Intuition of Protocols 5 and 6. We propose two protocols for input sharing, $\Pi_{\text{input−I}}$ and $\Pi_{\text{input−II}}$. When the input dealer is P_0, the input protocol is $\Pi_{\text{input−I}}$, i.e., Protocol 5. When the input dealer is other than P_0, the input protocol is $\Pi_{\text{input−II}}$, i.e., Protocol 6. We explain Protocol 5, $\Pi_{\text{input−I}}$ as follows.

In the offline phase of $\Pi_{\text{input−I}}$, for $j' = 1, \ldots, 4$ in parallel, parties in $\mathcal{P} \setminus \{P_{j'}\}$ compute $\lambda_{j'}$ by using F_L, $\text{uid}_{j'}$, and the pre-shared key $\text{k}_{\{0,1,2,3,4\}\setminus\{j'\}}$ held by parties except $P_{j'}$. Then, parties can compute $\lambda_{j'}$ without communications and letting $P_{j'}$ know about it.

In the online phase of $\Pi_{\text{input−I}}$, the input dealer P_0 computes m_x by using the actual input value x and the computed values in the offline phase, $\lambda_{x,j'}$ ($j' = 1, 2, 3, 4$) at Step 6. After computing m_x, P_0 sends m_x to parties in $\mathcal{P} \setminus \{P_0\}$ at Step 7. Then, at Step 8, parties in $\mathcal{P} \setminus \{P_0\}$ mutually exchange the received m_x and determine if the received values match by majority vote. If the majority vote works correctly, at Steps 9 and 10, parties set $[x]$ locally. If not, parties in $\mathcal{P} \setminus \{P_0\}$ engage in semi-honest 4PC excluding P_0 with a default input for P_i. Therefore, $\Pi_{\text{input−I}}$ can achieve PR because we assume that there is at most a single (static) corruption.

Protocol 6, $\Pi_{\text{input−II}}$ is almost the same as $\Pi_{\text{input−I}}$, except that the input dealer P_i is in $\mathcal{P} \setminus \{P_0\}$. The P_0's share of x can be computed without communications in the offline phase because of $[x]_0 = (\lambda_{x,1}, \lambda_{x,2}, \lambda_{x,3}, \lambda_{x,4})$. Hence, the amount of communication of $\Pi_{\text{input−II}}$ in the online phase is half of that of $\Pi_{\text{input−I}}$. Note that, all parties including the input dealer P_i can compute $\lambda_{x,i}$ by using k held among parties at Steps 3, 4, and 5 in Protocol 6 because the input dealer P_i can know $\lambda_{x,i}$.

3.5 Protocols in Evaluation Stage

Protocol 7

Share multiplication protocol Π_{mult}

Input: $[x], [y]$

Output: $[z]$ such that $z = x \cdot y \bmod L$

1: /*** Offline phase ***/
2: **for** $i' = 1, 2, 3, 4;\ j' = 1, 2, 3, 4$ **do in parallel**
3:    **if** $i' \neq j'$ **then**
4:        Three parties, P_a, P_b, and P_0 in $\mathcal{P} \setminus \{P_{i'}, P_{j'}\}$ $(a < b)$ run $\Pi_{\mathsf{RRS-I}}(\{P_a, P_b, P_0\}, \lambda_{x,i'} \cdot \lambda_{y,j'})$. Then, parties obtain $[\lambda_{x,i'} \cdot \lambda_{y,j'}]$.
5:    **else**
6:        Three parties, P_a, P_b, and P_c in $\mathcal{P} \setminus \{P_{i'}, P_0\}$ $(a < b < c)$ run $\Pi_{\mathsf{RRS-II}}(\{P_a, P_b, P_c\}, \lambda_{x,i'} \cdot \lambda_{y,j'})$. Then, parties obtain $[\lambda_{x,i'} \cdot \lambda_{y,j'}]$.
7:    **end if**
8: **end for**
9: /*** Online phase ***/
10: **for** $j' = 1, 2, 3, 4$ **do in parallel**
11:    Three parties P_a, P_b, and P_c in $\mathcal{P} \setminus \{P_{j'}, P_0\}$ $(a < b < c)$ run $\Pi_{\mathsf{RRS-II}}(\{P_a, P_b, P_c\}, -m_x \cdot \lambda_{y,j'} - m_y \cdot \lambda_{x,j'})$. Parties then obtain $[-m_x \cdot \lambda_{y,j'} - m_y \cdot \lambda_{x,j'}]$.
        // 1 round & $\log_2 L$ bits, i.e., 1 ring element
12: **end for**
13: Each party P_i sets $[m_x \cdot m_y]_i$ by $[x]_i$ and $[y]_i$ without communications as follows.

$$[m_x \cdot m_y]_0 = (0,\ 0,\ 0,\ 0)$$
$$[m_x \cdot m_y]_1 = (m_x \cdot m_y,\ 0,\ 0,\ 0)$$
$$[m_x \cdot m_y]_2 = (m_x \cdot m_y,\ 0,\ 0,\ 0)$$
$$[m_x \cdot m_y]_3 = (m_x \cdot m_y,\ 0,\ 0,\ 0)$$
$$[m_x \cdot m_y]_4 = (m_x \cdot m_y,\ 0,\ 0,\ 0)$$

14: Parties compute $[z]$ as follows.

$$
\begin{aligned}
[z] &= [x \cdot y] \\
&= \left[\left(m_x - \sum_{j'=1}^{4} \lambda_{x,j'} \right)\left(m_y - \sum_{j'=1}^{4} \lambda_{y,j'} \right) \right] \\
&= [m_x \cdot m_y] + \sum_{j'=1}^{4} [-m_x \cdot \lambda_{y,j'} - m_y \cdot \lambda_{x,j'}] + \sum_{i'=1}^{4}\sum_{j'=1}^{4} [\lambda_{x,i'} \lambda_{y,j'}]
\end{aligned}
$$

Protocol 8. DP protocol Π_{DP}

Input: $[\boldsymbol{x}] = ([x_0], \ldots, [x_{M-1}]), [\boldsymbol{y}] = ([y_0], \ldots, [y_{M-1}])$
Output: $[z]$ such that $z = \sum_{k=0}^{M-1} x_k \cdot y_k \bmod L$
1: /*** Offline phase ***/
2: **for** $i' = 1, 2, 3, 4$; $j' = 1, 2, 3, 4$ **do in parallel**
3:    **if** $i' \neq j'$ **then**
4:       Three parties, P_a, P_b, and P_0 in $\mathcal{P} \setminus \{P_{i'}, P_{j'}\}$ $(a < b)$ run $\Pi_{\mathsf{RRS-I}}($
      $\{P_a, P_b, P_0\}, \sum_{k=0}^{M-1} \lambda_{x_k, i'} \cdot \lambda_{y_k, j'})$. Then, parties obtain $[\sum_{k=0}^{M-1} \lambda_{x_k, i'} \cdot \lambda_{y_k, j'}]$.
5:    **else**
6:       Three parties, P_a, P_b, and P_c in $\mathcal{P} \setminus \{P_{i'}, P_0\}$ $(a < b < c)$ run $\Pi_{\mathsf{RRS-II}}(\{$
      $P_a, P_b, P_c\}, \sum_{k=0}^{M-1} \lambda_{x_k, i'} \cdot \lambda_{y_k, j'})$. Then, parties obtain $[\sum_{k=0}^{M-1} \lambda_{x_k, i'} \cdot \lambda_{y_k, j'}]$.
7:    **end if**
8: **end for**
9: /*** Online phase ***/
10: **for** $j' = 1, 2, 3, 4$ **do in parallel**
11:    Three parties P_a, P_b, and P_c in $\mathcal{P} \setminus \{P_{j'}, P_0\}$ $(a < b < c)$ run $\Pi_{\mathsf{RRS-II}}(\{$
   $P_a, P_b, P_c\}, \sum_{k=0}^{M-1} (-\mathsf{m}_{x_k} \cdot \lambda_{y_k, j'} - \mathsf{m}_{y_k} \cdot \lambda_{x_k, j'}))$.
   Parties then obtain $[\sum_{k=0}^{M-1} (-\mathsf{m}_{x_k} \cdot \lambda_{y_k, j'} - \mathsf{m}_{y_k} \cdot \lambda_{x_k, j'})]$. // 1 round &
   $\log_2 L$ bits, i.e., 1 ring element
12: **end for**
13: Each party P_i sets $[\sum_{k=0}^{M-1} \mathsf{m}_{x_k} \cdot \mathsf{m}_{y_k}]_i$ by $[x_k]_i$ and $[y_k]_i$ without communications as follows.

$$[\sum_{k=0}^{M-1} \mathsf{m}_{x_k} \cdot \mathsf{m}_{y_k}]_0 = (0, \ 0, \ 0, \ 0)$$

$$[\sum_{k=0}^{M-1} \mathsf{m}_{x_k} \cdot \mathsf{m}_{y_k}]_1 = (\sum_{k=0}^{M-1} \mathsf{m}_{x_k} \cdot \mathsf{m}_{y_k}, \ 0, \ 0, \ 0)$$

$$[\sum_{k=0}^{M-1} \mathsf{m}_{x_k} \cdot \mathsf{m}_{y_k}]_2 = (\sum_{k=0}^{M-1} \mathsf{m}_{x_k} \cdot \mathsf{m}_{y_k}, \ 0, \ 0, \ 0)$$

$$[\sum_{k=0}^{M-1} \mathsf{m}_{x_k} \cdot \mathsf{m}_{y_k}]_3 = (\sum_{k=0}^{M-1} \mathsf{m}_{x_k} \cdot \mathsf{m}_{y_k}, \ 0, \ 0, \ 0)$$

$$[\sum_{k=0}^{M-1} \mathsf{m}_{x_k} \cdot \mathsf{m}_{y_k}]_4 = (\sum_{k=0}^{M-1} \mathsf{m}_{x_k} \cdot \mathsf{m}_{y_k}, \ 0, \ 0, \ 0)$$

14: Parties compute $[z]$ as follows.

$$[z] = [\sum_{k=0}^{M-1} x_k \cdot y_k]$$

$$= [\sum_{k=0}^{M-1} (\mathsf{m}_{x_k} - \sum_{j'=1}^{4} \lambda_{x_k,j'})(\mathsf{m}_{y_k} - \sum_{j'=1}^{4} \lambda_{y_k,j'})]$$

$$= [\sum_{k=0}^{M-1} \mathsf{m}_{x_k} \cdot \mathsf{m}_{y_k}]$$

$$+ \sum_{j'=1}^{4} [\sum_{k=0}^{M-1} (-\mathsf{m}_{x_k} \cdot \lambda_{y_k,j'} - \mathsf{m}_{y_k} \cdot \lambda_{x_k,j'})]$$

$$+ \sum_{i'=1}^{4} \sum_{j'=1}^{4} [\sum_{k=0}^{M-1} \lambda_{x_k,i'} \lambda_{y_k,j'}]$$

Intuitions of Protocols 7 and 8. In the share multiplication protocol Π_{mult} (Protocol 7), parties compute $[z] = [x \cdot y]$ by using $[x]$ and $[y]$. To compute $[z]$, we first focus on the following equation.

$$z = x \cdot y$$

$$= (\mathsf{m}_x - \sum_{j'=1}^{4} \lambda_{x,j'})(\mathsf{m}_y - \sum_{j'=1}^{4} \lambda_{y,j'})$$

$$= \mathsf{m}_x \cdot \mathsf{m}_y + \sum_{j'=1}^{4} (-\mathsf{m}_x \cdot \lambda_{y,j'} - \mathsf{m}_y \cdot \lambda_{x,j'}) + \sum_{i'=1}^{4} \sum_{j'=1}^{4} \lambda_{x,i'} \lambda_{y,j'} \qquad (2)$$

From Eq. (2) and Sect. 2.2, we can observe that parties are able to compute the term $\sum_{i'=1}^{4} \sum_{j'=1}^{4} \lambda_{x,i'} \lambda_{y,j'}$ in the offline phase because the sub-shares $\lambda_{x,i'}$ and $\lambda_{y,j'}$ are independent of the actual inputs. Hence, we divide the computation of $[z]$ into an offline phase to compute $\sum_{i'=1}^{4} \sum_{j'=1}^{4} [\lambda_{x,i'} \lambda_{y,j'}]$ and an online phase to compute $[\mathsf{m}_x \cdot \mathsf{m}_y]$ and $\sum_{j'=1}^{4} [-\mathsf{m}_x \cdot \lambda_{y,j'} - \mathsf{m}_y \cdot \lambda_{x,j'}]$.

In the offline phase of Π_{mult}, three parties in $\mathcal{P} \setminus \{P_{i'}, P_{j'}\}$ first compute the cross-term $\lambda_{x,i'} \cdot \lambda_{y,j'}$ without communications for $i' = 1, \dots, 4$; $j' = 1, \dots, 4$ in parallel when $i' \neq j'$. They can do it because any $\lambda_{x,i'}$ and $\lambda_{y,j'}$ are always held by three parties in $\mathcal{P} \setminus \{P_{i'}, P_{j'}\}$ as explained in Sect. 2.2. When $i' = j'$, three parties in $\mathcal{P} \setminus \{P_{i'}, P_0\}$ also compute the cross-term $\lambda_{x,i'} \cdot \lambda_{y,j'}$ without communications. Then, three parties computing the cross-term run $\Pi_{\mathsf{RRS-I}}$ or $\Pi_{\mathsf{RRS-II}}$ and reshare it as $[\lambda_{x,i'} \lambda_{y,j'}]$ robustly.

In the online phase of Π_{mult}, at Steps 10, 11, and 12, three parties in $\mathcal{P} \setminus \{P_{j'}, P_0\}$ compute $-\mathsf{m}_x \cdot \lambda_{y,j'} - \mathsf{m}_y \cdot \lambda_{x,j'}$ without communication for $j' = 1, \dots, 4$ in parallel. After that, they reshare it as $[-\mathsf{m}_x \cdot \lambda_{y,j'} - \mathsf{m}_y \cdot \lambda_{x,j'}]$ by $\Pi_{\mathsf{RRS-II}}$

robustly. We note that three parties in $\mathcal{P} \setminus \{P_{j'}, P_0\}$ can do these operations because they can compute the cross-terms $\mathsf{m}_x \cdot \lambda_{y,j'}$ and $\mathsf{m}_y \cdot \lambda_{x,j'}$ as explained in Sect. 2.2.

We emphasize that the communication cost of our Π_{mult} to achieve PR after cheating has occurred is independent of circuit size, unlike previous studies [8,9]. During the execution of Π_{mult}, if cheating were to occur, the cheating would be detected in Π_{EJMP} that is invoked in $\Pi_{\mathsf{RRS-I}}$ or $\Pi_{\mathsf{RRS-II}}$. After detection, one of the three senders is identified as the honest party. Since the identification of the honest party can only occur in as many combinations as there are three senders, it can happen at most $\binom{5}{3} = 10$ times. Therefore, the amount of communication required to achieve PR is 10 ring elements, regardless of the circuit size.

Finally, parties compute $[\mathsf{m}_x \cdot \mathsf{m}_y]$ without communications at Step 13. Then, they obtain $[z]$ by using the shares that are computed in the previous steps.

In the DP protocol Π_{DP} (Protocol 8), parties compute $[z] = [\sum_{k=0}^{M-1} x_k \cdot y_k]$ by using $[\boldsymbol{x}] = ([x_0], \ldots, [x_{M-1}])$ and $[\boldsymbol{y}] = ([y_0], \ldots, [y_{M-1}])$. The computation strategy for Π_{DP} is almost identical to that of Π_{mult} except the messages are sent in batches for the dimensions. Hence, Π_{DP} requires the same (amortized) communication cost as Π_{mult}.

3.6 Protocols in Output Reconstruction Stage

Protocol 9. Opening protocol for one party Π_{openOne}

Input: Receiver P_i, share of x $[x] = ([x]_0, [x]_1, [x]_2, [x]_3, [x]_4)$ where

$$[x]_0 = (\lambda_{x,1}, \ \lambda_{x,2}, \ \lambda_{x,3}, \ \lambda_{x,4})$$
$$[x]_1 = (\mathsf{m}_x, \ \lambda_{x,2}, \ \lambda_{x,3}, \ \lambda_{x,4})$$
$$[x]_2 = (\mathsf{m}_x, \ \lambda_{x,1}, \ \lambda_{x,3}, \ \lambda_{x,4})$$
$$[x]_3 = (\mathsf{m}_x, \ \lambda_{x,1}, \ \lambda_{x,2}, \ \lambda_{x,4})$$
$$[x]_4 = (\mathsf{m}_x, \ \lambda_{x,1}, \ \lambda_{x,2}, \ \lambda_{x,3})$$

Output: P_i reconstructs $x \in \mathbb{Z}_L$.

1: **if** $i = 0$ **then**
2:   P_0, P_1, P_2, and P_3 run $\Pi_{\mathsf{EJMP}}(\{P_1, P_2, P_3\}, \mathsf{m}_x, P_0)$. // 1 round & $\log_2 L$ bits
3: **else**
4:   Let any three parties in $\mathcal{P} \setminus \{P_i\}$ be P_a, P_b, and P_c. P_i, P_a, P_b, and P_c run $\Pi_{\mathsf{EJMP}}(\{P_a, P_b, P_c\}, \lambda_{x,i}, P_i)$. // 1 round & $\log_2 L$ bits
5: **end if**
6: P_i computes $x = \mathsf{m}_x - \sum_{j'=1}^{4} \lambda_{x,j'} \bmod L$ by using $[x]_i$ and the received value in previous steps.

Intuition of Protocol 9. In the opening protocol for one party Π_{openOne}, the reconstructing party P_i reconstructs x by receiving the sub-share required for reconstruction via Π_{EJMP} to achieve PR. As described in Steps 1 through 4, if P_i is P_0, then the receiving value required for reconstruction is m_x. If not, it is $\lambda_{x,i}$.

The protocol for all parties to reconstruct x, Π_{open}, can be constructed by running multiple executions of Π_{openOne} while changing P_i in parallel. Note that $\lambda_{x,j'}$ (for $j' = 1, \ldots, 4$) is generated independent of actual inputs. Hence, Π_{openOne} in the case in which $P_i \neq P_0$ can be run in the offline phase.

4   Security Proof Sketch

We employ the ideal/real simulation paradigm [5], which compares an execution in the ideal world where a trusted third party computes the functionality for parties achieving PR with an execution in the real world, where parties run our protocol.

The protocol securely computes the functionality if adversaries in the ideal world can simulate executions of the real-world protocol. We prove that the security of our 5PC can be reduced to the security of the pseudo-random function F_L in a hybrid model [5] because our protocols consist solely of local computation and communication masked by random numbers generated by F_L and pre-shared keys. Moreover, we also prove that our 5PC can achieve PR, as it utilizes Π_{EJMP} for transmitting values and compute $\mathcal{F}_{\mathsf{5PC}}$ securely under the assumption of a single corruption.

To prove that our 5PC protocol is secure within the *Universal Composability* (UC) framework [6], we assume that our 5PC has *input availability* [18], i.e., the inputs of all parties are fixed before the execution of the protocol begins. As shown in [18, Theorem 1.5], any protocol that is proven secure with a black-box non-rewinding simulator and has input availability, is also secure under UC. As well as [2,11,12], since input availability holds for all of our protocols, including subprotocols, it is sufficient to prove security in the classic stand-alone setting and automatically derives UC from [18].

5   Conclusion

We proposed the maliciously secure 5PC with PR based on the $(2, 5)$-RSS. Our 5PC protocol exhibits superior communication efficiency for share multiplication in the online phase compared to existing methods.

Additionally, we also proposed the DP protocol with PR that has better communication efficiency in the online phase than existing methods. The DP protocol is a fundamental building block for various machine learning algorithms that are popular applications based on SS-MPC. Consequently, applications and services utilizing our 5PC protocol can achieve both efficient communication and security simultaneously.

Acknowledgments. This work was supported in part by JSPS KAKENHI Grant Number 23K18459, and The Telecommunications Advancement Foundation.

References

1. Araki, T., et al.: Optimized honest-majority mpc for malicious adversaries-breaking the 1 billion-gate per second barrier. In: 2017 IEEE Symposium on Security and Privacy (SP), pp. 843–862. IEEE (2017)
2. Araki, T., Furukawa, J., Lindell, Y., Nof, A., Ohara, K.: High-throughput semi-honest secure three-party computation with an honest majority. In: Proceedings of the 2016 ACM SIGSAC Conference on Computer and Communications Security, pp. 805–817 (2016)
3. Ben-Or, M., Goldwasser, S., Wigderson, A.: Completeness theorems for non-cryptographic fault-tolerant distributed computation (extended abstract). In: STOC, pp. 1–10. ACM (1988)
4. Byali, M., Chaudhari, H., Patra, A., Suresh, A.: FLASH: fast and robust framework for privacy-preserving machine learning. Proc. Priv. Enhan. Technol. **2020**(2), 459–480 (2020)
5. Canetti, R.: Security and composition of multiparty cryptographic protocols. J. Cryptol. **13**(1), 143–202 (2000)
6. Canetti, R.: Universally composable security: a new paradigm for cryptographic protocols. In: FOCS, pp. 136–145. IEEE Computer Society (2001)
7. Chaudhari, H., Rachuri, R., Suresh, A.: Trident: efficient 4pc framework for privacy preserving machine learning. In: NDSS. The Internet Society (2020)
8. Dalskov, A.P.K., Escudero, D., Keller, M.: Fantastic four: honest-majority four-party secure computation with malicious security. In: USENIX Security Symposium, pp. 2183–2200. USENIX Association (2021)
9. Dalskov, A.P.K., Escudero, D., Nof, A.: Fast fully secure multi-party computation over any ring with two-thirds honest majority. In: CCS, pp. 653–666. ACM (2022)
10. Damgård, I., Orlandi, C., Simkin, M.: Yet another compiler for active security or: efficient MPC over arbitrary rings. In: Shacham, H., Boldyreva, A. (eds.) CRYPTO 2018. LNCS, vol. 10992, pp. 799–829. Springer, Cham (2018). https://doi.org/10.1007/978-3-319-96881-0_27
11. Furukawa, J., Lindell, Y.: Two-thirds honest-majority mpc for malicious adversaries at almost the cost of semi-honest. In: Proceedings of the 2019 ACM SIGSAC Conference on Computer and Communications Security, pp. 1557–1571 (2019)
12. Furukawa, J., Lindell, Y., Nof, A., Weinstein, O.: High-throughput secure three-party computation for malicious adversaries and an honest majority. In: Coron, J.-S., Nielsen, J.B. (eds.) EUROCRYPT 2017. LNCS, vol. 10211, pp. 225–255. Springer, Cham (2017). https://doi.org/10.1007/978-3-319-56614-6_8
13. Goldreich, O., Micali, S., Wigderson, A.: How to play any mental game or a completeness theorem for protocols with honest majority. In: STOC, pp. 218–229. ACM (1987)
14. Gordon, S.D., Ranellucci, S., Wang, X.: Secure computation with low communication from cross-checking. In: Peyrin, T., Galbraith, S. (eds.) ASIACRYPT 2018. LNCS, vol. 11274, pp. 59–85. Springer, Cham (2018). https://doi.org/10.1007/978-3-030-03332-3_3
15. Koti, N., Kukkala, V.B., Patra, A., Raj Gopal, B.: Pentagod: stepping beyond traditional god with five parties. In: Proceedings of the 2022 ACM SIGSAC Conference on Computer and Communications Security, pp. 1843–1856 (2022)
16. Koti, N., Pancholi, M., Patra, A., Suresh, A.: SWIFT: super-fast and robust privacy-preserving machine learning. In: USENIX Security Symposium, pp. 2651–2668. USENIX Association (2021)

17. Koti, N., Patra, A., Rachuri, R., Suresh, A.: Tetrad: actively secure 4pc for secure training and inference. In: NDSS. The Internet Society (2022)
18. Kushilevitz, E., Lindell, Y., Rabin, T.: Information-theoretically secure protocols and security under composition. SIAM J. Comput. **39**(5), 2090–2112 (2010)
19. Mohassel, P., Rindal, P.: Aby^3: a mixed protocol framework for machine learning. In: ACM Conference on Computer and Communications Security, pp. 35–52. ACM (2018)
20. Patra, A., Suresh, A.: BLAZE: blazing fast privacy-preserving machine learning. In: NDSS. The Internet Society (2020)
21. Rabin, T., Ben-Or, M.: Verifiable secret sharing and multiparty protocols with honest majority (extended abstract). In: STOC, pp. 73–85. ACM (1989)
22. Yao, A.C.: How to generate and exchange secrets (extended abstract). In: FOCS, pp. 162–167. IEEE Computer Society (1986)

Model Extraction Attack on MPC Hardened Vertical Federated Learning

Xinqian Wang, Xiaoning Liu, and Xun Yi[(✉)]

RMIT University, Melbourne, VIC 3000, Australia
s3965998@student.rmit.edu.au, {xiaoning.liu,xun.yi}@rmit.edu.au

Abstract. Multi-Party Computation (MPC) based Vertical federated learning (VFL) provides a promising solution for privacy-preserving machine learning. With this approach, fragmented dataset owners can collaborate to conduct neural network inference without disclosing their data and local model parameters. However, the current MPC-based VFL frameworks only provide semi-honest security, assuming all involved parties will consistently follow the protocol. We believe this assumption may not always hold true in reality. To enhance the security of MPC-based VFL protocols, it is essential to examine potential malicious behaviours within the semi-honest protocol execution that could lead to the leakage of model parameters. Drawing upon the model extraction attack of Muse, we demonstrate a novel model extraction attack specifically tailored for MPC-based VFL protocols with semi-honest security. To demonstrate the feasibility of our attack, we provide a detailed, step-by-step example illustrating how a malicious party in the MPC-based VFL can steal the entire model's parameters. In experiments, we simulate the run time cost and total queries of our attack on multiple VFL structures, validating its applicability to real-world datasets.

Keywords: Privacy preservation · Secure multi-party computation · Vertical federated learning · Model stealing attack

1 Introduction

Federated learning (FL) [30] is emerged as a promising machine learning framework that enables privacy-aware training on large amounts of dispersed data across multiple parties. In FL, parties train local models on their datasets; only model updates (e.g., weights or gradients) are aggregated into a global model without exchanging any raw training data. FL can be categorized into horizontal federated learning (HFL) [30] and vertical federated learning (VFL) [28] based on how the training data are partitioned. HFL is applicable in scenarios where each data owner has data with different IDs but shares the same attributes. VFL is applicable in scenarios where each data owner has data with different attributes but shares the same IDs. Currently, the research domain of HFL has attained significant attention while the research domain of VFL is less-studied [28].

© The Author(s), under exclusive license to Springer Nature Singapore Pte Ltd. 2025
J. K. Liu et al. (Eds.): ProvSec 2024, LNCS 14903, pp. 63–82, 2025.
https://doi.org/10.1007/978-981-96-0954-3_4

Our study concentrates on the context of VFL. The participants of VFL are divided into one active party and multiple passive parties. In Fig. 1, we plot a basic example of VFL where an active party and a passive party collaboratively conduct the neural network prediction over the data that share the same IDs (ids of 0,1, and 2) but with different attributes (passive party owns attributes of P-1, P-2... and active party owns attributes of A-1...). For example, an internet e-commerce platform can serve as the active party and a bank can serve as the passive party. In this scenario, the e-commerce platform aims to combine data from the bank to use machine learning inference to predict whether users are eligible for loan approval. At first, each party deploys a local model to transform their locally stored attributes into embeddings, which are the latent representations of those attributes. Then, these embeddings are transferred to the active party's global model to compute the final predictions. Finally, the active party naturally receives the final predictions, while the passive party receives nothing. Typically, the passive party is assumed to contribute additional attributes driven solely by the incentive of money. Apparently, VFL enables parties to conduct neural network predictions by exchanging intermediate values, eliminating the need for direct data transformation.

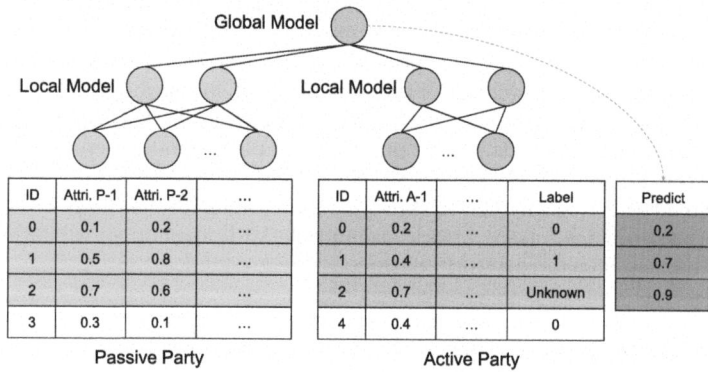

Fig. 1. An Illustration of Vertical Federated Learning.

However, further research on VFL demonstrates that a party with access to its model parameters can launch inference attacks, compromising the privacy of other parties. Specifically, an active party can conduct attribute inference attacks to infer the input attributes of the passive parties [22,29], while a passive party can launch label inference attacks to infer the prediction results [16]. Therefore, several studies propose hiding the model parameters by employing Multi-party Computation (MPC) to securely compute the VFL prediction [11,17,19,27,36–38]. With the use of MPC, it guarantees that both the activate party and the passive party learn nothing about the model parameters and only the activate party can learn the final prediction.

Current MPC-based VFL works [11,17,19,27,36–38] assume that all parties involved in the computation will continuously behave semi-honestly, which may not always happen in practice. Passive parties, who do not receive the final predictions, participate in VFL inference solely for the financial benefits provided by the active party. This financial incentive implies that they will likely to follow the protocol Conversely, the active party, which receives the final predictions, might be motivated to infer the model parameters and attributes from the passive parties, thereby reducing its reliance on the local models of the passive parties. Once the active party successfully infers the entire model parameters, it can further apply the inference attacks mentioned above, resulting in a breach of privacy that damages the passive parties.

Table 1. Comparison of Models

	plaintext ML		Privacy-preserving ML	
	[21,34]	[7,8]	[6,10,26]	Ours
High-accuracy	×	✓	✓	✓
High-efficiency	✓	×	✓	✓
Knowledge-limited	×	×	×	✓

Thus, we argue that it is possible for the active party to initiate model extraction attacks to steal the passive parties' model parameters. Model extraction attacks pose significant threats to both model owners and data owners, resulting in substantial damage to privacy. Table 1 compares our attack with existing representative model extraction attacks. The first column of Table 1 shows traditional model extraction attacks [21,34], which involve training a machine learning model to mimic the behaviour of the target model. These approaches typically struggle to accurately reproduce the exact model parameters of the target model, resulting in lower accuracy compared to the target parameters. The second column of Table 1 shows model extraction attacks that can replicate the same model parameters [7,8]. Specifically, Carlini formalized the problem as a crypt-analytic challenge, where an adversary learns model parameters through numerous adaptive queries, though with low efficiency [7]. The third column of Table 1 shows the works that analyzing the extraction of model parameters in the context of privacy-preserving machine learning. This setting differs from plaintext scenarios due to the adversary's knowledge, behaviours, and the used computation operations, which are defined by the protocol in MPC. The work of Muse [26] firstly applies model extraction attacks into MPC, showing how a malicious party can steal the model parameters of all the models in the setting of 2PC computation that achieves semi-honest security. Meanwhile, Muse [26] achieves an efficiency improvement that is at least 24 times faster than the work of Nicholas [7]. However, in these works [6,10,26], the adversary is typically assumed to be capable of controlling the entire input in the inference.

In this paper, we attempt to show the potential for active parties to infer model parameters in the context of the current progress of MPC-based VFL that only guarantees semi-honest security. To steal the model parameters, we take the attack proposed by Muse [26] as our starting point. Nevertheless, the attack of Muse [26] can not be directly applied to the scenario of privacy-preserving VFL. In VFL, the adversary (active party) can only access a part of the input which is different from the scenario described by Muse [26]. The adversary of Muse can manipulate its input; for instance, setting the input to all zeros can make it easy to predict the intermediate values between each layer. However, in the setting of VFL, the adversary can only manipulate partial inputs, making it more challenging to infer the parameters.

The main contribution of this work is introducing model extraction attacks within the context of MPC-based VFL inference with semi-honest security. We assume a two-party VFL scenario in which one active party and one passive party jointly perform the task of tabular data classification. Notably, our scenario can be generalized to include multiple passive parties, as each passive party can independently run a two-party protocol with the active party. We utilize the technique of Secret Sharing to construct our VFL protocol. The VFL protocol we established consists of the computations of ReLU and linear layers, following the same setup as in the previous work Muse. Then, we assume the active party is compromised by a malicious adversary and demonstrate how the adversary can extract model parameters through adaptive queries. Our contributions can be summarized as follows:

1. We introduce a novel attack targeting the MPC-based VFL inference framework, highlighting the limitations of existing VFL protocols that only achieve semi-honest security.
2. We demonstrate the feasibility of our attack by providing a concrete example, and the results of the attack are promising.
3. Through experiments, we assess the efficacy of our attack on various VFL structures, validating its applicability to real-world datasets.

2   Related Work

2.1   Privacy-Preserving Neural Network Inference

To safeguard data privacy, numerous studies leverage Secure Multi-Party Computation (MPC) for machine learning applications. MPC mainly contains three domains, Homomorphic Encryption (HE) [13], Secret Sharing (SS) [1,15], and Garbled Circuits (GC) [4]. Some studies [17,31] utilize HE for multiplication, strategically moving heavy computations to the pre-processing phase to boost efficiency. In general, the computational overhead of HE is higher than that of SS, and HE-based secure neural network inference faces challenges in supporting non-linear operations.

The techniques mentioned above are used to achieve privacy-preserving machine learning against semi-honest adversaries and malicious adversaries. In our paper, we opt for SS due to its simplicity and efficiency. However, our fundamental concept can be extended to any MPC protocols of privacy-preserving machine learning that only achieve semi-honest security.

2.2 Privacy-Preserving Vertical Federated Learning

Our work is closely in line with privacy-preserving vertical federated learning [11,12,17,18,20,27,36,38]. These approaches fall into two categories: traditional machine learning algorithms and neural network methods. Traditional algorithms include secure linear regression [18] based on SS and GC, secure logistic regression [11,20,38] based on HE, and secure XGBoost [12] based on HE. The neural network approach for secure inference [17,27,36] often involves transitioning encrypted data from HE to SS to perform non-linear operations. Besides, GC can also be used to compute the non-linear operation, however, due to its high computation cost, so far, less work of VFL has explored this approach. In our paper, we opt for achieving secure neural network inference.

2.3 Model Extraction Attacks

Several studies [7,8,21,23,34] have explored attacks on neural networks with black-box access to steal the model parameters. Unlike these attacks, which assume neural network inference is conducted on a single trusted server, the attack proposed by Muse [26] is the only model extraction attack that assumes a secure neural network inference scenario. Besides, the works [6,10] share a similar scenario as Muse [26], however, their focus is on how to defend the attack in privacy-preserving neural network inference. We would like to emphasize that the scenario in Muse's work is different from our setting. In our work, we extend Muse's attack to the scenario of privacy-preserving vertical federated learning (VFL).

3 Preliminary

(See Table 2).

Table 2. Notations

Symbol	Description
$x, \boldsymbol{x}, \boldsymbol{X}$	Scalar, vector, matrix
$\boldsymbol{x}_i$	The ith entry of vector $\boldsymbol{x}$
$\boldsymbol{X}_{ij}$	the entry in the ith row and jth column of matrix $\boldsymbol{X}$
e_i	Unit vector with the ith entry as 1 and the rest entries as 0
θ^i	The local model from the ith party
ψ	The global model
l_i	The number of linear layers from the ith party's local model
$\boldsymbol{x}^i$	The input vector from the ith party
$\boldsymbol{W}^{i,j}$	The parameters of linear layer from the jth linear layer of the ith party
$\langle x \rangle_i$	The share of x held by the ith party such that $x = \sum_{i=0}^{k-1} \langle x \rangle_i$
δ	A random value sampled from $\mathbb{Z}_{2^n}$

3.1   Vertical Federated Learning

Vertical federated learning (VFL) facilitates collaborative learning of a distributed model by involving one active party and multiple passive parties. Let a set $K := \{0, 1, ..., k-1\}$ be the index of all the parties, the active party holds the index of $k-1$. In VFL, the input vector x is vertically partitioned into k parts where each party $i \in K$ holds x^i such that $x = (x^0, x^1, ..., x^k)$. Let ψ and $\theta^i, i \in K$ represent the parameters of the global model held by the active party and local models held by the ith party. Define $f_{\theta^i}(\cdot)$ as the function representing the local model of the ith party, which maps the input vector to its latent representation, with $f_\psi(\cdot)$ following the same pattern. The operations in these mappings actually vary across different model structures. Our assumed VFL scenario aligns with the Vertical SplitNN [9], where each party jointly computes predictions as $F_\psi(f_{\theta^0}(x^0) + f_{\theta^1}(x^1) + ... + f_{\theta^{k-1}}(x^{k-1}))$.

3.2   Additive Secret Sharing

A 2-out-of-2 additive secret sharing [2] shares an n-bit secret integer x as $\langle x \rangle_0 + \langle x \rangle_1 \equiv x \pmod{2^n}$, where $\mathbb{Z}_{2^n}$ denote the ring. Addition or subtraction over shares $\langle z \rangle_i = \langle x \rangle_i \pm \langle y \rangle_i$ can be performed by each party P_i locally, where $i \in \{0, 1\}$ denotes the party number. Similarly, scalar multiplication by a public value $\langle z \rangle_i = \eta \cdot \langle x \rangle_i$ can be performed by P_i locally. Multiplication over two shares $\langle z \rangle = \langle x \rangle \cdot \langle y \rangle$ is supported by Beaver's multiplication technique [3]. Given the secret shared triple $\langle \alpha \rangle_i, \langle \beta \rangle_i, \langle \gamma \rangle_i$ subject to $\gamma = \alpha \cdot \beta$. To multiplying two shares, each party P_i sets $\langle e \rangle_i = \langle x \rangle_i - \langle \alpha \rangle_i$ and $\langle f \rangle_i = \langle y \rangle_i - \langle \beta \rangle_i$. The parties exchange to reconstruct the public values e and f. At the end, P_i locally computes $\langle z \rangle_i = i \cdot e \cdot f + f \cdot \langle \alpha \rangle_i + e \cdot \langle \beta \rangle_i + \langle \gamma \rangle_i$. Note that in the subsequent paper, all secure computations are performed under mod 2^n unless explicitly mentioned.

4   Problem Formulation

4.1   Scenario

Figure 2 illustrates the context of our work. We consider a scenario involving two parties: one active party and one passive party. By the way, it's important to note that our framework can be extended to accommodate one active party and multiple passive parties. **Firstly**, the active party, motivated by combining data from other parties to make more accurate predictions, sends the data's ID to the passive party for alignment. **Secondly**, after finishing the alignment, parties input their aligned data in the form of secret shares and execute MPC-based VFL inference protocols. Each party processes its data using a local model and sends the resulting outputs (the embeddings) to the global model. The global model then aggregates these transferred values and performs the linear mapping. The structure of the model is shown in Fig. 3). The model is pre-trained, and its parameters are stored as secret shares to hide them from both parties due to

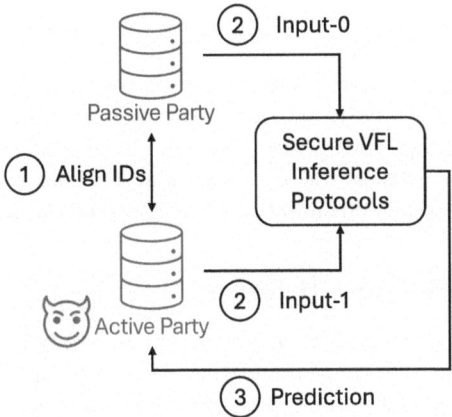

Fig. 2. The VFL system that we targeted.

privacy concerns. To conduct VFL inference, the active party and passive party turn their data into secret shares and send a part of the shares to each other. **Thirdly**, when the protocol ends, it outputs the final prediction and sends it to the Active party. Similarly, the final prediction is in the form of secret shares. To reconstruct the final prediction, the passive party sends its own shares to the active party. Thus, with the use of MPC, input values and intermediate values are split into two secret shares, with each party receiving one share. Such a scheme prevents any party from learning the data during computation.

4.2 Adversary Assumption

The adversary assumption we assumed here is similar to Muse [26] and SIMC [10]. In this setting, either a passive party is corrupted by a semi-honest adversary, or the active party is corrupted by a malicious adversary. Our focus in this paper is on exploring the behavior of malicious adversaries, as the MPC-based VFL inference protocol can defend against semi-honest adversaries. In Fig. 2, we let a malicious adversary corrupt the active party. A malicious adversary implies that it can arbitrarily deviate from the protocol of VFL inference. In construct to the active party, the passive party remains semi-honestly in the whole computation, following the protocols all the time.

Besides, we assume the active party seeks to infer the entire model parameters. Once all the model parameters are revealed, the passive parties' input attributes are also going to be disclosed. For extracting the model parameters, the adversary keeps conducting malicious behaviours based on its knowledge of the secure inference system. **Firstly**, each party involved in the computation can inherently access the computation pattern, which includes the model structure, the protocol used, and the sizes of intermediate computed values. By noticing the model structure, it is better for the adversary to extract the model parameters in a bottom-up fashion, starting from the back layer to the front layer.

Secondly, the active party would always receive the final prediction since it is the one who uses the inference service. Thus, the active party can monitor changes in the final prediction when it dynamically alters its input. **Thirdly**, the adversary can only modify its own input; it does not have access to the input attributes of the passive party. Since the local models from both parties are independent of each other, the adversary may initially attempt to extract its own model parameters and ultimately expose those of the passive party.

4.3   Adversary's Malicious Behaviour

Here, we discuss the adversary's malicious behaviour to infer the model parameters, starting from the method of malleation derived from Muse [26]. Our starting point is Muse [26], which targets a 2PC computation, a client and a server jointly compute the machine learning inference using MPC. Muse demonstrates how malicious clients extract the model parameters by using malleation. For a secret shares of x, let the server holds $\langle x \rangle_0$ and the client holds $\langle x \rangle_1$. The malicious client can add an arbitrary value δ to $\langle x \rangle_1$, changing the secret shares into $(\langle x \rangle_0, \langle x \rangle_1 + \delta)$. For example, the secret shares of 0 can be represented as $(-5, 5)$, where -5 is held by the server and 5 is held by the client. The client can locally add a value of 1 to 5, causing the shares of 0 to be perturbed into the shares of 1 which is $(-5, 6)$. Therefore, detecting such malicious behaviour proves challenging for MPC protocols which are limited to achieving semi-honest security. One important assumption of semi-honest security is presuming the absence of such behaviours. Nevertheless, as previously noted, this assumption may not consistently hold in real-world scenarios. When malleation occurs, distinguishing between a normal shared value and a malleated shared value becomes hard, as any single party can't tell any difference between a normal shared value and a malleated shared value.

5   Our Model Extraction Attack

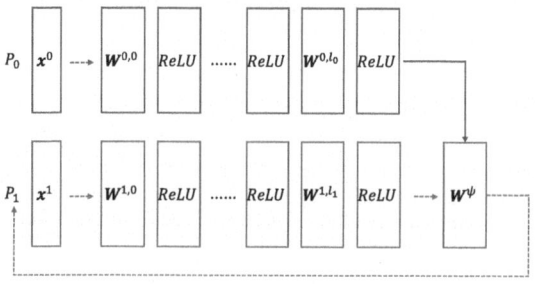

Fig. 3. The VFL system that we targeted.

5.1   Overview

In Fig. 3, we illustrate the VFL system targeted in our problem. As mentioned in Sect. 4, we only have two parties with the index set as $K = \{0, 1\}$. The index of 0 stands for the passive party P_0 and the index of 1 stands for the active party P_1. The passive party holds one local model θ^0 and the active party holds one local model θ^1 and one global model ψ.

The structure of these models is a combination of linear and non-linear layers. The local models from P_0, P_1 are equipped with l_0 and l_1 linear layers respectively, while the global model is set with one single linear layer. By omitting the bias term, we define the linear layer as a dense layer, which is computed as $\boldsymbol{W}^{i,j}\boldsymbol{x}$ with the input $\boldsymbol{x}$. We let the non-linear to be the ReLU layer, which is computed as $max(0, \boldsymbol{x}_i)$ for each element in $\boldsymbol{x}_i$. The dense layer is parameterized by $\boldsymbol{W}^{i,j}, i \in \{0, 1\}, j \in [0, l_i]$ and $\boldsymbol{W}^{\psi}$, while the ReLU layer is non-parameterized. It's important to note that there exist other linear and non-linear layers in various model architectures, such as batch normalization layers (a form of linear layer used for normalizing the distribution of intermediate values) and max-pooling layers (a type of non-linear layer commonly employed in image data processing). For the sake of simplicity and without loss of generality, we omit consideration of these layers. However, our solution can be generalized to accommodate these layers as well.

The adversary who compromises the active party would face three challenges, making it hard to capture the input-output relationship.

1. ReLU layer introduces non-linear relations between the input and the output.
2. Multiple hidden layers nested together.
3. Only a portion of the input can be accessed, specifically the input belonging to the active party.

In Sect. 5.2, based on the studies of Muse [26] and Nicholas [7], we summarize three types of malicious behaviours, where all of them are based on the malleation. The **first** malicious behaviour provides the adversary with arbitrary control over the output of the ReLU function. The **second** malicious behaviour utilizes the unit vector to reveal the linear layers' parameters through multiplication. The **third** malicious behaviour leverages the changes between two correlated queries to make the inference. In Sect. 5.3, we provide a detailed example of extracting parameters of the model in Fig. 3. Additionally, we discuss the solutions when the model prediction space is smaller than the targeted space of parameters for inference. Next, we malleate the secret shares of y by adding an arbitrary value δ', such that the shares of the resulting output $y + \delta'$ become equivalent to the shares of δ'. Considering the context of machine learning inference, where both input and model parameters fall within the range of $[-1, 1]$ [26], it becomes highly probable to identify suitable values for δ.

5.2   Attack Strategy

In Fig. 4, for secret shares of a single input x, the adversary from the active party adds a well-designed value δ to perturb its secret shares into $(\langle x \rangle_0, \langle x \rangle_1 + \delta)$.

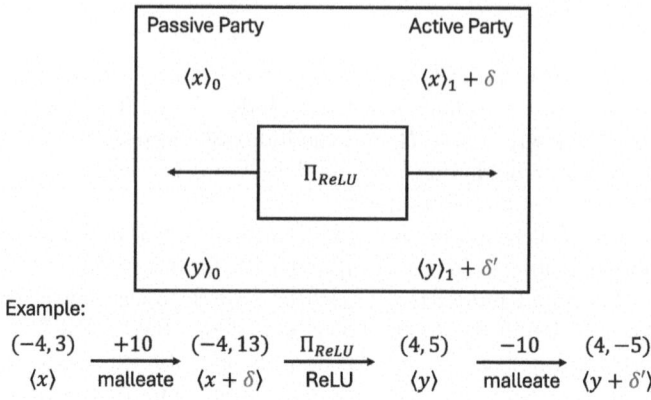

Fig. 4. Malleate the ReLU function.

Then, the ReLU protocol $\Pi_{\text{ReLU}}(x + \delta)$ sets $x + \delta$ to zero if it is negative, otherwise retaining its value if it is greater than or equal to zero. Lastly, the adversary adds another well-designed value δ' to perturb the secret shares of y into $(\langle y \rangle_0, \langle y \rangle_1 + \delta')$. By carefully selecting values for δ, δ', the adversary can transform the ReLU function into an identity mapping. The adversary can make $x + \delta \geq 0$, the protocol Π_{ReLU} is expected to output shares of $y = x + \delta$. Then, to restore the shares of x, the adversary malleates the secret shares of y by adding $\delta' = -\delta$, ensuring that the shares of the output $y + \delta'$ are equivalent to the shares of the input x. Moreover, the adversary can also craft δ, δ' to modify the secret shares of y into arbitrary value. It can make the value of $x + \delta \leq 0$, the protocol Π_{ReLU} is expected to output shares of $y = 0$. Then, it malleates the secret shares of y by adding an arbitrary value δ', such that the shares of the resulting output $y + \delta'$ become equivalent to the shares of δ'. The method is agnostic to the specific computation of the ReLU protocol and it is applicable to all ReLU protocols that attain semi-honest security [25, 35]. Considering the context of machine learning inference, where both input and model parameters fall within the range of $[-1, 1]$ [26], it becomes highly probable to identify suitable values for δ.

In Fig. 5, the adversary infers the model parameters of one linear layer column by column by malleating the layer's input, the secret shares of $\boldsymbol{x}$. Denote the parameters of the linear layer as $\boldsymbol{W}^{i,j}$, where $i \in \{0, 1\}$ and $j \in [0, l_i]$ (abbreviated as $\boldsymbol{W}$) Initially, the adversary introduces a well-designed vector $\boldsymbol{\delta}$ into $\boldsymbol{x}$. Then, the parties jointly execute the secure multiplication protocol Π_{mult}, using multiplication triplets $\boldsymbol{\alpha}, \boldsymbol{\beta}, \boldsymbol{\gamma}$, to obtain the secret shares of $\boldsymbol{W} \cdot \boldsymbol{x}$. As the result of $\boldsymbol{W} \cdot \boldsymbol{x}$ reflects the column combination of $\boldsymbol{W}$, accumulating sufficient combinations through multiple queries enables the inference of the model parameter $\boldsymbol{W}$. Assume we know the value of vector $\boldsymbol{x}$ that is shared, then we can add the vector of $\boldsymbol{\delta}$ to make $\boldsymbol{x} + \boldsymbol{\delta}$ (element-wise addition) into a unit vector such that $\boldsymbol{x} + \boldsymbol{\delta} = \boldsymbol{e}_i$ for some entry i. Then, the malleated vector is inputted

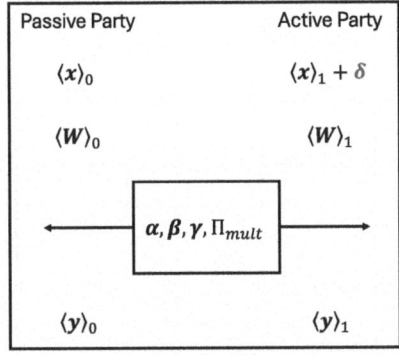

Example:

$$\Pi_{mult}(\langle W \rangle, \langle x + \delta \rangle) = \begin{bmatrix} \langle W_{0,0} \rangle & \langle W_{0,1} \rangle & \langle W_{0,2} \rangle \\ \langle W_{1,0} \rangle & \langle W_{1,1} \rangle & \langle W_{1,2} \rangle \\ \langle W_{2,0} \rangle & \langle W_{2,1} \rangle & \langle W_{2,2} \rangle \end{bmatrix} \begin{bmatrix} \langle 1 \rangle \\ \langle 0 \rangle \\ \langle 0 \rangle \end{bmatrix} = \begin{bmatrix} \langle W_{0,0} \rangle \\ \langle W_{1,0} \rangle \\ \langle W_{2,0} \rangle \end{bmatrix}$$

Fig. 5. Malleate the Linear function with one query.

into the current linear layer with parameter W. Thus, the $i-th$ column of W is revealed.

In Fig. 6, if the adversary does not know the passive party's input x^0, it cannot determine how to inject malleation to perturb the shares of x^0 into e_i. In this case, the adversary has to calculate the partial differential function of $W \cdot x$ with respect to x, such that $\frac{\partial W \cdot x}{\partial x} = \frac{W \cdot (x+\delta) - W \cdot x}{x+\delta-x} = W$. The perturbation of $\delta = e_i$ can extract the ith column of matrix W.

5.3 Demonstration of the Model Extraction Attack

Based on the target model structure in Fig. 3, we now provide a concrete example to show how we use the malleation to extract the target VFL model's parameters. As the discussion in Sect. 4.2, we let the adversary adopt a bottom-up strategy in our attack. Firstly, the adversary attempts to infer the global model's parameters. Secondly, the adversary infers its own local model parameters θ^1. Finally, the adversary infers the parameters of the passive party's local model θ^0.

Infer the Global Model ψ. The global model only has one linear layer with parameters W^ψ. Note that the input to the global model is derived from aggregating the output of both parties' local models. Since both parties' local models employ the ReLU layer as the final layer, we can utilize the malleation technique illustrated in Fig. 4 to transform these outputs into secret shares of zero. This involves adding a δ to each element to perturb it into a negative value secret share. Then, we keep doing malleation in the way which Fig. 5 does, malleating the vector of zero into a unit vector e_i to reveal the ith column of W^ψ. In Eq. 1, as each local

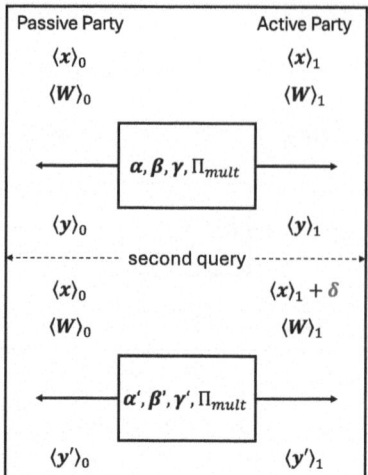

Fig. 6. Differential inference inference.

model's last layer is a ReLU layer, we can add $\delta = -10, \delta' = 0$, where the δ makes the output of Π_{ReLU} into all 0.

$$\begin{bmatrix} 1.7 \\ 2 \\ 3.3 \end{bmatrix} \xrightarrow[\delta = -10]{\text{malleate}} \begin{bmatrix} -8.3 \\ -8 \\ -6.7 \end{bmatrix} \xrightarrow{\text{ReLU}(\cdot)} \begin{bmatrix} 0 \\ 0 \\ 0 \end{bmatrix} \xrightarrow[\delta' = 0]{\text{malleate}} \begin{bmatrix} 0 \\ 0 \\ 0 \end{bmatrix} \tag{1}$$

Once we make the input of the global model as a zero vector, we consistently apply malleation of $\delta = e_0$ to convert it into a vector represented by e_0, subsequently deducing the initial column of the global model's parameters as per Eq. 2.

$$\overbrace{\begin{bmatrix} 0.1 \ 0.2 \ 0.3 \\ 0.4 \ 0.5 \ 0.6 \end{bmatrix}}^{W^{\psi}} \overbrace{\begin{bmatrix} 1 \\ 0 \\ 0 \end{bmatrix}}^{x+\delta} = \overbrace{\begin{bmatrix} 0.1 \\ 0.4 \end{bmatrix}}^{\text{final prediction}} \tag{2}$$

Infer the Active Party's Layer. Once the adversary has extracted the parameters of the global model, it will then start to infer the parameters of the active party, which is its own. To eliminate the impact from the output of the passive party's local model in the aggregation, the adversary ensures that the passive party's outputs remain **0**. However, the information of parameters from the intermediate layers, as is revealed column by column, may become lost through the computation. Here, we present an example illustrating the adversary's attempt to extract the first column of the active party's final linear layer (parameterized by W^{1,l_1}). In Eq. 3, the adversary has transformed the ReLU function from the last layer into an identical function through malleation.

$$\overbrace{\begin{bmatrix} 0.1 & 0.2 & 0.3 \\ 0.4 & 0.5 & 0.6 \end{bmatrix}}^{W^{\psi}} \overbrace{\begin{bmatrix} W_{0,0} & W_{0,1} & W_{0,2} \\ W_{1,0} & W_{1,1} & W_{1,2} \\ W_{2,0} & W_{2,1} & W_{2,2} \end{bmatrix}}^{W^{1,l_1}} \overbrace{\begin{bmatrix} 1 \\ 0 \\ 0 \end{bmatrix}}^{x+\delta}$$

$$= \overbrace{\begin{bmatrix} 0.1 & 0.2 & 0.3 \\ 0.4 & 0.5 & 0.6 \end{bmatrix}}^{W^{\psi}} \overbrace{\begin{bmatrix} W_{0,0} \\ W_{1,0} \\ W_{2,0} \end{bmatrix}}^{W^{1,l_1} \cdot x} = \begin{bmatrix} 0.1 \cdot W_{0,0} + 0.2 \cdot W_{1,0} + 0.3 \cdot W_{2,0} \\ 0.4 \cdot W_{0,0} + 0.5 \cdot W_{1,0} + 0.6 \cdot W_{2,0} \end{bmatrix} \tag{3}$$

The output of Eq. 3 is the VFL model's result, which will be sent to the adversary. Although the adversary is aware of the parameters of W^{ψ}, inferring the first column of W^{1,l_1} is challenging due to the existence of multiple solutions for the equation. To address this issue, the adversary uses the ReLU function to cut a part of parameters from the first column of W^{1,l_1}, aligning the number of parameters awaiting extraction with the number of prediction elements:

$$\overbrace{\begin{bmatrix} W_{0,0} \\ W_{1,0} \\ W_{2,0} \end{bmatrix}}^{W^{1,l_1} \cdot x} \xrightarrow[\delta = [10, 10, -10]]{\text{malleate}} \overbrace{\begin{bmatrix} W_{0,0} + 10 \\ W_{1,0} + 10 \\ W_{2,0} - 10 \end{bmatrix}}^{W^{1,l_1} \cdot x} \xrightarrow{\text{ReLU}(\cdot)} \overbrace{\begin{bmatrix} W_{0,0} + 10 \\ W_{1,0} + 10 \\ 0 \end{bmatrix}}^{W^{1,l_1} \cdot x}$$

$$\xrightarrow[\delta' = [-10, -10, 0]]{\text{malleate}} \overbrace{\begin{bmatrix} W_{0,0} \\ W_{1,0} \\ 0 \end{bmatrix}}^{W^{1,l_1} \cdot x} \xrightarrow{\text{multiply with } W^{\psi}} \begin{bmatrix} 0.1 \cdot W_{0,0} + 0.2 \cdot W_{1,0} \\ 0.4 \cdot W_{0,0} + 0.5 \cdot W_{1,0} \end{bmatrix} \tag{4}$$

Equation 4 also implies that the matrix of $\begin{bmatrix} 0.1 & 0.2 \\ 0.4 & 0.5 \end{bmatrix}$ is linear independent. Rarely, solving Eq. 4 would encounter linear dependence. In such cases, an additional query may be necessary.

Infer the First Layer from the Passive Party. After extracting the parameters of the global model and the active party's local model, the adversary proceeds to infer the parameters of the passive party. Since the adversary cannot access the input of the passive party, it first employs malleation to make the output of the local model's first ReLU layer become $\mathbf{0}$. Then, it uses malleation to extract the model parameters from the second linear to the last layer of the passive party's local model. However, it is hard for the adversary to infer the first layer. This difficulty arises because the adversary cannot ascertain which noise vector $\boldsymbol{\delta}$ to add to perturb the input vector x^0 from the active party to e_i. Thus, malleation of Fig. 6 is required, by adding a unit vector of e_i, the adversary can reveal the values of the passive party's first layer's parameter such that:

$$
\overbrace{\begin{bmatrix} W_{0,0} & W_{0,1} & W_{0,2} & W_{0,3} \\ W_{1,0} & W_{1,1} & W_{1,2} & W_{1,3} \\ W_{2,0} & W_{2,1} & W_{2,2} & W_{2,3} \\ W_{3,0} & W_{3,1} & W_{3,2} & W_{3,3} \end{bmatrix}}^{W^{0,0}} \left(\overbrace{\begin{bmatrix} x_0 + 1 \\ x_1 \\ x_2 \\ x_3 \end{bmatrix}}^{x^0 + \delta} - \overbrace{\begin{bmatrix} x_0 \\ x_1 \\ x_2 \\ x_3 \end{bmatrix}}^{x^0} \right) = \begin{bmatrix} W_{0,0} \\ W_{1,0} \\ W_{2,0} \\ W_{3,0} \end{bmatrix} \tag{5}
$$

6   Experiments on Model Extraction Attack

6.1   Implementation

We deploy our attack across both settings of MPC and plaintext. For implementing the plaintext, we use PyTorch to simulate our attack and compute the number of queries we need. For implementing the MPC, we use the MPC scheme of OTSemi2k from the MP-SPDZ library [24] and computed over 64 bits. OTSemi2k is a semi-honest adaption of SPDZ2K [14], which omits the steps of SPDZ2K that provide malicious security. In our MPC implementation, the active and passive parties are configured to communicate over a LAN connection. All experiments were conducted on the CPU of an Intel(R) Xeon(R) Silver 4309Y CPU @ 2.80 GHz with 32 cores.

As mentioned before, we set the architecture of the models as the full-connected neural networks. In experiments, we make both parties' local models share the same structure. In Table 3, to distinguish between the structure of local models and the global model, we use the "|" symbol as a separator. For instance, the notation '784-128 | 1' represents that the local models have a shape of 784-128, accepting input vectors of 784 entries and producing output vectors with 128 entries. The global model, on the other hand, has a shape of 1, receiving input from both parties' local models and generating a single output value.

Table 3. A list of model structures

Indexes	Model Structures	Local models	Global models
A	784-128 | 1	784-128	128-1
B	784-32 | 1	784-32	32-1
C	10-10-10 | 1	10-10-10	10-1
D	10-20-20 | 1	10-20-20	20-1
E	40-20-10-10 | 1	40-20-10-10	10-1
F	80-40-20 | 1	80-40-20	20-1
G	400-40-20 | 1	400-40-20	20-1
H	1000-500 | 1	1000-500	500-1
I	1000-500 | 10	1000-500	500-10
J	4000-1000 | 100	4000-1000	1000-100
K	2000-320-20 | 10	2000-320-20	20-10

6.2 Attack Complexity (Empirical)

Table 4. Query complexity of our attack

Index	# Parameters	# Queries	Time (h)
A	200,832	301,184	670.97
B	50,208	75,296	23.63
C	410	510	0.01
D	1,220	1,420	0.11
E	2,210	3,010	0.26
F	8,020	11,220	1.90
G	33,620	49,620	19.57
H	1,000,500	1,500,500	12,800.09
I	1,005,000	150,500	1,119.55
J	8,100,000	121,000	8,402.77
K	1,293,000	193,300	2,576.79

In Table 4, we compare the total number of queries and the total time costs required for extraction across various model structures indexed from A to K. The total number of queries is calculated from the plaintext, and we measure the total time by multiplying the time required for a single secure VFL inference by the total number of queries.

Table 4 demonstrates that the total time cost for our attack remains considerable. As illustrated in the last four rows of Table 4, inferring a typical VFL system with a moderate number of layers can require thousands of hours. Deploying such a cost is not feasible for the adversary in real-world scenarios. On the other hand, our attack can prove beneficial for certain lightweight VFL systems with model parameters totalling fewer than 50,000 (it is still feasible to extract the model with the index of A to G).

6.3 Compare the Total Execution Time of Our Attacks with Different Model Structures

In Fig. 7, we investigate how the depth of the model would influence the total number of queries to extract the whole VFL system. From the x-axis, we define four different basic model structures of 0 zero as "10-10 | 10", "20-20 | 20", "30-30 | 30", and "40-40 | 40". Whenever the depth increases by one, we incorporate an additional layer with the same dimension as the current layer into the model structure. For instance, the base model at a depth of 1 would be represented as "10-10-10 | 10".

In Fig. 7, we note that as the model's depth increases, regardless of its structure, the total number of queries required by the adversary increases linearly.

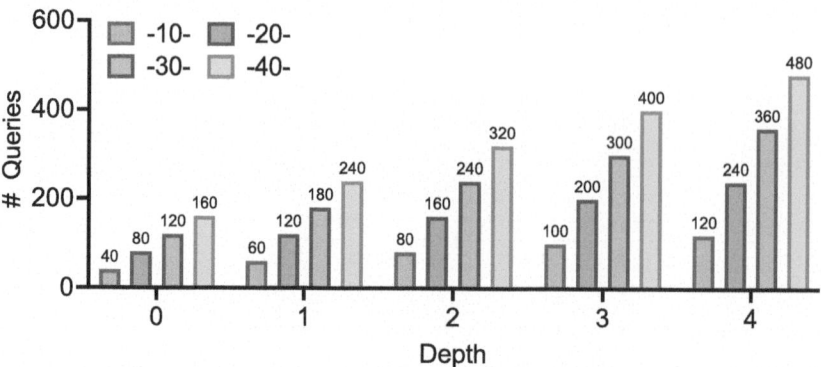

Fig. 7. Comparisons of attack queries and execution time per query across different depth and model structures.

Besides, as the depth of the model increases, the gap between different model structures at the same depth also grows linearly.

Next, we measure how the size of the output affects the total number of queries that the adversary requires to extract the system. In Fig. 8, we observe that when the output shape increases, the total number of query that used to infer the model parameters would drop significantly.

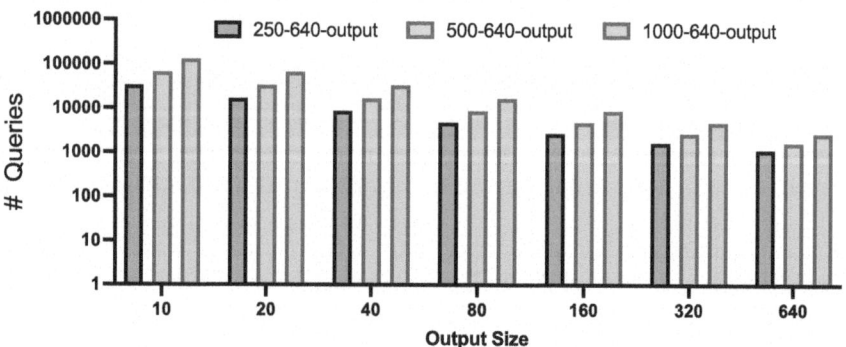

Fig. 8. Comparisons of attack queries across different output shapes and model structures.

7   Conclusion and Discussion

Limitations. We emphasize that the feasibility of our work depends on using a sufficiently large ring size ($\mathbb{Z}_{2^n}$) for the MPC-based computation of the VFL. The success of our approach relies on the selection of the random value δ that is used for malleation. Under such large ring sizes, it would be easy for us to find a δ. When the ring size is small and close to the range of the model parameters, it becomes difficult to select a feasible δ as desired. Consequently, we infer that our approach may not work well on some resource-constrained devices, such as IoT devices, which typically possess over smaller bit lengths. Moreover, the effectiveness of our malleation hinges on our prior understanding of the distribution of model parameters, assumed to be $[-1, 1]$. Given few studies are studying the parameter distributions of a trained network, our assumption may not always be valid in the future.

We address the efficiency bottleneck of our work to the output size of the model. For every extraction, the maximum number of parameters we can extract is determined by the size of the final prediction. As detailed in Table 4, when the model's final prediction is limited to one, to extract every one parameter, our attack requires at least one query.

Defense. Our attack is only applicable to security systems designed to defend against semi-honest adversaries. To defend our attacks, using conventional approaches such as zero-knowledge proofs [5] and cut-and-choose techniques [39] usually imply high communication and computation costs. To boost efficiency, efforts have been made to develop lightweight protocols [6,10,26]. However, while these protocols are useful, they fail to protect systems against Distributed Denial of Service attacks.

In addition to cryptographic protocols, alternative methods like secure dropout layers [33] and differential privacy [32] can also help thwart attacks by introducing randomness into the inference system. The secure dropout layers randomly set certain input elements to zero with a defined probability, changing the connections within the layers and making it difficult for adversaries to precisely deduce the model structure. Differential privacy introduces sophisticated random noise vectors to perturb the final predictions, providing provable security guarantees but potentially degrading the utility of the models.

Future Works. A promising extension of our solution involves applying our attack to a secure VFL inference system with diverse inputs. For example, within a secure VFL inference system, an active party might process image data while passive parties handle text data. Because such models that tend to have large input and output space, may be more vulnerable to our attack.

Conclusion. In this paper, we introduce a novel model extraction attack designed to steal model parameters during the execution of VFL secure inference protocols with semi-honest security. Our findings highlight the importance of addressing malicious behaviour among parties in current privacy-preserving VFL research. We formalize three malicious behaviours based on malleation which then be modelized by the adversary to conduct the model extraction attack. Then, to demonstrate the effectiveness of our attack, we offer a systematic example of how model parameters can be progressively revealed through simple matrix multiplication and ReLU functions. In our experiments, we quantify the total time required for the adversary to execute the model-extraction attack and text how different model structures influence the attack's efficiency. We envision our attack as an initial stride toward realizing privacy-preserving vertical federated learning in the face of malicious adversaries.

References

1. Araki, T., Furukawa, J., Lindell, Y., Nof, A., Ohara, K.: High-throughput semi-honest secure three-party computation with an honest majority. In: Proceedings of the 2016 ACM SIGSAC Conference on Computer and Communications Security, pp. 805–817 (2016)
2. Atallah, M., Bykova, M., Li, J., Frikken, K., Topkara, M.: Private collaborative forecasting and benchmarking. In: Proceedings of the of WPES (2004)
3. Beaver, D.: Efficient multiparty protocols using circuit randomization. In: Advances in Cryptology-CRYPTO 1991: Proceedings 2011, pp. 420–432. Springer (1992)
4. Bellare, M., Hoang, V.T., Rogaway, P.: Foundations of garbled circuits. In: Proceedings of the 2012 ACM Conference on Computer and communications security, pp. 784–796 (2012)
5. Bitansky, N., Canetti, R., Chiesa, A., Tromer, E.: Recursive composition and bootstrapping for snarks and proof-carrying data. In: Proceedings of the Forty-Fifth Annual ACM Symposium on Theory of Computing, pp. 111–120 (2013)
6. Brüggemann, A., Schick, O., Schneider, T., Suresh, A., Yalame, H.: Don't eject the impostor: fast three-party computation with a known cheater. In: 2024 IEEE Symposium on Security and Privacy (SP), pp. 164–164. IEEE Computer Society (2024)
7. Carlini, N., Jagielski, M., Mironov, I.: Cryptanalytic extraction of neural network models. In: Annual International Cryptology Conference, pp. 189–218. Springer (2020)
8. Carlini, N., et al.: Stealing part of a production language model (2024)
9. Ceballos, I., et al.: SplitNN-driven vertical partitioning. arXiv preprint arXiv:2008.04137 (2020)
10. Chandran, N., Gupta, D., Obbattu, S.L.B., Shah, A.: {SIMC}:{ML} inference secure against malicious clients at {Semi-Honest} cost. In: 31st USENIX Security Symposium (USENIX Security 22), pp. 1361–1378 (2022)
11. Chen, C., et al.: When homomorphic encryption marries secret sharing: secure large-scale sparse logistic regression and applications in risk control. In: Proceedings of the 27th ACM SIGKDD Conference on Knowledge Discovery & Data Mining, pp. 2652–2662 (2021)
12. Cheng, K., et al.: SecureBoost: a lossless federated learning framework. IEEE Intell. Syst. **36**(6), 87–98 (2021)
13. Cheon, J.H., Kim, A., Kim, M., Song, Y.: Homomorphic encryption for arithmetic of approximate numbers. In: Advances in Cryptology–ASIACRYPT 2017: 23rd Model Extraction Attack on MPC Hardened Vertical Federated Learning 19 International Conference on the Theory and Applications of Cryptology and Information Security, Part I, Hong Kong, China, 3–7 December 2017, pp. 409–437. Springer (2017)
14. Cramer, R., Damgård, I., Escudero, D., Scholl, P., Xing, C.: SPDZ2k: efficient MPC mod 2k for dishonest majority. In: Annual International Cryptology Conference, pp. 769–798. Springer (2018)

15. David, B., Dowsley, R., Katti, R., Nascimento, A.C.: Efficient unconditionally secure comparison and privacy preserving machine learning classification protocols. In: International Conference on Provable Security, pp. 354–367. Springer (2015)

16. Fu, C., et al.: Label inference attacks against vertical federated learning. In: 31st USENIX Security Symposium (USENIX Security 2022), pp. 1397–1414 (2022)

17. Fu, F., Xue, H., Cheng, Y., Tao, Y., Cui, B.: BlindFL: vertical federated machine learning without peeking into your data. In: Proceedings of the 2022 International Conference on Management of Data, pp. 1316–1330 (2022)

18. Gascón, A., et al.: Privacy-preserving distributed linear regression on high-dimensional data. Cryptology ePrint Archive (2016)

19. Gong, M., et al.: A multi-modal vertical federated learning framework based on homomorphic encryption. IEEE Trans. Inf. Forensics Secur. (2023)

20. Hardy, S., et al.: Private federated learning on vertically partitioned data via entity resolution and additively homomorphic encryption. arXiv preprint arXiv:1711.10677 (2017)

21. Jagielski, M., Carlini, N., Berthelot, D., Kurakin, A., Papernot, N.: High accuracy and high fidelity extraction of neural networks. In: 29th USENIX Security Symposium (USENIX Security 2020), pp. 1345–1362 (2020)

22. Jiang, X., Zhou, X., Grossklags, J.: Comprehensive analysis of privacy leakage in vertical federated learning during prediction. Proc. Priv. Enhanc. Technol. **2022**(2), 263–281 (2022)

23. Juuti, M., Szyller, S., Marchal, S., Asokan, N.: PRADA: protecting against DNN model stealing attacks. In: 2019 IEEE European Symposium on Security and Privacy (EuroS&P), pp. 512–527. IEEE (2019)

24. Keller, M.: MP-SPDZ: a versatile framework for multi-party computation. In: Proceedings of the 2020 ACM SIGSAC Conference on Computer and Communications Security, pp. 1575–1590 (2020)

25. Keller, M., Sun, K.: Secure quantized training for deep learning. In: International Conference on Machine Learning, pp. 10912–10938. PMLR (2022)

26. Lehmkuhl, R., Mishra, P., Srinivasan, A., Popa, R.A.: Muse: secure inference resilient to malicious clients. In: 30th USENIX Security Symposium (USENIX Security 2021), pp. 2201–2218 (2021)

27. Li, S., Yao, D., Liu, J.: FedVS: straggler-resilient and privacy-preserving vertical federated learning for split models. In: Proceedings of the 40th International Conference on Machine Learning, ICML 2023. JMLR.org (2023)

28. Liu, Y., et al.: Vertical federated learning: concepts, advances, and challenges. IEEE Trans. Knowl. Data Eng. (2024)

29. Luo, X., Wu, Y., Xiao, X., Ooi, B.C.: Feature inference attack on model predictions in vertical federated learning. In: 2021 IEEE 37th International Conference on Data Engineering (ICDE), pp. 181–192. IEEE (2021)

30. McMahan, B., Moore, E., Ramage, D., Hampson, S., y Arcas, B.A.: Communication-efficient learning of deep networks from decentralized data. In: Artificial Intelligence and Statistics, pp. 1273–1282. PMLR (2017)

31. Mishra, P., Lehmkuhl, R., Srinivasan, A., Zheng, W., Popa, R.A.: Delphi: a cryptographic inference service for neural networks. In: 29th USENIX Security Symposium (USENIX Security 2020), pp. 2505–2522. USENIX Association (2020). https://www.usenix.org/conference/usenixsecurity20/presentation/mishra

32. Ruan, W., Xu, M., Fang, W., Wang, L., Wang, L., Han, W.: Private, efficient, and accurate: protecting models trained by multi-party learning with differential privacy. In: 2023 IEEE Symposium on Security and Privacy (SP), pp. 1926–1943. IEEE (2023)

33. Shao, J., Sun, Y., Li, S., Zhang, J.: DRES-FL: Dropout-resilient secure federated learning for non-IID clients via secret data sharing. Adv. Neural. Inf. Process. Syst. **35**, 10533–10545 (2022)
34. Tramèr, F., Zhang, F., Juels, A., Reiter, M.K., Ristenpart, T.: Stealing machine learning models via prediction {APIs}. In: 25th USENIX Security Symposium (USENIX Security 2016), pp. 601–618 (2016)
35. Wagh, S., Gupta, D., Chandran, N.: SecureNN: 3-party secure computation for neural network training. In: Proceedings on Privacy Enhancing Technologies (2019)
36. Wu, Y., et al.: Falcon: a privacy-preserving and interpretable vertical federated learning system. Proc. VLDB Endow. **16**(10), 2471–2484 (2023)
37. Xu, R., Baracaldo, N., Zhou, Y., Anwar, A., Joshi, J., Ludwig, H.: FedV: privacy-preserving federated learning over vertically partitioned data. In: Proceedings of the 14th ACM Workshop on Artificial Intelligence and Security, pp. 181–192 (2021)
38. Zhao, J., et al.: VFLR: An efficient and privacy-preserving vertical federated framework for logistic regression. IEEE Trans. Cloud Comput. (2023)
39. Zhu, R., Huang, Y., Katz, J., Shelat, A.: The {Cut-and-Choose} game and its application to cryptographic protocols. In: 25th USENIX Security Symposium (USENIX Security 2016), pp. 1085–1100 (2016)

Searchable Encryption

Verifiable Conjunctive Searchable Symmetric Encryption with Result Pattern Hiding

Huy-Hoang Chung-Nguyen[1]([✉]), Dandan Yuan[2], and Shujie Cui[1]

[1] Monash University, Clayton, VIC, Australia
cnhhoang.sec@gmail.com, Shujie.Cui@monash.edu
[2] Centrum Wiskunde & Informatica (CWI), Amsterdam, Netherlands
dandan.yuan@cwi.nl

Abstract. Symmetric Searchable Encryption (SSE) guarantees the security of outsourced data without sacrificing search capability. Supporting conjunctive multi-keyword search makes the SSE more practical. However, existing conjunctive SSE schemes commonly face two issues: leaking the Keyword Pair Result Pattern (KPRP) and works only when the server is honest.

This paper presents the first Verifiable Conjunctive Searchable Symmetric Encryption (VCSSE) without the KPRP leakage. Our approach considers any VSSE scheme as a black box and deploys a customized iteration of the recent Result-Hiding Filter, referred to as the Verifiable Result-Hiding Filter, to develop a VCSSE that prevents the disclosure of KPRP. In addition to successfully integrating both verifiability and KPRP-hiding, our scheme also avoids non-negligible false positives, in contrast to approaches that deploy the Bloom Filter.

Furthermore, we introduce an extension to our solution that supports dynamic databases. In addition to the aforementioned security properties, our approach achieves forward privacy and backward privacy in dynamic settings, while also ensuring fault-tolerance for verifiability. This implies that our scheme remains resilient to incorrect updates originating from incautious clients in the malicious server setting. While ensuring all the mentioned security properties, our schemes deliver optimal sublinear complexity performance.

Keywords: Security and Privacy Protection · Verification · Database Management · Information Search and Retrieval

1 Introduction

Outsourcing data to the cloud is becoming increasingly popular. Despite numerous advantages, there is a downside to this approach: the potential exposure of sensitive data to the cloud service provider. Unfortunately, conventional encryption methods hinder the data owner's ability to search within encrypted data.

© The Author(s), under exclusive license to Springer Nature Singapore Pte Ltd. 2025
J. K. Liu et al. (Eds.): ProvSec 2024, LNCS 14903, pp. 85–105, 2025.
https://doi.org/10.1007/978-981-96-0954-3_5

In other words, the client must download and decrypt the entire database to search for a specific document. This straightforward approach is excessively time-consuming and burdensome, especially in scenarios involving frequent searches. In light of this, extensive research efforts have been dedicated to exploring Searchable Symmetric Encryption (SSE) as an efficient solution to address this issue. SSE enables clients to securely outsource the data to an untrusted server without compromising the search capability. The data owner typically encrypts the database, often employing a specialized data structure consisting of keyword-document pairs, and sends it to the server. When searching for a keyword, the server retrieves all encrypted documents containing that keyword, having limited knowledge of the queried keyword and the resulting documents itself.

1.1   Related Work

Since its introduction in 2000 by Song et al. [16], Symmetric Searchable Encryption has garnered interest from both the academic and industrial sectors. Many studies have been proposed to thoroughly investigate and enhance the performance and security of SSE [2,4,5,8]. Moreover, in the pursuit of improving the practicality of SSE, researchers are exploring additional functionalities. Among the notable features are dynamic SSE [2,4,5], range queries [1,14], conjunctive queries [1,6,12], and verifiability [7,10,11]. Nevertheless, there is a trade-off between performance, security, and functionality. Selecting the right balance among these three aspects is crucial when developing an SSE scheme.

Conjunctive SSE. A practical SSE scheme should support multi-keyword searches. Cash et al. [6] introduced the first non-generic sublinear SSE scheme supporting boolean queries, OXT, marking a significant advancement in conjunctive SSE research. Unfortunately, OXT leaks the Keyword Pair Result Pattern (KPRP) to the server, i.e., the server knows if documents contain any two keywords in the search query. Formally, let $DB(w)$ be the list of documents contains keyword w. Given a conjunction query of n keywords $con(w_1, ..., w_n)$, the KPRP discloses $DB(w_i) \cap DB(w_j), \forall i, j \in \{1, ..., n\} : i < j$. Subsequent research shows that file-injection attacks [21] can exploit this leakage to reveal a significant amount of data with guaranteed success. By injecting carefully constructed documents into the database during the Setup phase, the attacker can take advantage of the KPRP leakage to uncover all keywords in conjunctive queries and document identifiers associated with each searched keyword. Therefore, it is crucial to design an SSE scheme that can avoid the leakage of KPRP [12,22].

Verifiable SSE. Most studies on SSE operate under the assumption that the server is honest-but-curious. In other words, the server attempts to acquire information about queries and the database but faithfully executes the protocol as requested. In a more realistic scenario, a malicious server may provide inaccurate and/or incomplete search results, yet traditional SSE schemes are incapable to detect such issues. Therefore, Verifiable SSE was first proposed by [10], and later works [3,7,10,11] have been studied to guarantee the correctness and completeness of search queries, even in the presence of a malicious server. To the best of our knowledge, existing Verifiable Conjunctive SSE scheme reveals the KPRP, making them susceptible to File-Injection attacks.

Dynamic SSE. Another challenging aspect of SSE involves efficiently updating the specialized database. Kamara et al. [9] were the first to propose a Dynamic SSE (DSSE) scheme with sub-linear performance and defined the adaptive security for DSSE. After this breakthrough, the academic sector focuses on improving security, with the most prominent being forward privacy and backward privacy [17]. Informally, forward privacy obfuscates the correlation between an update query and previous searches, whereas backward privacy guarantees that search queries do not disclose any information about deleted documents. Failure to ensure forward privacy enables file-injection attack [21] to extract valuable information about keywords. A recent attack on backward privacy decreases the target's security level and exposes its deletion history [18]. Although the severity may vary, attaining both privacy properties is advantageous for enhancing security.

1.2   Our Contribution

In this paper, we first enhance the recently proposed Result-hiding Filter [20] by integrating verifiability into the cryptographic primitive, which we refer to as Verifiable Result-hiding Filter, or VRHF. We subsequently utilize the VRHF to develop the initial Verifiable Conjunctive Symmetric Searchable Encryption scheme, which prevents KPRP leakage. Our scheme concurrently eliminates non-negligible false positives and maintains sublinear performance. Lastly, we introduce an extension of the previous scheme to accommodate update queries. This extension not only preserves the forward and backward privacy of a black-box VDSSE but also achieves fault tolerance, ensuring resilience against inadvertent client errors.

1.3   Organization

The remaining sections of the paper are structured as follows. We will commence with a concise examination of the preliminaries employed in this study. Subsequently, an essential building block for our scheme, Verifiable Result-Hiding Filter, will be presented in Sect. 3. Section 4 will introduce our proposed SSE scheme, VCPH, which is the first Verifiable Conjunctive SSE with KPRP hiding. The expansion of our scheme to accommodate dynamic settings will be outlined in Sect. 5. Lastly, Sect. 6 delivers the concluding thoughts of our research.

2   Preliminaries

Throughout this paper, $\{0,1\}^l$ denotes the set of all binary strings length l. $\{0,1\}^*$ denotes the set of all binary strings of arbitrary length. $a_1 \leftarrow a_2$ is assigning value a_2 to a_1. $x \xleftarrow{\$} S$ means x is uniformly sampled from set S. $|X|$ is the cardinality of a set/list/map X. W represents the set of all keywords in the database. Given a single or multi-keyword query q, $\mathrm{DB}(q)$ denotes the list of documents satisfies q.

2.1 Authenticated Encryption

Authenticated Encryption (AE) scheme [15] is an encryption scheme that ensures both confidentiality and integrity of the data, consisting of three algorithms: $AE.KeyGen$, $AE.Enc$, and $AE.Dec$. Generally, $AE.KeyGen$ is a probabilistic algorithm that takes a security parameter λ as input and outputs secret key k. $AE.Enc$ is a deterministic encryption algorithm that takes as input secret key k, a nonce non, a message M, and outputs a ciphertext C. The decryption algorithm, $AE.Dec$, takes secret key k, a nonce non, and a ciphertext C. If the nonce non is correct, it outputs the original message M, or produces a string "invalid" otherwise.

2.2 VSSE and VDSSE

Verifiable Symmetric Searchable Encryption (VSSE) scheme enables the client to verify whether the server has executed all protocols honestly or tampered with the results maliciously, returning incorrect information. A VSSE scheme consists of 2 protocols:

- **Setup**$(\lambda, \mathrm{DB}; \perp) \rightarrow (K, s; \mathrm{EDB})$: Takes the security parameter λ and a database DB as input. The client outputs secret key K and a secret state s, while the server outputs an encrypted database EDB.
- **Search**$(K, s, w; \mathrm{EDB}) \rightarrow (s', \mathrm{DB}(w)$ or "Reject"; EDB'): The client inputs the secret key K and a single keyword w, whereas the server inputs EDB. **Search** protocol verifies the results returned by the server. If the server is not honest, the protocol outputs a string "Reject". Otherwise, the client outputs documents that contain the keyword w and a new state s', while the server outputs an updated encrypted database EDB'.

In addition to **Setup** and **Search** protocols, VDSSE has an **Update** protocol to support the dynamic setting, enabling clients to efficiently add and/or delete keyword-document pairs from the database.

- **Update**$(K, s, op, w, id; \mathrm{EDB}) \leftarrow (s'; \mathrm{EDB'})$: On input the secret key K, a state s, an operation $op \in \{add, del\}$ corresponding to add and delete, a keyword w, and a document identifier id, the client outputs a new state s'. The server takes the encrypted database EDB as input and outputs an updated encrypted database EDB'.

A VSSE scheme should satisfy three fundamental properties: correctness, soundness, and confidentiality.

Correctness. When the server honestly performs all the protocols and returns the correct result for every query, we say that a VCSSE achieves correctness. In other words, for each query $\psi(\overline{w})$, where $\overline{w}$ is the set of input keywords, the server should be able to return the correct search result $DB(\psi(\overline{w}))$ by following designed protocols.

Soundness. Informally, soundness property ensures that the malicious server cannot deceive the client into accepting invalid search results. To elaborate, the client should be able to detect incorrect and/or incomplete search results if the server did not perform queries honestly.

Confidentiality. The server should be unable to acquire any non-trivial information from the outsourced database and queries. Within the conjunctive SSE setting, it is crucial that the server does not acquire knowledge of the KPRP, as such leakage can lead to severe attacks [21] and disclose other information.

Apart from the aforementioned properties, VDSSE has extra security properties that need to be satisfied under the dynamic setting, such as forward privacy [2,17], backward privacy [4,17], and recently fault-tolerance [19].

Forward Privacy. Forward privacy prevents the information leakage regarding updated keywords. Informally, the server cannot link the update operation with previous searched queries to exploit information. Forward privacy is essential to prevent File-Injection attacks [21]. Formally, a $\mathcal{L}$-adaptively-secure SSE scheme Σ is forward private if the update leakage function $\mathcal{L}^{Update}$ can be written as:

$$\mathcal{L}^{Update}(DB,\, op, id, w) = \mathcal{L}'(op, id)$$

Backward Privacy. Backward privacy ensures that once data is deleted, it does not reveal any information thereafter. Stefonov initially introduced backward privacy [17], which was later formally classified into three types by Bost et al. [4]. The types of privacy are arranged in decreasing order of strength from I to III. Upon a search query on w, each type leaks $DB(w)$, their insertion time, and additional information as follows:

- **Type I:** leaks total number of updates on w.
- **Type II:** leaks the timing of each update on w (excluding their content).
- **Type III:** leaks the timing of each update on w, and identifies which deletion update nullified which insertion update.

Fault-Tolerance. A fault-tolerant SSE scheme can preserve its functionalities and properties even after incorrect updates. As discussed in [19], small errors from negligent clients can lead to the malfunctioning of many incremental-hash-based methods, jeopardizing their correctness and soundness. An update operation (op, id, w) is considered *incorect* if it falls into either of the two cases:

- $op = add$ and $id \in DB(w)$
- $op = del$ and $id \notin DB(w)$

3 Verifiable Result-Hiding Filter

Result-Hiding Filter [20] is beneficial for CSSE as it aids in concealing the Keyword-Pair Result Pattern (KPRP). In essence, the membership between a keyword and a document is stored in a map, and the map is encrypted into ES and stored on the server. Only the client that holds the secret key can initiate membership checking, revealing only the final result pattern to the server, thereby effectively preventing KPRP leakage. Nevertheless, to attain verifiability, a slight modification is necessary. In particular, in its **RHFEncrypt** algorithm, for each element $ES[i]$, after finishing adding dummy values, we further encrypt $ES[i]$ using Authenticated Encryption. This minor change enables the client to verify the honesty of the server in the subsequent search phase. If the server either modifies $ES[i]$ or returns incorrect position $ES[i']$, $AE.Dec$ will return "invalid", notifying the client of the malicious behavior.

3.1 Construction

The pseudo code for VRHF is illustrated in Fig. 1. To emphasize the distinctions from the original RHF, our modifications are showcased in red text.

3.2 Correctness of VRHF

Define $In(\delta, \Delta)$ as a function that outputs 1 if $\delta \in \Delta$, and 0 otherwise.

Definition 1 (Correctness of VRH-Filter). *We say an implementation of VRHF, Π, satisfies correctness if for any security parameter λ and PPT adversary $\mathcal{A}$, there exists a negligible function negl such that:*

$$\Pr[\text{VRHFCorr}_{\mathcal{A}}^{\Pi}(\lambda) = 1] \leq negl(\lambda)$$

Where $\text{VRHFCorr}_{\mathcal{A}}^{\Pi}(\lambda)$ *is defined in Fig. 2.*

Theorem 1. *If both the Result-Hiding Filter and the authenticated encryption scheme AE satisfy correctness, VRHF achieves correctness in Definition 1.*

Proof. As discussed in [20], RHF achieves correctness if the probability of **RHFTest**(K_F, δ, res) producing incorrect results for $\delta \in res$ is negligible. Since AE satisfies correctness, and we use AE to encrypt $ES[i]$ (**VRHF.Encrypt**, line 20), applying AE.Dec to decrypt res (**VRHF.Test**, line 3) should yield the original $ES[i]$ or an invalid value "invalid". After decrypting res, the subsequent logical flow should mirror that of RHF, resulting in the correct outcome with negligible false positives.

3.3 Soundness of VRHF

Theorem 2. *If the authenticated encryption AE satisfies authenticity in 2.1, VRHF achieves soundness.*

VRHF.Encrypt(K_F, Δ):

1: $(k_{f1}, k_{f2}, k_v) \leftarrow K_F$
2: Choose a constant φ
   and set $\zeta \leftarrow \varphi|\Delta|$
3: Choose a hash $H : \{0,1\}* \rightarrow [1, \zeta]$
4: $ES \leftarrow$ empty array
5: **for** $1 \leq i \leq \zeta$ **do**
6:    $ES[i] \leftarrow$ empty set
7: **end for**
8: **for** each $\delta \in \Delta$ **do**
9:    $tag_1 \leftarrow F(k_{f1}, \delta)$
10:   $pos \leftarrow H(tag_1)$
11:   $tag_2 \leftarrow F(k_{f2}, \delta)$
12:   $ES[pos] \leftarrow ES[pos] \cup \{tag_2\}$
13: **end for**
14: Find the position j with $|ES[j]|$
    being the largest among all the
    sets in ES
15: $\pi \leftarrow |ES[j]|$
16: **for** $1 \leq i \leq \zeta$ **do**
17:   **while** $|ES[i]| < \pi$ **do**
18:     $tag_2 \xleftarrow{\$} \{0,1\}^\lambda$
19:     $ES[i] \leftarrow ES[i] \cup \{tag_2\}$
20:   **end while**
21:   $ES[i] \leftarrow$ AE.Enc($k_v, i, ES[i]$)
22: **end for**
23: **return** ES

VRHF.Setup(1^λ):

1: $k_{f1} \xleftarrow{\$} \{0,1\}^\lambda$, $k_{f2} \xleftarrow{\$} \{0,1\}^\lambda$,
2: $k_v \leftarrow$ AE.KeyGen(1^λ)
3: **return** $K_F = (k_{f1}, k_{f2}, k_v)$

VRHF.GetTok(K_F, δ):

1: $(k_{f1}, -, -) \leftarrow K_F$
2: **return** $etok = F(k_{f1}, \delta)$

VRHF.Respond($etok, ES$):

1: $pos \leftarrow H(etok)$
2: **return** $res = ES[pos]$

VRHF.Test(K_F, δ, res):

1: $(-, k_{f2}, k_v) \leftarrow K_F$
2: $tag_2 = F(k_{f2}, \delta)$
3: $res \leftarrow$ AE.Dec(k_v, pos, res)
4: **if** $res = "invalid"$ **then**
5:    **return** -1, and **exit** protocol
6: **end if**
7: **if** $tag_2 \in res$ **then**
8:    **return** 1
9: **else**
10:   **return** 0
11: **end if**

Fig. 1. Verifiable Result Hiding Filter

1) Generate key K_F by running **VRHFSetup**(1^λ).
2) $\mathcal{A}$ chooses a set Δ, and receives the encrypted structure $ES \leftarrow$ **VRHFEncrypt**(K_F, Δ).
3) $\mathcal{A}$ makes queries adaptively as follows:
   $\mathcal{A}$ chooses element δ.
   $\mathcal{A}$ receives a token $etok \leftarrow$ **RHFGetTok**(K_F, δ).
   $\mathcal{A}$ performs **RHFRespond**($etok, ES$) to retrieve res.
   $\mathcal{A}$ receives the result $b_\delta \leftarrow$ **RHFTest**(K_F, δ, res).
4) If, during step 3, $\mathcal{A}$ selects any δ for which $b_\delta \neq In(\delta, \Delta)$, the game outputs 1; otherwise, it outputs 0.

Fig. 2. VRHFCorr$^\Pi{}_{\mathcal{A}}(\lambda)$

To achieve soundness, VRHF should be able to identify any malicious actions performed by the server. In the construction we discuss later, the server executes only the **VRHF**.Respond protocol. Therefore, any malicious behavior from the server would involve sending an incorrect res. Since the server lacks the secret key k_v, it cannot create a valid AE-encrypted $ES[i]$. Therefore, decrypting res and obtaining the result "invalid" would indicate its dishonesty. If the server chooses to return a valid element of ES from an incorrect position, let's say $ES[i']$, then AE.Dec($k_v, i, ES[i']$) would also result in "invalid" due to the mismatched nonce i' instead of i. If AE satisfies authenticity, the only way for the server to bypass its verification is returning the unaltered element of ES at the correct position i, consequently ensuring the soundness of the VRHF.

3.4   Security of VRHF

Our VRHF is built upon the concepts of PRF F, Hash function H, with the addition of Authenticated Encryption AE. The security proof of our scheme is similar to RH-filter: If F is a secure PRF, H is modeled as a random oracle, AE satisfies the privacy and authenticity definition, then our VRHF construction is semantically secure. We provide a full security analysis in Appendix A.

3.5   Performance of VRHF

Given that the only distinction between VRHF and RHF is the additional authenticated encryption layer, their performance is comparable. Let's assume that the maximum number of elements in Δ mapped by H to the same hash is t. The computational time and space complexity of **VRHFSetup** in creating ES are both $O(\varphi t|\Delta|)$. **RHFGetTok** generates $etok$ in $O(1)$ time and space complexity. **VRHFRespond** retrieves res, which is of size $O(t)$, with $O(1)$ computational overhead. **VRHFTest** requires $O(\log t)$ computational overhead for membership checking, using binary search. Given that H is uniformly random, the expected value of t remains relatively small, exhibiting logarithmic growth with ζ when φ is fixed [13]. According to [20], with δ containing tens of millions of elements, t is only 11 and 8 for φ values of 1 and 2, respectively.

4   VCPHprotocol

This section presents VCPH, a KPRP-hiding Verifiable Conjunctive Searchable Encryption. Through the use of a VSSE scheme as a black-box, along with VRHF, our scheme stands out as the first VCSSE capable of preventing KPRP leakage while simultaneously avoiding non-negligible false positives. To keep things simple, we assume that the conjunction queries are in the form of $w_1 \wedge con(w_2, ..., w_n)$. Here, con represents an arbitrary conjunction that may include negated terms.

4.1   Overview

Our scheme VCPH consists of two protocols, corresponding to two phases, VCPH.Setup and VCPH.Search. In the Setup phase, the client generates two encrypted structures, EDB1 and EDB2, using VSSE and VDSSE and Verifiable Result Hiding Filter, respectively. During the Search phase, we use the Search algorithm of VSSE on EDB1 to obtain ids, the set of indexes for documents matching w_1. For each identifier in ids, we then check whether they match the query by utilizing VRHF on EDB2. The server's integrity is examined at each step, either through VSSE or VRHF, to ensure the client only accepts correct and complete results.

4.2   Construction Details

Setup Protocol. During the Setup phase, the client first runs the Setup protocol to generate encrypted database EDB_1 and key K_E. Additionally, the client creates a set S containing all keyword-document pairs in the database. S is then encrypted using VRHF to generate a second structured EDB_2 and key K_F. The client keeps the key pair $K = (K_E, K_F)$ and sends the encrypted database EDB = (EDB_1, EDB_2) to the server (Fig. 3).

Client:
1: K_E, EDB_1 ← VSSE.Setup(λ, DB)
2: S ← empty set
3: **for** each $w \in$ W **do**
4:    **for** each $id \in$ DB(w) **do**
5:       S ← S $\cup$ $\{(w, id)\}$
6:    **end for**
7: **end for**
8: K_F ← VRHF.Setup(λ)
9: EDB_2 ← VRHF.Encrypt(K_F, S)
10: **return** $K = (K_E, K_F)$

Server:
11: **return** EDB = (EDB_1, EDB_2)

Fig. 3. VCPH.Setup

Search Protocol. Given a search query $w_1 \wedge con(w_2, ..., w_n)$, both the client and server execute the single-keyword Search protocol of VSSE to obtain ids, the set of identifiers for documents that match the *s-term* w_1. Unlike the original VSSE, in our scheme, the outcome of VSSE.Search(K_E, w_1; EDB_1) is not conclusive, as we still need to account for the *x-terms*, i.e., $\{w_2, ..., w_n\}$. Therefore, ids will solely be the set of indexes, rather than the set of encrypted documents. The resulting *ids* are guaranteed to be accurate and comprehensive by the protocols of VSSE, as elaborated in Sect. 2.2.

For every document identifier in *ids*, we will check whether it satisfies the query. The client creates $token_c$ ($1 \leq c \leq |ids|$), comprising $n - 1$ smaller tokens $tok_{c,i}$ ($2 \leq i \leq n$), each is produced by VRHF.GetTok with the pair $(ids[c], w_i)$ as input. In essence, $tok_{c,i}$ is the encrypted token that represents $ids[c]$ and w_i. Its presence in ES indicates that document $ids[c]$ contains keyword w_i. These tokens are added to a $|ids| \times (n - 1)$ dimensional matrix Tokens and sent to the server to retrieve its corresponding matrix Responds in EDB_2. For each element Responds$[c][i]$ in the matrix, the client invokes VRHF.Test for verifying and membership checking. The result is stored in variable b with three possibilities:

- $b = -1$: The server is detected to be malicious. Thus, the algorithm outputs **"Reject"** and halts the protocol.
- $b = 0$: The server is honest, and $tok_{c,i}$ does not exist in EDB_2.
- $b = 1$: The server is honest, and $tok_{c,i}$ exists in EDB_2.

Considering b and the type of term (negated or non-negated), we can determine whether the c-th document satisfies the i-th term in the query or not. Should the document meet every term, the client includes it in the list for subsequent retrieval. Finally, the client sends the request, and the server returns the list of encrypted documents back to the client.

If the malicious server does not faithfully execute the Search protocol and provides incorrect or incomplete results, the Search protocol of VCPH should be capable of identifying this, outputting **"Reject"**, and stopping the protocol. On the contrary, if the server performs honestly, the client outputs **"Accept"** at the end of the protocol, confirming the receipt of the correct and complete result from the server.

4.3   Correctness of VCPH

Theorem 3. *If the black-box VSSE scheme is correct, and VRHF satisfy both correctness and soundness, VCPH achieves correctness.*

Our scheme is correct when the client accepts search result, indicating that the server has honestly executed the protocols, and the returned documents align with the query. In the Setup phase of our scheme, we generated two encrypted databases: EDB_1 for verifiable single-keyword search and EDB_2 to verify the existence of keyword-document pairs. During the Search phase, both the client and server perform the single-keyword search protocol from VSSE to retrieve documents that contain w_1. Because the black-box VSSE is correct, the retrieved result is $DB(w_1)$. Afterward, for each document in $DB(w_1)$, the client sends tokens representing the desired keyword-document pair to the server to obtain the corresponding *res*. In the case of the server acting maliciously and providing incorrect results, the client will be informed because of the Soundness of VRHF. Otherwise, the client can precisely verify whether the keyword-document pair of

Client:
1: $(K_E, K_F) \leftarrow K$

Client and Server:
2: Runs VSSE.Search(K_E, w_1; EDB_1) to get *ids*

Client:
3: Tokens $\leftarrow$ empty list
4: **for** $c = 1$ to $|ids|$ **do**
5:     $token_c \leftarrow$ empty list
6:     **for** $i = 2$ to n **do**
7:       $\delta \leftarrow (ids[c], w_i)$
8:       $tok_{c,i} \leftarrow$ VRHF.GetTok(K_F, δ)
9:       $token_c \leftarrow token_c \cup \{tok_{c,i}\}$
10:     **end for**
11:     Tokens $\leftarrow$ Tokens $\cup \{token_c\}$
12: **end for**
13: Send Tokens to the server

Server:
14: Responds $\leftarrow$ empty list
15: **for** $c = 1$ to $|$Tokens$|$ **do**
16:     $respond_c \leftarrow$ empty list
17:     **for** $i = 1$ to n **do**
18:       $res \leftarrow$ VHRF.Respond(Tokens$[c][i]$, EDB_2)
19:       $respond_c \leftarrow respond_c \cup \{res\}$
20:     **end for**

21:     Add $respond_c$ to Responds
22: **end for**
23: Send Responds to the client

Client:
24: R $\leftarrow$ empty list
25: **for** $c = 1$ to $|$Tokens$|$ **do**
26:     $match_c \leftarrow true$
27:     **for** $i = 1$ to n **do**
28:       $\delta \leftarrow (ids[c], w_i)$
29:       $b \leftarrow$ VRHF.Test($K_F, \delta,$ Responds$[c][i]$)
30:       **if** $b = -1$ **then**
31:         **return "Reject"**
32:         **exit protocol**
33:       **end if**
34:       **if** ($b = 1$ and w_i is a negated term) or ($b = 0$ and w_i is a non-negated term) **then**
35:         $match_c \leftarrow false$
36:         Break the loop for i
37:       **end if**
38:     **end for**
39:     **if** $match_c = true$ **then**
40:       R $\leftarrow$ R $\cup \{id_c\}$
41:     **end if**
42: **end for**

Fig. 4. VCPH.Search

interest exists in the database EDB_2 or not, as VRHF can accurately check membership with negligible false-positive (Correctness of VRHF). With the acquired information, the client can determine which document matches the query, allowing them to create a correct and complete list for the request (Fig. 4).

4.4 Soundness of VCPH

Theorem 4. *If both VSSE and VRHF satisfy soundness, VCPH achieves soundness.*

When the client and server initially execute the Search protocol of VSSE, if the malicious party is dishonest, the client will be notified as long as the black-box VSSE scheme is sound. In the subsequent steps, apart from receiving the final result containing matched documents, the client only receives a list of *res*, each corresponding to a document in DB(w_1). Soundness of VRHF ensures that if the server chooses to manipulate any of the *res*, the client will be notified, thereby guaranteeing the soundness of VCPH. In line with established practices in SSE literature, it is assumed that the client has a mechanism for verifying the integrity of the final results, and this particular aspect is not explicitly addressed.

4.5 Security of VCPH

In this section, we represent the query as $q = q[1] \wedge con(q[2], ..., q[n])$. The client first executes the Setup protocol offline and sends EDB = $(\text{EDB}_1, \text{EDB}_2)$ to the server, leaking the size of EDB, denoted as N. During Search phase, the VSSE.Search protocol is first executed to receive $\text{DB}(q[1])$, thereby exposing Search leakage of VSSE. Subsequently, for each $id \in \text{DB}(q[1])$, the client forges a corresponding token. Using the c-th token, the server can execute VRHF.Respond to retrieve $n - 1$ elements of *res*, containing the information about the existence of (id_c, w_i). Similar to RHF, our VRHF only reveals whether the same keyword-document pair has been queried before. Nevertheless, the server cannot extract the information due to not having the secret key K_F. The examination is done offline by the client, thus preventing KPRP leakage. Finally, similar to all other previous SSE schemes, our solution reveals the whole result pattern $\text{DB}(q)$.

Theorem 5. *If VSSE is a secure SSE scheme, and VRHF satisfies security properties outlined in Sect. 3, then VCPH is $\mathcal{L}_{VCPH}$-adaptively secure where*

- $\mathcal{L}_{VCPH}^{Setup}(DB) = N$
- $\mathcal{L}_{VCPH}^{Search}(DB, q) = (\mathcal{L}_{VSSE}^{Search}, DB(q), DB(q[1]), EP(q[1]), IP(q[1]))$

4.6 Performance of VCPH

Setup. The setup phase generates the encrypted structure ES, which encrypts N keyword-document pairs and pads each position to t elements. Therefore, both the computational and storage overhead have a complexity of $O(tN)$.

Search. In the search phase, after invoking **VSSE.Search** to retrieve $\text{DB}(w_1)$, the client needs to check whether $(n-1)|\text{DB}(w_1)|$ keyword-document pairs exist in the database. Let c be the cardinality of $\text{DB}(w_1)$. The process of generating tokens at client side and responding at server side incurs communication overheads of $O(nc)$ and $O(nct)$ respectively, while both have a time complexity of $O(nc)$. The membership-checking process requires $O(nc \cdot \log t)$ computational cost. Overall, the search process incurs $O(nc \cdot \log t)$ and $O(nct)$ computation and communication overhead, respectively.

5 Extension to Support Dynamic Database

This section discusses the expansion into a dynamic database setting. We present a solution to accommodate update functionality into VCPH, resulting in a Dynamic VCSSE (VCDSSE). Our solution not only prevents the KPRP leakage but also addresses additional security challenges in the dynamic setting.

5.1   Overview

Our solution resembles to DHBS [20], a Conjunctive DSSE that employs RH-filter and leverages a DSSE Σ as a black-box. DHBS prevents KPRP leakage and inherits forward and backward secured from Σ. In comparison to our goal, DHBS lacks verifiability and fault-tolerance. By substituting Σ and RHF in DHBS with a fault-tolerant VDSSE scheme and VRHF, respectively, we can establish a fault-tolerant VCSSE scheme in a dynamic setting, while simultaneously maintaining essential properties like forward and backward privacy.

5.2   Detailed Construction

Selecting the appropriate external VDSSE is of utmost importance, as both the security and performance of our scheme depend on this black-box. To achieve forward privacy, backward privacy and fault-tolerance, the selected VDSSE should also possess these properties. For instance, the approach presented by [19,20] introduces a fault-tolerant, forward-private and backward-private VDSSE scheme that exhibits improved storage efficiency and performance compared to earlier forward-secured DSSE schemes. In this section, we consider their work as a black-box in our solution, denoted as Σ.

The significant difference lies in the update phase. The client possesses a table T for local updates. After every ρ updates, an encrypted structure ES is generated from T and sent to the server, after which T is cleared empty. On the server side, we utilize a filter list ESS to keep track of cnt encrypted structures ES received from the client. The search phase, simply put, is similar to that of VCPH. By inspecting T and ESS, one can verify whether a pair $(w_i,\ id)$ $(2 \leq i \leq n$ and $id \in \mathrm{DB}(w_1))$ exists in the database.

The pseudo code for our construction is provided in Figs. 5, 6, and 7. In the figures, $DTok_c[i, 0, \perp]$, $DTok_c[i, j, op]$ are the tokens for querying the response of whether ES_0 includes (w_i, id), ES_j includes $(w_i||id, op)$, respectively. $DR_c[i, j, op]$ is the response for $DTok_c[i, j, op] \in \mathrm{ESS}[j + 1]$.

Client:
1: K_Σ, EDB$_\Sigma$ $\leftarrow$ Σ.Setup(λ, DB)
2: S $\leftarrow$ empty set
3: **for** each $w \in$ W **do**
4:     **for** each $id \in$ DB(w) **do**
5:         S $\leftarrow$ S $\cup \{(w, id)\}$
6:     **end for**
7: **end for**
8: $K_F \leftarrow$ VRHF.Setup(λ)
9: $ES_0 \leftarrow$ VRHF.Encrypt(K_F, S)

10: Send EDB$_\Sigma$, ES_0 to the server
11: $cnt \leftarrow 0$, $T \leftarrow$ empty table
12: Choose ρ as the size of T
13: **return** $K = (K_\Sigma, K_F)$ and
      $s = (s_\Sigma, cnt, T, \rho)$

Server:
14: ESS $\leftarrow$ empty list
15: ESS $\leftarrow$ ESS $\cup \{ES_0\}$
16: **return** EDB $= ($EDB$_\Sigma$, ESS$)$

Fig. 5. DVCPH.Setup

1: Client and server jointly execute
   Σ.Update($K_\Sigma, s_\Sigma, op, w, id$; EDB$_\Sigma$)

   Client:
2: $T[w||id] \leftarrow op$
3: **if** $|T| = \rho$ **then**
4: $\quad cnt \leftarrow cnt + 1$
5: $\quad (k_{f1}, k_{f2}, k_v) \leftarrow K_F$
6: $\quad k'_{f1} \leftarrow F(k_{f1}, cnt)$
7: $\quad k'_{f2} \leftarrow F(k_{f2}, cnt)$
8: $\quad K'_F \leftarrow (k'_{f1}, k'_{f2})$

9: $\quad ES_{cnt} \leftarrow$ VRHFEncrypt(K'_F, T)
10: $\quad$ Send ES_{cnt} to the server
11: $\quad$ Clear T
12: **end if**
13: **return** $s = (s_\Sigma, cnt, T, \rho)$

   Server:
14: **if** receives ES_{cnt} **then**
15: $\quad$ ESS $\leftarrow$ ESS $\cup \{ES_{cnt}\}$
16: **end if**
17: **return** EDB $=$ (EBD$_\Sigma$, ESS)

Fig. 6. DVCPH.Update

1: Run Σ.Search(K_Σ, s_Σ, w_1; EDB$_\Sigma$), where client gets DB(w_1)

   Client:
2: $I \leftarrow$ empty list
3: Insert elements in DB(w_1) into I in random order
4: $(k_{f1}, k_{f2}) \leftarrow K_F$
5: **for** $j = 1$ to cnt **do**
6: $\quad k'_{f1} \leftarrow F(k_{f1}, j), k'_{f2} \leftarrow F(k_{f2}, j), K_{F_j} \leftarrow (k'_{f1}, k'_{f2})$
7: **end for**
8: **for** $c = 1$ to $|I|$ **do**
9: $\quad id \leftarrow I[i]$
10: $\quad DTok_c \leftarrow$ empty table
11: $\quad$ **for** $i = 2$ to n **do**
12: $\quad\quad DTok_c[i, 0, \bot] \leftarrow$ VRHF.GetTok($K_F, (w_i, id)$)
13: $\quad\quad$ **for** $j = 1$ to cnt **do**
14: $\quad\quad\quad DTok_c[i, j, add] \leftarrow$ VRHF.GetTok($K_{F_j}, (w_i||id, add)$)
15: $\quad\quad\quad DTok_c[i, j, del] \leftarrow$ VRHF.GetTok($K_{F_j}, (w_i||id, del)$)
16: $\quad\quad$ **end for**
17: $\quad$ **end for**
18: $\quad$ Send $DTok_c$ to the server
19: **end for**

   Server
20: **while** receives $DTok_c$ **do**
21: $\quad DR_c \leftarrow$ empty table
22: $\quad$ **for** each $DTok_c[i, j, op]$ **do**
23: $\quad\quad DR_c[i, j, op] \leftarrow$ VRHF.Respond($DTok_c[i, j, op]$, ESS$[j + 1]$)
24: $\quad$ **end for**
25: $\quad$ Send DR_c to the client
26: **end while**
   Continue in the next figure...

Fig. 7. DVCPH.Search

```
      Client
27: while receives $DR_c$ do
28:    $id \leftarrow I[c]$
29:    for $i = 2$ to $n$ do
30:       if $T[w_i||id]$ exists then
31:          if $T[w_i||id] = add$ then
32:             Continue with next iteration for $i$ (Line 31)
33:          else if $T[w_i||id] = del$ then
34:             Break loop $i$, continue with next iteration for $DR_c$ (Line 29)
35:          end if
36:       else
37:          for $j = cnt$ down to 1 do
38:             $r_a \leftarrow$ VRHF.Test$(K_{F_j}, (w_i||id, add), DR_c[i, j, add])$
39:             $r_d \leftarrow$ VRHF.Test$(K_{F_j}, (w_i||id, del), DR_c[i, j, del])$
40:             if $r_a = 1$ then
41:                Break loop $j$, continue with next iteration for $i$ (Line 31)
42:             end if
43:             if $r_d = 1$ then
44:                Break loop $j$, continue with next iteration for $DR_c$ (Line 29)
45:             end if
46:          end for
47:          $r \leftarrow$ VRHF.Test$(K_F, (w_i, id), DR_c[i, 0, \bot])$
48:          if $r = 0$ then
49:             Break loop $i$, continue with next iteration for $DR_c$ (Line 29)
50:          end if
51:       end if
52:    end for
53:    $R \leftarrow R \cup \{id\}$
54: end while
```

Fig. 7. (*continued*)

5.3 Security of DVCPH

The security analysis of DVCPH shares similarity with that of VCPH in the Setup and Search phases. DVCPH exposes N in the Setup phase, and $\mathrm{DB}(q[1])$, $\mathrm{IP}(q)$, $\mathrm{EP}(q[1])$, the leakage of Σ in the Search phase. During Update phase, Σ.Update is executed to update EDB_Σ, revealing $\mathcal{L}_\Sigma^{Update}$. In regard to ESS, the updates are stored locally in T. When T reaches its capacity, a VRH-filter is created and sent to the server, revealing nothing but the size of the filter. Formally, the search leakage of DVCPH can be written as:

- $\mathcal{L}_{DVCPH}^{Setup}(\mathrm{DB}) = N$
- $\mathcal{L}_{DVCPH}^{Search}(\mathrm{DB}, q) = (\mathcal{L}_\Sigma^{Search}, \mathrm{DB}(q), \mathrm{DB}(q_1), \mathrm{EP}(q_1), \mathrm{IP}(q_1))$
- $\mathcal{L}_{DVCPH}^{Update}(\mathrm{DB}, op, w, id) = (\mathcal{L}_\Sigma^{Update}, |\mathrm{ES}_{cnt}|)$

Forward and Backward Privacy. Given that the VRH-filter discloses only its size, and updates are stored locally on the client's machine, the server is incapable of connecting an update to previous queries or utilizing information from deleted entries. Consequently, as long as Σ achieves forward and/or backward privacy, DVCPH satisfies equivalent properties.

Fault-Tolerance. Our system can withstand incorrect updates since, for each keyword-document pair, T retains only the latest update operation. Deleting a non-existent pair or adding multiple keyword-document pairs would have no impact on our scheme. Therefore, if Σ is fault-tolerant, our scheme would also achieve fault-tolerance.

5.4   Performance of DVCPH

Update. For each query, the cost for updating the local cache T is $O(1)$. When T reaches its full capacity ρ, the client creates and sends a new filter of VRHF to the server, costing $O(t\rho)$ computational and communication overheads. Since we need ρ updates to trigger this event, the average cost of each update is $O(t)$.

Setup. Compared to VCPH, in addition to generating ES, DVCPH also initializes an empty table T at $O(1)$. As a result, the overall computational and storage complexity is $O(tN)$.

Search. The client needs to check the existence of $(n-1)|\mathrm{DB}(w_1)|$ keyword-document pairs in the database. For each pair, **VRHF.Test** is executed at most $1 + 2cnt$ times. Consequently, the computation and communication overheads are $O(n|\mathrm{DB}(w_1)|\log t \cdot cnt)$ and $O(n|\mathrm{DB}(w_1)|t \cdot cnt)$, respectively.

Since $cnt = N^+/\rho$, where N^+ is the number of updates queries, the efficiency of the search function decreases linearly with the increase of cnt. As such, our scheme is better suited for databases with infrequent updates.

6   Conclusion

In this paper, we introduced the first Verifiable Conjunctive SSE scheme capable of concealing the Keyword Pair Result Pattern. By integrating Authenticated Encryption with the recently introduced Result Hiding Filter and implementing a VSSE scheme as a black-box, our system achieves multi-keyword search, verifiability, KPRP-hiding, and non-negligible false-positives. We further expand our research to accommodate dynamic databases, demonstrating that our solution achieves forward and backward privacy, along with resilience against incorrect updates from careless clients. Despite the notable enhancement in security, our scheme maintains sub-linear performance. Potential areas for future research includes multi-client settings, completely hiding the reveal of the *s-term* w_1, or improving the performance by reducing communication overhead.

A   Security of VRHF

Since **VRHFGetTok**(K_F, δ) is a deterministic algorithm, the generated token *etok* reveals the repetition of δ. We define such leakage as token pattern, and is captured by the function *tp*. Formally, consider a sequence of queried element $\{\delta_1, \delta_2, ...\}$, where δ_i represents the chosen element in the i-th query. Given an element δ, we have $tp(\delta) = \{i | \delta = \delta_i\}$.

VRHFReal$_{\mathcal{A}}^{\varPi}(\lambda)$
1) **VRHFSetup**(1^λ) outputs K_F.
2) $\mathcal{A}$ adaptively chooses elements. For each chosen element δ, $\mathcal{A}$ receives $etok \leftarrow$ **VRHF.GetTok**(K_F, δ).
3) $\mathcal{A}$ picks a set Δ, and receives $ES \leftarrow$ **VRHF.Encrypt**(K_F, Δ).
4) $\mathcal{A}$ repeats step 2.
5) $\mathcal{A}$ outputs a bit b.

VRHFIdeal$_{\mathcal{A},\mathcal{S}}^{\varPi}(\lambda)$
1) $\mathcal{S}(\lambda)$ outputs nothing.
2) $\mathcal{A}$ adaptively chooses elements. For each chosen element δ, $\mathcal{A}$ receives $etok \leftarrow \mathcal{S}(tp(\delta))$.
3) $\mathcal{A}$ picks a set Δ, and gets $ES \leftarrow \mathcal{S}(|\Delta|)$.
4) $\mathcal{A}$ repeats step 2.
5) $\mathcal{A}$ outputs a bit b.

Fig. 8. Real and ideal games for VRHF

Definition 2 (Security of VRHF). *An implementation $\varPi$ of VRHF is sementically secure if for every security parameter λ and PPT adversary $\mathcal{A}$, there exists a simulator $\mathcal{S}$ and a negligible function negl such that:*

$$|\Pr[\text{VRHFReal}_{\mathcal{A}}^{\varPi}(\lambda)] - \Pr[\text{VRHFIdeal}_{\mathcal{A},\mathcal{S}}^{\varPi}(\lambda)]| \leq negl(\lambda)$$

where VRHFReal$_{\mathcal{A}}^{\varPi}(\lambda)$ and VRHFIdeal$_{\mathcal{A},\mathcal{S}}^{\varPi}(\lambda)$ are the games defined in Fig. 8.

Theorem 6. *If F is a secure PRF, H is a hash function modeled as a random oracle, and AE satisfies the privacy and authenticity definition, then VRHF is semantically secure as defined in Definition 2.*

Proof. First, we define simulator $\mathcal{S}$ as in Fig. 9.

---

1) $S(\lambda)$ creates an empty table F1.
2) $\mathcal{A}$ selects elements adaptively. For the i-th element δ, $S(tp(\delta))$ does as follows:

   2.1) If $tp(\delta)$ is not empty, S sets $etok \leftarrow$F1$[j]$ where j is the minimum value in $tp(\delta)$.

   2.2) Otherwise, S sets $etok \xleftarrow{\$} \{0,1\}^\lambda$ and F1$[i] = etok$.

   2.3) S sends $etok$ to $\mathcal{A}$.
3) $\mathcal{A}$ selects a set Δ. $S(|\Delta|)$ does as follows:

   3.1) S chooses a constant φ, sets $\zeta \leftarrow \varphi|\Delta|$, and creates ES as an array consisting of ζ empty sets.

   3.2) S computes $tag_2 \xleftarrow{\$} \{0,1\}^\lambda$, $pos \xleftarrow{\$} [1,\zeta]$, and $ES[pos] \leftarrow ES[pos] \cup \{tag_2\}$

   3.3) S pads ES in the same manner as in **VRHF.Encrypt**, and then assigns $ES[i] \leftarrow$ AE.Enc$(k_v, i, ES[i])$. 3.4) S sends ES to $\mathcal{A}$.
4) $\mathcal{A}$ repeats step 2). However, in step 2.2), instead of updating F1$[i]$, S updates F1$[total + i] \leftarrow etok$ where $total$ is the total number of queries performed in step 2).
5) $\mathcal{A}$ outputs a bit b.

Fig. 9. VRHF Simulator S

To show that this simulation experiment is indistinguishable from the real one, we define four games as follows:

Game $G_0^{\mathcal{L}}$: This is the real experiment VRHFReal$_{\mathcal{A}}^{\mathcal{L}}(\lambda)$

Game $G_1^{\mathcal{L}}$: We initialize an empty table F1 and replace every call to $F(k_{f1}, \delta)$ with the procedure as follows: if δ is a repeated input to $F(k_{f1}, .)$, we output F1$[\delta]$. Otherwise, we set F1$[\delta] \xleftarrow{\$} \{0,1\}^\lambda$ and output F1$[\delta]$. Because the input to $F(k_{f2}, .)$ is unique in this scenario, we replace each invocation with a uniformly random output from $\{0,1\}^\lambda$. In order to differentiate between $G_0^{\mathcal{L}}$ and $G_1^{\mathcal{L}}$, the adversary must break the PRF security of $F(k_{f_1}, .)$ or $F(k_{f_2}, .)$. As such:

$$|\Pr[G_0^{\mathcal{L}}(\lambda) = 1] - \Pr[G_1^{\mathcal{L}}(\lambda) = 1]| \leq 2.Adv_{F,\mathcal{B}}^{PRF}$$

Game $G_2^{\mathcal{L}}$: In this game, we replace each call to hash function H with uniformly random output from $[1,\zeta]$. Since H is modeled as a random oracle, it is impossible to distinguish between $G_1^{\mathcal{L}}$ and $G_2^{\mathcal{L}}$.

$$\Pr[G_1^{\mathcal{L}}(\lambda) = 1] = \Pr[G_2^{\mathcal{L}}(\lambda) = 1]$$

Game $G_3^{\mathcal{L}}$: Let lb be the bit length of a ciphertext generated by $AE.Enc$. After creating an empty table T, we replace every call to authenticated encryption schemes $AE.Enc(.,.,.)$ (**VRHF.Encrypt**, line 20, Fig. 1) with the following pseudo-codes:

$$
\begin{aligned}
&1:\ ES[i] \xleftarrow{\$} \{0,1\}^{lb} \\
&2:\ M[ES[i]] \leftarrow (k_v, i, ES[i])
\end{aligned}
$$

and $AE.Dec(.,.,.,.)$ (**VRHF.Test**, line 3, Fig. 1) with:

```
 1: if M[res] does not exist then
 2:     res ← "invalid"
 3: else
 4:     (k, nonce, mes) ← M[res]
 5:     if k ≠ k_v or nonce ≠ i then
 6:         res ← "invalid"
 7:     else
 8:         res ← mes
 9:     end if
10: end if
```

The probability of distinguishing $G_2^{\mathcal{L}}$ from $G_3^{\mathcal{L}}$ is the advantage of a PPT adversary $\mathcal{B}_2$ cracks the privacy or authenticity of AE.

$$
|\Pr[G_2^{\mathcal{L}}(\lambda) = 1] - \Pr[G_3^{\mathcal{L}}(\lambda) = 1]| \leq Adv_{AE,\mathcal{B}_2}^{Priv} + Adv_{AE,\mathcal{B}_2}^{Auth}
$$

The only difference between $G_3^{\mathcal{L}}$ and ideal experiment is the replacement of of every key δ in F1 with the sequence number of the earliest query on δ. As the adversary cannot differentiate between the two experiments since they have identical views, we conclude that:

$$
|Pr[VRHFReal_{\mathcal{A}}^{\Pi}(\lambda)] - Pr[VRHFIdeal_{\mathcal{A},\mathcal{S}}^{\Pi}(\lambda)]| \leq 2.Adv_{F,\mathcal{B}}^{PRF} + Adv_{AE,\mathcal{B}_2}^{Priv} + \\
Adv_{AE,\mathcal{B}_2}^{Auth}
$$

References

1. Boneh, D., Waters, B.: Conjunctive, subset, and range queries on encrypted data. In: Vadhan, S.P. (ed.) TCC 2007. LNCS, vol. 4392, pp. 535–554. Springer, Heidelberg (2007). https://doi.org/10.1007/978-3-540-70936-7_29
2. Bost, R.: σοφος: Forward secure searchable encryption. In: Proceedings of the 2016 ACM SIGSAC Conference on Computer and Communications Security, pp. 1143–1154 (2016)
3. Bost, R., Fouque, P.A., Pointcheval, D.: Verifiable dynamic symmetric searchable encryption: optimality and forward security. Cryptology ePrint Archive (2016)

4. Bost, R., Minaud, B., Ohrimenko, O.: Forward and backward private searchable encryption from constrained cryptographic primitives. In: Proceedings of the 2017 ACM SIGSAC Conference on Computer and Communications Security, pp. 1465–1482 (2017)

5. Cash, D., et al.: Dynamic searchable encryption in very-large databases: data structures and implementation. Cryptology ePrint Archive (2014)

6. Cash, D., Jarecki, S., Jutla, C., Krawczyk, H., Roşu, M.-C., Steiner, M.: Highly-scalable searchable symmetric encryption with support for Boolean queries. In: Canetti, R., Garay, J.A. (eds.) CRYPTO 2013, Part I. LNCS, vol. 8042, pp. 353–373. Springer, Heidelberg (2013). https://doi.org/10.1007/978-3-642-40041-4_20

7. Chai, Q., Gong, G.: Verifiable symmetric searchable encryption for semi-honest-but-curious cloud servers. In: 2012 IEEE International Conference on Communications (ICC), pp. 917–922. IEEE (2012)

8. Curtmola, R., Garay, J., Kamara, S., Ostrovsky, R.: Searchable symmetric encryption: improved definitions and efficient constructions. In: Proceedings of the 13th ACM Conference on Computer and Communications Security, pp. 79–88 (2006)

9. Kamara, S., Papamanthou, C., Roeder, T.: Dynamic searchable symmetric encryption. In: Proceedings of the 2012 ACM Conference on Computer and Communications Security, pp. 965–976 (2012)

10. Kurosawa, K., Ohtaki, Y.: UC-secure searchable symmetric encryption. In: Keromytis, A.D. (ed.) FC 2012. LNCS, vol. 7397, pp. 285–298. Springer, Heidelberg (2012). https://doi.org/10.1007/978-3-642-32946-3_21

11. Kurosawa, K., Ohtaki, Y.: How to update documents *verifiably* in searchable symmetric encryption. In: Abdalla, M., Nita-Rotaru, C., Dahab, R. (eds.) CANS 2013. LNCS, vol. 8257, pp. 309–328. Springer, Cham (2013). https://doi.org/10.1007/978-3-319-02937-5_17

12. Lai, S., et al.: Result pattern hiding searchable encryption for conjunctive queries. In: Proceedings of the 2018 ACM SIGSAC Conference on Computer and Communications Security, pp. 745–762 (2018)

13. Larson, P.Å.: Expected worst-case performance of hash files. Comput. J. **25**(3), 347–352 (1982)

14. Pham, V.A., Hoang, D.H., Chung-Nguyen, H.H., Tran, M.K., Tran, M.T.: Privacy preserving visual log service with temporal interval query using interval tree-based searchable symmetric encryption. In: Proceedings of the 10th International Symposium on Information and Communication Technology, pp. 425–432 (2019)

15. Rogaway, P., Bellare, M., Black, J.: OCB: a block-cipher mode of operation for efficient authenticated encryption. ACM Trans. Inf. Syst. Secur. (TISSEC) **6**(3), 365–403 (2003)

16. Song, D.X., Wagner, D., Perrig, A.: Practical techniques for searches on encrypted data. In: Proceeding 2000 IEEE Symposium on Security and Privacy, S&P 2000, pp. 44–55. IEEE (2000)

17. Stefanov, E., Papamanthou, C., Shi, E.: Practical dynamic searchable encryption with small leakage. Cryptology ePrint Archive (2013)

18. Yoon, H., Yu, M., Kwak, C., Hahn, C., Koo, D., Hur, J.: Shedding light on blind spot of backward privacy in dynamic searchable symmetric encryption. IEEE Access (2023)

19. Yuan, D., Cui, S., Russello, G.: We can make mistakes: Fault-tolerant forward private verifiable dynamic searchable symmetric encryption. In: 2022 IEEE 7th European Symposium on Security and Privacy (EuroS&P), pp. 587–605. IEEE (2022)

20. Yuan, D., Cui, S., Russello, G.: Result pattern hiding Boolean searchable encryption: achieving negligible false positive rates in low storage overhead. Cryptology ePrint Archive, Paper 2024/865 (2024). https://eprint.iacr.org/2024/865
21. Zhang, Y., Katz, J., Papamanthou, C.: All your queries are belong to us: the power of {File-Injection} attacks on searchable encryption. In: 25th USENIX Security Symposium (USENIX Security 2016), pp. 707–720 (2016)
22. Zuo, C., Sun, S.F., Liu, J.K., Shao, J., Pieprzyk, J., Wei, G.: Forward and backward private dynamic searchable symmetric encryption for conjunctive queries. Cryptology ePrint Archive (2020)

Compressed Cookies: Practical Wildcard Symmetric Searchable Encryption with Optimized Storage

Jiaojiao Wu[1], Kai Du[1], Jianfeng Wang[1(✉)], Shi-Feng Sun[2(✉)], Yunling Wang[3], Yong Li[4], Wenyuan Tian[5], and Yusen Wang[5]

[1] School of Cyber Engineering, Xidian University, Xi'an, China
{jiaojiaowujj,kaidu}@stu.xidian.edu.cn, jfwang@xidian.edu.cn
[2] School of Cyber Science and Engineering, Shanghai Jiao Tong University, Shanghai, China
shifeng.sun@sjtu.edu.cn
[3] School of Cyberspace Security, Xi'an University of Posts and Telecommunications, Xi'an, China
ylwang@xupt.edu.cn
[4] Huawei Technologies Düsseldorf GmbH, Düsseldorf, Germany
yong.li1@huawei.com
[5] Beijing Huawei Digital Technologies Co., Ltd., Beijing, China
{tianwenyuan,wangyusen9}@huawei.com

Abstract. Wildcard symmetric searchable encryption enables the server to perform efficient wildcard keyword search over encrypted data while preserving data privacy. Currently, one of the most promising wildcard SSE framework can achieve sublinear search complexity by combining characteristic extraction techniques with the traditional membership test structure Bloom filter. However, all existing constructions consume significant storage space due to the storage expansion inherent in Bloom filters. In this paper, we initially consider the storage compression for wildcard SSE based on characteristic extraction while maintaining its sublinear search efficiency. Specifically, we propose a new practical wildcard SSE scheme, XorWSSE, which achieves optimized storage by using xor filter. On average, each characteristic saves 15% storage overhead compared to Bloom filter-based schemes. Moreover, we address the security threats of search tokens introduced by the combination of xor filter and characteristic extraction by proposing a "PRF-then-Hash" method. We further conduct a rigorous security analysis for XorWSSE. Finally, we implement and compare our proposed scheme XorWSSE to the state-of-the-art scheme presented by Zhang et al. XorWSSE obtains an 86% storage saving, accelerates setup time by 22×, and speeds up search time by three orders of magnitude.

Keywords: Data Privacy · Symmetric Searchable Encryption · Wildcard Keyword

1 Introduction

Data privacy is essential for secure storage and access of data. To this end, numerous organizations and individuals outsource their encrypted data to servers

J. K. Liu et al. (Eds.): ProvSec 2024, LNCS 14903, pp. 106–126, 2025.
https://doi.org/10.1007/978-981-96-0954-3_6

while simultaneously expecting to perform searches privately on the encrypted data. Symmetric searchable encryption (SSE) [16] emerges as a cryptographic primitive enabling the client to search over encrypted data, while also preserving the privacy of both the data and queries. The most existing researches in the field of SSE has primarily focused on *exact keyword search*. However, numerous practical applications require us to support *wildcard keyword search*, particularly for fuzzy matching and fast locating relevant files. We consider two types of typical wildcards "?" and "*", where

- "?" matches a single character, i.e., a single-character wildcard.
- "*" matches zero or multiple characters, i.e., a multiple-character wildcard.

For example, in a library database, searching for a keyword *"cry?t*"* will find out matches such as *"cryptography"*, *"cryptanalysis"*, and *"cryotron"*.

So far, several works focus on wildcard keyword search on encrypted data [3, 11,14,15,19,21–24]. Among these, the most promising construction for practical wildcard SSE is based on characteristic extraction and Bloom filters, which is initially proposed by Suga et al. [19] and further extended by others [11,23,24]. The essential idea is to create a Bloom filter (a membership test data structure) for each keyword's characteristics. However, these Bloom filter-based wildcard SSE schemes are all susceptible to the storage expansion stemming from Bloom filters, which may result in significant server storage overhead. Specifically, each characteristic element in the Bloom filter incurs at least a storage overhead of $1.44 \log_2(1/\epsilon)$ bits, where $\log_2(1/\epsilon)$ bits is the theoretical lower bound of storage per element at the desired false-positive probability ϵ.

In this paper, we initiatively investigate the storage compression of wildcard SSE. We introduce the utilization of xor filter [10], a faster and smaller alternative to Bloom filter, to achieve nearly optimal storage efficiency and efficient search. According to our observation, integrating xor filter directly may compromise the semantic security of queries. Therefore, we will explore the following question in this paper:

How to design a secure and practical wildcard SSE scheme that achieves nearly optimal storage overhead?

1.1 Our Contributions

In this paper, we provide a positive answer to the above question. Roughly, we propose a new practical wildcard SSE scheme, named XorWSSE, which achieves optimized storage and practical search by using xor filter. We also prove that the search tokens satisfy semantic security. In the following, we will detail our contributions.

- We propose XorWSSE, a practical wildcard SSE scheme with optimized storage, utilizing xor filter as the underlying data structure. XorWSSE only requires $1.23 \log_2(1/\epsilon)$ bits per characteristic element, resulting in a 15% reduction in storage compared to Bloom filter-based solutions. Additionally, we provide a formal description of keyword characteristic extraction and select four characteristic types to support wildcard queries with high accuracy.

- We present a "PRF-then-Hash" method to guarantee the security of search tokens. Concretely, we employ a cryptographically secure PRF for generating search tokens and then transfer the token-based location computation to the server side, where the latter relies only on the fast non-cryptographical hash function native to the xor filter.
- We rigorously analyze the security of XorWSSE. Furthermore, we implement our proposed scheme XorWSSE in Java and compare it with the state-of-the-art scheme proposed by Zhang et al. [23] The result shows that our storage is reduced by 86%, and the setup time and search time are accelerated by 22× and three orders of magnitude, respectively.

1.2   Related Work

Song et al. [16] introduced the notion of symmetric searchable encryption (SSE). Since then, plenty of works have been investigated for expressive query functionality [6,12,13], high-level security [1,4,5,7,8,18], and performance optimization [17,20]. However, most existing SSE schemes are designed for exact keyword search while not supporting wildcard keyword search. Sedghi et al. [15] initialized the study of wildcard keyword search on encrypted data. They proposed the first wildcard searchable encryption scheme using hidden vector encryption (HVE), but it is hindered by the inefficiency of asymmetric operations.

To achieve efficient wildcard keyword query, Bösch et al. [3] proposed the first wildcard SSE scheme by constructing Bloom filter for each document. This scheme only works for single-character wildcards and requires enumerating all possible wildcard keywords during index generation and traversing all documents to obtain the matching results, resulting in significant storage and computation overhead. Later, Suga et al. [19] introduced the keyword characteristic extraction method, and combined it with Bloom filter to design a new wildcard SSE scheme based on the inverted index, which achieves sublinear search complexity and optimal trapdoor communication $O(1)$. However, this scheme also only allows wildcard queries with single-character wildcards. To address this issue, Hu et al. [11] extended Suga et al.'s scheme [19] by introducing different characteristic types (normal order, reverse order, and existence), enabling a flexible multiple-character wildcard SSE. Meanwhile, Zhao et al. [24] devised a novel Bloom filter-based wildcard SSE scheme supporting wildcard queries with both single- and multiple-character wildcards. This scheme achieves enhanced query accuracy by incorporating other characteristics such as character distance and appearance frequency. After that, Zhang et al. [23] introduced a tree-based index to improve search performance. Specifically, this scheme layers different characteristics (such as A-layer, AB-layer, and BF-layer) to accelerate queries. Within the BF-layer, Bloom filters still need to be constructed for keyword characteristics. Unfortunately, the storage of all aforementioned Bloom filter-based schemes increases with the expansion of Bloom filter. In this paper, we construct a novel practical wildcard SSE scheme with optimized storage based on xor filter [10].

So far, some researchers have focused on other aspects of wildcard keyword search, such as eliminating false positives [14], improving security [21], and han-

Table 1. Notations

Notation	Description
S	A set from the universe $\mathcal{U}$, i.e., $S \subseteq \mathcal{U}$
k	The fingerprint size in the xor filter
B	The filter array B of the xor filter
L	The filter array length, i.e., $|B| = L$
r	The number of hash functions
λ	The security parameter
DB	A database $\mathsf{DB} = \left\{ (w_i, \mathsf{DB}(w_i)) \right\}_{i=1}^{m}$
W	The set of all keywords in DB, i.e., $\mathsf{W} = \{w_i\}_{i=1}^{m}$
DB(w)	The identifiers of documents containing keyword $w \in \mathsf{W}$
m	The number of keywords in DB, i.e. $|\mathsf{W}| = m$
F	Pseudorandom function (PRF)
?	The single-character wildcard
*	The multiple-character wildcard

dling dynamic scenarios [22]. Li et al. [14] presented a fully wildcard searchable encryption schemes by utilizing inner product encryption (IPE). Although this scheme eliminates false positives and achieves high security and functionality, it requires computationally expensive pairing operations. Very recently, Wang et al. [21] proposed a new wildcar keyword search scheme that supports highly flexible wildcard queries (single/multi-character wildcard) and resists correlation and composition attacks. This scheme also relies on public-key primitives, key aggregate searchable encryption (KASE), leading to significant computational overhead. Additionally, Weener et al. [22] designed a dynamic wildcard searchable scheme that satisfies backward privacy based on [24].

2 Preliminaries

In this section, we outline the cryptographic tools required for this paper, including pseudorandom function, symmetric searchable encryption, xor filter, and characteristic extraction. The notations are described in Table 1.

2.1 Pseudorandom Function

For all probabilistic polynomial-time (PPT) adversaries $\mathcal{A}$, a function $F : \mathcal{K} \times \mathcal{X} \to \mathcal{Y}$ is called a pseudorandom function (PRF) if there is a negligible function $\mathsf{negl}(\lambda)$ such that:

$$\left| \Pr[\mathcal{A}^{F_k(\cdot)}(1^\lambda) = 1] - \Pr[\mathcal{A}^{f(\cdot)}(1^\lambda) = 1] \right| \leq \mathsf{negl}(\lambda),$$

where $f : \mathcal{X} \to \mathcal{Y}$ is a random function.

2.2 Symmetric Key Encryption

A symmetric key encryption (SKE) scheme consists of three polynomial-time algorithms $\mathsf{SKE} = (\mathsf{Gen}, \mathsf{Enc}, \mathsf{Dec})$.

- Gen(1^λ): The key generation algorithm takes a security parameter λ as input and outputs a secret key $K \in \mathcal{K}$, where $\mathcal{K}$ is key space.
- Enc(K, m): The encryption algorithm takes as inputs the secret key $K \in \mathcal{K}$ and a plaintext message $m \in \mathcal{M}$, and outputs the ciphertext $c \in \mathcal{C}$, where $\mathcal{M}$ and $\mathcal{C}$ are message space and ciphertext space, respectively.
- Dec(K, c): The decryption algorithm takes as inputs the secret key $K \in \mathcal{K}$ and the ciphertext $c \in \mathcal{C}$, and outputs the plaintext message m.

Correctness. A SKE scheme is perfectly correct if for all $m \in \mathcal{M}$, $K \leftarrow \mathsf{Gen}(1^\lambda)$ and $c \leftarrow \mathsf{Enc}(K, m)$, it holds that $\Pr[\mathsf{Dec}(K, c) = m] = 1$.

Security. Informally, a standard CPA-secure SKE scheme ensures that an adversary, with the capability to adaptively query an encryption oracle, cannot gain any meaningful information about the plaintext from the ciphertext. In this work, we focus on a stronger security notion, random-ciphertext-secure against chosen-plaintext attacks (RCPA). A SKE scheme is considered RCPA-secure if the ciphertexts it outputs are computationally indistinguishable from random value to an adversary that can adaptively query an encryption oracle. The formal definition of an RCPA-secure SKE scheme is as follows.

Definition 1. *A SKE scheme* SKE = (Gen, Enc, Dec) *is RCPA-secure if for all probabilistic polynomial time (PPT) adversary* $\mathcal{A}$*, its advantage*

$$Adv_{\mathsf{SKE},\mathcal{A}}^{\mathsf{RCPA}}(\lambda) = |\Pr[\mathsf{Exp}_{\mathsf{SKE},\mathcal{A}}^{\mathsf{RCPA}}(\lambda) = 1] - 1/2|$$

is negligible in λ*, where the experiment* $\mathsf{Exp}_{\mathsf{SKE},\mathcal{A}}^{\mathsf{RCPA}}(\lambda)$ *between a challenger and an adversary* $\mathcal{A}$ *is defined as follows.*

- Setup: The challenger generates a key $K \leftarrow \mathsf{Gen}(1^\lambda)$.
- Query Phase 1: The adversary $\mathcal{A}$ adaptively accesses the encryption oracle, meaning that when $\mathcal{A}$ queries on $m \in \mathcal{M}$, the challenger returns $c \leftarrow \mathsf{Enc}(K, m)$.
- Challenge: The adversary $\mathcal{A}$ sends a message m to the challenger. Then the challenger generates two ciphertexts $c_0 \leftarrow \mathsf{Enc}(K, m)$ and $c_1 \overset{\$}{\leftarrow} \mathcal{C}$. After that, the challenger chooses a bit $b \in \{0, 1\}$ randomly and gives c_b to $\mathcal{A}$.
- Query Phase 2: The adversary $\mathcal{A}$ adaptively accesses the encryption oracle again, similar to Phase 1, and subsequently it outputs a bit $b' \in \{0, 1\}$.
- Guess: The adversary $\mathcal{A}$ outputs a bit $b' \in \{0, 1\}$. The experiment returns 1 if $b' = b$ and 0 otherwise.

2.3 Symmetric Searchable Encryption

Symmetric searchable encryption (SSE) [8,16] allows the client to encrypt a document collection DB = $(D_{id_1}, D_{id_2}, \ldots, D_{id_d})$ and store the encrypted documents on the server. Later, the client can perform private keyword query on the encrypted document collection without revealing any information to the server beyond a well-defined and "reasonable" leakage function. Following the structure-based SSE [6], we decouple the storage of documents and index structures, meaning the database can be represented as keyword/identifier-set pairs, i.e., $\mathsf{DB} = \left\{ \left(w_i, \mathsf{DB}(w_i) \right) \right\}_{i=1}^{m}$, where $\mathsf{DB}(w)$ refers to the set of identifiers of documents containing the keyword w. In the following content, we denote d as the number of documents (identifiers) in the database DB, m as the number of keywords in DB. Formally, an SSE scheme consists of a setup algorithm and a search protocol, denoted as $\mathsf{SSE} = (\mathsf{Setup}, \mathsf{Search})$, defined as follows:

- $\mathsf{Setup}(1^\lambda, \mathsf{DB})$: It takes a security parameter λ and a database DB as inputs and outputs $(\mathsf{SK}, \mathsf{EDB})$, where the secret key SK is stored by the client and the encrypted database EDB is outsourced to the server.
- $\mathsf{Search}(\mathsf{SK}, w; \mathsf{EDB})$: This protocol is performed by the client and the server. Concretely, the client inputs the secret key SK and the queried keyword w, and then generates a search token tk_w and sends it to the server. Upon receiving the search token tk_w, the the server retrieves the identifiers of the documents containing keyword w from the encrypted database EDB.

Correctness. The correctness of an SSE scheme implies that the server returns the correct query result for every query. The formal definition is provided in the reference [6].

Security. A secure SSE scheme ensures the privacy of both data and queries, revealing only well-defined and "reasonable" leakage and no other information about the database and queries to the adversary [8]. We define the leakage function of an SSE scheme as $\mathcal{L}(\mathsf{DB}, \mathsf{q}) = (\mathcal{L}^{\mathsf{Setup}}, \mathcal{L}^{\mathsf{Search}})$, where $\mathcal{L}^{\mathsf{Setup}}(\mathsf{DB})$ captures the leakage of the database DB during the setup phase and $\mathcal{L}^{\mathsf{Search}}(\mathsf{q})$ represents the leakage from q queries $\mathsf{q} = (\mathsf{q}[1], \mathsf{q}[2], \ldots, \mathsf{q}[q])$ during the search phase. Thus, the formal definition of a secure SSE scheme is described as follows:

Definition 2. *An SSE scheme* $\mathsf{SSE} = (\mathsf{Setup}, \mathsf{Search})$ *is $\mathcal{L}$-adaptively secure if for any PPT adversaries $\mathcal{A}$ with the leakage function $\mathcal{L} = (\mathcal{L}^{\mathsf{Setup}}, \mathcal{L}^{\mathsf{Search}})$, there exists a PPT simulator $\mathcal{S}$ such that*

$$\left| \Pr[\mathbf{Real}_{\mathcal{A}}^{\mathsf{SSE}}(\lambda) = 1] - \Pr[\mathbf{Ideal}_{\mathcal{A},\mathcal{S}}^{\mathsf{SSE}}(\lambda) = 1] \right| \leq \mathsf{negl}(\lambda),$$

where the real and ideal experiments $\mathbf{Real}_{\mathcal{A}}^{\mathsf{SSE}}, \mathbf{Ideal}_{\mathcal{A},\mathcal{S}}^{\mathsf{SSE}}$ *are defined as follows.*

- $\mathbf{Real}_{\mathcal{A}}^{\mathsf{SSE}}(\lambda)$: The adversary $\mathcal{A}$ selects a database DB. The experiment then runs $\mathsf{Setup}(1^\lambda, \mathsf{DB})$ and returns EDB to $\mathcal{A}$. $\mathcal{A}$ adaptively chooses queries $\mathsf{q} = (\mathsf{q}[1], \mathsf{q}[2], \ldots, \mathsf{q}[q])$. The experiment thus runs $\mathsf{Search}(\mathsf{q})$ and returns the transcript to $\mathcal{A}$. Finally, $\mathcal{A}$ outputs a bit $b \in \{0, 1\}$.
- $\mathbf{Ideal}_{\mathcal{A},\mathcal{S}}^{\mathsf{SSE}}(\lambda)$: The adversary $\mathcal{A}$ chooses a database DB. The experiment simulates and returns the encrypted database EDB by using $\mathcal{S}(\mathcal{L}^{\mathsf{Setup}}(\mathsf{DB}))$. $\mathcal{A}$ then adaptively selects a series queries $\mathsf{q} = (\mathsf{q}[1], \mathsf{q}[2], \ldots, \mathsf{q}[q])$, and the experiment runs $\mathcal{S}(\mathcal{L}^{\mathsf{Search}}(\mathsf{q}))$ and returns the transcript to $\mathcal{A}$. Finally, $\mathcal{A}$ outputs a bit $b \in \{0, 1\}$.

2.4 Xor Filter

Xor filter (XF), proposed by Graf and Lemire [10], is a compact data structure used for approximate membership queries. XF are faster than the classical data structure (Bloom filter [2] and cuckoo filter [9]), while simultaneously achieves almost optimal storage overhead $\approx 1.23n$, where n is the number of distinct elements in a given set.

For a formal definition, an xor filter consists of the following three algorithms such as $\mathsf{XF} = (\mathsf{XF.Setup}, \mathsf{XF.Update}, \mathsf{XF.Query})$, and the details are described in Algorithm 1 (refer to the reference [10, 20]).

- $\mathsf{XF.Setup}(n, k)$: The setup algorithm takes the parameters n and k as inputs, where n is the size of a given set S and k is the bit size of a fingerprint. Thus, this algorithm generates an empty array B with size of $L = \lfloor 1.23n \rfloor + \beta$, a fingerprint function $f : \mathcal{U} \to \{0,1\}^k$ and a collection of hash functions $\mathcal{H} = \{h_t : \mathcal{U} \to [\frac{t}{r}L, \frac{t+1}{r}L)\}$, where $t \in [0, r-1]$. Finally, this algorithm outputs $(B, f, \mathcal{H})$.
- $\mathsf{XF.Update}(\mathcal{H}, f, B, S)$: The update algorithm takes as inputs the set of hash functions $\mathcal{H}$, the fingerprint function f, the empty array B, and a dataset $S \subseteq \mathcal{U}$. Firstly, this algorithm runs $\mathsf{MappingStep}$ to push the elements in the set S into a stack, thereby determining the order in which the elements pop out of the stack. For each element $(x, i) \in Stack$, $B[i]$ is initially set to $f(x)$, and if any of the other $r-1$ positions corresponding to x is $null$, then those positions are padded with random strings. Thus, we further set $B[i] = f(x) \bigoplus\limits_{t \in [0, r-1] \setminus \{t'\}} B[h_t(x)]$, where $h_{t'}(x) = i$. Finally, this algorithm outputs the array B.
- $\mathsf{XF.Query}(\mathcal{H}, f, B, x)$: The query algorithm takes as inputs the hash functions $\mathcal{H}$, the array B, and the element x to be queried. Finally, it outputs the bitwise exclusive or (xor) value of r positions, i.e., $B[h_0(x)] \oplus B[h_1(x)] \oplus \cdots \oplus B[h_{r-1}(x)]$.

Here is an example of an xor filter for a set $S = \{a, b, c, d\}$. Initially, we set the array size $|B| = 6$. Thus, we choose three hash functions, i.e., $r = 3$, and $h_0 : \mathcal{U} \to [0, 1]$, $h_1 : \mathcal{U} \to [2, 3]$, and $h_2 : \mathcal{U} \to [4, 5]$.

When inserting all elements $x \in S$ into an xor filter, we first execute the mapping step. Concretely, we initialize a temporary array T with equal size $L = 6$. Then we compute $h_0(x)$, $h_1(x)$, and $h_2(x)$ for all $x \in S$, and insert the elements into the corresponding locations in T. For example, we insert x into $T[h_0(x)]$, $T[h_1(x)]$, and $T[h_2(x)]$. After that, we select any entry $T[i]$ that has only one element, and push its corresponding element/location pair (x, i) into the stack $Stack$ P, and delete the remaining $r-1$ elements about x in T. The process is repeated until all elements $x \in S$ are pushed into $Stack$ P. Assume that $Stack$ P contains entries $(b, 1)$, $(a, 3)$, $(d, 4)$, and $(c, 0)$. Next, we pop element/location from $Stack$ P one by one following the last-in-first-out (LIFO) principle. For each element $x \in S$, we insert its fingerprint $f(x)$ into the corresponding location i in the array B, ensuring that the xor value of the

Algorithm 1. Xor Filter (XF)

XF.Setup(n, k)
```
1: B ← ∅, where |B| = L = ⌊1.23n⌋ + β
2: f : U → {0,1}^k
3: H = {h_t : U → [t/r L, t+1/r L)}, where t ∈ [0, r−1]
4: return (H, f, B)
```

XF.Update(H, f, B, S)
```
 1: Stack ← MappingStep(H, S)
 2: for (x, i) ∈ Stack do
 3:     B[i] ← f(x)
 4:     for t = 0 to r − 1 do
 5:         if h_t(x) ≠ i then
 6:             if B[h_t(x)] = null then
 7:                 B[h_t(x)] ←$ {0,1}^k
 8:             end if
 9:             B[i] ← B[i] ⊕ B[h_t(x)]
10:         end if
11:     end for
12: end for
13: for j ∈ [|B|] do
14:     if B[j] = null then
15:         B[j] ←$ {0,1}^k
16:     end if
17: end for
18: return B
```

XF.Query(H, B, x)
```
1: R ← 0^k
2: for t = 0 to r − 1 do
3:     R ← R ⊕ B[h_t(x)]
4: end for
5: return R
```

MappingStep(H, S)
```
 1: Stack P, Q ← ∅
 2: T ← ∅, where |T| = L
 3: for x ∈ S do
 4:     for t = 0 to r − 1 do
 5:         T[h_t(x)] ← T[h_t(x)] ∪ {x}
 6:     end for
 7: end for
 8: for i = 0 to L − 1 do
 9:     if |T[i]| = 1 then
10:         Push i into Stack Q
11:     end if
12: end for
13: while Stack Q ≠ null do
14:     i ← Stack Q
15:     if |T[i]| = 1 then
16:         Push (x, i) into Stack P
17:         for t = 0 to r − 1 do
18:             T[h_t(x)] ← T[h_t(x)]\{x}
19:         end for
20:     end if
21: end while
22: if |P| ≠ |S| then return Failure
23: end if
24: return Success and Stack P
```

three locations corresponding to the element equals its fingerprint value, i.e., $B[h_0(x)] \oplus B[h_1(x)] \oplus B[h_2(x)] = f(x)$. Specifically, if any position is empty, it is padded with a random string.

For a query for an element x', we compute the three locations using similar methods and perform xor operations for the values at these three positions to obtain $R = B[h_0(x')] \oplus B[h_1(x')] \oplus B[h_2(x')]$. Finally, if the equation $R = f(x')$ holds, then x' belongs to the set S; otherwise, it does not.

2.5 Characteristic Extraction

Characteristic extraction refers to the process of extracting specific characters from a string based on certain pattern, such as position, frequency, and so on. This method enables wildcard queries, allowing for the queried keywords containing wildcard characters (such as "?" and "*"), which has been applied to wildcard queries on encrypted data.

Suga et al. [19] proposed the first wildcard SSE scheme based on characteristic extraction; however, only *normal order* characteristic is used in this scheme, resulting in support for only single-character wildcard keyword queries. Later, Hu et al. [11] further utilized *reverse order* and *existence* characteristics, enabling

---

Algorithm 2. Index/Trapdoor Keyword Characteristic Extraction

---

IKCE(w)

1: $w = (w[1], \ldots, w[l])$, where $w[i]$ is the i-th character of keyword w ($i \in \{1, \ldots, l\}$)
2: Type-I (Normal order): $C_w^{\mathrm{I}} = \{w[1]||1, w[2]||2, \ldots, w[l]||l\}$
3: Type-II (Reverse order): $C_w^{\mathrm{II}} = \{w[1]|| - l, w[2]|| - (l-1), \ldots, w[l]|| - 1\}$
4: Type-III (2-gram): $C_w^{\mathrm{III}} = \{w[1]||w[2], w[2]||w[3], \ldots, w[l-1]||w[l]\}$
5: Type-IV (Single-character skip): $C_w^{\mathrm{IV}} = \{w[1]||w[3], w[2]||w[4], \ldots, w[l-2]||w[l]\}$
6: $C_w \leftarrow C_w^{\mathrm{I}} \cup C_w^{\mathrm{II}} \cup C_w^{\mathrm{III}} \cup C_w^{\mathrm{IV}}$
7: **return** C_w

TKCE($\hat{w}$)

1: $\hat{w}$ is a queried keyword containing wildcards "?" and "*",
   e.g., $\hat{w} = (\hat{w}[1], \ldots, ?, \ldots, \hat{w}[l_1], *, \ldots, *, \hat{w}[-l_2], \ldots, ?, \ldots, \hat{w}[-1])$
2: Type-I (Normal order): $C_{\hat{w}}^{\mathrm{I}} = \{(\hat{w}[1], 1), \ldots, (\hat{w}[l_1], l_1)\}$ (before the first "*")
3: Type-II (Reverse order): $C_{\hat{w}}^{\mathrm{II}} = \{(\hat{w}[-l_2], -l_2), \ldots, (\hat{w}[-1], -1)\}$ (after the last "*")
4: Type-III (2-gram) $C_{\hat{w}}^{\mathrm{III}}$ and Type-IV (Single-character skip) $C_{\hat{w}}^{\mathrm{IV}}$: Similar to Type-III and Type-IV character extraction of the algorithm IKCE
5: $C_{\hat{w}} \leftarrow C_{\hat{w}}^{\mathrm{I}} \cup C_{\hat{w}}^{\mathrm{II}} \cup C_{\hat{w}}^{\mathrm{III}} \cup C_{\hat{w}}^{\mathrm{IV}}$
6: **return** $C_{\hat{w}}$

---

support for multiple-character wildcard keyword queries. After that, many wild-card SSE schemes [23,24] diversify the types of characteristics, such as *n-gram*, *substring, character distance*, to enrich query expressiveness. Generally, the characteristic types can be chosen flexibly based on the specific requirements for wildcard query accuracy. In this paper, we consider four types of characteristics: *normal order, reverse order, 2-gram*, and *single-character skip*, achieving a tunable trade-off between query accuracy and server storage. A smaller set of characteristics trades off for better performance. Specifically, these four types of characteristics are sufficient for achieving our practical wildcard SSE scheme that supports single- and multiple-character wildcard keyword queries.

Next, we describe the formal characteristic extraction algorithms IKCE(w) and TKCE($\hat{w}$) for index and trapdoor keywords, as shown in Algorithm 2. In more detail, we provide examples to illustrate four types of characteristic sets.

Index Keyword Characteristic Extraction. For an index keyword $w =$ "*adefxes*", we obtain the characteristic set $C_w \leftarrow C_w^{\mathrm{I}} \cup C_w^{\mathrm{II}} \cup C_w^{\mathrm{III}} \cup C_w^{\mathrm{IV}}$ by running the algorithm IKCE(w).

(1) Type-I (Normal order): $C_w^{\mathrm{I}} = \{a||1, d||2, e||3, f||4, x||5, e||6, s||7\}$
(2) Type-II (Reverse order): $C_w^{\mathrm{II}} = \{a|| - 7, d|| - 6, e|| - 5, f|| - 4, x|| - 3, e|| - 2, s|| - 1\}$
(3) Type-III (2-gram): $C_w^{\mathrm{III}} = \{a||d, d||e, e||f, f||x, x||e, e||s\}$
(4) Type-IV (Single-character skip): $C_w^{\mathrm{IV}} = \{a||e, d||f, e||x, f||e, x||s\}$

Trapdoor Keyword Characteristic Extraction. For a queried keyword $\hat{w} =$ "*a?e * x * es*", we generate its characteristic set $C_{\hat{w}} \leftarrow C_{\hat{w}}^{\mathrm{I}} \cup C_{\hat{w}}^{\mathrm{II}} \cup C_{\hat{w}}^{\mathrm{III}} \cup C_{\hat{w}}^{\mathrm{IV}}$ by running the algorithm TKCE($\hat{w}$).

(1) Type-I (Normal order): $C_{\hat{w}}^{\mathrm{I}} = \{a||1, e||3\}$
(2) Type-II (Reverse order): $C_{\hat{w}}^{\mathrm{II}} = \{e|| - 2, s|| - 1\}$
(3) Type-III (2-gram): $C_{\hat{w}}^{\mathrm{III}} = \{e||s\}$
(4) Type-IV (Single-character skip): $C_{\hat{w}}^{\mathrm{IV}} = \{a||e\}$

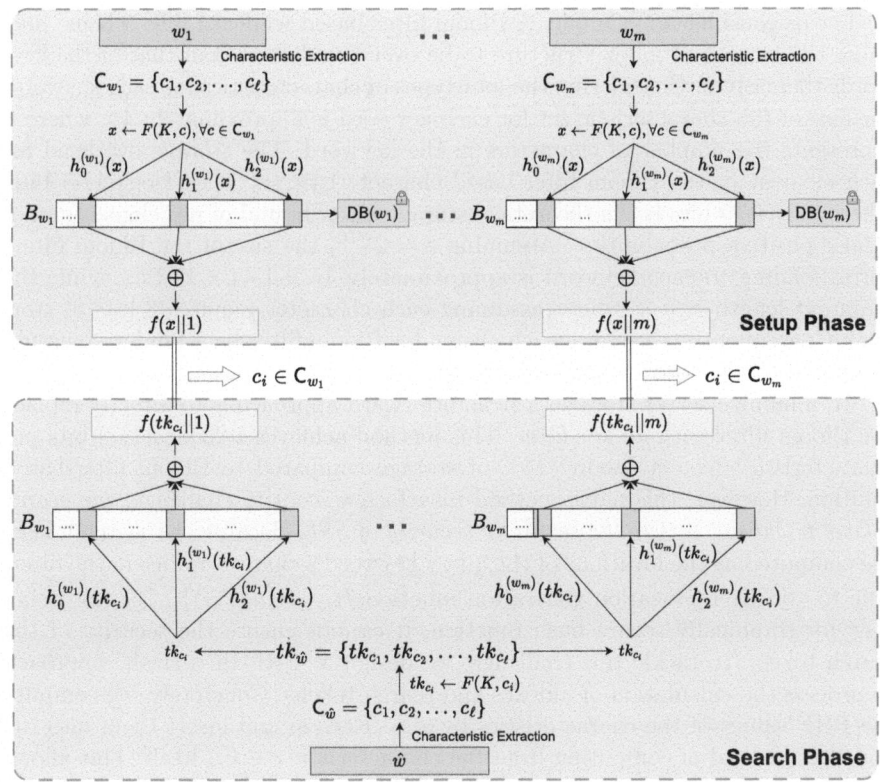

Fig. 1. Overview of our proposed scheme XorWSSE

3 The Proposed Construction

In this section, we propose a new practical wildcard SSE scheme, named XorWSSE, which achieves optimized storage by using xor filter. We give a technical overview, the detailed description and security analysis for our proposed scheme.

3.1 Technical Overview

The basic idea of our wildcard SSE scheme XorWSSE is similar to that of Bloom filter-based construction. Both solutions construct a membership test data structure (i.e., Bloom filter or xor filter) for the characteristic set of each keyword in database. When querying a keyword containing wildcards, we identify matching keywords by finding those keywords whose characteristic sets contain all the characteristics of the queried wildcard keyword. So far, all wildcard SSE schemes based on characteristic extraction [11,23,24] rely on Bloom filters to build index structures. However, the storage expansion of these indexes is entirely determined by Bloom filter expansion, which suffers from a large server storage.

Let us consider an example. A Bloom filter-based wildcard SSE scheme may cause the storage of index structure to be over $10\times$ larger than that of the keywords themselves. Considering the four types of characteristics for each keyword, the size of the characteristic set for each keyword is approximately $4n$, where n represents the number of characters in the keyword. The storage overhead for each element in the Bloom filter-based characteristic set is $1.44\log_2(1/\epsilon)$ bits, where $\log_2(1/\epsilon)$ bits is the theoretical storage lower bound of per element under a false-positive probability ϵ. Assuming $\epsilon = 2^{-16}$, the size of the Bloom filters corresponding to each keyword is approximately $4n \times 1.44 \times 16$ bits, while the plaintext length is $n \times 8$ bits (assuming each character requires 8 bits of storage). Consequently, the storage expansion for Bloom filter-based index structure compared to keyword storage exceeds $10\times$.

To minimize server storage, a straightforward approach is to directly replace the Bloom filter with an xor filter. This method achieves $1.23\log_2(1/\epsilon)$ bits per characteristic element, saving 15% of storage compared to Bloom filter-based solution. However, this naive method may face a security challenge: *the search tokens might not satisfy the semantic security of SSE*. Because the search tokens are computed as the locations of the query keyword's characteristics in the filter. Due to xor filter's location generation function $\mathcal{H}_w = \{h_t^{(w)}(\cdot)\}_{t\in[0,2]}$ not being a cryptographically secure hash function, it cannot ensure the security of the search token. To tackle this challenge, we design a "PRF-then-Hash" approach to process the calculation of indexes and search tokens. Concretely, we compute the PRF values of the characteristics by $x \leftarrow F(K,c)$ and insert them into the xor filter instead of computing from the characteristic $c \in \mathsf{C}_w$ itself. This allows the client use a cryptographically secure PRF to generate the search token. Additionally, the server finally handles the computation of the locations, also reducing the query computation overhead on the client side. The overview of XorWSSE is shown in Fig. 1.

3.2   The Concrete Construction

Algorithm 3 details our proposed scheme, where $\mathsf{SKE} = (\mathsf{Gen}, \mathsf{Enc}, \mathsf{Dec})$ represents an RCPA-secure symmetric key encryption scheme with a key space $\mathcal{K} = \{0,1\}^\lambda$ and ciphertext space $\mathcal{C}$. Additionally, $F : \{0,1\}^\lambda \times \{0,1\}^* \rightarrow \{0,1\}^\lambda$ is a PRF and f is a fingerprint function with k-bit outputs in an xor filter. A database denotes $\mathsf{DB} = \big\{\big(w_j, \mathsf{DB}(w_j)\big)\big\}_{j=1}^m$ according to the inverted index, and the total keyword set is represented as $\mathsf{W} = \{w_j\}_{j=1}^m$. Concretely, our proposed scheme works as follows.

- Setup($1^\lambda, k, \mathsf{DB}$): The client first chooses a key K_e for the encryption algorithm SKE and a PRF key K, and initializes an empty map EDB for the database DB. Then, for each keyword $w \in \mathsf{W}$, the client mainly performs three steps: it extracts the characteristics of w, inserts them into the corresponding xor filter, and encrypts all identifiers of documents containing the keyword w. The details are shown as follows.

Algorithm 3. Wildcard SSE from Xor Filter (XorWSSE)

Setup($1^\lambda, k, \mathsf{DB}$)

Client:

1: $K_e \leftarrow \mathsf{Gen}(1^\lambda)$, $K \xleftarrow{\$} \{0,1\}^\lambda$

2: $\mathsf{DB} = \left\{(w_j, \mathsf{DB}(w_j))\right\}_{j=1}^m$, $\mathsf{W} = \{w_j\}_{j=1}^m$

3: $\mathsf{EDB} \leftarrow \emptyset$

4: $j \leftarrow 1$

5: **for** $w \in \mathsf{W}$ **do**

6:    $\mathsf{C}_w \leftarrow \mathsf{IKCE}(w)$

7:    $(\mathcal{H}_w, f, B_w) \leftarrow \mathsf{XF.Setup}(|\mathsf{C}_w|, k)$

     ▷ $\mathcal{H}_w = \{h_t^{(w)}(\cdot)\}_{t \in [0,2]}$,

     ▷ $f : \mathcal{U} \to \{0,1\}^k$,

     ▷ $|B_w| = \lfloor 1.23|\mathsf{C}_w| \rfloor + \beta$

8:    $Stack_w \leftarrow \mathsf{MappingStep}(\mathcal{H}_w, \mathsf{C}_w)$

9:    **for** $(c, i) \in Stack_w$ **do**   ▷ $c \in \mathsf{C}_w$

10:      $x \leftarrow F(K, c)$

11:      $B_w[i] \leftarrow f(x\|j)$

12:      **for** $t \in [0,2]$ **do**

13:        **if** $h_t^{(w)}(x) \neq i$ **then**

14:          **if** $B_w[h_t^{(w)}(x)] = null$ **then**

15:            $B_w[h_t^{(w)}(x)] \xleftarrow{\$} \{0,1\}^k$

16:          **end if**

17:          $B_w[i] \leftarrow B_w[i] \oplus B_w[h_t^{(w)}(x)]$

18:        **end if**

19:      **end for**

20:    **end for**

21:    **for** $s \in [|B_w|]$ **do**

22:      **if** $B_w[s] = null$ **then**

23:        $B_w[s] \xleftarrow{\$} \{0,1\}^k$

24:      **end if**

25:    **end for**

26:    $\mathsf{EDB}[B_w] \leftarrow \mathsf{Enc}(K_e, \mathsf{DB}(w))$

27:    $j \leftarrow j + 1$

28: **end for**

29: $\mathsf{SK} \leftarrow (K_e, K)$

30: **return** $(\mathsf{SK}, \mathsf{EDB})$

Search($\mathsf{SK}, \hat{w}; \mathsf{EDB}$)

Client:

1: Parse $\mathsf{SK} = (K_e, K)$

2: $\mathsf{C}_{\hat{w}} \leftarrow \mathsf{TKCE}(\hat{w})$

3: $\mathsf{tk}_{\hat{w}} \leftarrow \emptyset$

4: **for** $c \in \mathsf{C}_{\hat{w}}$ **do**

5:    $tk_c \leftarrow F(K, c)$

6:    $\mathsf{tk}_{\hat{w}} \leftarrow \mathsf{tk}_{\hat{w}} \cup \{tk_c\}$

7: **end for**

8: **return** $\mathsf{tk}_{\hat{w}}$

Server:

9: Parse $\mathsf{tk}_{\hat{w}} = \{\mathsf{tk}_{\hat{w}}[1], \ldots, \mathsf{tk}_{\hat{w}}[|\mathsf{C}_{\hat{w}}|]\}$

10: $\mathsf{Res} \leftarrow \emptyset$, $X \leftarrow 0$

11: **for** $j \in [m]$ **do**

12:    $v \leftarrow 1$

13:    **for** $i \in [|\mathsf{C}_{\hat{w}}|]$ **do**

14:      **for** $t \in [0,2]$ **do**

15:        $X \leftarrow X \oplus B_{w_j}[h_t^{(w_j)}(\mathsf{tk}_{\hat{w}}[i])]$

16:      **end for**

17:      **if** $X = f(\mathsf{tk}_{\hat{w}}[i]\|j)$ **then**

18:        $v \leftarrow v \&\& 1$

19:      **else**

20:        $v \leftarrow v \&\& 0$ **break**

21:      **end if**

22:    **end for**

23:    **if** $v = 1$ **then**

24:      $\mathsf{Res} \leftarrow \mathsf{Res} \cup \{\mathsf{EDB}[B_{w_j}]\}$

25:    **end if**

26: **end for**

27: **return** Res

Client:

28: Parse $\mathsf{SK} = (K_e, K)$, $\mathsf{Res} = \{\mathsf{ct}_1, \ldots, \mathsf{ct}_{|\mathsf{Res}|}\}$

29: $\mathsf{R} \leftarrow \emptyset$

30: **for** $i \in [|\mathsf{Res}|]$ **do** $\mathsf{R} \leftarrow \mathsf{R} \cup \{\mathsf{Dec}(K_e, \mathsf{ct}_i)\}$

31: **end for**

32: **return** R

---

(1) The client extracts the characteristic set C_w of each keyword w by running $\mathsf{C}_w \leftarrow \mathsf{IKCE}(w)$. (Line 6)

(2) Given a characteristic set C_w and a fingerprint size parameter k, the client invokes $\mathsf{XF.Setup}(|\mathsf{C}_w|, k)$ (see Algorithm 1) to initialize an empty array B_w with size $1.23|\mathsf{C}_w| + \beta$ and sample three hash functions $\mathcal{H}_w = $

$\{h_0^{(w)}, h_1^{(w)}, h_2^{(w)}\}$ and a fingerprint function f that outputs in $\{0,1\}^k$. Then, the client runs MappingStep($\mathcal{H}_w, C_w$) (see Algorithm 1) to determine the order of inserting all characteristics $c \in C_w$, and pushes these ordered characteristics (c,i) into a *Stack*. After that, the client inserts the fingerprint of each characteristic c associated with $(c,i) \in Stack$ into B_w. In particular, the fingerprint and three array locations are computed based on $x \leftarrow F(K,c)$. (Lines 7–25)

(3) The client encrypts the identifiers of documents containing the keyword w, i.e., Enc(K_e, DB(w)), and then stores it in EDB[B_w]. (Line 26)

Finally, the client stores the secret key SK $\leftarrow (K_e, K)$ locally and outsources the encrypted database EDB to the server.

- Search(SK, $\hat{w}$; EDB): The search protocol takes as inputs a wildcard keyword $\hat{w}$ and the secret key SK from the client, as well as the encrypted database EDB from the server, and outputs the query result R matching $\hat{w}$. This process also involves three steps: the client generates a token, the server performs a wildcard search, and the client decrypts the results. The following are the specific details:

(1) When performing search on $\hat{w}$, the client first extracts the characteristic set $C_{\hat{w}} \leftarrow$ TKCE($\hat{w}$), and then computes $F(K,c)$ for all characteristics $c \in C_{\hat{w}}$ and stores these PRF values into a token set $\mathsf{tk}_{\hat{w}}$. Finally, the client sends the search token $\mathsf{tk}_{\hat{w}}$ to the server. (Lines 2–8)

(2) Upon receiving the search token $\mathsf{tk}_{\hat{w}} = \{\mathsf{tk}_{\hat{w}}[1], \ldots, \mathsf{tk}_{\hat{w}}[\|C_{\hat{w}}\|]\}$, the server traverses $\{B_{w_j}\}_{j=1}^m$ over the encrypted database EDB to find all the matched xor filters and returns their corresponding ciphertexts. Concretely, for each xor filter B_{w_j} ($j \in [m]$), the server checks whether all characteristics of queried keyword $\hat{w}$ are belongs to B_{w_j} ($j \in [m]$) using $\{\mathsf{tk}_{\hat{w}}[i]\}_{i=1}^{|C_{\hat{w}}|}$ by following the query process of xor filter. If all characteristics of $\hat{w}$ match the xor filter B_{w_j}, the server stores its corresponding ciphertext EDB[B_{w_j}] into the result set Res. Finally, the server returns the result Res. (Lines 11–27)

(3) The client decrypts Res by using the secret key K_e to obtain all identifiers R matching the query $\hat{w}$. (Lines 30–32)

3.3   Security Analysis

In this section, we describe the leakage profile of our wildcard SSE scheme and give a detailed security analysis.

Leakage Function. We start by describing the leakage function $\mathcal{L}$ to be used in security analysis of our wildcard SSE scheme. A database denotes DB $= \{(w_j, \text{DB}(w_j))\}_{j=1}^m$ and a sequence of q queries is represented by $\mathsf{q} = \{\mathsf{q}[1], \ldots, \mathsf{q}[q]\}$, where each $\mathsf{q}[i]$ is a queried keyword containing wildcard characters. The leakage function $\mathcal{L}(\text{DB}, \mathsf{q})$ contains the following defined information.

- m is the number of keyword in DB.
- $\{c_w\}$ includes the number of the characteristics for each keyword ($w \in [m]$).

- $\overline{q}$ is the characteristic equality pattern of the queries.
- AP is the access pattern of the queries, i.e., matching filter.
- RP is the result pattern of the queries, i.e., matching document identifiers.

Theorem 1. *Assuming that* SKE $=$ (Gen, Enc, Dec) *is an RCPA-secure symmetric encryption scheme and F is a secure PRF, our proposed wildcard SSE scheme* XorWSSE *achieves $\mathcal{L}$-semantically secure against adaptive attacks, where $\mathcal{L}$ is the leakage function as defined above.*

Proof. The proof of this theorem is conducted by two steps: we analyze $\mathcal{L}$-semantically non-adaptive security of our scheme, and then it can be extended to $\mathcal{L}$-semantically security against adaptive attacks (it invokes the adaptive EDB simulator, we omit here).

We prove non-adaptive security of our scheme by several games Game_0, Game_1, Game_2, and Simulator (more game details are shown in the Appendix A). In each game, the adversary $\mathcal{A}$ provides DB and q, which are processed by an Initialize of our scheme to produce an output. $\mathcal{A}$ then outputs the game's result (a bit) based on this output. The proof starts with the real game $\mathbf{Real}_{\mathcal{A}}^{\mathsf{XorWSSE}}$ and ends with a game $\mathbf{Ideal}_{\mathcal{A},\mathcal{S}}^{\mathsf{XorWSSE}}$ that can be efficiently simulated with the leakage $\mathcal{L} = (m, \{c_w\}, \overline{q}, \mathsf{AP}, \mathsf{RP})$.

- Game_0: This game is identical to the real game $\mathbf{Real}_{\mathcal{A}}^{\mathsf{XorWSSE}}$, which represents an instantiation of the real game as shown in Algorithm 4. In this game, the adversary $\mathcal{A}$ provides (DB, q) and the simulator $\mathcal{S}$ simulates the Setup and Search phases. Here, the sub-algorithm Serversearch is utilized for the server's computations within the Search phase, and its output serves as the response message. We have that

$$\Pr[\mathsf{Game}_0 = 1] = \Pr[\mathbf{Real}_{\mathcal{A}}^{\mathsf{XorWSSE}}(\lambda) = 1].$$

- Game_1: In this game, we replace the encryption scheme with a random function. We can reduce the distinguishing advantage between Game_1 and Game_0 to the RCPA security of the symmetric key encryption scheme SKE. Thus, there exists a reduction algorithm $\mathcal{B}_1$ such that

$$\left| \Pr[\mathsf{Game}_1 = 1] - \Pr[\mathsf{Game}_0 = 1] \right| \leq m \cdot \mathbf{Adv}_{\mathsf{SKE},\mathcal{B}_1}^{\mathsf{RCPA}}(\lambda).$$

- Game_2: In this game, we modify the evaluation of PRF $F(K, \cdot)$ with the evaluation of independent random function with identical domain and range.

$$\left| \Pr[\mathsf{Game}_2 = 1] - \Pr[\mathsf{Game}_1 = 1] \right| \leq \mathbf{Adv}_{F,\mathcal{B}_2}^{\mathsf{PRF}}(\lambda).$$

- Simulator: We build a simulator from Game_2, which takes as input $\mathcal{L} = (m, \{c_w\}, \overline{q}, \mathsf{AP}, \mathsf{RP})$ and outputs a simulated (EDB, tk, Res, ResIds). We can see that Game_2 is efficiently simulated by the simulator with the leakage function $\mathcal{L}$, so we get that

$$\Pr[\mathbf{Ideal}_{\mathcal{A},\mathcal{S}}^{\mathsf{XorWSSE}} = 1] = \Pr[\mathsf{Game}_2 = 1].$$

Combining the above analysis, we can conclude that the advantage of any non-adaptive PPT adversary against our scheme is

$$|\Pr[\mathbf{Real}_{\mathcal{A}}^{\text{XorWSSE}}(\lambda) = 1] - \Pr[\mathbf{Ideal}_{\mathcal{A},\mathcal{S}}^{\text{XorWSSE}} = 1]|$$
$$\leq m \cdot \mathbf{Adv}_{\text{SKE},\mathcal{B}_1}^{\text{RCPA}}(\lambda) + \mathbf{Adv}_{F,\mathcal{B}_2}^{\text{PRF}}(\lambda) \leq \text{negl}(\lambda).$$

4   Performance Evaluation

In this section, we give a thorough experimental evaluation of our proposed scheme XorWSSE. Firstly, we describe the configuration of the experimental environment and parameter selection. We then compare our scheme with Zhang et al. [23] in terms of computation and storage overhead. Note that the state-of-the-art scheme [23], similar to our scheme XorWSSE, is a (Bloom) filter-based wildcard SSE scheme designed for both single and multi-wildcard queries in static settings.

4.1   Implementation Setup

Both our scheme and Zhang et al. [23] are implemented with JAVA and we employ JDK library to realize cryptographic primitives such as AES and SHA-256. We run the experiments on the machine with Intel i5-11500 CPU @ 2.70 GHz and 16 GB RAM. To accurately measure both client and server costs, all experiments are conducted on the same device. The implemention of XorWSSE and Zhang et al. [23] consists of two steps Setup and Search. Specifically, the reported running times of Setup and Search are the average of 10 and 100 experiments, respectively.

In our experiments, the characteristics sets are stored in xor filters for our scheme and Bloom filter for Zhang et al.' scheme [23], respectively. In the following experiments, the false positive rate of xor filter and Bloom filter is 2^{-8}. For each xor filter, the total storage capacity is $\lfloor 1.23n \rfloor + \beta$, where n is the length of the characteristic set. The parameter β is a constant in xor filter according to [10]. We perform several experiments to choose the minimum parameter to construct each xor filter, where β is almost 0 or 1.

4.2   Evaluation and Comparison

Storage Evaluation. The storage overhead of encrypted indexes is related to database size and keyword length. As shown in Fig. 2, the encryption indexes storage overhead of both schemes increases with the amount of database increases. Note that we choose the keyword length as 12. However, our scheme has a smaller storage overhead compared to the large storage requirements of Zhang et al.'s scheme. When the database size is 2^{18}, our scheme only requires a storage overhead of 13.6 MB, while Zhang et al.'s scheme requires 103 MB. Even

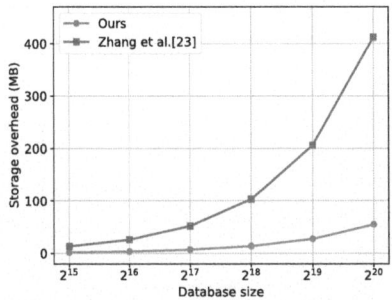

Fig. 2. Storage overhead with database size

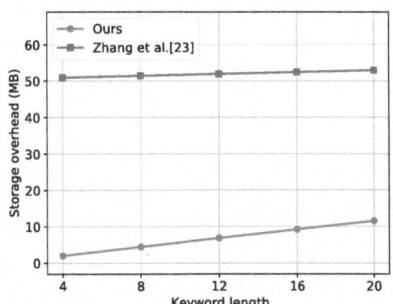

Fig. 3. Storage overhead with keyword length

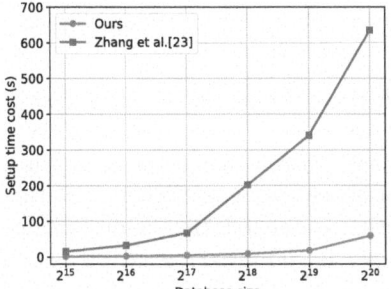

Fig. 4. Setup time with database size

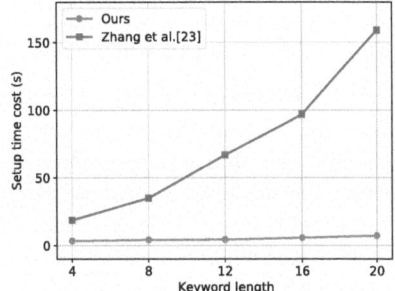

Fig. 5. Setup time with keyword length

if the data size increases to 2^{20}, the storage overhead of our scheme still does not exceed 60 MB. We also analyze the impact of keyword length on storage overhead. Figure 3 demonstrates that our scheme consistently outperforms Zhang et al.'s scheme in terms of storage overhead across all keyword lengths, with the database size fixed at 2^{17}. Compare to Zhang et al.'s scheme, our scheme with 12 keyword length brings a saving of 86% in server storage.

Setup Evaluation. The cost of setup is also dominated by database size and keyword length. As shown in Fig. 4, we choose 12 as keyword length for different database size. With the database size increases, our scheme generates more xor filters and Zhang et al.'s scheme needs to generate more leaf nodes, therefore the setup time for Zhang et al.'s scheme increases rapidly. Given a database size of 2^{15}, our scheme takes 1.1 s for setup, while Zhang et al.'s scheme takes 15.2 s. Our scheme achieves a 13.8× speedup in setup time compared to Zhang et al.'s scheme. For database size of 2^{19}, our scheme takes 17.5 s in setup phase, while Zhang et al.'s scheme takes 340.6 s, thus we obtain a speed up of 19.5×. Figure 5 illustrates illustrates how the setup time increases for both schemes as the keyword length changes. Note that we set database size as 2^{17}. Figure 5 depicts that the setup time cost of our scheme is much smaller than that of

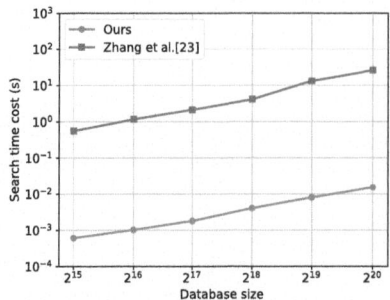
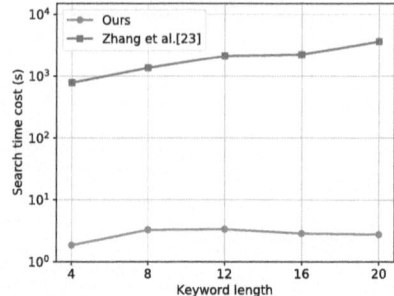

Fig. 6. Search time with database size   **Fig. 7.** Search time with keyword length

Zhang et al.'s scheme, i.e. 3.3 s–7.1 s v.s. 18.61 s–58.8 s. Our scheme achieves a speedup of 22× in setup when keyword length equals to 20.

Search Evaluation. We compare the search time of our scheme with that of Zhang et al.'s scheme in various parameter settings, i.e., database size and keyword length. For fairness in both scheme, we set keyword length both 12 when analyzing the impact of database size, and database size as 2^{17} when exploring the impact of keyword length. Figure 6 shows that the search time of our scheme is less than 1ms when the database size is 2^{15}. As the database size grows, search times for both schemes increase. Zhang et al.'s scheme becomes less efficient due to ineffective character filtering rules at larger database sizes. When the database size reaches 2^{20}, our scheme takes only 15.3ms for search, whereas Zhang et al.'s scheme requires 25 s, resulting in a speedup of 1634×. This indicates that our scheme is better suited for large databases. As illustrated in Fig. 7, the search time cost of Zhang et al.'s scheme increases as keyword length increases, but our scheme is independent on keywords length. The underlying reason is that Zhang et al.'s scheme must verify more possibilities when a wildcard "*" is present in the search keyword, leading to increased time as keyword length grows. In contrast, our scheme only requires computing hash values from extracted characteristics, making it more efficient. Therefore, our scheme outperforms Zhang et al.'s scheme in terms of query efficiency.

5   Conclusion

In this paper, we initially investigate storage compression of wildcard SSE. We design a novel, practical, and secure wildcard SSE scheme, named XorWSSE, utilizing xor filter instead of the traditional Bloom filter-based index structure. XorWSSE achieves optimal storage, requiring only $1.23 \log_2(1/\epsilon)$ bits per characteristic, which is 15% less than $1.44 \log_2(1/\epsilon)$ bits required by Bloom filters. Moreover, XorWSSE outperforms the state-of-the-art scheme [23] in setup and query efficiency. However, the existing dynamic and conjunctive wildcard SSE schemes still suffer from storage expansion due to Bloom filters. Therefore, our future research focuses on wildcard SSE schemes that support dynamic updates and conjunctive wildcard keyword queries.

Acknowledgments. This work was supported by the National Key Research and Development (R&D) Program Young Scientist Scheme (No. 2022YFB3102400), the Key Research and Development Program of Shaanxi (No. 2022KWZ-01), and the National Natural Science Foundation of China (Nos. 62072357, 62272294, and 62102313).

A   Game Details of Proof for Theorem 1

Algorithm 4. Game_0

Initialize(DB, q)

1: $K_e, K \xleftarrow{\$} \{0,1\}^\lambda$
2: $\{(w_j, \text{DB}(w_j))\}_{j=1}^m \leftarrow \text{DB}, \text{EDB} \leftarrow \emptyset, j \leftarrow 1$
3: **for** $w \in W$ **do**
4:     $C_w \leftarrow \text{IKCE}(w)$
5:     $(\mathcal{H}_w, f, B_w) \leftarrow \text{XF.Setup}(|C_w|, k)$
6:     $Stack_w \leftarrow \text{MappingStep}(\mathcal{H}_w, C_w)$
7:     **for** $(c, i) \in Stack_w$ **do**
8:         $x \leftarrow F(K, c), B_w[i] \leftarrow f(x||j)$
9:         **for** $t = 0$ *to* 2 **do**
10:            **if** $h_t^{(w)}(x) \neq i$ **then**
11:                **if** $B_w[h_t^{(w)}(x)] = null$ **then**
12:                    $B_w[h_t^{(w)}(x)] \xleftarrow{\$} \{0,1\}^k$
13:                **end if**
14:                $B_w[i] \leftarrow B_w[i] \oplus B_w[h_t^{(w)}(x)]$
15:            **end if**
16:        **end for**
17:    **end for**
18:    **for** $s \in [|B_w|]$ **do**

19:        **if** $B_w[s] = null$ **then** $B_w[s] \xleftarrow{\$} \{0,1\}^k$
20:        **end if**
21:    **end for**
22:    $\text{EDB}[B_w] \leftarrow \text{Enc}(K_e, \text{DB}(w))$
23:    $j \leftarrow j + 1$
24: **end for**
25: **for** $i = 1, \ldots, q$ **do**
26:    $C_{q[i]} \leftarrow \text{TKCE}(q[i])$
27:    **for** $c \in C_{q[i]}$ **do**
28:        $tk_c \leftarrow F(K, c), \text{tk}[i] \leftarrow \text{tk}[i] \cup \{tk_c\}$
29:    **end for**
30:    $\text{Res}[i] \leftarrow \text{ServerSearch}(\text{EDB}, \text{tk}[i])$
31:    **for** $w \in W$ **do**
32:        $C_w \leftarrow \text{IKCE}(w)$
33:        **if** $C_{q[i]} \subseteq C_w$ **then**
34:            $\text{ResIds}[i] \leftarrow \text{ResIds}[i] \cup \text{DB}(w)$
35:        **end if**
36:    **end for**
37: **end for**
38: **return** $(\text{EDB}, \text{tk}, \text{Res}, \text{ResIds})$

Algorithm 5. Game$_1$

Initialize(DB, q)

1: $K_e, K \xleftarrow{\$} \{0,1\}^\lambda$
2: $\{(w_j, \mathsf{DB}(w_j))\}_{j=1}^m \leftarrow \mathsf{DB}, \mathsf{EDB} \leftarrow \emptyset,$
  $j \leftarrow 1$
3: **for** $w \in \mathsf{W}$ **do**
4:   $\mathsf{C}_w \leftarrow \mathsf{IKCE}(w)$
5:   $(\mathcal{H}_w, f, B_w) \leftarrow \mathsf{XF.Setup}(|\mathsf{C}_w|, k)$
6:   $Stack_w \leftarrow \mathsf{MappingStep}(\mathcal{H}_w, \mathsf{C}_w)$
7:   **for** $(c, i) \in Stack_w$ **do**
8:     $x \leftarrow F(K, c), B_w[i] \leftarrow f(x\|j)$
9:     **for** $t = 0$ *to* 2 **do**
10:       **if** $h_t^{(w)}(x) \neq i$ **then**
11:         **if** $B_w[h_t^{(w)}(x)] = null$ **then**
12:           $B_w[h_t^{(w)}(x)] \xleftarrow{\$} \{0,1\}^k$
13:         **end if**
14:         $B_w[i] \leftarrow B_w[i] \oplus B_w[h_t^{(w)}(x)]$
15:       **end if**
16:     **end for**
17:   **end for**
18:   **for** $s \in [|B_w|]$ **do**
19:     **if** $B_w[s] = null$ **then** $B_w[s] \xleftarrow{\$}$ $\{0,1\}^k$
20:     **end if**
21:   **end for**
22:   $\boxed{\mathsf{EDB}[B_w] \xleftarrow{\$} \{0,1\}^\lambda}$
23:   $j \leftarrow j + 1$
24: **end for**
25: **for** $i = 1, \ldots, q$ **do**
26:   $\mathsf{C}_{\mathsf{q}[i]} \leftarrow \mathsf{TKCE}(\mathsf{q}[i])$
27:   **for** $c \in \mathsf{C}_{\mathsf{q}[i]}$ **do**
28:     $tk_c \leftarrow F(K, c), \mathsf{tk}[i] \leftarrow \mathsf{tk}[i] \cup \{tk_c\}$
29:   **end for**
30:   $\mathsf{Res}[i] \leftarrow \mathsf{ServerSearch}(\mathsf{EDB}, \mathsf{tk}[i])$
31:   **for** $w \in \mathsf{W}$ **do**
32:     $\mathsf{C}_w \leftarrow \mathsf{IKCE}(w)$
33:     **if** $\mathsf{C}_{\mathsf{q}[i]} \subseteq \mathsf{C}_w$ **then**
34:       $\mathsf{ResIds}[i] \leftarrow \mathsf{ResIds}[i] \cup \mathsf{DB}(w)$
35:     **end if**
36:   **end for**
37: **end for**
38: **return** $(\mathsf{EDB}, \mathsf{tk}, \mathsf{Res}, \mathsf{ResIds})$

Algorithm 6. Game$_2$

Initialize(DB, q)

1: $K_e, K \xleftarrow{\$} \{0,1\}^\lambda$
2: $\{(w_j, \mathsf{DB}(w_j))\}_{j=1}^m \leftarrow \mathsf{DB}, \mathsf{EDB} \leftarrow \emptyset,$
  $j \leftarrow 1$
3: $\mathsf{C_W} \leftarrow \emptyset$
4: **for** $w \in \mathsf{W}$ **do**
5:   $\mathsf{C}_w \leftarrow \mathsf{IKCE}(w), \mathsf{C_W} \leftarrow \mathsf{C_W} \cup \mathsf{C}_w$
6: **end for**
7: **for** $c \in \mathsf{C_W}$ **do** $\boxed{X[c] \leftarrow \{0,1\}^\lambda}$
8: **end for**
9: **for** $w \in \mathsf{W}$ **do**
10:   $(\mathcal{H}_w, f, B_w) \leftarrow \mathsf{XF.Setup}(|\mathsf{C}_w|, k)$
11:   $Stack_w \leftarrow \mathsf{MappingStep}(\mathcal{H}_w, \mathsf{C}_w)$
12:   **for** $(c, i) \in Stack_w$ **do**
13:     $x \leftarrow X[c], B_w[i] \leftarrow f(x\|j)$
14:     **for** $t = 0$ *to* 2 **do**
15:       **if** $h_t^{(w)}(x) \neq i$ **then**
16:         **if** $B_w[h_t^{(w)}(x)] = null$ **then**
17:           $B_w[h_t^{(w)}(x)] \xleftarrow{\$} \{0,1\}^k$
18:         **end if**
19:         $B_w[i] \leftarrow B_w[i] \oplus B_w[h_t^{(w)}(x)]$
20:       **end if**
21:     **end for**
22:   **end for**
23:   **for** $s \in [|B_w|]$ **do**
24:     **if** $B_w[s] = null$ **then** $B_w[s] \xleftarrow{\$}$ $\{0,1\}^k$
25:     **end if**
26:   **end for**
27:   $\mathsf{EDB}[B_w] \xleftarrow{\$} \{0,1\}^\lambda$
28:   $j \leftarrow j + 1$
29: **end for**
30: **for** $i = 1, \ldots, q$ **do**
31:   $\mathsf{C}_{\mathsf{q}[i]} \leftarrow \mathsf{TKCE}(\mathsf{q}[i])$
32:   **for** $c \in \mathsf{C}_{\mathsf{q}[i]}$ **do**
33:     $tk_c \leftarrow \boxed{X[c]}, \mathsf{tk}[i] \leftarrow \mathsf{tk}[i] \cup \{tk_c\}$
34:   **end for**
35:   $\mathsf{Res}[i] \leftarrow \mathsf{ServerSearch}(\mathsf{EDB}, \mathsf{tk}[i])$
36:   **for** $w \in \mathsf{W}$ **do**
37:     $\mathsf{C}_w \leftarrow \mathsf{IKCE}(w)$
38:     **if** $\mathsf{C}_{\mathsf{q}[i]} \subseteq \mathsf{C}_w$ **then**
39:       $\mathsf{ResIds}[i] \leftarrow \mathsf{ResIds}[i] \cup \mathsf{DB}(w)$
40:     **end if**
41:   **end for**
42: **end for**
43: **return** $(\mathsf{EDB}, \mathsf{tk}, \mathsf{Res}, \mathsf{ResIds})$

Algorithm 7. Simulator

Initialize($m, \{c_w\}, \overline{\mathbf{q}}, \mathsf{AP}, \mathsf{RP}$)
1: $\mathsf{EDB} \leftarrow \emptyset$
2: **for** $c \in \overline{\mathbf{q}}$ **do** $X[c] \leftarrow \{0,1\}^\lambda$
3: **end for**
4: **for** $w \in [m]$ **do**
5:     $\mathsf{C}_w \leftarrow \emptyset$
6:     **while** $|\mathsf{C}_w| < c_w$ **do**
7:         **if** $w \in \bigcup_{i=1}^q \mathsf{AP}[i]$ **then**
8:             $\mathsf{C}_w \leftarrow \mathsf{C}_w \cup \{X[c]\}$
9:         **else**
10:             $x \leftarrow \{0,1\}^\lambda$, $\mathsf{C}_w \leftarrow \mathsf{C}_w \cup \{x\}$
11:         **end if**
12:     **end while**
13:     $(\mathcal{H}_w, f, B_w) \leftarrow \mathsf{XF.Setup}(c_w, k)$
14:     $Stack_w \leftarrow \mathsf{MappingStep}(\mathcal{H}_w, \mathsf{C}_w)$
15:     **for** $(x, i) \in Stack_w$ **do**
16:         $B_w[i] \leftarrow f(x\|j)$
17:         **for** $t = 0$ to 2 **do**
18:             **if** $h_t^{(w)}(x) \neq i$ **then**
19:                 **if** $B_w[h_t^{(w)}(x)] = null$ **then**
20:                     $B_w[h_t^{(w)}(x)] \overset{\$}{\leftarrow} \{0,1\}^k$
21:                 **end if**
22:                 $B_w[i] \leftarrow B_w[i] \oplus B_w[h_t^{(w)}(x)]$
23:             **end if**
24:         **end for**
25:     **end for**
26:     **for** $s \in [|B_w|]$ **do**
27:         **if** $B_w[s] = null$ **then** $B_w[s] \overset{\$}{\leftarrow} \{0,1\}^k$
28:         **end if**
29:     **end for**
30:     $\mathsf{EDB}[B_w] \overset{\$}{\leftarrow} \{0,1\}^\lambda$
31:     $j \leftarrow j + 1$
32: **end for**
33: **for** $i = 1, \ldots, q$ **do**
34:     **for** $c \in \overline{q}[i]$ **do**
35:         $tk_c \leftarrow X[c]$, $\mathsf{tk}[i] \leftarrow \mathsf{tk}[i] \cup \{tk_c\}$
36:     **end for**
37:     $\mathsf{Res}[i] \leftarrow \mathsf{ServerSearch}(\mathsf{EDB}, \mathsf{tk}[i])$
38:     $\mathsf{ResIds}[i] \leftarrow \mathsf{RP}[i]$
39: **end for**
40: **return** $(\mathsf{EDB}, \mathsf{tk}, \mathsf{Res}, \mathsf{ResIds})$

References

1. Amjad, G., Kamara, S., Moataz, T.: Injection-secure structured and searchable symmetric encryption. In: Guo, J., Steinfeld, R. (eds.) ASIACRYPT 2023. LNCS, vol. 14443, pp. 232–262. Springer, Cham (2023). https://doi.org/10.1007/978-981-99-8736-8_8

2. Bloom, B.H.: Space/time trade-offs in hash coding with allowable errors. Commun. ACM **13**(7), 422–426 (1970)

3. Bösch, C., Brinkman, R., Hartel, P., Jonker, W.: Conjunctive wildcard search over encrypted data. In: Jonker, W., Petković, M. (eds.) SDM 2011. LNCS, vol. 6933, pp. 114–127. Springer, Heidelberg (2011). https://doi.org/10.1007/978-3-642-23556-6_8

4. Bost, R.: $\sum o\varphi o\varsigma$: forward secure searchable encryption. In: CCS, pp. 1143–1154. ACM (2016)

5. Bost, R., Minaud, B., Ohrimenko, O.: Forward and backward private searchable encryption from constrained cryptographic primitives. In: CCS, pp. 1465–1482. ACM (2017)

6. Cash, D., Jarecki, S., Jutla, C., Krawczyk, H., Roşu, M.-C., Steiner, M.: Highly-scalable searchable symmetric encryption with support for Boolean queries. In:

Canetti, R., Garay, J.A. (eds.) CRYPTO 2013. LNCS, vol. 8042, pp. 353–373. Springer, Heidelberg (2013). https://doi.org/10.1007/978-3-642-40041-4_20

7. Chen, T., et al.: The power of bamboo: On the post-compromise security for searchable symmetric encryption. In: NDSS. The Internet Society (2023)

8. Curtmola, R., Garay, J.A., Kamara, S., Ostrovsky, R.: Searchable symmetric encryption: improved definitions and efficient constructions. In: CCS, pp. 79–88. ACM (2006)

9. Fan, B., Andersen, D.G., Kaminsky, M., Mitzenmacher, M.: Cuckoo filter: practically better than bloom. In: CoNEXT, pp. 75–88. ACM (2014)

10. Graf, T.M., Lemire, D.: XOR filters: faster and smaller than bloom and cuckoo filters. ACM J. Exp. Algorithmics **25**, 1.5:1–1.5:16 (2020)

11. Hu, C., Han, L.: Efficient wildcard search over encrypted data. Int. J. Inf. Sec. **15**(5), 539–547 (2016)

12. Kamara, S., Moataz, T.: SQL on structurally-encrypted databases. In: Peyrin, T., Galbraith, S. (eds.) ASIACRYPT 2018. LNCS, vol. 11272, pp. 149–180. Springer, Cham (2018). https://doi.org/10.1007/978-3-030-03326-2_6

13. Kamara, S., Papamanthou, C., Roeder, T.: Dynamic searchable symmetric encryption. In: CCS, pp. 965–976. ACM (2012)

14. Li, Y., Ning, J., Chen, J.: Secure and practical wildcard searchable encryption system based on inner product. IEEE Trans. Serv. Comput. **16**(3), 2178–2190 (2023)

15. Sedghi, S., van Liesdonk, P., Nikova, S., Hartel, P., Jonker, W.: Searching keywords with wildcards on encrypted data. In: Garay, J.A., De Prisco, R. (eds.) SCN 2010. LNCS, vol. 6280, pp. 138–153. Springer, Heidelberg (2010). https://doi.org/10.1007/978-3-642-15317-4_10

16. Song, D.X., Wagner, D.A., Perrig, A.: Practical techniques for searches on encrypted data. In: S&P, pp. 44–55. IEEE Computer Society (2000)

17. Song, X., Dong, C., Yuan, D., Xu, Q., Zhao, M.: Forward private searchable symmetric encryption with optimized I/O efficiency. IEEE Trans. Dependable Secure Comput. **17**(5), 912–927 (2020)

18. Stefanov, E., Papamanthou, C., Shi, E.: Practical dynamic searchable encryption with small leakage. In: NDSS. The Internet Society (2014)

19. Suga, T., Nishide, T., Sakurai, K.: Secure keyword search using bloom filter with specified character positions. In: Takagi, T., Wang, G., Qin, Z., Jiang, S., Yu, Y. (eds.) ProvSec 2012. LNCS, vol. 7496, pp. 235–252. Springer, Heidelberg (2012). https://doi.org/10.1007/978-3-642-33272-2_15

20. Wang, J., Sun, S., Li, T., Qi, S., Chen, X.: Practical volume-hiding encrypted multi-maps with optimal overhead and beyond. In: CCS, pp. 2825–2839. ACM (2022)

21. Wang, Q., Hu, D., Li, M., Yang, G.: Secure and flexible wildcard queries. IEEE Trans. Inf. Forensics Secur. 1 (2024). https://doi.org/10.1109/TIFS.2024.3430056

22. Weener, J., Hahn, F., Peter, A.: Libertas: Backward private dynamic searchable symmetric encryption supporting wildcards. In: Sural, S., Lu, H. (eds.) DBSec 2022. LNCS, vol. 13383, pp. 215–235. Springer, Cham (2022). https://doi.org/10.1007/978-3-031-10684-2_13

23. Zhang, X., Zhao, B., Qin, J., Hou, W., Su, Y., Yang, H.: Practical wildcard searchable encryption with tree-based index. Int. J. Intell. Syst. **36**(12), 7475–7499 (2021)

24. Zhao, F., Nishide, T.: Searchable symmetric encryption supporting queries with multiple-character wildcards. In: Chen, J., Piuri, V., Su, C., Yung, M. (eds.) NSS 2016. LNCS, vol. 9955, pp. 266–282. Springer, Cham (2016). https://doi.org/10.1007/978-3-319-46298-1_18

Encryption

PPA-DCA: A Privacy-Preserving and Accountable Data Collection and Analysis Scheme Using Decentralized Multi-client Functional Encryption

Meixin Chen⬥, Jie Chen⁽⊠⁾⬥, Guang Zhang, and Qiaohan Chu⬥

Shanghai Key Laboratory of Trustworthy Computing, Software Engineering Institute,
East China Normal University, Shanghai 200062, China
s080001@e.ntu.edu.sg

Abstract. In the digital age, collecting and analyzing product data via cloud computing is crucial for product improvement. However, current solutions do not guarantee the protection of each client's data from misuse, and there is no assurance that the information collected by third parties is from a reliable source. In this paper, we propose a new scheme for privacy-preserving and accountable data collection and analysis (called PPA-DCA for short), which uses decentralized multi-client functional encryption. This scheme addresses malicious data misuse by clients and provides a reliable method for third-party companies to collect and analyze data. With a verify-first-encrypt approach, we ensure that only verified clients can encrypt and transmit data, make our scheme more efficient than other works. Additionally, the scheme introduces a monitoring mechanism as a system monitor, capable of detecting any abnormal or malicious behavior of clients in real-time. Upon discovering unauthorized or malicious activities, the system can promptly identify and take corresponding punitive measures. Based on the standard assumptions on bilinear groups, the scheme satisfies static indistinguishable security, simultaneously ensuring the unforgeability, accountability, and privacy of signatures.

Keywords: Inner Product Functional Encryption · Threshold Signature · Cloud Computing · Multi-Client

1 Introduction

Cloud computing has been widely used to enable cloud users to share private data to cloud servers with elastic resources at a low maintenance cost. In today's digital age, it is common for companies to collect and analyze product data through cloud computing in order to improve their products.

For example, TV stations or film and television platforms like YouTube gather user ratings for movies and TV shows, evaluate the popularity of these

J. K. Liu et al. (Eds.): ProvSec 2024, LNCS 14903, pp. 129–147, 2025.
https://doi.org/10.1007/978-981-96-0954-3_7

productions, analyze users' preferences and trends, and use this information to make decisions about which productions to invest in, promote, and broadcast. In the financial industry, third-party firms can collect business data from various companies in the same sector to assess risk and manage it, understand the competitive situation, and predict future industry trends. This information can then be used to provide strategic decision-making suggestions to the government. Similarly, in the pharmaceutical industry, medical institutions can collect and analyze treatment outcome data for patients using a particular drug. This data is crucial in evaluating the effectiveness and safety of the drug, and can greatly inform the regulation and clinical application of the drug, as well as the decision-making of doctors.

The applications mentioned above can be summarized as a third-party company that collects and analyzes information from various customers, and analyzes it using the aggregated results. Inner-Product Functional Encryption (IPFE) [1] is well-suited for this real-world scenario require aggregated results due to its simplicity and adaptability. The key holder can obtain the information related to the inner-product of a specific vector in the encrypted data, rather than directly obtaining the decryption result of the encrypted data. However, IPFE has two potential problems: key escrow issues and malicious abuse. In IPFE schemes, keys are generated and distributed by a central authority, which has the problem of having too much power. The central authority can decrypt or calculate all ciphertext, endangering user privacy. Currently, Chotard et al. have proposed a decentralized multi-client IPFE (DMC-IPFE) scheme, [15] that can address key escrow issues. The central authority is removed and each client has complete control over their individual data and the functional keys they authorize the generation of. Malicious abuse refers to the presence of dishonest clients who submit false information that affects the results of the analysis. By adding each client's identifier to the message during the encryption, if an exception is found later, client's identifier can be traced after the decryption phase.

However, it does not completely protect against malicious abuse, there are two challenges to face:

- When there are malicious clients involved, we must find them immediately; otherwise, they can pretend to be normal clients to sending a large number of invalid requests or outright denial of service.
- The third party still needs to bear the cost of encryption, because it can only figure clients who give the fake data out at the decryption stage. Before decryption, it still need to encrypt messages for any client including the underlying malicious one.

So we want to find a more efficient solution to address above problems. We hope: 1) Participating clients can be authenticated at the beginning, and only those that pass the verification can send data to the third party to reduce the communication overhead. 2) If the verification fails, no private data will be leaked. That is, any client's data remains private, between other clients and the third-party companies. 3) Also, be able to find and hold accountable the dishonest client that failed the validation to prevent the client from continuing to participate in subsequent information collection.

1.1 Contributions

In order to deal with problems mentioned above, we propose a novel scheme called PPA-DCA. This scheme offers a secure and privacy-preserving solution for companies in the same industry to submit data and a reliable way for third-party firms to collect and analyze data via cloud computing. We demonstrate the effectiveness of our scheme through a series of experiments and simulations, and compare it to existing solutions in terms of security, efficiency, and scalability.

Our contributions can be summarized as follows:

1. We add a threshold verification mechanism before encryption. Clients that meet the threshold, not all clients, generate signatures for verification. Only after the verification is passed can the next steps take place, otherwise they will be interrupted.
2. We add a third tracer to play the role of a monitor, discouraging clients from engaging in malicious behavior. Once the malicious clients are found in the beginning, they will no longer be able to participate.
3. Based on the previous two points, we propose a new solution for data collection and analysis. We enhance DMC-IPFE to reduce communication overhead by verifying first and encrypting later, the runtime of each algorithm is greatly reduced. The identifier only appears at the time of signature, not all the time in the message.
4. We realize the concrete algorithms of our system using Rust language to test the effect and compare with prior similar works.

1.2 Organization

The rest of this paper is organized as follows. Section 2 provides an overview of preliminaries. Section 3 introduces the system model and discusses threat models as well as security models. Section 4 describes our proposed scheme in detail and analyse the security of our scheme. Section 5 presents the results of our experiments and simulations, and compares our scheme to existing solutions. Finally, Sect. 6 concludes the paper.

1.3 Related Work

Functional encryption (FE), first introduced by Boneh, Sahai and Waters [11], is an extension of traditional public key cryptography [12]. It enables the key holder to calculate the functional value of encrypted data rather than anything else, overcoming the all-or-nothing release limitations of traditional public-key cryptography schemes [23]. With the development of FE, the research on it can be classified into two types [16, 33]: (1) to construct schemes to support expressive and general functions; (2) to design efficient schemes for specific functions [23].

Focusing on schemes constructed to support expressive and general functions, Multi-Client FE (MCFE) schemes have been introduced in [20]. However, none of the cryptographic assumptions they rely on, such as indistinguishability obfuscation [18], single-input FE for circuits [21], or multi-linear maps [6], are standard [15]. Building FE for specific function classes that meet standard security definitions is a challenge.

Targeting on specific functions, in 2015, Abdalla, Bourse, De Caro, and Pointcheval [1] considered the question of building FE for inner-product functions (IPFE). Their schemes satisfy standard security definitions, under well-understood assumptions like the Decisional Diffie-Hellman (DDH) [3] and Learning With Errors [28]. Furthermore, the security also gradually enhancement, from selective secure [1] to fully secure [5]. Considering privacy issues, function-hiding IPFE schemes were proposed [8].

To support computation over encrypted data from multiple authorities, Abdalla et al. [4] proposed a Multi-Input IPFE (MI-IPFE) scheme and a function-hiding MI-IPFE scheme [2] to extend the privacy of functions. In order to reduce dependence on central authority (CA), Chotard et al. [15] introduced the decentralized scheme.

Threshold Signatures with Private Accountability (TAPS) is introduced by Boneh and Komlo [10]. It can be regarded as a combination of Private Threshold Signature (PTS) [32] and Accountable Threshold Signature (ATS) [29]. PTS requires the signature reveals nothing about the threshold and the identities of the signers participating in the signing phase [32]. ATS requires that all the signers who participate in the signing phase can be found out, from the public signature [29].

2   Preliminaries

In this section, we introduce the group, the assumptions and a signature scheme we rely on.

2.1   Bilinear Group

Bilinear groups are a set of three cyclic groups $\mathbb{G}_1$, $\mathbb{G}_2$ and $\mathbb{G}_T$ of a prime order p along with a bilinear map $e : \mathbb{G}_1 \times \mathbb{G}_2 \to \mathbb{G}_T$ with the following properties [9]:

- *bilinear* : for all $g \in \mathbb{G}_1$, $\tilde{g} \in \mathbb{G}_2$ and $a, b \in \mathbb{Z}_p$, $e\left(g^a, \tilde{g}^b\right) = e\left(g, \tilde{g}\right)^{a \cdot b}$;
- *non-degenerate* : for $g \neq 1_{\mathbb{G}_1}$ and $\tilde{g} \neq 1_{\mathbb{G}_2}$, $e\left(g, \tilde{g}\right) \neq 1_{\mathbb{G}_T}$;
- *computable* : the map e is computable efficiently.

Let $\mathcal{BG}\left(1^\lambda\right) \to (e, p, \mathbb{G}_1, \mathbb{G}_2, \mathbb{G}_T)$ be a generator of bilinear groups. It takes as input a security parameter 1^λ and outputs bilinear groups $(e, p, \mathbb{G}_1, \mathbb{G}_2, \mathbb{G}_T)$ with prime order p and $e : \mathbb{G}_1 \times \mathbb{G}_2 \to \mathbb{G}_T$.

According to the performance and implementation in [17] and [14], we make use of the pairing explained by [23] and [15]. Let $\mathcal{PG} = (\mathbb{G}_1, \mathbb{G}_2, p, P_1, P_2, e)$ be a generator of pairing group, where $\mathbb{G}_1 \neq \mathbb{G}_2$ and there is no efficient isomorphism

$\psi : \mathbb{G}_2 \rightarrow \mathbb{G}_1$. $\mathbb{G}_1, \mathbb{G}_2, \mathbb{G}_T$ are additive cyclic groups of order p for a 2λ-bit prime p, P_1 and P_2 are generators of $\mathbb{G}_1$ and $\mathbb{G}_2$, respectively, and $e : \mathbb{G}_1 \times \mathbb{G}_2 \rightarrow \mathbb{G}_T$ is an efficiently computable (non-degenerate) bilinear map. Define $P_T := e(P_1, P_2)$, which is a generator of $\mathbb{G}_T$.

2.2 Assumptions

Decisional Diffie-Hellman Assumption. The Decisional Diffie-Hellman assumption (DDH) [25] says that for all ppt adversaries $\mathcal{A}$, the following advantage function $\mathsf{Adv}_{\mathcal{A}}^{DDH}(\lambda)$ is negligible in λ:

$$\Pr[\mathcal{A}(G, g^a, g^b, g^c) = 1] - \Pr[\mathcal{A}(G, g^a, g^b, g^{ab}) = 1],$$

where G is a cyclic group of prime order p, $a, b, c \leftarrow \mathbb{Z}_p$.

Symmetric eXternal Diffie-Hellman Assumption. The Symmetric eXternal Diffie-Hellman Assumption (SXDH) [30] states that, in a pairing group, the DDH assumption holds in both $\mathbb{G}_1$ and $\mathbb{G}_2$.

2.3 Signature Scheme

A signature scheme $\mathcal{SIG}$ [22] is a triple of PPT algorithms comprised of (KeyGen, Sign, Verify), with message space $\mathcal{M}$ and signature space $\mathcal{S}$:

- KeyGen(1^λ) $\leftarrow$ (pk, sk): The key generation algorithm takes as input the security parameter λ. Output a pair of keys including a public verification key pk and a secret signing key sk.
- Sign(sk, m) $\leftarrow \sigma$: The signature generation algorithm takes as input the signing key sk and a message $m \in \mathcal{M}$. Output a signature $\sigma \in \mathcal{S}$.
- Verify(pk, m, σ) $\leftarrow$ 0/1: The verification algorithm takes as input the public verification key pk, a message $m \in \mathcal{M}$, and a signature σ. If the signature is valid, output 1. Otherwise output 0.

We say a signature scheme is secure [24] if it is existentially unforgeable against chosen message attacks (EUF-CMA). More concretely, if for all PPT adversaries $\mathcal{A}$, the following function $\mathsf{Adv}_{\mathcal{A},\mathcal{SIG}}^{EUF-CMA}$ holds:

$$\Pr\left[\begin{array}{l} \mathsf{Verify}(\mathsf{pk}, m, \sigma) = 1 \\ (m, \sigma) \notin \{(m_i, \sigma_i)\}_{i=1}^{q} \end{array} : \begin{array}{l} (\mathsf{pk}, \mathsf{sk}) \xleftarrow{\$} \mathsf{KeyGen}\left(1^\lambda\right) \\ (m, \sigma) \xleftarrow{\$} \mathcal{A}^{\mathsf{SIGN}(\cdot)}(\mathsf{pk}) \end{array} \right] = \mathsf{negl}(\lambda)$$

where $\mathsf{SIGN}(m_i)$ returns $\sigma_i \leftarrow \mathsf{Sign}(\mathsf{sk}, m_i)$ for $i = 1, \cdots, q$.

3 System Model

In this section, we introduce the system model and security model of our proposed PPA-DCA. We define various entities and give a description of their interactions in our system model. We analyze the security requirement of each entities and present some possible attacks in our model.

3.1   Entities in Our System

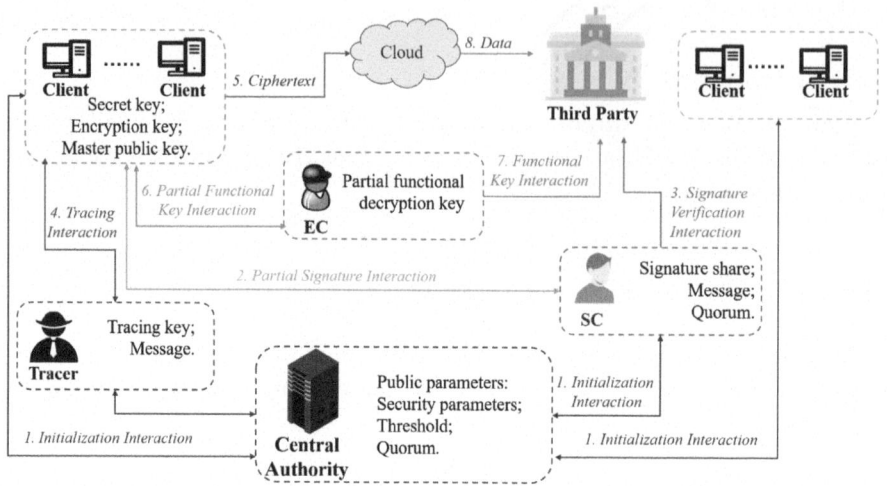

Fig. 1. System model in our article.

We present a description figure of our system framework in Fig. 1, which consists of six entities: 1)Central Authority(CA); 2) Client; 3) Combiner for DMC-IPFE (Encryption Combiner, or EC); 4) Combiner for TAPS (Signature Combiner, or SC); 5) Tracer and 6) Third Party. The detailed description of characteristics and functionalities of each entity is given below:

– The CA initializes the system parameters first and distributes them to the Client, SC, Tracer and Third Party through specific protocols, and these entities are confidential from each other, only knowing the parameters they get and know nothing about other entities.
– Each Client initializes the parameters needed for encryption, they first generate the secret key, encryption key and public parameters through interaction. Except for the public parameters that can be disclosed, the others are known only to the Client. The data is encrypted by using the encryption key, and then the partial functional decryption key is generated.
– The EC only interacts with Clients and Third Party in one direction. The EC receives a portion of the functional decryption keys generated by each Client and aggregates them into a complete decryption key for the system to send to a Third Party.
– The SC is the aggregator of signatures. It interacts with each Client to get a partial signature, and then aggregates the signatures of the Clients participating in the threshold signature and sends them to Third Party and Tracer.
– The Tracer is the guardian against malicious users. It records the signers' paths at the end of the signature, and it is the first line of defense for security,

which can be used to track down malicious clients when the next steps of data collection and analysis become problematic.

- Third Party is the terminal of cloud computing. After the signature is verified, it receives encrypted data from other Client and obtains the calculated result using the function key sent by EC.

3.2 Definition of the System

We nest threshold signatures before the encryption phase. Hence, the system we proposed is comprised of a set of the key functions:

- **Setup**(λ_1): Takes as input the system security parameter λ_1, generate secret keys sk_i and encryption keys ek_i, as well as the public parameters mpk.
- **TAPS_KeyGen**(λ_2, n, t): Takes as input a security parameter λ_2, the number of signers n and the threshold t. Output a public key pk, signer keys $(sk_1, \ldots, sk_n)$, a combiner secret key sk_c and a tracing secret key sk_t.
- **TAPS_Sign**(sk_j, m, C): Takes as input secret key sk_j, where $j \subseteq [n]$, the message $m \in \mathcal{M}$ and an optional input, identities of the signing quorum $C \subseteq [n]$. Output the corresponding signature share δ_j.
- **TAPS_Combine**$\left(sk_C, m, C, \{\delta_j\}_{i \in C}\right)$: Takes as input secret key of the signers participated in signing, a message m, a description of the signing quorum $C \subseteq [n]$ where $|C| = t$ and t valid signature shares by members of C. In the case of valid input, it outputs a TAPS signature σ.
- **TAPS_Verify** (pk, m, σ): Takes as input the public key pk, a message m and the signature σ. It the signature is valid, output 1. Else output 0.
- **TAPS_Trace** (sk_t, m, σ): Takes as input the tracer's secret key sk_t, a message m and a signature σ. Output a set $C \subseteq [n]$, where $|C| \geq t$ or a special meaasge fail. Supposing that the algorithm outputs a set C, then the set is intended to be a set of signers whose keys must have been used to generates σ.
- **Encrypt** (ek_i, x_i, ℓ): Takes as input a client encryption key ek_i, a value x_i to encrypt, and a label ℓ, and outputs the ciphertext $C_{\ell,i}$.
- **DKeyGenShare** (sk_i, ℓ_f): Takes as input a client secret key sk_i and a label ℓ_f, and outputs the partial functional decryption key $dk_{f,i}$ for a function $f : \mathcal{M}^n \to \mathcal{R}$ that is described in ℓ_f.
- **DKeyComb** $\left((dk_{f,i})_i, \ell_f\right)$: Takes as input the partial functional decryption keys and eventually outputs the functional decryption key dk_f.
- **Decrypt** ($dk_f, \ell, \mathbf{C}$): Takes as input a functional decryption key dk_f, a label ℓ, and an n-vector ciphertext $\mathbf{C}$, and outputs $f(\mathbf{x})$, if $\mathbf{C}$ is a valid encryption of $\mathbf{x} = (x_i)_i \in \mathcal{M}^n$ for the label ℓ, or $\perp$ otherwise.

3.3 Threat Model

Since the collection of information is often initiated by a credible company or popped up within the official software, we assume the Third Party is a trustworthy entity here. The CA is regarded as a credible entity because it generates the system parameters and interact keys via the secure protocol. The SC, EC and Tracer is semi-trusted, who faithfully carries out system operations but may launch any passive attacks. The Clients are untrustworthy, who can launch any attacks. So we can summarize the possible attacks in our PPA-DCA system, which may not cover all potential real-world threat scenarios.

Client Malicious Attacks. This attack means that the client is dishonest and sends false data to a third party. Or it is possible to tamper with its input vectors or keys in order to obtain incorrect calculations or compromise the security of the system.

Identity Forgery Attack. Unauthorized clients may forge identities or impersonate other legitimate parties in order to gain unauthorized access or perform malicious actions.

Eavesdropping Attack. An adversary has access to transcripts of the communications in the public channels and can make some senders play maliciously to learn the sensitive information.

Collusion Attack. The unauthorized parties can get together to launch the above attacks. For example, since the senders do not trust each other, and they can collude and give their secret keys to the adversary who will play on their behalf.

3.4 Security Model

In this part, we describe three security models. The first one is the static indistinguishability (sta-IND) to cover eavesdropping attack and collusion attack. The second one is existential unforgeability against a chosen message attack (EUF-CMA) to cover client malicious attack and identity forgery attack. The last one is privacy to cover eavesdropping attack. The security games can refer to [15] and [10], here merely to provide the definitions but not additional information.

Definition 1. *We say this DMC-IPFE is sta-IND-secure if for any adversary $\mathcal{A}$, the following advantage is negligible.*

$$\mathsf{Adv}^{IND}(\mathcal{A}) = |P[\beta = 1 \mid b = 1] - P[\beta = 1 \mid b = 0]|$$

Definition 2. *Provided that for all probabilistic polynomial time adversaries $\mathcal{A} = (\mathcal{A}_0, \mathcal{A}_1)$, the function $\mathsf{Adv}^{forg}_{\mathcal{A},S}(\lambda)$ is a negligible function of λ, then we say that a TAPS scheme S is EUF-CMA with accountability.*

Besides, privacy is one of the most important properties of our scheme. Privacy for a threshold signature scheme is often defined by requiring that a threshold signature on a message m be indistinguishable from a signature on m generated by some standard (non-threshold) signature scheme [19]. This property guarantees that a threshold signature reveals nothing about the threshold and the quorum that produced the signature. To define privacy as an intrinsic property of the TAPS, the scheme need to satisfy two privacy requirements: **Privacy against the public** (priv1) and **Privacy against signers** (priv2) [10].

Definition 3. *If for all probabilistic poly-nominal time public adversaries $\mathcal{A} = (\mathcal{A}_0, \mathcal{A}_1)$, the function $\mathsf{Adv}_{\mathcal{A},\mathcal{S}}^{priv1}(\lambda)$ and $\mathsf{Adv}_{\mathcal{A},\mathcal{S}}^{priv2}(\lambda)$ are negligible functions of λ, a TAPS scheme $\mathcal{S}$ is private.*

4   Proposed Scheme and Its Security

Based on DMC-IPFE and TAPS, we proposed the PPA-DCA. Refer to Sect. 3, in this section, we will mainly explain the algorithms that the system entities run.

- *System Setup*$(\lambda) \rightarrow (n, t, \mathsf{sk}_i, \mathsf{ek}_i, \mathsf{mpk})$. The setup algorithm generates $\mathcal{PG} := (\mathbb{G}_1, \mathbb{G}_2, p, P_1, P_2, e) \xleftarrow{\$} PGGen\left(1^\lambda\right)$. Samples two full-domain hash functions $\mathcal{H}_1$ and $\mathcal{H}_2$ onto $\mathbb{G}_1^2$ and $\mathbb{G}_2^2$ respectively. Each sender $\mathcal{S}_i$ generates $\boldsymbol{s}_i \xleftarrow{\$} \mathbb{Z}_p^2$ for all $i \in [n]$, and interactively generates $\mathbf{T}_i \xleftarrow{\$} \mathbb{Z}_p^{2\times2}$ such that $\sum_{i\in[n]} \mathbf{T}_i = \mathbf{0}$. The algorithm returns the number of clients n, the quorum t, the master public key mpk, encryption keys ek_i and secret keys sk_i for $i = 1, \ldots, n$,

$$\mathsf{mpk} \leftarrow (\mathcal{PG}, \mathcal{H}_1, \mathcal{H}_2), \mathsf{ek}_i = \boldsymbol{s}_i, \mathsf{sk}_i = (\boldsymbol{s}_i, \mathbf{T}_i)$$

- *TAPS_KeyGen*$(1^\lambda, n, t) \rightarrow (\mathsf{pk}, (\mathsf{sk}_1, \ldots, \mathsf{sk}_n), \mathsf{sk}_c, \mathsf{sk}_t)$. The keygen algorithm generates $\mathcal{G} := (G, q, g) \xleftarrow{\$} GGen(1^\lambda)$. Choose $\mathsf{sk}_1, \cdots, \mathsf{sk}_n \xleftarrow{\$} \mathbb{Z}_q$ and set $\mathsf{pk}_i \leftarrow g^{\mathsf{sk}_j}$ for $j \in [n]$, $\mathsf{pk}' \leftarrow (\mathsf{pk}_1, \cdots, \mathsf{pk}_n)$. Encrypt t with ElGamal: $\psi \xleftarrow{\$} \mathbb{Z}_q$ and $(T_0, T_1) \leftarrow (g^\psi, g^t h^\psi)$. Generate $(\mathsf{sk}_{cs}, \mathsf{pk}_{cs}) \xleftarrow{\$} \mathcal{SIG}.\mathsf{KeyGen}(\lambda)$, where $\mathcal{SIG}$ is a signature scheme presented in Sect. 2.3. Sample $\mathsf{sk}_e \xleftarrow{\$} \mathbb{Z}_q$ and set $\mathsf{pk}_t \leftarrow g^{\mathsf{sk}_e} \in \mathbb{G}$.
  The algorithm returns TAPS's public key pk, client keys $(\mathsf{sk}_1, \ldots, \mathsf{sk}_n)$, a combiner secret key sk_c and a tracing secret key sk_t where

$$\mathsf{pk} \leftarrow \left(\mathsf{pk}', \mathsf{pk}_t, \mathsf{pk}_{cs}, T_0, T_1\right), \mathsf{sk}_c \leftarrow (\mathsf{pk}, \mathsf{sk}_{cs}, t, \psi), \mathsf{sk}_t \leftarrow (\mathsf{pk}, \mathsf{sk}_e, t)$$

  The verifier's public key pk is published by the CA in public. While the client's secret key sk_i, the combiner's secret key sk_c and the tracing secret key sk_t will be sent by the CA respectively to the Client, the Combiner and the Tracer.

- *TAPS_Sign*$(\mathsf{sk}_j, m, C) \rightarrow \delta_j$. This algorithm takes as input the Clients' secret key sk_j who pertain to the quorum set C and the message m that need to be signed. The Combiner and signer j interact through a protocol, so that the Combiner obtains a signature share $\delta_j \leftarrow (R_j, z_j) \in \mathbb{G} \times \mathbb{Z}_q$, where (R_j, z_j) satisfies $g^{z_j} = \mathsf{pk}_j^c \cdot R_j$ for $c \leftarrow H(\mathsf{pk}, R, m) \in \mathbb{Z}_q$. Here $R \in \mathbb{G}$ is defined as $R := \prod_{j\in C} R_j$. The algorithm returns each participating client's signature $\delta_j, j \in C$.

- *TAPS_Comb*$\left(\mathsf{sk}_C, m, C, \{\delta_j\}_{j\in C}\right) \rightarrow \sigma$. This algorithm takes as input the combiner's secret key sk_c, the message m, the collection of clients who participate in signing along with their t signature shares. If $|C| \neq t$, abort. With $|C| = t$ and $\delta_j = (R_j, z_j)$, the coordinator compute $R \leftarrow \prod_{j\in C} R_j \in \mathbb{G}$ and

$z \leftarrow \sum_{j \in C} z_j \in \mathbb{Z}_q$, set $c \leftarrow H(\mathsf{pk}, R, m) \in \mathbb{Z}_q$, then $g^z = \left[\prod_{j \in C} \mathsf{pk}_j\right]^c \cdot R$. Encrypt z with ElGamal: $\rho \xleftarrow{\$} \mathbb{Z}_q, ct := (c_0, c_1) \leftarrow (g^\rho, g^z \mathsf{pk}_t^\rho)$. Set $(b_1, \ldots, b_n) \in \{0, 1\}^n$, such that $b_j = 1$ if and only if $j \in C$, then $g^z = \left[\prod_{j=1}^n (\mathsf{pk}_j)^{b_j}\right]^c \cdot R$. Generate a zero knowledge proof π for the relation $\mathcal{R}_S$ using Bulletproof protocol [13]. Sign with Combiner's key $tg \xleftarrow{\$} \mathcal{SIG}.\mathsf{Sign}$ $(\mathsf{sk}_{cs}, (m, R, ct, \pi))$. The algorithm returns the combined TAPS signature $\sigma \leftarrow (R, ct, \pi, tg)$.

- *TAPS_Verify* $(\mathsf{pk}, m, \sigma) \rightarrow 0/1$. Parse $\mathsf{pk} = (\mathsf{pk}', \mathsf{pk}_t, \mathsf{pk}_{cs}, T_0, T_1)$ and set $c \leftarrow H(\mathsf{pk}, R, m)$. Verify the following requirements:
  - $\mathcal{SIG}.\mathsf{Ver}(\mathsf{pk}_{cs}, (m, R, ct, \pi), tg) = 1$, and
  - π is a valid proof for the relation $\mathcal{R}_S$ with respect to the statement $(g, h, \mathsf{pk}', \mathsf{pk}_t, T_0, T_1, R, c, ct = (c_0, c_1))$.

  The algorithm returns 1 if the verification passes, otherwise returns 0.

- *TAPS_Trace* $(\mathsf{sk}_t, m, \sigma) \rightarrow C/\mathsf{fail}$. Parse $\mathsf{sk}_t = (\mathsf{pk}, \mathsf{sk}_t, t)$ where $\mathsf{pk} \leftarrow (\mathsf{pk}', \mathsf{pk}_t, \mathsf{pk}_{cs}, T_0, T_1)$ and $\mathsf{pk}' \leftarrow (\mathsf{pk}_1, \cdots, \mathsf{pk}_n)$. Firstly, ensure that (m, σ) is a valid signature, abort if *TAPS_Verify*(pk, m, σ) rejects. Parse σ as (R, ct, π, tg) and $ct = (c_0, c_1)$. Set $c \leftarrow H(\mathsf{pk}, R, m)$. ElGamal decrypt $ct = (c_0, c_1)$ as $g^{(z')} \leftarrow c_1/c_0^{\mathsf{sk}_e} \in \mathbb{G}$. Find a set $C \subseteq [n]$, where $|C| = t$ and $g^{(z')} = R \cdot \left(\prod_{i \in C} \mathsf{pk}_i\right)^c$. The algorithm returns C and records the log, if such a set $C \subseteq [n]$ is found. Otherwise, the algorithm return fail.

- *Encrypt* $(\mathsf{ek}_i, x_i, \ell) \rightarrow C_{\ell,i}$. Takes as input the value x_i to encrypt, under the key $\mathsf{ek}_i = s_i$ and the label ℓ. It computes $[u_\ell]_1 := \mathcal{H}_1(\ell) \in \mathbb{G}_1^2$. This algorithm returns the ciphertext $[c_i]_1 = [u_\ell^\top s_i + x_i]_1 \in \mathbb{G}_1$.

- *DKeyGenShare* $(\mathsf{sk}_i, \ell_f) \rightarrow \mathsf{dk}_{f,i}$. Parse $y \in \mathbb{Z}_p^n$ that defines the function $f_y(x) = \langle x, y \rangle$, and the secret key $\mathsf{sk}_i = (s_i, T_i)$, it computes $[v_y]_2 := \mathcal{H}_2(y) \in \mathbb{G}_2^2, [d_i]_2 := [y_i \cdot s_i + T_i v_y]_2$. This algorithm returns the partial decryption key as $\mathsf{dk}_{y,i} := ([d_i]_2)$.

- *DKeyComb* $((\mathsf{dk}_{f,i})_i, \ell_f) \rightarrow \mathsf{dk}_f$. Parse the partial decryption keys $\mathsf{dk}_{y,i} = ([d_i]_2)_{i \in [n]}$. The algorithm returns the whole decryption key $\mathsf{dk}_y := (y, [d]_2)$, where $[d]_2 = \sum_{i \in [n]} [d_i]_2$.

- *Decrypt* $(\mathsf{dk}_f, \ell, C) \rightarrow f(x)$. Parse the decryption key $\mathsf{dk}_y = [d]_2$, the label ℓ, and ciphertexts $([c_i]_1)_{i \in [n]}$, it computes $[\alpha]_T := \sum_{i \in [n]} e([c_i]_1, [y_i]_2) - e([u_\ell]_1^\top, [d]_2)$. The algorithm eventually solves the discrete logarithm in basis $[1]_T$ to extract and returns the results α.

4.1 Correctness

Note that TAPS only serves as a verification function and does not affect our results, so the correctness of the results depends on the DMC-IPFE scheme. So let $x, y \in \mathbb{Z}_p^n$, we have:

$$[d]_2 = \sum_{i \in [n]} [d_i]_2 = \sum_{i \in [n]} [y_i \cdot s_i + \mathbf{T}_i v_y]_2$$

$$= \left[\sum_{i \in [n]} y_i \cdot s_i \right]_2 + [v_y]_2 \cdot \sum_{i \in [n]} \mathbf{T}_i = \left[\sum_{i \in [n]} y_i \cdot s_i \right]_2.$$

Thus:

$$[\alpha]_T := \sum_{i \in [n]} e\left([c_i]_1, [y_i]_2\right) - e\left([u_\ell]_1^\top, [d]_2\right)$$

$$= \sum_i \left[(u_\ell^\top s_i + x_i) y_i \right]_T - \left[\sum_{i \in [n]} y_i u_\ell^\top s_i \right]_T = \left[\sum_i x_i y_i \right]_T.$$

4.2 Security Analysis

Theorem 1. *Our PPA-DCA scheme is sta-IND secure, and supports client signature unforgeability, accountability, and privacy. Namely, the advantage function of our scheme* $\mathsf{Adv}_A^{PPA-DCA}$ *is negligible. And in addition, the advantage for unforgeability and accountability* $\mathsf{Adv}_{A,PPA-DCA}^{forg}(\lambda)$, *the advantage function for privacy against the public* $\mathsf{Adv}_{A,PPA-DCA}^{priv1}(\lambda)$ *and the advantage function for privacy against the signing clients* $\mathsf{Adv}_{A,PPA-DCA}^{priv2}(\lambda)$ *are negligible functions.*

We have introduced the security models in Sect. 3.4, and these models cover all possible attacks in our scheme. To prove Theorem 1, we introduce some useful theorems and lemmas in [15] and [10].

Theorem 2. *The DMC-IPFE is sta-IND secure under the SXDH assumption, in the random oracle model.*

Theorem 3. *The TAPS scheme is unforgeable, accountable, and private, assuming the underlying Schnorr ATS scheme is secure, the signature scheme* Sig *is strongly unforgeable, DDH assumption holds in G, and the bulletproofs protocol proof for* $\mathcal{R}_S$ *is an non-interactive argument of knowledge and HVZK.*

Note that Theorem 2 is actually the security of the decentralized multi-client functional encryption for Inner Product (DMC-IPFE) in [15], except that third parties receives a single signature from the combiner for TAPS, instead of receiving signatures from each client. Then, if we can prove that the single signature from the combiner for TAPS is unforgeable as the signatures from each client, we can say that our PPA-DCA scheme is secure, which is implied by Theorem 2. Proving that the single signature from the combiner for TAPS is unforgeable as well as the signatures from each client, is equivalent to prove that our scheme is unforgeable. The signature is unforgeable can be implied by Theorem 3. Therefore, our scheme is secure and supports client signature unforgeability. The rest is to prove that our scheme also supports client signature accountability and privacy, and this can also be implied by Theorem 3. Then, we complete our proof for Theorem 1. So far, we have completed the whole security proof for our scheme.

5   Performance Evaluation

We need to consider two main parts in our scheme: (i.) realize a concrete implementation of the earlier mentioned threshold signature scheme proposed in [10]; (ii.) integrate this signature scheme implementation into the decentralized multi-client functional encryption for inner product in order to support for users who need to sign. We proceed our performance evaluation with the theoretical analysis and the experimental analysis.

5.1   Theoretical Analysis

Practical construction of functional encryption for specific classes of functions is of high interest. We first concentrate on the outer layer Inner-Product Functional Encryption in the Decentralized Multi-Client setting:

Table 1. Functionalities comparison of different solutions to linearly aggregating private multi-client data.

Scheme	Multiple Inner Products	Non Interactive Setup	Non Interactive Encrypt	Non Interactive KeyGen	Decentralized
PSA [31]	×	✓	✓	×	×
FE [1]	✓	✓	×	✓	×
MCFE [5]	✓	✓	✓	✓	×
Ours	✓	×	✓	✓	✓

1 **Functionality:** The functionality of our scheme can be seen in Table 1, focusing on the core functionalities relevant to inner-product functional encryption schemes. Our scheme has a key generation protocol that does not require interactions and makes the system decentralized.
2 **Efficiency:** the proposed scheme is highly practical as their efficiency is comparable to that of the DDH-based IP-FE scheme from [5]. A value x_i is encrypted as a unique group element C_i. The setup phase, key generation and decryption all take time linear in the number of participants, and encryption takes time linear in its input according to [15].
3 **Security:** our scheme is sta-IND-secure under the standard SXDH assumption in the random oracle model.

Table 2. Communication comparison among existing signatures with tracing capability

Scheme	Public Keys	Signature Size	Accountability	Involved Party
LGS [34]	$n\|G\| + 2\|\mathbb{Z}_p\|$	$4n\|G\| + 6\|\mathbb{Z}_p\|$	✓	all
SLTGS [7]	$n\|G\|$	$3n\|G\| + 7\|\mathbb{Z}_p\|$	✓	all
DDT-LGS [26]	$(n+2)\|G\|$	$4n\|G\| + 6\|\mathbb{Z}_p\|$	✓	all
Ours	$(2n+1)\|G\|$	$(n + \log n)\|G\| + 4\|\mathbb{Z}_p\|$	✓	partially

Then we turn to focus on the signature component of our scheme. Compared to previous signature schemes with similar tracing capability, Table 2 illustrate the public keys size, signature size and functions between them, where $|G|$ denotes the number of all single element in the group G, and $|\mathbb{Z}_p|$ denotes the number of all single element in the ring $\mathbb{Z}_p$, n denotes the number of the attribute authorities. As we can see from Table 2, although the cost of our public key is large, the signature size is relatively small and our signature does not require the participation of all clients.

5.2   Experimental Analysis

In this part, we evaluate the performance of the proposed scheme presented in Sect. 4. The simulation is built on a laptop with the following specification: Intel Core i7-10510U, 2.30 GHz, 16-GB RAM and Windows 10 operation system. We choose to realize Bulletproofs [13] to accommodate our scheme due to its small computational communications.

We first implement the signature scheme, adding necessary extensions and modifications to suit our construction. The programming language used is Rust in order to make use of some publicly available implementation building blocks. The most suitable foundations implementation framework for signature is bulletproofs [13], relying on cryptography library curve25519-dalek which provides group operations. In addition, cryptography library blake2 which provides hash functions with security parameter $\lambda = 256$ is used for the outer encryption framework.

We make a comparison by replacing the number of clients and the quorum signers. Here we can make a reference according to the Figs. 2a and 2b. In Fig. 2a, we set the quorum fixed, and change the number of clients. While in Fig. 2b, we switch the setting. From the above figures, it can be seen intuitively that the number of clients has a significant impact on the growth of time cost, while the growth of time cost is still relatively slow regardless of the number of quorum signers.

We also compare our scheme with other accountable works in terms of runtime and memory overhead. The efficiency of signature part is shown in the Table 3. Here we fix the number of clients $n = 27$ and the threshold $t = 6$. Though the verification part takes some time, the signing and tracing are still

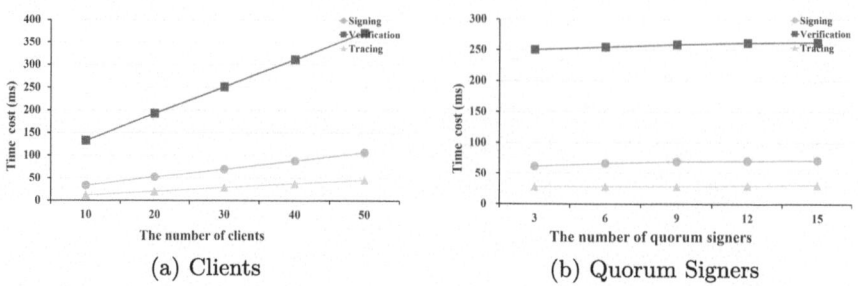

Fig. 2. Average time cost of signature part with different numbers of (a) clients. (b) signers.

Table 3. Performance comparison with other signatures

Scheme	Sign (ms)	Verify (ms)	Trace (ms)	Signatures (bits)
LGS [34]	196.5	297.7	29.6	1874
SLTGS [7]	100.5	64.4	39.8	2080
DDT-LGS [26]	201.6	291.8	51.0	–
Ours	66.3	254.4	28.2	1040

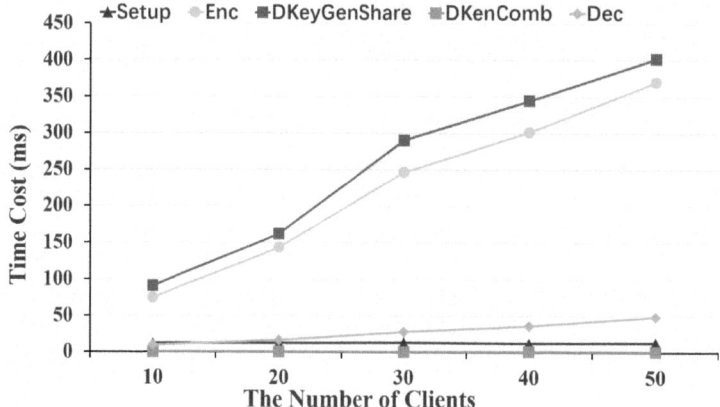

Fig. 3. Average time cost of outer encryption framework with different numbers of clients

well done. Moreover, the overhead of our signature is the smallest among these schemes.

We then turn the target to our outer encryption framework. We realize the concrete implementation of [15] and the results of our experiment are illustrated in Fig. 3. Our scheme is time-consuming in generating the partial functional decryption key and encrypting. Of the remaining three steps, the operation is relatively fast.

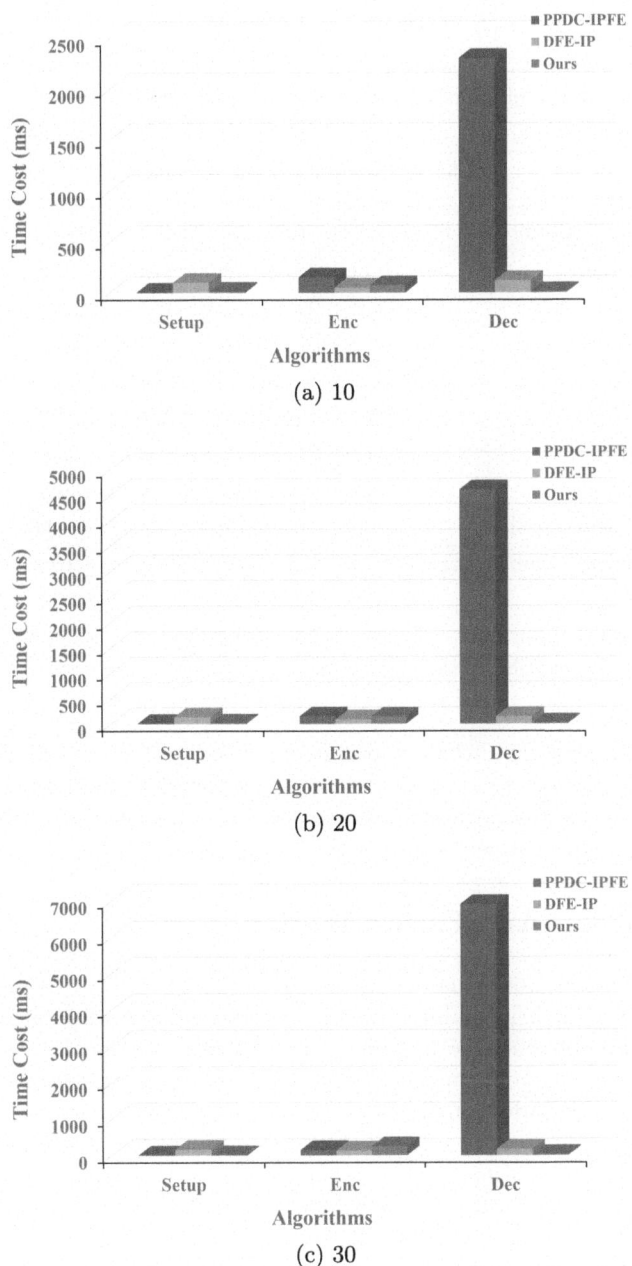

Fig. 4. Average time cost of algorithms with different numbers of values (a) 10. (b) 20. (c) 30.

Also, we give the comparison between other IPFE schemes for aggregation analysis and ours in Fig. 4. Considering the number of values need to be encrypted, we choose PPDC-IPFE [27] and DFE-IP [23] to compare with our scheme. The runtime of our scheme at *Setup* and *Enc* is comparable to the other two schemes, but the efficiency at *Dec* is quite surprising.

Table 4. Scalability of our scheme

The Number of Clients	10	20	30	40	50
Setup	11.60	12.20	12.90	11.90	13.30
KeyGen	7.12	12.00	14.80	16.97	21.16
Comb	22.82	35.37	44.18	60.35	74.55
Sign	33.28	54.81	65.98	85.60	106.01
Verify	132.44	210.14	251.34	311.32	371.17
Trace	11.65	20.24	28.65	37.32	45.26
Enc	74.00	143.20	246.70	301.30	369.80
DKeyGenShare	90.40	161.90	290.30	344.20	401.90
DKenComb	0.20	0.40	0.60	0.80	1.10
Dec	8.90	16.40	27.60	35.90	48.40
Total Runtime	392.41	666.66	983.05	1205.66	1452.65

[a] The runtime of the algorithms are measured in millisecond.

At last, we show the whole experimental results of our system in Table 4. We evaluate how our system performance is impacted as the number of clients increases. Here we compare the average time and see that the whole system performance stays relatively stable with increasing clients.

6   Conclusion And Future Work

In this paper, we propose a new scheme called PPA-DCA, which aims to address the challenges of malicious abuse during data sharing and analysis in the cloud computing environment. By utilizing decentralized functional encryption and threshold signature, we have successfully mitigated the problem of data abuse of multiple clients. Additionally, the tracking mechanism serves as a monitor to ensure the accuracy and credibility of the data source. Through a series of experiments and simulations, we verify the effectiveness of the PPA-DCA scheme and compare it with existing solutions. The results demonstrate that our scheme has significant advantages in terms of efficiency and scalability.

Through the PPA-DCA scheme, enterprises can securely share and analyze data in the cloud computing environment, ensuring the accuracy of client data while improving the efficiency of data processing. Our scheme has a wide range of applications and can drive data-driven decision making and business development in various industries. However, we are also aware that the PPA-DCA scheme may have limitations for more complex data analysis tasks and specific application scenarios, and further research and improvement are necessary.

Acknowledgements. This work was supported by National Natural Science Foundation of China (62372180) and Innovation Program of Shanghai Municipal Education Commission (2021-01-07-00-08-E00101).

References

1. Abdalla, M., Bourse, F., De Caro, A., Pointcheval, D.: Simple functional encryption schemes for inner products. In: Katz, J. (ed.) PKC 2015. LNCS, vol. 9020, pp. 733–751. Springer, Heidelberg (2015). https://doi.org/10.1007/978-3-662-46447-2_33
2. Abdalla, M., Catalano, D., Fiore, D., Gay, R., Ursu, B.: Multi-input functional encryption for inner products: function-hiding realizations and constructions without pairings. In: Shacham, H., Boldyreva, A. (eds.) CRYPTO 2018, Part I. LNCS, vol. 10991, pp. 597–627. Springer, Cham (2018). https://doi.org/10.1007/978-3-319-96884-1_20
3. Abdalla, M., Catalano, D., Gay, R., Ursu, B.: Inner-product functional encryption with fine-grained access control. In: Moriai, S., Wang, H. (eds.) ASIACRYPT 2020, Part III. LNCS, vol. 12493, pp. 467–497. Springer, Cham (2020). https://doi.org/10.1007/978-3-030-64840-4_16
4. Abdalla, M., Gay, R., Raykova, M., Wee, H.: Multi-input inner-product functional encryption from pairings. In: Coron, J.-S., Nielsen, J.B. (eds.) EUROCRYPT 2017, Part I. LNCS, vol. 10210, pp. 601–626. Springer, Cham (2017). https://doi.org/10.1007/978-3-319-56620-7_21
5. Agrawal, S., Libert, B., Stehlé, D.: Fully secure functional encryption for inner products, from standard assumptions. In: Robshaw, M., Katz, J. (eds.) CRYPTO 2016. LNCS, vol. 9816, pp. 333–362. Springer, Heidelberg (2016). https://doi.org/10.1007/978-3-662-53015-3_12
6. Ananth, P., Sahai, A.: Projective arithmetic functional encryption and indistinguishability obfuscation from degree-5 multilinear maps. In: Coron, J.-S., Nielsen, J.B. (eds.) EUROCRYPT 2017, Part I. LNCS, vol. 10210, pp. 152–181. Springer, Cham (2017). https://doi.org/10.1007/978-3-319-56620-7_6
7. Bao, Z., He, D., Wang, H., Luo, M., Peng, C.: A group signature scheme with selective linkability and traceability for blockchain-based data sharing systems in e-health services. IEEE Internet Things J. **10**(23), 21115–21128 (2023). https://doi.org/10.1109/JIOT.2023.3284968
8. Bishop, A., Jain, A., Kowalczyk, L.: Function-hiding inner product encryption. In: Iwata, T., Cheon, J.H. (eds.) ASIACRYPT 2015, Part I. LNCS, vol. 9452, pp. 470–491. Springer, Heidelberg (2015). https://doi.org/10.1007/978-3-662-48797-6_20
9. Boneh, D., Franklin, M.: Identity-based encryption from the weil pairing. In: Kilian, J. (ed.) CRYPTO 2001. LNCS, vol. 2139, pp. 213–229. Springer, Heidelberg (2001). https://doi.org/10.1007/3-540-44647-8_13
10. Boneh, D., Komlo, C.: Threshold signatures with private accountability. In: Dodis, Y., Shrimpton, T. (eds.) CRYPTO 2022. LNCS, vol. 13510, pp. 551–581. Springer, Cham (2022). https://doi.org/10.1007/978-3-031-15985-5_19
11. Boneh, D., Sahai, A., Waters, B.: Functional encryption: definitions and challenges. In: Ishai, Y. (ed.) TCC 2011. LNCS, vol. 6597, pp. 253–273. Springer, Heidelberg (2011). https://doi.org/10.1007/978-3-642-19571-6_16

12. Boneh, D., Sahai, A., Waters, B.: Functional encryption: a new vision for public-key cryptography. Commun. ACM **55**(11), 56–64 (2012). https://doi.org/10.1145/2366316.2366333

13. Bünz, B., Bootle, J., Boneh, D., Poelstra, A., Wuille, P., Maxwell, G.: Bulletproofs: short proofs for confidential transactions and more. In: 2018 IEEE Symposium on Security and Privacy (SP), pp. 315–334 (2018). https://doi.org/10.1109/SP.2018.00020

14. Chatterjee, S., Menezes, A.: On cryptographic protocols employing asymmetric pairings - the role of Ψ revisited. Discret. Appl. Math. **159**(13), 1311–1322 (2011)

15. Chotard, J., Dufour Sans, E., Gay, R., Phan, D.H., Pointcheval, D.: Decentralized multi-client functional encryption for inner product. In: Peyrin, T., Galbraith, S. (eds.) ASIACRYPT 2018. LNCS, vol. 11273, pp. 703–732. Springer, Cham (2018). https://doi.org/10.1007/978-3-030-03329-3_24

16. Dupont, P., Pointcheval, D.: Functional encryption with oblivious helper. In: Proceedings of the 2017 ACM on Asia Conference on Computer and Communications Security, AsiaCCS 2017, Abu Dhabi, United Arab Emirates, 2–6 April 2017, pp. 205–214. ACM (2017). https://doi.org/10.1145/3052973.3052996

17. Galbraith, S.D., Paterson, K.G., Smart, N.P.: Pairings for cryptographers. Discret. Appl. Math. **156**(16), 3113–3121 (2008)

18. Garg, S., Gentry, C., Halevi, S., Raykova, M., Sahai, A., Waters, B.: Candidate indistinguishability obfuscation and functional encryption for all circuits. In: 54th Annual IEEE Symposium on Foundations of Computer Science, FOCS 2013, 26–29 October 2013, Berkeley, CA, USA, pp. 40–49. IEEE Computer Society (2013). https://doi.org/10.1109/FOCS.2013.13

19. Gennaro, R., Jarecki, S., Krawczyk, H., Rabin, T.: Robust threshold DSS signatures. Inf. Comput. **164**(1), 54–84 (2001)

20. Goldwasser, S., Gordon, S.D., Goyal, V., Jain, A., Katz, J., Liu, F.-H., Sahai, A., Shi, E., Zhou, H.-S.: Multi-input functional encryption. In: Nguyen, P.Q., Oswald, E. (eds.) EUROCRYPT 2014. LNCS, vol. 8441, pp. 578–602. Springer, Heidelberg (2014). https://doi.org/10.1007/978-3-642-55220-5_32

21. Goldwasser, S., Kalai, Y.T., Popa, R.A., Vaikuntanathan, V., Zeldovich, N.: Reusable garbled circuits and succinct functional encryption. In: Symposium on Theory of Computing Conference, STOC 2013, Palo Alto, CA, USA, 1–4 June 2013, pp. 555–564. ACM (2013). https://doi.org/10.1145/2488608.2488678

22. Goldwasser, S., Micali, S., Yao, A.C.: Strong signature schemes. In: Proceedings of the 15th Annual ACM Symposium on Theory of Computing, 25–27 April, 1983, Boston, Massachusetts, USA, pp. 431–439. ACM (1983). https://doi.org/10.1145/800061.808774

23. Han, J., Chen, L., Susilo, W., Chen, L., Wu, G.: DFE-IP: delegatable functional encryption for inner product. Inf. Sci. **647**, 119425 (2023)

24. Hofheinz, D., Jager, T.: Tightly secure signatures and public-key encryption. In: Safavi-Naini, R., Canetti, R. (eds.) CRYPTO 2012. LNCS, vol. 7417, pp. 590–607. Springer, Heidelberg (2012). https://doi.org/10.1007/978-3-642-32009-5_35

25. Lewko, A., Meiklejohn, S.: A profitable sub-prime loan: obtaining the advantages of composite order in prime-order bilinear groups. In: Katz, J. (ed.) PKC 2015. LNCS, vol. 9020, pp. 377–398. Springer, Heidelberg (2015). https://doi.org/10.1007/978-3-662-46447-2_17

26. Li, Z., Zhao, B., Guo, H., Zhai, F., Li, L.: Multi-party audit and regulatory mechanism for P2P electricity transaction based on distributed traceable linkable group signature. IEEE Access **11**, 128410–128420 (2023). https://doi.org/10.1109/ACCESS.2023.3333032

27. Ligier., D., Carpov., S., Fontaine., C., Sirdey., R.: Privacy preserving data classification using inner-product functional encryption. In: Proceedings of the 3rd International Conference on Information Systems Security and Privacy - ICISSP, pp. 423–430. INSTICC, SciTePress (2017). https://doi.org/10.5220/0006206704230430

28. Mera, J.M.B., Karmakar, A., Marc, T., Soleimanian, A.: Efficient lattice-based inner-product functional encryption. In: Hanaoka, G., Shikata, J., Watanabe, Y. (eds) PKC 2022. LNCS, vol. 13178, pp. 163–193. Springer, Cham (2022). https://doi.org/10.1007/978-3-030-97131-1_6

29. Micali, S., Ohta, K., Reyzin, L.: Accountable-subgroup multisignatures: extended abstract. In: CCS 2001, Proceedings of the 8th ACM Conference on Computer and Communications Security, Philadelphia, Pennsylvania, USA, 6–8 November 2001, pp. 245–254. ACM (2001). https://doi.org/10.1145/501983.502017

30. Rothblum, R.D.: On the circular security of bit-encryption. In: Sahai, A. (ed.) TCC 2013. LNCS, vol. 7785, pp. 579–598. Springer, Heidelberg (2013). https://doi.org/10.1007/978-3-642-36594-2_32

31. Shi, E., Chan, T.H., Rieffel, E.G., Chow, R., Song, D.: Privacy-preserving aggregation of time-series data. In: Proceedings of the Network and Distributed System Security Symposium, NDSS 2011, San Diego, California, USA, 6th–9th February 2011. The Internet Society (2011). https://www.ndss-symposium.org/ndss2011/privacy-preserving-aggregation-of-time-series-data

32. Stinson, D.R., Strobl, R.: Provably secure distributed Schnorr signatures and a (t, n) threshold scheme for implicit certificates. In: Varadharajan, V., Mu, Y. (eds.) ACISP 2001. LNCS, vol. 2119, pp. 417–434. Springer, Heidelberg (2001). https://doi.org/10.1007/3-540-47719-5_33

33. Wee, H.: Functional encryption and its impact on cryptography. In: Abdalla, M., De Prisco, R. (eds.) SCN 2014. LNCS, vol. 8642, pp. 318–323. Springer, Cham (2014). https://doi.org/10.1007/978-3-319-10879-7_18

34. Zhang, L., Li, H., Li, Y., Yu, Y., Au, M.H., Wang, B.: An efficient linkable group signature for payer tracing in anonymous cryptocurrencies. Futur. Gener. Comput. Syst. **101**, 29–38 (2019)

Ideal Public Key Encryption, Revisited

Yao Cheng[1,2], Xianhui Lu[1,2(✉)], and Ziyi Li[1,2]

[1] Key Laboratory of Cyberspace Security Defense, Institute of Information Engineering, Chinese Academy of Sciences, Beijing 100049, China
{chengyao,luxianhui,liziyi}@iie.ac.cn
[2] School of Cyber Security, University of Chinese Academy of Sciences, Beijing 100049, China

Abstract. To capture all reasonable security properties of public key encryption (PKE), the notion of ideal public key encryption is proposed by Zhandry and Zhang (CRYPTO 20). Informally, an ideal primitive is a minimal structured random function constrained by its definite functionality, that is, it has nothing more than its indispensable functionality. In Zhandry and Zhang's definition, the decryption algorithm returns a rejection symbol for an invalid ciphertext which seems additional to decryption correctness, the indispensable functionality of ideal PKE. So, we propose to replace the property of explicit rejection of invalid ciphertexts with implicit rejection of invalid ciphertexts which seems more compact and suitable to the definition of ideal PKE. We aim to explore the relationship between them by investigating the existence of an efficient transformation between them.

As a first step, we explore the implication from the situation of implicit rejection to that of explicit rejection by providing a transformation from the former to the latter. For the other direction, we provide only an intuitive separation conjecture at this point. Additionally, we discuss the construction of ideal PKE with implicit rejection to demonstrate its feasibility.

Keywords: Ideal Primitives · Public Key Encryption · Indifferentiability

1 Introduction

For a given cryptographic concept, various security models are devised to capture different scenarios, necessitating distinct constructions for different applications. Rarely are multiple security models considered simultaneously for a PKE scheme, until Zhang and Zhandry [9] developed an ideal PKE construction that simultaneously captures any reasonable security property and can be composed to work in any reasonable larger protocol.

The definition of an ideal PKE is proposed in a manner analogous to the definition of ideal hash functions, specifically the random oracle (RO) model [3]. To enhance understanding, we begin with the RO. In the random oracle model,

J. K. Liu et al. (Eds.): ProvSec 2024, LNCS 14903, pp. 148–167, 2025.
https://doi.org/10.1007/978-981-96-0954-3_8

the hash function is a truly random function, accessible through queries to the function. Precisely, an RO is uniformly sampled from the set of all possible functions. A similar approach needs to be defined for an ideal PKE. Due to the fundamental requirement of decryption correctness, the elements of this set are selected from all function tuples that satisfy this condition. An ideal PKE is uniformly sampled from such a set, achieving the maximum possible randomness. Access to the ideal PKE is through a black-box interface, providing information solely about the core functionality without revealing any additional details.

In Zhandry and Zhang's definition of ideal PKE, the decryption algorithm explicitly rejects invalid ciphertexts by returning a rejection symbol $\perp$, for ciphertexts not generated through the encryption algorithm. This property seems to be in addition to the decryption correctness functionality. If we eliminate the explicit rejection property while retaining decryption correctness, we obtain an ideal PKE with implicit rejection, where the decryption algorithm returns a random string for invalid ciphertexts.

PKE schemes with implicit rejection and explicit rejection are both used in practice, each suited to different scenarios. For instance, the finalist of the NIST PQC KEMs adopts implicit rejection, which releases less information to adversaries. Conversely, security notions such as robustness [1] require explicit rejection. Regarding specific security for PKE, such as IND-qCCA security, Ge et al. [6] proved the equivalence of implicit and explicit rejection even in the presence of quantum adversaries. However, from the perspective of ideal security, the relationship between an ideal PKE with explicit rejection and one with implicit rejection has not been explored.

1.1 Our Results

This paper focuses on the relationship between ideal PKE with explicit rejection and ideal PKE with implicit rejection. We demonstrate that ideal PKE with implicit rejection implies ideal PKE with explicit rejection. Conversely, we conjecture that no such implication exists in the opposite direction, and that ideal PKE with implicit rejection is stronger. A formal proof of this conjecture is a topic for future work. Additionally, we provide a construction of ideal PKE with implicit rejection to illustrate its existence.

1.2 Technical Overview

To demonstrate the implication, we build a construction based on one ideal primitive and show that it behaves equivalently to the other ideal primitive. The proof is established within the indifferentiability framework introduced by Maurer et al. [8], which generalizes indistinguishability and ensures that the construction performs as well as the ideal primitive in many settings. The formal definition of indifferentiability can be found in Sect. 2.3.

In the indifferentiability framework, the differentiator interacts with either the real construction or the ideal primitive through both honest and adversarial interfaces. The differentiator can access the internal components of the construction via adversarial interfaces. Indifferentiability means that no probabilistic polynomial-time (PPT) differentiator can determine whether it is interacting with the real construction or the ideal primitive, even with access to the internal components. This implies that the real construction performs indifferentiably from the ideal one, ensuring that the only reasonable attacks are those that use black-box access, without gaining any advantage from exploiting the specific design.

This paper primarily constructs an ideal PKE with explicit rejection based on an ideal PKE with implicit rejection and designs an ideal PKE with implicit rejection. When designing these constructions, besides the underlying ideal primitive, additional components can also be used. The first component we consider is the random oracle (RO), a fundamental ideal primitive to achieve the functionality of deterministic mapping only. Since ideal primitives in public-key cryptography, such as ideal PKE, imply the existence of ROs, it is reasonable to include random oracles as components. Another viable option is to incorporate random permutations, which have been shown to be equivalent to random oracles by Coron et al. [5].

Implication. The key to designing the construction of an ideal PKE with explicit rejection based on an ideal PKE with implicit rejection lies in determining the validity of the ciphertext. Noting that an ideal deterministic PKE (DPKE) inherently implies explicit rejection since the decryption algorithm can determine the validity of a ciphertext by re-encryption, we use ideal DPKE as an intermediate step in our design.

The transformation from an ideal PKE with implicit rejection to an ideal DPKE refers to the Encrypt-with-Hash construction [2], which converts an encryption scheme and a hash function into a deterministic encryption scheme, adapted to take indifferentiability into account. Combining this with the construction from an ideal DPKE to an ideal PKE with explicit rejection provided by Zhandry and Zhang [9], we establish that an ideal PKE with implicit rejection implies an ideal PKE with explicit rejection.

Existence. The construction of ideal non-interactive key exchange (NIKE) and the transformation from ideal NIKE to ideal DPKE to ideal PKE with explicit rejection are outlined by Zhandry and Zhang [9]. Since ideal PKE with implicit rejection does not require determining the validity of ciphertexts, we directly construct an ideal PKE with implicit rejection from an ideal NIKE, without the intermediary step of de-randomization to obtain an ideal DPKE.

To recover the plaintext, unlike Zhang and Zhang's approach of using random permutations ($c_2 = P(pk, m) \oplus k$), we utilize an ideal cipher ($E(k, m, str)$), where k is the shared key generated by NIKE and $str = H(pk, m, r)$, and later use a permutation $P(c_1, c_2)$ where c_1 is generated by NIKE and c_2 is generated by E, for the sake of indifferentiability.

2 Preliminaries

2.1 Notations

Throughout this paper, $\{0,1\}^*$ denotes the set of all finite-length bit strings. For two bit strings, X and Y, $X\|Y$ denotes string concatenation. The length of a string X is denoted by $|X|$. For a finite set S, we denote $s \leftarrow S$ the process of sampling s uniformly from S. If A's running time is polynomial in the parameter, then A is called probabilistic polynomial time (PPT).

2.2 Ideal Primitives

An ideal primitive is defined by a set of function tuples with functionality constraints. The security of the ideal primitive is inherent in the uniform sampling from this set, rather than being defined by cryptographic games. We recall some definitions of ideal primitives.

Definition 1 (Random Oracle [3]). *Let $\mathcal{X}$, $\mathcal{Y}$ be the sets such that $|\mathcal{X}| \geq 2^{\omega(log\lambda)}$, $|\mathcal{Y}| \geq 2^{\omega(log\lambda)}$. We denote $\mathcal{H}[\mathcal{X} \to \mathcal{Y}]$ as the set of all functions that map from $\mathcal{X}$ to $\mathcal{Y}$. We say H is a random oracle if H is randomly sampled from $\mathcal{H}$.*

Definition 2 (Random Permutation [4]). *Let $\mathcal{Z}$ be the sets such that $|\mathcal{Z}| \geq 2^{\omega(log\lambda)}$. We denote $\mathcal{P}[\mathcal{Z} \to \mathcal{Z}]$ as the set of all permutations that map from $\mathcal{Z}$ to $\mathcal{Z}$. We say $P(P^{-1})$ is a random permutation if P is randomly sampled from $\mathcal{P}$ and P^{-1} is its inverse.*

Definition 3 (Ideal Cipher [4]). *Let $\mathcal{K}, \mathcal{Z}$ be the sets such that $|\mathcal{K}| \geq 2^{\omega(log\lambda)}, |\mathcal{Z}| \geq 2^{\omega(log\lambda)}$. We denote $\mathcal{E}[\mathcal{K} \times \mathcal{Z} \to \mathcal{Z}]$ as the set of functions that every $E(k, \cdot), (E \in \mathcal{E}, k \in \mathcal{K})$ is a permutation that map from $\mathcal{Z}$ to $\mathcal{Z}$. We say $E(E^{-1})$ is an ideal cipher if E is randomly sampled from $\mathcal{E}$ and $E^{-1}(k, \cdot)$ is the inverse of $E(k, \cdot)$.*

Definition 4 (Ideal NIKE [9]). *Let $\mathcal{SK}, \mathcal{PK}, \mathcal{K}$ be the sets such that: $|\mathcal{SK}| \geq^{\omega(log\lambda)}, |\mathcal{PK}| \geq^{\omega(log\lambda)}, |\mathcal{K}| \geq^{\omega(log\lambda)}, |\mathcal{SK}| \leq |\mathcal{PK}|, |\mathcal{PK}| \times |\mathcal{SK}| \leq |\mathcal{K}|$. We denote $\mathcal{F}[\mathcal{SK} \to \mathcal{PK}]$ as the set of all injections that map from $\mathcal{SK}$ to $\mathcal{PK}$; $\mathcal{G}[\mathcal{PK} \times \mathcal{SK} \to \mathcal{K}]$ as the set of all injections that map from $\mathcal{PK} \times \mathcal{SK}$ to $\mathcal{K}$; We define $\mathcal{T}$ as the set of all function tuples (Gen, Shk) such that:*

- *$Gen \in \mathcal{F}, Shk \in \mathcal{G}$;*
- *$\forall sk_1, sk_2 \in \mathcal{SK}, Shk(Gen(sk_1), sk_2) = Shk(Gen(sk_2), sk_1)$;*
- *If $Shk(pk_1, sk_1) = Shk(pk_2, sk_2)$, then $(pk_1, sk_1) = (pk_2, sk_2)$ or $pk_1 = Gen(sk_2) \wedge pk_2 = Gen(sk_1)$.*

We say that a NIKE scheme $\Pi_{\mathsf{NIKE}} = (\mathsf{NKG}, \mathsf{NSK})$ associated with secret key space $\mathcal{SK}$, public key space $\mathcal{PK}$, and shared key space $\mathcal{K}$, is an ideal NIKE, denoted as INIKE, if Π_{NIKE} is sampled from $\mathcal{T}$ uniformly.

2.3 Indifferentiability

In the indifferentiability framework [8], the differentiator $\mathcal{D}$ is employed to distinguish between the real-world construction $\mathcal{C}$ and the ideal primitive $\mathcal{I}$ as depicted in Fig. 1. Honest parties access $\mathcal{C}$ or $\mathcal{I}$ via the honest interfaces, precisely, blackbox access the primitive. Adversaries access via the adversarial interfaces to access the inner components.

In the left case, $\mathcal{D}$ has direct access to both the honest (index 1) and adversarial (index 2) interfaces of $\mathcal{C}$. In the right case, the interaction with the adversarial interface of $\mathcal{I}$ is replaced by a simulator $\mathcal{S}$. An indifferentiable construction ensures that no differentiator can discern which entity they are connected to. The formal definition of indifferentiability is stated as follows.

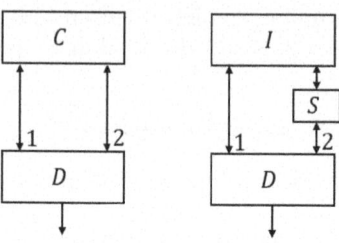

Fig. 1. Indifferentiability.

Definition 5 (Indifferentiability [8]). *Let $\mathcal{Q}$ and $\mathcal{P}$ be two primitives. G is a PPT construction that uses $\mathcal{Q}$ to construct $\mathcal{P}$. $G(\mathcal{Q})$ is strongly indifferentiable from $\mathcal{P}$, if there exists a PPT simulator $\mathcal{S}$ such that for any PPT differentiator $\mathcal{D}$, there exists a negligible function $\mu(\lambda)$*

$$Adv_{G,\mathcal{Q},\mathcal{P},\mathcal{S},\mathcal{D}}(1^\lambda) = |Pr[\mathcal{D}^{G(\mathcal{Q}),\mathcal{Q}} = 1] - Pr[\mathcal{D}^{\mathcal{P},\mathcal{S}^\mathcal{P}} = 1]| \leq \mu(\lambda).$$

Moreover, we say $G(\mathcal{Q})$ is weakly indifferentiable from $\mathcal{P}$, if for any PPT differentiator $\mathcal{D}$, there exists a PPT simulator $\mathcal{S}_\mathcal{D}$ and a negligible function $\mu(\lambda)$

$$Adv_{G,\mathcal{Q},\mathcal{P},\mathcal{S}_\mathcal{D},\mathcal{D}}(1^\lambda) = |Pr[\mathcal{D}^{G(\mathcal{Q}),\mathcal{Q}} = 1] - Pr[\mathcal{D}^{\mathcal{P},\mathcal{S}_\mathcal{D}^\mathcal{P}} = 1]| \leq \mu(\lambda).$$

3 Ideal PKE

Definition 6 (Ideal PKE with Explicit Rejection [9][1]). *Let $\mathcal{SK}$, $\mathcal{PK}$, $\mathcal{M}$, $\mathcal{R}$, $\mathcal{C}$ be the sets such that $|\mathcal{SK}| \geq 2^{\omega(log\lambda)}$, $|\mathcal{PK}| \geq 2^{\omega(log\lambda)}$, $|\mathcal{R}| \geq 2^{\omega(log\lambda)}$, $|\mathcal{C}| \geq 2^{\omega(log\lambda)}$, and $\frac{|\mathcal{C}|}{|\mathcal{M}|\times|\mathcal{R}|} \geq poly$. We denote $\mathcal{G}[\mathcal{SK} \rightarrow \mathcal{PK}]$ as the set of all functions that map from $\mathcal{SK}$ to $\mathcal{PK}$, $\mathcal{E}[\mathcal{PK} \times \mathcal{M} \times \mathcal{R} \rightarrow \mathcal{C}]$ as the set of all functions that map from $\mathcal{PK} \times \mathcal{M} \times \mathcal{R}$ to $\mathcal{C}$, and $\mathcal{D}[\mathcal{SK} \times \mathcal{C} \rightarrow \mathcal{M} \cup \perp]$ as the set of all functions that map from $\mathcal{SK} \times \mathcal{C}$ to $\mathcal{M} \cup \perp$. We define $\mathcal{T}$ as the set of all function tuples (Gen, Enc, Dec) such that:*

– $Gen \in \mathcal{G}$, $Enc \in \mathcal{E}$, $Dec \in \mathcal{D}$;
– $\forall sk \in \mathcal{SK}, m \in \mathcal{M}, r \in \mathcal{R}, Dec(sk, Enc(Gen(sk), m, r)) = m;$

---

[1] We have replaced the original requirement of injections with functions and relaxed the requirement for set size. In the modified definition, the valid ciphertext remains sparse, and a random sample results in an invalid ciphertext. The definitions before and after the modification are indistinguishable.

– $\forall sk \in \mathcal{SK}, c \in \mathcal{C}$, if there is no $(m, r) \in \mathcal{M} \times \mathcal{R}$ such that $Enc(Gen(sk),$ $m, r) = c$, then $Dec(sk, c) = \bot$.

We say that a PKE scheme $\Pi_{\mathsf{PKE}}=(\mathsf{Gen}, \mathsf{Enc}, \mathsf{Dec})$ associated with secret key space $\mathcal{SK}$, public key space $\mathcal{PK}$, message space $\mathcal{M}$, nonce space $\mathcal{R}$, and ciphertext space $\mathcal{C}$, is an ideal PKE with explicit rejection, denoted as $\mathsf{IPKE}^{\perp}$, if Π_{PKE} is sampled from $\mathcal{T}$ uniformly. Moreover, if the nonce space is empty, then we say such a scheme is an ideal DPKE, denoted as IDPKE.

Definition 7 (Ideal PKE with Implicit Rejection). Let $\mathcal{SK}$, $\mathcal{PK}$, $\mathcal{M}$, $\mathcal{R}$, $\mathcal{C}$ be the sets such that $|\mathcal{SK}| \geq 2^{\omega(\log \lambda)}$, $|\mathcal{PK}| \geq 2^{\omega(\log \lambda)}$, $|\mathcal{R}| \geq 2^{\omega(\log \lambda)}$, $|\mathcal{C}|$ $\geq 2^{\omega(\log \lambda)}$, and $\frac{|\mathcal{C}|}{|\mathcal{M}| \times |\mathcal{R}|} \geq poly$. We denote $\mathcal{G}[\mathcal{SK} \to \mathcal{PK}]$ as the set of all functions that map from $\mathcal{SK}$ to $\mathcal{PK}$, $\mathcal{E}[\mathcal{PK} \times \mathcal{M} \times \mathcal{R} \to \mathcal{C}]$ as the set of all functions that map from $\mathcal{PK} \times \mathcal{M} \times \mathcal{R}$ to $\mathcal{C}$, and $\mathcal{D}[\mathcal{SK} \times \mathcal{C} \to \mathcal{M}]$ as the set of all functions that map from $\mathcal{SK} \times \mathcal{C}$ to $\mathcal{M}$. We define $\mathcal{T}$ as the set of all function tuples (Gen, Enc, Dec) such that:

– $Gen \in \mathcal{G}$, $Enc \in \mathcal{E}$, $Dec \in \mathcal{D}$;
– $\forall sk \in \mathcal{SK}, m \in \mathcal{M}, r \in \mathcal{R}, Dec(sk, Enc(Gen(sk), m, r)) = m$.

We say that a PKE scheme $\Pi_{\mathsf{PKE}}=(\mathsf{Gen}, \mathsf{Enc}, \mathsf{Dec})$ associated with secret key space $\mathcal{SK}$, public key space $\mathcal{PK}$, message space $\mathcal{M}$, nonce space $\mathcal{R}$, and ciphertext space $\mathcal{C}$, is an ideal PKE with implicit rejection, denoted as $\mathsf{IPKE}^{\not\perp}$, if Π_{PKE} is sampled from $\mathcal{T}$ uniformly.

3.1 Intuition of Separation

The separation implies that no construction based on ideal PKE with explicit rejection can be indifferentiable from an ideal PKE with implicit rejection. In this context, the differentiator is computationally unbounded and capable of polynomial queries. This stems from the fact that computational assumptions with random oracles (ROs) lead to computationally indifferentiable ideal PKE with implicit rejection directly, without needing to utilize ideal PKE with explicit rejection.

Next, we explain why we believe that an ideal PKE with explicit rejection cannot construct an ideal PKE with implicit rejection. It has been noted in [7] that an ideal PKE with implicit rejection cannot be constructed solely based on random oracles (ROs). Therefore, the decryption structure must be established based on ideal PKE with explicit rejection, which leads to a correlation regarding the validity of ciphertexts between ideal PKE with implicit rejection and explicit rejection. This correlation raises the issue that ideal PKE with explicit rejection leaks information about the validity of ciphertexts through adversarial interfaces, more so than through honest interfaces.

The intuition behind this analysis scrutinizes constructions in various scenarios, and the challenge in providing a formal proof lies in extracting commonalities across all constructions utilizing components of ideal PKE with explicit rejection and ROs. The formal proof of this separation will be the focus of our future work.

4   Implication

Construction[IPKE$^{\not\perp}$ $\Rightarrow$ IDPKE]. Let $\mathsf{PKE} = (\mathsf{Gen}^{\not\perp}, \mathsf{Enc}^{\not\perp}, \mathsf{Dec}^{\not\perp})$ be an implicit rejected PKE scheme with nonce space $\mathcal{R}$, $H_0 : \{0,1\}^* \to \mathcal{R}$ be a random oracle, the algorithms of the DPKE scheme $\mathsf{DPKE} = T_{\mathsf{IPKE}^{\not\perp} \Rightarrow \mathsf{IDPKE}}[\mathsf{PKE}, H_0] = (\mathsf{Gen}_0, \mathsf{Enc}_0, \mathsf{Dec}_0)$ are defined as:

- $pk := \mathsf{Gen}_0(sk) = \mathsf{Gen}^{\not\perp}(sk)$;
- $c := \mathsf{Enc}_0(pk, m) = \mathsf{Enc}^{\not\perp}(pk, m, H_0(pk, m))$;
- $\mathsf{Dec}_0(sk, c)$: On inputs secret key sk and ciphertext c, the algorithm runs $m' = \mathsf{Dec}^{\not\perp}(sk, c)$ and $pk = \mathsf{Gen}^{\not\perp}(sk)$. If $\mathsf{Enc}^{\not\perp}(pk, m', H_0(pk, m')) = c$, then the algorithm outputs m', else it aborts.

Construction[IDPKE $\Rightarrow$ IPKE$^\perp$][9, B.3]. Let $\mathsf{DPKE} = (\mathsf{Gen}_0, \mathsf{Enc}_0, \mathsf{Dec}_0)$ be a DPKE scheme, $H_1 : \{0,1\}^* \to \mathcal{R}$ be a random oracle, the algorithms of the PKE scheme $\mathsf{PKE} = T_{\mathsf{IDPKE} \Rightarrow \mathsf{IPKE}^\perp}[\mathsf{DPKE}, H_1] = (\mathsf{Gen}^\perp, \mathsf{Enc}^\perp, \mathsf{Dec}^\perp)$ are defined as:

- $pk := \mathsf{Gen}^\perp(sk) = \mathsf{Gen}_0(sk)$;
- $c := \mathsf{Enc}^\perp(pk, m, r) = \mathsf{Enc}_0(pk, m\|H_1(pk, m, r)\|0^{|\mathcal{N}|})$;
- $\mathsf{Dec}^\perp(sk, c)$: On inputs secret key sk and ciphertext c, the algorithm runs $m'\|str = \mathsf{Dec}^{\not\perp}(sk, c)$. If $m' \neq \perp$ and the last $|\mathcal{N}|$ bits are $0^{|\mathcal{N}|}$, then the algorithm outputs m', else it aborts.

Lemma 1 (IPKE$^{\not\perp}$ $\Rightarrow$ IDPKE). *Let* $\mathsf{PKE} = (\mathsf{Gen}^{\not\perp}, \mathsf{Enc}^{\not\perp}, \mathsf{Dec}^{\not\perp})$ *be an* IPKE$^{\not\perp}$ *scheme. Then* $\mathsf{DPKE} = T_{\mathsf{IPKE}^{\not\perp} \Rightarrow \mathsf{IDPKE}}[\mathsf{PKE}, H_0] = (\mathsf{Gen}_0, \mathsf{Enc}_0, \mathsf{Dec}_0)$ *is indifferentiable from an* IDPKE *scheme.*

Proof (sketch). To prove indifferentiability, we need to build an efficient simulator $\mathcal{S}$ to respond to the adversarial interfaces. Precisely, it responds just by keeping several tables and calling the honest interfaces. In this case, the adversary has three honest interfaces $\mathsf{Gen}_0, \mathsf{Enc}_0, \mathsf{Dec}_0$ and four adversarial interfaces $H_0, \mathsf{Gen}^{\not\perp}, \mathsf{Enc}^{\not\perp}, \mathsf{Dec}^{\not\perp}$.

The simulator records queries in the form of tables. If an item already exists in the table, the simulator consistently responds with the corresponding entry. For a new query (i.e., one not present in the table), the simulator responds according to specific rules, which are outlined here, and adds this new item into the table. Full details of the proof can be found in Appendix A in the full version.

- For $\mathsf{Gen}^{\not\perp}$ query with sk, the simulator calls the interface Gen_0 and responds with its return value.
- For a new H_0 query with pk, m, the simulator responds with a random value.
- For a new $\mathsf{Enc}^{\not\perp}$ query with pk, m, r, the simulator searches items with pk, m, r in the H_0 table. If there exists such an item, simulator responds with $c = \mathsf{Enc}_0(pk, m)$, and responds with a random value otherwise.
- For a new $\mathsf{Dec}^{\not\perp}$ query with sk, c, the simulator searches items with sk, c in the $\mathsf{Enc}^{\not\perp}$ table to gets the corresponding m. Otherwise it calls the interface Dec_0, responds with m if it returns m and responds with a random message otherwise.

Lemma 2 (IDPKE $\Rightarrow$ IPKE$^\perp$ [9]). *Let* DPKE $= (\mathsf{Gen}_0, \mathsf{Enc}_0, \mathsf{Dec}_0)$ *be an* IDPKE *scheme. Then* PKE $= T_{\mathsf{IDPKE}\Rightarrow\mathsf{IPKE}^\perp}[\mathsf{DPKE}, H_1] = (\mathsf{Gen}^\perp, \mathsf{Enc}^\perp, \mathsf{Dec}^\perp)$ *is indifferentiable from an* IPKE$^\perp$ *scheme.*

Theorem 1 (IPKE$^{\not\perp}$ $\Rightarrow$ IPKE$^\perp$). *Let* PKE$_0 = (\mathsf{Gen}^{\not\perp}, \mathsf{Enc}^{\not\perp}, \mathsf{Dec}^{\not\perp})$ *be an* IPKE$^{\not\perp}$ *scheme. Then* PKE$_1 = T_{\mathsf{IDPKE}\Rightarrow\mathsf{IPKE}^\perp}[T_{\mathsf{IPKE}^{\not\perp}\Rightarrow\mathsf{IDPKE}}[\mathsf{PKE}, H_0], H_1] = (\mathsf{Gen}^\perp, \mathsf{Enc}^\perp, \mathsf{Dec}^\perp)$ *is indifferentiable from an* IPKE$^\perp$ *scheme.*

5 Existence

Construction[INIKE $\Rightarrow$ IPKE$^{\not\perp}$]. Let NIKE $= (\mathsf{NKG}, \mathsf{NSK})$ be an NIKE scheme with secret key space $\mathcal{SK}$ and shared key space $\mathcal{K}$, $H_0 : \{0,1\}^* \to \mathcal{SK}$, $H_1 : \{0,1\}^* \to \mathcal{SK}$, $H_2 : \{0,1\}^* \to \mathcal{R}$ be random oracles, $P : \mathcal{C} \to \mathcal{C}$ is a random permutation, and $E : \mathcal{K} \times \mathcal{M} \times \mathcal{R} \to \mathcal{M} \times \mathcal{R}$ is an ideal cipher. The algorithms of the PKE scheme PKE$^{\not\perp} = T_{\mathsf{INIKE}\Rightarrow\mathsf{IPKE}^{\not\perp}}[\mathsf{NIKE}, H_0, H_1, H_2, E, P] = (\mathsf{Gen}^{\not\perp}, \mathsf{Enc}^{\not\perp}, \mathsf{Dec}^{\not\perp})$ are defined as:

- $pk := \mathsf{Gen}^{\not\perp}(sk) = \mathsf{NKG}(H_0(sk))$;
- $c := \mathsf{Enc}^{\not\perp}(pk, m, r) = P(\mathsf{NKG}(H_1(pk, m, r)), E(k, m, H_2(pk, m, r)))$, where $k = \mathsf{NSK}(pk, H_1(pk, m, r))$;
- $\mathsf{Dec}^{\not\perp}(sk, c)$: On inputs secret key sk and ciphertext c, the algorithm computes $(c_1, c_2) = P^{-1}(c)$, $k = \mathsf{NSK}(c_1, H_0(sk))$, $m' \| str = E^{-1}(k, c_2)$. Then the algorithm outputs m'.

Theorem 2 (INIKE $\Rightarrow$ IPKE$^{\not\perp}$). *Let* NIKE $= (\mathsf{NKG}, \mathsf{NSK})$ *be an* INIKE *scheme. Then* PKE$^{\not\perp} = T_{\mathsf{INIKE}\Rightarrow\mathsf{IPKE}^{\not\perp}}[\mathsf{NIKE}, H_0, H_1, H_2, E, P] = (\mathsf{Gen}^{\not\perp}, \mathsf{Enc}^{\not\perp}, \mathsf{Dec}^{\not\perp})$ *is indifferentiable from an* IPKE$^{\not\perp}$ *scheme.*

To prove indifferentiability, we need to build an efficient simulator $\mathcal{S}$ to respond to the adversarial interfaces $(H_0, H_1, H_2, E, E^{-1}, P, P^{-1}, \mathsf{NKG}, \mathsf{NSK})$. Precisely, it responds just by keeping several tables and calling the honest interfaces $(\mathsf{Gen}^{\not\perp}, \mathsf{Enc}^{\not\perp}, \mathsf{Dec}^{\not\perp})$. Full details of the proof can be found in Appendix B in the full version.

The simulator keeps tables to record queries and updates tables when responding a new query. The necessity and simulation method of H_0, H_1, NKG and NSK are implied in the proof of Theorem 7 in [9, F], so we will not elaborate on them here. H_2 is used to hide the information r, so that the decryption algorithm cannot recovery it. E is used to recovery the message m. Here we emphasize the role of P in the construction. Without P, i.e., if $c := \mathsf{Enc}^{\not\perp}(pk, m, r) = \mathsf{NKG}(H_1(pk, m, r)), E(k, m, H_2(pk, m, r))$, where $k = \mathsf{NSK}(pk, H_1(pk, m, r))$, the simulator cannot simulate E correctly. Specifically, if the adversary gets $pk = \mathsf{Gen}^{\not\perp}(sk)$ via the honest interface, $H_1(pk, m, r), c_1 = \mathsf{NKG}(H_1(pk, m, r)), k = \mathsf{NSK}(c_1, H_0(sk))$ via the adversarial interface, then if the adversary queries $E(k, m', str)$ where $m' \neq m$, the simulator can not respond with the correct c_2 to satisfy $\mathsf{Dec}^{\not\perp}(sk, c_1, c_2) = m'$ in the ideal world, while the real construction always meets this relationship. With the addition of the random permutation, the simulator can respond more flexibly. To address the issue just mentioned, the simulator can reply with a random c_2, then compute a valid ciphertext c encrypted from m' and program $P(c_1, c_2)$ to be c. Thus the adversary will get $\mathsf{Dec}^{\not\perp}(sk, P(c_1, c_2)) = m'$. Another reason why this method works is that the adversary cannot distinguish between valid and invalid ciphertexts.

A   Proof of Lemma 1

Lemma 1 ($\mathsf{IPKE}^{\not\perp} \Rightarrow \mathsf{IDPKE}$). *Let* $\mathsf{PKE} = (\mathsf{Gen}^{\not\perp}, \mathsf{Enc}^{\not\perp}, \mathsf{Dec}^{\not\perp})$ *be an* $\mathsf{IPKE}^{\not\perp}$ *scheme. Then* $\mathsf{DPKE} = T_{\mathsf{IPKE}^{\not\perp} \Rightarrow \mathsf{IDPKE}}[\mathsf{PKE}, H_0] = (\mathsf{Gen}_0, \mathsf{Enc}_0, \mathsf{Dec}_0)$ *is indifferentiable from an* IDPKE *scheme.*

Proof. According to the definition of indifferentiability, the adversary has access to three honest interfaces $(\mathsf{Gen}_0, \mathsf{Enc}_0, \mathsf{Dec}_0)$ and four adversarial interfaces $(H_0, \mathsf{Gen}^{\not\perp}, \mathsf{Enc}^{\not\perp}, \mathsf{Dec}^{\not\perp})$. Therefore, we need to build an efficient simulator $\mathcal{S}$ to properly simulate the behavior of these four adversarial interfaces. This ensures that for any PPT differentiator $\mathcal{D}$, the view of $\mathcal{D}$ in the real game is statistically close to the view in the ideal game. To achieve this, we proceed with a sequence of hybrid games, where each game introduces a system that responds to all queries (both honest and adversarial) in a slightly different manner. We construct our simulator $\mathcal{S}$ as the system in the last game of this sequence.

Game G_0: This game is identical to the real game except that the system maintains three tables to record queries via adversarial interfaces, referring to H_0-table, $\mathsf{Enc}^{\not\perp}$-table, and $\mathsf{Dec}^{\not\perp}$-table. The system responds to the queries the same as in the real world and maintains three tables as follows:

- H_0-table: Initially empty, consists of tuples with form of (pk, m, r). If the adversary queries H_0 with (pk, m), which does not exist in H_0-table (no tuple that the first two elements of it is (pk, m)), inserts $(pk, m, H_0(pk, m))$ into H_0-table.
- $\mathsf{Enc}^{\not\perp}$-table: Initially empty, consists of tuples with form of (pk, m, r, c). If the adversary queries $\mathsf{Enc}^{\not\perp}$ with (pk, m, r), which does not exist in $\mathsf{Enc}^{\not\perp}$-table (no tuple that the first three elements of it is (pk, m, r)), inserts $(pk, m, r, \mathsf{Enc}^{\not\perp}(pk, m, r))$ into $\mathsf{Enc}^{\not\perp}$-table.
- $\mathsf{Dec}^{\not\perp}$-table: Initially empty, consists of tuples with form of (sk, c, m). If the adversary queries $\mathsf{Dec}^{\not\perp}$ with (sk, c), which does not exist in $\mathsf{Dec}^{\not\perp}$-table (no tuple that the first two elements of it is (sk, c)), inserts $(sk, c, \mathsf{Dec}^{\not\perp}(sk, c))$ into $\mathsf{Dec}^{\not\perp}$-table.

All queries are responded to by the real oracles, and these tables are used solely to keep track of the adversary's queries to the adversarial interfaces. These tables are completely hidden from the adversary. Hence the view in real game is identical to the one in in G_0.

Notations. For ease of exposition, we use the following notations.

- $Q := (sk; \mathsf{Gen}^{\not\perp})$ denotes query to $\mathsf{Gen}^{\not\perp}$ with sk.
- $Q := (pk, m; H_0)$ denotes query to H_0 with (pk, m). We say $Q \in H_0$ if there is a tuple $T = (T_1, T_2, T_3)$ in H_0-table such that $T_1 = pk, T_2 = m$.

- $Q := (pk, m, r; \mathsf{Enc}^{\cancel{}})$ denotes query to $\mathsf{Enc}^{\cancel{}}$ with (pk, m, r). We say $Q \in \mathsf{Enc}^{\cancel{}}$ if there is a tuple $T = (T_1, T_2, T_3, T_4)$ in $\mathsf{Enc}^{\cancel{}}$-table such that $T_1 = pk, T_2 = m, T_3 = r$.
- $Q := (sk, c; \mathsf{Dec}^{\cancel{}})$ denotes query to $\mathsf{Dec}^{\cancel{}}$ with (sk, c). We say $Q \in \mathsf{Dec}^{\cancel{}}$ if there is a tuple $T = (T_1, T_2, T_3)$ in $\mathsf{Dec}^{\cancel{}}$-table such that $T_1 = sk, T_2 = c$.
- Q_k: the k-th query.

Game G_1: This game is identical to G_0, except the way of maintaining the tables and responding to the queries. The system responds to part queries in an alternative way, which is only using the tables and accessing to the honest interfaces. Specifically,

$\mathsf{Gen}^{\cancel{}}$-Query: Suppose $Q_k = (sk, \mathsf{Gen}^{\cancel{}})$, then the system responds with $\mathsf{Gen}_0(sk)$.

H_0-Query: Suppose $Q_k = (pk, m; H_0)$, then the system responds as follows:

- Case 1. If $Q_k \in H_0$ corresponding to $T = (T_1, T_2, T_3)$ (T is in H_0-table such that $T_1 = pk, T_2 = m$), then the system responds with T_3;
- Case 2. Otherwise, the system responds with $H_0(pk, m)$ and inserts $(pk, m, H_0(pk, m))$ into H_0-table.

$\mathsf{Enc}^{\cancel{}}$-Query: Suppose $Q_k = (pk, m, r; \mathsf{Enc}^{\cancel{}})$, then the system responds as follows:

- Case 1. If $Q_k \in \mathsf{Enc}^{\cancel{}}$ corresponding to $T = (T_1, T_2, T_3, T_4)$ then the system responds with T_4;
- Case 2. If $Q_k \notin \mathsf{Enc}^{\cancel{}}$, but there is a tuple $T = (T_1, T_2, T_3) \in H_0$ such that $T_1 = pk, T_2 = m, T_3 = r$, then the system responds with $\mathsf{Enc}_0(pk, m)$ and inserts $(pk, m, \mathsf{Enc}_0(pk, m))$ into $\mathsf{Enc}^{\cancel{}}$-table;
- Case 3. Otherwise, the system responds with $\mathsf{Enc}^{\cancel{}}(pk, m, r)$ and inserts $(pk, m, r, \mathsf{Enc}^{\cancel{}}(pk, m, r))$ into $\mathsf{Enc}^{\cancel{}}$-table.

$\mathsf{Dec}^{\cancel{}}$-Query: Suppose $Q_k = (sk, c; \mathsf{Dec}^{\cancel{}})$, then the system responds as follows:

- Case 1. If $Q_k \in \mathsf{Dec}^{\cancel{}}$ corresponding to $T = (T_1, T_2, T_3)$, then the system responds with T_3;
- Case 2. If $Q_k \notin \mathsf{Dec}^{\cancel{}}$, but there is a tuple $T = (T_1, T_2, T_3, T_4) \in \mathsf{Enc}^{\cancel{}}$ such that $T_1 = \mathsf{Enc}_0(sk), T_4 = c$, then the system responds with T_2 and inserts (sk, c, T_2) into $\mathsf{Dec}^{\cancel{}}$-table;
- Case 3. Otherwise, the system queries $(sk, c; \mathsf{Dec}_0)$.
  a. if $\mathsf{Dec}_0(sk, c) = m$, then the system responds with m and inserts (sk, c, m) into $\mathsf{Dec}^{\cancel{}}$-table;
  b. if $\mathsf{Dec}_0(sk, c) = \perp$, the system responds with $\mathsf{Dec}^{\cancel{}}(sk, c)$ and inserts $(sk, c, \mathsf{Dec}^{\cancel{}}(sk, c))$ into $\mathsf{Dec}^{\cancel{}}$-table.

The adversary's view in this game is identical to the view in G_0. However, the system can only answer some queries using tables and honest interfaces; for the remaining queries, it must call the real oracles. Therefore, in the subsequent hybrid games, we will demonstrate alternative methods to respond to these queries without invoking the real oracles, while ensuring that the adversary's view does not change significantly.

Game G_2: This game is identical to G_1 except for responding to H_0 queries.

H_0-Query: Suppose $Q_k = (pk, m; H_0)$, then the system responds as follows:

- Case 1. If $Q_k \in H_0$, same as in $\mathbf{G_1}$;
- Case 2. Otherwise, the system samples $r \leftarrow \mathcal{R}$, responds with r and inserts (pk, m, r) into H_0-table.

The only difference occurs in case 2. The response is indistinguishable unless there is a tuple $T = (T_1, T_2, T_3, T_4) \in \mathsf{Enc}^{\not{L}}$ such that $T_1 = pk, T_2 = m, T_4 = \mathsf{Enc}_0(pk, m), T_3 \neq r$, which occurs with negligible probability.

Game $\mathbf{G_3}$: This game is identical to $\mathbf{G_2}$ except for responding to $\mathsf{Enc}^{\not{L}}$ queries. $\mathsf{Enc}^{\not{L}}$-Query: Suppose $Q_k = (pk, m, r; \mathsf{Enc}^{\not{L}})$, then the system responds as follows:

- Case 1. If $Q_k \in \mathsf{Enc}^{\not{L}}$, same as in $\mathbf{G_2}$;
- Case 2. If $Q_k \notin \mathsf{Enc}^{\not{L}}$, but there is a tuple $T = (T_1, T_2, T_3) \in H_0$ such that $T_1 = pk, T_2 = m, T_3 = r$, same as in $\mathbf{G_2}$;
- Case 3. Otherwise, the system samples $c \leftarrow \mathcal{C} \backslash \{\mathsf{Enc}_0(pk, m)\}$, responds with c and inserts (pk, m, r, c) into $\mathsf{Enc}^{\not{L}}$-table.

The only difference occurs in case 3. The response is indistinguishable unless $r = H_0(pk, m)$ but there is no tuple $T = (T_1, T_2, T_3)$ such that $T_1 = pk, T_2 = m$, which occurs with negligible probability.

Game $\mathbf{G_4}$: This game is identical to $\mathbf{G_3}$ except for responding to $\mathsf{Dec}^{\not{L}}$ queries. $\mathsf{Dec}^{\not{L}}$-Query: Suppose $Q_k = (sk, c; \mathsf{Dec}^{\not{L}})$, then the system responds as follows:

- Case 1. If $Q_k \in \mathsf{Dec}^{\not{L}}$, same as in $\mathbf{G_3}$;
- Case 2. If $Q_k \notin \mathsf{Dec}^{\not{L}}$, but there is a tuple $T = (T_1, T_2, T_3, T_4) \in \mathsf{Enc}^{\not{L}}$ such that $T_1 = \mathsf{Enc}_0(sk), T_4 = c$, same as in $\mathbf{G_3}$;
- Case 3. Otherwise, the system queries $(sk, c; \mathsf{Dec}_0)$.
    a. if $\mathsf{Dec}_0(sk, c) = m$, same as in $\mathbf{G_3}$;
    b. if $\mathsf{Dec}_0(sk, c) = \perp$, the system samples $m \leftarrow \mathcal{M}$, responds with m and inserts (sk, c, m) into $\mathsf{Dec}^{\not{L}}$-table.

The only difference occurs in case 3.b. There are two cases: 1) c is an invalid ciphertext for $\mathsf{Enc}^{\not{L}}$. 2) $r \neq H_0(pk, m)$, where $\mathsf{Gen}^{\not{L}}(sk) = pk; \mathsf{Enc}^{\not{L}}(pk, m, r) = c$. In both cases, the system can respond with a random message.

Game $\mathbf{G_5}$: In this game, the queries to the adversarial interfaces are answered using tables maintained by the system, supplemented by queries to honest interfaces. At this stage, we replace the honest interfaces with their ideal versions. The system in this game operates efficiently by maintaining several tables and utilizing the ideal honest interfaces to respond to adversarial queries. Therefore, we can construct a simulator that precisely mimics the behavior of the system in $\mathbf{G_5}$, responding to adversarial queries. The view in $\mathbf{G_5}$ is identical to the ideal world.

B   Proof of Theorem 2

Theorem 2 (INIKE $\Rightarrow$ IPKE$^{\not{L}}$). *Let* $\mathsf{NIKE} = (\mathsf{NKG}, \mathsf{NSK})$ *be an* INIKE *scheme. Then* $\mathsf{PKE}^{\not{L}} = T_{\mathsf{INIKE} \Rightarrow \mathsf{IPKE}^{\not{L}}}[\mathsf{NIKE}, H_0, H_1, H_2, E, P] = (\mathsf{Gen}^{\not{L}}, \mathsf{Enc}^{\not{L}}, \mathsf{Dec}^{\not{L}})$ *is indifferentiable from an* $\mathsf{IPKE}^{\not{L}}$ *scheme.*

Proof. According to the definition of indifferentiability, we immediately observe that the adversary has three honest interfaces $(\text{Gen}^{\swarrow}, \text{Enc}^{\swarrow}, \text{Dec}^{\swarrow})$ and nine adversarial interfaces $(\text{NKG}, \text{NSK}, H_0, H_1, H_2, E, E^{-1}, P, P^{-1})$. Therefore, we need to build an efficient simulator $\mathcal{S}$ to properly simulate the behavior of these four adversarial interfaces. This ensures that for any PPT differentiator $\mathcal{D}$, the view of $\mathcal{D}$ in the real game is statistically close to the view in the ideal game. To achieve this, we proceed with a sequence of hybrid games, where each game introduces a system that responds to all queries (both honest and adversarial) in a slightly different manner. We construct our simulator $\mathcal{S}$ as the system in the last game of this sequence.

Game G_0: This game is identical to the real game except that the system maintains tables to record queries via adversarial interfaces, referring to NKG-table, NSK-table, H_0-table, H_1-table, H_2-table, E-table, E^{-1}-table, P-table, and P^{-1}-table. We first define the following notations for ease of exposition.

- $Q := (sk; H_0)$ denotes query to H_0 with sk. We say $Q \in H_0$ if there is a tuple $T = (T_1, T_2)$ in H_0-table such that $T_1 = sk$.
- $Q := (pk, m, r; H_1)$ denotes query to H_1 with (pk, m, r). We say $Q \in H_1$ if there is a tuple $T = (T_1, T_2, T_3, T_4)$ in H_1-table such that $T_1 = pk, T_2 = m, T_3 = r$.
- $Q := (pk, m, r; H_2)$ denotes query to H_2 with (pk, m, r). We say $Q \in H_2$ if there is a tuple $T = (T_1, T_2, T_3, T_4)$ in H_2-table such that $T_1 = pk, T_2 = m, T_3 = r$.
- $Q := (k, m, str; E)$ denotes query to E with (k, m, str). We say $Q \in E$ if there is a tuple $T = (T_1, T_2, T_3, T_4)$ in E-table such that $T_1 = k, T_2 = m, T_3 = str$.
- $Q := (k, c_2; E^{-1})$ denotes query to E^{-1} with k, c_2. We say $Q \in E^{-1}$ if there is a tuple $T = (T_1, T_2, T_3, T_4)$ in P^{-1}-table such that $T_1 = k, T_4 = c_2$.
- $Q := (c_1, c_2; P)$ denotes query to P with c_1, c_2. We say $Q \in P$ if there is a tuple $T = (T_1, T_2, T_3)$ in P-table such that $T_1 = c_1, T_2 = c_2$.
- $Q := (c; P^{-1})$ denotes query to P^{-1} with c. We say $Q \in P^{-1}$ if there is a tuple $T = (T_1, T_2, T_3)$ in P^{-1}-table such that $T_3 = c$.
- $Q := (SK; \text{NKG})$ denotes query to NKG with SK. We say $Q \in \text{NKG}$ if there is a tuple $T = (T_1, T_2)$ in NKG-table such that $T_1 = SK$.
- $Q := (PK_1, SK_1; \text{NSK})$ denotes query to NSK with PK_1, SK_1. We say $Q \in \text{NSK}$ if there is a tuple $T = (T_1, T_2, T_3)$ in NSK-table such that $T_1 = PK_1, T_2 = SK_1$.
- Q_k: the k-th query.

The system responds to the queries the same as in the real world and maintains tables as follows:

- H_0-table: Initially empty, consists of tuples with form of (sk, SK). If the adversary makes a query $Q = (sk, H_0)$ that $Q \notin H_0$, inserts $(sk, H_0(sk))$ into H_0-table.
- H_1-table: Initially empty, consists of tuples with form of (pk, m, r, SK). If the adversary makes a query $Q = (pk, m, r, H_1)$ that $Q \notin H_1$, inserts $(pk, m, r, H_1(pk, m, r))$ into H_1-table.

- H_2-table: Initially empty, consists of tuples with form of (pk, m, r, str). If the adversary makes a query $Q = (pk, m, r, H_2)$ that $Q \notin H_2$, inserts $(pk, m, r, H_2(pk, m))$ into H_2-table.
- E-table: Initially empty, consists of tuples with form of (k, m, str, c_2). If the adversary makes a query $Q = (k, m, str, E)$ that $Q \notin E$, inserts $(k, m, str, E(k, m, str))$ into E-table.
- E^{-1}-table: Initially empty, consists of tuples with form of (k, m, str, c_2). If the adversary makes a query $Q = (k, c_2, E^{-1})$ that $Q \notin E^{-1}$, inserts $(k, E^{-1}(k, c_2), c_2)$ ($E^{-1}(k, c_2)$ denotes two elements here.) into E^{-1}-table.
- P-table: Initially empty, consists of tuples with form of (c_1, c_2, c). If the adversary makes a query $Q = (c_1, c_2, P)$ that $Q \notin P$, inserts $(c_1, c_2, P(c_1, c_2))$ into P-table.
- P^{-1}-table: Initially empty, consists of tuples with form of (c_1, c_2, c). If the adversary makes a query $Q = (c, P^{-1})$ that $Q \notin P^{-1}$, inserts $(P^{-1}(c), c)$ ($P^{-1}(c)$ denotes two elements here.) into P^{-1}-table.
- NKG-table: Initially empty, consists of tuples with form of (SK, pk). If the adversary makes a query $Q = (SK, \mathsf{NKG})$ that $Q \notin \mathsf{NKG}$, inserts $(SK, \mathsf{NKG}(SK))$ into NKG-table.
- NSK-table: Initially empty, consists of tuples with form of (PK_1, SK_2, k). If the adversary makes a query $Q = (PK_1, SK_2, \mathsf{NSK})$ that $Q \notin \mathsf{NSK}$, inserts $(PK_1, SK_2, \mathsf{NSK}(PK_1, SK_2))$ into NSK-table.

All queries are responded to by the real oracles, and these tables are used only to keep track of the adversary's queries to the adversarial interfaces, remaining completely hidden from the adversary. Hence the view in real game is identical to the one in in $\mathbf{G_0}$.

Game $\mathbf{G_1}$: This game is identical to $\mathbf{G_0}$, except the way of maintaining the tables and responding to the queries. The system responds to part queries in an alternative way, which is only using the tables and accessing to the honest interfaces. Specifically,

H_0-Query: Suppose $Q_k = (sk; H_0)$, then the system responds as follows:

- Case 1. If $Q_k \in H_0$ corresponding to (T_1, T_2), then the system responds with T_2;
- Case 2. Otherwise, the system responds with $H_0(sk)$, inserts $(sk, H_0(sk))$ into H_0-table and inserts $(H_0(sk), \mathsf{Gen}^{\nparallel}(sk))$ into NKG-table.

H_1-Query: Suppose $Q_k = (pk, m, r; H_1)$, then the system responds as follows:

- Case 1. If $Q_k \in H_1$ corresponding to (T_1, T_2, T_3, T_4), then the system responds with T_4;
- Case 2. Otherwise, the system responds with $H_1(pk, m, r)$ and inserts $(pk, m, r, H_1(pk, m, r))$ into H_1-table. Then the system computes $c = \mathsf{Enc}^{\nparallel}(pk, m, r)$ if there is a tuple $(T_1, T_2, T_3) \in P \cup P^{-1}$ such that $T_3 = c$, the system inserts $(H_1(pk, m, r), T_1)$ into NKG-table.

P^{-1}-Query: Suppose $Q_k = (c; P^{-1})$, then the system responds as follows:

- Case 1. If $Q_k \in P \cup P^{-1}$ corresponding to (T_1, T_2, T_3), then the system responds with T_1, T_2;
- Case 2. If $Q_k \notin P \cup P^{-1}$, but there is a tuple $(T_1, T_2, T_3, T_4) \in H_1$ such that $\mathsf{Enc}^{\not\perp}(T_1, T_2, T_3) = c$,
    a. if there is a tuple $(\dot{T}_1, \dot{T}_2) \in \mathsf{NKG}$,
        i. if there are tuples $(T_1', T_2', T_3', T_4') \in H_2, (\hat{T}_1, \hat{T}_2, \hat{T}_3) \in \mathsf{NSK}, (\tilde{T}_1, \tilde{T}_2, \tilde{T}_3, \tilde{T}_4) \in E \cup E^{-1}$ such that $T_1' = T_1 = \hat{T}_1, T_2' = T_2 = \tilde{T}_2, T_3' = T_3, T_4 = \dot{T}_1 = \hat{T}_2, \hat{T}_3 = \tilde{T}_1, \tilde{T}_3 = T_4'$, then the system responds with $\dot{T}_2, \tilde{T}_4$ and inserts $(\dot{T}_2, \tilde{T}_4, c)$ into P^{-1}-table;
        ii. if there are tuples $(T_1', T_2', T_3', T_4') \in H_2, (T_1'', T_2'') \in H_0, (\hat{T}_1, \hat{T}_2, \hat{T}_3) \in \mathsf{NSK}, (\tilde{T}_1, \tilde{T}_2, \tilde{T}_3, \tilde{T}_4) \in E \cup E^{-1}$ such that $\mathsf{Gen}^{\not\perp}(T_1'') = T_1' = T_1, T_2' = T_2 = \tilde{T}_2, T_3' = T_3, T_4 = \dot{T}_1, \dot{T}_2 = \hat{T}_1, T_2'' = \hat{T}_2, \hat{T}_3 = \tilde{T}_1, \tilde{T}_3 = T_4'$, then the system responds with $\dot{T}_2, \tilde{T}_4$ and inserts $(\dot{T}_2, \tilde{T}_4, c)$ into P^{-1}-table;
        iii. otherwise, the system responds with $\dot{T}_2, c_2$ where $c_1, c_2 := P^{-1}(c)$, and inserts $(\dot{T}_2, c_2, c)$ into P^{-1}-table;
    b. else if there are tuples $(T_1', T_2', T_3', T_4') \in H_2, (\hat{T}_1, \hat{T}_2, \hat{T}_3) \in \mathsf{NSK}, (\tilde{T}_1, \tilde{T}_2, \tilde{T}_3, \tilde{T}_4) \in E \cup E^{-1}$ such that $T_1' = T_1 = \hat{T}_1, T_2' = T_2 = \tilde{T}_2, T_3' = T_3, T_4 = \hat{T}_2, \hat{T}_3 = \tilde{T}_1, \tilde{T}_3 = T_4'$, then the system responds with $c_1, \tilde{T}_4$ where $c_1, c_2 = P^{-1}(c)$, inserts $(c_1, \tilde{T}_4, c)$ into P^{-1}-table, and inserts (T_4, c_1) into NKG-table;
    c. otherwise, the system responds with c_1, c_2 where $c_1, c_2 = P^{-1}(c)$, inserts (c_1, c_2, c) into P^{-1}-table, and inserts (T_4, c_1) into NKG-table;
- Case 3. Otherwise, the system responds with $P^{-1}(c)$ and inserts $(P^{-1}(c), c)$ into P^{-1}-table.

NKG-Query: Suppose $Q_k = (SK; \mathsf{NKG})$, then the system responds as follows:

- Case 1. If $Q_k \in \mathsf{NKG}$ corresponding to (T_1, T_2), then the system responds with T_2;
- Case 2. Otherwise, the system responds with $\mathsf{NKG}(SK)$ and inserts $(SK, \mathsf{NKG}(SK))$ into NKG-table.

Remark 1. Replies to H_0 already add an item to the table list of NKG, and replies to P^{-1} and H_1 may add an item to the table list of NKG, thus we need not repeatedly research these tables when replying NKG-Query. In addition, we search the NKG table only for such information in the later queries.

NSK-Query: Suppose $Q_k = (PK_1, SK_2; \mathsf{NSK})$, then the system responds as follows:

- Case 1. If $Q_k \in \mathsf{NSK}$ corresponding to (T_1, T_2, T_3), then the system responds with T_3;
- Case 2. If $Q_k \notin \mathsf{NSK}$, but there are tuples $(T_1, T_2), (T_1', T_2') \in \mathsf{NKG}, (\hat{T}_1, \hat{T}_2, \hat{T}_3) \in \mathsf{NSK}$ such that $T_1 = SK_2, T_2' = PK_1, \hat{T}_1 = T_2, \hat{T}_2 = T_1'$, then the system responds with $\hat{T}_3$ and inserts $(PK_1, SK_2, \hat{T}_3)$ into NSK-table;
- Case 3. Otherwise, the system responds with $\mathsf{NSK}(PK_1, SK_2)$ and inserts $(PK_1, SK_2, \mathsf{NSK}(PK_1, SK_2))$ into NSK-table.

H_2-Query: Suppose $Q_k = (pk, m, r; H_2)$, then the system responds as follows:

- Case 1. If $Q_k \in H_2$ corresponding to (T_1, T_2, T_3, T_4), then the system responds with T_4;
- Case 2. If $Q_k \notin H_2$, but there are tuples $(T_1, T_2, T_3, T_4) \in H_1, (T_1', T_2', T_3', T_4') \in E \cup E^{-1}, (\hat{T}_1, \hat{T}_2, \hat{T}_3) \in$ NSK, $(\tilde{T}_1, \tilde{T}_2, \tilde{T}_3) \in P \cup P^{-1}$ such that $T_1 = \hat{T}_1 = pk, T_2 = T_2' = m, T_3 = r, T_4 = \hat{T}_2, T_1' = \hat{T}_3, T_4' = \tilde{T}_2, \tilde{T}_3 = \mathsf{Enc}^{\not{\mathrel{}}}(pk, m, r)$, the system responds with T_3' and inserts (pk, m, r, T_3') into H_2-table;
- Case 3. If $Q_k \notin H_2$, but there are tuples $(T_1, T_2) \in H_0, (T_1', T_2', T_3', T_4') \in E \cup E^{-1}, (\hat{T}_1, \hat{T}_2, \hat{T}_3) \in$ NSK, $(\tilde{T}_1, \tilde{T}_2, \tilde{T}_3) \in P \cup P^{-1}$ such that $\mathsf{Gen}^{\not{\mathrel{}}}(T_1) = pk, T_2 = \hat{T}_2, T_1' = \hat{T}_3, T_2' = m, T_4' = \tilde{T}_2, \hat{T}_1 = \tilde{T}_1, \tilde{T}_3 = \mathsf{Enc}^{\not{\mathrel{}}}(pk, m, r)$, the system responds with T_3' and inserts (pk, m, r, T_3') into H_2-table;
- Case 4. Otherwise, the system responds with $H_2(pk, m, r)$ and inserts $(pk, m, r, H_2(pk, m, r))$ into H_2-table.

E-Query: Suppose $Q_k = (k, m, str; E)$, then the system responds as follows:

- Case 1. If $Q_k \in E \cup E^{-1}$ corresponding to $T = (T_1, T_2, T_3, T_4)$, then the system responds with T_4;
- Case 2. If $Q_k \notin E \cup E^{-1}$,
    - a. if there is a tuple $(T_1, T_2, T_3, T_4) \in H_2$ such that $T_2 = m, T_4 = str$,
        - i. if there are tuples $(T_1', T_2', T_3', T_4') \in H_1, (\hat{T}_1, \hat{T}_2, \hat{T}_3) \in$ NSK, $(\tilde{T}_1, \tilde{T}_2, \tilde{T}_3) \in P \cup P^{-1}$ such that $T_1' = T_1 = \hat{T}_1, T_2' = T_2, T_3' = T_3, \hat{T}_2 = T_4', \hat{T}_3 = k, \tilde{T}_3 = \mathsf{Enc}^{\not{\mathrel{}}}(T_1, T_2, T_3)$, then the system responds with $\tilde{T}_2$ and inserts $(k, m, str, \tilde{T}_2)$ into E-table;
        - ii. if there are tuples $(T_1', T_2') \in H_0, (\hat{T}_1, \hat{T}_2, \hat{T}_3) \in$ NSK, $(\tilde{T}_1, \tilde{T}_2, \tilde{T}_3) \in P \cup P^{-1}$ such that $\mathsf{Gen}^{\not{\mathrel{}}}(T_1') = T_1, \hat{T}_1 = \tilde{T}_1, \hat{T}_2 = T_2', \hat{T}_3 = k, \tilde{T}_3 = \mathsf{Enc}^{\not{\mathrel{}}}(T_1, T_2, T_3)$, then the system responds with $\tilde{T}_2$ and inserts $(k, m, str, \tilde{T}_2)$ into E-table;
    - b. else if there are tuples $(T_1, T_2, T_3, T_4) \in H_1, (\hat{T}_1, \hat{T}_2, \hat{T}_3) \in$ NSK such that $T_1 = \hat{T}_1, \hat{T}_2 = T_4', \hat{T}_3 = k$, then the system responds with $E(k, m, str)$ and inserts $(k, m, str, E(k, m, str))$ into E-table;
    - c. else if there are tuples $(T_1, T_2) \in H_0, (\hat{T}_1, \hat{T}_2, \hat{T}_3) \in$ NSK such that $T_2 = \hat{T}_1, \hat{T}_3 = k$, then the system responds with $E(k, m, str)$ and inserts $(k, m, str, E(k, m, str))$ into E-table;
    - d. otherwise, the system responds with $E(k, m, str)$ and inserts $(k, m, str, E(k, m, str))$ into E-table.

P-Query: Suppose $Q_k = (c_1, c_2; P)$, then the system responds as follows:

- Case 1. If $Q_k \in P \cup P^{-1}$ corresponding to (T_1, T_2, T_3), then the system responds with T_3;
- Case 2. If $Q_k \notin P \cup P^{-1}$, but there are tuples $(T_1, T_2, T_3, T_4) \in H_2, (T_1', T_2', T_3', T_4') \in H_1, (\hat{T}_1, \hat{T}_2) \in$ NKG, $(\hat{T}_1, \hat{T}_2, \hat{T}_3) \in$ NSK, $(\tilde{T}_1, \tilde{T}_2, \tilde{T}_3, \tilde{T}_4) \in E \cup E^{-1}$ such that $T_1' = T_1 = \hat{T}_1, T_2' = T_2 = \tilde{T}_2, T_3' = T_3, T_4' = \hat{T}_1 = \hat{T}_2, \hat{T}_2 = c_1, \hat{T}_3 = \tilde{T}_1, \tilde{T}_3 = T_4, \tilde{T}_4 = c_2$, then the system responds with $\mathsf{Enc}^{\not{\mathrel{}}}(T_1, T_2, T_3, T_4)$ and inserts $(c_1, c_2, \mathsf{Enc}^{\not{\mathrel{}}}(T_1, T_2, T_3, T_4))$ into P-table;

- Case 3. If $Q_k \notin P \cup P^{-1}$, but there are tuples $(T_1, T_2, T_3, T_4) \in H_2, (T_1', T_2', T_3', T_4') \in H_1, (T_1'', T_2'') \in H_0, (\dot{T}_1, \dot{T}_2) \in \mathsf{NKG}, (\hat{T}_1, \hat{T}_2, \hat{T}_3) \in \mathsf{NSK}, (\tilde{T}_1, \tilde{T}_2, \tilde{T}_3, \tilde{T}_4) \in E \cup E^{-1}$ such that $\mathsf{Gen}^{\not{k}}(T_1'') = T_1' = T_1, T_2' = T_2 = \tilde{T}_2, T_3' = T_3, T_4' = \dot{T}_1, \dot{T}_2 = \hat{T}_1 = c_1, T_2'' = \hat{T}_2, \hat{T}_3 = \tilde{T}_1, \tilde{T}_3 = T_4, \tilde{T}_4 = c_2$, then the system responds with $\mathsf{Enc}^{\not{k}}(T_1, T_2, T_3, T_4)$ and inserts $(c_1, c_2, \mathsf{Enc}^{\not{k}}(T_1, T_2, T_3, T_4))$ into P-table;
- Case 4. Otherwise, the system responds with $P(c_1, c_2)$ and inserts $(c_1, c_2, P(c_1, c_2))$ into P-table.

E^{-1}-Query: Suppose $Q_k = (k, c_2; E^{-1})$, then the system responds as follows:

- Case 1. If $Q_k \in E \cup E^{-1}$ corresponding to (T_1, T_2, T_3, T_4), then the system responds with T_2, T_3;
- Case 2. If $Q_k \notin E \cup E^{-1}$, but there are tuples $T = (T_1, T_2, T_3, T_4) \in H_1, \hat{T} = (\hat{T}_1, \hat{T}_2, \hat{T}_3) \in \mathsf{NSK}, (\tilde{T}_1, \tilde{T}_2, \tilde{T}_3) \in P \cup P^{-1}$ such that $T_1 = \hat{T}_1, T_4 = \hat{T}_2, \hat{T}_3 = k, c_2 = \tilde{T}_2, \tilde{T}_3 = \mathsf{Enc}^{\not{k}}(T_1, T_2, T_3)$,
    - a. if there is a tuple $T' = (T_1', T_2', T_3', T_4') \in H_2$ such that $T_1' = T_1, T_2' = T_2, T_3' = T_3$, the system responds with T_2, T_4' and inserts (k, T_2, T_4', c_2) into E^{-1}-table;
    - b. else, the system responds with T_2, str where $m, str = E^{-1}(k, c_2)$, and inserts (k, T_2, str, c_2) into E^{-1}-table;
- Case 3. If $Q_k \notin E \cup E^{-1}$, but there are tuples $T = (T_1, T_2) \in H_0, \hat{T} = (\hat{T}_1, \hat{T}_2, \hat{T}_3) \in \mathsf{NSK}, (\tilde{T}_1, \tilde{T}_2, \tilde{T}_3) \in P \cup P^{-1}$ such that $T_2 = \hat{T}_2, \hat{T}_1 = \tilde{T}_1, \hat{T}_3 = k, c_2 = \tilde{T}_2$, the system computes $m' = \mathsf{Dec}^{\not{k}}(T_1, \tilde{T}_3)$,
    - a. if there is a tuple $T' = (T_1', T_2', T_3', T_4') \in H_2$ such that $T_1' = \mathsf{Gen}^{\not{k}}(T_1), T_2' = m', \tilde{T}_3 = \mathsf{Enc}^{\not{k}}(T_1', T_2', T_3')$, the system responds with m', T_4' and inserts (k, m', T_4', c_2) into E^{-1}-table;
    - b. else, the system responds with m', str where $m, str = E^{-1}(k, c_2)$, and inserts (k, m', str, c_2) into E^{-1}-table;
- Case 4. Otherwise, the system responds with with m', str where $m', str = E^{-1}(k, c_2)$, and inserts (k, m', str, c_2) into E^{-1}-table.

The adversary's view in this game is identical to that in $\mathbf{G_0}$. However, the system can only respond to some queries using tables and honest interfaces; for the remaining queries, it must invoke the real oracles. Therefore, in the following hybrid games, we will demonstrate alternative methods (not calling the real oracles) to handle the remaining queries, ensuring negligible change to the adversary's view.

Game $\mathbf{G_2}$: This game is identical to $\mathbf{G_1}$ except for responding to H_0 queries in case 2.

- Case 2. Otherwise, the system samples $SK \leftarrow \mathcal{SK}$, responds with SK, inserts (sk, SK) into H_0-table and inserts $(SK, \mathsf{Gen}^{\not{k}}(sk))$ into NKG-table.

In case 2, the adversary knows nothing of the real response. Thus the response can be replied with a random string. The response is indistinguishable unless there already exits a tuple $T = (T_1, T_2) \in \mathsf{NKG}$ such that $T_1 = SK, T_2 \neq \mathsf{Gen}^{\not{k}}(sk)$, which occurs with negligible probability.

Game G_3: This game is identical to G_2 except for responding to H_1 queries in case 2.

- Case 2. Otherwise, the system samples $SK \leftarrow \mathcal{SK}$, responds with SK and inserts (pk, m, r, SK) into H_1-table. Then the system computes $c = \mathsf{Enc}^{\not{\ell}}(pk, m, r)$ if there is a tuple $(T_1, T_2, T_3) \in P \cup P^{-1}$ such that $T_3 = c$, the system inserts (SK, T_1) into NKG-table.

The response is indistinguishable unless there are tuples $T = (T_1, T_2, T_3) \in P \cup P^{-1}$ and $T' = (T_1', T_2') \in$ NKG such that $T_3 = \mathsf{Enc}^{\not{\ell}}(pk, m, r), T_1' = SK, T_2' \neq T_1$, which occurs with negligible probability.

Game G_4: This game is identical to G_3 except for responding to P^{-1} queries in case 2.a.iii, case 2.b, case 2.c and case 3.

- Case 2. If $Q_k \notin P \cup P^{-1}$, but there is a tuple $(T_1, T_2, T_3, T_4) \in H_1$ such that $\mathsf{Enc}^{\not{\ell}}(T_1, T_2, T_3) = c$,
    - a. if there is a tuple $(\dot{T}_1, \dot{T}_2) \in$ NKG,
        - iii. otherwise, the system samples $c_2 \leftarrow \mathcal{C}_2$, responds with $\dot{T}_2, c_2$, and inserts $(\dot{T}_2, c_2, c)$ into P^{-1}-table;
    - b. else if there are tuples $(T_1', T_2', T_3', T_4') \in H_2, (\hat{T}_1, \hat{T}_2, \hat{T}_3) \in$ NSK, $(\tilde{T}_1, \tilde{T}_2, \tilde{T}_3, \tilde{T}_4) \in E \cup E^{-1}$ such that $T_1' = T_1 = \hat{T}_1, T_2' = T_2 = \tilde{T}_2, T_3' = T_3, T_4 = \hat{T}_2, \hat{T}_3 = \tilde{T}_1, \tilde{T}_3 = T_4'$, then the system samples $c_1 \leftarrow \mathcal{C}_1$, responds with $c_1, \tilde{T}_4$, inserts $(c_1, \tilde{T}_4, c)$ into P^{-1}-table, and inserts (T_4, c_1) into NKG-table;
    - c. otherwise, the system samples $c_1, c_2 \leftarrow \mathcal{C}$, responds with c_1, c_2, inserts (c_1, c_2, c) into P^{-1}-table, and inserts (T_4, c_1) into NKG-table;
- Case 3. Otherwise, the system samples $c_1, c_2 \leftarrow \mathcal{C}$, responds with c_1, c_2, and inserts (c_1, c_2, c) into P^{-1}-table.

Cases where the adversary queries P^{-1} with a new c can be divided into two categories. For the first one, c is encrypted from pk, m, r, and the adversary knows sk, pk, m, r. If the adversary gets $H_1(pk, m, r), \mathsf{NKG}(H_1(pk, m, r))$, the adversary can predict $c_1 = \mathsf{NKG}(H_1(pk, m, r))$ (case 2.a). If the adversary further gets $k = \mathsf{NSK}(pk, H_1(pk, m, r))/\mathsf{NSK}(c_1, H_0(sk))$ and $H_2(pk, m, r)$, $Ek, m, H_2(pk, m, r)$, the adversary can predict $c_2 = Ek, m, H_2(pk, m, r)$. If the adversary cannot predict c_1 but gets $H_1(pk, m, r), k = \mathsf{NSK}(pk, H_1(pk, m, r)), H_2(pk, m, r), Ek, m, H_2(pk, m, r)$, the adversary can predict $c_2 = Ek, m, H_2(pk, m, r)$(case 2.b). For the part where the adversary can predict, the system answer it correctly. For the others, the system can answer it randomly. For the second one, the adversary knows nothing about sk, pk, m, r and the system can answer it randomly.

Game G_5: This game is identical to G_4 except for responding to NKG queries in case 2.

- Case 2. Otherwise, the system samples $sk \in \mathcal{SK}$, responds with $\mathsf{Gen}^{\not{\ell}}(sk)$ and inserts $(SK, \mathsf{Gen}^{\not{\ell}}(sk))$ into NKG-table and (sk, SK) into H_0-table.

sk is independent of the adversary's view, so $\mathsf{Gen}^{\not\perp}(sk)$ is well-distributed.
Game $\mathbf{G_6}$: This game is identical to $\mathbf{G_5}$ except for responding to NSK queries in case 3.

- Case 3. Otherwise, the system samples $k \leftarrow \mathcal{K}$, responds with k, and inserts (PK_1, SK_2, k) into NSK-table.

In case 3, the adversary cannot predict $\mathsf{NSK}(PK_1, SK_2)$, which implies that the system can answer it randomly.
Game $\mathbf{G_7}$: This game is identical to $\mathbf{G_6}$ except for responding to H_2 queries in case 4.

- Case 4. Otherwise, the system samples $str \leftarrow \mathcal{R}$, responds with str and inserts (pk, m, r, str) into H_2-table.

In this case, the adversary cannot predict $H_2(pk, m, r)$, which implies the system can answer it randomly.
Game $\mathbf{G_8}$: This game is identical to $\mathbf{G_7}$ except for responding to E queries in case 2.b, case 2.c, and case 2.d.

- Case 2. If $Q_k \notin E \cup E^{-1}$,
    b. else if there are tuples $T = (T_1, T_2, T_3, T_4) \in H_1, \hat{T} = (\hat{T}_1, \hat{T}_2, \hat{T}_3) \in \mathsf{NSK}$ such that $T_1 = \hat{T}_1, \hat{T}_2 = T'_4, \hat{T}_3 = k$, then the system samples $c_2 \leftarrow \mathcal{C}_2, r \leftarrow \mathcal{R}$, responds with c_2 and inserts (k, m, str, c_2) into E-table and (T_1, m, r, str) into H_2-table. If there is a tuple $T' = (T'_1, T'_2) \in \mathsf{NKG}$ such that $T'_1 = T_4$, then the system inserts $(c_1, c_2, \mathsf{Enc}^{\not\perp}(T_1, m, r))$ into P-table, else the system samples $c_1 \leftarrow \mathcal{C}_1$, inserts (T_4, c_1) into NKG-table and $(c_1, c_2, \mathsf{Enc}^{\not\perp}(T_1, m, r))$ into P-table;
    c. else if there are tuples $T = (T_1, T_2) \in H_0, \hat{T} = (\hat{T}_1, \hat{T}_2, \hat{T}_3) \in \mathsf{NSK}$ such that $T_2 = \hat{T}_1, \hat{T}_3 = k$, then the system compute $pk = \mathsf{Gen}^{\not\perp}(T_1)$, samples $c_2 \leftarrow \mathcal{C}_2, r \leftarrow \mathcal{R}$, responds with c_2 and inserts (k, m, str, c_2) into E-table, and $(\hat{T}_1, c_2, \mathsf{Enc}^{\not\perp}(pk, m, r))$ into P-table;
    d. otherwise, the system samples $c_2 \leftarrow \mathcal{C}_2$ responds with c_2 and inserts (k, m, str, c_2) into E-table.

For cases where the adversary makes a new query (k, m, str), if k is not obtained from $\mathsf{NSK}(pk, H_1(pk, m, r))$ or $\mathsf{NSK}(c_1, H_0(pk))$, the system can respond it randomly. Else if the adversary gets str from $H_2(pk, m, r)$, and knows $P(c_1, c_2) = \mathsf{Enc}^{\not\perp}(pk, m, r)$, the system can answer with the correct c. For the other cases, the system can answer it randomly. Noting that the case 2.b and case 2.c are addressed a little differently, this is to deal with consistency for invalid ciphertexts. After such handling, $\mathsf{Dec}^{\not\perp}(sk, P(c_1, c_2)) = m$.
Game $\mathbf{G_9}$: This game is identical to $\mathbf{G_8}$ except for responding to P queries in case 4.

- Case 4. Otherwise, the system responds with $P(c_1, c_2)$ and inserts $(c_1, c_2, P(c_1, c_2))$ into P-table.

Noting that some cases to respond E queries in **Game G_8** may add an item to the table list of P, such cases can be included in case 1 in this game. In case 4, the adversary cannot predict $P(c_1, c_2)$ and it's proper for the system to respond with a random string.

Game G_{10}: This game is identical to G_9 except for responding to E^{-1} queries in case 2.b, case 3.b and case 4.

- Case 2. If $Q_k \notin E \cup E^{-1}$, but there are tuples $T = (T_1, T_2, T_3, T_4) \in H_1, \hat{T} = (\hat{T}_1, \hat{T}_2, \hat{T}_3) \in \mathsf{NSK}, (\tilde{T}_1, \tilde{T}_2, \tilde{T}_3) \in P \cup P^{-1}$ such that $T_1 = \hat{T}_1, T_4 = \hat{T}_2, \hat{T}_3 = k, c_2 = \tilde{T}_2, \tilde{T}_3 = \mathsf{Enc}^{\not{k}}(T_1, T_2, T_3)$,
  - b. else, the system samples $str \leftarrow \mathcal{R}$, responds with T_2, str, and inserts (k, m', str, c_2) into E^{-1}-table;
- Case 3. If $Q_k \notin E \cup E^{-1}$, but there are tuples $T = (T_1, T_2) \in H_0, \hat{T} = (\hat{T}_1, \hat{T}_2, \hat{T}_3) \in \mathsf{NSK}, (\tilde{T}_1, \tilde{T}_2, \tilde{T}_3) \in P \cup P^{-1}$ such that $T_2 = \hat{T}_2, \hat{T}_1 = \tilde{T}_1, \hat{T}_3 = k, c_2 = \tilde{T}_2$, the system computes $m' = \mathsf{Dec}^{\not{k}}(T_1, \tilde{T}_3)$,
  - b. else, the system samples $str \leftarrow \mathcal{R}$, responds with m', str, and inserts (k, m', str, c_2) into E^{-1}-table;
- Case 4. Otherwise, the system samples $m', str \leftarrow \mathcal{M} \times \mathcal{R}$, responds with with m', str, and inserts (k, m', str, c_2) into E^{-1}-table.

In case 2.b and case 3.b, the adversary knows nothing about str, which implies that the system can answer it randomly. In case 4, the adversary cannot predict $E^{-1}(k, z)$ and it's proper for the system to respond with a random string.

Game G_{11}: In this game, queries to adversarial interfaces are answered using tables maintained by the system and by querying honest interfaces. At this stage, we replace the honest interfaces with their ideal versions. The system in this game is efficient; it responds to adversarial interfaces by maintaining several tables and invoking the honest interfaces. Consequently, we can construct a simulator to handle adversarial queries exactly as the system does in G_{11}. The view in G_{11} is identical to the ideal world.

References

1. Abdalla, M., Bellare, M., Neven, G.: Robust encryption. In: Micciancio, D. (ed.) TCC 2010. LNCS, vol. 5978, pp. 480–497. Springer, Heidelberg (2010). https://doi.org/10.1007/978-3-642-11799-2_28
2. Bellare, M., Boldyreva, A., O'Neill, A.: Deterministic and efficiently searchable encryption. In: Menezes, A. (ed.) CRYPTO 2007. LNCS, vol. 4622, pp. 535–552. Springer, Heidelberg (2007). https://doi.org/10.1007/978-3-540-74143-5_30
3. Bellare, M., Rogaway, P.: Random oracles are practical: a paradigm for designing efficient protocols. In: CCS, pp. 62–73. ACM (1993)
4. Black, J.: The ideal-cipher model, revisited: an uninstantiable blockcipher-based hash function. In: Robshaw, M. (ed.) FSE 2006. LNCS, vol. 4047, pp. 328–340. Springer, Heidelberg (2006). https://doi.org/10.1007/11799313_21
5. Coron, J.-S., Patarin, J., Seurin, Y.: The random oracle model and the ideal cipher model are equivalent. In: Wagner, D. (ed.) CRYPTO 2008. LNCS, vol. 5157, pp. 1–20. Springer, Heidelberg (2008). https://doi.org/10.1007/978-3-540-85174-5_1

6. Ge, J., Shan, T., Xue, R.: Tighter qcca-secure key encapsulation mechanism with explicit rejection in the quantum random oracle model. In: CRYPTO (5). Lecture Notes in Computer Science, vol. 14085, pp. 292–324. Springer, Heidelberg (2023). https://doi.org/10.1007/978-3-031-38554-4_10

7. Impagliazzo, R., Rudich, S.: Limits on the provable consequences of one-way permutations. In: Goldwasser, S. (ed.) CRYPTO 1988. LNCS, vol. 403, pp. 8–26. Springer, New York (1990). https://doi.org/10.1007/0-387-34799-2_2

8. Maurer, U., Renner, R., Holenstein, C.: Indifferentiability, impossibility results on reductions, and applications to the random oracle methodology. In: Naor, M. (ed.) TCC 2004. LNCS, vol. 2951, pp. 21–39. Springer, Heidelberg (2004). https://doi.org/10.1007/978-3-540-24638-1_2

9. Zhandry, M., Zhang, C.: Indifferentiability for public key cryptosystems. In: Micciancio, D., Ristenpart, T. (eds.) CRYPTO 2020. LNCS, vol. 12170, pp. 63–93. Springer, Cham (2020). https://doi.org/10.1007/978-3-030-56784-2_3

Simple Construction of PEKS from LWE-Based IBE in the Standard Model

Hirotomo Shinoki[✉], Hisayoshi Sato, and Masayuki Yoshino

Hitachi, Ltd., Chiyoda City, Japan
{hirotomo.shinoki.sw,hisayoshi.sato.th,masayuki.yoshino.aa}@hitachi.com

Abstract. Public key encryption with keyword search (PEKS) enables one to perform search on encrypted data. In 2005, Abdalla et al. proved that PEKS can be generically constructed from anonymous identity-based encryption (IBE) schemes. To the best of our knowledge, all existing lattice-based PEKS schemes have been constructed by this conversion. In this paper, we simplify the generically constructed PEKS schemes when the underlying IBE is the lattice-based scheme proposed by Agrawal et al. (EUROCRYPT 2010) or its variants. Then, we prove that the new construction satisfies the essential properties for PEKS. Our framework includes the most efficient new LWE-based PEKS in the standard model. Moreover, our methodology can be applied to PEKS with advanced functionalities.

Keywords: Public Key Encryption with Keyword Search · PEKS · Searchable Encryption · Lattice · LWE

1 Introduction

Public key encryption with keyword search (PEKS) is a kind of public key cryptosystem which allows keyword search on encrypted data. In PEKS, a data sender encrypts a keyword using the public key. To search for a keyword, a data receiver generates a trapdoor from the keyword using the secret key. Then, by running the test algorithm, anyone can check whether a ciphertext and a trapdoor have been generated from the same keyword.

In 2004, Boneh et al. [8] proposed the first PEKS scheme, which is based on the Bilinear Diffie-Hellman (BDH) assumption. This scheme has the similar structure to the Identity Based Encryption (IBE) scheme by Boneh and Franklin [9]. Also, they showed that PEKS implies IBE and suggested that PEKS is closely related to IBE. Conversely, in 2005, Abdalla et al. [1] proposed a generic conversion from anonymous IBE to PEKS. To the best of our knowledge, all of the existing PEKS schemes are constructed using this conversion. In particular, Boneh et al. PEKS can be constructed by applying it to Boneh-Franklin IBE.

© The Author(s), under exclusive license to Springer Nature Singapore Pte Ltd. 2025
J. K. Liu et al. (Eds.): ProvSec 2024, LNCS 14903, pp. 168–186, 2025.
https://doi.org/10.1007/978-981-96-0954-3_9

Recently, lattice-based encryption schemes have become increasingly attractive for post-quantum cryptography. In 2008, Gentry et al. [13] proposed the first lattice-based anonymous IBE scheme in the random oracle model. Since then, many lattice-based anonymous IBE schemes have been proposed [2,3,6,11,14,22,23,26]. Lattice-based PEKS schemes can be constructed by applying the generic conversion to these schemes. Behnia et al. [7] implemented the lattice-based PEKS which is generically constructed from Agrawal-Boneh-Boyen IBE (ABB-IBE) [3].

1.1 Our Contributions

In this paper, we propose a new lattice-based PEKS framework. This construction is mainly based on the Learning with Errors (LWE) assumption. In preparation, we formulate the IBE framework which we call ABB-class IBE. ABB-class IBE includes Agrawal-Boneh-Boyen IBE and its variant schemes [2,3,6,11,14,22,23,26]. All efficient LWE-based anonymous IBE schemes in the standard model are ABB-class. Then, we propose a new conversion method from ABB-class IBE to PEKS. This construction is more efficient than applying Abdalla et al. conversion to ABB-class IBE schemes. Thus, our PEKS framework includes the most efficient new LWE-based PEKS in the standard model.

We show that our PEKS satisfies essential properties for PEKS: IND-CKA security, correctness, and consistency. Intuitively, IND-CKA security ensures that no information on the keyword is leaked from a ciphertext. Correctness (resp. consistency) means that the test algorithm outputs the correct result when the ciphertext and the trapdoor have been generated from the same keyword (resp. different keywords). Moreover, many lattice-based functional PEKS schemes [19–21,24,25,27] are based on the similar structure to ABB-class IBE. Our methodology can be applied to these functional PEKS schemes.

1.2 Technical Overview

We represent a rough sketch of our simplification method in the representative case. In the existing construction[1], the ciphertext of a keyword w is

$$\{c_{0,i} = u_i^\top s + \mathsf{error}_i\}_{i=1}^\kappa, \quad c_1 = M(w)^\top s + \mathsf{error}$$

where s is a random vector chosen in the encryption algorithm. $u_1, \ldots, u_\kappa$ are random vectors included in the public key, and $M(w)$ is a matrix. The trapdoor corresponding to w' is the set of short vectors $e_1, \ldots, e_\kappa$ such that $M(w')e_i = u_i$ for each i. Then, $|c_{0,i} - e_i^\top c_1|$ is relatively small (e.g. smaller than $q/4$) if $w = w'$, whereas it is almost random if $w \neq w'$. Thus, when $w \neq w'$, the probability that $|c_{0,i} - e_i^\top c_1| < q/4$ for every i is about $2^{-\kappa}$. The keyword search can be performed by checking whether or not $|c_{0,i} - e_i^\top c_1| < q/4$ for every i.

About this construction, we can consider the following question:

---

[1] To be exact, this is a slightly simplified version of the existing scheme constructed by Abdalla et al. conversion.

Are the parameters $u_1, \ldots, u_\kappa$ really effectual in this PEKS scheme?

In this paper, we showed that they are not. Consider using short vectors $e_1, \ldots, e_\kappa$ such that $M(w')e_i = 0$ for each i as the trapdoor. Then, the keyword search can be performed by computing $|e_i^\top c_1|$ for each i. In this way, $\{u_i\}_{i=1}^\kappa$ can be removed from the public key, and $\{c_{0,i}\}_{i=1}^\kappa$ can be removed from the ciphertext.

The main difficulty in this simplification is to guarantee consistency. In the case of the existing construction,

$$|c_{0,1} - e_1^\top c_1|, |c_{0,2} - e_2^\top c_1|, \ldots, |c_{0,\kappa} - e_\kappa^\top c_1|$$

are almost independent and random when $w \neq w'$ since $c_{0,1}, \ldots, c_{0,\kappa}$ are (computationally) random and independent from the other variables. However, in the case of our construction, it is unclear whether

$$|e_1^\top c_1|, |e_2^\top c_1|, \ldots, |e_\kappa^\top c_1|$$

can be regarded as independent since it depends on the way $e_1, \ldots, e_\kappa$ are chosen. Thus, we analyzed the sampling algorithm of $e_1, \ldots, e_\kappa$. By showing that $|e_1^\top c_1|, \ldots, |e_\kappa^\top c_1|$ are close to independent, we proved that our simplified construction satisfies consistency.

2 Preliminaries

We summarize the basic notations used in this paper here.

"Probabilistic polynomial-time" is abbreviated to "PPT". For a finite set S, $x \xleftarrow{\$} S$ means that x is sampled uniformly at random from S, and $\mathrm{Unif}(S)$ denotes the uniform distribution over S. For a vector v, $\|v\|$ denotes its L^2 norm. We use the following notations for matrix concatenation:

$$[A|B] := \begin{pmatrix} A & B \end{pmatrix}, \quad [A;C] := \begin{pmatrix} A \\ C \end{pmatrix}.$$

We say that a function $f : \mathbb{N} \to \mathbb{R}$ is negligible and write $f(n) = \mathsf{negl}(n)$ if for any positive integer k there exists an integer n_k such that $|f(n)| < n^{-k}$ for any $n > n_k$. Let $\mathbb{Z}_q$ denote the quotient ring $\mathbb{Z}/q\mathbb{Z}$. Let $\log x$ denote $\log_2 x$.

2.1 Lattices

Let $b_1, \ldots, b_k \in \mathbb{R}^n$ be linearly independent vectors and $B = [b_1| \cdots |b_k] \in \mathbb{R}^{n \times k}$.

$$\mathcal{L}(B) = \{Bx : x \in \mathbb{Z}^k\}$$

is called the lattice generated by $b_1, \ldots, b_k$. When $n = k$, it is called full-rank. In this paper, we only deal with full-rank lattices. We introduce the basic notations for lattices below.

Definition 1. *Let m, n, q be positive integers. For $A \in \mathbb{Z}_q^{n \times m}$ and $u \in \mathbb{Z}_q^n$, we define the m-dimensional lattices $\Lambda_q(A)$, $\Lambda_q^\perp(A)$, and a discrete set $\Lambda_q^u(A)$ as follows:*

$$\Lambda_q(A) = \{y \in \mathbb{Z}^m : y = A^\top s \bmod q \quad \text{for some } s \in \mathbb{Z}^n\},$$
$$\Lambda_q^\perp(A) = \{e \in \mathbb{Z}^m : Ae = 0 \bmod q\},$$
$$\Lambda_q^u(A) = \{e \in \mathbb{Z}^m : Ae = u \bmod q\}.$$

Note that $\Lambda_q^u(A) = t + \Lambda_q^\perp(A)$ holds for any $t \in \Lambda_q^u(A)$.

Definition 2 (Determinant). *Let $\Lambda = \mathcal{L}(B)$ be a lattice. The determinant of Λ is defined as*
$$\det(\Lambda) = \mathrm{vol}(\{Bx : x \in [0, 1)^k\}).$$

This definition is independent of the choice of B.
    For any rank n matrix $A \in \mathbb{Z}_q^{n \times m}$,

$$\det(\Lambda_q^\perp(A)) = q^n, \quad \det(\Lambda_q(A)) = q^{m-n}.$$

Definition 3 (Dual Lattice). *Let $\Lambda \subset \mathbb{R}^n$ be any full-rank lattice. The dual lattice Λ^* of Λ denotes the lattice defined as $\{x \in \mathbb{R}^n : x^\top v \in \mathbb{Z} \text{ for any } v \in \Lambda\}$.*
    For any matrix $A \in \mathbb{Z}_q^{n \times m}$,

$$\Lambda_q^\perp(A) = q \cdot \Lambda_q(A)^*, \quad \Lambda_q(A) = q \cdot \Lambda_q^\perp(A)^*.$$

2.2   Discrete Gaussian Distribution

For a real parameter $s > 0$ and a center $c \in \mathbb{R}^m$, the Gaussian function on $\mathbb{R}^m$ is defined as
$$\rho_{s,c}(x) = \exp(-\pi \|x - c\|^2 / s^2).$$

For a discrete set $\Lambda \subset \mathbb{R}^m$, we set $\rho_{s,c}(\Lambda) := \sum_{x \in \Lambda} \rho_{s,c}(x)$. The discrete Gaussian distribution on Λ with a parameter s and a center c is defined as

$$\mathcal{D}_{s,c}(\Lambda)(x) = \frac{\rho_{s,c}(x)}{\rho_{s,c}(\Lambda)}$$

for $x \in \Lambda$. We omit the description of c when $c = 0$.
    Micciancio and Regev [16] introduced the notion of the smoothing parameter.

Definition 4 (Smoothing Parameter). *Let Λ be a lattice and $\epsilon > 0$ be a real number. The smoothing parameter $\eta_\epsilon(\Lambda)$ is the smallest $s > 0$ such that $\rho_{1/s}(\Lambda^* \backslash \{0\}) \leq \epsilon$.*

We use the following upper bound for the smoothing parameter.

Lemma 1 ([13,17])**.** *For a lattice Λ, let $\lambda_1^\infty(\Lambda) := \min_{0 \neq x \in \Lambda} \|x\|_\infty$. Then, for any m-dimensional lattice Λ and $\epsilon > 0$,*

$$\eta_\epsilon(\Lambda) \leq \frac{\sqrt{\ln(2\,m(1 + 1/\epsilon))/\pi}}{\lambda_1^\infty(\Lambda^*)}.$$

2.3   Sampling Algorithms on Lattices

We introduce some sampling algorithms on lattices. For each positive integer n, let $q(n) \geq 3$ be an integer and $m'(n)$ be a non-negative integer.

Definition 5 ([5,10,13,15]). *There exist the following PPT algorithms for some $m = \Omega(n \log q)$ and $\sigma = \omega(\sqrt{n \log q \log m})$.*

- *The PPT algorithm* TrapGen$(1^n, 1^m, q)$ *outputs a matrix $A \in \mathbb{Z}_q^{n \times m}$ and a trapdoor T_A such that A is statistically close to uniform.*
- *For an overwhelming fraction of $A \in \mathbb{Z}_q^{n \times m}$ and any $u \in \mathbb{Z}_q^n$, the PPT algorithm* SamplePre(A, T_A, u, σ) *outputs $e \in \mathbb{Z}^m$ from a distribution statistically close to $\mathcal{D}_\sigma(\Lambda_q^u(A))$.*
- *For an overwhelming fraction of $A \in \mathbb{Z}_q^{n \times m}$, any $A' \in \mathbb{Z}_q^{n \times m'}$ and $u \in \mathbb{Z}_q^n$, the PPT algorithm* SampleLeft(A, A', T_A, u, σ) *outputs $e \in \mathbb{Z}^{m+m'}$ from a distribution statistically close to $\mathcal{D}_\sigma(\Lambda_q^u([A|A']))$. The concrete construction is as follows:*
  1. *Samples a vector e_2 from $\mathcal{D}_\sigma(\mathbb{Z}^{m'})$.*
  2. *Runs $e_1 \leftarrow$ SamplePre$(A, T_A, u - A'e_2, \sigma)$.*
  3. *Outputs $e := [e_1; e_2] \in \mathbb{Z}^{m+m'}$.*

2.4   Leftover Hash Lemma

We introduce the Leftover Hash Lemma. This lemma is used in the consistency proof of our scheme.

Definition 6 (Statistical Distance). *For random variables X, Y on a finite set S, the statistical distance $\Delta(X; Y)$ is defined as follows:*

$$\Delta(X; Y) := \frac{1}{2} \sum_{s \in S} \left| \Pr[X = s] - \Pr[Y = s] \right|.$$

Definition 7 (Guessing Probability). *For a random variable X on a finite set S, we define the guessing probability as $\gamma(X) := \max_{s \in S} \Pr[X = s]$.*

Definition 8 (Universal Hash Family). *A hash family $\mathcal{H} = \{h_k : X \to Y\}_k$ is called universal when for any distinct elements $x_1, x_2 \in X$,*

$$\Pr_{h \xleftarrow{\$} \mathcal{H}} [h(x_1) = h(x_2)] = \frac{1}{|Y|}.$$

Lemma 2 (Leftover Hash Lemma [3]). *Let $\mathcal{H} = \{h : X \to Y\}$ be a universal hash family, H be a random variable uniformly distributed over $\mathcal{H}$, and $T_1, \ldots, T_k$ be independent random variables taking values in X. Let γ denote $\max_{i=1,\ldots,k} \gamma(T_i)$. Then the following inequality holds:*

$$\Delta\left((H, H(T_1), \ldots, H(T_k)); \mathrm{Unif}(\mathcal{H} \times Y^k)\right) \leq \frac{k}{2} \sqrt{\gamma \cdot |Y|}.$$

2.5 Learning with Errors (LWE)

The schemes we consider in this paper are mainly based on the learning with errors assumption.

Definition 9 (Learning with Errors Assumption [18]). *For each positive integer n, let $q(n) \geq 3$ be an integer and $\chi(n)$ be an error distribution on $\mathbb{Z}_q$. For $s \in \mathbb{Z}_q^n$, let $\mathcal{O}_s$ be the oracle which samples a $\xleftarrow{\$} \mathbb{Z}_q^n$, $x \leftarrow \chi$ and outputs $(a, a^\top s + x)$. Let $\mathcal{O}_\$$ be the oracle which outputs $(a, b) \xleftarrow{\$} \mathbb{Z}_q^n \times \mathbb{Z}_q$. We say that the Learning with Errors (LWE) assumption holds if for any PPT algorithm $\mathcal{A}$,*

$$\left| \Pr[1 \leftarrow \mathcal{A}^{\mathcal{O}_s}(1^n)] - \Pr[1 \leftarrow \mathcal{A}^{\mathcal{O}_\$}(1^n)] \right|$$

is negligible for a randomly chosen secret $s \xleftarrow{\$} \mathbb{Z}_q^n$.

2.6 Identity-Based Encryption (IBE)

Identity-Based Encryption (IBE) consists of the following four PPT algorithms.

- Setup(1^λ): Given a security parameter λ, it outputs a public parameter pp and a master secret key msk.
- Extract(pp, msk, id): Given a public parameter pp, a master secret key msk, and an identity id, it outputs a secret key $\mathsf{sk}_{\mathsf{id}}$.
- Enc(pp, id, m): Given a public parameter pp, an identity id, and a plaintext m, it outputs a ciphertext C.
- Dec(pp, $\mathsf{sk}_{\mathsf{id}}$, C): Given a public parameter pp, a secret key $\mathsf{sk}_{\mathsf{id}}$, and a ciphertext C, it outputs a plaintext m.

For simplicity, we often omit the description of pp from the input. The IBE scheme is called correct if the minimum value of

$$\Pr[(\mathsf{pp}, \mathsf{msk}) \leftarrow \mathsf{Setup}(1^\lambda); \mathsf{sk}_{\mathsf{id}} \leftarrow \mathsf{Extract}(\mathsf{msk}, \mathsf{id}) : \mathsf{Dec}(\mathsf{sk}_{\mathsf{id}}, \mathsf{Enc}(\mathsf{id}, m)) = m]$$

with respect to id and m is overwhelming (i.e. $1 - \mathsf{negl}(\lambda)$).

We introduce INDr-ID-CPA security [3] for IBE. Intuitively, INDr-ID-CPA security means that a ciphertext is indistinguishable from a random data.

Definition 10 (INDr-ID-CPA Security). *Let $\mathsf{CGen}(\mathsf{pp}, \mathsf{id}, m, b)$ denote the PPT algorithm which outputs $C \leftarrow \mathsf{Enc}(\mathsf{id}, m)$ if $b = 0$ and outputs $C \xleftarrow{\$} \mathcal{C}_\lambda$ if $b = 1$ where $\mathcal{C}_\lambda$ is the ciphertext space. We say that an IBE scheme is INDr-ID-CPA secure if for any PPT adversary $\mathcal{A}$, the advantage*

$$\left| \Pr[(\mathsf{pp}, \mathsf{msk}) \leftarrow \mathsf{Setup}(1^\lambda); (\mathsf{id}^*, m^*, \mathsf{st}) \leftarrow \mathcal{A}^{\mathcal{O}_{\mathsf{ext}}(\mathsf{msk}, \cdot)}(\mathsf{find}, \mathsf{pp}); \right.$$

$$\left. b \xleftarrow{\$} \{0, 1\}; C^* \leftarrow \mathsf{CGen}(\mathsf{pp}, \mathsf{id}^*, m^*, b); b' \leftarrow \mathcal{A}^{\mathcal{O}_{\mathsf{ext}}(\mathsf{msk}, \cdot)}(\mathsf{guess}, \mathsf{st}, C^*) : b = b'] - \frac{1}{2} \right|$$

is negligible in λ. Here, the extract oracle $\mathcal{O}_{\mathsf{ext}}(\mathsf{msk}, \cdot)$ outputs $\mathsf{sk}_{\mathsf{id}} \leftarrow \mathsf{Extract}(\mathsf{msk}, \mathsf{id})$ given an identity id as input. It is required that id^* should not have been input in the find phase and should not be input in the guess phase.

2.7   Public Key Encryption with Keyword Search (PEKS)

Public key Encryption with Keyword Search (PEKS) consists of the following four PPT algorithms.

- KeyGen(1^λ): Given a security parameter λ, it outputs a public key pk and a secret key sk.
- Enc(pk, w): Given a public key pk and a keyword w, it outputs a ciphertext C.
- Trapdoor(sk, w): Given a secret key sk, and a keyword w, it outputs a trapdoor T. We omit the description of pk for simplicity.
- Test(T, C): Given a trapdoor T and a ciphertext C, it outputs a bit $b \in \{0, 1\}$.

The PEKS scheme is said to be correct if Test(T, C) algorithm almost always outputs 1 when T and C have been generated from the same keyword. The PEKS scheme is said to be consistent if Test(T, C) algorithm almost always outputs 0 when T and C have been generated from different keywords. We describe the formal definitions below.

Definition 11 (Correctness). *We say that a PEKS scheme is correct if the minimum value of*

$$\Pr[(\mathsf{pk}, \mathsf{sk}) \leftarrow \mathsf{KeyGen}(1^\lambda); C \leftarrow \mathsf{Enc}(\mathsf{pk}, w); T \leftarrow \mathsf{Trapdoor}(\mathsf{sk}, w) : \mathsf{Test}(T, C) = 1]$$

with respect to w is overwhelming.

Definition 12 (Consistency). *We say that a PEKS scheme is (computationally) consistent if for any PPT algorithm $\mathcal{A}$,*

$$\Pr[(\mathsf{pk}, \mathsf{sk}) \leftarrow \mathsf{KeyGen}(1^\lambda); (w, w') \leftarrow \mathcal{A}(\mathsf{pk}); C \leftarrow \mathsf{Enc}(\mathsf{pk}, w);$$
$$T \leftarrow \mathsf{Trapdoor}(\mathsf{sk}, w') : \mathsf{Test}(T, C) = 0 \vee w = w']$$

is overwhelming.

Additionally, PEKS schemes are required to satisfy Indistinguishability under Chosen Keyword Attack (IND-CKA security).

Definition 13 (IND-CKA Security). *We say that a PEKS scheme is IND-CKA secure if for any PPT adversary $\mathcal{A}$, the advantage*

$$\left| \Pr[(\mathsf{pk}, \mathsf{sk}) \leftarrow \mathsf{KeyGen}(1^\lambda); (w_0^*, w_1^*, \mathsf{st}) \leftarrow \mathcal{A}^{\mathcal{O}_{\mathsf{td}}(\mathsf{sk}, \cdot)}(\mathsf{find}, \mathsf{pk}); \right.$$
$$\left. b \xleftarrow{\$} \{0, 1\}; C^* \leftarrow \mathsf{Enc}(\mathsf{pk}, w_b^*); b' \leftarrow \mathcal{A}^{\mathcal{O}_{\mathsf{td}}(\mathsf{sk}, \cdot)}(\mathsf{guess}, \mathsf{st}, C^*) : b = b'] - \frac{1}{2} \right|$$

is negligible in λ. Here, the trapdoor oracle $\mathcal{O}_{\mathsf{td}}(\mathsf{sk}, \cdot)$ outputs $T \leftarrow$ Trapdoor(sk, w) given a keyword w as input. It is required that either w_0^* or w_1^* should not have been input in the find phase and should not be input in the guess phase.

In this paper, we consider the stronger security notion which we call INDr-CKA security. INDr-CKA security means that a ciphertext is indistinguishable from random. This property is used in the consistency proof of our scheme.

Definition 14 (INDr-CKA Security). *Let* CGen(pk, w, b) *denote the PPT algorithm which outputs* $C \leftarrow$ Enc(pk, w) *if* $b = 0$ *and outputs* $C \xleftarrow{\$} C_\lambda$ *if* $b = 1$ *where* C_λ *is the ciphertext space. We say that a PEKS scheme is INDr-CKA secure if for any PPT adversary* $\mathcal{A}$, *the advantage*

$$\left| \Pr[(\mathsf{pk}, \mathsf{sk}) \leftarrow \mathsf{KeyGen}(1^\lambda); (w^*, \mathsf{st}) \leftarrow \mathcal{A}^{\mathcal{O}_{\mathsf{td}}(\mathsf{sk}, \cdot)}(\mathsf{find}, \mathsf{pk}); \right.$$

$$\left. b \xleftarrow{\$} \{0, 1\}; C^* \leftarrow \mathsf{CGen}(\mathsf{pk}, w^*, b); b' \leftarrow \mathcal{A}^{\mathcal{O}_{\mathsf{td}}(\mathsf{sk}, \cdot)}(\mathsf{guess}, \mathsf{st}, C^*) : b = b'] - \frac{1}{2} \right|$$

is negligible in λ. *Here, the trapdoor oracle* $\mathcal{O}_{\mathsf{td}}(\mathsf{sk}, \cdot)$ *outputs* $T \leftarrow$ Trapdoor(sk, w) *given a keyword* w *as input. It is required that* w^* *should not have been input in the find phase and should not be input in the guess phase.*

2.8 Generic Construction of PEKS

Abdalla et al. [1] proposed a method of converting anonymous IBE to PEKS. Note that INDr-ID-CPA security implies anonymity.

- PEKS.KeyGen(1^λ): It runs (pp, msk) $\leftarrow$ IBE.Setup(1^λ). Then it outputs a public key pk = pp and a secret key sk = msk.
- PEKS.Enc(pk, w): It samples $R \xleftarrow{\$} \{0, 1\}^{\kappa(\lambda)}$ and runs $C \leftarrow$ IBE.Enc(pk, w, R). Then it outputs a ciphertext (C, R). κ is a function such that $2^{-\kappa}$ is negligible (e.g. $\kappa(\lambda) = \lambda$).
- PEKS.Trapdoor(sk, w): It runs $\mathsf{sk}_w \leftarrow$ IBE.Extract(sk, w) and outputs a trapdoor $T = \mathsf{sk}_w$.
- PEKS.Test(T, (C, R)): It runs $R' \leftarrow$ IBE.Dec(T, C). Then it outputs 1 if $R = R'$ and outputs 0 otherwise.

If the original IBE is correct and INDr-ID-CPA secure, the PEKS scheme is correct, consistent, and INDr-CKA secure.

3 Existing Lattice-Based PEKS Schemes

Agrawal et al. [3] proposed a lattice-based IBE scheme in the standard model (ABB-IBE). It is INDr-ID-CPA secure under the LWE assumption. We review the construction of ABB-IBE and its conversion to PEKS.

3.1 Agrawal-Boneh-Boyen IBE

In this section, we review the construction of ABB-IBE [3]. Some research [2,6, 14,22,23,26] has made the public key size of ABB-IBE smaller. The following framework captures both the original ABB-IBE and these variant schemes. We call this framework ABB-class IBE.

The following components depend on the concrete scheme $\mathcal{E}_{\mathsf{ABB}}$: a PPT algorithm $\mathsf{PubGen}_{\mathcal{E}_{\mathsf{ABB}}}$, a function $F_{\mathcal{E}_{\mathsf{ABB}}}$ which outputs an element of $\mathbb{Z}_q^{n \times m'}$, and a distribution $\chi'_{\mathcal{E}_{\mathsf{ABB}}}(n)$ on $\mathbb{Z}_q^{m+m'}$.

- $\mathsf{Setup}(1^n)$:
  1. Sets the parameters m, m', q, σ.
     m, m' are positive integers, q is a prime number, and σ is a positive real number.
  2. Runs $(A, T_A) \leftarrow \mathsf{TrapGen}(1^n, 1^m, q)$.
  3. Samples $u \xleftarrow{\$} \mathbb{Z}_q^n$.
  4. Runs $P \leftarrow \mathsf{PubGen}_{\mathcal{E}_{\mathsf{ABB}}}(1^n, 1^m, 1^{m'}, q)$.
  5. Outputs the public parameter $\mathsf{pp} = (A, P, u)$ and the master secret key $\mathsf{msk} = T_A$.
- $\mathsf{Extract}(\mathsf{msk}, \mathsf{id})$:
  1. Runs $e \leftarrow \mathsf{SampleLeft}(A, F_{\mathcal{E}_{\mathsf{ABB}}}(P, \mathsf{id}), T_A, u, \sigma)$.
  2. Outputs $\mathsf{sk}_{\mathsf{id}} = e \in \mathbb{Z}^{m+m'}$.
- $\mathsf{Enc}(\mathsf{id}, b \in \{0, 1\})$:
  1. Samples $s \xleftarrow{\$} \mathbb{Z}_q^n$.
  2. Samples $x \leftarrow \chi$ and $y \leftarrow \chi'_{\mathcal{E}_{\mathsf{ABB}}}$.
     Computes $c_0 \leftarrow u^\top s + x + b\lfloor q/2 \rfloor$ and $c_1 \leftarrow [A | F_{\mathcal{E}_{\mathsf{ABB}}}(P, \mathsf{id})]^\top s + y$.
  3. Outputs $(c_0, c_1) \in \mathbb{Z}_q \times \mathbb{Z}_q^{m+m'}$.
- $\mathsf{Dec}(\mathsf{sk}_{\mathsf{id}}, C = (c_0, c_1))$:
  1. Computes $t \leftarrow c_0 - \mathsf{sk}_{\mathsf{id}}^\top c_1 \in \mathbb{Z}_q$.
  2. Treats t as an integer in $[-q/2, q/2]$. Outputs 0 if $-\lfloor q/4 \rfloor < t < \lfloor q/4 \rfloor$, otherwise outputs 1.

As an example, we briefly review the construction of the original (adaptively secure) ABB-IBE. In ABB-IBE, m' is equal to m. The identity space is $\{-1, 1\}^l$ where l is a parameter. P consists of $l + 1$ random matrices $A_1, A_2, \ldots, A_l, B \in \mathbb{Z}_q^{n \times m}$, and $F_{\mathcal{E}_{\mathsf{ABB}}}(P, (b_1, \ldots, b_l)) = B + \sum_{i=1}^{l} b_i A_i$. $\chi'_{\mathcal{E}_{\mathsf{ABB}}}$ samples $y' \leftarrow \chi^m$, $R \leftarrow \mathbb{Z}_q^{m \times m}$ and outputs $y = [y'; R^\top y']$ where each element of R is chosen as the sum of l independent coins in $\{-1, 1\}$.

The existing ABB-class IBE schemes have the following property. This is a variant of INDr-ID-CPA security for ABB-class IBE.

Definition 15. *Suppose that the INDr-ID-CPA adversary of ABB-class IBE has access to the following oracle instead of the extract oracle:*

Given an identity id*, it outputs* $e \leftarrow \mathsf{SampleLeft}(A, F_{\mathcal{E}_{\mathsf{ABB}}}(P, \mathsf{id}), T_A, 0, \sigma)$*.*
The challenge identity cannot be input to this oracle.

We call this oracle the zero-extract oracle. If the advantage in this game is negligible for any PPT adversary, we say this scheme is INDr-ID$_0$-CPA secure.

Remark 1. INDr-ID$_0$-CPA security can be proved in the exactly same way as INDr-ID-CPA security in all existing ABB-class IBE schemes. Indeed, in the proof of INDr-ID-CPA security, the randomness of u is used only when embedding an LWE instance $(a, b) \in \mathbb{Z}_q^n \times \mathbb{Z}_q$ to (u, c_0^*) where c_0^* is the first component of the challenge ciphertext, and it is irrelevant to the queries in the find/guess phase. This modification of u to 0 has been used to construct signature schemes in the full version of [3] and [11].

3.2 Conversion to PEKS

The above ABB-class IBE framework assumes that the plaintext is 1-bit. However, when constructing PEKS, it is essential to use IBE schemes with multi-bit plaintexts. A simple way to achieve this is to encrypt the plaintext bit-by-bit. Let ABB-PEKS1 denote the PEKS framework constructed using this method. Behnia et al. PEKS [7] is a kind of ABB-PEKS1 which uses ABB-IBE.

However, in this method, the ciphertext size becomes N times larger to encrypt a N-bit plaintext. Another way [3,13] is to fix c_1 for each message bit. Setup samples uniformly random $u_1, \ldots, u_N \in \mathbb{Z}_q^n$ instead of u. c_0 for each message bit b_i is computed as $c_{0,i} = u_i^\top s + x_i + b_i \lfloor q/2 \rfloor$. Thus, the ciphertexts have the form of $(c_0, c_1) \in \mathbb{Z}_q^N \times \mathbb{Z}_q^{m+m'}$ where $c_0 = (c_{0,1}, \ldots, c_{0,N})$. The secret key is the tuple of N keys in the original scheme, each corresponding to each u_i. Let ABB-PEKS2 denote the PEKS framework constructed using this method.

These PEKS frameworks are INDr-CKA secure, correct, and consistent since they are converted from INDr-ID-CPA secure correct IBE schemes. For constructing more efficient LWE-based PEKS schemes, there are two research directions: constructing a more efficient ABB-class IBE scheme and improving the conversion method from ABB-class IBE. Much research has been done on the former, but none on the latter. We focus on the latter in this paper.

4 Construction of Our Simpler Lattice-Based PEKS

We propose a new PEKS framework based on ABB-class IBE. As described in Sect. 1.2, the main idea is removing c_0 from ciphertexts and setting $u = 0$ in the generically constructed PEKS.

4.1 Description of Algorithms and Security Analysis

Let $\mathcal{E}_{\mathsf{ABB}}$ be an ABB-class IBE scheme. Let $\kappa_{\mathsf{td}}, \kappa_{\mathsf{ct}} : \mathbb{N} \to \mathbb{N}$ be polynomially-bounded and polynomial-time computable functions such that $2^{-\kappa_{\mathsf{td}}\kappa_{\mathsf{ct}}}$ is negligible. We propose a new PEKS scheme $\mathsf{ABBtoPEKS}_{\kappa_{\mathsf{td}},\kappa_{\mathsf{ct}}}(\mathcal{E}_{\mathsf{ABB}})$. This scheme consists of the following algorithms.

- KeyGen(1^n):
  1. Sets the parameters m, m', q, σ.
  2. Runs $(A, T_A) \leftarrow \mathsf{TrapGen}(1^n, 1^m, q)$.
  3. Runs $P \leftarrow \mathsf{PubGen}_{\mathcal{E}_{\mathsf{ABB}}}(1^n, 1^m, 1^{m'}, q)$.
  4. Outputs the public key $\mathsf{pk} = (A, P)$ and the secret key $\mathsf{sk} = T_A$.
- Enc(pk, w):
  1. Samples $s_j \xleftarrow{\$} \mathbb{Z}_q^n$ and $y_j \leftarrow \chi'_{\mathcal{E}_{\mathsf{ABB}}}$ for $j = 1, \ldots, \kappa_{\mathsf{ct}}(n)$.
  2. Computes $c_j \leftarrow [A|F_{\mathcal{E}_{\mathsf{ABB}}}(P, w)]^\top s_j + y_j$.
  3. Outputs $\{c_j\}_{j=1}^{\kappa_{\mathsf{ct}}(n)}$.
- Trapdoor(sk, w):
  1. Runs $e_i \leftarrow \mathsf{SampleLeft}(A, F_{\mathcal{E}_{\mathsf{ABB}}}(P, w), T_A, 0, \sigma)$ for $i = 1, \ldots, \kappa_{\mathsf{td}}(n)$.
  2. Outputs $\{e_i\}_{i=1}^{\kappa_{\mathsf{td}}(n)}$.
- Test($\{e_i\}_{i=1}^{\kappa_{\mathsf{td}}(n)}, \{c_j\}_{j=1}^{\kappa_{\mathsf{ct}}(n)}$):
  1. Computes $k_{i,j} \leftarrow e_i^\top c_j \in \mathbb{Z}_q$ for each $(i, j) \in [1, \kappa_{\mathsf{td}}(n)] \times [1, \kappa_{\mathsf{ct}}(n)]$.
  2. Treats each $k_{i,j}$ as an integer in $[-q/2, q/2]$. Outputs 1 if $-\lfloor q/4 \rfloor < k_{i,j} < \lfloor q/4 \rfloor$ for every (i, j), otherwise outputs 0.

It is easy to see that $\mathsf{ABBtoPEKS}_{\kappa_{\mathsf{td}}, \kappa_{\mathsf{ct}}}(\mathcal{E}_{\mathsf{ABB}})$ is INDr-CKA secure if $\mathcal{E}_{\mathsf{ABB}}$ is INDr-ID$_0$-CPA secure. By the hybrid argument, it is sufficient to consider the case $\kappa_{\mathsf{td}}(n) = \kappa_{\mathsf{ct}}(n) = 1$ for all n.[2] In this case, the ciphertext is a part of that in $\mathcal{E}_{\mathsf{ABB}}$, and the trapdoor oracle in the INDr-CKA game corresponds to the zero-extract oracle in the INDr-ID$_0$-CPA game.

Also, $\mathsf{ABBtoPEKS}_{\kappa_{\mathsf{td}}, \kappa_{\mathsf{ct}}}(\mathcal{E}_{\mathsf{ABB}})$ is correct since the range of the error $e^\top y$ is smaller than that of the original error $x - e^\top y$.

To sum up, the following theorem holds.

Theorem 1. *Assume that an ABB-class IBE scheme $\mathcal{E}_{\mathsf{ABB}}$ is correct and INDr-ID$_0$-CPA secure. Then the PEKS scheme $\mathsf{ABBtoPEKS}_{\kappa_{\mathsf{td}}, \kappa_{\mathsf{ct}}}(\mathcal{E}_{\mathsf{ABB}})$ is correct and INDr-CKA secure.*

Now, it is left to be shown that the proposed scheme is consistent. We give the consistency proof in the next section.

4.2 Consistency Proof

In this section, we prove that $\mathsf{ABBtoPEKS}_{\kappa_{\mathsf{td}}, \kappa_{\mathsf{ct}}}(\mathcal{E}_{\mathsf{ABB}})$ is consistent provided that this scheme is INDr-CKA secure. We do not describe the detailed parameter setting for ABB-class IBE since it depends on the concrete schemes, but we use the following common conditions to prove consistency.

$$\begin{cases} m = \Omega(n \log q) & \text{(in order that TrapGen can be run)} \\ m' = O(m) & \text{(since } m' \text{ should be small for efficiency)} \\ \sigma = \omega(\sqrt{m \log m}) & \text{(in order that SampleLeft can be run)} \\ q = \Omega(\sigma \sqrt{m}) & \text{(for correctness)} \end{cases}$$

We also use the following lemmas for proof.

---

[2] Note that this case does not satisfy consistency since $2^{-\kappa_{\mathsf{td}} \kappa_{\mathsf{ct}}}$ is not negligible.

Lemma 3 ([16]). *For any lattice Λ, real number $s > 0$, and vector $c \in \text{span}(\Lambda)$, $\rho_{s,c}(\Lambda) \leq \rho_s(\Lambda)$ holds.*

Lemma 4 ([12]). *Let Λ be any m-dimensional lattice. For any $\epsilon \in (0,1)$, $s \geq \eta_\epsilon(\Lambda)$ and $c \in \mathbb{R}^m$,*

$$\rho_{s,c}(\Lambda) \in [1-\epsilon, 1+\epsilon] \cdot s^m \det(\Lambda^*).$$

In particular,

$$\rho_{s,c}(\Lambda) \in \left[\frac{1-\epsilon}{1+\epsilon}, 1\right] \cdot \rho_s(\Lambda).$$

Lemma 5 ([12]). *For each positive integer n, let $q(n)$ be a prime number and $m(n)$ be a positive integer such that $m = \Omega(n \log q)$. Let $s(n)$ be any $\omega(\sqrt{\log m})$ function. Then, there exists a negligible function ϵ_s such that the following condition holds for an overwhelming fraction of $A \in \mathbb{Z}_q^{n \times m}$:*

$$\eta_{\epsilon_s(n)}(\Lambda_q^\perp(A)) \leq s(n).$$

Lemma 6 ([13,15]). *Suppose that $\sigma = \omega(\sqrt{n \log q \log m})$. Then, there exists a negligible function ϵ such that for an overwhelming fraction of $A \in \mathbb{Z}_q^{n \times m}$ and for any $u \in \mathbb{Z}_q^n, e \in \Lambda_q^u(A)$, we have*

$$\Pr[e \leftarrow \mathsf{SamplePre}(A, T_A, u, \sigma))] \in \left[\frac{1-\epsilon}{1+\epsilon}, \frac{1+\epsilon}{1-\epsilon}\right] \cdot \Pr[e \leftarrow \mathcal{D}_\sigma(\Lambda_q^u(A))].$$

The following lemma is the concrete version of Theorem 3.4 in [10].

Lemma 7. *Suppose that $\sigma = \omega(n \log q \log m)$, and let ϵ denote the function defined in Lemma 6. Suppose that a real number ϵ' satisfies $\sigma \geq \eta_{\epsilon'}(\Lambda_q^\perp(A))$. Then, for an overwhelming fraction of $A \in \mathbb{Z}_q^{n \times m}$ and for any $M \in \mathbb{Z}_q^{n \times m'}, u \in \mathbb{Z}_q^n, e \in \Lambda_q^u(A)$, we have*

$$\Pr[e \leftarrow \mathsf{SampleLeft}(A, M, T_A, u, \sigma)] \leq \frac{1+\epsilon}{1-\epsilon} \cdot \frac{1+\epsilon'}{1-\epsilon'} \cdot \Pr[e \leftarrow \mathcal{D}_\sigma(\Lambda_q^u([A|M]))].$$

Proof. By Lemma 4 and Lemma 6, for any $e = [e_1; e_2] \in \mathbb{Z}^m \times \mathbb{Z}^{m'}$,

$$\Pr[e \leftarrow \mathsf{SampleLeft}] = \frac{\rho_\sigma(e_2)}{\rho_\sigma(\mathbb{Z}^{m'})} \Pr[e_1 \leftarrow \mathsf{SamplePre}(A, T_A, u - Me_2, \sigma)]$$

$$\in \left[\frac{1-\epsilon}{1+\epsilon}, \frac{1+\epsilon}{1-\epsilon}\right] \cdot \frac{\rho_\sigma(e_2)}{\rho_\sigma(\mathbb{Z}^{m'})} \cdot \frac{\rho_\sigma(e_1)}{\rho_\sigma(\Lambda_q^{u-Me_2}(A))}$$

$$\subset \left[\frac{1-\epsilon}{1+\epsilon}, \frac{1+\epsilon}{1-\epsilon} \cdot \frac{1+\epsilon'}{1-\epsilon'}\right] \cdot \frac{\rho_\sigma(e)}{\rho_\sigma(\mathbb{Z}^{m'})\rho_\sigma(\Lambda_q^\perp(A))}.$$

Moreover,

$$\rho_\sigma(\Lambda_q^u([A|M])) = \sum_{x \in \mathbb{Z}^{m'}} \rho_\sigma(x)\rho_\sigma(\Lambda_q^{u-Mx}(A))$$

$$\in \left[\frac{1-\epsilon'}{1+\epsilon'}, 1\right] \sum_{x \in \mathbb{Z}^{m'}} \rho_\sigma(x)\rho_\sigma(\Lambda_q^\perp(A))$$

$$= \left[\frac{1-\epsilon'}{1+\epsilon'}, 1\right] \rho_\sigma(\mathbb{Z}^{m'})\rho_\sigma(\Lambda_q^\perp(A)).$$

This completes the proof. $\qquad\qquad\qquad\qquad\qquad\qquad\qquad\qquad\qquad\qquad\qquad\square$

By Lemma 5, in the ABB-class IBE parameter settings, there exists a negligible function $\epsilon'(n)$ such that $\sigma \geq \eta_{\epsilon'}(\Lambda_q^\perp(A))$ holds for an overwhelming fraction of $A \in \mathbb{Z}_q^{n \times m}$.

Next, we compute an upper bound of $\Pr[e \leftarrow \mathcal{D}_\sigma(\Lambda_q^u([A|M])) \bmod q\mathbb{Z}^{m+m'}]$.

Lemma 8. *Let σ, μ be positive real numbers, and let $c \in \mathbb{R}^m$. If $q \geq \sigma \cdot \eta_\mu(\mathbb{Z}^m)$, then $\rho_{\sigma,c}(q\mathbb{Z}^m) \leq 1 + \mu$ holds.*

Proof. By Lemma 3, it is enough to prove the case of $c = 0$. Since $(\mathbb{Z}^m)^* = \mathbb{Z}^m$, by the definition of smoothing parameter,

$$\rho_{\sigma/q}(\mathbb{Z}^m \setminus \{0\}) \leq \mu.$$

Using $\rho_{\sigma/q}(0) = 1$ and $\rho_{\sigma/q}(x) = \rho_\sigma(qx)$, it follows that

$$\rho_\sigma(q\mathbb{Z}^m) \leq 1 + \mu.$$

$\qquad\qquad\qquad\qquad\qquad\qquad\qquad\qquad\qquad\qquad\qquad\qquad\qquad\qquad\qquad\square$

Lemma 9. *Let $A \in \mathbb{Z}_q^{n \times m}$ be a rank n matrix. Suppose that $0 < \epsilon' < 1$, $\sigma \geq \eta_{\epsilon'}(\Lambda_q^\perp(A))$, and $q \geq \sigma \cdot \eta_\mu(\mathbb{Z}^{m+m'})$. Then, for any $M \in \mathbb{Z}_q^{n \times m'}$, $u \in \mathbb{Z}_q^n$, and $x \in \Lambda_q^u([A|M])$,*

$$\mathcal{D}_\sigma(\Lambda_q^u([A|M]))(x + q\mathbb{Z}^{m+m'}) \leq \frac{q^n(1+\mu)}{\sigma^m(1-\epsilon')}.$$

In other words, for any $M \in \mathbb{Z}_q^{n \times m'}$ and $u \in \mathbb{Z}_q^n$,

$$\gamma(\mathcal{D}_\sigma(\Lambda_q^u([A|M])) \bmod q\mathbb{Z}^{m+m'}) \leq \frac{q^n(1+\mu)}{\sigma^m(1-\epsilon')}.$$

Proof. Since A is rank n, there exists $c \in \mathbb{Z}^m$ such that $Ac = -u \pmod q$. Then we have

$$\rho_\sigma(\Lambda_q^u([A|M])) \geq \sum_{[y;0^{m'}]\in\Lambda_q^u([A|M])} \rho_\sigma([y;0^{m'}])$$

$$= \sum_{y\in\Lambda_q^u(A)} \rho_\sigma(y)$$

$$= \rho_{\sigma,c}(\Lambda_q^\perp(A)).$$

Therefore, by Lemma 4 and Lemma 8 we have

$$\mathcal{D}_\sigma(\Lambda_q^u([A|M]))(x + q\mathbb{Z}^{m+m'}) = \frac{\rho_\sigma(x + q\mathbb{Z}^{m+m'})}{\rho_\sigma(\Lambda_q^u([A|M]))}$$

$$= \frac{\rho_{\sigma,-x}(q\mathbb{Z}^{m+m'})}{\rho_\sigma(\Lambda_q^u([A|M]))}$$

$$\leq \frac{1+\mu}{\rho_{\sigma,c}(\Lambda_q^\perp(A))}$$

$$\leq \frac{1+\mu}{\sigma^m \det(\Lambda_q^\perp(A)^*)(1-\epsilon')}$$

$$= \frac{1+\mu}{\sigma^m q^{-m} \det(\Lambda_q(A))(1-\epsilon')}$$

$$= \frac{q^n(1+\mu)}{\sigma^m(1-\epsilon')}.$$

□

By Lemma 1, small μ such as $1/2$ satisfies $q \geq \sigma \cdot \eta_\mu(\mathbb{Z}^{m+m'})$ for sufficiently large n since $q = \Omega(\sigma\sqrt{m})$ and $m' = O(m)$. As mentioned before, in the ABB-class IBE parameter settings, $\epsilon'(n)$ can be a negligible function. Thus,

$$\frac{q^n(1+\mu)}{\sigma^m(1-\epsilon')} \leq 2q^n\sigma^{-m}$$

holds for large n. By using Lemma 7, for an overwhelming fraction of $A \in \mathbb{Z}_q^{n\times m}$,

$$\max_{M,u} \gamma\left(\mathsf{SampleLeft}(A, M, T_A, u, \sigma) \bmod q\mathbb{Z}^{m+m'}\right) \leq 3q^n\sigma^{-m}$$

holds.

Now, we prove that the proposed scheme is consistent.

Theorem 2. *For a PPT adversary $\mathcal{A}$, let $P_{\mathcal{A}}(n)$ denote the advantage in the consistency game of our scheme:*

$$P_{\mathcal{A}}(n) := \Pr[(\mathsf{pk}, \mathsf{sk}) \leftarrow \mathsf{KeyGen}(1^n); (w, w') \leftarrow \mathcal{A}(\mathsf{pk});$$

$$\{c_j\}_{j=1}^{\kappa_{\mathsf{ct}}(n)} \leftarrow \mathsf{Enc}(\mathsf{pk}, w);$$

$$\{e_i\}_{i=1}^{\kappa_{\mathsf{td}}(n)} \leftarrow \mathsf{Trapdoor}(\mathsf{sk}, w') :$$

$$\{e_i^\top c_j\}_{i,j} \in (-\lfloor q/4\rfloor, \lfloor q/4\rfloor]^{\kappa_{\mathsf{td}}(n)\times\kappa_{\mathsf{ct}}(n)} \wedge w \neq w'].$$

Assume that $\mathsf{ABBtoPEKS}_{\kappa_{td},\kappa_{ct}}(\mathcal{E}_{ABB})$ *is INDr-CKA secure. Then, for any* $\mathcal{A}$, $P_{\mathcal{A}}(n) \leq 2^{-\kappa_{td}(n)\kappa_{ct}(n)} + \mathsf{negl}(n)$ *holds. In particular,* $\mathsf{ABBtoPEKS}_{\kappa_{td},\kappa_{ct}}(\mathcal{E}_{ABB})$ *is consistent if* $2^{-\kappa_{td}\kappa_{ct}}$ *is negligible.*

Proof. Let

$$P_{\mathcal{A}}'(n) := \Pr[(\mathsf{pk},\mathsf{sk}) \leftarrow \mathsf{KeyGen}(1^n); (w,w') \leftarrow \mathcal{A}(\mathsf{pk});$$

$$c_j \xleftarrow{\$} \mathbb{Z}_q^{m+m'} (j = 1,\ldots,\kappa_{ct}(n));$$

$$e_i \leftarrow \mathsf{SampleLeft}(A, F_{\mathcal{E}_{ABB}}(P,w'), T_A, 0, \sigma) \; (i = 1,\ldots,\kappa_{td}(n)):$$

$$\{e_i^{\top} c_j\}_{i,j} \in (-\lfloor q/4 \rfloor, \lfloor q/4 \rfloor)^{\kappa_{td}(n) \times \kappa_{ct}(n)} \wedge w \neq w'].$$

$|P_{\mathcal{A}}(n) - P_{\mathcal{A}}'(n)|$ is negligible in n since we can construct a PPT adversary in the INDr-CKA game of $\mathsf{ABBtoPEKS}_{\kappa_{td},\kappa_{ct}}(\mathcal{E}_{ABB})$ with the advantage $|P_{\mathcal{A}}(n) - P_{\mathcal{A}}'(n)|/2$. Then it suffices to show that $P_{\mathcal{A}}'(n) \leq 2^{-\kappa_{td}(n)\kappa_{ct}(n)} + \mathsf{negl}(n)$. Now we set $\kappa_{ct}'(n) := \min\{n, \kappa_{ct}(n)\}$. By fixing the inputs of $\mathsf{SampleLeft}$ and applying Leftover Hash Lemma to the function

$$h : \mathbb{Z}_q^{m+m'} \ni x \mapsto [c_1^{\top}; \cdots ; c_{\kappa_{ct}'(n)}^{\top}] x \in \mathbb{Z}_q^{\kappa_{ct}'(n)},$$

it follows that

$$\Delta(\{e_i^{\top} c_j\}_{(i,j) \in [1,\kappa_{td}(n)] \times [1,\kappa_{ct}'(n)]}; \mathsf{Unif}(\mathbb{Z}_q^{\kappa_{td}(n) \times \kappa_{ct}'(n)})) \leq \frac{\kappa_{td}(n)}{2}\sqrt{3q^n \sigma^{-m} \cdot q^{\kappa_{ct}'(n)}}$$

$$< \kappa_{td}(n) q^n \sigma^{-\frac{m}{2}}$$

for any matrix $F_{\mathcal{E}_{ABB}}(P,w')$ and for an overwhelming fraction of $A \in \mathbb{Z}_q^{n \times m}$. Thus, the probability that $e_i^{\top} c_j \in (-\lfloor q/4 \rfloor, \lfloor q/4 \rfloor)$ holds for any $(i,j) \in [1,\kappa_{td}(n)] \times [1,\kappa_{ct}(n)]$ is bounded above by

$$2^{-\kappa_{td}(n)\kappa_{ct}'(n)} + \kappa_{td}(n) q^n \sigma^{-\frac{m}{2}} \leq 2^{-\kappa_{td}(n)\kappa_{ct}(n)} + 2^{-n\kappa_{td}(n)} + \kappa_{td}(n) q^n \sigma^{-\frac{m}{2}}.$$

Since $m = \Omega(n \log q)$ and $\sigma = \omega(\sqrt{m \log m})$, $\kappa_{td}(n) q^n \sigma^{-\frac{m}{2}} = q^{-\omega(n \log m)}$ is negligible. This completes the proof. $\qquad\square$

Remark 2. When considering practical parameters, $\kappa_{td}(n)\kappa_{ct}(n) \leq n$ holds. In these cases, $\kappa_{ct}'(n) = \kappa_{ct}(n)$ holds, and $\kappa_{td}(n) q^n \sigma^{-\frac{m}{2}}$ is much smaller than $2^{-\kappa_{td}(n)\kappa_{ct}(n)}$. Thus, the false positive rates in our scheme with $(\kappa_{td}, \kappa_{ct}) = (1, \kappa)$ and $(\kappa_{td}, \kappa_{ct}) = (\kappa, 1)$ are close to those in ABB-PEKS1 and ABB-PEKS2 respectively. This guarantees the validity of the comparison in the next section.

4.3 Comparison to Existing PEKS

In this section, we compare our PEKS scheme with the existing LWE-based PEKS schemes: ABB-PEKS1 and ABB-PEKS2. The matrix $F_{\mathcal{E}_{ABB}}(P, w)$ is abbreviated to F_w. In our scheme, the public key size is $|P| + mn \log q$, the ciphertext size is $\kappa_{ct}(m + m') \log q$, and the trapdoor size is $\kappa_{td}\ell_{m+m'}$. The false positive rate of ABB-PEKS1 or ABB-PEKS2 is about $2^{-\kappa}$, and that of our scheme is about $2^{-\kappa_{td}\kappa_{ct}}$. As shown in Fig. 1 and Table 1, when we set $(\kappa_{td}, \kappa_{ct}) = (1, \kappa)$, our scheme becomes an improved version of ABB-PEKS1. In addition, when we set $(\kappa_{td}, \kappa_{ct}) = (\kappa, 1)$, our scheme becomes an improved version of ABB-PEKS2. Alternatively, one may use the intermediate parameter settings such as $(\kappa_{td}, \kappa_{ct}) = (\lceil\sqrt{\kappa}\rceil, \lceil\sqrt{\kappa}\rceil)$.

	ABB-PEKS1	Ours ($\kappa_{td} = 1, \kappa_{ct} = \kappa$)
Public key	$A \quad P \quad \boxed{u \in \mathbb{Z}_q^n}$	$A \quad P \quad \boxed{}$
Ciphertext	$\boxed{\begin{array}{c} (b_1, \ldots, b_\kappa) \in \{0,1\}^\kappa \\ u^\top s_1 + \mathsf{error}_1 + b_1\lfloor q/2\rfloor \in \mathbb{Z}_q \\ \vdots \\ u^\top s_\kappa + \mathsf{error}_\kappa + b_\kappa\lfloor q/2\rfloor \in \mathbb{Z}_q \end{array}}$ $[A|F_w]^\top s_1 + \mathsf{error}_1' \in \mathbb{Z}_q^{m+m'}$ $\vdots$ $[A|F_w]^\top s_\kappa + \mathsf{error}_\kappa' \in \mathbb{Z}_q^{m+m'}$	$\boxed{}$ $[A|F_w]^\top s_1 + \mathsf{error}_1' \in \mathbb{Z}_q^{m+m'}$ $\vdots$ $[A|F_w]^\top s_\kappa + \mathsf{error}_\kappa' \in \mathbb{Z}_q^{m+m'}$
Trapdoor	$e \leftarrow \mathsf{SampleLeft}(A, F_w, T_A, u, \sigma)$	$e \leftarrow \mathsf{SampleLeft}(A, F_w, T_A, 0, \sigma)$

	ABB-PEKS2	Ours ($\kappa_{td} = \kappa, \kappa_{ct} = 1$)
Public key	$A \quad P \quad \boxed{U \in \mathbb{Z}_q^{n\times\kappa}}$	$A \quad P \quad \boxed{}$
Ciphertext	$\boxed{\begin{array}{c} b \in \{0,1\}^\kappa \\ U^\top s + \mathsf{error} + b\lfloor q/2\rfloor \in \mathbb{Z}_q^\kappa \end{array}}$ $[A|F_w]^\top s + \mathsf{error}' \in \mathbb{Z}_q^{m+m'}$	$\boxed{}$ $[A|F_w]^\top s + \mathsf{error}' \in \mathbb{Z}_q^{m+m'}$
Trapdoor	$e_1 \leftarrow \mathsf{SampleLeft}(A, F_w, T_A, u_1, \sigma)$ $\vdots$ $e_\kappa \leftarrow \mathsf{SampleLeft}(A, F_w, T_A, u_\kappa, \sigma)$	$e_1 \leftarrow \mathsf{SampleLeft}(A, F_w, T_A, 0, \sigma)$ $\vdots$ $e_\kappa \leftarrow \mathsf{SampleLeft}(A, F_w, T_A, 0, \sigma)$

Fig. 1. Comparison of the existing schemes and our scheme

Since all existing efficient PEKS from LWE assumption in the standard model is generically constructed from ABB-class IBE, our construction is the most efficient among these PEKS schemes.

Our methodology can be applied also to many LWE-based functional PEKS [19–21,24,25,27]. Some of them are based on the structure of fixed dimension

Table 1. Comparison of communication costs

	Public key	Ciphertext	Trapdoor
ABB-PEKS1 [7]	$\|P\| + (m+1)n\log q$	$\kappa((m+m'+1)\log q + 1)$	$\ell_{m+m'}$
Ours $(\kappa_{td}=1, \kappa_{ct}=\kappa)$	$\|P\| + mn\log q$	$\kappa(m+m')\log q$	$\ell_{m+m'}$
ABB-PEKS2	$\|P\| + (m+\kappa)n\log q$	$(m+m'+\kappa)\log q + \kappa$	$\kappa\ell_{m+m'}$
Ours $(\kappa_{td}=\kappa, \kappa_{ct}=1)$	$\|P\| + mn\log q$	$(m+m')\log q$	$\kappa\ell_{m+m'}$

$|P|$ denotes the bit size of P. $\ell_{m+m'}$ denotes the bit size of the short vector in $\mathbb{Z}^{m+m'}$.

hierarchical identity-based encryption [4] rather than ABB-class IBE, but the proofs of consistency are similar.

5 Conclusion

We proposed a new construction method of PEKS from Agrawal-Boneh-Boyen IBE or its variants. Our schemes are more efficient than those constructed by applying Abdalla et al. conversion method to these IBE schemes. As a result, our construction includes the most efficient LWE-based PEKS scheme in the standard model. In addition, our technique can be applied to many other schemes based on the similar structure. It would be helpful to construct simple LWE-based functional PEKS schemes.

References

1. Abdalla, M., Bellare, M., Catalano, D., Kiltz, E., Kohno, T., Lange, T., Malone-Lee, J., Neven, G., Paillier, P., Shi, H.: Searchable encryption revisited: consistency properties, relation to anonymous ibe, and extensions. In: Shoup, V. (ed.) CRYPTO 2005. LNCS, vol. 3621, pp. 205–222. Springer, Heidelberg (2005). https://doi.org/10.1007/11535218_13
2. Abla, P.: Identity-based encryption from LWE with more compact master public key. In: Oswald, E. (ed.) CT-RSA 2024. LNCS, vol. 14643, pp. 319–353. Springer, Cham (2024). https://doi.org/10.1007/978-3-031-58868-6_13
3. Agrawal, S., Boneh, D., Boyen, X.: Efficient lattice (H)IBE in the standard model. In: Gilbert, H. (ed.) EUROCRYPT 2010. LNCS, vol. 6110, pp. 553–572. Springer, Heidelberg (2010). https://doi.org/10.1007/978-3-642-13190-5_28
4. Agrawal, S., Boneh, D., Boyen, X.: Lattice basis delegation in fixed dimension and shorter-ciphertext hierarchical IBE. In: Rabin, T. (ed.) CRYPTO 2010. LNCS, vol. 6223, pp. 98–115. Springer, Heidelberg (2010). https://doi.org/10.1007/978-3-642-14623-7_6
5. Alwen, J., Peikert, C.: Generating shorter bases for hard random lattices. Theory Comput. Syst. **48**, 535–553 (2011)
6. Apon, D., Fan, X., Liu, F.: Compact identity based encryption from LWE. Cryptology ePrint Archive, 2016/125 (2016)

7. Behnia, R., Ozmen, M.O., Yavuz, A.A.: Lattice-based public key searchable encryption from experimental perspectives. IEEE Trans. Dependable Secure Comput. **17**(6), 1269–1282 (2018)

8. Boneh, D., Di Crescenzo, G., Ostrovsky, R., Persiano, G.: Public key encryption with keyword search. In: Cachin, C., Camenisch, J.L. (eds.) EUROCRYPT 2004. LNCS, vol. 3027, pp. 506–522. Springer, Heidelberg (2004). https://doi.org/10.1007/978-3-540-24676-3_30

9. Boneh, D., Franklin, M.: Identity-based encryption from the weil pairing. In: Kilian, J. (ed.) CRYPTO 2001. LNCS, vol. 2139, pp. 213–229. Springer, Heidelberg (2001). https://doi.org/10.1007/3-540-44647-8_13

10. Cash, D., Hofheinz, D., Kiltz, E.: How to delegate a lattice basis. Cryptology ePrint Archive, 2009/351 (2009)

11. Cash, D., Hofheinz, D., Kiltz, E., Peikert, C.: Bonsai trees, or how to delegate a lattice basis. In: Gilbert, H. (ed.) EUROCRYPT 2010. LNCS, vol. 6110, pp. 523–552. Springer, Heidelberg (2010). https://doi.org/10.1007/978-3-642-13190-5_27

12. Gentry, C., Peikert, C., Vaikuntanathan, V.: Trapdoors for hard lattices and new cryptographic constructions. Cryptology ePrint Archive, 2007/432 (2007)

13. Gentry, C., Peikert, C., Vaikuntanathan, V.: Trapdoors for hard lattices and new cryptographic constructions. In: ACM STOC 2008, pp. 197–206 (2008)

14. Jager, T., Kurek, R., Niehues, D.: Efficient adaptively-secure IB-KEMs and VRFs via near-collision resistance. In: Garay, J.A. (ed.) PKC 2021. LNCS, vol. 12710, pp. 596–626. Springer, Cham (2021). https://doi.org/10.1007/978-3-030-75245-3_22

15. Micciancio, D., Peikert, C.: Trapdoors for lattices: simpler, tighter, faster, smaller. In: Pointcheval, D., Johansson, T. (eds.) EUROCRYPT 2012. LNCS, vol. 7237, pp. 700–718. Springer, Heidelberg (2012). https://doi.org/10.1007/978-3-642-29011-4_41

16. Micciancio, D., Regev, O.: Worst-case to average-case reductions based on gaussian measures. SIAM J. Comput. **37**(1), 267–302 (2007)

17. Peikert, C., Rosen, A.: Efficient collision-resistant hashing from worst-case assumptions on cyclic lattices. In: Halevi, S., Rabin, T. (eds.) TCC 2006. LNCS, vol. 3876, pp. 145–166. Springer, Heidelberg (2006). https://doi.org/10.1007/11681878_8

18. Regev, O.: On lattices, learning with errors, random linear codes, and cryptography. J. ACM **56**(6), 1–40 (2009)

19. Tang, Y., Ba, Y., Li, L., Wang, X., Yan, X.: Lattice-based public-key encryption with conjunctive keyword search in multi-user setting for IIoT. Clust. Comput. **25**(4), 2305–2316 (2022)

20. Wang, P., Xiang, T., Li, X., Xiang, H.: Public key encryption with conjunctive keyword search on lattice. J. Inf. Secur. Appl. **51**, 102433 (2020)

21. Xu, L., Yuan, X., Steinfeld, R., Wang, C., Xu, C.: Multi-writer searchable encryption: an LWE-based realization and implementation. In: ASIACCS 2019, pp. 122-133 (2019)

22. Yamada, S.: Adaptively secure identity-based encryption from lattices with asymptotically shorter public parameters. In: Fischlin, M., Coron, J.-S. (eds.) EUROCRYPT 2016. LNCS, vol. 9666, pp. 32–62. Springer, Heidelberg (2016). https://doi.org/10.1007/978-3-662-49896-5_2

23. Yamada, S.: Asymptotically compact adaptively secure lattice IBEs and verifiable random functions via generalized partitioning techniques. In: Katz, J., Shacham, H. (eds.) CRYPTO 2017. LNCS, vol. 10403, pp. 161–193. Springer, Cham (2017). https://doi.org/10.1007/978-3-319-63697-9_6

24. Yang, X., Chen, X., Huang, J., Li, H., Huang, Q.: FS-IBEKS: forward secure identity-based encryption with keyword search from lattice. Comput. Stand. Interfaces **86**, 103732 (2023)
25. Yang, Y., Zheng, X., Chang, V., Ye, S., Tang, C.: Lattice assumption based fuzzy information retrieval scheme support multi-user for secure multimedia cloud. Multimed. Tools Appl. **77**, 9927–9941 (2018)
26. Yamada, S.: Asymptotically compact adaptively secure lattice IBEs and verifiable random functions via generalized partitioning techniques. In: Katz, J., Shacham, H. (eds.) CRYPTO 2017. LNCS, vol. 10403, pp. 161–193. Springer, Cham (2017). https://doi.org/10.1007/978-3-319-63697-9_6
27. Zhang, X., Xu, C., Wang, H., Zhang, Y., Wang, S.: FS-PEKS: lattice-based forward secure public-key encryption with keyword search for cloud-assisted industrial internet of things. IEEE Trans. Dependable Secure Comput. **18**(3), 1019–1032 (2019)

Signature

Traceable Ring Signatures: Logarithmic-Size, Without Any Setup, from Standard Assumptions

Xuan Thanh Khuc[1(✉)], Willy Susilo[1], Dung Hoang Duong[1], Fuchun Guo[1], Kazuhide Fukushima[2], and Shinsaku Kiyomoto[2]

[1] Institute of Cybersecurity and Cryptology, School of Computing and Information Technology, University of Wollongong, Wollongong, NSW 2522, Australia
xtk929@uowmail.edu.au, {wsusilo,hduong,fuchun}@uow.edu.au
[2] Information Security Laboratory, KDDI Research, Inc., Fujimino, Japan
{ka-fukushima,kiyomoto}@kddi-research.jp

Abstract. A traceable ring signature is a variant of ring signatures that allows public traceability of a user's identity if they have produced two signatures for the same issue. Fujisaki and Suzuki first proposed traceable ring signatures at PKC'2007. They have numerous applications in e-coupons, e-voting, and blockchain. While several traceable ring signatures exist in both classical and post-quantum settings, most are proven in the (quantum) random oracle or common reference string models. These models require impractical or inefficient assumptions, such as the heuristic of random oracles or a trusted setup.

In this paper, we present the first generic construction of traceable ring signature schemes that do not rely on a trusted setup or the random oracle heuristic. Specifically, our scheme can be instantiated from standard assumptions, and the size of the signatures is only logarithmic in the number of ring members.

Keywords: Verifiable random function · NIWI · Traceable ring signatures · Ring signatures · Plain model · Standard model

1 Introduction

Ring signatures allow a person to sign a message on behalf of a group of users, but no one (including users of that ring) can know exactly who signed that message. In a ring signature, there is no group manager, no particular setup for secret sharing among group members, and the dynamics of group choice. This indicates that no individual or group can exclusively escrow a signer's identity.

This work is partially supported by the ARC Linkage Project LP190100984. Willy Susilo is supported by the ARC Australian Laureate Fellowship FL230100033. Fuchun Guo is supported by the ARC Future Fellowship FT220100046. Dung Hoang Duong is partially supported by the AEGiS 2023 grant from the University of Wollongong.

J. K. Liu et al. (Eds.): ProvSec 2024, LNCS 14903, pp. 189–208, 2025.
https://doi.org/10.1007/978-981-96-0954-3_10

Rivest *et al.* [12] introduced the first ring signature in 2001. A traceable ring signature is a variant that still maintains the flexibility properties of a ring signature. A traceable ring signature has a tag $T = (R, issue)$, where R is the set of public keys of the ring members, and the issue refers to, for instance, an election or some social issue. A ring member can sign a message using his secret key. The verifier can verify the signature on the message with respect to tag T, but the verifier cannot know who generated the signature among all the possible ring members in R. Assume the signer signs a message again with the same tag; everyone can determine that the two signatures are linked. However, if he signs two different messages with the same tag, it is evident that these signatures are linked, and the signer's anonymity is revoked.

Traceable ring signatures are ideal for anonymous voting in online discussions on bulletin boards. Consider a group of individuals discussing a particular issue and wanting to cast anonymous votes. They avoid involving a trusted party or setting up a complex protocol. Additionally, some group members may abstain from voting. Standard ring signatures are unsuitable because they do not restrict members to a single vote.

1.1 Previous Works

The first classical traceable ring signature scheme (TRS) was proposed by Fujisaki *et al.* [8]. Based on the DDH assumption, this scheme was proved secure in the random oracle model (ROM), where hash functions are modelled as random oracles. A random oracle is an idealised black-box function that produces truly random outputs for each unique input. Real hash functions do not perfectly emulate random oracles, leading to a gap between theoretical security and practical implementation. In [5], they show that several protocols are secure in ROM but trivially insecure whenever the random oracle is instantiated with a real hash function. In [10], Hu *et al.* gave a version of TRS with forward security, where even if the signer's secret key is exposed, the generated signatures are still secure. This scheme has linear signature sizes with the number of users in the ring and is secure in ROM. A new security definition has been given by Bultel *et al.* [4]. In Bultel's scheme, the signer's identity is revealed only when he signs multiple k messages on the same tag. This scheme is proven secure in the ROM based on DDH assumption and bilinear pairing. Branco *et al.* [3] built the first code-based TRS scheme using the Fiat-Shamir transformation and Stern protocol. However, this scheme has some flaws in the proof of security that were pointed out in [6]. Based on (linkable) ring signature framework [2], Wei *et al.* [14] construct two TRS schemes from group actions that can be instantiated with isogenies and lattices. These schemes have a logarithmic signature size and are secure in the ROM.

In 2011, Fujisaki [7] introduced a version of TRS proven secure using DDH assumption and bilinear pairing in the common reference string model (CRS). A trusted setup phase generates a common reference string (CRS) available to all parties in the CRS model. However, the CRS must be generated and distributed in a trusted manner, which can be challenging to achieve in practice.

Moreover, the need for a trusted setup phase can complicate deployment and use in decentralised environments. Recently, Feng *et al.* [6] has built a lattice-based TRS with security in quantum random oracle (QROM). The QROM extends the ROM to adversaries with quantum capabilities. In particular, we also require the assumption of a quantum oracle in which all parties are involved in a scheme. Now, qubits represent the output and input of QROM. This scheme uses non-interactive zero-knowledge proof, a family of hash functions, and pseudorandom functions with some additional properties. This scheme used the Unruh transformation technique [13] to claim security to achieve a non-interactive protocol in QROM.

As far as we know, the construction of TRS has yet to be known to be secure in the plain model. This is the most basic and realistic model. It assumes no trusted setup or idealised components; everything must work based on standard, practical assumptions without additional trust or idealisation. The plain model closely represents real-world conditions, making protocols designed in this model more useful. Therefore, this model is the most desirable one to achieve but also the most difficult to construct cryptographic schemes due to the lack of additional assumptions. Table 1 compares our scheme with other TRS.

Table 1. Comparison of our TRS with other schemes in the ring of l users.

Traceable Ring Signatures	Signature size	Hardness assumption	Security model
Fujisaki *et al.* [8]	$O(l)$	DDH[a]	ROM
Hu *et al.* [10]	$O(l)$	DDH	ROM
Fujisaki [7]	$O(\sqrt{l})$	DDH	CRS
Branco *et al.* [3]	$O(\log(l))$	SD[b]	ROM
Feng *et al.* [6]	$O(\log(l))$	SIS[c], LWE[d]	ROM, QROM
Wei *et al.* [14]	$O(\log(l))$	MSIS[c], MLWE[d], CSIDH[e]	ROM
This work	$O(\log(l))$	**Generic assumption**	**Plain**

[a] DDH: Decisional Diffie Hellman.
[b] SD: Syndrome Decoding
[c] SIS: Short Integer Solution, MSIS: Module Short Integer Solution
[d] LWE: Learning with Errors, MLWE: Module Learning with Errors
[e] CSIDH: Commutative Supersingular Isogeny Diffie Hellman

1.2   Our Contribution

The notable contributions and innovations of our work can be summarised as follows:

- In this work, we introduce the first generic construction of traceable ring signatures that are secure in the plain model and have a logarithmic signature size. Our scheme can be built from falsifiable standard assumptions without the random oracle heuristic or trusted setup assumptions. Hence, our research successfully resolves the longstanding open challenge of constructing logarithmic-size traceable ring signatures in the plain model.

- Our proposed generic scheme achieves public traceability. It ensures that two signatures are linked if signed by the same signer on the same message with the same tag. However, the signer who generates two signatures for distinct messages with the same tag can be traced. Anyone can trace by utilising message/signature pairs and the tag.
- Our scheme achieves exculpability. It guarantees that an honest ring user cannot be falsely accused of signing twice using the same tag. More precisely, an adversary can't create a ring signature that can be traced back to the specific target using a publicly traceable algorithm. Even if the attacker can corrupt all ring members except the target, this task should still be considered infeasible.
- Our scheme achieves anonymity. It guarantees that the signer's identity cannot be distinguished from any of the potential ring members as long as the signer does not sign two messages using the same tag. Furthermore, it is impossible to establish a link between any two signatures produced with two separate tags. It is impossible to ascertain whether the same signer makes them.
- Our scheme achieves tag-linkability. It ensures that every two signatures generated by the same signer for the same tag are linked. If any two signatures are not linked, the total number of signatures with respect to the same tag cannot exceed the total number of ring members in the tag.

2   Techniques Overview

Non-interactive zero-knowledge proof (NIZK) is crucial in various cryptographic protocols. In particular, the zero-knowledge property in NIZK is precious for proving security in traceable ring signatures. Informally speaking, this property requires the existence of a simulator that can generate a simulated proof without needing a witness. The probability that an adversary can distinguish a real proof from a simulated one is negligible. To prove anonymity, we replace the actual signer with a simulator algorithm, ensuring that the adversary cannot determine who generates a signature. To prove tag-linkability and exculpability, we embed an underlying hardness assumption into a statement within the scheme. Then, we create a simulator algorithm for the scheme. Now, the adversary interacts with this simulator instead of the actual signer. Based on valid forgery signatures and the soundness of NIZK, we can extract a solution to the underlying hardness assumption. However, NIZK requires a hash function to act as a random oracle or necessitate a common reference string, making them unsuitable for the plain model.

Non-interactive witness-indistinguishable proof (NIWI) differs from NIZK in its security guarantees and setup assumptions. NIWI does not necessarily require a trusted setup like a common reference string (CRS) or a random oracle, making them more suitable for use in the plain model. However, NIWI provides weaker security guarantees (witness indistinguishability) wherein the adversary cannot distinguish which witness was used to generate the proof instead of offering the stronger zero-knowledge property found in NIZK. This entails significant challenges in constructing TRS schemes and proving their security in the plain model, where only minimal assumptions and weaker security guarantees are provided. This is also the biggest challenge we have to overcome.

Our construction is motivated by a sequence of publications [1,6,8,9]. We use several cryptographic building blocks, including one-way functions, commitment schemes (CS), public-key encryption (PKE), verifiable random functions (VRF), somewhere perfectly binding hash functions (SPB), and NIWI. At a high level, our construction is based on the sign-then-encrypt-then-prove paradigm that is typically used for building group/ring signatures.

Before presenting our constructions, we recall a simple approach from [1] to build a ring signature in the plain model. In framework [1], every user's public key $\mathsf{VK} = (\mathsf{pk}, \mathsf{vk})$ is composed of the public key encryption pk and the verification key vk of a signature scheme. Now, consider a ring of l users $R = (\mathsf{VK}_1, \ldots, \mathsf{VK}_l)$ and a message $\mathsf{m} \in \{0,1\}^*$, and assume the signer has a signing secret key sk_i and the corresponding public key $\mathsf{VK}_i = (\mathsf{pk}_i, \mathsf{vk}_i)$. To generate a signature for the message m, the signer uses the secret key sk_i to obtain the signature σ and then encrypts σ using the key pk_i to obtain a ciphertext ct_i. For any $j \neq i$, since the signer does not know the other user's secret keys, he computes the ciphertext ct_j using pk_j to encrypt a string 0. Finally, the signer uses a non-interactive witness-indistinguishable proofs π for a language $\mathcal{L}$ with the statement $(\mathsf{m}, \mathsf{ct}_1, \ldots, \mathsf{ct}_l, \mathsf{VK}_1, \ldots, \mathsf{VK}_l)$ to prove that there is an index i such that ct_i encrypts a signature σ and σ is a valid signature of message m under the verification key vk_i. The ring signature Σ includes the ciphertexts and the NIWI transcript, i.e., $\Sigma = (\mathsf{ct}_1, \ldots, \mathsf{ct}_l, \pi)$. To verify signature Σ, the verifier uses the verification process of NIWI to prove that the statement $(\mathsf{m}, \mathsf{ct}_1, \ldots, \mathsf{ct}_l, \mathsf{VK}_1, \ldots, \mathsf{VK}_l)$ has π as a proof.

1. Constructing Traceability for Ring Signatures in the Plain Model. In order to construct a traceable ring signature, we must enable traceability for the corresponding ring signature. Our traceable technique is motivated by the results from [6]. However, the approach in [6] uses a NIZK in the random oracle; it is not directly applicable to the plain model as we use a NIWI.

Our general idea requires each user to have some associated value to detect whether a signer has signed twice on the same or different messages for the same tag. Now, the signer computes a set containing exactly l elements by using the signer's secret key, message, and tag, where l is the number of users in the ring R. In order for anyone to trace a signature, this set is published as part of the signature. In the same tag case, if two signatures are generated by the same signer on the same message, then two sets are identical. Hence, two signatures are linked in this case. However, if two signatures are generated by the same signer on two different messages, then these sets have only one similar element.

Since the index of the same element is exactly the index of the signer in the ring, the identity of the signer is revealed in this case. These sets are totally different when different users generate these signatures. Specifically, we denote $T = (R, \text{issue})$ as a tag. The signer will first compute two values $v_0 = \text{Hash}(T, m)$, $v_i = E(\text{sk}_i, T)$, where sk_i is a signer secret key, Hash is a collision resistance hash function and E is a pseudorandom function. For correctness, we require that the Hash and E functions have the same output domain. Moreover, we require the output of E function to be unique (to avoid two users having the same value of v), randomness (to ensure anonymity for the signer), and intersection-free range properties (to ensure public traceability). Informally speaking, the domain $\mathcal{Y}$ is the intersection-free range if for every $v_1, v_2 \in \mathcal{Y}$ and z_1, z_2 is chosen uniformly random from $\mathcal{Y}$, the probability that there exists $c_1, c_2, d_1, d_2 \leq \text{poly}(\lambda)$ such that $c_1 \cdot v_1 + d_1 \cdot z_1 = c_2 \cdot v_2 + d_2 \cdot z_2$ is negligible.

Now, the signer computes $\mu = (v_i - v_0)/i$. For every $j \in [l]$ and $j \neq i$, the signer computes $v_j = v_0 + j \cdot \mu$. To ensure correctness in computing μ and v_i for all $i \in [l]$, we require that the output domain of E is well defined with addition operation (if v, w belongs to the output of E then $v + w$ also belongs the output of E) and scalar multiplication (if v belongs to the output of E and $a = j/i$, where $i, j \in [l]$ then $a \cdot v$ also belong output domain of E. In [6], they require output of E is a vector space over $\mathbb{Q}$. This is a strong requirement. Since the output of E deals with a finite field, we cannot use a finite field to present an infinite element in $\mathbb{Q}$.) Set $V = (v_1, \ldots, v_l)$. The signer also uses a NIWI for language $\mathcal{L}$ with the statement $(m, T, \text{ct}_1, \ldots, \text{ct}_l, \text{VK}_1, v_1 \ldots, \text{VK}_l, v_l)$ to prove that there is an index i not only satisfies the same conditions as the above RS scheme but also satisfies $E(\text{sk}_i, T) = v_i$. The signature is $\Sigma = (\mu, \text{ct}_1, \ldots, \text{ct}_l, \pi)$. We do not need to add all v_i to the signature as by using μ, T, m; anyone can recompute the set V. To check the signature, the verifier first recomputes the set V. Then, the verifier uses the NIWI's verification to check the correctness of the statement x.

The tracing algorithm works as follows: with inputs (m, Σ, T) and (m', Σ', T), anyone can completely recover v_0, v_0' and sets V, V'. We have some cases as follows:

- If two signatures are generated by the same signer on the same message, then we have $v_0 = v_0'$ and $v_i = v_i'$, $\forall i \in [l]$. Hence, we have $V \equiv V'$. The algorithm returns linked, i.e. two signatures signed by the same signer. However, no one can know who generated these signatures.
- If two signatures are generated by the same signer on two different messages, then we have $v_0 \neq v_0'$ and $v_i = v_i'$. In this case, we have $V \cap V' = v_i$. Then, the algorithm returns the signer's identifier as VK_i.
- If two different signers generate two signatures, then we have $v_i \neq v_i'$. Since the output of E is the intersection-free range, we can prove that $V \cap V' = \emptyset$. The algorithm returns accept in this case.

2. Proving Security by Using Weaker Properties in the Plain Model. In the random oracle or common reference string, proving anonymity is not a hard task. We can generate a ring signature without using the signer secret by using a simulation in the zero-knowledge property. Hence, the adversary cannot know who generated a ring signature. However, anonymity is the most challenging task in constructing ring signatures in the plain model since we no longer have zero knowledge property. As a standard technique, in order to prove anonymity, we must transform a signature computed with user VK_1 into a signature computed with user VK_2 via a sequence of hybrids. A statement claims that a signature is generated by user VK_1 or VK_2. The transformation can done by using three hybrids $\mathcal{H}_0, \mathcal{H}_1$ and $\mathcal{H}_2$. We denote the hybrid $\mathcal{H}_0$ ($\mathcal{H}_2$) is an experiment where signature is generated by user VK_1 (VK_2) using relation $\mathcal{R}_1$ ($\mathcal{R}_2$). The hybrid $\mathcal{H}_1$ is true for users VK_1 and VK_2. The indistinguishability between hybrid $\mathcal{H}_0$ and $\mathcal{H}_1$ is based on the assumption of underlying primitives. The difference between $\mathcal{H}_1$ and $\mathcal{H}_2$ is negligible as NIWI has witness indistinguishability.

Unfortunately, we cannot apply this technique directly to our TRS since we do not achieve hybrid $\mathcal{H}_1$. Specifically, our signature contains traceable element μ, which depends on the message m, tag T and the signer's secret key. If the adversary requests signing two times on the same message, then we can return the different μ for each time. In other words, the difference between $\mathcal{H}_0$ and $\mathcal{H}_1$ is non-negligible. To achieve anonymity, our proving must not contain a hybrid that is true with both relations $\mathcal{R}_1$ and $\mathcal{R}_2$. Specifically, we will add one more relation in the NIWI. This relationship would be unlikely in an actual key generation algorithm. However, we need the above relationship to happen in the anonymity proof. Now, each user will choose a random value nonce and add it to the signer secret key in the key generation algorithm. Then, the user computes the commitment value com on nonce and adds com to the signer public key. The additional relation said that there exist two users in the ring whose nonce values satisfy the condition $F(nonce_i) = nonce_j$, where $i \neq j \in [l]$ and F are one-way functions. We can easily see that this relation is unlikely in an actual key generation algorithm because the nonce values are uniformly random. However, we can choose two users who satisfy the above relation in the anonymity experiment. Therefore, we can avoid a hybrid game where the total relation is true with both users VK_1 and VK2.

However, adding a new relation also slightly affects proving tag-linkability, exculpability and anonymity. Specifically, we must restrict the adversary from adding his generated public key to the ring R in the tag-linkability and exculpability experiment. Indeed, we assume that the adversary can add his public keys. In this case, the adversary trivially generates a valid forged signature by choosing two public keys whose nonce values satisfy the newly added relation. In the anonymity experiment, we restrict the adversary to querying each message only once to the signing oracle for each tag T. Since the adversary will obtain a different set of V than the previous one, the adversary can distinguish between the hybrid experiments. Previous works such as [9] also had to overcome similar situations. However, they add one more relation by using public key encryption instead of a commitment scheme as our construction.

3. Shortening Signature Size to Logarithmic. Our signature size is still linear in l. There are two main obstacles to reducing the signature size. Firstly, the ring signature Σ containing all the ciphertexts $ct_1, \ldots, ct_l$. Secondly, the witnesses for the π protocol are also linear in l. Since we add another relation to $\mathcal{L}$ and do not directly switch witnesses over the ct ciphertext in the proving anonymity, we only need to use one ciphertext ct instead of two one as in construction [1] where the real signer generates one ciphertext and another is chosen randomly. The π protocol then proves the statement $(\mathsf{m}, \mathsf{ct}, \mathsf{VK}_1, \mathsf{v}_1, \ldots, \mathsf{VK}_l, \mathsf{v}_l)$ that there are indices i, j such that ct is a ciphertext using the public key pk_i of the signature σ, where signature σ is a signature of message m by using secret key sk_i with the corresponding public key pk_i or all above computation is done by signer j or two signers i, j have nonces such that $\mathsf{F}(\mathsf{nonce}_i) = \mathsf{nonce}_j$. Now, the ring signature is $\Sigma = (\mu, \mathsf{ct}, \pi)$. For witness compression, we use the somewhere perfect binding hash function SPB to compress the $\mathsf{G} = (\mathsf{VK}_1, \mathsf{v}_1, \ldots, \mathsf{VK}_l, \mathsf{v}_l)$ into h_i and h_j, where the value h_i and h_j is tied to the index i of the real signer and index j of a random user in the ring.

4. Reducing Underlying Primitives: We use a Sig signature scheme with EU-CMA security and a pseudorandom function E with unique output in the above construction. However, we can completely replace the use of both Sig and E by using the only function VRF. Given a secret key sk as input and a message m, the VRF function outputs a pseudorandom evaluation v and a proof p. The verifier can check the correctness of evaluation v by using the message m, proof p and the corresponding public key vk. Furthermore, if p is unknown, the output v is still pseudorandom. Since VRF is a deterministic algorithm, using v can guarantee distinction between users in the ring. The value v is considered a unique value for each signer. Hence, we require the VRF function to be key collision resistance to ensure that the same output will not be produced with different secret keys and the same T. We use the ciphertext of p instead of encrypting signature σ.

5. The Efficiency of Our Construction: Our signature includes $(\mu, \mathsf{ct}, \mathsf{hk}_i, \mathsf{hk}_j, \pi)$. The ciphertext ct and μ are logarithmic in size and independent of the number of users in the ring. Using an efficiency SPB hashing scheme, the hashing key $\mathsf{hk}_i, \mathsf{hk}_j$ and the proof π are logarithmic sizes. Hence, our signature is logarithmic size.

3   Preliminaries

This section will recall some cryptographic primitives that are building blocks for our construction. We will use λ as a main security parameter. We will write $y \leftarrow \mathcal{A}(x, \mathsf{r})$ to denote that y is the output of the probabilistic algorithm $\mathcal{A}$ with input x and random coin r. We denote $[l]$ as the set $\{1, 2, \ldots, l\}$. Let $\mathsf{r} \leftarrow_s \mathsf{S}$ denote r be chosen uniformly random from the set S.

Definition 1 (Public Key Encryption, [1,9]). *A public key encryption scheme* PKE *consists of 3 PPT algorithms* (PKE.KeyGen, PKE.Enc, PKE.Dec) *with the following syntax:*

- $(\mathsf{pk}, \mathsf{sk}) \leftarrow$ PKE.KeyGen(1^λ). *On input of a security parameter* 1^λ, *this PPT algorithm outputs a pair of public and secret keys* (pk, sk).

- ct ← PKE.Enc(pk, m). *On input of a public key* pk *and a message* m, *this PPT algorithm outputs a ciphertext* ct.
- m ← PKE.Dec(sk, ct). *On input of a secret key* sk *and a ciphertext* ct, *this deterministic algorithm outputs a message* m.

We consider the following properties of a PKE scheme. Firstly, the property of *perfect correctness* guarantees that the original plaintext can be obtained through decryption if the keys and ciphertexts were generated honestly. Secondly, *pseudorandom public keys* ensure that public keys are computationally indistinguishable from uniform. Thirdly, *key privacy* guarantees that the adversary, without knowledge about the secret keys, cannot determine for which public key a ciphertext has been computed. Fourthly, IND-CPA guarantees that knowing only the public key, it is computationally infeasible to decide which message is contained in a ciphertext.

Definition 2 (Commitment Schemes, [1]). *A commitment scheme* CS *consists of two algorithms* (CS.Com, CS.Verify) *defined the following:*

- (com, γ) ← CS.Com(1^λ, m): *On input a security parameter* 1^λ, *a message* m, *this PPT algorithm outputs a commitment value* com *and unveil information* γ.
- b ← CS.Verify(com, m, γ): *On input a commitment value com, a message m, and unveil information* γ, *this deterministic algorithm outputs a single bit* $b \in \{0, 1\}$.

We consider the following properties of a commitment scheme. Firstly, the property of *correctness* guarantees that for any message m, if a commitment and an opening are honestly generated, the verification process should always confirm the commitment as valid for that message. Secondly, *perfect binding* guarantees that it should be impossible for any adversary to produce two different messages that correspond to the same commitment and both verify as valid. Last, *computational hiding* guarantees that for any two different messages, their corresponding commitments should be computationally indistinguishable.

Definition 3 (Somewhere Perfectly Binding Hashing, [1]). *A somewhere perfectly binding hash family with private local opening* SPB *consists of four algorithms* (SPB.Gen, SPB.Hash, SPB.Open, SPB.Verify) *defined the following:*

- (hk, shk) ← SPB.Gen(1^λ, n, ind). *On input of a security parameter* 1^λ, *a database size n and an index* ind, *this PPT algorithm outputs public hashing key* hk *and corresponding secret hashing key* shk.
- h ← SPB.Hash(hk, db). *On input a hashing key* hk, *a database* db *of size n, this deterministic algorithm outputs a hash value* h.
- τ ← SPB.Open(hk, shk, db, ind). *On input a hashing key* hk, *private hashing key* shk, *a database* db *of size n, and index* ind, *this algorithm outputs a witness* τ.
- b ← SPB.Verify(hk, h, ind, x, τ). *On input a hashing key* hk, *a hash value* h, *and an index* ind, *this algorithm outputs a single bit* $b \in \{0, 1\}$.

We consider several following properties. Firstly, *correctness* ensures that the verification process will be successful if the keys, hashes, and openings are generated truthfully. Secondly, *efficiency* ensures that the size of public hashing hk and witnesses τ is logarithmic with the number of ring users. Moreover, the Verify algorithm can be computed by a circuit of size $\log(n) \cdot \text{poly}(\lambda)$. Thirdly, *somewhere perfectly binding* ensures that if a particular index i and value x pass verification, all valid openings for that index must result in x. Lastly, *index hiding* means that an efficient attacker cannot determine the index i from the public hashing key.

Let $\mathcal{R}$ be an efficiently computable binary relation, where for $(\mathbf{x}, \mathbf{w}) \in \mathcal{R}$ ($\mathbf{x}$ is a statement and $\mathbf{w}$ is the witness). The language $\mathcal{L}_\mathcal{R}$ is defined as all statements that have a valid witness in $\mathcal{R}$, i.e. $\mathcal{L}_\mathcal{R} := \{\mathbf{x} \mid \exists \mathbf{w} : (\mathbf{x}, \mathbf{w}) \in \mathcal{R}\}$.

Definition 4 (Non-Interactive Proof System, [1]). *Let $\mathcal{R}$ be an efficiently computable witness relation, and $\mathcal{L}_\mathcal{R}$ be the language accepted by $\mathcal{R}$. A non-interactive witness-indistinguishable proof system NIWI for $\mathcal{L}_\mathcal{R}$ includes two algorithms* (NIWI.Prove, NIWI.Verify) *with the following syntax:*

- $\pi \leftarrow$ NIWI.Prove$(1^\lambda, \mathbf{x}, \mathbf{w})$. *On input a statement $\mathbf{x}$ and a witness $\mathbf{w}$, output a proof π or $\bot$.*
- $b \leftarrow$ NIWI.Verify$(\mathbf{x}, \pi)$. *Given a statement $\mathbf{x}$ and a proof π, it outputs a bit b.*

We consider the following properties. Firstly, *perfect completeness* ensures that correct statements can always be proven. Secondly, *perfect soundness* prevents the generation of valid proofs for false statements. Thirdly, *witness indistinguishability* states that given two valid witnesses for a statement, no efficient adversary can determine which witness was used to compute the proof.

Definition 5 (Verifiable Random Function, [9]). *A verifiable random function is 4-tuple* (VRF.Gen, VRF.Eval, VRF.Prove, VRF.Verfify) *with the following syntax:*

- (vk, sk) $\leftarrow$ VRF.Gen(1^λ) : *On input a security parameter 1^λ, this PPT algorithm outputs a public verification key vk and corresponding secret key sk.*
- v $\leftarrow$ VRF.Eval(sk, x) : *On input the secret key sk and an input value $x \in \{0,1\}^{a(\lambda)}$, this deterministic algorithm outputs a value $v \in \{0,1\}^{b(\lambda)}$ ($a(\lambda)$ and $b(\lambda)$ are polynomial bounded and efficiently computable function in λ). Moreover, we require $\{0,1\}^{b(\lambda)}$ is well defined with addition operation (if $v, w \in \{0,1\}^{b(\lambda)}$ then $v + w \in \{0,1\}^{b(\lambda)}$) and scalar multiplication operation (if $c = j/i$, where $i, j \in [N], N$ is some integer, $v \in \{0,1\}^{b(\lambda)}$ then $c \cdot v \in \{0,1\}^{b(\lambda)}$).*
- p $\leftarrow$ VRF.Prove(sk, x) : *On input a secret key sk and an input value x, this PPT algorithm outputs a proof p.*
- $b \leftarrow$ VRF.Verify(vk, x, v, p). *On input a verification key vk, an input value x, a value v, and a proof p, this deterministic algorithm outputs a single bit b.*

We consider several following properties for VRFs. Firstly, *complete provability* ensures that outputs and proofs generated from consistent inputs will verify each other. Secondly, *unique provability* provides only one valid proof for each input. Thirdly, *residual unpredictability* ensures that an adversary cannot predict outputs. Fourthly, *key privacy* ensures that the public key cannot be determined from the output values. Fifthly, *key collision resistance* guarantees that the same output will not be produced with different secret keys. Sixthly, *residual pseudorandomness* ensures that the adversary cannot distinguish between outputs and random values. *Last one*, we also require the output domain of VRF to be *intersection-free range and well-defined with addition and scalar multiplication operations*. These properties are somewhat restrictive. However, in [Sect. 3.5.1, [6]], they show that Fujisaki's construction [8] based on DDH satisfies these requirements. In addition, in [Sect. 4, [6]], they introduce another instantiation based on lattice assumption that fully satisfies these requirements. Following the same argument in [6], VRF schemes that meet all the above requirements can be constructed from DDH [11].

Definition 6 (One-Way Function, [9]). *A one-way function* $y \leftarrow \mathsf{F}(1^\lambda, x)$ *with input the security* λ *and* $x \in \{0, 1\}^\lambda$, *is a deterministic algorithm that computes an output* $y \in \{0, 1\}^\lambda$.

We require F to be *efficiently computable*, and *hard to invert* function. Let $(x_1, \ldots, x_l)$, where $x_i \leftarrow_\$ \{0, 1\}^\lambda$ and $l = \mathsf{poly}(\lambda)$. The probability that there exists a pair (x_i, x_j) such that $\mathsf{F}(x_i) = x_j$ is negligible in λ [Lemma 1, [9]].

4 Traceable Ring Signatures

In this section, we first recall the definition and security model for traceable ring signatures in Sect. 4.1. Our construction of the compact traceable ring signature in the plain model is presented in Sect. 4.2, and Sect. 4.3 is devoted to the security proof.

4.1 Definition

Definition 7 (Traceable Ring Signatures). *A traceable ring signature* TRS *scheme is given by 4-tuple algorithm* (TRS.KeyGen, TRS.Sign, TRS.Verify, TRS.Trace) *defined as follows:*

- (VK, SK) ← TRS.KeyGen(1^λ). *On input of the public parameter* 1^λ, *this PPT algorithm generates a public verification key* VK *and a corresponding secret key* SK *for a signer.*
- Σ ← TRS.Sign(SK, T, m). *On input a signing key* SK, *a tag* T = (R = (VK$_i$)$_{[l]}$, issue) *and a message* m $\in \{0, 1\}^*$, *this PPT algorithm outputs a signature* Σ *on* m.
- b ← TRS.Verify(T, Σ, m). *On input a tag* T, *a signature* Σ *and a message* m $\in \{0, 1\}^*$, *this deterministic algorithm outputs a bit* b.
- γ ← TRS.Trace(T, m, Σ, m', Σ'). *On input a tag* T *and two message/signature pair* (m, Σ) *and* (m', Σ'), *this deterministic algorithm outputs* γ, *where* $\gamma \in$ {accept, reject, linked, VK}.

We require the following properties for traceable ring signatures. First, the correctness guarantees that a signature generated by honest users will pass the verification algorithm with all but negligible probability.

Definition 8 (Correctness). *We say that a traceable ring signature* TRS *is correct, if for all* $\lambda \in \mathbb{N}$, *all* $l = \mathsf{poly}(\lambda)$, *all* $i \in [l]$ *and all message* $\mathsf{m} \in \{0,1\}^*$ *that if for* $i \in [l]$, $(\mathsf{VK}_i, \mathsf{SK}_i) \leftarrow \mathsf{TRS.KeyGen}(1^\lambda)$, $\mathsf{T} = (\mathsf{R} = (\mathsf{VK}_i)_{[l]}, \mathsf{issue})$ *for some* issue, $\Sigma \leftarrow \mathsf{TRS.Sign}(\mathsf{SK}, \mathsf{T}, \mathsf{m})$, *then it holds that*

$$\Pr[\mathsf{TRS.Verify}(\mathsf{T}, \Sigma, \mathsf{m}) = 1] = 1 - \mathsf{negl}(\lambda).$$

where the probability is taken over the coin tosses of algorithms TRS.Setup, TRS.KeyGen *and* TRS.Sign.

Second, it ensures that two signatures are linked if they are signed by the same signer on the same message and have the same tag. However, the signer who generates two signatures for distinct messages with the same tag can be traced. Anyone can conduct the tracing by utilising message/signature pairs and the tag.

Definition 9 (Public Traceability). *We say that a traceable ring signature* TRS *is public traceable, if for all* $\lambda \in \mathbb{N}$, *all* $l = \mathsf{poly}(\lambda)$, *all* $\mathsf{m}, \mathsf{m}', \mathsf{issue}$, *for all* $i \in [l]$, $(\mathsf{VK}_i, \mathsf{SK}_i) \leftarrow \mathsf{TRS.KeyGen}(1^\lambda)$, *tag* $\mathsf{T} = (\mathsf{R} = (\mathsf{VK}_i)_{[l]}, \mathsf{issue})$, *signatures* $\Sigma \leftarrow \mathsf{TRS.Sign}(\mathsf{SK}_i, \mathsf{T}, \mathsf{m})$ *and* $\Sigma' \leftarrow \mathsf{TRS.Sign}(\mathsf{SK}_j, \mathsf{T}, \mathsf{m}')$, *it holds that if* $\mathsf{TRS.Verify}(\mathsf{T}, \Sigma, \mathsf{m}) = 1$ *and* $\mathsf{TRS.Verify}(\mathsf{T}, \Sigma', \mathsf{m}') = 1$ *then*

$$\mathsf{TRS.Trace}(\mathsf{T}, \mathsf{m}, \Sigma, \mathsf{m}', \Sigma') = \begin{cases} \text{accepted} & \text{if } i \neq j \\ \text{linked} & \text{else if } \mathsf{m} = \mathsf{m}' \\ \mathsf{VK}_i & \text{otherwise } \mathsf{m} \neq \mathsf{m}' \end{cases}$$

with overwhelming probability. Otherwise, it returns reject. *The probability is taken over the coin tosses of algorithms* TRS.Setup, TRS.KeyGen *and* TRS.Sign.

Third, an honest ring user cannot be accused of signing twice with respect to the same tag. Specifically, an adversary cannot generate a traceable ring signature that can be used to identify the target signer using a publicly traceable algorithm when combined with a signature generated by the target user. In our exculpability experiment, all user's keys are generated by the experiment. After that, the adversary can learn some of the users' secrets. However, the adversary cannot add his key to the user's ring.

Definition 10 (Exculpability). *We say that a trace ring signature* TRS *is exculpable if, for every PPT adversary* $\mathcal{A}$, *it holds that* $\mathcal{A}$ *has a negligible advantage in the following experiment.*
$\mathsf{Exp}_{\mathsf{TRS-Excul}}$:

1. *For all* $i = 1, \ldots, l$, *generate* $(\mathsf{VK}_i, \mathsf{SK}_i) \leftarrow \mathsf{TRS.KeyGen}(1^\lambda, \mathsf{r}_i)$ *by using random coins* r_i. *The experiment sets* $\mathsf{R} = (\mathsf{VK}_1, \ldots, \mathsf{VK}_l)$.
2. *The adversary chooses a public key* $\mathsf{VK} \in \mathsf{R}$ *and provides it to the experiment.*

3. *Excepting a random coin used to generate the pair of keys* $(\mathsf{VK}, \mathsf{SK})$, *the experiment provides all other random coins to the adversary* $\mathcal{A}$.

4. *The* $\mathcal{A}$ *can access the signing oracle with respect to* SK, $\mathsf{TRS.Sign}_{\mathsf{SK}}$ *to query signing any* $(\mathsf{T}, \hat{\mathsf{m}})$, *where* $\mathsf{T} = (\mathsf{R}, \mathsf{issue})$.

5. *In the end, the adversary* $\mathcal{A}$ *outputs two pairs,* $(\mathsf{T}, \mathsf{m}, \Sigma)$ *and* $(\mathsf{T}, \mathsf{m}', \Sigma')$, *where* $\mathsf{T} = (\mathsf{R}, \mathsf{issue})$ *and* $\mathsf{VK} \in \mathsf{R}$.

6. *The experiment outputs 1 if the following conditions hold:*
   i. $\mathsf{TRS.Verify}(\mathsf{T}, \mathsf{m}, \Sigma) = 1$ *and* $\mathsf{TRS.Verify}(\mathsf{T}, \mathsf{m}', \Sigma') = 1$
   ii. $\mathsf{TRS.Trace}(\mathsf{T}, \mathsf{m}, \Sigma, \mathsf{m}', \Sigma') = \mathsf{VK}$
   iii. *At least of* $(\mathsf{T}, \mathsf{m}, \Sigma)$ *and* $(\mathsf{T}, \mathsf{m}', \Sigma')$ *is not linked to any* $(\mathsf{T}, \hat{\mathsf{m}}, \hat{\Sigma})$ *in query/answer list between* $\mathcal{A}$ *and* $\mathsf{TRS.Sign}_{\mathsf{SK}}$.

Fourth, the signer's identity is indistinguishable from any of the possible ring members as long as a signer does not sign on two different messages with respect to the same tag. Moreover, any two signatures generated with respect to two distinct tags cannot be linked. Namely, no one can determine whether the same signer generates them. In our experiment on anonymity, the adversary is limited to querying the signing oracle for each tag T only once per message.

Definition 11 (Anonymity). *We say that a trace ring signature* TRS *is anonymous if every PPT adversary* $\mathcal{A}$, *it holds that* $\mathcal{A}$ *has a negligible advantage in the following experiment.*
$\mathsf{Exp}_{\mathsf{TRS\text{-}Anon}}(\mathcal{A})$:

1. *For* $i = 1, 2$, *the experiment generates* $(\mathsf{VK}_i, \mathsf{SK}_i) \leftarrow \mathsf{TRS.KeyGen}(1^\lambda)$.

2. *Sample* $b \leftarrow_{\$} \{1, 2\}$.

3. *The experiment provides* $\mathsf{VK}_1, \mathsf{VK}_2$ *to* $\mathcal{A}$. *The adversary* $\mathcal{A}$ *can append new keys to the global public key list* R. *The experiment requires* VK_1, *and* VK_2 *must be included in* R. *Moreover,* $\mathcal{A}$ *can access three signing oracles* $\mathsf{TRS.Sign}_{\mathsf{SK}_b}, \mathsf{TRS.Sign}_{\mathsf{SK}_1}$ *and* $\mathsf{TRS.Sign}_{\mathsf{SK}_2}$, *where*
   i. $\mathsf{TRS.Sign}_{\mathsf{SK}_b}$ *is challenge signing oracle with respect to* SK_b *for signing* (T, m). *The experiment requires if* (T, m) *and* $(\mathsf{T}', \mathsf{m}')$ *are two queries of* $\mathcal{A}$ *to the challenge signing oracle* $\mathsf{TRS.Sign}_{\mathsf{SK}_b}$ *then* $\mathsf{T}' \neq \mathsf{T}$.
   ii. $\mathsf{TRS.Sign}_{\mathsf{SK}_1}$ *(resp.* $\mathsf{TRS.Sign}_{\mathsf{SK}_2}$*) is the signing oracle with respect to* SK_1 *(resp.* SK_2*) for signing* (T, m). *The experiment requires if* (T, m) *is a query of* $\mathcal{A}$ *to* $\mathsf{TRS.Sign}_{\mathsf{SK}_b}$ *and* $(\mathsf{T}', \mathsf{m}')$ *is a query of* $\mathcal{A}$ *to* $\mathsf{TRS.Sign}_{\mathsf{SK}_1}$ *or* $\mathsf{TRS.Sign}_{\mathsf{SK}_2}$ *then* $\mathsf{T}' \neq \mathsf{T}$.

4. $\mathcal{A}$ *outputs a guess* $b' \in \{1, 2\}$. *The experiment outputs 1 if* $b' = b$. *Otherwise, it outputs 0.*

Fifth, it guarantees the link between every pair of signatures generated by the same signer for the same tag. If any two signatures are not linked, the maximum number of signatures with the same tag cannot be greater than the total number of members in the tag. In our tag-linkability, the experiment generates all keys on the ring for users. Subsequently, the adversary may uncover certain user secrets. Nevertheless, the adversary is prohibited from appending their key to those of the users.

Definition 12 (Tag-linkability). *We say that a traceable ring signature TRS is tag-linkable if every PPT adversary $\mathcal{A}$, it holds that $\mathcal{A}$ has at most negligible advantage in the following experiment.*
$\mathsf{Exp}_{\mathsf{TRS\text{-}TagL}}(\mathcal{A})$:

1. *For all $i = 1, \ldots, l$, generate $(\mathsf{VK}_i, \mathsf{SK}_i) \leftarrow \mathsf{TRS.KeyGen}(1^\lambda, \mathsf{r}_i)$ by using random coins r_i. The experiment sets $\mathsf{R} = (\mathsf{VK}_1, \ldots, \mathsf{VK}_l)$.*
2. *The experiment provides all random coins r_i for all $i = 1, \ldots, l$ used to generate the keys to the adversary $\mathcal{A}$.*
3. *Adversary outputs $\mathsf{T} = (\mathsf{R}, \mathsf{issue})$ and $(l + 1)$ message/signature pairs, $(\mathsf{m}_1, \Sigma_1), \ldots, (\mathsf{m}_{l+1}, \Sigma_{l+1})$, where $\mathsf{R} = (\mathsf{VK}_1, \ldots, \mathsf{VK}_l)$.*
4. *If the experiment outputs 1 if the following conditions hold:*
   i. $\mathsf{TRS.Verify}(\mathsf{T}, \mathsf{m}_i, \Sigma_i) = 1, \forall i \in [l + 1]$
   ii. $\mathsf{TRS.Trace}(\mathsf{T}, \mathsf{m}_i, \Sigma_i, \mathsf{m}_j, \Sigma_j) = \mathsf{accepted}, \forall i, j \in [l + 1]$ s.t. $i \neq j$.
   Otherwise, the experiment outputs 0.

A traceable ring signature is unforgeable if it is tag-linkable and exculpable [Theorem 2.6, [8]].

4.2   Our Traceable Ring Signature Construction

In this section, we will present a construction of a traceable ring signature scheme. Let

- $\mathsf{VRF} = (\mathsf{VRF.Gen}, \mathsf{VRF.Eval}, \mathsf{VRF.Prove}, \mathsf{VRF.Verfify})$ be a verifiable random function.
- $\mathsf{PKE} = (\mathsf{PKE.Gen}, \mathsf{PKE.Enc}, \mathsf{PKE.Dec})$ be a public encryption scheme.
- $\mathsf{SPB} = (\mathsf{SPB.Gen}, \mathsf{SPB.Hash}, \mathsf{SPB.Open}, \mathsf{SPB.Verify})$ be a somewhere perfectly binding hash function.
- Hash be a collision-resistant hash function with the same output range of the VRF function.
- $\mathsf{CS} = (\mathsf{CS.Com}, \mathsf{CS.Verfify})$ be a commitment scheme.
- F be a one-way function.
- $\mathsf{NIWI} = (\mathsf{NIWI.Prove}, \mathsf{NIWI.Verify})$ be a NIWI proof system for the language $\mathcal{L}$ defined as in Eq. (1).

Firstly, we define relation $\mathcal{R}_1$ consisting of the statement $\mathbf{x}_1$ and witness $\mathbf{w}_1$, where

$$\mathbf{x}_1 = (\mathsf{m}, \mathsf{T}, \mathsf{V}, \mathsf{ct}, \mathsf{hk}_i, \mathsf{h}_i), \text{ where } \mathsf{T} = ((\mathsf{VK}_1, \ldots, \mathsf{VK}_l), \mathsf{issue}), \mathsf{V} = (\mathsf{v}_1, \ldots, \mathsf{v}_l)$$
$$\mathbf{w}_1 = (\mathsf{VK}_i, i, \mathsf{p}_i, \mathsf{r}_{\mathsf{ct}}, \tau_i), \text{ where } \mathsf{VK}_i = (\mathsf{vk}_i, \mathsf{pk}_i, \mathsf{com}_i), \text{ for some index } i \in [l].$$

satisfying the following:

$$\mathsf{SPB.Verfify}(\mathsf{hk}_i, \mathsf{h}_i, i, (\mathsf{VK}_i, \mathsf{v}_i), \tau_i) = 1$$
$$\text{and } \mathsf{PKE.Enc}(\mathsf{pk}_i, \mathsf{p}_i, \mathsf{r}_{\mathsf{ct}}) = \mathsf{ct}$$
$$\text{and } \mathsf{VRF.Verify}(\mathsf{vk}_i, \mathsf{T}, \mathsf{v}_i, \mathsf{p}_i) = 1$$

We define relation $\mathcal{R}_2$ as the same $\mathcal{R}_1$ except that it is true for index j and $j \neq i$. Namely, the relation $\mathcal{R}_2$ contains $(\mathbf{x}_2, \mathbf{w}_2)$, where

$\mathbf{x}_2 = (\mathsf{m}, \mathsf{T}, \mathsf{V}, \mathsf{ct}, \mathsf{hk}_j, \mathsf{h}_j)$, where $\mathsf{T} = ((\mathsf{VK}_1, \dots, \mathsf{VK}_l), \mathsf{issue})$, $\mathsf{V} = (\mathsf{v}_1, \dots, \mathsf{v}_l)$
$\mathbf{w}_2 = (\mathsf{VK}_j, j, \mathsf{p}_i, \mathsf{r}_{\mathsf{ct}}, \tau_j)$, where $\mathsf{VK}_j = (\mathsf{vk}_j, \mathsf{pk}_j, \mathsf{com}_j)$, for some index $j \in [l]$.

Let $\mathcal{L}_1, \mathcal{L}_2$ be the language accepted by $\mathcal{R}_1$ and $\mathcal{R}_2$ (respectively). Next, we consider relation $\mathcal{R}_3$ consisting of $(\mathbf{x}_3, \mathbf{w}_3)$, where

$\mathbf{x}_3 = (\mathsf{m}, \mathsf{T}, \mathsf{V}, \mathsf{h}_i, \mathsf{h}_j, \mathsf{hk}_i, \mathsf{hk}_j)$, where $\mathsf{T} = ((\mathsf{VK}_1, \dots \mathsf{VK}_l), \mathsf{issue})$, $\mathsf{V} = (\mathsf{v}_1, \dots, \mathsf{v}_l)$
$\mathbf{w}_3 = (\mathsf{VK}_i, \mathsf{VK}_j, i, j, \tau_i, \tau_j, \mathsf{nonce}_i, \mathsf{nonce}_j, \gamma_i, \gamma_j)$, for some index $i \neq j \in [l]$.

satisfying the following:

$$\mathsf{SPB.Verfify}(\mathsf{hk}_i, \mathsf{h}_i, i, (\mathsf{VK}_i, \mathsf{v}_i), \tau_i) = 1$$
$$\text{and } \mathsf{SPB.Verfify}(\mathsf{hk}_j, \mathsf{h}_j, j, (\mathsf{VK}_j, \mathsf{v}_j), \tau_j) = 1$$
$$\text{and } \mathsf{CS.Verify}(\mathsf{com}_i, \mathsf{nonce}_i, \gamma_i) = 1$$
$$\text{and } \mathsf{CS.Verify}(\mathsf{com}_j, \mathsf{nonce}_j, \gamma_j) = 1$$
$$\text{and } \mathsf{F}(\mathsf{nonce}_i) = \mathsf{nonce}_j$$

Let $\mathcal{L}_3$ be the language accepted by $\mathcal{R}_3$. Define the language $\mathcal{L}$ as

$$\mathcal{L} := \mathcal{L}_1 \vee \mathcal{L}_2 \vee \mathcal{L}_3. \tag{1}$$

The statements and witness for $\mathcal{L}$ are of the form:

$\mathbf{x} = (\mathsf{m}, \mathsf{T}, \mathsf{V}, \mathsf{ct}, \mathsf{h}_i, \mathsf{h}_j, \mathsf{hk}_i, \mathsf{hk}_j)$, where $\mathsf{T} = ((\mathsf{VK}_1, \dots, \mathsf{VK}_l), \mathsf{issue})$, $\mathsf{V} = (\mathsf{v}_1, \dots, \mathsf{v}_l)$
$\mathbf{w} = (\mathsf{VK}_i, \mathsf{VK}_j, i, j, \mathsf{p}_i, \mathsf{r}_{\mathsf{ct}}, \tau_i, \tau_j, \mathsf{nonce}_i, \mathsf{nonce}_j, \gamma_i, \gamma_j)$.

Our traceable ring signature $\mathsf{TRS} = (\mathsf{TRS.KeyGen}, \mathsf{TRS.Sign}, \mathsf{TRS.Verify}, \mathsf{TRS.Trace})$ consists of four algorithms defined as follows:

$\mathsf{TRS.KeyGen}(1^\lambda)$: On input a security parameter 1^λ, it does as follows.
  - Compute $(\mathsf{vk}, \mathsf{sk}) \leftarrow \mathsf{VRF.Gen}(1^\lambda)$
  - Choose $\mathsf{pk}, \mathsf{nonce}$ uniformly at random
  - Compute $(\mathsf{com}, \gamma) \leftarrow \mathsf{CS.Com}(1^\lambda, \mathsf{nonce})$
  - Set $\mathsf{VK} := (\mathsf{vk}, \mathsf{pk}, \mathsf{com})$ and $\mathsf{SK} := (\mathsf{sk}, \mathsf{nonce}, \gamma)$
  - Return $(\mathsf{VK}, \mathsf{SK})$
$\mathsf{TRS.Sign}(\mathsf{SK}_i, \mathsf{T}, \mathsf{m})$: On input a secret key SK_i of the user i, a tag T, and a message m do the following.
  - Parse $\mathsf{VK}_i = (\mathsf{vk}_i, \mathsf{pk}_i, \mathsf{com}_i)$ and $\mathsf{SK}_i = (\mathsf{sk}_i, \mathsf{nonce}_i, \gamma_i)$
  - Compute $\mathsf{v}_0 \leftarrow \mathsf{Hash}(\mathsf{T}, \mathsf{m})$, $\mathsf{v}_i \leftarrow \mathsf{VRF.Eval}(\mathsf{sk}_i, \mathsf{T})$
  - Compute $\mathsf{p}_i \leftarrow \mathsf{VRF.Prove}(\mathsf{sk}_i, \mathsf{T})$
  - Compute $\mu = (\mathsf{v}_i - \mathsf{v}_0)/i$ and $\mathsf{v}_j = \mathsf{v}_0 + \mu \cdot j$ for all $j \in [l]$ and $j \neq i$
  - Compute $\mathsf{ct} \leftarrow \mathsf{PKE.Enc}(\mathsf{pk}_i, \mathsf{p}_i, \mathsf{r}_{\mathsf{ct}})$,
  - Set $\mathsf{G} := (\mathsf{g}_1, \dots, \mathsf{g}_l)$, where $\mathsf{g}_i := (\mathsf{VK}_i, \mathsf{v}_i)$

- Compute $(\mathsf{hk}_i, \mathsf{skh}_i) \leftarrow \mathsf{SPB}.\mathsf{Gen}(1^\lambda, |\mathsf{G}|, i)$, $\mathsf{h}_i \leftarrow \mathsf{SPB}.\mathsf{Hash}(\mathsf{hk}_i, G)$
- Compute $\tau_i \leftarrow \mathsf{SPB}.\mathsf{Open}(\mathsf{hk}_i, \mathsf{shk}_i, \mathsf{G}, i)$
- Choose uniformly at random index $j \in [l]$ such that $(j \neq i)$
- Choose uniformly at random γ_j, nonce_j
- Compute $(\mathsf{hk}_j, \mathsf{skh}_j) \leftarrow \mathsf{SPB}.\mathsf{Gen}(1^\lambda, |\mathsf{G}|, j)$, and $\mathsf{h}_j \leftarrow \mathsf{SPB}.\mathsf{Hash}(\mathsf{hk}_j, \mathsf{G})$
- Compute $\tau_j \leftarrow \mathsf{SPB}.\mathsf{Open}(\mathsf{hk}_j, \mathsf{shk}_j, \mathsf{G}, j)$
- Set $\mathbf{x} = (\mathsf{m}, \mathsf{T}, \mathsf{V}, \mathsf{ct}, \mathsf{h}_i, \mathsf{h}_j, \mathsf{hk}_i, \mathsf{hk}_j)$, where $\mathsf{T} = ((\mathsf{VK}_1, \ldots, \mathsf{VK}_l), \mathsf{issue})$ and $\mathsf{V} = (\mathsf{v}_1, \ldots, \mathsf{v}_l)$
- Set witness $\mathbf{w} = (\mathsf{VK}_i, \mathsf{VK}_j, i, j, \mathsf{p}_i, \mathsf{r}_{\mathsf{ct}}, \tau_i, \tau_j, \mathsf{nonce}_i, \mathsf{nonce}_j, \gamma_i, \gamma_j)$
- Compute $\pi \leftarrow \mathsf{NIWI}.\mathsf{Prove}(\mathbf{x}, \mathbf{w})$
- Output $\Sigma \leftarrow (\mu, \mathsf{ct}, \mathsf{hk}_i, \mathsf{hk}_j, \pi)$

$\mathsf{TRS}.\mathsf{Verify}(\mathsf{T}, \Sigma, \mathsf{m})$: On input a tag T, a signature Σ and a message m, do the following.

- Parse $\Sigma = (\mu, \mathsf{ct}, \mathsf{hk}_i, \mathsf{hk}_j, \pi)$
- Compute $\mathsf{v}_0 = \mathsf{Hash}(\mathsf{T}, \mathsf{m})$ and $\mathsf{v}_i = \mathsf{v}_0 + i \cdot \mu$ for all $i \in [l]$
- Set $\mathsf{G} = (\mathsf{g}_1, \ldots, \mathsf{g}_l)$, where $\mathsf{g}_i = (\mathsf{VK}_i, \mathsf{v}_i)$ for all $i \in [l]$
- Compute $\mathsf{h}'_i \leftarrow \mathsf{SPB}.\mathsf{Hash}(\mathsf{hk}_i, \mathsf{G})$ and $\mathsf{h}'_j \leftarrow \mathsf{SPB}.\mathsf{Hash}(\mathsf{hk}_j, \mathsf{G})$
- Set $\mathbf{x} = (\mathsf{m}, \mathsf{T}, \mathsf{V}, \mathsf{ct}, \mathsf{h}'_i, \mathsf{h}'_j, \mathsf{hk}_i, \mathsf{hk}_j)$
- Output $\mathsf{NIWI}.\mathsf{Verify}(\mathbf{x}, \pi)$

$\mathsf{TRS}.\mathsf{Trace}(\mathsf{T}, \mathsf{m}, \Sigma, \mathsf{m}', \Sigma')$: On input an tag T and two pairs of message-signature (m, Σ) and (m', Σ'), do the following.

- If $\mathsf{TRS}.\mathsf{Verify}(\mathsf{T}, \Sigma, \mathsf{m}) = 0$ or $\mathsf{TRS}.\mathsf{Verify}(\mathsf{T}, \Sigma', \mathsf{m}) = 0$, then return reject
- Parse $\Sigma = (\mu, \mathsf{ct}, \mathsf{hk}_i, \mathsf{hk}_j, \pi)$ and $\Sigma' = (\mu', \mathsf{ct}', \mathsf{hk}'_i, \mathsf{hk}'_j, \pi')$.
- For all $i \in [l]$, compute $\mathsf{v}_i = \mathsf{v}_0 + i \cdot \mu$, where $\mathsf{v}_0 = \mathsf{Hash}(\mathsf{T}, \mathsf{m})$. Set $\mathsf{V} = (\mathsf{v}_1, \ldots, \mathsf{v}_l)$
- For all $i \in [l]$, compute $\mathsf{v}'_i = \mathsf{v}'_0 + i \cdot \mu'$, where $\mathsf{v}'_0 = \mathsf{Hash}(\mathsf{T}, \mathsf{m}')$. Set $\mathsf{V}' = (\mathsf{v}'_1, \ldots, \mathsf{v}'_l)$
- If $\mathsf{v}_i = \mathsf{v}'_i$, for all $i \in [l]$, it outputs Linked
- If there is only one index $i \in [l]$ such that $\mathsf{v}_i = \mathsf{v}'_i$ then it outputs the verification key VK_i
- Otherwise, it outputs accept

Theorem 1 (Correctness). *If the* $\mathsf{NIWI}, \mathsf{VRF}, \mathsf{PKE}$ *and* SPB *scheme are correct then* TRS *is correct. Moreover, our scheme has a logarithmic signature size.*

Proof. The proof of correctness follows directly from the construction. □

Theorem 2 (Public Traceability). *If* VRF *has residual pseudorandomness, key collision resistance, unique provability and intersection-free range, then* TRS *is public traceability.*

Proof. We consider two traceable ring signatures $\Sigma = (\mu, \mathsf{ct}, \mathsf{hk}_i, \mathsf{hk}_j, \pi)$ and $\Sigma' = (\mu', \mathsf{ct}', \mathsf{hk}'_i, \mathsf{hk}'_j, \pi')$ for two messages m and m' with the same tag T. We have two cases as follows:

1. If $i = i'$ then we have $\mathsf{v}_i = \mathsf{VRF}.\mathsf{Eval}(\mathsf{sk}_i, \mathsf{T}) = \mathsf{VRF}.\mathsf{Eval}(\mathsf{sk}_i, \mathsf{T}) = \mathsf{v}'_i$.

- If $m = m'$ then we have $v_0 = \mathsf{Hash}(T, m) = \mathsf{Hash}(T, m') = v'_0$. This implies $v_j = v'_j$ for all $j \in [l]$. In this case, the $\mathsf{TRS}.\mathsf{Trace}(T, m, \Sigma, m', \Sigma)$ algorithm returns linked.
- If $m \neq m'$ then we have $v_0 = \mathsf{Hash}(T, m) \neq \mathsf{Hash}(T, m') = v'_0$. This implies $\mu \neq \mu'$. Hence, we have $v_j \neq v'_j$ for all $j \in [l]$, $j \neq i$. In this case, there is only one index $i \in [l]$ such that $v_i = v'_i$. The public traceable algorithm returns VK_i.

2. If $i \neq i'$, we have $v_i = \mathsf{VRF}.\mathsf{Eval}(sk_i, T) \neq \mathsf{VRF}.\mathsf{Eval}(sk_{i'}, T) = v'_{i'}$ since VRF has key collision resistance and unique provability. Moreover, by residual pseudorandomness of VRF, we have $v_i, v'_{i'}$ to be pseudorandomness in $\{0, 1\}^{b(\lambda)}$. We consider two following cases:

- If $m \neq m'$ then we have $v_0 = \mathsf{Hash}(T, m) \neq \mathsf{Hash}(T, m') = v'_0$. Assume that the public traceable algorithm does not return accept. In other words, there must exists index $s \in [l]$ such that $v_s = v'_s$, i.e., $\mathsf{Hash}(T, m) + s \cdot \mu = \mathsf{Hash}(T, m') + s \cdot \mu'$. By definition, we have $\mu = \frac{v_i - v_0}{i}$ and $\mu' = \frac{v'_{i'} - v'_0}{i'}$. This implies $(ii' - si') \cdot v_0 + si' \cdot v_i = (ii' - si) \cdot v'_0 + si \cdot v'_{i'}$. Set $c_1 = (ii' - si')$, $d_1 = si'$, $c_2 = (ii' - si)$ and $d_2 = si$. Hence, we have $c_1 \cdot v_0 + d_1 \cdot v_i = c_2 \cdot v'_0 + d_2 \cdot v'_{i'}$. This contradicts the intersection-free range property of the VRF function. Therefore, the $\mathsf{TRS}.\mathsf{Trace}(T, m, \Sigma, m', \Sigma)$ algorithm returns accept in this case.
- If $m = m'$ then we have $v_0 = \mathsf{Hash}(T, m) = \mathsf{Hash}(T, m') = v'_0$. Using the same argument as the above case, we can show that $v_j \neq v'_j$ for all $j \in [l]$. Indeed, assume that the $\mathsf{TRS}.\mathsf{Trace}(T, m, \Sigma, m', \Sigma)$ algorithm does not return accept. In other words, there must exists index $s \in [l]$ such that $v_s = v'_s$, i.e., $v_0 + s \cdot \mu = v'_0 + s \cdot \mu'$. Since $v_0 = v'_0$, this implies $\mu = \mu'$. We have $-i' \cdot v_0 + i' \cdot v_i = -i \cdot v'_0 + i \cdot v'_{i'}$. Let $c_1 = -i'$, $d_1 = i'$, $c_2 = -i$ and $d_2 = i$. Hence, we have $c_1 \cdot v_0 + d_1 \cdot v_i = c_2 \cdot v'_0 + d_2 \cdot v'_{i'}$. This also contradicts the intersection-free range property of the VRF function. Therefore, the public traceable algorithm also returns accept. □

4.3   Security Proofs

This section will present formal security proofs for our traceable ring signature.

Theorem 3 (Exculpability). *If* VRF *has residual unpredictability, intersection-free range,* CS *is perfect binding,* NIWI *has perfect soundness,* SPB *is somewhere perfectly binding,* F *is a one-way function,* PKE *has pseudorandom public keys then* TRS *is exculpable.*

We see that there are two ways the adversary can win the $\mathsf{Exp}_{\mathsf{TRS}\text{-}\mathsf{Excul}}$ experiment. Let $s \in [l]$ be index such that $\mathsf{VK}_s = \mathsf{VK}$. The first way is the adversary can give a valid forgery traceable ring signature with respect to public key VK_s for any message. The second way is the adversary can find two distinct users $i, i' \in [l]$ and $(i \neq i')$ such that $v_0 + \mu \cdot s = v'_0 + \mu' \cdot s$ where $v_0 = \mathsf{Hash}(T, m)$, $v'_0 = \mathsf{Hash}(T, m')$, $\mu = (v_i - v_0)/i$ and $\mu' = (v'_i - v'_0)/i'$. In the first case, we can use the adversary to break the residual unpredictability of the VRF function. In the latter case, we can break the intersection-free range of the VRF function.

Proof. Let $\mathcal{A}$ be a PPT adversary against the exculpability experiment of TRS. We consider the following hybrids:

- Hybrid $\mathcal{H}_0$: This is the real experiment.
- Hybrid $\mathcal{H}_1$: The experiment is the same as $\mathcal{H}_0$, expect that for all $i \in [l]$ the challenger generates the public keys pk_i in VK_i by using $((\mathsf{pk}_i, \hat{\mathsf{sk}}_i)) \leftarrow \mathsf{PKE.KeyGen}(1^\lambda)$ instead of choosing pk_i uniformly at random. Moreover, the challenger stores all the secret keys $\hat{\mathsf{sk}}_{i \in [l]}$. As the public keys of PKE are pseudorandom, $\mathcal{H}_0$ and $\mathcal{H}_1$ are computationally indistinguishable.
- Hybrid $\mathcal{H}_2$: The same as $\mathcal{H}_1$, except that all nonce generated in $\mathsf{TRS.KeyGen}(1^\lambda)$ is chosen in a way there does not exist a pair $(\mathsf{nonce}_i, \mathsf{nonce}_j)$ such that either $\mathsf{nonce}_j = \mathsf{F}(\mathsf{nonce}_i)$ or $\mathsf{nonce}_i = \mathsf{F}(\mathsf{nonce}_j)$ for all $i, j \in [l]$. By the one-way property of F, the probability that such a pair exists is negligible. Hence, the probability of distinguishing between $\mathcal{H}_1$ and $\mathcal{H}_2$ is negligible. Next, we prove that there exists a reduction R such that $\mathsf{R}^{\mathcal{A}}$ breaks the residual unpredictability or intersection-free range of VRF.

Reduction $\mathsf{R}^{\mathcal{A}}(\mathsf{vk})$:

- Guess index $s \in [l]$ that will be chosen by the adversary to insert vk from $\mathsf{Exp}_{\mathsf{VRF-UR}}$. Now, we have $\mathsf{VK} = \mathsf{VK}_s = (\mathsf{vk}, \mathsf{pk}_s, \mathsf{com}_s)$. For all $i \neq s$, generate $(\mathsf{VK}_i, \mathsf{SK}_i)$ as in Hybrid $\mathcal{H}_2$.
- If $\mathcal{A}$ sends signature queries $(\mathsf{m}, \mathsf{VK}, \mathsf{T})$, send T to oracle $\mathsf{VRF.Eval}(\mathsf{sk}, \cdot)$ to obtain (v, p). Then, the challenger computes a signature Σ normally as in the signing algorithm.
- The adversary $\mathcal{A}$ output $(\mathsf{m}, \Sigma, \mathsf{T}), (\mathsf{m}', \Sigma', \mathsf{T})$. We have
  i. $\mathsf{TRS.Verify}(\mathsf{T}, \mathsf{m}, \Sigma) = 1$ and $\mathsf{TRS.Verify}(\mathsf{T}, \mathsf{m}', \Sigma') = 1$
  ii. $\mathsf{TRS.Trace}(\mathsf{T}, \mathsf{m}, \Sigma, \mathsf{m}', \Sigma') = \mathsf{VK} = \mathsf{VK}_s$.
- Parse $\Sigma = (\mu, \mathsf{ct}, \mathsf{hk}_i, \mathsf{hk}_j, \pi)$, $\Sigma' = (\mu', \mathsf{ct}', \mathsf{hk}'_i, \mathsf{hk}'_j, \pi')$,
- Compute $\mathsf{v}_s = \mathsf{v}_0 + s \cdot \mu$ and $\mathsf{v}'_s = \mathsf{v}'_0 + s \cdot \mu'$, where $\mathsf{v}_0 = \mathsf{Hash}(\mathsf{T}, \mathsf{m})$, $\mathsf{v}'_0 = \mathsf{Hash}(\mathsf{T}, \mathsf{m}')$, $\mu = \frac{\mathsf{v}_i - \mathsf{v}_0}{i}$ and $\mu' = \frac{\mathsf{v}'_i - \mathsf{v}'_0}{i'}$. By knowing all secret keys sk_i for all $i \in [l]$ except $i \neq s$, the challenger computes $\mathsf{v}_i = \mathsf{VRF.Eval}(\mathsf{sk}_i, \mathsf{T})$ then checks two cases as follows:
  - If there does not exist two distinct users $i, i' \in [l]$ such that $\mathsf{v}_0 + s \cdot \mu = \mathsf{v}'_0 + s \cdot \mu'$. This implies $i = i' = s$. Then, compute $\mathsf{p}_s \leftarrow \mathsf{PKE.Dec}(\hat{\mathsf{sk}}_s, \mathsf{ct})$ and output $(\mathsf{v}_s, \mathsf{p}_s)$ a break for the residual unpredictability of VRF.
  - If there exist two distinct users $i, i' \in [l]$ such that $\mathsf{v}_0 + s \cdot \mu = \mathsf{v}'_0 + s \cdot \mu'$ then $(ii' - si') \cdot \mathsf{v}_0 + si' \cdot \mathsf{v}_i = (ii' - si) \cdot \mathsf{v}'_0 + si \cdot \mathsf{v}'_{i'}$. Set $c_1 = (ii' - si')$, $d_1 = si'$, $c_2 = (ii' - si)$ and $d_2 = si$. Hence, we have $c_1 \cdot \mathsf{v}_0 + d_1 \cdot \mathsf{v}_i = c_2 \cdot \mathsf{v}'_0 + d_2 \cdot \mathsf{v}'_{i'}$. This breaks the intersection-free range of VRF.

Now, we prove that $\mathsf{VRF.Verify}(\mathsf{vk}, \mathsf{T}, \mathsf{v}_s, \mathsf{p}_s) = 1$. In Hybrid $\mathcal{H}_2$, since CS is perfect binding, the adversary cannot use the relation $\mathcal{R}_3$ to prove the NIWI scheme. In other words, the adversary must use a witness for one of two first relations. By the perfect soundness of the NIWI, it holds that $(m, T, V, ct, hk_i, h_i) \in \mathcal{L}_1$ or $(m, T, V, ct, hk_j, h_j) \in \mathcal{L}_2$, where $T = ((VK_1, \ldots, VK_l), issue)$, $V = (v_1, \ldots, v_l)$. Assume w.l.o.g that $(m, T, V, ct, hk_i, h_i) \in \mathcal{L}_1$. Moreover, as the public traceable algorithm returns VK_s, there exists $(VK, s, p_s, r_{ct}, \tau_s)$ with $VK = (vk, pk_s, com_s)$ such that $SPB.Verfify(hk_s, h_s, s, (VK, v_s), \tau_s) = 1$ and $PKE.Enc(pk_s, p_s, r_{ct}) = ct$ and $VRF.Verify(vk, T, v_s, p_s) = 1$. By the somewhere perfect binding of SPB, we have $h_s = SPB.Hash(hk_s, G)$ and $SPB.Verfify(hk_s, h_s, s, (VK, v_s), \tau_s) = 1$. This implies $VK = VK_s$ and $v_s = VRF.Eval(sk_s, T)$. Moreover, it also holds that $PKE.Enc(pk_s, p_s, r_{ct}) = ct$ and $VRF.Verify(vk, T, v_s, p_s) = 1$. $\square$

Theorem 4 (Anonymity). *If* VRF *has residual pseudorandomness and key privacy,* NIWI *is computationally witness-indistinguishable,* PKE *is IND-CPA and key privacy,* CS *is computational hiding,* SPB *is index hiding, then* TRS *is anonymous.*

Proof. The full version contains detailed proof. $\square$

Theorem 5 (Tag-linkability). *If* VRF *has unique provability,* NIWI *has perfect soundness,* SPB *is somewhere perfectly binding,* CS *is perfectly binding,* PKE *is perfectly correct and* F *is one-way function then* TRS *is tag-linkable.*

To prove tag-linkability, we need to show that an adversary $\mathcal{A}$ who knows up to l secret keys cannot output $(l + 1)$ message-signature pairs with respect to tag T. Informal speaking, to generate a valid message-signature pair, $\mathcal{A}$ needs to provide a valid NIWI proof in the signature. Because NIWI is perfect soundness, the claimed statement must be true. Since the challenger generates l secret keys and F is a one-way function, the probability that there exists a pair $nonce_i$ and $nonce_j$ such that $F(nonce_i) = nonce_j$ is negligible. Even if $\mathcal{A}$ can know l secret key, $\mathcal{A}$ is impossible to find a pair $nonce_i$ and $nonce_j$ in relation $\mathcal{R}_3$. Now, the adversary $\mathcal{A}$ must find another strategy. Namely, $\mathcal{A}$ needs to know a witness of one in two first relations. The somewhere perfect binding property of SPB holds that the adversary must have used a member's identity in the ring. The perfect correctness of the PKE scheme holds that ct must contain a valid proof for respective VRF. Due to the unique provability of the VRF, the adversary cannot generate $(l + 1)$ different evaluated values from l secret keys with respect to tag T.

Proof. The full version contains detailed proof. $\square$

5 Conclusion

A ring signature is a well-studied cryptographic primitive with numerous applications. A traceable ring signature is an enhanced version that retains the flexibility of a ring signature while providing additional security features. This paper presents the first construction of a traceable ring signature in the plain model.

Our scheme achieves a logarithmic signature size relative to the number of ring members, relies only on standard assumptions, and does not require a trusted setup. Since our construction is generic and based on underlying primitives, creating a concrete instantiation may involve making several choices and optimising the primitives, which we identify as a direction for future research.

References

1. Backes, M., Döttling, N., Hanzlik, L., Kluczniak, K., Schneider, J.: Ring signatures: logarithmic-size, no setup-from standard assumptions. In: EUROCRYPT 2019, pp. 281–311. Springer, 2019
2. Beullens, W., Katsumata, S., Pintore, F.: Calamari and falafl: logarithmic (linkable) ring signatures from isogenies and lattices. In: Moriai, S., Wang, H. (eds.) Advances in Cryptology - ASIACRYPT 2020. pp, pp. 464–492. Springer International Publishing, Cham (2020)
3. Branco, P., Mateus, P.: A traceable ring signature scheme based on coding theory. In: PQCrypto 2019, pp. 387–403. Springer, 2019
4. Bultel, X., Lafourcade, P.: k-times full traceable ring signature. In: 2016 11th International Conference on Availability, Reliability and Security (ARES), pp. 39–48. IEEE (2016)
5. Canetti, R., Goldreich, O., Halevi, S.: The random oracle methodology, revisited. J. ACM (JACM) **51**(4), 557–594 (2004)
6. Feng, H., Liu, J., Li, D., Li, Y., Wu, Q.: Traceable ring signatures: general framework and post-quantum security. Des. Codes Cryptogr. **89**(6), 1111–1145 (2021)
7. Fujisaki, E.: Sub-linear size traceable ring signatures without random oracles. In: Cryptographers' Track at the RSA Conference, pp. 393–415. Springer, 2011
8. Fujisaki, E., Suzuki, K.: Traceable ring signature. In: International Workshop on Public Key Cryptography, pp. 181–200. Springer, 2007
9. Haque, A., Krenn, S., Slamanig, D., Striecks, C.: Logarithmic-size (linkable) threshold ring signatures in the plain model. In: Public-Key Cryptography–PKC 2022: 25th IACR International Conference on Practice and Theory of Public-Key Cryptography, Virtual Event, 8–11 March 2022, Proceedings, Part II, pp. 437–467. Springer, 2022
10. Hu, C., Li, D.: Forward-secure traceable ring signature. In: Eighth ACIS International Conference on Software Engineering, Artificial Intelligence, Networking, and Parallel/Distributed Computing (SNPD 2007), vol. 3, pp. 200–204. IEEE (2007)
11. Papadopoulos, D., et al.: Making nsec5 practical for dnssec. Cryptology ePrint Archive, 2017
12. Rivest, R.L., Shamir, A., Tauman, Y.: How to leak a secret. In: Advances in Cryptology - ASIACRYPT 2001, 7th International Conference on the Theory and Application of Cryptology and Information Security, Gold Coast, Australia, 9–13 December 2001, Proceedings, pp. 552–565 (2001)
13. Unruh, D.: Non-interactive zero-knowledge proofs in the quantum random oracle model. In: Annual International Conference on the Theory and Applications of Cryptographic Techniques, pp. 755–784. Springer, 2015
14. Wei, W., Luo, M., Bao, Z., Peng, C., He, D.: Traceable ring signatures from group actions: logarithmic, flexible, and quantum resistant. In: International Conference on Selected Areas in Cryptography (2022)

Tightly Secure Identity-Based Signature from Cryptographic Group Actions

Xuan Thanh Khuc[1]([✉]), Willy Susilo[1], Dung Hoang Duong[1], Fuchun Guo[1], Hyungrok Jo[2], and Tsuyoshi Takagi[3]

[1] Institute of Cybersecurity and Cryptology, School of Computing and Information Technology, University of Wollongong, Wollongong, NSW 2522, Australia
xtk929@uowmail.edu.au, {wsusilo,hduong,fuchun}@uow.edu.au
[2] Institute of Advanced Sciences, Yokohama National University, Yokohama, Kanagawa, Japan
jo-hyungrok-xz@ynu.ac.jp
[3] Department of Mathematical Informatics, Graduate School of Information Science and Technology, The University of Tokyo, Bunkyo, Japan
takagi@mist.i.u-tokyo.ac.jp

Abstract. Identity-based Signatures (IBS) are a form of digital signature scheme that enables the generation and verification of signatures based on a user's identity, such as an email address, social security number, or any other unique identifier. Recent advancements in post-quantum cryptography have further strengthened IBS schemes, making them resilient against quantum computing threats and ensuring their applicability in future secure communications. At ProvSec'21, Shaw and Dutta introduced an identity-based signature obtained from the isogeny-based signature scheme CSI-FiSh by Beullens et al. at ASIACRYPT'19. Later, at PQCrypto'23, Chen et al. proposed a tightly secure IBS by utilising the tightly secure variant of CSI -FiSh, called Lossy CSI -FiSh, by Kaafarani et al. at PKC'20.

In this paper, we generalise those results to obtain a framework for constructing an IBS scheme from cryptographic (non-abelian) group actions. Under the pseudorandom assumption of underlying group actions, we prove that our IBS is tightly secure in the random oracle model. Moreover, we also generalise a Forward-Secure Identity-based Signature (FSIBS) scheme from group actions. This scheme ensures past signatures remain unforgeable even if the current signing key is compromised. Our schemes can be instantiated from existing NIST's post-quantum signature candidates such as MEDS, LESS and ALTEQ.

This research is partially supported by the ARC Linkage Project LP220100332. Willy Susilo is supported by the ARC Australian Laureate Fellowship FL230100033. Fuchun Guo is supported by the ARC Future Fellowship FT220100046. Tsuyoshi Takagi is supported by JST CREST Grant Number JPMJCR2113. Hyungrok Jo conducted this research under a contract of "Research and development on new generation cryptography for secure wireless communication services" among "Research and Development for Expansion of Radio Wave Resources (JPJ000254)", which was supported by the Ministry of Internal Affairs and Communications, Japan.

J. K. Liu et al. (Eds.): ProvSec 2024, LNCS 14903, pp. 209–228, 2025.
https://doi.org/10.1007/978-981-96-0954-3_11

Keywords: Tight security · Group Actions · Identity-based Signatures · Forward-Secure Identity-based Signatures

1   Introduction

1.1   Group Actions in Cryptography

Group actions have been introduced in cryptography first by Brassard and Yung [11] in terms of *one-way group actions*. It has then been studied for commutative groups by Couveignes [16] in terms of *hard homogeneous spaces* and then formulated by Stolbunov [38] in terms of *isogeny-based cryptography*, one of the promising candidates for post-quantum cryptography (PQC). The problem with Stolbunov's scheme is the requirement of an efficient method to sample in the class group and the fact that each class group member should have an efficiently computable unique representation. This problem was solved by De Feo and Galbraith by employing the Fiat-Shamir with Aborts method of Lyubashevsky [30], resulting in an efficient signature instantiation called SeaSign [20]. Later, Beullens et al. [9] returned to Stolbunov's original method and proposed an efficient algorithm to compute the class group action of random class group elements, which yielded an efficient instantiation called CSI-FiSh. Since then, many efficient schemes have been constructed based on CSI-FiSh such as ring signature [8], threshold signature [18].

In terms of non-commutative group actions, several PQC candidates (e.g., signatures) have been introduced. Ji et al. [25] initialized this direction by introducing general linear group actions on tensors and provided some cryptographic constructions, from which general linear group actions on alternating trilinear forms have been studied [39] that results in the signature scheme ALTEQ [10]- a candidate for a recent call by NIST for additional post-quantum signatures [31]. Another direction involves code equivalence which results in two NIST candidates MEDS [15] and LESS [3]. It is worth noted that the underlying mathematical problems of ALTEQ, MEDS, and LESS are polynomial-time equivalent; see [35] and references therein. Due to the non-commutativity of the group actions, all existing cryptographic constructions only consist of signatures [3,10,15], ring signatures [4,13] and threshold signatures [5]. However, the underlying mathematical problems in the non-commutative group action settings can be formalised as the *Hidden Subgroup Problem* for general linear groups, which provides strong security support against quantum attacks; see [39] for further detailed discussions. Another advantage of non-commutative group actions is the flexibility in choosing parameters for designed security level, as opposed to isogeny-based cryptography that is limited to CSIDH-512 parameter computed in CSI-FiSh only [9].

1.2   Identity-Based Signatures

Digital signatures are one of the most basic building blocks in cryptography, and they provide authenticity, integrity, and non-repudiation. In standard schemes, each user creates their key pair, which includes a public key and a secret key that only they know. The public key is used to identify each user. The users aren't usually recognised by randomly generated keys in the real world, though. Instead, their names or email addresses are used. A public-key infrastructure (PKI) must be set up so that public keys can be linked to real-world identities. One way to do this is to have a hierarchy of trusted certification authorities (CAs) that can certify public keys as belonging to a specific person. In order to reduce the need for such big infrastructures, Shamir suggested in his essential work [36] using identity-based signatures, in which a user's public key is his identity. A trusted authority gives out the matching secret key. The trusted authority gets it from a master secret that only the trusted authority knows, and they are thought to have a way to check the user's identity. This relaxes several requirements that come with PKI and certificates, making it possible for schemes to work better. In such a scheme, an honest user with identity id can sign a message M using its secret key usk_{id}, and its signature Σ can be publicly verified, given the master public key mpk and its identity id.

In most cryptographic schemes, including identity-based signatures, security is maintained as long as the secret keys remain confidential. Once a secret key is exposed, the security of both past and future signatures is compromised. Although frequent key revocation could address the key exposure issue, it is inefficient and does not ensure the security (unforgeability) of past signatures. Another potential solution involves secret sharing schemes, but these are costly in terms of computational and communication overhead, as noted in [6]. A promising approach to this problem is to combine forward-secure signatures (FSS) [6] with identity-based signatures to create a forward-secure IBS (FSIBS).

In the group action settings, there have been several IBS proposals. The first isogeny-based IBS (CSIibs) was proposed by Peng et al. [32], but Shaw and Dutta [37] pointed out a flaw in the main structure of CSIibs. To address this issue, they proposed a new ID-based signature scheme incorporating forward secrecy. Subsequently, Chen et al. [12] proposed a scheme with tight security proofs corresponding to a generic construction. In terms of non-commutative group actions, Barenghi et al. [4] proposed an instantiation of IBS based on LESS. Their construction follows the generic framework proposed by Kiltz and Neven [26] in which an IBS can be efficiently generated from a secure digital signature.

1.3   Tight Security Reduction

The Fiat-Shamir transformation [21] uses a cryptographic hash function modelled as a random oracle to convert an identification scheme into a digital signature scheme. This method provides for an easy-to-understand and straightforward construction in the random oracle model (ROM). However, it has a loose reduction, i.e., if an adversary can break the Fiat-Shamir signature with advantage ϵ, the reduction shows that it is possible to break the underlying hard problem with advantage ϵ^2/q_h, where q_h is the number of hash evaluations an adversary can query. Therefore, in order to instantiate the Fiat-Shamir signature with provably secure parameters, we must assume the hardness of the underlying hard problem for a security level that is much higher than expected. This affects all standard Fiat-Shamir signatures, and IBS is no exception. Some evidence exists that the non-tight schemes did not actually attain their claimed security level; see [27, Section 5] for some concrete examples and details.

In [1], Abdalla et al. studied a so-called *lossy identification scheme* from which the corresponding Fiat-Shamir signature is proved to be tightly secure. They also provide instantiations in both classical and post-quantum (lattices) settings. Following this technique, El Kaafarani et al. in [19] proposed a lossy identification from CSI-FiSh [9], which yielded a tightly secure signature scheme from isogenies. At PQCrypto'23, Chen et al. [12] utilised the lossy CSI -FiSh by El Kaafarani et al. [19] to propose a tightly secure IBS from isogeny. In terms of non-commutative group actions, Chen et al. [13] studied lossy identification schemes obtained from non-commutative group actions and proved that the Fiat-Shamir signature is tightly secure under the pseudo-randomness of the underlying group actions.

1.4 Our Contribution

In this paper, we present a tightly secure identity-based signature (IBS) for non-commutative group actions, generalising previous works in the setting of commutative group actions (i.e., isogenies) by Shaw-Dutta [37] and Chen et al. [12], following the proof framework by Fukumitsu and Hasegawa [22]. Due to the (assumed) intransitivity of the non-commutative group actions, our scheme is similar to that by Shaw-Dutta [37], as opposed to the tightly secure one by Chen et al. [12]. The reason is that the class group action on the classes of elliptic curves is transitive. Hence, it is necessary to have two copies in the public key to achieve tight security reduction [19]. We prove that under the pseudorandom assumption of the underlying group actions, our IBS is tightly secure.

We also introduce a forward-secure identity-based signature (FSIBS) scheme based on group action, which ensures the security of past signatures even if the signing key for the current time period is compromised. The primary components of our FSIBS scheme are a group action-based standard signature scheme, our group action-based IBS scheme, and a forward-secure pseudo-random generator. Our FSIBS scheme does not achieve a tight security proof.

1.5 Technique Overview

Let's first recall how a standard signature can be constructed from cryptographic group actions. It follows the framework of the GMW [24] for graph isomorphisms, which can be found in [5,13].

Let X be a finite set and G be a group acting on X. We denote by $\star$ the action of G on X. A GMW-style Sigma protocol can be constructed as in Fig. 1. Here $x_0 \xleftarrow{\$} X$ is uniformly sampled from X, and $g_1, \ldots, g_S \xleftarrow{\$} G$, where $S > 0$ is a positive integer. Set $g_0 = 1_G$ to be the identity of G, and for each $i \in [S] := \{1, \ldots, S\}$, compute $x_i := g_i \star x_0$. The public key is $\mathsf{pk} = (x_0, \ldots, x_S)$ and the secret key is $\mathsf{sk} = (g_0, \ldots, g_S)$. The group action-based sigma protocol has a framework as in Fig. 1.

Prover$(x_0, \ldots, x_S, g_0, \ldots, g_S)$ **Verifier**$(x_0, \ldots, x_S)$

$h \xleftarrow{\$} G, R := h \star x_0$ $\xrightarrow{\quad R \quad}$

                        $\xleftarrow{\quad \alpha \quad}$ $\alpha \xleftarrow{\$} \{0, 1, \ldots, S\}$

$f := hg_\alpha^{-1}$ $\xrightarrow{\quad f \quad}$ Check whether $R \overset{?}{=} f \star x_\alpha$

Fig. 1. A group action-based sigma protocol

For correctness, we can see that $R = hg_\alpha^{-1} \star x_\alpha = (hg_\alpha^{-1} g_\alpha) \star x_0 = h \star x_0$. This scheme has soundness error $\frac{1}{S+1}$, and hence it needs to be repeated several times, say T, to attain the required security level. A signature scheme, called FS$[\Sigma]$ for convenience, is hence obtained through the Fiat-Shamir transformation [21]: a signature for a message M is computed as follows:

- Sample $h_1, \ldots, h_T \xleftarrow{\$} G$ and compute $R_i = h_i \star x_0$ for $i = 1, \ldots, T$
- Compute $(\alpha_1, \ldots, \alpha_T) = H_1(R_1, \ldots, R_T, M) \in \{0, 1, \ldots, S\}^T$
- Compute $f_i := h_i g_{\alpha_i}^{-1}$ for $i = 1, \ldots, T$.

The signature will be $(R_1, \ldots, R_T, f_1, \ldots, f_T)$. For verification, the verifier can compute $(\alpha_1, \ldots, \alpha_T) = H_1(R_1, \ldots, R_T, M)$. Then, the verifier returns 1 only if $R_i = f_i \star x_{\alpha_i}$ for all $i \in [T]$.

In [26], the authors presented two generic methods for constructing an IBS scheme from a standard signature scheme. The first method is straightforward and involves creating a certificated IBS directly from a signature scheme. The second method is more efficient but comes with certain conditions. In particular, more efficient construction cannot be applied universally to all signature schemes. It requires the underlying signature scheme to have a specific feature known as the *samplable property*. This property ensures the existence of a trapdoor, which allows for the extraction of a secret key from a uniformly sampled public key. Generally, for group action-based signature schemes, the approach described in [26] for the second construction is not feasible. This is because there is no known trapdoor that can extract an element in G from an element in X. Hence, we follow a modified construction based on [22], which yields a tight security reduction IBS.

Our construction is as follows. First of all, a master public key mpk $=$ $(x_0, \ldots, x_S)$ and master secret key msk $=$ $(g_0 = 1_G, g_1, \ldots, g_S)$ are generated as Sigma protocol in the Fig. 1. The secret key for a user with identity id is a signature FS$[\Sigma]$, which is generated from the message to be id under (mpk, msk). Namely, we have usk$_{\mathsf{id}} = (R_1, \ldots, R_T, f_1, \ldots, f_T)$, where $(\alpha_1, \ldots, \alpha_T) = H_1(R_1, \ldots, R_T, \mathsf{id})$. As in [22], for a given message M, the user id can generate a signature by only using another sigma protocol for the secret key usk$_{\mathsf{id}}$. In particular, we have

- For $i \in [T]$, sample $h_i \xleftarrow{\$} G$ and compute $A_i := u_i \star x_i$.
- Compute $(c_1, \ldots, c_T) = H_2((R_i, A_i)_{i \in [T]}, \mathsf{id}, M) \in \{0, 1, \ldots, S\}^T$, where H_2 is a secure hash function.

Now if we followed the way to generate a signature in the $\mathsf{FS}(\Sigma)$ above, then for each $i \in [T]$, we would have $\sigma_i = u_i f_{c_i}^{-1}$. But then, we cannot verify the validity of a signature since $\sigma_i \star x_{c_i} = u_i f_{c_i}^{-1} \star (g_{c_i} \star x_0) = (u_i f_{c_i}^{-1} g_{c_i}) \star x_0$ which is not equal to $A_i = u_i \star x_i = (u_i g_i) \star x_0$. In addition, the scheme in [22] also used $(\alpha_1, \ldots, \alpha_T)$ as parts of the signing process, while the aforementioned normal process does not use it at all.

In order to fix this, we have a double layer of $\mathsf{FS}[\Sigma]$ within the user secret key generation as well as in the signature generation process. In particular, the secret key of a user id will be $\mathsf{usk}_{\mathsf{id}} = (R_{ij}, f_{ij})_{i \in [T], j \in [S]}$ with $(\alpha_i)_{i \in [T_1 T_2]} = H_1((R_{ij})_{i \in [T_1], j \in [T_2]}, \mathsf{id})$, where $T_1 = T$ to be the number of repetitions of the sigma protocol in Fig. 1, and $T_2 = S$ is equal to the parameter of the master public key.

Now, a signature for a message M is computed as follows:

- For $i \in [T_1], j \in [T_2]$, the commitment A_{ij} is computed by $u_{ij} \star x_{\alpha_i}$ with $u_{ij} \xleftarrow{\$} G$.
- Compute $(c_{ij})_{i \in [T_1], j \in [T]} = H_2((R_{ij}, A_{ij})_{i \in [T_1], j \in [T_2]}, \mathsf{id}, M)$
- For $i \in [T_1], j \in [T_2]$, compute $\sigma_{ij} = u_{ij} f_{ic_{ij}}^{-1}$.

Then, a signature will be $\Sigma = ((R_{ij}, c_{ij}, \sigma_{ij})_{i \in [T_1], j \in [T_2]})$.

In order to verify a signature, for all $i \in [T_1], j \in [T_2]$, the verifier computes $A_{ij} = \sigma_{ij} \star x_{\alpha_i}$ when $c_{ij} = 0$. If $c_{ij} > 0$, then verifier computes $A_{ij} = \sigma_{ij} \star R_{ic_{ij}}$. The verifier outputs 1 if $(c_{ij})_{i \in [T_1], j \in [T_2]} = H_2((A_{ij})_{i \in [T_1], j \in [T_2]}, \mathsf{id}, M)$. We easy can see that if $c_{ij} = 0$ then $\sigma_{ij} = u_{ij} \star f_{i0}^{-1} = u_{ij}$. This implies $A_{ij} = \sigma_{ij} \star x_{\alpha_i} = u_{ij} \star x_{\alpha_i}$. If $c_{ij} > 0$, we have $f_{ic_{ij}}^{-1} \star R_{ic_{ij}} = x_{\alpha_i}$. This implies $A_{ij} = \sigma_{ij} \star R_{ic_{ij}} = u_{ij} f_{ic_{ij}}^{-1} \star R_{ic_{ij}} = u_{ij} \star x_{\alpha_i}$. Therefore, a signature generated by an honest signer will pass the verification algorithm.

Note that Shaw and Dutta in [37], followed by Chen et al. [12], also use this method to overcome this problem. However, they only work in an isogeny-based setting, which is a commutative group. Moreover, our scheme needs choosing T_1, T_2 opposed to that founded [12] and [37]. Namely, their construction set $T_1 = S$ is equal to the parameter of the master public key, and $T_2 = T$ is the number of repetitions of the sigma protocol. We also note that the proof in Chen et al. [12] has some typos and confusion, which we will fix and show in our proof; see Sect. 3 for the details.

Our construction of an FSIBS involves two main components: an IBS scheme and a standard signature scheme, both of which leverage a Forward-Secure Pseudo-Random Generator (FSPRG). The FSPRG is used to generate secret and public keys for the standard signature scheme. It ensures that keys for different time periods are generated in a manner that maintains forward security, meaning the compromise of the key for the current period does not affect the security of keys for previous periods. The IBS scheme is used to authenticate auxiliary parameters that include an identifier id and the associated time periods P. This adds a layer of security by linking the identity of the signer and the specific time periods to the signature. This scheme is used to sign the actual messages using the signing key of the current time periods. The public and secret keys for this scheme are generated by the FSPRG, ensuring forward security. Namely, we generalise as follows [2,37]:

- At the initial setup, a master secret key msk and master public key mpk are generated for the IBS scheme. For each time period $p \in [P]$, the FSPRG generates a unique secret key psk and public key ppk for the standard signature scheme.
- For each message M to be signed, the signer uses the current time period's secret key generated by the FSPRG. The message, along with the identifier id and time period, is then authenticated using the IBS scheme. The resulting FSIBS signature comprises two parts: the signature from the standard signature scheme and the authentication from the IBS scheme.
- To verify a signature, both parts of the FSIBS signature are checked. The standard signature part is verified using the public key corresponding to the time period. The IBS part is verified to ensure that the identifier and time period are correctly authenticated.

2 Background

2.1 Notation

We denote by $\mathbb{F}_q$ the field of q elements, where q in this paper is always a prime number. We denote by $\mathrm{GL}(n,q)$ the group of all $n \times n$ invertible matrices over $\mathbb{F}_q$. For a finite set S, $s \xleftarrow{\$} S$ means that s is uniform-randomly sampled from S. We denote by $|S|$ the cardinality of S. For a positive integer k, we denote by $[k]$ the set $\{1, \ldots, k\}$. For a positive integer T, we denote $(s_1, \ldots, s_T) = (s_i)_{i \in [T]}$. For an $n \times m$ matrix A, we write A^t for its transpose.

2.2 Cryptographic Group Actions

Definition 1 (Group action). *A group G is said to act on a set X if there is a map $\star : G \times X \to X$ that satisfies the following two properties:*

1. *Identity: If e is the identity element of G, then for any $x \in X$, we have $e \star x = x$.*
2. *Compatibility: For any $g, h \in G$ and any $x \in X$, we have $g \star (h \star x) = (gh) \star x$.*

We use the abbreviated notation $(G, X, \star)$ to denote a group action. Given a group action $(G, X, \star)$ for a set element $x \in X$, we may define its orbit as $\mathcal{O}(x) := \{g \star x | g \in G\}$. The stabiliser of an element $x \in X$ is $\mathsf{Stab}(x) := \{g \in G | g \star x = x\}$ which is a subgroup of G. If G is finite then we have $|G| = |\mathcal{O}(x)| \cdot |\mathsf{Stab}(x)|$.

We consider group actions that satisfy one or more of the following properties:

– Transitive: A group action $(G, X, \star)$ is said to be *transitive* if for every $x, y \in X$, there exists a group element $g \in G$ such that $y = g \star x$.
– Faithful: A group action $(G, X, \star)$ is said to be *faithful* if there does not exist a $g \in G$ such that $x = g \star x$ for all $x \in X$ other than the identity element.
– Free: A group action $(G, X, \star)$ is said to be *free* if for each group element $g \in G$, g is the identity element if and only if there exists some set element $x \in X$ such that $x = g \star x$.
– Regular: A group action $(G, X, \star)$ is said to be *regular* if it is both *free* and *transitive*.

In group action-based cryptography, we focus on regular actions. If a group action is regular, then for any $x \in X$, the map $f_x : g \mapsto g \star x$ defines a bijection between G and X. In particular, we have $|G| = |X|$ if G (or X) is finite. We define an effective group action (EGA) as follows.

Definition 2 (Effective Group Action). *A group action $(G, X, \star)$ is effective if the following properties are satisfied:*

1. *The group G is finite, and there exists an efficient (PPT) algorithm for:*
    i. *Membership testing, i.e., to decide if a given bit string represents a valid group element in G.*
    ii. *Equality testing, i.e., to decide if two-bit strings represent the same group element in G.*
    iii. *Sampling, i.e., to sample an element g from a distribution that are statistically close to uniform on G.*
    iv. *Operation, i.e., to compute gh for any $g, h \in G$.*
    v. *Inversion, i.e., to compute g^{-1} for any $g \in G$.*
2. *The set X is finite, and there exist efficient algorithms for:*
    i. *Membership testing, i.e., to decide if a bit string represents a valid set element.*
    ii. *Unique representation, i.e., given any arbitrary set element $x \in X$, compute a string $\hat{x}$ that canonically represents x.*
3. *There exists a distinguished element $x_0 \in X$, called the origin, such that its bit-string representation is known.*
4. *There exists an efficient algorithm that, given (some bit-string representations of) any $g \in G$ and any $x \in X$, outputs $g \star x$.*

Group Action Inverse Problem (GAIP) is a problem that arises from group action.

Definition 3 (GAIP). *Let $(X, G, \star)$ be a group action. Given x and y in X, find, if there exists, an element $g \in G$ such that $y = g \star x$.*

In order for a solution g to exist, we require that x, y belong to the same orbit. In other words, given the public parameter $x \in X$, the function $f_x : G \to X$ with $f_x(g) := g \star x$ are a one-way function family. One important thing about the problems that are derived from group actions is that they are hard on average. This means that any given case is likely to be as hard as the hardest one. In

[17], they proved that the GAIP is hard on the average case. A meet-in-the-middle graph walk method from Pohl [33] is the most famous traditional GAIP algorithm. Galbraith et al. [23] also made a low-memory version of this method. Both of them run in time $O(\sqrt{|G|})$. In [14], they showed GAIP can be formulated as a hidden shift problem. Hence, it can be solved by Kuperberg's quantum algorithm and its variants [28,29,34], provided a quantum oracle to evaluate the group action. All these algorithms have subexponential complexity.

In group action constructions, we use generalised K instances of GAIP, call K-GAIP stated the following. Here, we restrict the set X into one orbit.

Definition 4 (K-GAIP). *Given $x_0 \xleftarrow{\$} X$ and $x_1, \ldots, x_{K-1} \xleftarrow{\$} \mathcal{O}(x_0)$, find, if there exists, an element $g \in G$ such that there exists $i, j \in \{0, \ldots, K-1\}$ with $i \neq j$ such that $g \star x_i = x_j$.*

Another problem that is useful for our work is the *pseudorandomness* of the group actions. In particular, it is defined as follows.

Definition 5 (K-Pseudorandomness). *The K-pseudorandom problem asks to distinguish between the following distributions:*

- *The random distribution: $(x_0, \ldots, x_{K-1}) \xleftarrow{\$} X^K$, where $x_i \xleftarrow{\$} X$ for $i = \{0, \ldots, K-1\}$; and*
- *The pseudorandom distribution: $(x_0, \ldots, x_{K-1}) \xleftarrow{\$} X^K$, where $x_0 \xleftarrow{\$} X$ and $x_i \xleftarrow{\$} \mathcal{O}(x_0)$ for $i = \{0, \ldots, K-1\}$.*

Under the assumption of the hardness of K-Pseudorandomness, it is proven in [13] that the signature scheme $\mathsf{FS}[\Sigma]$ as mentioned in the introduction, and hence ALTEQ, is in fact secure in quantum random oracle model (QROM).

2.3 Identity-Based Signature

In the following, we provide a formal definition and the security properties of identity-based signatures.

Definition 6. *For a security parameter λ, let $\mathcal{ID} = \mathcal{ID}(\lambda)$ be the identity space, let $\mathcal{M} = \mathcal{M}(\lambda)$ be the message space, and let $\mathcal{USK} = \mathcal{USK}(\lambda)$ be the user secret key space. An identity-based signature IBS scheme is given by 4-tuple polynomial-time algorithm $(\mathsf{IBS.Setup}, \mathsf{IBS.KeyDer}, \mathsf{IBS.Sign}, \mathsf{IBS.Verify})$ defined as follows:*

1. $(\mathsf{mpk}, \mathsf{msk}) \leftarrow \mathsf{IBS.Setup}(1^\lambda)$. *On input of the security parameter 1^λ, this PPT algorithm generates a master public key mpk and a corresponding master secret key msk.*
2. $\mathsf{usk_{id}} \leftarrow \mathsf{IBS.KeyDer}(\mathsf{mpk}, \mathsf{msk}, \mathsf{id})$. *On input a master public key mpk, a master secret key msk, and an identity $\mathsf{id} \in \mathcal{ID}$, this PPT algorithm outputs a user secret key $\mathsf{usk_{id}} \in \mathcal{USK}$.*
3. $\Sigma \leftarrow \mathsf{IBS.Sign}(\mathsf{mpk}, \mathsf{usk_{id}}, M)$. *On input, a master public key mpk, a user secret key $\mathsf{usk_{id}} \in \mathcal{USK}$, and message $M \in \mathcal{M}$, this PPT algorithm outputs a signature Σ.*

4. $1/0 \leftarrow$ IBS.Verify(mpk, id, M, Σ). *On input a master public key* mpk, *an identity* id $\in \mathcal{ID}$, *a message* $M \in \mathcal{M}$, *and a signature* Σ, *this deterministic algorithm outputs 1 (accept) and 0 (reject).*

In an IBS scheme, we consider the following properties. First, the correctness guarantees that a signature generated by an honest signer will pass the verification algorithm with all but negligible probability.

Definition 7 (Correctness). *We say that an identity-based signature* IBS *is correct, if for all* $\lambda \in \mathbb{N}$, *all identity* id $\in \mathcal{ID}$ *and all message* $M \in \mathcal{M}$ *that if* (mpk, msk) $\leftarrow$ IBS.Setup(1^λ), uskid $\leftarrow$ IBS.KeyDer(mpk, msk, id), *and* $\Sigma \leftarrow$ IBS.Sign(mpk, uskid, M) *then it holds that*

$$\Pr[\text{IBS.Verify}(\text{mpk}, \text{id}, \Sigma, M) = 1] = 1 - \text{negl}(\lambda).$$

Second, this property makes sure that an adversary cannot create a new tuple (id, message, signature) for an identity and a message that has not been queried before, even if the adversary gets a set of secret keys for some identities and signatures for a certain number of tuples (identity, message) of its choice.

Definition 8 (EUF-IBS-CMA). *We say that an IBS is EUF-IBS-CMA if, for every PPT adversary* $\mathcal{A}$, *it holds that* $\mathcal{A}$ *has a negligible advantage in the following experiment.*
$\text{Exp}_{\mathcal{A}}^{\text{EUF-IBS-CMA}}(\lambda)$:

1. *The challenger generates* (mpk, msk) $\leftarrow$ IBS.Setup(1^λ) *and sets* $\mathcal{Q}_{\text{id}} \leftarrow \emptyset$, *and* $\mathcal{Q}_M \leftarrow \emptyset$.
2. *The challenger gives* mpk *to the adversary* $\mathcal{A}$. *Moreover,* $\mathcal{A}$ *can access two oracles* $\mathcal{O}_{\text{IBS.KeyDer}}$, $\mathcal{O}_{\text{IBS.Sign}}$, *where*
   i. *Key derivation oracle* $\mathcal{O}_{\text{IBS.KeyDer}}$: *On input a key derivation query* id $\in \mathcal{ID}$, *the oracle* $\mathcal{O}_{\text{IBS.KeyDer}}$ *computes* uskid $\leftarrow$ IBS.KeyDer(mpk, msk, id). *Then, it returns* uskid *and adds* id *to* $\mathcal{Q}_{\text{id}}$ *set.*
   ii. *Signing oracle* $\mathcal{O}_{\text{IBS.Sign}}$: *On input a signing query* (id, M) $\in \mathcal{ID} \times \mathcal{M}$, *the oracle* $\mathcal{O}_{\text{IBS.Sign}}$ *computes* $\Sigma \leftarrow$ IBS.Sign(mpk, uskid, M). *It returns signature* Σ *and sets* $\mathcal{Q}_M \leftarrow \mathcal{Q}_M \cup \{(\text{id}, M)\}$.
3. *In the end, the adversary outputs a forgery* (id*, M^*, Σ^*).
4. *The challenger outputs 1 if the following three conditions hold:*
   - id* $\notin \mathcal{Q}_{\text{id}}$,
   - (id*, M^*) $\notin \mathcal{Q}_M$,
   - IBS.Verify(mpk, id*, M^*, Σ^*) = 1.
   Otherwise, it outputs 0.

The advantage of $\mathcal{A}$ *is defined by* $\text{Adv}_{\mathcal{A}}^{\text{EUF-IBS-CMA}}(\lambda) = \Pr[\text{Exp}_{\mathcal{A}}^{\text{EUF-IBS-CMA}}(\lambda) = 1]$.

2.4   Forward-Secure Identity-Based Signatures

In this section, we provide a formal definition and the security properties of forward-secure identity-based signatures (FSIBS).

Definition 9 (FSIBS). *For a security parameter λ, let $\mathcal{ID} = \mathcal{ID}(\lambda)$ be the identity space, $\mathcal{P} = \mathcal{P}(\lambda)$ be the pre-specified number of time period space, let $\mathcal{M} = \mathcal{M}(\lambda)$ be the message space, and let $\mathcal{USK} = \mathcal{USK}(\lambda)$ be the user secret key space. A forward-secure identity-based signature FSIBS scheme is given by 6-tuple polynomial-time algorithm* (FSIBS.Setup, FSIBS.KeyDer, FSIBS.Initialize, FSIBS.Update, FSIBS.Sign, FSIBS.Verify) *defined as follows:*

1. (mpk, msk) $\leftarrow$ FSIBS.Setup(1^λ). *On input of the security parameter 1^λ, this PPT algorithm generates a master public key* mpk *and a corresponding master secret key* msk.
2. usk$_{\mathsf{ID}}$ $\leftarrow$ FSIBS.KeyDer(mpk, msk, ID). *On input a master public key* mpk, *a master secret key* msk, *and an identity* id $= (\mathsf{id}\|P) \in (\mathcal{ID}\|\mathcal{P})$, *this PPT algorithm outputs a user secret key* usk$_{\mathsf{ID}} \in \mathcal{USK}$.
3. (sk$_{\mathsf{ID},0}$, τ_{ID}) $\leftarrow$ FSIBS.Initialize(mpk, usk$_{\mathsf{ID}}$, ID). *On input, a master public key* mpk, *a user secret key* usk$_{\mathsf{ID}} \in \mathcal{USK}$, *and an identity* ID $= (\mathsf{id}\|P) \in (\mathcal{ID}\|\mathcal{P})$, *this PPT algorithm outputs a initial signing secret key* sk$_{\mathsf{ID},0}$ *and auxiliary information* τ_{ID}.
4. sk$_{\mathsf{ID},p}$ $\leftarrow$ FSIBS.Update(mpk, τ_{ID}, p, sk$_{\mathsf{id},p-1}$, ID). *On input the master public key* mpk, *auxiliary information* τ_{ID}, *a time period* $1 \leq p \leq P \in \mathcal{P}$, *a secret key* sk$_{\mathsf{ID},p-1} \in \mathcal{USK}$ *of previous time period* $(p-1)$, *and an identity* ID $= (\mathsf{id}\|P) \in (\mathcal{ID}\|\mathcal{P})$, *this PPT algorithm outputs a signing secret key* sk$_{\mathsf{ID},p}$ *at time period p.*
5. Σ $\leftarrow$ FSIBS.Sign(mpk, τ_{ID}, ID, p, sk$_{\mathsf{ID},p}$, M). *On input, a master public key* mpk, *auxiliary information* τ_{ID}, *an identity* ID $= (\mathsf{id}\|P) \in (\mathcal{ID}\|\mathcal{T})$, *a time period* $p < P \in \mathcal{P}$, *a user secret key* sk$_{\mathsf{ID},p} \in \mathcal{USK}$ *at time period p, and message* $M \in \mathcal{M}$, *this PPT algorithm outputs a signature Σ for message M associated with* ID *and time period p.*
6. 1/0 $\leftarrow$ FSIBS.Verify(mpk, ID, p, M, Σ). *On input a master public key* mpk, *an identity* ID $= (\mathsf{id}\|T) \in (\mathcal{ID}\|\mathcal{T})$, *a time period* $p < P \in \mathcal{P}$, *a message* $M \in \mathcal{M}$, *and a signature Σ, this deterministic algorithm outputs 1 (accept) and 0 (reject).*

First, the correctness guarantees that a signature generated by an honest signer will pass the verification algorithm with all but negligible probability.

Definition 10 (Correctness). *We say that a forward secure identity-based signature FSIBS is correct if for all $\lambda \in \mathbb{N}$, all identity* ID $= (\mathsf{id}\|P) \in (\mathcal{ID}\|P)$ *and all message $M \in \mathcal{M}$ that if* (mpk, msk) $\leftarrow$ FSIBS.Setup(1^λ), usk$_{\mathsf{ID}}$ $\leftarrow$ FSIBS.KeyDer(mpk, msk, ID), (sk$_{\mathsf{ID},0}$, τ_{ID}) $\leftarrow$ FSIBS.Initialize(mpk, usk$_{\mathsf{ID}}$, ID), sk$_{\mathsf{ID},p}$ $\leftarrow$ FSIBS.Update(mpk, τ_{ID}, p, sk$_{\mathsf{id},p-1}$, ID), *then it holds that*

$$\Pr[\mathsf{FSIBS.Verify}(\mathsf{mpk}, \mathsf{ID}, p, M, \mathsf{FSIBS.Sign}(\mathsf{mpk}, \tau_{\mathsf{ID}}, \mathsf{ID}, p, \mathsf{sk}_{\mathsf{ID},p}, M))] = 1 - \mathsf{negl}(\lambda).$$

Second, this property makes sure that an adversary cannot create a new tuple (id, message, signature) for an identity and a message that has not been queried before, even if the adversary gets a set of secret keys for some identities and signatures for a certain number of tuples (identity, message) of its choice.

Definition 11 (EUF-FSIBS-CMA). *We say that a forward secure identity-based signature* FSIBS *is* EUF-FSIBS-CMA *if, for every PPT adversary* $\mathcal{A}$, *it holds that* $\mathcal{A}$ *has a negligible advantage in the following experiment.* $\mathsf{Exp}_{\mathcal{A}}^{\mathsf{EUF\text{-}FSIBS\text{-}CMA}}(\lambda)$:

1. *The challenger generates* $(\mathsf{mpk}, \mathsf{msk}) \leftarrow \mathsf{FSIBS.Setup}(1^\lambda)$ *and sets* $\mathcal{Q}_{\mathsf{ID}} \leftarrow \emptyset$, $\mathcal{Q}_M \leftarrow \emptyset$, $\mathcal{Q}_R \leftarrow \emptyset$, $\mathcal{Q}_\tau \leftarrow \emptyset$ *and* $\mathcal{Q}_{\mathsf{psk}} \leftarrow \emptyset$.
2. *The challenger gives* mpk *to the adversary* $\mathcal{A}$. *Moreover,* $\mathcal{A}$ *can access three oracles* $\mathcal{O}_{\mathsf{FSIBS.KeyDer}}$, $\mathcal{O}_{\mathsf{FSIBS.Sign}}$, $\mathcal{O}_{\mathsf{Reveal}}$ *where*
   i. *Key derivation oracle* $\mathcal{O}_{\mathsf{FSIBS.KeyDer}}$: *On input a key derivation query* $\mathsf{ID} = (\mathsf{id}\|P)$, *the oracle* $\mathcal{O}_{\mathsf{FSIBS.KeyDer}}$ *computes* $\mathsf{usk}_{\mathsf{ID}} \leftarrow \mathsf{FSIBS.KeyDer}(\mathsf{mpk}, \mathsf{msk}, \mathsf{ID})$. *It returns* $\mathsf{usk}_{\mathsf{ID}}$ *and adds* ID *to* $\mathcal{Q}_{\mathsf{ID}}$ *set. Then, it computes* $(\mathsf{sk}_{\mathsf{ID},0}, \tau_{\mathsf{ID}}) \leftarrow \mathsf{FSIBS.Initialize}(\mathsf{mpk}, \mathsf{usk}_{\mathsf{ID}}, \mathsf{ID})$ *and* $\mathsf{sk}_{\mathsf{ID},p} \leftarrow \mathsf{FSIBS.Update}(\mathsf{mpk}, \tau_{\mathsf{ID}}, p, \mathsf{sk}_{\mathsf{ID},p-1}, \mathsf{ID})$ *for all* $p \in [P]$. *Then, it sets* $\mathcal{Q}_\tau = \mathcal{Q}_\tau \cup \tau_{\mathsf{ID}}$ *and* $\mathcal{Q}_{\mathsf{psk}} = \mathcal{Q}_{\mathsf{psk}} \cup (\mathsf{psk}_{\mathsf{ID},p})_{p\in[P]}$.
   ii. *Reveal oracle* $\mathcal{O}_{\mathsf{Reveal}}$: *On input a query* (ID, p), *where* $\mathsf{ID} = \mathsf{id}\|P$ *and* $p \leq P$, *the* $\mathcal{O}_{\mathsf{Reveal}}$ *returns* $\mathsf{psk}_{\mathsf{ID},p}$, *where* $\mathsf{psk}_{\mathsf{ID},p}$ *is retrieved from* $\mathcal{Q}_{\mathsf{psk}}$. *It sets* $\mathcal{Q}_R = \mathcal{Q}_R \cup (\mathsf{ID}, p)$.
   iii. *Signing oracle* $\mathcal{O}_{\mathsf{FSIBS.Sign}}$: *On input a signing query* (ID, p, M), *the oracle* $\mathcal{O}_{\mathsf{FSIBS.Sign}}$ *retrieves* τ_{ID} *from* $\mathcal{Q}_\tau$ *and* $\mathsf{psk}_{\mathsf{ID},p}$ *retrieves from* $\mathcal{Q}_{\mathsf{psk}}$. *Then, it computes* $\Sigma \leftarrow \mathsf{FSIBS.Sign}(\mathsf{mpk}, \tau_{\mathsf{ID}}, \mathsf{ID}, p, \mathsf{sk}_{\mathsf{ID},p}, M)$. *It returns signature* Σ *and sets* $\mathcal{Q}_M \leftarrow \mathcal{Q}_M \cup \{(\mathsf{ID}, p, M)\}$.
3. *In the end, the adversary outputs a forgery* $(\mathsf{ID}^*, p^*, M^*, \Sigma^*)$.
4. *The challenger outputs 1 if the following conditions hold:*
   - $\mathsf{ID}^* \notin \mathcal{Q}_{\mathsf{ID}}$,
   - $(\mathsf{ID}^*, p^*, M^*) \notin \mathcal{Q}_M$,
   - *If* $\mathsf{ID}^* = \mathsf{ID}$ *for some* $(\mathsf{ID}, p) \in \mathcal{Q}_R$, *then* $p^* < p$.
   - $\mathsf{FSIBS.Verify}(\mathsf{mpk}, \mathsf{ID}^*, p^*, M^*, \Sigma^*) = 1$.
   Otherwise, it outputs 0.

The advantage of $\mathcal{A}$ *is defined by*

$$\mathsf{Adv}_{\mathcal{A}}^{\mathsf{EUF\text{-}FSIBS\text{-}CMA}}(\lambda) = \Pr[\mathsf{Exp}_{\mathcal{A}}^{\mathsf{EUF\text{-}FSIBS\text{-}CMA}}(\lambda) = 1].$$

3 Tightly Secure IBS from Group Actions

In this section, we present our generic construction for a tightly secure IBS.

For the system parameters, we let $T, S > 0$ be a positive integer, to be specified later, $H_1 : \{0,1\}^* \rightarrow \{0,\ldots,S\}^{TS}$ and $H_2 : \{0,1\}^* \rightarrow \{0,\ldots,S\}^{TS}$ be secure hash functions, modelled as random oracles. Let $\mathcal{ID} = \{0,1\}^*$ and $\mathcal{M} = \{0,1\}^*$ be the identity space and message space respectively. Let G be a group acting on a finite set X.

Our IBS $=$ (IBS.Setup, IBS.KeyDer, IBS.Sign, IBS.Verify) scheme consists of four polynomial time algorithms constructed as follows.

1. $(\mathsf{mpk}, \mathsf{msk}) \leftarrow \mathsf{IBS}.\mathsf{Setup}(1^\lambda)$: On input a security parameter λ, do the following:

   1.1. Sample $x_0 \overset{\$}{\leftarrow} X$, $g_1, \ldots, g_S \overset{\$}{\leftarrow} G$, set also $g_0 = 1_G$ to be the identity element of G.

   1.2. For $i \in [S]$ compute $x_i := g_i \star x_0$.

   1.3. Output $\mathsf{mpk} = (x_0, x_1, \ldots, x_S)$ and $\mathsf{msk} = (g_1, \ldots, g_S)$.

2. $\mathsf{usk_{id}} \leftarrow \mathsf{IBS}.\mathsf{KeyDer}(\mathsf{mpk}, \mathsf{msk}, \mathsf{id})$: On input the master public key mpk, master secret key msk and an identity id of a user, do the following:

   2.1. For $i \in [T], j \in [S]$, choose $h_{ij} \overset{\$}{\leftarrow} G$ and compute $R_{ij} = h_{ij} \star x_0$.

   2.2. Compute $(\alpha_i)_{i \in [TS]} = H_1((R_{ij})_{i \in [T], j \in [S]}, \mathsf{id})$.

   2.3. For $i \in [T], j \in [S]$ compute $f_{ij} = h_{ij} g_{\alpha_i}^{-1}$.

   2.4. Return $\mathsf{usk_{id}} = ((R_{ij}, f_{ij})_{i \in [T], j \in [S]})$.

3. $\Sigma \leftarrow \mathsf{IBS}.\mathsf{Sign}(\mathsf{mpk}, \mathsf{usk_{id}}, \mathsf{id}, M)$: On input the master public key mpk, an identity id together with her secret key $\mathsf{usk_{id}}$ and a message M, do the following:

   3.1. For $i \in [T]$, set $f_{i0} = g_0 = 1_G$.

   3.2. Compute $(\alpha_i)_{i \in [TS]} = H_1((R_{ij})_{i \in [T], j \in [S]}, \mathsf{id})$.

   3.3. For $i \in [T], j \in [S]$, choose $u_{ij} \overset{\$}{\leftarrow} G$ and compute $A_{ij} = u_{ij} \star x_{\alpha_i}$.

   3.4. Compute $(c_{ij})_{i \in [T], j \in [S]} = H_2((A_{ij})_{i \in [T], j \in [S]}, \mathsf{id}, M)$.

   3.5. For $i \in [T], j \in [S]$ compute $\sigma_{ij} := u_{ij} f_{ic_{ij}}^{-1}$.

   3.6. Output a signature $\Sigma = ((R_{ij}, c_{ij}, \sigma_{ij})_{i \in [T], j \in [S]})$.

4. $0/1 \leftarrow \mathsf{IBS}.\mathsf{Verify}(\mathsf{mpk}, \mathsf{id}, \Sigma, M)$: On input the master public key mpk, an identity $\mathsf{usk_{id}}$, a message M together with a signature Σ, do the following:

   4.1. Parse Σ as $((R_{ij})_{i \in [T], j \in [S]}, (c_{ij})_{i \in [T], j \in [S]}, (\sigma_{ij})_{i \in [T], j \in [S]})$.

   4.2. Compute $(\alpha_i)_{i \in [TS]} = H_1((R_{ij})_{i \in [T], j \in [S]}, \mathsf{id})$.

   4.3. For $i \in [T], j \in [S]$
   - If $c_{ij} = 0$ then compute $A'_{ij} := \sigma_{ij} \star x_{\alpha_i}$.
   - If $c_{ij} > 0$ then compute $A'_{ij} := \sigma_{ij} \star R_{ic_{ij}}$.

   4.4. Output 1 if $(c_{ij})_{i \in [T], j \in [S]} = H_2((A'_{ij})_{i \in [T], j \in [S]}, \mathsf{id}, M)$, and 0 otherwise.

Proposition 1. *The* IBS *scheme described above is correct.*

Proof. Let $\Sigma = ((R_{ij})_{i \in [T], j \in [S]}, (c_{ij})_{i \in [T], j \in [S]}, (\sigma_{ij})_{i \in [T], j \in [S]})$ is a signature of a message M, and $(\alpha_i)_{i \in [TS]} = H_1((R_{ij})_{i \in [T], j \in [S]}, \mathsf{id})$.

For $i \in [T], j \in [S]$, we have that:

- If $c_{ij} = 0$ then $\sigma_{ij} = u_{ij} f_{i0}^{-1} = u_{ij}$, and hence

$$A'_{ij} = \sigma_{ij} \star x_{\alpha_i} = u_{ij} \star x_{\alpha_i} = A_{ij}.$$

- If $c_{ij} > 0$, then by the construction of $\mathsf{usk_{id}}$, we have that $f_{ic_{ij}}^{-1} \star R_{ic_{ij}} = x_{\alpha_i}$. And hence

$$A'_{ij} = \sigma_{ij} \star R_{ic_{ij}} = u_{ij} f_{ic_{ij}}^{-1} \star R_{ic_{ij}} = u_{ij} \star x_{\alpha_i} = A_{ij}.$$

Then, it is clear that

$$(c_{ij})_{i \in [T], j \in [S]} = H_2((A_{ij})_{i \in [T], j \in [S]}, \mathsf{id}, M) = H_2((A'_{ij})_{i \in [T], j \in [S]}, \mathsf{id}, M)$$

and the verifier accepts this signature. □

Theorem 1. *If the* (S+1)-*pseudorandomness problem is hard, then the* IBS *scheme constructed above is* EUF-IBS-CMA *secure in the random oracle model.*

Proof. The full version contains detailed proof. □

4 Forward-Secure IBS from Group Actions

For the system parameters, we let $T, S > 0$ be a positive integer, which will be specified later. Let $H : \{0,1\}^* \to \{0,\ldots,S\}^T$, $H_1 : \{0,1\}^* \to \{0,\ldots,S\}^{TS}$ and $H_2 : \{0,1\}^* \to \{0,\ldots,S\}^{TS}$ be secure hash functions, modelled as random oracles. Let $F : \{0,1\}^{m_r} \to \{0,1\}^{m_l+m_r}$ be a forward-secure pseudo-random generator, where $m_l, m_r \in \mathbb{N}^*$. Let PRG $: \{0,1\}^{m_l} \to G^S$ be a pseudo-random generator. Let $\mathcal{P} \in \mathbb{N}^*$, $\mathcal{ID} = \{0,1\}^*$ and $\mathcal{M} = \{0,1\}^*$ be the time period space, identity space and message space respectively. Let G be a group acting on a finite set X. Our framework also uses IBS in Sect. 3 and a standard signature FS[Σ].

Our FSIBS = (FSIBS.Setup, FSIBS.KeyDer, FSIBS.Initialize, FSIBS.Update, FSIBS.Sign, FSIBS.Verify) scheme consists of four polynomial time algorithms constructed as follows.

1. (mpk, msk) ← FSIBS.Setup(1^λ): On input a security parameter λ, do the following:
   1.1. Sample $x_0 \xleftarrow{\$} X$, $g_1, \ldots, g_S \xleftarrow{\$} G$, set also $g_0 = 1_G$ to be the identity element of G.
   1.2. For $i \in [S]$ compute $x_i := g_i \star x_0$.
   1.3. Output mpk $= (x_0, x_1, \ldots, x_S)$ and msk $= (g_1, \ldots, g_S)$.
2. uskID ← FSIBS.KeyDer(mpk, msk, ID): On input the master public key mpk, master secret key msk and ID $= (\mathsf{id}\|P)$ of identity user id with pre-specified number of time periods P, do the following:
   2.1. For $i \in [T], j \in [S]$, choose $h_{ij} \xleftarrow{\$} G$ and compute $R_{ij} = h_{ij} \star x_0$.
   2.2. Compute $(\alpha_i)_{i \in [TS]} = H_1((R_{ij})_{i \in [T], j \in [S]}, \mathsf{ID})$.
   2.3. For $i \in [T], j \in [S]$ compute $f_{ij} = h_{ij} g_{\alpha_i}^{-1}$.
   2.4. Return uskID $= ((R_{ij}, f_{ij})_{i \in [T], j \in [S]})$.
3. (pskID,0, τ_{ID}) ← FSIBS.Initialize(mpk, ID, uskID): On input the master public key mpk, ID $= (\mathsf{id}\|P)$ together with her secret key uskID, do the following:
   3.1. Sample a seed $\gamma_0 \xleftarrow{\$} \{0,1\}^{m_r}$.
   3.2. For $k \in [P]$ do as follow:
      3.2.1. Compute $(\beta_k, \gamma_k) = F(\gamma_{k-1})$, where $\beta_k \in \{0,1\}^{m_l}$ and $\gamma_k \in \{0,1\}^{m_r}$.
      3.2.2. Compute $(d_{k1}, \ldots, d_{kS}) = \mathsf{PRG}(\beta_k)$.

3.2.3. Generate a pair of public and secret keys $(\mathsf{ppk}_k, \mathsf{psk}_k)$ using the Sig.KeyGen algorithm of signature $\mathsf{FS}[\Sigma]$.

- For $i \in [S]$, compute $y_{ki} = d_{ki} \star x_0$.
- Set public key $\mathsf{ppk}_k = (y_{k1}, \ldots, y_{kS})$ and signing secret key $\mathsf{psk}_k = (d_{k1}, \ldots, d_{kS})$

3.2.4. Compute $\Sigma_k \leftarrow \mathsf{IBS.Sign}(\mathsf{mpk}, \mathsf{usk}_{\mathsf{ID}}, \mathsf{ID}, (\mathsf{ID}\|k\|\mathsf{ppk}_k))$ as follows:

- For $i \in [T]$, set $f_{i0} = g_0 = 1_G$.
- Compute $(\alpha_i)_{i \in [TS]} = H_1((R_{ij})_{i \in [T], j \in [S]}, \mathsf{ID})$.
- For $i \in [T], j \in [S]$, choose $u_{kij} \xleftarrow{\$} G$ and compute $A_{kij} = u_{kij} \star x_{\alpha_i}$.
- Compute
  $(c_{kij})_{i \in [T], j \in [S]} = H_2((A_{kij})_{i \in [T], j \in [S]}, \mathsf{ID}, (\mathsf{ID}\|k\|\mathsf{ppk}_k))$.
- For $i \in [T], j \in [S]$ compute $\sigma_{kij} := u_{kij} f_{ic_{kij}}^{-1}$.
- Output a signature $\Sigma_k = ((R_{ij}, c_{kij}, \sigma_{kij})_{i \in [T], j \in [S]})$.

3.2.5. Set $\tau_{\mathsf{ID},k} = (\mathsf{ID}, \mathsf{ppk}_k, k, \Sigma_k)$.

3.4. Delete $\mathsf{usk}_{\mathsf{ID}}, \mathsf{psk}_k, \beta_k, \gamma_k$ for all $k \in [P]$.

3.3. Return $\mathsf{psk}_{\mathsf{ID},0} = \gamma_0$ and $\tau_{\mathsf{ID}} = \{\tau_{\mathsf{ID},k}\}_{k \in [P]}$.

4. $\mathsf{sk}_{\mathsf{ID},p} \leftarrow \mathsf{FSIBS.Update}(\mathsf{mpk}, \tau_{\mathsf{ID}}, p, \mathsf{sk}_{\mathsf{id},p-1}, \mathsf{ID})$. On input the master public key mpk, auxiliary information τ_{ID}, a time period $1 \leq p < P$, a secret key $\mathsf{sk}_{\mathsf{ID},p-1}$ of previous time period $(p-1)$, and an identity $\mathsf{ID} = (\mathsf{id}\|P)$, do follows:

4.1. If $p = 1$, parse $\mathsf{psk}_{\mathsf{ID},p-1} = \gamma_0$. Otherwise, parse $\mathsf{psk}_{\mathsf{ID},p-1} = (\mathsf{psk}_{p-1}, \gamma_{p-1})$.

4.2. Compute $(\beta_p, \gamma_p) = F(\gamma_{p-1})$.

4.3. Compute $(d_{p1}, \ldots, d_{pS}) = \mathsf{PRG}(\beta_{p-1})$.

4.4. Generate a pair of public and secret keys $(\mathsf{ppk}_p, \mathsf{psk}_k p)$ using the Sig.KeyGen algorithm of signature $\mathsf{FS}[\Sigma]$.

- For $i \in [S]$, compute $y_{pi} = d_{pi} \star x_0$.
- Set public key $\mathsf{ppk}_p = (y_{p1}, \ldots, y_{pS})$ and signing secret key $\mathsf{psk}_p = (d_{p1}, \ldots, d_{pS})$

4.5. Parse $\tau_{\mathsf{ID},p} = (\mathsf{ID}, \mathsf{ppk}_p, p, \Sigma_p)$ and run $\mathsf{IBS.Verify}(\mathsf{mpk}, \mathsf{ID}, \Sigma_p, (\mathsf{ID}\|p\|\mathsf{ppk}_p))$ as follows:

- Parse Σ_p as $((R_{ij})_{i \in [T], j \in [S]}, (c_{pij})_{i \in [T], j \in [S]}, (\sigma_{pij})_{i \in [T], j \in [S]})$
- Compute $(\alpha_i)_{i \in [TS]} = H_1((R_{ij})_{i \in [T], j \in [S]}, \mathsf{ID})$.
- For $i \in [T], j \in [S]$, do
  * If $c_{pij} = 0$ then compute $A'_{pij} := \sigma_{pij} \star x_{\alpha_i}$.
  * If $c_{pij} > 0$ then compute $A'_{pij} := \sigma_{pij} \star R_{ic_{pij}}$.
- If $(c_{pij})_{i \in [T], j \in [S]} = H_2((A'_{pij})_{i \in [T], j \in [S]}, \mathsf{ID}, (\mathsf{ID}\|p\|\mathsf{ppk}_p))$ then set check = 1. Otherwise, set check = 0.

4.7. If check = 1, return $\mathsf{psk}_{\mathsf{ID},p} = (\mathsf{psk}_p, \gamma_p)$ and erase $\mathsf{psk}_{\mathsf{ID},p-1}$. Otherwise, return abort.

5. $\Sigma \leftarrow \mathsf{FSIBS.Sign}(\mathsf{mpk}, \tau_{\mathsf{ID}}, \mathsf{ID}, p, \mathsf{psk}_{\mathsf{ID},p}, M)$: On input the master public key mpk, auxiliary information τ_{ID}, an identity $\mathsf{ID} = \mathsf{id}\|P$, time period p, secret key $\mathsf{psk}_{\mathsf{ID},p}$, a message M together with a signature Σ, do the following:

5.1. Parse $\mathsf{psk}_{\mathsf{ID},p} = (\mathsf{psk}_p, \gamma_p)$, where $\mathsf{psk}_p = (d_{p1}, \ldots, d_{pS})$.

5.2. Compute a signature σ_p for message M by using Sig.Sign algorithm of signature $FS[\Sigma]$ under signing key psk_p.
   - Set $d_{p0} = 1_G$.
   - For $i \in [T]$, sample $l_{pi} \xleftarrow{\$} G$ and compute $Q_{pi} = l_{pi} \star x_0$
   - Compute $(\mu_{p1}, \ldots, \mu_{pT}) = H(Q_{p1}, \ldots, Q_{pT}, M)$
   - For $i \in [T]$, compute $w_{pi} = l_{pi} d_{\mu_{pi}}^{-1}$.
   - Set $\sigma_p = (Q_{p1}, \ldots, Q_{pT}, w_{p1}, \ldots, w_{pT})$.
   - Return $\Sigma = (\sigma_p, \tau_{\mathsf{ID},p})$.

6. $0/1 \leftarrow$ FSIBS.Verify($\mathsf{mpk}, \mathsf{ID}, p, M, \Sigma$): On input the master public key mpk, an identity ID, time period p, a message M together with a signature Σ, do the following:

6.1. Check the validity of the signature σ_p for message M by using the Sig.Verify algorithm of signature $FS[\Sigma]$ under the public key ppk_p.
   - Parse $\sigma_p = (Q_{p1}, \ldots, Q_{pT}, w_{p1}, \ldots, w_{pT})$.
   - Compute $(\mu_{p1}, \ldots, \mu_{pT}) = H(Q_{p1}, \ldots, Q_{pT}, M)$.
   - If $Q_{pi} = w_{pi} \star x_{\mu_{pi}}$ for all $i \in [T]$, then set $\mathsf{check}_1 = 1$. Otherwise, set $\mathsf{check}_1 = 0$.

6.2. Parse $\tau_{\mathsf{ID},p} = (\mathsf{ID}, \mathsf{ppk}_p, p, \Sigma_p)$ and run IBS.Verify($\mathsf{mpk}, \mathsf{ID}, \Sigma_p, (\mathsf{ID}\|p\| \mathsf{ppk}_p)$) as follows:
   - Parse Σ_p as $((R_{ij})_{i\in[T],j\in[S]}, (c_{pij})_{i\in[T],j\in[S]}, (\sigma_{pij})_{i\in[T],j\in[S]})$
   - Compute $(\alpha_i)_{i\in[TS]} = H_1((R_{ij})_{i\in[T],j\in[S]}, \mathsf{ID})$.
   - For $i \in [T], j \in [S]$, do
     * If $c_{pij} = 0$ then compute $A'_{pij} := \sigma_{pij} \star x_{\alpha_i}$.
     * If $c_{pij} > 0$ then compute $A'_{pij} := \sigma_{pij} \star R_{ic_{pij}}$.
   - If $(c_{pij})_{i\in[T],j\in[S]} = H_2((A'_{pij})_{i\in[T],j\in[S]}, \mathsf{ID}, (\mathsf{ID}\|p\|\mathsf{ppk}_p))$ then set $\mathsf{check}_2 = 1$. Otherwise, set $\mathsf{check}_2 = 0$.

6.3. If $\mathsf{check}_1 = 1$ and $\mathsf{check}_2 = 1$, return 1. Otherwise, return 0.

Proposition 2. *Our* FSIBS *scheme described above is correct.*

Proof. The correctness of our FSIBS scheme directly follows from the correctness of standard signature $FS[\Sigma]$ scheme and our IBS scheme. □

Theorem 2. *If the forward-secure pseudorandom generator F is* ROR *secure, our* IBS *scheme is* EUF-IBS-CMA *secure and standard signature $FS[\Sigma]$ scheme is* EUF-CMA *secure, then our* FSIBS *scheme is* EUF-FSIBS-CMA *secure in the random oracle.*

The proof idea can be summarised as follows: Assume there is an adversary $\mathcal{A}$ that can compromise the EUF-FSIBS-CMA security of our group action-based FSIBS scheme. We will use $\mathcal{A}$ as a subroutine to create an adversary $\mathcal{F}_{FS[\Sigma]}$ against the EUF-CMA security of $FS[\Sigma]$, an adversary $\mathcal{F}_{IBS}$ against the EUF-IBS-CMA security of IBS, and a distinguisher $\mathcal{F}_{FSPRG}$ against the ROR security of the FSPRG F.

The $\mathcal{F}_{FS[\Sigma]}$ is constructed as follows: First, $\mathcal{F}_{FS[\Sigma]}$ will guess a time period $p^* \in [P]$ where during which it thinks the adversary $\mathcal{A}$ will create a forged signature. Then, the $\mathcal{F}_{FS[\Sigma]}$ replace pk^* from EUF-CMA experiment to public key at time period p^*. Now, $\mathcal{F}_{\mathsf{FS}[\Sigma]}$ will interact with $\mathcal{A}$ as a challenger in the EUF-FSIBS-CMA experiment. Specifically, $\mathcal{F}_{\mathsf{FS}[\Sigma]}$ can respond to all queries at periods $p \neq p^*$ as usual. For the period p^*, if it encounters a signature query, $\mathcal{F}_{\mathsf{FS}[\Sigma]}$ will query the signing oracle of $\mathsf{FS}[\Sigma]$ to obtain a signature and then create an FSIBS signature as usual. If a secret key query is made for the time period p^*, $\mathcal{F}_{\mathsf{FS}[\Sigma]}$ will stop because it does not know the secret key for that period. From the forgery signature produced by the adversary $\mathcal{A}$ against the FSIBS scheme, $\mathcal{F}_{\mathsf{FS}[\Sigma]}$ can extract a signature for the signature scheme $\mathsf{FS}[\Sigma]$ to submit to EUF-CMA experiment. Since $\mathcal{F}_{\mathsf{FS}[\Sigma]}$ has to guess the correct time period, its success probability is approximately $\frac{1}{P}$ times the success probability of the adversary $\mathcal{A}$.

The adversaries $\mathcal{F}_{\mathsf{FS}[\Sigma]}$ and $\mathcal{F}_{\mathsf{FSPRG}}$ can be constructed in a similar manner. They will guess a position where they think the adversary $\mathcal{A}$ will launch an attack. Then, they will respond to queries at other positions in the usual way. At the guessed position, they may call supporting oracle queries or abort if it does not know the secret information. From the forged FSIBS signature, $\mathcal{F}$ can achieve success in the corresponding experiments. Since, in each case, we have to guess the position where the forgery will occur, we lose a factor in the success probability, meaning our FSIBS scheme does not achieve a tight security proof.

Proof. The full version contains detailed proof.   □

In addition to the IBS and FSIBS schemes [12,37] established with CSI -FiSh, we next present some candidates of group actions underlying existing PQC candidates ALTEQ [10], MEDS [15], LESS [3].

Group Action Underlying MEDS. The Matrix Equivalence Digital Signature (MEDS) scheme is a digital signature scheme based on the difficulty of finding an isometry between two equivalent matrix rank-metric codes. Let $n_1, n_2, n_3 \in \mathbb{N}$. The set S is $\mathbb{F}_q^{n_1} \otimes \mathbb{F}_q^{n_2} \otimes \mathbb{F}_q^{n_3}$. The group $G = \mathrm{GL}(n_1, q) \times \mathrm{GL}(n_2, q) \times \mathrm{GL}(n_3, q)$. The action defined as $(A_1, A_2, A_3) \in G$ sending $u_1 \otimes u_2 \otimes u_3$ to $A_1(u_1) \otimes A_2(u_2) \otimes A_3(u_3)$ and then linearly extending this to the whole $\mathbb{F}_q^{n_1} \otimes \mathbb{F}_q^{n_2} \otimes \mathbb{F}_q^{n_3}$.

Group Action Underlying LESS. This scheme relies on the idea of finding some kind of isomorphism between linear codes. For $1 \leq d \leq n$, let $M(d \times n, \mathbb{F}_q)$ be the linear space of $d \times n$ matrices over $\mathbb{F}_q$. Let $\mathrm{Mon}(n, q)$ be the group of $n \times n$ monomial matrices over $\mathbb{F}_q$. The group $G = \mathrm{GL}(n, q) \times \mathrm{Mon}(n, q)$, the set $S = \mathrm{M}(d \times n, \mathbb{F}_q)$, and the action is defined as $(A, C) \in \mathrm{GL}(n, q) \times \mathrm{Mon}(n, q)$ sending $B \in \mathrm{M}(d \times n, q)$ to $ABC^\top$.

Group Action Underlying ALTEQ. Let $\mathbb{F}_q$ be the finite field of order q. A trilinear form $\phi : \mathbb{F}_q^n \times \mathbb{F}_q^n \times \mathbb{F}_q^n \to \mathbb{F}_q$ is alternating if ϕ evaluates to 0 whenever two arguments are the same. We use $\mathrm{ATF}(n, q)$ to denote the set of all alternating trilinear forms defined over $\mathbb{F}$. Let A be an invertible matrix of size $n \times n$ over $\mathbb{F}_q$. Then A sends ϕ to another alternating trilinear form $\phi \circ A$, defined as $(\phi \circ A)(u, v, w) := \phi(A^\top(u), A^\top(v), A^\top(w))$.

Group Action Underlying HAWK. This scheme is based on the lattice isomorphism problem (LIP). Informally, its search version aims to find an isomorphism between two given isomorphic lattices. In [7], they proved that lattice isomorphism in the quadratic form setting as a group action.

5   Conclusion

This paper advances the field of identity-based signature schemes by generalising the framework to accommodate non-commutative group actions, building upon the foundational work of Shaw-Dutta and Chen et al. Through the pseudorandom assumption of the underlying group actions, we have demonstrated that our proposed IBS scheme is tightly secure in the random oracle model. Additionally, we have introduced a forward-secure identity-based signature scheme that ensures the integrity of past signatures even if the current signing key is compromised. By utilising group action-based standard signature schemes, our group action-based IBS scheme, and a forward-secure pseudo-random generator, our constructions offer robust security measures. Furthermore, the ability to instantiate our schemes from existing NIST post-quantum signature candidates, such as MEDS, LESS, and ALTEQ, enhances the versatility and applicability of IBS in secure communications. These contributions provide a significant step forward in the development of secure cryptographic systems resistant to quantum computing threats.

References

1. Abdalla, M., Fouque, P.-A., Lyubashevsky, V., Tibouchi, M.: Tightly-secure signatures from lossy identification schemes. In: Pointcheval, D., Johansson, T. (eds.) EUROCRYPT 2012. LNCS, vol. 7237, pp. 572–590. Springer, Heidelberg (2012). https://doi.org/10.1007/978-3-642-29011-4_34
2. Al Ebri, N., Baek, J., Shoufan, A., Vu, Q.H., Center, E.B.T.I.: Forward-secure identity-based signature: new generic constructions and their applications. J. Wirel. Mob. Networks Ubiquitous Comput. Dependable Appl. 4(1), 32–54 (2013)
3. Baldi, M.,et al.: NIST PQC Submission (2023). Accessed 06 Feb 2024
4. Barenghi, A., Biasse, J.-F., Ngo, T., Persichetti, E., Santini, P.: Advanced signature functionalities from the code equivalence problem. Int. J. Comput. Math. Comput. Syst. Theory 7(2), 112–128 (2022)
5. Battagliola, M., Borin, G., Meneghetti, A., Persichetti, E.: Cutting the GRASS: threshold group action signature schemes. IACR Cryptol. ePrint Arch., p. 859 (2023)
6. Bellare, M., Miner, S.K.: A forward-secure digital signature scheme. In: Wiener, M. (ed.) CRYPTO 1999. LNCS, vol. 1666, pp. 431–448. Springer, Heidelberg (1999). https://doi.org/10.1007/3-540-48405-1_28
7. Benčina, B., Budroni, A., Chi-Domínguez, J.-J., Kulkarni, M.: Properties of lattice isomorphism as a cryptographic group action. In: Saarinen, M.-J., Smith-Tone, D. (eds.) Post-Quantum Cryptography, pp. 170–201. Springer, Cham (2024). https://doi.org/10.1007/978-3-031-62743-9_6
8. Beullens, W., Katsumata, S., Pintore, F.: Calamari and falafl: logarithmic (linkable) ring signatures from isogenies and lattices. In: Moriai, S., Wang, H. (eds.) ASIACRYPT 2020. LNCS, vol. 12492, pp. 464–492. Springer, Cham (2020). https://doi.org/10.1007/978-3-030-64834-3_16

9. Beullens, W., Kleinjung, T., Vercauteren, F.: CSI-FiSh: efficient isogeny based signatures through class group computations. In: Galbraith, S.D., Moriai, S. (eds.) ASIACRYPT 2019. LNCS, vol. 11921, pp. 227–247. Springer, Cham (2019). https://doi.org/10.1007/978-3-030-34578-5_9

10. Bläser, M., et al.: The ALTEQ signature scheme: algorithm specifications and supporting documentation. In: NIST PQC Submission (2023). Accessed 06 Feb 2024

11. Brassard, G., Yung, M.: One-way group actions. In: Menezes, A.J., Vanstone, S.A. (eds.) CRYPTO 1990. LNCS, vol. 537, pp. 94–107. Springer, Heidelberg (1991). https://doi.org/10.1007/3-540-38424-3_7

12. Chen, J., Jo, H., Sato, S., Shikata, J.: A tightly secure identity-based signature scheme from isogenies. In: Johansson, T., Smith-Tone, D. (eds.) Post-Quantum Cryptography - 14th International Workshop, PQCrypto 2023, College Park, MD, USA, August 16-18, 2023, Proceedings, vol. 14154, pp. 141–163. Springer, Heidelberg (2023)

13. Chen, Z., Duong, D. H., Nguyen, T.N., Qiao, Y., Susilo, W., Tang, G.: On digital signatures based on isomorphism problems: QROM security and ring signatures. IACR Cryptol. ePrint Arch., 1184 (2022)

14. Childs, A., Jao, D., Soukharev, V.: Constructing elliptic curve isogenies in quantum subexponential time. J. Math. Cryptol. $8(1)$, 1–29 (2014)

15. Chou, T., et al.: The Matrix Equivalence Digital Signature (MEDS). In: NIST PQC Submission (2023). Accessed 06 Feb 2024

16. Couveignes, J.M.: Hard homogeneous spaces. IACR Cryptol. ePrint Arch. (2006)

17. D'Alconzo, G.: A note on the hardness of problems from cryptographic group actions. arXiv preprint arXiv:2202.13810 (2022)

18. De Feo, L., Meyer, M.: Threshold schemes from isogeny assumptions. In: Kiayias, A., Kohlweiss, M., Wallden, P., Zikas, V. (eds.) PKC 2020. LNCS, vol. 12111, pp. 187–212. Springer, Cham (2020). https://doi.org/10.1007/978-3-030-45388-6_7

19. El Kaafarani, A., Katsumata, S., Pintore, F.: Lossy CSI-FiSh: efficient signature scheme with tight reduction to decisional CSIDH-512. In: Kiayias, A., Kohlweiss, M., Wallden, P., Zikas, V. (eds.) PKC 2020. LNCS, vol. 12111, pp. 157–186. Springer, Cham (2020). https://doi.org/10.1007/978-3-030-45388-6_6

20. De Feo, L., Galbraith, S.D.: SeaSign: compact isogeny signatures from class group actions. In: Ishai, Y., Rijmen, V. (eds.) EUROCRYPT 2019. LNCS, vol. 11478, pp. 759–789. Springer, Cham (2019). https://doi.org/10.1007/978-3-030-17659-4_26

21. Fiat, A., Shamir, A.: How to prove yourself: practical solutions to identification and signature problems. In: Odlyzko, A.M. (ed.) CRYPTO 1986. LNCS, vol. 263, pp. 186–194. Springer, Heidelberg (1987). https://doi.org/10.1007/3-540-47721-7_12

22. Fukumitsu, M., Hasegawa, S.: A galindo-garcia-like identity-based signature with tight security reduction, revisited. In: Sixth International Symposium on Computing and Networking, CANDAR 2018, Takayama, Japan, 23–27 November 2018, pp. 92–98. IEEE Computer Society (2018)

23. Galbraith, S.D., Hess, F., Smart, N.P.: Extending the GHS weil descent attack. In: Knudsen, L.R. (ed.) EUROCRYPT 2002. LNCS, vol. 2332, pp. 29–44. Springer, Heidelberg (2002). https://doi.org/10.1007/3-540-46035-7_3

24. Goldreich, O., Micali, S., Wigderson, A.: Proofs that yield nothing but their validity for all languages in NP have zero-knowledge proof systems. J. ACM $38(3)$, 691–729 (1991)

25. Ji, Z., Qiao, Y., Song, F., Yun, A.: General linear group action on tensors: a candidate for post-quantum cryptography. In: Hofheinz, D., Rosen, A. (eds.) TCC

2019. LNCS, vol. 11891, pp. 251–281. Springer, Cham (2019). https://doi.org/10.1007/978-3-030-36030-6_11

26. Kiltz, E., Neven, G.: Identity-based signatures. In: Joye, M., Neven, G. (eds.) Identity-Based Cryptography, vol. 2 of Cryptology and Information Security Series, pp. 31–44. IOS Press (2009)

27. Koblitz, N., Menezes, A.: Critical perspectives on provable security: fifteen years of "another look" papers. Adv. Math. Commun. **13**(4), 517–558 (2019)

28. Kuperberg, G.: A subexponential-time quantum algorithm for the dihedral hidden subgroup problem. SIAM J. Comput. **35**(1), 170–188 (2005)

29. Kuperberg, G.: Another subexponential-time quantum algorithm for the dihedral hidden subgroup problem. In: 8th Conference on the Theory of Quantum Computation, Communication and Cryptography, p. 20 (2013)

30. Lyubashevsky, V.: Fiat-shamir with aborts: applications to lattice and factoring-based signatures. In: Matsui, M. (ed.) ASIACRYPT 2009. LNCS, vol. 5912, pp. 598–616. Springer, Heidelberg (2009). https://doi.org/10.1007/978-3-642-10366-7_35

31. National Institute of Standards and Technology. Call for additional digital signature schemes for the post-quantum cryptography standardization process (2022)

32. Peng, C., Chen, J., Zhou, L., Choo, K.-K.R., He, D.: Csiibs: a post-quantum identity-based signature scheme based on isogenies. J. Inf. Secur. Appl. **54**, 102504 (2020)

33. Pohl, I.: Bidirectional and heuristic search in path problems. Technical Report 104 Stanford Linear Accelerator Center, Stanford, California (1969)

34. Regev, O.: A subexponential time algorithm for the dihedral hidden subgroup problem with polynomial space. arXiv preprint quant-ph/0406151 (2004)

35. Samardjiska, S., Qiao, Y.: Digital signatures from equivalence problems - a closer look at MEDS and ALTEQ. In: NIST Post-Quantum Cryptography Seminars (2023)

36. Shamir, A.: Identity-based cryptosystems and signature schemes. In: Blakley, G.R., Chaum, D. (eds.) CRYPTO 1984. LNCS, vol. 196, pp. 47–53. Springer, Heidelberg (1985). https://doi.org/10.1007/3-540-39568-7_5

37. Shaw, S., Dutta, R.: Identification scheme and forward-secure signature in identity-based setting from isogenies. In: Huang, Q., Yu, Yu. (eds.) ProvSec 2021. LNCS, vol. 13059, pp. 309–326. Springer, Cham (2021). https://doi.org/10.1007/978-3-030-90402-9_17

38. Stolbunov, A.: Cryptographic schemes based on isogenies. PhD thesis, Norwegian University of Science and Technology (2012)

39. Tang, G., Duong, D.H., Joux, A., Plantard, T., Qiao, Y., Susilo, W.: Practical post-quantum signature schemes from isomorphism problems of trilinear forms. In: Dunkelman, O., Dziembowski, S. (eds.) Advances in Cryptology - EUROCRYPT 2022 - 41st Annual International Conference on the Theory and Applications of Cryptographic Techniques, Trondheim, Norway, 30 May–3 June 2022, Proceedings, Part III, vol. 13277 of Lecture Notes in Computer Science, pp. 582–612. Springer, Heidelberg (2022)

Generic Construction of Withdrawable Signature from Hash-Then-One-Way Signature

Xin Liu$^{(\boxtimes)}$, Willy Susilo , and Joonsang Baek

Institute of Cybersecurity and Cryptology, School of Computing and Information Technology, University of Wollongong, Wollongong, Australia
xl879@uowmail.edu.au, {wsusilo,baek}@uow.edu.au

Abstract. Withdrawable signature, a recently introduced variant of digital signature, addresses the need for flexibility in existing digital signatures by allowing signers to retract their signatures securely and efficiently. The retraction can be attained by having a withdrawable signature scheme initially create an "unverifiable" signature on the signer's public key, which can later be converted into a conventional one, verifiable only by the signer. Previously, there were only two specific constructions of withdrawable signature based on Schnorr and pairing. Recognizing the practical importance of the RSA signature, we aim to provide a generic construct of the withdrawable signature from the hash-then-one-way type (Type-H) signature, with RSA being a concrete instantiation.

To achieve our goal, we revisit and extend the definition and security notions of the existing withdrawable signature, introducing the concept of the "extended withdrawable signature" that extends the verification of the withdrawable signature from certain verifiers only to allow universal verification - a feature not achieved by previous work. We provide formal security analysis to demonstrate that our generic construction satisfies the revisited security notions of the withdrawable signature. This approach broadens the applicability and enhances the security of withdrawable signatures in various cryptographic applications.

Keywords: Digital Signatures · Withdrawable Signature · Hash-Then-One-Way Signature

1 Introduction

The concept of the withdrawable signature was first introduced by Liu et al. in [22]. Withdrawable signatures primarily address the essential need for flexibility in traditional digital signatures by enabling signers to retract their signatures securely and efficiently. Traditional digital signature schemes ensure integrity and

This work is partly supported by the Australian Research Council (ARC) Discovery Project DP200100144. W. Susilo is supported by the ARC Laureate Fellowship FL230100033.

authenticity, but *lack the capability for retraction*, as once a digital signature is generated by the signer, it remains permanently valid and cannot be revoked. This limitation is particularly challenging in dynamic and decentralized environments such as e-voting, blockchain-based smart contracts, and escrow services, where the ability to withdraw or alter earlier consents is necessary.

Building on the highlighted challenges, withdrawable signature, this primitive uniquely addresses the gap in traditional digital signatures by enabling the retraction of signatures without compromising security or integrity-an important achievement that no previous work has accomplished. As a concrete application, the withdrawable signature is necessary for e-voting systems [2], where voters can submit their votes through digital signatures. By using withdrawable signatures, voters can retract or change their votes before the election deadline, making the submitted votes retractable. Additionally, the withdrawable signature is essential in escrow services, where funds or assets are held by a third party until conditions are met. This allows parties to retract their consents before payment finalization, ensuring flexibility and security in financial transactions.

To achieve this, in [22], Liu et al. proposed a solution for retracting traditional digital signatures with the following idea: instead of directly generating a permanently verifiable signature, a withdrawable signature scheme should contain two phases. In the first phase, a signer creates a signature that can be considered "unverifiable" on its public key if it needs to withdraw it. This "unverifiable" signature is called the "withdrawable signature". This withdrawable signature provides the signer with the following flexibility: if the signer wishes to retract the signature, it can do so without taking action. This "unverifiability" on the signer's public key only property is the most important feature of a withdrawable signature, called *withdrawability*. The second phase is optional for the signer. It can convert this withdrawable signature into a verifiable one on its public key using its secret key when necessary. Once converted, the signature becomes a conventional signature that cannot be withdrawn again. Importantly, this newly generated verifiable signature must remain traceable to the original withdrawable signature. This connection ensures that only the signer can convert the withdrawable signature into a verifiable one, thereby guaranteeing the signature scheme's *unforgeability*.

With this core idea, they provided two constructions based on pairing and Schnorr signature, respectively. Considering the versatility of RSA signatures, one would ask: *"is it possible to construct a withdrawable signature from RSA?"*

Despite potential future quantum threats posed by Shor's quantum factoring algorithm [28], RSA remains widely used in practical applications. RSA-PKCS #1 v1.5 [19,24] remains the most widely used digital signature scheme in practice, especially in TLS [7,17]. Given that RSA-based public keys are the most common in practical applications, RSA-based signature schemes have the greatest practical relevance in the context of TLS 1.3 [7,26]. Even recent research in [6], Chevignard et al. indicated that a circuit with less than 1700 qubits could be proposed for factoring RSA-2048. While quantum computers with a small number of qubits (less than 100) have been developed by various organizations, including IBM and Google, the capabilities required to break RSA-2048 are still beyond current technology. Therefore, RSA is an ideal cryptographic primitive for implementing the withdrawable signature in versatile, practical applications.

To construct the "withdrawable signature", Liu et al. [22] proposed a solution for generating an "unverifiable" signature based on the strong designated-verifier signature (SDVS) [18]. In this approach, an SDVS is applied as a withdrawable signature by ensuring that a withdrawable signature is verifiable by a specific (designated) verifier only. Consequently, this withdrawable signature is "unverifiable" to anyone other than the signer and the designated verifier, achieving *withdrawability*. Meanwhile, the *unforgeability* of the withdrawable signature scheme is considered *unforgeability under insider corruption*, as the withdrawable signature shouldn't be confirmed without the signer's secret key, even by the designated verifier.

Revisiting Withdrawable Signature. There is occasionally a situation where a third party needs to verify the validity of a withdrawable signature. How do we ensure that the universally verifiable withdrawable signature remains "unverifiable" on the signer's public key? To achieve this, instead of limiting the verification capability between the signer and the certain verifier, we must ensure a withdrawable signature still holds the signer ambiguity between the signer and other possible signers. In the context of the aforementioned SDVS-based withdrawable signature, the designated verifier in the withdrawable signature can be considered as one of two possible signers (the signer and the certain verifier). Given a message-withdrawable signature pair, it becomes computationally infeasible for anyone other than the signer and the designated verifier to determine who signed the message without access to the signer's secret key. This is achieved because once the signer generates a withdrawable signature, the verifier can generate the same one using its secret key. This ambiguity ensures that a third party considers the signature still "unverifiable" on the signer's public key only.

With these considerations, this paper aims to revisit and extend the definition and security notions of withdrawable signature. We introduce the concept called extended withdrawable signature, in which withdrawability is not restricted by employing the SDVS. As we have mentioned, any signature scheme, when equipped with signer ambiguity property, can achieve the aforementioned withdrawability. We call this property "extended withdrawability".

The Definition of Extended Withdrawable Signature. In an extended withdrawable signature scheme, the signer can produce an extended withdrawable signature with any signature scheme that holds signer ambiguity between the public key set γ. The signer first to declare the public key set γ that contains all potential signer's public keys (including pk), and generate aux $= \gamma \subseteq$ pk from algorithm "Shuffle(pk, γ)". The withdrawable signature σ is generated with its secret key sk and the public key set aux of all other users that could also be a signer through algorithm "WSign". The withdrawable signature σ contains two parts: ω generated from the corresponding signature scheme and the public key set aux. The verification algorithm of the extended withdrawable signature can be performed by anyone who obtains σ through the WSVerify algorithm with the corresponding public key set aux, the signer's public key pk, and the message m. If the signer wants to withdraw σ, it merely takes no action.

Later, if the signer wants to transform the extended withdrawable signature, it then executes the algorithm, "Confirm", to lift the ambiguity on σ and yield a signature $\tilde{\sigma}$ that identifies pk as the real signer of σ. This unambiguous signature is referred to as the "confirmed signature", and can be verified through the "confirmed signature verification" algorithm CVerify with m and pk. Note that $\tilde{\sigma}$ should be deterministically traced back to the original σ. This connection is established through the checking algorithm Check, which verifies whether σ and $\tilde{\sigma}$ form a valid withdrawable/confirmed signature pair.

Based on the definition and security notions, we have one comprehensive generic construction for extended withdrawable signature through a 1-out-of-n signature scheme derived from the hash-then-one-way type (Type-H) signatures, where RSA is the most important concrete instantiation of Type-H signatures.

1.1 Technical Overview

We provide a technical overview of our extended withdrawable signature, focusing on the technical challenges to realizing the generic construction from the Type-H signature we had to face.

The Definition of 1-Out-of-n Signature. To construct our generic construction on the withdrawable signature, we first revisit the concept of the "1-out-of-n signature" that was first mentioned in [1], which addresses the required extended withdrawability property. In a 1-out-of-n signature scheme, a signer can create a verifiable signature ω not only with its public key pk but also with $n - 1$ potential user's public key set, where $n \geq 2$. With the potential signers' public keys as auxiliary information aux in the withdrawable signature $\sigma = (\omega, \text{aux})$, anyone who obtains σ can verify through both pk and aux while can not decide whether the signer "or" any other signer concluded in aux generated this 1-out-of-n signature. Thus, the withdrawable signature generated from this 1-out-of-n signature σ can be verifiable through pk and aux. Meanwhile, σ can directly be adapted into verifiable through $\overline{\text{pk}} \in \text{aux}$ and $\overline{\text{aux}} = \text{aux} \cup \text{pk} \setminus \overline{\text{pk}}$. This property can be derived from many variants of signatures, including but not limited to ring signatures and DVS.

Constructing 1-Out-of-n Signature from Type-H *Signature.* Generally, a 1-out-of-n signature scheme should have a public key set that includes the public keys of all potential signers $\gamma = \{\text{pk}_j\}_{j=1}^n$. Without loss of generality, assume that $\text{pk}_i, i \in [1, n]$ is the signing user's public key, and its public/secret key pair is denoted as $(\text{pk}_i, \text{sk}_i)$. Within the construction of 1-out-of-n signature, we explore Type-H signature, which serves as foundational elements in constructing 1-out-of-n signature signature. (Note that this concept was first introduced in [1]).

We now describe the Type-H signature. For readability, we will use the RSA signature instantiation in square brackets, "[" and "]", for each step.

Let F be a trapdoor one-way function and I be its inverse function. A Type-H signature contains two fundamental functions I and a hash function $H_i : \{0,1\}^* \rightarrow \Delta_i$ in the signing stage with signing algorithm H.Sign. Let $\Delta_i [\mathbb{Z}_{N_i}]$ be the randomness domain decided by the signer's public key pk $[e_i, N_i]$. First, the hash function H_i generates h with message m and auxiliary information A through $H_i [h = H_i(m, A)]$. The function I then produces s with signer's secret key d through $I(\mathsf{sk}, h) [s = h^d]$. The resulting Type-H signature is a tuple consisting of s and auxiliary information A where $\sigma = (s, A)$. The signature σ is verified by using the function F, H_i, and pk_i through the verification algorithm H.Verify. Specifically, h' is computed through $F(\mathsf{pk}, s) [h' = s^e]$. To validate the correctness of h', H_i ensures that $h = H_i(m, A)$ matches h'.

If we take the 1-out-of-n signature from the RSA signature where $n = 2$ as the concrete instantiation, considering the public key set $\gamma = \{\mathsf{pk}_j\}_{j=1}^2 = \{(e_j, N_j)\}_{j=1}^2$ and the signer's public key is denoted as $\mathsf{pk}_i = (e_i, N_i)$ where $i \xleftarrow{\$} \{1, 2\}$. With two hash functions in RSA signature as $H_j : \{0,1\}^* \rightarrow \mathbb{Z}_{N_j}, j \in [1, 2]$ for pk_j. This 1-out-of-2 signature scheme is demonstrated as follows: for $j \neq i$, the signer picks randomnesses s_j, h, z, $R \leftarrow \mathbb{Z}_{N_i}$ and computes $k_i = z^R$. Then the signer computes c_j as: $c_j = H_j(m, \gamma, k_i)$. After that, the signer can compute k_j through $k_j = c_j + s_j^{e_j} + z^R$. Then c_i is computed by $c_i = H_j(m, \gamma, k_i)$, $s_i = (h - c_i)^{e_i}$ and the 1-out-of-2 signature with γ is $\omega = (c_1, s_1, s_2, z, R)$.

From 1-Out-of-n Signature to Extended Withdrawable Signature. As mentioned above, a 1-out-of-n signature can directly serve as an extended withdrawable signature, as the extended withdrawability is ensured by the ambiguity between the signer and other potential signers whose public key is listed in aux.

Another technical challenge emerges in the "confirmed signature" generation phrase: how can the signer convert a 1-out-of-n signature into one directly verifiable with its public key, perhaps along with some extra public parameters? One simple approach is to let the signer re-sign the message using its secret key, effectively resolving the ambiguity of the signer's identity. However, this re-signing introduces a drawback, as the new signature doesn't maintain any relationship to the original extended withdrawable signature.

Our solution with 1-out-of-2 signature from RSA signature is illustrated as follows: the R in the 1-out-of-2 signature is not a directly generated randomness. It should generated from the message m, the signer's secret key d_i with the chosen randomness set $\{s_j\}_{j \neq i}$. The R now is generated as $R = H_i(m, s_j^{d_i})$. The extended withdrawable signature $\sigma = (\omega, \mathsf{aux})$ then needs to contain the 1-out-of-2 signature ω with $\mathsf{aux} = \{\mathsf{pk}_j\}_{j \neq i}$.

The verification algorithm of σ is performed using the public key of the signer pk_i and aux as follows: for any verifier, it first reconstructs γ through $\gamma = \{\mathsf{pk}_j\}_{j=1}^n$, and $k_1' = c_1 + s_1^{e_1} + z^R$, $c_2' = H_2(m, \gamma, k_1')$, $k_2' = c_2 + s_2^{e_2} + z^R$, $c_1' = H_1(m, \gamma, k_2')$. If $c_1' = c_1$, then the verification of σ is successful.

This extended withdrawable signature scheme achieves withdrawability leveraging the signer ambiguity in the 1-out-of-2 signature and holds the universal verifiability, as σ can also be verifiable through pk_j with $\overline{\mathsf{aux}} = \{\mathsf{pk}_i\}$. As a result, even when other users complete the withdrawable signature verification algorithm of σ, they remain uncertain about whether the signer is the real signer.

Suppose the signer wants to transform a withdrawable signature σ into a confirmed signature $\tilde{\sigma}$ associated with σ. While the signer holds the secret key sk_i, it can easily reconstruct $S_j = s'^{d_i}_j$ with $s'_j = s_j$ obtained from σ. With the three fundamental algorithms of RSA signature RSA.DS denoted as RSA.DS = (KeyGen, RSA.Sign, RSA.Verify), the signer can re-sign message $\{m, \sigma\}$ with its secret key sk_i to get $\delta_1 = \mathsf{RSA.Sign}(\{m, \sigma\}, \mathsf{sk}_i)$. The confirmed signature $\tilde{\sigma}$ that contains δ_1, S_j and s'_j now can be verified as a conventional signature on $\mathsf{pk}_i = (e_i, N_i)$ through $1 = \mathsf{RSA.Verify}(\{m, \sigma\}, \mathsf{pk}_i, \delta_1)$ and $s'_j = S^{e_i}_j$. During the checking stage, $\tilde{\sigma}$ can easily be linked with the extended withdrawable signature $\sigma = (\omega, \mathsf{aux})$ through $s'_j = s_j = \{s_1, s_2\} \setminus \{s_i\}$ and $R = H_i(m, S_j)$.

With the revisited definition and security notions in Sect. 3, our generic construction of extended withdrawable signatures is detailed in Sect. 4, and the security analysis is in Sect. 5. The concrete instantiation from the RSA signature and performance evaluation are provided in Sect. 6 and Sect. 7.

1.2   Our Contributions

Motivated by the absence of a withdrawable signature scheme based on RSA that is publicly verifiable and suitable for various applications, we present the concept of the "extended withdrawable signature". This extended withdrawable signature ensures that the generated withdrawable signature is publicly verifiable. Our contributions in this paper can be summarized as follows:

1. We extend the definition of a *withdrawable signature* scheme and provide the concept of *extended withdrawable signature*, which provides *extended withdrawability*. The *extended withdrawable signature* ensures an extended withdrawable signature holds universal verifiability through n possible signers while keeping signer ambiguity until the real signer confirms it.
2. We propose a generic construction of the extended withdrawable signature from the Type-H signature. We also give a concrete instantiation from the RSA signature with a 1-out-of-2 signature scheme.

2   Related Work

In this section, we review relevant works that could be used as the foundation for our extended withdrawable signature scheme to construct 1-out-of-n signature schemes, particularly focusing on the DVS and the ring signature.

Designated-Verifier Signature Scheme. The concept of designated-verifier signatures (DVS) was first presented by Jakobsson et al. in [18] and independently by Chaum in 1995 [5]. Since then, the field has been studied extensively for several decades, with various assumptions leading to different instantiations. Notable contributions in this area include the following works [21, 32–35].

DVS has multiple variations; one notable variation is universal designated-verifier signature schemes (UDVS). The establishment of the first UDVS scheme was carried out by Steinfeld et al. in [29] with the bilinear group, and two more UDVS schemes were later developed in [30], which expanded the conventional Schnorr/RSA signature techniques. Following the work by Steinfeld et al. [29], several UDVS schemes have been proposed in literatures [16,31,36]. Additionally, the first lattice-based UDVS was proposed in [20].

Ring Signature Scheme. The concept of ring signature was first proposed by Rivest, Shamir, and Tauman in [27]. In a ring signature scheme, a signer can select a set of public keys, including their own, and create a signature on behalf of that public key set. For instance, in the public key setting, include RSA-based [27], discrete logarithm-based [15], pairing-based [4] and lattice-based [9, 10]. Ring signatures can be generically constructed through zero-knowledge proof on a signer index, particularly through a one-out-of-many proof, as demonstrated in [14,23]. The logarithmic-size constructions are also suggested in [3,11,13].

Claimable Ring Signature Scheme and Claimable Designated Verifier Signature Scheme. The concept of claimable ring signatures (CRS) was first introduced by Park et al. in [25]. CRS allows a user to sign a message anonymously while retaining the ability to reveal their identity if needed. This is similar to withdrawable signatures, where signatures are initially considered revoked and can be confirmed when necessary. A withdrawable signature can only be verified using the signer's public key after confirmation by the signer. This state of withdrawability is maintained through the signer's ambiguity property. Therefore, a claimable ring signature can be viewed as a specific type of withdrawable signature, achieving withdrawability through signer ambiguity.

The concept of claimable designated verifier signatures (CDVS) was later proposed by Yamashita et al. in [35], building on the idea of claimable ring signatures from [25]. CDVS allows a signer to claim they created a designated verifier signature when necessary. Like CRS, a CDVS is another form of withdrawable signature that maintains signer ambiguity.

3   Notations and Definitions

The detailed original definition of the withdrawable signature is illustrated in [22]. As described in the syntax of the withdrawable signature, a withdrawable signature scheme $\mathcal{WS}$ involves two parties in the signing phase: the signer pk_i and a designated verifier pk_j. In the "withdrawable signing" algorithm WSign, the signer generates the withdrawable signature σ using the signer's secret key sk_i and the designated verifier's public key pk_j. Our extended withdrawable signature $\mathcal{EWS}$ still involves two parties during the signing phase but expands pk_j by replacing only one single verifier pk_j into a group of potential signers aux, where aux must contain at least one public key different from signer's public key pk.

In the "withdrawable signature verification" algorithm WSVerify, as outlined in [22], verification can only be performed using the designated verifier's secret key sk_j, limiting verification to the designated verifier. We then extend the WSVerify algorithm to allow anyone who obtains the withdrawable signature σ to verify it using the signer's public key pk.

We also rephrase the definition of the "confirmed signature verification" algorithm, CVerify. According to [22], CVerify involves two stages: verifying the confirmed signature $\widetilde{\sigma}$ using the two public keys pk_i and pk_j, and checking whether $\widetilde{\sigma}$ corresponds to the withdrawable signature σ. To clarify, we redefine CVerify as $CVerify(m, pk, \widetilde{\sigma})$, indicating that $\widetilde{\sigma}$ is a valid signature of pk on m. Additionally, we introduce a new algorithm, $Check(m, pk, \sigma, \widetilde{\sigma})$, to ensure that $\widetilde{\sigma}$ correctly traces back to its corresponding withdrawable signature σ.

According to security notions of the withdrawable signature, *withdrawability*, as defined in [22], ensures that a PPT adversary $\mathcal{A}$, given a message m and an unconfirmed withdrawable signature σ, cannot feasibly determine whether pk_i or pk_j created σ. In our extended withdrawable signature, *withdrawability* is extended to *extended withdrawability* as in Definition 3. Given a message m and its corresponding unconfirmed withdrawable signature σ, it should be infeasible for an adversary $\mathcal{A}$ to determine whether pk or any other potential signer $\overline{pk} \neq pk$ where $\overline{pk} \in aux$ created the withdrawable signature.

The detailed syntax and security notions of our extended withdrawable signature are presented as follows.

3.1   Extended Withdrawable Signature: Definition

Notation and Terminology. Throughout this paper, we use λ as the security parameter. By $a \xleftarrow{\$} \gamma$, we denote an element a is chosen uniformly at random from a set γ. Let $\gamma = \{pk_j\}_{j=1}^n$ be a set of public keys chosen by the signer, where each public key pk_j is generated by the same key generation algorithm $KeyGen(1^k)$ and $n = |\gamma|$. The signer's public key pk_i is included in γ where $i \in [1, n]$. The corresponding secret key of pk_j is denoted as sk_j, and the signer's corresponding secret key is sk_i.

To create a withdrawable signature, the signer first selects a set of public keys γ, which includes the public keys of all potential signers, including the signer's own public key pk where $pk \in \gamma$. The signer then announces the auxiliary information aux through the "shuffling algorithm" Shuffle for the corresponding extended withdrawable signature. This auxiliary information comprises the set of public keys belonging to all other potential signers, defined as $aux = \gamma \setminus \{pk\}$.

An extended withdrawable signature scheme $\mathcal{EWS}$ consists of seven polynomial time algorithms, (KeyGen, Shuffle, WSign, WSVerify, Confirm, CVerify, Check), each of which is described below:

– $(pk, sk) \leftarrow KeyGen(1^k)$: The key generation algorithm takes the security parameters 1^k as input to return a public/secret key pair (pk, sk).
– $aux \leftarrow Shuffle(pk, \gamma)$: The shuffling algorithm takes the signer's public key pk and the pubic key set of all possible signers γ ($pk \in \gamma$) as input, to return the auxiliary information $aux = \gamma \setminus \{pk\}$.

- $\sigma \leftarrow$ WSign$(m, \mathsf{sk}, \mathsf{aux})$: The "withdrawable signing" algorithm takes as input a message m, signer's secret key sk and auxiliary information aux, to return a new extended withdrawable signature σ on m of pk.
- $1/0 \leftarrow$ WSVerify(m, pk, σ): The "extended withdrawable signature verification" algorithm takes as input an extended withdrawable signature σ on m of pk with auxiliary information aux, to return either 1 or 0.
- $\widetilde{\sigma} \leftarrow$ Confirm(m, sk, σ): The "confirm" algorithm takes as input an extended withdrawable signature σ on m of pk where WSVerify$(m, \mathsf{pk}, \sigma) = 1$ and σ is the withdrawable signature generated by the signer, to return a confirmed signature $\widetilde{\sigma}$ on m of pk.
- $1/0 \leftarrow$ CVerify$(m, \mathsf{pk}, \widetilde{\sigma})$: The "confirmed signature verification" algorithm takes as input a confirmed signature $\widetilde{\sigma}$ on m of pk, to return either $1/0$.
- $1/0 \leftarrow$ Check$(m, \mathsf{pk}, \sigma, \widetilde{\sigma})$: The "checking" algorithm takes as input a confirmed signature $\widetilde{\sigma}$ on m of pk where CVerify$(m, \mathsf{pk}, \widetilde{\sigma}) = 1$ and a withdrawable signature σ on m of pk where WSVerify$(m, \mathsf{pk}, \sigma) = 1$, to returns 1 if σ is the corresponding withdrawable signature of $\widetilde{\sigma}$. Otherwise, it returns 0.

3.2 Security Notions of the Extended Withdrawable Signature

The security notion of an extended withdrawable signature scheme $\mathcal{EWS}$ covers the properties of correctness, unforgeability under insider corruption, and extended withdrawability in three aspects.

Correctness. As long as the extended withdrawable signature σ is verifiable through the extended withdrawable signature verification algorithm WSVerify, it can be concluded that the corresponding confirmed signature $\widetilde{\sigma}$ is also verifiable through the confirm verification algorithm CVerify. Additionally, the withdrawable/confirmed signature pair σ and $\widetilde{\sigma}$ will pass the checking algorithm Check.

Unforgeability Under Insider Corruption. Nobody except the signer can transform a verifiable extended withdrawable signature σ generated from sk with respect to pk into corresponding confirmed signature $\widetilde{\sigma}$, even the adversary can always obtain the secret key sk_i of potential signer $\mathsf{pk}_i \in \mathsf{aux}$.

Extended Withdrawability. The extended withdrawability means that, for a withdrawable signature σ that WSVerify$(m, \mathsf{pk}, \mathsf{aux}, \sigma) = 1$, it must satisfy the signer ambiguity property. The withdrawable signature σ can be verifiable with a different signer $\overline{\mathsf{pk}} \in \mathsf{aux}$ where WSVerify$(m, \overline{\mathsf{pk}}, \overline{\mathsf{aux}}, \sigma) = 1$ and $\overline{\mathsf{aux}} = \gamma \setminus \overline{\mathsf{pk}}$.

We call an extended withdrawable signature scheme $\mathcal{EWS}$ *secure* if it is *correct, unforgeable under insider corruption,* and *extended withdrawable.* Below, we provide formal security definitions of correctness, unforgeability under insider corruption, and extended withdrawability.

Definition 1 (Correctness). *An $\mathcal{EWS}$ is considered correct for any security parameter k, any public key set γ, and any message $m \in \{0,1\}^*$. For $\gamma = \{\mathsf{pk}_j\}_{j=1}^n$ where $\mathsf{pk} \in \gamma$, if with following algorithms:* $(\mathsf{pk}, \mathsf{sk}) \leftarrow$ KeyGen(1^k), $\mathsf{aux} \leftarrow$ Shuffle(pk, γ), $\sigma \leftarrow$ WSign$(m, \mathsf{sk}, \mathsf{aux})$ *and* $\widetilde{\sigma} \leftarrow$ Confirm(m, sk, σ).

It holds with an overwhelming probability (in k) that the corresponding verification algorithms: $1 \leftarrow$ WSVerify(m, pk, σ), $1 \leftarrow$ CVerify$(m, \mathsf{pk}, \widetilde{\sigma})$ *and* $1 \leftarrow$ Check$(m, \mathsf{pk}, \sigma, \widetilde{\sigma})$.

Definition 2 (Unforgeability under insider corruption). *Considering an unforgeability under insider corruption experiment* $\mathrm{Exp}_{\mathcal{EWS},\mathcal{A}}^{\mathrm{EUF\text{-}CMA}}(1^k)$ *for a PPT adversary* $\mathcal{A}$ *and security parameter k. The three oracles we use to build the* $\mathrm{Exp}_{\mathcal{EWS},\mathcal{A}}^{\mathrm{EUF\text{-}CMA}}(1^k)$ *are shown as follows.*

Oracle$\mathcal{O}_j^{\mathrm{Corrupt}}(\cdot)$	Oracle$\mathcal{O}_{\mathsf{sk},\mathsf{aux}}^{\mathrm{WSign}}(\cdot)$	Oracle$\mathcal{O}_{\mathsf{sk},\sigma}^{\mathrm{Confirm}}(\cdot)$
if $j \neq i$,	if $\mathsf{pk} = \mathsf{pk}_i \wedge i \notin \mathcal{CO} \wedge \mathsf{pk}_i \notin \mathsf{aux}$	if $\sigma \in \mathcal{W}$
$\mathcal{CO} \leftarrow \mathcal{CO} \cup \mathsf{sk}_j$	$\sigma \leftarrow$ WSign$(m, \mathsf{sk}, \mathsf{aux})$	$\mathcal{M} \leftarrow \mathcal{M} \cup \{m\}$
return sk_j	$\mathcal{W} \leftarrow \mathcal{W} \cup \{\sigma\}$	$\widetilde{\sigma} \leftarrow$ Confirm(m, sk, σ)
else return $\perp$	return σ	return $\widetilde{\sigma}$
	else return $\perp$	else return $\perp$

With oracles $\mathcal{O}_j^{\mathrm{Corrupt}}(\cdot)$, $\mathcal{O}_{\mathsf{sk},\mathsf{aux}}^{\mathrm{WSign}}(\cdot)$ *and* $\mathcal{O}_{\mathsf{sk},\sigma}^{\mathrm{Confirm}}(\cdot)$, *we have the following experiment* $\mathrm{Exp}_{\mathcal{EWS},\mathcal{A}}^{\mathrm{EUF\text{-}CMA}}(1^k)$ *for the proof of unforgeability under corruption:*

$\mathrm{Exp}_{\mathcal{EWS},\mathcal{A}}^{\mathrm{EUF}}\text{-}\mathrm{CMA}(1^k)$
for $j = 1$**to** μ**do**
$\quad$ $(\mathsf{pk}_j, \mathsf{sk}_j) \leftarrow$ KeyGen(1^k);
$\quad$ $\mathcal{P} = \{\mathsf{pk}_j\}_{j=1}^{\mu}$, $(\mathsf{pk}, \mathsf{sk}) \leftarrow (\mathsf{pk}_i, \mathsf{sk}_i)$, $i \in [1, \mu]$, $\gamma \subseteq \mathcal{P}$, $|\gamma| = n$;
$\quad$ $\mathsf{aux}_i \leftarrow$ Shuffle(pk, γ_i), $\mathsf{pk} \in \gamma_i, \mathcal{CO}, \mathcal{W}, \mathcal{M} \leftarrow \emptyset$;
$\quad$ $(m^*, \sigma^*, \widetilde{\sigma}^*) \leftarrow \mathcal{A}^{\mathcal{O}_j^{\mathrm{Corrupt}}(\cdot), \mathcal{O}_{\mathsf{sk},\mathsf{aux}}^{\mathrm{WSign}}(\cdot), \mathcal{O}_{\mathsf{sk},\sigma}^{\mathrm{Confirm}}(\cdot)}(1^k, \gamma^*)$
if $\gamma^* \subseteq \mathcal{P}$, $\mathsf{pk}_i \in \gamma^*, i \notin \mathcal{CO} \wedge \mathsf{aux}^* = \gamma^* \setminus \mathsf{pk}_i \wedge m^* \notin \mathcal{M}$
$\quad \wedge 1 \leftarrow$ WSVerify$(m^*, \mathsf{pk}^*, \sigma^*) \wedge 1 \leftarrow$ CVerify$(m^*, \mathsf{pk}^*, \widetilde{\sigma}^*) \wedge 1 \leftarrow$
Check$(m^*, \mathsf{pk}^*, \sigma^*, \widetilde{\sigma}^*)$
$\quad$ **return** 1
else return 0

An extended withdrawable signature scheme $\mathcal{EWS}$ *is unforgeable under insider corruption of EUF-CMA security if, for all PPT adversary* $\mathcal{A}$, *there exists a negligible function* negl *such that:* $\Pr[\mathrm{Exp}_{\mathcal{EWS},\mathcal{A}}^{\mathrm{EUF\text{-}CMA}}(1^k) = 1] \leq$ negl(1^k).

Definition 3 (Extended Withdrawability). *Let* $\gamma = \{\mathsf{pk}_j\}_{j=1}^{n}$, $\mathsf{pk} \in \gamma$, $\mathsf{aux} = \gamma \setminus \mathsf{pk}$, *considering an extended withdrawability experiment* $\mathrm{Exp}_{\mathcal{EWS},\mathcal{A}}^{\mathrm{Withdraw}}(1^k)$ *for a PPT adversary* $\mathcal{A}$ *and security parameter k. The oracle we use to build our withdrawability experiment* $\mathrm{Exp}_{\mathcal{EWS}}^{\mathrm{Withdraw}}(1^k)$ *is shown as follows.*

Oracle$\mathcal{O}_{\mathsf{sk},\mathsf{aux}}^{\mathrm{WSign}}(\cdot)$
if $m \notin \mathcal{M}$
$\quad$ $\sigma \leftarrow$ WSign$(m, \mathsf{sk}, \mathsf{aux})$, $\mathcal{M} \leftarrow \mathcal{M} \cup \{m\}$
$\quad$ **return** σ
else return $\perp$

With oracle Oracle $\mathcal{O}^{\mathsf{WSign}}_{\mathsf{sk},\mathsf{aux}}(\cdot)$, we have the following experiment $\mathsf{Exp}^{\mathsf{Withdraw}}_{\mathcal{EWS}}(1^k)$:

$$
\begin{array}{l}
\hline
\mathsf{Exp}^{\mathsf{Withdraw}}_{\mathcal{EWS},\mathcal{A}}(1^k) \\
\hline
\quad \textbf{for } i = 1 \textbf{ to } n \textbf{ do} \\
\qquad (\mathsf{pk}_i, \mathsf{sk}_i) \leftarrow \mathsf{KeyGen}(1^k), \gamma = \{\mathsf{pk}_i\}_{i=1}^n;, \mathcal{M} \leftarrow \emptyset; \\
\qquad (\overline{\mathsf{pk}}, \overline{\mathsf{aux}}) \leftarrow \mathcal{A}^{\mathcal{O}^{\mathsf{WSign}}_{\mathsf{sk},aux}(\cdot)}(1^k, m^*, \gamma, \sigma^*) \\
\quad \textbf{if } m^* \in \mathcal{M} \wedge \overline{\mathsf{aux}} = \gamma \setminus \overline{\mathsf{pk}} \wedge 1 \leftarrow \mathsf{WSVerify}(m^*, \overline{\mathsf{pk}}, \sigma^*) \\
\qquad \textbf{return } 1 \\
\quad \textbf{else return } 0 \\
\hline
\end{array}
$$

An extended withdrawable signature achieves extended withdrawability if, for any PPT adversary $\mathcal{A}$, as long as the Confirm *algorithm hasn't been executed, there exists a negligible function* negl *such that:* $\Pr[\mathsf{Exp}^{\mathsf{Withdraw}}_{\mathcal{EWS},\mathcal{A}}(1^k) = 1] = 1.$

4   Our Construction

4.1   Preliminaries

Hash-then-One-Way Type Signature [1]. In a Type-H signature scheme H.DS, let F be a trapdoor one-way function and I be its inverse function. For any h taken from the randomness domain Δ_i, computing $h = F(\mathsf{pk}, s)$ is easy, but any pre-image of s cannot be computed in polynomial time. Trapdoor information sk allows one to efficiently compute one of the pre-images of s.

One Type-H signature scheme H.DS consists of four algorithms: Setup, KeyGen, H.Sign, and H.Verify. With hash function $H_i : \{0,1\}^* \to \Delta_i$, the detailed signature scheme is defined as follows.

- $(\mathsf{pk}, \mathsf{sk}) \leftarrow \mathsf{KeyGen}(1^k)$: On input system parameters 1^k, it returns a public and secret key pair (pk, sk).
- $\sigma \leftarrow \mathsf{H.Sign}(m, \mathsf{sk})$: On input the signer's secret key sk and message m, it returns the signature $\sigma = (s, \mathsf{aux})$ where $h = H_i(m, \mathsf{aux})$, $s = I(\mathsf{sk}, h)$.
- $1/0 \leftarrow \mathsf{H.Verify}(m, \mathsf{pk}, \sigma)$: On input the (m, pk, σ), it returns 1, which indicates a valid signature of pk on m if the following equation holds, such that: $h = h'$ where $h = H_i(m, \mathsf{aux})$ and $h' = F(\mathsf{pk}, s)$. Otherwise, it returns 0.

1-Out-of-n Signature. To build our generic construction of the extended withdrawable signature, we first revisit the definition of 1-out-of-n signature in [1]. Considering a public key set $\gamma = \{\mathsf{pk}_j\}_{j=1}^n$, let $i \xleftarrow{\$} \{1, \cdots, n\}$, and $(\mathsf{pk}_i, \mathsf{sk}_i)$ denotes the signer's public/secret key pair. The statement chosen by the signer, which serves as an additional input during the signing stage, is denoted by state. A 1-out-of-n signature scheme consists of the following three PPT algorithms:

$$
\mathsf{Ambi.DS} = \begin{cases}
(\mathsf{pk}_i, \mathsf{sk}_i) \leftarrow & \mathsf{Ambi.KeyGen}(1^k) \\
\sigma \leftarrow & \mathsf{Ambi.Sign}(m, \mathsf{sk}_i, \gamma, \mathsf{state}) \\
1/0 \leftarrow & \mathsf{Ambi.Verify}(m, \gamma, \sigma)
\end{cases}
$$

The security of Ambi.DS holds two aspects: *signer ambiguity* (Definition 4) and *unforgeability*. We then revisit the definition of signer ambiguity as follows.

Definition 4 (Signer Ambiguity). *Assume n public/secret key pairs are generated as $(\mathsf{pk}_1, \mathsf{sk}_1), \cdots, (\mathsf{pk}_n, \mathsf{sk}_n) \leftarrow \mathsf{Ambi.KeyGen}(1^k)$. Let $\mathcal{P} = \{\mathsf{pk}_j\}_{j=1}^n$, the signer's public/secret key pair is denoted as $(\mathsf{pk}_s, \mathsf{sk}_i)$ where $i \xleftarrow{s} \{1, n\}$. Considering an experiment $\mathsf{Exp}_{\mathsf{Ambi.DS}, \mathcal{A}}^{\mathsf{SigAmbi}}(1^k)$ for a PPT adversary $\mathcal{A}$ and security parameter k. The oracle we use to build our extended withdrawability experiment $\mathsf{Exp}_{\mathsf{Ambi.DS}, \mathcal{A}}^{\mathsf{SigAmbi}}(1^k)$ is shown as follows.*

$\mathsf{Oracle}\mathcal{O}_{\mathsf{sk}_i, \gamma, \mathsf{state}}^{\mathsf{Ambi.Sign}}(\cdot)$

---

if $\gamma \subseteq \mathcal{P}, \mathsf{pk}_s \in \gamma$

    $\sigma \leftarrow \mathsf{Ambi.Sign}(m, \mathsf{sk}_i, \gamma, \mathsf{state}), \mathcal{M} \leftarrow \mathcal{M} \cup \{m\}$

    return σ

else return $\perp$

With $\mathcal{O}_{\mathsf{sk}_i, \gamma, \mathsf{state}}^{\mathsf{Ambi.Sign}}(\cdot)$, we have the experiment $\mathsf{Exp}_{\mathsf{Ambi.DS}, \mathcal{A}}^{\mathsf{SigAmbi}}(1^k)$:

$\mathsf{Exp}_{\mathsf{Ambi.DS}, \mathcal{A}}^{\mathsf{SigAmbi}}(1^k)$

---

  for $j = 1$ **to** n **do**

    $(\mathsf{pk}_j, \mathsf{sk}_j) \leftarrow \mathsf{KeyGen}(1^k), \mathcal{P} = \{\mathsf{pk}_j\}_{j=1}^n, i \xleftarrow{s} \{1, n\},$

    $b \xleftarrow{s} \{0, 1\};$

    $\mathcal{M} \leftarrow \emptyset;$

  if $\gamma^* \subseteq \mathcal{P}, \overline{\mathsf{pk}_0}, \overline{\mathsf{pk}_1} \in \gamma^* \wedge m^* \notin \mathcal{M} \wedge 1 \leftarrow \mathsf{Ambi.Verify}(m^*, \gamma^*, \sigma_i^*)$

    $\sigma_b^* \leftarrow \mathsf{Ambi.Sign}(m^*, \overline{\mathsf{sk}_b}, \gamma^*, \mathsf{state})$

    $b' \leftarrow \mathcal{A}^{\mathcal{O}_{\mathsf{sk}_i, \gamma, \mathsf{state}}^{\mathsf{Ambi.Sign}}(\cdot)}(1^k, m^*, \overline{\mathsf{pk}_0}, \overline{\mathsf{pk}_1}, \sigma_b^*)$

  if $b = b'$

    return 1

    else return 0

A 1-out-of-n signature scheme achieves signer ambiguous if, for any PPT adversary $\mathcal{A}$, there exists a negligible function negl *such that:*

$$\Pr[\mathsf{Exp}_{\mathsf{Ambi.DS}, \mathcal{A}}^{\mathsf{SigAmbi}}(1^k) = 1] \leq \frac{1}{n} + \mathsf{negl}(1^k).$$

A 1-out-of-n signature scheme can be derived from specialized variants of existing signature schemes, specifically, the ring signature and the designated-verifier signature, where the *signer ambiguity* can rely on the *anonymity* provided by the ring signature and the designated-verifier signature.

4.2   A Generic Construction from Type-H Signature

We first describe the new notations introduced to construct the generic construction of our extended withdrawable signature from Type-H signature:

- We have $H_i : \{0,1\}^* \to \Delta_i$ being a hash function. Domain Δ_i depends on the corresponding public key pk_i. For $h_1, h_2 \in \Delta_i$, let $h_1 + h_2$ be the group operation for the domain Δ_i. We then use $h_1 - h_2$ to represent the group operation on h_1 with an inverse of h_2 for the domain Δ_i.
- We use the symbol $\odot$ to represent consecutive "+" operations: $\odot_{i=1}^n h_i := h_1 + \cdots + h_n$.
- If h_1 and h_2 are uniformly distributed within Δ_i, the operation $h_1 + h_2$ and $h_1 - h_2$ also maintains uniform distribution within Δ_i.

Then, the signer sets the group of all possible signers as $\gamma = \{\mathsf{pk}_j\}_{j=1}^n$ with hash functions $\{H_j\}_{j=1}^n$, and sets $\mathsf{pk}_i = \mathsf{pk}$ where $i \xleftarrow{\$} \{1,n\}$ with its public key pk.

The constructed 1-out-of-n signature scheme from Type-H signature $\mathsf{H.DS} = (\mathsf{KeyGen}, \mathsf{H.Sign}, \mathsf{H.Verify})$ is detailed as follows.

1-out-of-n Signature Scheme from Type-H Signature

$\mathsf{Ambi.Sign}(m, \mathsf{sk}_i, \gamma, \mathsf{state})$	$\mathsf{Ambi.Verify}(m, \gamma, \sigma)$
parse $\gamma = \{\mathsf{pk}_j\}_{j=1}^n$,	parse $\sigma = (c_1, s_1, \cdots, s_n, z, R)$,
parse $\mathsf{state} = \{\{s_j\}_{j \neq i}, R\}$	parse $\gamma = \{\mathsf{pk}_j\}_{j=1}^n$
$\quad h, z \xleftarrow{\$} \Delta_i, k_i = h + F(R, z)$	For all $j = \{1, \cdots, n\}$:
$\quad c_{i+1} = H_{i+1}(m, \gamma, k_i)$	$\quad k'_j = c_j + F(\mathsf{pk}_j, s_j) + F(R, z),$
For all $j \neq i$:	$\quad c'_{j+1} = H_{j+1}(m, \gamma, k'_j)$
$\quad k_j = c_j + F(\mathsf{pk}_j, s_j) + F(R, z)$	if $c_1 \neq c'_1$
$\quad c_{j+1} = H_{j+1}(m, \gamma, k_j)$	$\quad\quad$ **return** 0
$\quad s_i = I(h - c_i, \mathsf{sk}_i)$	**else return** 1
$\quad \sigma = (c_1, s_1, \cdots, s_n, z, R)$	
return σ	

Our generic construction from Type-H signature is detailed as follows.

KeyGen(1^k)	Shuffle(pk, γ)
return (pk, sk)	define $\gamma = \{\mathsf{pk}_j\}_{j=1}^n$,
	$\mathsf{pk}_s \leftarrow \mathsf{pk}, i \xleftarrow{\$} \{1, n\}, \mathsf{aux} = \gamma \setminus \mathsf{pk}_s$
	return aux

WSign($m, \mathsf{sk}, \mathsf{aux}$)	WSVerify(m, pk, σ)
$\gamma = \mathsf{aux} \cup \mathsf{pk}$	parse $\sigma = (\sigma_1, \mathsf{aux})$
For all $j \neq i$:	parse $\gamma = \mathsf{aux} \cup \mathsf{pk}$
$s_j \xleftarrow{\$} \Delta_i, R = H_i(m, \bigodot_{j \neq i} I(s_j, \mathsf{sk}))$	**if** $1 \leftarrow \boxed{\mathsf{Ambi.Verify}(m, \gamma, \sigma_1)}$
state $= \{\{s_j\}_{j \neq i}, R\}, \mathsf{sk}_i = \mathsf{sk}$	**return** 1
$\sigma_1 \leftarrow \boxed{\mathsf{Ambi.Sign}(m, \mathsf{sk}_i, \gamma, \mathsf{state})}$	**else return** 0
$\sigma = (\sigma_1, \mathsf{aux})$	
return σ	

Confirm(m, sk, σ)	CVerify($m, \mathsf{pk}, \widetilde{\sigma}$)
parse $\sigma = (\sigma_1, \mathsf{aux})$	parse $\widetilde{\sigma} = (\delta_1, \delta_2, \delta_3)$
parse $\sigma_1 = (c_1, \{s_j\}_{j=1}^n, z, R)$	parse $\delta_2 = \{S_j\}_{j \neq i}, \delta_3 = \{s_j\}_{j \neq i}$
$\{S_j\}_{j \neq i} = \{I(s_j, \mathsf{sk})\}_{j \neq i}$	**if** $1 \leftarrow \mathsf{H.Verify}(\{m, \sigma\}, \mathsf{pk}, \delta_1)$,
$\delta_1 \leftarrow \mathsf{H.Sign}(\{m, \sigma\}, \mathsf{sk})$	$\{s_j\}_{j \neq i} = F(\mathsf{pk}, \{S_j\}_{j \neq i})$
$\delta_2 \leftarrow \{S_j\}_{j \neq i}, \delta_3 \leftarrow \{s_j\}_{j \neq i}$	**return** 1
$\widetilde{\sigma} = (\delta_1, \delta_2, \delta_3)$	**else return** 0
return $\widetilde{\sigma}$	

Check($m, \mathsf{pk}, \sigma, \widetilde{\sigma}$)
parse $\sigma = (\sigma_1, \mathsf{aux}), \sigma_1 = (c_1, \{s_j\}_{j=1}^n, z, R)$
parse $\widetilde{\sigma} = (\delta_1, \delta_2, \delta_3), \delta_2 = \{S_j\}_{j \neq i}, \delta_3 = \{s_j\}_{j \neq i}$
if $1 \leftarrow \mathsf{WSVerify}(m, \mathsf{pk}, \sigma), 1 \leftarrow \mathsf{CVerify}(m, \mathsf{pk}, \widetilde{\sigma})$,
$\{s_j\}_{j \neq i} = \{s_j\}_{j=1}^n \setminus \{s_i\}$
$R = H_i(m, \bigodot_{j \neq i} S_j)$
return 1
else return 0

5   Security Analysis

5.1   Unforgeability Under Insider Corruption of Our Extended Withdrawable Signature Scheme from **Type-H** Signature

Theorem 1. *If the underlying* Type-H *signature scheme H.DS is secure against EUF-CMA* [12] *in random oracle model, our generic construction for the extended withdrawable signature from* Type-H *signature presented in Sect. 4.2 is unforgeable under insider corruption (Definition 2) in the random oracle model with reduction loss $L = q_{H_i}$ where q_{H_i} denotes the number of hash queries to the random oracle H_i.*

Proof. Let $\mathcal{C}$ be an algorithm that breaks EUF-CMA of underlying Type-H signature scheme H.DS. We build a simulator $\mathcal{B}$ that runs adversary $\mathcal{A}$, which breaks unforgeability under insider corruption, to help $\mathcal{C}$ break EUF-CMA of H.DS in the random oracle model.

Setup. $\mathcal{B}$ has access to the algorithm $\mathcal{C}$. Suppose $\mathcal{C}$ executes the EUF-CMA game of H.DS, denoted as $\mathsf{Exp}_{\mathcal{A}}^{\mathrm{EUF\text{-}CMA}}$ which includes a signing oracle denoted as $\mathcal{O}_{\mathsf{sk}}^{\mathsf{H.Sign}}(\cdot)$, where $\mathcal{O}_{\mathsf{sk}}^{\mathsf{H.Sign}}(\cdot) : \omega_i \leftarrow \mathsf{H.Sign}(m, \mathsf{sk}_i)$. $\mathcal{C}$ first generates $(\mathsf{pk}, \mathsf{sk}) \leftarrow \mathsf{KeyGen}(1^k)$. Then, $\mathcal{B}$ gains pk from $\mathcal{C}$ and sets $\mathcal{P} = \{\mathsf{pk}_j\}_{j=1}^n$ where $\mathsf{pk}_i = \mathsf{pk} \in \mathcal{P}, i \in [1, n]$. $\mathcal{B}$ provides $\mathcal{P}$ to $\mathcal{A}$.

$\mathcal{A}$ now can set the public key set $\gamma_i \subseteq \mathcal{P}$ where $\mathsf{pk}_i \in \gamma_i$ and provide γ_i to $\mathcal{B}$.

Oracle Simulation. $\mathcal{B}$ answers the oracle queries as follows.

Corruption Query. The adversary $\mathcal{A}$ makes secret key queries of $\mathsf{pk}_j, j \in [1, \mu]$ in this phase. If $\mathcal{A}$ queries for the secret key of pk_i, abort. Otherwise, $\mathcal{B}$ returns the corresponding sk_j to $\mathcal{A}$, and adds sk_j to the corrupted secret key list $\mathcal{CO}$.

H-Query. The adversary $\mathcal{A}$ makes hash queries in this phase.

$\mathcal{C}$ simulates H_i as a random oracle, $\mathcal{B}$ then answers the hash queries of H_i through $\mathcal{C}$. For hash queries of H_j where $j \neq i$, $\mathcal{B}$ directly returns H_j to $\mathcal{A}$.

Signature Query. $\mathcal{A}$ outputs a message m_i and queries for extended withdrawable signature with corresponding signer pk_i and $\gamma_i \subseteq \mathcal{P}$. If $\mathsf{pk}_i \notin \gamma_i$, $\mathcal{B}$ abort. Otherwise, for $j \neq i$, $\mathcal{B}$ chooses $r_{j,i} \xleftarrow{\$} \Delta_i$ and sets $\{r_{j,i}\}_{j=1}^n$ as inputs of random oracle H_i and obtains $s_{j,i} = H_i(r_{j,i})$. $\mathcal{B}$ then asks for the signing outputs of $r_{j,i}$ from $\mathcal{C}$ as $\tau_{j,i} \leftarrow \mathcal{O}_{\mathsf{sk}}^{\mathsf{H.Sign}}(r_{j,i})$. With $\{\tau_{j,i}\}_{j\neq i}$, $\mathcal{B}$ could respond to the signature query from $\mathcal{A}$ as follows:

- $\mathcal{O}_{\mathsf{sk},\mathsf{aux}}^{\mathsf{WSign}}(\cdot)$: $\mathcal{B}$ chooses $h_i, z_i, c_{1,i}, s_{i,i} \xleftarrow{\$} \Delta_i$. Then, with corresponding aux_i where $\mathsf{aux}_i = \gamma_i \setminus \mathsf{pk}_i$, $\mathcal{B}$ computes the following:
  1. $R_i = H_i(m, \gamma, \bigodot_{j=1}^n \tau_{j,i})$
  2. For all $j \in [1, n]$: $k_{j,i} = c_{j,i} + F(\mathsf{pk}_j, s_{j,i}) + F(R_i, z_i)$
  3. $c_{j+1,i} = H_{j+1}(m_i, \gamma, k_{j,i})$
  4. $\sigma_{1,i} = (c_{1,i}, s_{1,i}, \cdots, s_{n,i}, z_i, R_i)$
  5. $\sigma_i = (\sigma_{1,i}, \mathsf{aux}_i)$
- $\mathcal{O}_{\mathsf{sk},\sigma}^{\mathsf{Confirm}}(\cdot)$: $\mathcal{B}$ sets $\{m_i, \sigma_i\}$ as the input of $\mathcal{C}$ and asks for the signing output of $\mathcal{C}$ as $\omega_i \leftarrow \mathsf{H.Sign}(\{m_i, \sigma_i\}, \mathsf{sk})$. With $\omega_i, \{\tau_{j,i}\}_{j\neq i}$ from $\mathcal{C}$, aux_i and σ_i, $\mathcal{B}$ can respond the confirmed signature query for $\mathcal{A}$ as follows:
  1. $\delta_{2,i} = (\{\tau_{j,i}\}_{j\neq i}), \delta_{3,i} = (\{s_{j,i}\}_{j\neq i})$
  2. $\widetilde{\sigma}_i = (\omega_i, \delta_{2,i}, \delta_{3,i})$

Meanwhile, $\mathcal{B}$ sets $\mathcal{M} \leftarrow \mathcal{M} \cup m_i$ and $\mathcal{W} \leftarrow \mathcal{W} \cup \sigma_i$.

Forgery. On the forgery phase, $\mathcal{B}$ returns an extended withdrawable signature σ_m^* for pk with $\mathsf{aux}^* \subseteq \{\mathcal{P}\}$ on some m^* that has not been queried before. After $\mathcal{A}$ transforms σ_m^* into $\widetilde{\sigma}_{m^*}$, if $0 \leftarrow \mathsf{CVerify}(m, \mathsf{pk}, \widetilde{\sigma}_m^*)$ or $0 \leftarrow \mathsf{Check}(m, \mathsf{pk}, \sigma_m^*, \widetilde{\sigma}_m^*)$, abort. Otherwise, if $\widetilde{\sigma}_{m^*}$ is valid, $\mathcal{B}$ then can directly obtain a forged signature ω^* for pk_i on $\{m^*, \sigma_m^*\}$ from $\mathcal{A}$'s forged confirmed signature $\widetilde{\sigma}_m^* = (\omega^*, \delta_2^*)$.

Therefore, we can use the $\mathcal{A}$ to break the unforgeability in the EUF-CMA model of our underlying signature scheme H.DS, which contradicts the property of our underlying signature scheme.

Probability of Successful Simulation. All queried extended withdrawable signatures σ_i and corresponding confirmed signatures $\tilde{\sigma}_i$ are simulatable, and the forged signature is reducible because the message m^* cannot be chosen for a signature query as it will be used for the signature forgery. Therefore, the probability of successful simulation is $\frac{1}{q_{H_i}}$ for q_{H_i} queries.   □

To prove the extended withdrawability of our generic construction from Type-H signature, we first give the proof of the signer ambiguity in the random oracle for the underlying 1-out-of-n signature scheme.

Theorem 2. *Our 1-out-of-n signature scheme from* Type-H *signature in Sect. 4.2 satisfies the signer ambiguity (Definition 4) in the random oracle model.*

Proof. $\mathcal{B}$ sets the challenge public key set as $\mathcal{P} = \{\mathsf{pk}_j\}_{j=1}^n$ and associated secret key set as $\mathcal{R} = \{\mathsf{sk}_j\}_{j=1}^n$. The signer is denoted as pk_i where $i \in [1, n]$.

Oracle Simulation. $\mathcal{B}$ answers the oracle queries as follows.

H-Query. The adversary $\mathcal{A}$ makes hash queries in this phase. $\mathcal{B}$ simulates H_i as a random oracle.

Signature Query. The adversary $\mathcal{A}$ makes signature queries in this phase. $\mathcal{A}$ outputs a message m_i and queries for 1-out-of-n signature with corresponding public key set $\gamma_i \subseteq \mathcal{S}$, and signer $\mathsf{pk}_i \in \gamma_i$. $\mathcal{B}$ could respond to the signature query from $\mathcal{A}$ as follows:

- $\mathcal{O}_{\mathsf{sk}_i,\gamma}^{\mathsf{Ambi.Sign}}(\cdot)$: $\mathcal{B}$ returns $\sigma_i \leftarrow \mathsf{Ambi.Sign}(m_i, \mathsf{sk}_i, \gamma_i)$

Challenge. $\mathcal{A}$ gives $\mathcal{B}$ a challenge message m^* with corresponding public key set $\gamma^* \subseteq \mathcal{S}$, $\gamma^* = \{\mathsf{pk}_j\}_{j=1}^n$ and two public keys $\{\overline{\mathsf{pk}}_0, \overline{\mathsf{pk}}_1\} \subseteq \gamma^*$. The corresponding secret keys of $\{\overline{\mathsf{pk}}_0, \overline{\mathsf{pk}}_1\}$ are denoted as $\{\overline{\mathsf{sk}}_0, \overline{\mathsf{sk}}_1\}$.

$\mathcal{B}$ first randomly chooses $\{s_1, \cdots, s_n\} \xleftarrow{\$} \Delta_i$, and $h, z, R \xleftarrow{\$} \Delta_i$. Then, $\mathcal{B}$ randomly chooses $b \xleftarrow{\$} \{0, 1\}$ and computes $\sigma_b \leftarrow \mathsf{Ambi.Sign}(m^*, \overline{\mathsf{sk}}_b, \gamma^*)$ as: $\sigma_b = (c_1, s_1, \cdots, s_n, z, R)$ where $k_j = c_j + F(\mathsf{pk}_j, s_j) + F(R, z)$.

Output. Finally, $\mathcal{A}$ outputs a bit b'. Observe that b and $\overline{\mathsf{sk}}_b$ is not used in the generation phrase of σ_b. Therefore, $\mathcal{A}$ can only win with a probability of $1/2$.

Probability of Successful Simulation. There is no abort in our simulation, the probability of successful simulation is 1.

Thus, our underlying 1-out-of-n signature scheme Ambi.DS holds signer ambiguity in the random oracle.

Theorem 3. *Our generic construction of the extended withdrawable signature from* Type-H *signature presented in Sect. 4.2 satisfies the extended withdrawability (Definition 3) in the random oracle model.*

Proof. As the underlying 1-out-of-n signature scheme Ambi.DS holds the signer ambiguity, in our proof of Theorem 3, $\mathcal{B}$ sets the challenge public key set for $\mathcal{A}$ as $\gamma = \{pk_j\}_{j=1}^n$ where signer's public key is denoted as $pk_i \in \gamma$. The associated auxiliary information is $aux = \gamma \setminus pk_i$.

Oracle Simulation. $\mathcal{B}$ answers the oracle queries as follows.

H-Query. The adversary $\mathcal{A}$ makes hash queries in this phase. $\mathcal{B}$ simulates H_i as a random oracle.

Signature Query. $\mathcal{A}$ outputs a message m_i and queries for extended withdrawable signature with pk_i and aux, $\mathcal{B}$ responses the signature query of $\mathcal{A}$ as follows:

- $\mathcal{O}^{\mathsf{WSign}}_{sk,aux}(\cdot)$: $\mathcal{B}$ chooses $\{s_{j,i}\}_{j=1}^n \xleftarrow{\$} \Delta_i$, $R_i \xleftarrow{\$} \Delta_i$ and computes the following:
  1. parse $\gamma = aux \cup pk_i$, $state_i = \{\{s_{j,i}\}_{j=1}^n, R_i\}$
  2. $\sigma_{1,i} \leftarrow \mathsf{Ambi.Sign}(m_i, sk_i, \gamma, state_i)$
  3. $\sigma_i = (\sigma_{1,i}, aux)$

Meanwhile, $\mathcal{B}$ sets $\mathcal{M} \leftarrow \mathcal{M} \cup m_i$.

Challenge. On the challenge phrase, $\mathcal{A}$ gives $\mathcal{B}$ a message $m^* \notin \mathcal{M}$. $\mathcal{B}$ now chooses $\{s_j^*\}_{j=1}^n, R^* \xleftarrow{\$} \Delta_i$. $\mathcal{B}$ then computes the challenge withdrawable signature σ^* as follows: $\mathcal{B}$ first obtains $\gamma = aux \cup pk_i$ and $state^* = \{\{s_j^*\}_{j=1}^n, R^*\}$, then computes $\sigma_1^* \leftarrow \mathsf{Ambi.Sign}(m^*, sk_i, \gamma)$.

$\mathcal{B}$ now can set the challenge withdrawable signature as: $\sigma^* = (\sigma_1^*, aux)$.

Simulate. The adversary $\mathcal{A}$ then can simulate the withdrawable signature σ^* of pk_i on a new public key $\overline{pk}_i \in aux$ as: $\overline{\sigma}^* = (\sigma_1^*, \overline{aux})$ with different $\overline{aux} = \gamma \setminus \overline{pk}_i$.

Probability of Breaking the Extended Withdrawability Property. As the underlying Ambi.DS achieves signer ambiguity (Theorem 2), which means that given the challenge withdrawable signature, $\widetilde{\sigma}^*$ the adversary $\mathcal{A}$ only has a probability $1/n$ of guessing the real signer's identity pk_i correctly, thereby breaking the extended withdrawability. Meanwhile, $1 \leftarrow \mathsf{WSVerify}(m^*, \overline{pk}_i, \sigma^*)$ as the verification phrase remains the same as follows: the verifier obtains same $\gamma = \overline{aux} \cup \overline{pk}_i = aux \cup pk_i$ and $1 \leftarrow \mathsf{Ambi.Verify}(m^*, \gamma, \sigma_1^*)$.

Probability of Successful Simulation. There is no abort in our simulation, the probability of successful simulation is 1.   □

6   An Instantiation from RSA Signature

In this section, we present an instantiation of our generic construction in Sect. 4, relying on the following two building blocks:

1. The RSA signature scheme, which is secure under the RSA assumption, is a Type-H signature scheme. We use RSA.DS to denote the RSA signature scheme which contains three algorithms: (KeyGen, RSA.Sign, RSA.Verify).
2. A 1-out-of-2 signature scheme generated from the RSA signature, which holds the signer ambiguity among $n = 2$ signers.

With the public key (e, N), where $N = pq$ (with p and q being two distinct large prime numbers), its corresponding secret key d generated from KeyGen, and hash function $H : \{0,1\}^* \to \mathbb{Z}_N$, the RSA signature $\omega \leftarrow$ RSA.Sign(m, sk) is computed as $\omega = H(m)^d \bmod N$. The verification algorithm $1/0 \leftarrow$ RSA.Verify(m, pk, σ) checks the signature by verifying that $H(m) \equiv \omega^e \bmod N$.

Let $\gamma = \{(e_j, N_j)\}_{j=1}^2$, and $\mathsf{pk} = \mathsf{pk}_i = (e_i, N_i)$ where $i \xleftarrow{\$} \{1, 2\}$ denote the signer's RSA public key. The signer's corresponding secret key is d_i.

With hash functions $H_j : \{0,1\}^* \to \mathbb{Z}_{N_j}$ where $j \in [1, 2]$, the 1-out-of-2 signature scheme from RSA signature is as follows.

Ambi.Sign$(m, \mathsf{sk}_i, \gamma)$	Ambi.Verify(m, γ, σ)
parse $\gamma = \{\mathsf{pk}_1, \mathsf{pk}_2\}, i \xleftarrow{\$} \{1, 2\}$	parse $\sigma = (c_1, s_1, s_2, z, R)$,
For $j \neq i$: parse state $= \{s_j, R\}$	parse $\gamma = \{\mathsf{pk}_1, \mathsf{pk}_2\}$
$h, z \xleftarrow{\$} \mathbb{Z}_{N_i}, k_i = h + z^R$	$k_1' = c_1 + s_1^{e_1} + z^R, c_2' = H_2(m, \gamma, k_1')$
$c_j = H_j(m, \gamma, k_i), k_j = c_j + s_j^{e_j} + z^R$	$k_2' = c_2' + s_2^{e_2} + z^R, c_1' = H_1(m, \gamma, k_2')$
$c_i = H_i(m, \gamma, k_j), s_i = (h - c_i)^{d_i}$	if $c_1 \neq c_1'$
$\sigma = (c_1, s_1, s_2, z, R)$	return 0
return σ	else return 1

Following this, we have an instantiation of an extended withdrawable signature scheme based on RSA signatures as follows.

KeyGen(1^k)	Shuffle(pk, γ)
$N = pq, \phi(N) = (p-1)(q-1),$	define $\gamma = \{(e_1, N_1), (e_2, N_2)\}$
$e \xleftarrow{\$} \mathbb{Z}_N^*, d \equiv e^{-1} \bmod \phi(N)$	$\mathsf{pk}_i \leftarrow \mathsf{pk}, i \xleftarrow{\$} \{1, 2\}$
$\mathsf{pk} \leftarrow (e, N), \mathsf{sk} \leftarrow d$	aux $= \gamma \setminus \mathsf{pk}_i$
return $(\mathsf{pk}, \mathsf{sk})$	return aux

WSign$(m, \mathsf{sk}, \mathsf{aux})$	WSVerify(m, pk, σ)
$\gamma = \mathsf{aux} \cup \mathsf{pk}$	
For $j \neq i$:	
$s_j \xleftarrow{\$} \mathbb{Z}_{N_i}, R = H_i(m, s_j^{d_i})$	parse $\sigma = (\sigma_1, \mathsf{aux})$
state $= \{s_j, R\}, \mathsf{sk}_i = \mathsf{sk}$	parse $\gamma = \mathsf{aux} \cup \mathsf{pk}$
$\sigma_1 \leftarrow \boxed{\text{Ambi.Sign}(m, d_i, \gamma, \text{state})}$	if $1 \leftarrow \boxed{\text{Ambi.Verify}(m, \gamma, \sigma_1)}$
$\sigma = (\sigma_1, \mathsf{aux})$	return 1
return σ	else return 0

Confirm(m, sk, σ)	CVerify$(m, \mathsf{pk}, \widetilde{\sigma})$
parse $\sigma = (\sigma_1, \mathsf{aux})$	parse $\widetilde{\sigma} = (\delta_1, \delta_2, \delta_3)$
For $j \neq i : S_j = s_j^{\mathsf{sk}}$	parse $\delta_2 = S_j, \delta_3 = s_j$
$\delta_1 \leftarrow$ H.Sign$(\{m, \sigma\}, \mathsf{sk})$	if $1 \leftarrow$ H.Verify$(\{m, \sigma\}, \mathsf{pk}, \delta_1)$,
$\delta_2 \leftarrow S_j, \delta_3 \leftarrow s_j$	$s_j = S_j^{e_i}$
$\widetilde{\sigma} = (\delta_1, \delta_2, \delta_3)$	return 1
return $\widetilde{\sigma}$	else return 0

Check$(m, \mathsf{pk}, \sigma, \widetilde{\sigma})$
parse $\sigma = (\sigma_1, \mathsf{aux}), \sigma_1 = (c_1, s_1, s_2, z, R)$
parse $\widetilde{\sigma} = (\delta_1, \delta_2, \delta_3), \delta_2 = S_j, \ \delta_3 = s_j$
if $1 \leftarrow$ WSVerify$(m, \mathsf{pk}, \sigma), 1 \leftarrow$ CVerify$(m, \mathsf{pk}, \widetilde{\sigma})$,
$\quad s_j = \{s_1, s_2\} \setminus \{s_i\}$
$\quad R = H_i(m, S_j)$
return 1
else return 0

7 Performance Evaluation of Our Instantiation from the RSA Signature

In this section, we present the performance evaluation of our concrete instantiation based on the RSA signature, as illustrated in Sect. 6. We compare the computation cost of our RSA-based withdrawable signature with the withdrawable signature from the DVS using the Schnorr signature proposed in [22].

Communication Cost Analysis. We use $|\mathbb{Z}_N|$ to denote the size of the elements in $\mathbb{Z}_N$. In the key generation (KeyGen) phase, the communication cost is $2|\mathbb{Z}_N|$, reflecting the signer's public key length. During the withdrawable signature generation (WSign) stage, the communication cost is $2|\mathbb{Z}_N| + 3|\mathbb{Z}_N| + 2(2-1)|\mathbb{Z}_N| = 7|\mathbb{Z}_N|$, accounting for the message/withdrawable signature pair and the aux length. At the confirmation (Confirm) stage, since the confirmed signature generation algorithm requires the message/withdrawable signature pair as input, the communication cost increases to $7|\mathbb{Z}_N| + 3|\mathbb{Z}_N| = 10|\mathbb{Z}_N|$.

Computation Cost Analysis. In our RSA-based withdrawable signature scheme, we denote the RSA function and the inverse RSA function on $\mathbb{Z}_N$ by $|E(R)|$ and $|E(R^{-1})|$. In the withdrawable signature from the DVS using the Schnorr signature proposed in [22], we denote the exponentiation operations on the cyclic groups $\mathbb{G}$ by $|E_{\mathbb{G}}|$. The detailed computational cost analysis is in Table 1.

To achieve a 128-bit security level, we recommend the key size of our RSA-based withdrawable signature scheme, as well as the Schnorr-based withdrawable signature scheme, should be at least 3082 bits [8].

Table 1. Comparison of Computational Costs

Algorithm	WSign	WSVerify	Confirm	CVerify	Check
Ours with RSA	$2|E(R)| + 2|E(R^{-1})|$	$4|E(R)|$	$2|E(R^{-1})|$	$2|E(R)|$	$6|E(R)|$
In [22]	$4|E(\mathbb{G})|$	$2|E(\mathbb{G})|$	$3|E(\mathbb{G})|$	$5|E(\mathbb{G})|$	–

8 Conclusion

In this work, we extended the definition of the withdrawable signature to encompass a wider class of the withdrawable signature, including the construction from RSA. To achieve this, we utilized the Type-H signature and provided a generic construction of the extended withdrawable based on it. Our construction leverages a novel property called "extended withdrawability", which ensures that a withdrawable signature remains verifiable but cannot be directly linked to the original signer without the confirmed signature generation algorithm, thereby upholding the essence of extended withdrawability.

Note that our generic construction of extended withdrawable signatures from Type-H signature can be adapted with various cryptographic primitives, enhancing its practical relevance. Once we instantiate our generic construction with a post-quantum secure Type-H signature scheme, we can obtain a post-quantum withdrawable signature scheme, which is of independent interest, leading to the first construction of a post-quantum secure withdrawable signature scheme.

References

1. Abe, M., Ohkubo, M., Suzuki, K.: 1-out-of-n signatures from a variety of keys. In: Zheng, Y. (ed.) ASIACRYPT 2002, pp. 415–432. Springer, Heidelberg (2002)
2. Al-Maaitah, S., Qatawneh, M., Quzmar, A.: E-voting system based on blockchain technology: a survey. In: ICIT 2021, pp. 200–205. IEEE (2021)
3. Backes, M., Döttling, N., Hanzlik, L., Kluczniak, K., Schneider, J.: Ring signatures: logarithmic-size, no setup-from standard assumptions. In: EUROCRYPT 2019, pp. 281–311. Springer (2019)
4. Boneh, D., Gentry, C., Lynn, B., Shacham, H.: Aggregate and verifiably encrypted signatures from bilinear maps. In: EUROCRYPT 2003, pp. 416–432. Springer (2003)
5. Chaum, D., Van Heyst, E.: Group signatures. In: EUROCRYPT 1991, pp. 257–265. Springer (1991)
6. Chevignard, C., Fouque, P.A., Schrottenloher, A.: Reducing the number of qubits in quantum factoring. Cryptology ePrint Archive (2024)
7. Diemert, D., Jager, T.: On the tight security of TLS 1.3: theoretically sound cryptographic parameters for real-world deployments. J. Cryptol. 34(3), 30 (2021)
8. Elaine, B., Barker, W., Burr, W., Polk, W., Smid, M.: Recommendation for key management, part 1: General. NIST Spec. Publ. 800, 57 (2016)
9. Esgin, M.F., Steinfeld, R., Liu, J.K., Liu, D.: Lattice-based zero-knowledge proofs: new techniques for shorter and faster constructions and applications. In: CRYPTO 2019, pp. 115–146. Springer (2019)
10. Esgin, M.F., Steinfeld, R., Sakzad, A., Liu, J.K., Liu, D.: Short lattice-based one-out-of-many proofs and applications to ring signatures. In: ACNS 2019, pp. 67–88. Springer (2019)
11. Esgin, M.F., Steinfeld, R., Zhao, R.K.: MatRiCT+: more efficient post-quantum private blockchain payments. In: IEEE S&P 2022, pp. 1281–1298. IEEE (2022)
12. Goldwasser, S., Micali, S., Rivest, R.L.: A digital signature scheme secure against adaptive chosen-message attacks. SIAM J. Comput. 17(2), 281–308 (1988)
13. Gritti, C., Susilo, W., Plantard, T.: Logarithmic size ring signatures without random oracles. IET Inf. Secur. 10(1), 1–7 (2016)
14. Groth, J., Kohlweiss, M.: One-out-of-many proofs: or how to leak a secret and spend a coin. In: EUROCRYPT 2015, pp. 253–280. Springer (2015)
15. Herranz, J., Sáez, G.: Forking lemmas for ring signature schemes. In: INDOCRYPT 2003, pp. 266–279. Springer (2003)
16. Huang, X., Susilo, W., Mu, Y., Wu, W.: Secure universal designated verifier signature without random oracles. Int. J. Inf. Secur. 7, 171–183 (2008)
17. Jager, T., Kakvi, S.A., May, A.: On the security of the PKCS# 1 v1. 5 signature scheme. In: CCS 2018, pp. 1195–1208 (2018)
18. Jakobsson, M., Sako, K., Impagliazzo, R.: Designated verifier proofs and their applications. In: EUROCRYPT 1996, pp. 143–154. Springer (1996)

19. Kaliski, B.: PKCS# 1: RSA encryption version 1.5. RFC 2313 (1998). https://www.rfc-editor.org/rfc/rfc2313.txt

20. Li, B., Liu, Y., Yang, S.: Lattice-based universal designated verifier signatures. In: ICEBE 2018, pp. 329–334. IEEE (2018)

21. Li, Y., Susilo, W., Mu, Y., Pei, D.: Designated verifier signature: definition, framework and new constructions. In: UIC 2007, pp. 1191–1200. Springer (2007)

22. Liu, X., Baek, J., Susilo, W.: Withdrawable signature: how to call off a signature. In: ISC 2023, pp. 557–577. Springer (2023)

23. Lyubashevsky, V., Nguyen, N.K.: BLOOM: bimodal lattice one-out-of-many proofs and applications. In: ASIACRYPT 2022, pp. 95–125. Springer (2023)

24. Moriarty, K., Kaliski, B., Jonsson, J., Rusch, A.: PKCS# 1: RSA cryptography specifications version 2.2. RFC 8017 (Informational) (2016). https://www.rfc-editor.org/rfc/rfc8017.txt

25. Park, S., Sealfon, A.: It wasn't me! Repudiability and claimability of ring signatures. In: CRYPTO 2019, pp. 159–190. Springer (2019)

26. Rescorla, E.: The transport layer security (TLS) protocol version 1.3 (2018). https://datatracker.ietf.org/doc/html/rfc8446

27. Rivest, R.L., Shamir, A., Tauman, Y.: How to leak a secret. In: ASIACRYPT 2001, pp. 552–565. Springer (2001)

28. Shor, P.W.: Algorithms for quantum computation: discrete logarithms and factoring. In: FOCS 1994, pp. 124–134. IEEE (1994)

29. Steinfeld, R., Bull, L., Wang, H., Pieprzyk, J.: Universal designated-verifier signatures. In: ASIACRYPT 2003, pp. 523–542. Springer (2003)

30. Steinfeld, R., Wang, H., Pieprzyk, J.: Efficient extension of standard Schnorr/RSA signatures into universal designated-verifier signatures. In: PKC 2004, pp. 86–100. Springer (2004)

31. Thanalakshmi, P., Anbazhagan, N., Joshi, G.P., Yang, E.: A quantum resistant universal designated verifier signature proof. AIMS Math. 8(8), 18234–18250 (2023)

32. Thorncharoensri, P., Susilo, W., Baek, J.: Aggregatable certificateless designated verifier signature. IEEE Access 8, 95019–95031 (2020)

33. Tian, H., Chen, X., Li, J.: A short non-delegatable strong designated verifier signature. In: ACISP 2012, pp. 261–279. Springer (2012)

34. Xin, X., Ding, L., Li, C., Sang, Y., Yang, Q., Li, F.: Quantum public-key designated verifier signature. Quantum Inf. Process. 21(1), 33 (2022)

35. Yamashita, K., Hara, K., Watanabe, Y., Yanai, N., Shikata, J.: Designated verifier signature with claimability. In: APKC 2023, pp. 21–32 (2023)

36. Zhang, R., Furukawa, J., Imai, H.: Short signature and universal designated verifier signature without random oracles. In: ACNS 2005, pp. 483–498. Springer (2005)

Efficient Fork-Free BLS Multi-signature Scheme with Incremental Signing

Syh-Yuan Tan[1]([✉])[ID], Tiong-Sik Ng[2][ID], and Swee-Huay Heng[1][ID]

[1] Multimedia University, Melaka, Malaysia
{sytan,shheng}@mmu.edu.my
[2] Yonsei University, Seoul, South Korea
ngtiongsik@yonsei.ac.kr

Abstract. In this paper, we propose a new BLS multi-signature (MS) scheme that offers advantages compared to the state-of-the-art Boneh-Drijvers-Neven MS (BDN-MS) scheme. Firstly, the proposed scheme is provably secure without a forking lemma. Specifically, we show that it is unforgeable under chosen message attack (uf-cma) in the plain public key model if BLS signature is uf-cma. Moreover, the security against the rogue public key attacks of our MS scheme can be reduced to the binding security of a multi-set commitment scheme, stemming from the *commit-and-verify* technique underlying the proposed BLS-MS which is of independent interest. Secondly, the proposed scheme supports incremental signing, that is, a new BLS signature can be added to an existing multi-signature of the same message. Thirdly, the proposed MS scheme has a more efficient public key aggregation algorithm, resulting in approximately 42 times faster verification process than BDN-MS when considering 10,000 signers. Finally, we also show that the proposed MS scheme can be extended into an aggregate MS (AMS) scheme as in that of BDN-MS.

Keywords: BLS · multi-signature · rogue public key · splitting zero · attack

1 Introduction

The BLS signature scheme [8] is a classic short signature scheme based on the bilinear pairing function. In the Type-3 pairing setting with generators $g_1 \in \mathbb{G}_1$ and $g_2 \in \mathbb{G}_2$, its public-secret key pair is constructed as $(pk = g_2^x \in \mathbb{G}_2, sk = x \in \mathbb{Z}_q^*)$ while the short signature on a message m is generated as $s = H(m)^{sk} \in \mathbb{G}_1$. A verifier can verify the signature by computing $H(m)$ and checking whether the equation $e(s, g_2) = e(H(m), pk)$ holds. Due to its short signature size and efficient verification, BLS has been studied in the use cases which require simultaneous verification for multiple signatures from multiple signers on either the same or different messages.

The aggregated signatures (AS) version, namely, the BLS-AS scheme [7] was proposed soon after for signing on *distinct messages*. Specifically, given

© The Author(s), under exclusive license to Springer Nature Singapore Pte Ltd. 2025
J. K. Liu et al. (Eds.): ProvSec 2024, LNCS 14903, pp. 250–268, 2025.
https://doi.org/10.1007/978-981-96-0954-3_13

a sequence of individual signatures signed by n different individuals, BLS-AS aggregates these signatures into a single compact signature $\sigma = \prod_{i=1}^{n} s_i$ for verification, enabling simultaneous validation by checking if $e(\sigma, g_2) = \prod_{i=1}^{n} e(H(m_i), pk_i)$ holds.

On the contrary, the multi-signatures (MS) version, namely, the BLS-MS scheme [5] was proposed independently for signing on the *same message*. Compared to BLS-AS, public keys can be aggregated in BLS-MS as $apk = \prod_{i=1}^{n} pk_i$ and the verification is as efficient as that of the original BLS signature scheme such that $e(\sigma, g_2) = e(H(m), apk)$. This initial BLS-MS version, however, requires proof of possessions for user secret keys sk_i, or it is vulnerable to malicious key generation such as the rogue public key attack [3,5–7,9,12] and splitting zero attack [3,9,13,14]. In the context of BLS signature, a rogue public-key attacker crafts a malicious $pk' = g_2^{x'} \cdot pk^{-1}$ for a randomly selected $x' \in \mathbb{Z}_q^*$. Subsequently, the attacker can forge a valid MS $\sigma = H(m)^{x'}$ on behalf of the victim because the verification

$$\overbrace{e(\sigma, g_2) = e(H(m)^{x'-x+x}, g_2) = e(H(m), \underbrace{pk' \cdot pk}_{\text{Splitting zero attack}})}^{\text{Rogue PK attack}}$$

always returns true. A splitting zero attack works in a similar vein in which the attacker crafts at least two malicious $(pk = g_2^x, pk' = g_2^{x'})$ such that $x + x' = 0$. It is clear that the two attacks work when signing the same message only.

Years later, Boneh et al. [6] came up with an improved BLS-MS, which we term as BDN-MS, that does not require proof of possessions yet is proven to resist the rogue public key attacks. Basically, BDN-MS utilises a hash function to bind every signature s_i to its public key in the list of signers $pk_i \in L$, achieving the same effect of signing distinct messages, yet it is still able to preserve the aggregation features for signatures and public keys. BDN-MS is proposed as a replacement for the Schnorr-based MS [4,11] currently deployed in Bitcoin blockchains [6]. In addition to its smaller signature size, BDN-MS does not require interactions among signers to generate a multi-signature, that is, the signers do not have to be online simultaneously. Boneh et al. further showed that BDN-MS can be extended into an *aggregate multi-signature scheme* (AMS) that can aggregate multi-signatures for different messages into a single signature [6].

Instead of viewing an aggregated BLS as an AS or MS scheme, Camenisch et al. [9] analysed the use case as BLS signatures with a batch verifier (BLS-Batch) and it comes with a different approach in the security analysis. Essentially, BLS-Batch does not need an additional security analysis to prove resistance against rogue public key attacks as in BLS-AS [7] and BLS-MS [5,6]. However, if BLS-Batch is to be used as a BLS-AS or BLS-MS, it does not offer signature aggregations.

Recently, Baldimtsi et al. [2] showed that if the signers are static, the public key aggregation in BDN-MS can be pre-computed during setup to significantly reduce the multi-signature verification time. However, none of the previous works realise *incremental signing* for a BLS-based multi-signature scheme, that is, adding a new BLS signature to a BLS multi-signature in the aforementioned approaches.

1.1 Our Contribution

In this work, we construct a secure multi-signature (MS) scheme based on a uf-cma-secure signature scheme and a binding-secure multi-set commitment scheme using an approach that we term *commit-and-verify*. Specifically, we employ BLS signature [8] and MoniPoly multi-set commitment [16] as the building blocks. While BDN-MS binds $pk_i \in L$ to its signature s_i through hashing, we achieve the same purpose using the commitment mechanism. Besides avoiding hashing long bit strings L, this enables our MS scheme to achieve better efficiency by using the (committed messages as) exponents that can be significantly smaller than the hash output of fixed size $|\mathbb{Z}_q|$ as in BDN-MS. To the best of our knowledge, the proposed scheme is also the first BLS-based MS scheme that enables incremental signing, that is, adding a new BLS signature to an existing multi-signature. Finally, we extend our MS scheme into an aggregate MS (AMS) scheme, similar to the BDN-MS and BDN-AMS [6].

2 Preliminaries

2.1 Bilinear Pairing

Throughout this paper, let $\mathbb{G}_1$ and $\mathbb{G}_2$ be groups of prime order q based on an elliptic curve E. Then, let g_1 and g_2 be generators of $\mathbb{G}_1$ and $\mathbb{G}_2$ respectively. The bilinear pairing function e maps elements from the groups $\mathbb{G}_1$ and $\mathbb{G}_2$ to the group $\mathbb{G}_T$, i.e., $e : \mathbb{G}_1 \times \mathbb{G}_2 \to \mathbb{G}_T$, which requires the following properties:

1. Bilinearity: $e(g_1{}^a, g_2{}^b) = e(g_1, g_2)^{ab}$.
2. Non-degeneracy: $e(g_1, g_2) \neq 1$.
3. e is efficiently computable, i.e., there is an algorithm to compute $e(g_1, g_2)$ for any $g_1 \in \mathbb{G}_1$ and $g_2 \in \mathbb{G}_2$.

2.2 Signature Scheme

We first define a signature scheme by four algorithms SIG={Pg, Kg, Sign, Vf} below:

$\mathsf{Pg}(1^k) \to par$: This is run by a trusted party to generate the system parameter par.

$\mathsf{Kg}(par) \to (pk, sk)$: This is run by the signer to generate the public and secret key pair (pk, sk).

$\mathsf{Sign}(pk, sk, m) \to s$: This is run by the signer who holds the (pk, sk) key pair to sign a message m as s.

$\mathsf{Vf}(pk, m, s) \to (0 \text{ or } 1)$: If the message and signature pair (m, s) is valid under pk, output 1, and output 0 otherwise.

We consider the notion of unforgeability under chosen message attack (uf-cma) for SIG as in Table 1.

Table 1. The uf-cma game for signature schemes.

$\mathcal{O}^{\mathsf{Sign}(pk,sk,\cdot)}$:	$\mathbf{Game}_{\mathsf{SIG},\mathcal{F}}^{\mathsf{uf\text{-}cma}}$:
$s \leftarrow \mathsf{Sign}(pk, sk, m)$	$SIG \leftarrow \emptyset;\ (par) \leftarrow \mathsf{Pg}(1^k)$
$SIG \leftarrow SIG \cup \{m, s\}$	$(pk, sk) \leftarrow \mathsf{Kg}(par)$
Return (s)	$(m^*, s^*) \leftarrow \mathcal{F}^{\mathcal{O}^{\mathsf{Sign}}}(pk)$
	$b \leftarrow \mathsf{Vf}(pk, m^*, s^*)$
	If $(m^*, \cdot) \in SIG \lor b = 0$, then return LOSE
	Return WIN

Note: SIG: corrupted signature list, m^* : challenge message

Definition 1 (Signature Unforgeability). *An* SIG *is* $(\varepsilon_{sig}, t_{sig})$-*secure if there is no polynomial time forger* $\mathcal{F}$ *that can win in* $\mathbf{Game}_{\mathsf{SIG},\mathcal{F}}^{\mathsf{uf\text{-}cma}}$ *with non-negligible probability* ε_{sig}:

$$\Pr[\mathbf{Game}_{\mathsf{SIG},\mathcal{F}}^{\mathsf{uf\text{-}cma}} = \mathsf{WIN}] = \varepsilon_{sig}$$

in time t_{sig}.

BLS Signature Scheme. We recall the BLS signature in the Type-3 pairing setting [10], as defined by the following algorithms BLS={Pg, Kg, Sign, Verify}.

$\mathsf{Pg}(1^k)$: Choose a secure hash function $H : \{0, 1\}^* \to \mathbb{G}_1$. Generate a bilinear group parameter $(q, g_1 \in \mathbb{G}_1, g_2 \in \mathbb{G}_2, e : \mathbb{G}_1 \times \mathbb{G}_2 \to \mathbb{G}_T)$ and set the system parameter as $par = (q, g_1, g_2, e, H)$.

$\mathsf{Kg}(par)$: Generate $pk = g_2^{sk}$ where $sk \in \mathbb{Z}_q^*$ is randomly selected and output the public and secret key pair as (pk, sk).

$\mathsf{Sign}(pk, sk, m)$: Compute the signature as $\sigma = H(m)^{sk}$.

$\mathsf{Vf}(pk, m, \sigma)$: Output 1 if the following holds:

$$e(\sigma, g_2) = e(H(m), pk)$$

and output 0 otherwise.

2.3   Multi-set Commitment

Unlike a commitment scheme $C = (\mathsf{Setup}, \mathsf{Commit}, \mathsf{Open})$, a set commitment (SC) scheme also consists of $\mathsf{OpenIntersection}$, $\mathsf{VerifyIntersection}$, $\mathsf{OpenDifference}$ and $\mathsf{VerifyDifference}$ algorithms that allow openings based on set operations. When multiple SC are aggregated, it yields a multi-set commitment MSC (c.f. Appendix A) which consists the same algorithms as the former.

MoniPoly Multi-set Commitment Scheme. MoniPoly SC scheme [15,16] is perfectly hiding and proven to offer binding based on the co-SDH assumption. Let $h_1 \in \mathbb{G}_1$ and $h_2 \in \mathbb{G}_2$ be the generators, the public parameters is $pk = ((e, \mathbb{G}_1, \mathbb{G}_2, \mathbb{G}_T, q), \{g_j = h_1^{x^j}, X_j = h_2^{x^j}\}_{0 \leq j \leq n})$. To commit to a set $A = \{a_1, \ldots, a_n\} \in \mathbb{Z}_q^n$, compute the commitment as:

$$C = g_0^{o \prod_{a \in A}(x+a)} = \left(\prod_{j=0}^{n} g_j^{\mathsf{a}_j} \right)^o$$

where the randomly chosen $o \in \mathbb{Z}_q^*$ is the opening value and $\prod_{a \in A}(x + a) = \sum_{j=1}^{n} \mathsf{a}_j x^j$.

The aggregated version, namely, MoniPoly MSC scheme [16] is also perfectly hiding and proven to have multi-set binding based on the co-DLOG assumption. The public parameters are basically N-set of set commitment parameters $\{pk_1, \ldots, pk_N\}$ such that $PK = (e, \mathbb{G}_1, \mathbb{G}_2, \mathbb{G}_T, q, \{\{g_{i,j} = h_{i,1}^{x^j}, X_{i,j} = h_{i,2}^{x^j}\}_{0 \leq j \leq n}\}_{i=1}^N)$. The commitment on a multi-set $A = \{A_1, \ldots, A_N\} \in \mathbb{Z}_q^N$ is then computed as:

$$C = \prod_{i=1}^{N} C_j = \prod_{i=1}^{N} g_{i,0}^{o_i \prod_{a \in A_i}(x+a)} = \prod_{i=1}^{N} \left(\prod_{j=0}^{n} g_{i,j}^{\mathsf{a}_{i,j}} \right)^{o_i}$$

where the randomly chosen $O = \{o_1, \ldots, o_N\} \in \mathbb{Z}_q^N$ is the opening value and $\prod_{a \in A_i}(x + a) = \sum_{j=1}^{n} \mathsf{a}_{i,j} x^j$. The reader is directed to [15,16] for the detailed construction.

In this work, we consider only the binding property of MoniPoly MSC.

Definition 2 (Binding [16]). *MoniPoly MSC is $(\varepsilon_{bind}, t_{bind})$-secure if there is no polynomial time adversary $\mathcal{A}$ that can output two pairs $(A_1, O_1), (A_2, O_2)$ with non-negligible probability ε_{bind} such that:*

$$\Pr[\mathsf{Open}(pk, C, A_1, O_1) = \mathsf{Open}(pk, C, A_2, O_2) = 1] = \varepsilon_{bind}$$

in time t_{bind}.

2.4   Multi-signature Scheme

A multi-signature scheme [6] is defined by five algorithms $MS=\{Pg, Kg, Sign, KAg, Vf\}$ as the following:

$Pg(1^k) \rightarrow par$: This is run by a trusted party to generate the system parameter par.

$Kg(par) \rightarrow (pk, sk)$: This is run by a signer to generate the public and secret key pair (pk, sk).

$Sign(par, L, sk, m) \rightarrow \sigma$: This is an interactive algorithm run by signers, each with a public key $pk \in L$ and a secret key sk to collectively sign a message m as σ.

$KAg(par, L) \rightarrow (apk)$: Given a list of public key L, output an aggregate public key apk.

$Vf(par, apk, m, \sigma) \rightarrow (0$ or $1)$: If the message and multi-signature pair (m, σ) is valid under apk, output 1 and output 0 otherwise.

Different from a multi-signature scheme, an aggregate multi-signature scheme [6] $AMS=\{Pg, Kg, Sign, KAg, Vf, SAg, AVf\}$ contains two additional algorithms as the following:

$SAg(par, \{apk_j, m_j, \sigma_j\}_{j=1}^k) \rightarrow (apk)$: Given a list of triples $\{apk_j, m_j, \sigma_j\}$, output an aggregate multi-signature Σ.

$AVf(par, \{apk_j, m_j, \}_{j=1}^k, \Sigma) \rightarrow (0$ or $1)$: If the aggregate multi-signature Σ is valid under the tuple $\{apk_j, m_j\}_{j=1}^n$, output 1 and output 0 otherwise.

We adopt the uf-cma game used in BDN-MS and BDN-AMS [6] as depicted in Table 2. For the latter, it is an extension to the uf-cma game in multi-signature schemes [4,6,7]. The signing oracle $\mathcal{O}_X^{Sign}$ will simulate the honest signer to complete a signing protocol for a message m in either the scheme $X = MS$ or $X = AMS$ with the signers listed in L. The honest signer will be the combiner if it is listed as the first in the list L such that $pk^* = L[0]$.

Definition 3 (Multi-Signature Unforgeability). *An* MS *is* $(\varepsilon_{ms}, t_{ms})$-*secure if there is no polynomial time forger* $\mathcal{F}$ *that can win in* $\mathbf{Game}_{MS,\mathcal{F}}^{uf\text{-}cma}$ *with non-negligible probability* ε_{ms} *in time* t_{ms} *such that:*

$$\Pr[\mathbf{Game}_{MS,\mathcal{F}}^{uf\text{-}cma} = WIN] = \varepsilon_{ms}.$$

Definition 4 (Aggregate Multi-Signature Unforgeability). *An* AMS *is* $(\varepsilon_{ams}, t_{ams})$-*secure if there is no polynomial time forger* $\mathcal{F}$ *that can win in* $\mathbf{Game}_{AMS,\mathcal{F}}^{uf\text{-}cma}$ *with non-negligible probability* ε_{ams} *in time* t_{ams} *such that:*

$$\Pr[\mathbf{Game}_{AMS,\mathcal{F}}^{uf\text{-}cma} = WIN] = \varepsilon_{ams}.$$

Table 2. The uf-cma game for (A)MS schemes.

$\mathcal{O}_{\mathsf{X}}^{\mathsf{Sign}(par,\cdot,sk^*,\cdot)}$:	$\mathbf{Game}_{\mathsf{X},\mathcal{F}}^{\mathsf{uf\text{-}cma}}$:
If $pk^* \notin L$, then return $\perp$	$SIG \leftarrow \emptyset$; $(par) \leftarrow \mathsf{ParGen}(1^k)$
$s \leftarrow \mathsf{Sign}(par, L, sk^*, m)$	$(pk^*, sk^*) \leftarrow \mathsf{KeyGen}(par)$
$SIG \leftarrow SIG \cup \{L, m, s\}$	$(L^*, m^*, \sigma^*) \leftarrow \mathcal{F}^{\mathcal{O}_{\mathsf{X}}^{\mathsf{Sign}}}(par, pk^*)$
If $pk^* = L[0]$, then //is combiner	If $\mathsf{X} = \mathsf{MS}$, then
If $\mathsf{X} = \mathsf{MS}$, then	$\quad b \leftarrow \mathsf{Vf}(par, \mathsf{KAg}(par, L^*), m^*, \sigma^*)$
Return σ	If $\mathsf{X} = \mathsf{AMS}$, then
If $\mathsf{X} = \mathsf{AMS}$, then	$\quad b \leftarrow \mathsf{AVf}(par, \{apk_j, m_j\} \cup \{\mathsf{KAg}(par, L^*), m^*\}, \Sigma^*)$
Return Σ	If $(\cdot, m^*, \cdot) \in SIG \; \vee \; b = 0$, then return LOSE
Return s	Return WIN

Note: SIG: corrupted signature list, (L^*, m^*) : challenge

2.5 Batch Verification

As noted in the previous works [3,5,9,12], fulfilling Definition 3 (resp. Definition 4) indicates a multi-signature is valid but does not guarantee every signature that forms the multi-signature is also valid. On the other hand, although the batch verification notion does not allow an adversary to generate signature key pair, it covers this requirement on every single signature:

Definition 5 (Signature Batch Verification [9]). *Let SIG be a signature scheme, $\{(pk_1, sk_1), \ldots, (pk_N, sk_N)\}$ be the independent output of $\mathsf{Kg}(par)$, $L = \{pk_1, \ldots, pk_N\}$, $M = \{m_1, \ldots, m_N\}$ and $\sigma = \{s_1, \ldots, s_N\}$. Batch is a batch verification algorithm if:*

1. *$\forall pk_i \in L : \mathsf{SIG.Vf}(pk_i, m_i, \sigma_i) = 1$, then $\mathsf{Batch}(L, M, \sigma) = 1$.*
2. *$\exists pk_i \in L : \mathsf{SIG.Vf}(pk_i, m_i, \sigma_i) = 0$, then $\mathsf{Batch}(L, M, \sigma) = 0$ except with a negligible probability.*

We also briefly describe the BLS batch verification (BLS-Batch) proposed by Camenisch et al. [9] using the small exponent test [3]:

$\mathsf{Batch}(L, M, \sigma)$: Parse $L = \{pk_1, \ldots, pk_N\}, M = \{m_1, \ldots, m_N\}, \sigma = \{s_1, \ldots, s_N\}$ and generate a vector $\delta = \{\delta_1, \ldots, \delta_N\} \in \mathbb{Z}_q^*$ such that each $|\delta_i| \approx 60$ bits. Output 1 if the equation:

$$e\left(\prod_{i=1}^{N} s_i^{\delta_i}, g_2\right) = \prod_{i=1}^{N} e\left(H(m_i)^{\delta_i}, pk_i\right) \tag{1}$$

holds, output 0 otherwise.

Theorem 1 ([9]). *The algorithm above is a batch verification algorithm for BLS signatures.*

Commit-and-Verify. Our *commit-and-verify* approach, which is of independent interest, can be viewed as a variant of the small exponent test that does not need to draw random δ_i each time a batch verification is performed. We assume a batch verifier has a BLS key pair $(pk = g_2^x \in \mathbb{G}_2, sk = x \in \mathbb{Z}_q^*)$. Subsequently, while the small exponent test uses a random vector $\delta = \{\delta_1, \ldots, \delta_N\} \in \mathbb{Z}_q^*$, we use the vector $\delta = \{sk + 1, \ldots, sk + N\}$ and obtain the variant:

$\mathsf{Batch}(L, M, \sigma)$: Parse $L = \{pk_1, \ldots, pk_N\}, M = \{m_1, \ldots, m_N\}, \sigma = \{s_1, \ldots, s_N\}$ and generate a vector $\delta = \{sk + 1, \ldots, sk + N\}$ where sk is the verifier's secret key. Output 1 if the equation:

$$e\left(\prod_{i=1}^{N} s_i^{sk+i}, g_2\right) = \prod_{i=1}^{N} e\left(H(m_i)^{sk+i}, pk_i\right) \tag{2}$$

holds, output 0 otherwise.

Similar to the observation in the previous works [8,9], if there is only one signer, our Batch can be simplified into $e(\prod_{i=1}^{N} s_i^{sk+i}, g_2) = e(\prod_{i=1}^{N} H(m_i)^{sk+i}, pk)$ that uses two pairings only. On the contrary, if there are multiple signers but each signs on the same message, it can resemble a multi-signature scheme. Interestingly, the arithmetic sequence in δ makes possible the construction of a BLS-based multi-signature scheme that supports incremental signing as shown in the next section. Before that, we prove that the proposed Batch is secure.

Theorem 2. *The proposed Batch algorithm is a batch verification algorithm for BLS signatures.*

Proof. Recall that the MoniPoly multi-set commitment scheme [15] has a parameter $PK = (e, \mathbb{G}_1, \mathbb{G}_2, \mathbb{G}_T, q, \{\{g_{i,j} = h_{i,1}^{x^j}, X_{i,j} = h_{i,2}^{x^j}\}_{0 \leq j \leq n}\}_{i=1}^{N})$ and a commitment in the form $C = \prod_{i=1}^{N} g_{i,0}^{o_i \prod_{a \in A_i}(x+a)}$. If we view $h_{i,1} = H(m_i)^{sk_i}$ and therefore $g_{i,1} = h_{i,1}^x = (H(m_i)^{sk_i})^{sk}$, the product of signatures at the left hand side of the Eq. (2) subsumes a MoniPoly multi-set commitment:

$$\prod_{i=1}^{N} s_i^{sk+i} = \prod_{i=1}^{N} H(m_i)^{sk_i(sk+i)} \iff \prod_{i=1}^{N} g_{i,0}^{o_i \prod_{a \in A_i}(x+a)} = C$$

such that every committed set $A_i \in A$ contains only one message $A_i = \{i\}$ and the commitment secret is $x = sk$ with the opening value $o_i = 1$. Follows from the correctness of the commitment and BLS signatures, when $\mathsf{BLS.Vf}(pk_i, m_i, s_i) = 1$ for all $(pk_i \in L, m_i \in M, s_i \in \sigma)$, it is always the case $\mathsf{Batch}(L, M, \sigma) = 1$ in the proposed batch verifier.

Now we analyse the second condition in Definition 5. Without loss of generality, we consider the case when $\mathsf{BLS.Vf}(pk_N, m_N, s_N = H(m_N)^x) = 0$ but $\mathsf{Batch}(L, M, \sigma) = 1$ happens, that is, $x \neq sk_N \in \mathbb{Z}_q^*$. Let $\log_{H(m_N)}(\sigma) = \alpha$ and $\log_{H(m_N)}(H(m_i)) = \beta_i$ for $i \neq N$. From Eq. (2), we have:

$$\alpha \equiv \sum_{i=1}^{N-1} \beta_i(sk+i)sk_i + (sk+N)x \mod q$$

$$-(sk+N)x \equiv \sum_{i=1}^{N-1} \beta_i(sk+i)sk_i - \alpha \mod q$$

$$x \equiv \frac{\sum_{i=1}^{N-1} \beta_i(sk+i)sk_i - \alpha}{-(sk+N)} \mod q. \tag{3}$$

This indicates that for every set $X = (\alpha, sk, \beta_{i \neq N}, sk_{i \neq N}, \forall i : pk_i \in L) \in \mathbb{Z}_q^{3N}$, there is exactly one $s_N = x \in \mathbb{Z}_q^*$ for Eq. (3) to hold. Therefore, if $\mathsf{Batch}(L, M, \sigma) = 1$ and every i is distinct, $\mathsf{BLS.Vf}(pk_N, m_N, s_N = H(m_N)^x) = 0$ will not happen because it must be $x = sk_N$.

Moreover, if i does not need to be in an arithmetic sequence, the second condition still holds. In precise, given the same α and m_i yet $s_N \neq x$, there exists another valid set X' such that $L' \neq L$ for $L' \in X'$. This is equivalent to breaking the binding property in the MoniPoly set commitment. That is, finding a tuple $(i', o_{i'}) \in X' \neq (N, o_N = 1) \in X$ which leads to a success batch verification yet $s_{i'} = g_{i',0} = H(m_N)^{sk_{i'}} \neq g_{N,0}$ where $sk_{i'} = sk_N o_{i'}$. It is clear that even with this relaxation on i, we still have $\mathsf{BLS.Vf}(pk_{i'}, m_N, s_{i'}) = 1$.

□

3 New BLS Multi-signature Scheme

The idea behind the proposed signature aggregation technique continues from our *commit-and-verify* approach in the BLS batch verification (c.f. Section 2.5), that is, we uniquely "lock" each signature s_i in a multi-signature to its corresponding public key $pk_i \in L$ by committing to the index i. In precise, we let the signatures be the public keys in a multi-set commitment and the indices as the multi-set messages. For comparison in the subsequent sections, we follow the notation from BDN-MS scheme [6] which can be found in Appendix B. We present our construction below:

$\mathsf{Pg}(1^k)$: Choose two secure hash functions $H : \mathbb{G}_1 \to \{0, 1\}^\ell$ and $H_0 : \{0, 1\}^* \to \mathbb{G}_1$. Generate a bilinear group parameter $(q, g_1 \in \mathbb{G}_1, g_2 \in \mathbb{G}_2, e : \mathbb{G}_1 \times \mathbb{G}_2 \to \mathbb{G}_T)$ and set the system parameter as $par = (q, g_1, g_2, e, H, H_0)$.

$\mathsf{Kg}(par)$: Generate $pk = g_2^{sk}$ where $sk \in \mathbb{Z}_q^*$ is randomly selected and output the public and secret key pair as (pk, sk).

$\mathsf{Sign}(par, L, sk, m)$: In this single round protocol, every i-th signer sends the signature $s_i = H_0(m)^{sk_i}$ to a designated combiner which is one of the signers in the list $L = \{pk_1, \ldots, pk_N\}$ and his key pair is (pk, sk). To simplify the notation, we assume it is always $pk = pk_1 \in L$. The combiner outputs the final signature as

$$\sigma = \left(S_1 = \prod_{i=1}^{N} s_i^{sk+a_i}, S_2 = H_0(m)^{sk}\right) \tag{4}$$

where $a_i = H(S_2) + i$.

$\mathsf{KAg}(par, L)$: Given a list of public key $L = \{pk_1, \ldots, pk_N\}$ where the combiner's public key is always $pk = pk_1$, compute the aggregate public key as $apk = (K_1 = \prod_{i=1}^{N} pk_i, K_2 = pk \prod_{i=1}^{N} pk_i^i)$.

$\mathsf{Vf}(par, apk, m, \sigma)$: Output 1 if the following holds:

$$e\left(S_1 S_2, g_2\right) = e\left(\prod_{i=1}^{N} s_i^{sk+a_i}, g_2\right) e\left(H_0(m)^{sk}, g_2\right)$$

$$= \prod_{i=1}^{N} e\left(H_0(m)^{sk} H_0(m)^{H(S_2)+i}, g_2^{sk_i}\right) e\left(H_0(m), pk\right)$$

$$= e\left(H_0(m)^{sk+H(S_2)}, \prod_{i=1}^{N} pk_i\right) e\left(H_0(m), pk \prod_{i=1}^{N} pk_i^i\right)$$

$$= e\left(S_2 H_0(m)^{H(S_2)}, K_1\right) e\left(H_0(m), K_2\right) \tag{5}$$

and output 0 otherwise.

3.1 Relation to BDN-MS

Our proposed MS scheme can be viewed as a generalisation of Boneh et al.'s multi-signature (BDN-MS) scheme [6] (c.f. Appendix B) that uses $a_i = H_1(pk_i, L)$ and does not consider the combiner's key pair, i.e., $(pk = 1_{\mathbb{G}_1}, sk = 0)$. While BDN-MS relies on the way the exponents a_i are generated to resist rogue public key attack, ours relies on the combiner's signing key sk which acts as the commitment secret key.

Therefore, when $sk \in \mathbb{Z}_q^*$ is securely chosen, H_1 in BDN-MS can be as trivial as a function that outputs the index $a_i = i$ of $pk_i \in L$. The security is not affected as shown in the subsequent security analysis (c.f. Theorem 4) in which there is no special requirement in generating a_i except they must be consistent for (L, m), that is, be non-zero values and distinct from each other.

3.2 Hash Length ℓ

When the combiner's secret key sk is not securely chosen such as $sk = -a_i$ for small $1 \le a_i \le |L|$, it opens to a self-defeating attack. This is where $H : \mathbb{G}_1 \to \{0,1\}^\ell$ comes into the play, a similar security mechanism as the small exponent test to the BLS batch verification [9]. The use of the additional H makes sure $sk = -H(S_2) - i = -a_i$ now happens with a probability of $1/2^\ell$. We note that setting $\ell \approx 60$ as in the BLS batch verification [9] is sufficient to resist the self-defeating attack. In the situation where the self-defeating attack is not possible, for instance, length of sk is proven to be greater than $|L|$, we can safely set $\ell = 0$. We will analyse the performance degradation caused by ℓ in Sect. 4.

3.3 Incremental Signing

Our construction, different from BDN-MS's construction [6], allows *incremental signing*. After a multi-signature σ is generated, a new signer with key pair (pk_{n+1}, sk_{n+1}) can add a new signature $s_{n+1} = (S_2 H_0(m)^{H(S_2)+n+1})^{sk_{n+1}}$ to σ as a new multi-signature $\sigma' = (S_1 s_{n+1}, S_2)$ without needing to recompute from scratch. The new aggregated public key is then computed as $apk' = (K_1 pk_{n+1}, K_2 pk_{n+1}^{n+1})$. More importantly, the incremental signing preserves the lightweight scalar multiplications that speed up not only the signing protocol but also the public key aggregation, and subsequently the overall multi-signature verification.

3.4 Security Analysis

Although our proposed MS shares similarities with BDN-MS, we do not prove the uf-cma security using the forking lemma which yields loose reduction. We show that the proposed MS is uf-cma-secure as long as the BLS signature scheme is uf-cma-secure.

Theorem 3. *If BLS signature scheme is (ε', t')-uf-cma-secure, then our proposed multi-signature scheme is (ε, t)-uf-cma-secure such that:*

$$\varepsilon \geq N\varepsilon', t = t' - O(N)$$

where N is the total signers in the multi-signature scheme and $O(N)$ is the communication time required to answer multi-signature queries.

Proof. We show that if there exists a forger $\mathcal{F}_{ms}$ which breaks the uf-cma security of our proposed multi-signature scheme, then a BLS adversary $\mathcal{F}_{bls}$ can break the uf-cma security of BLS signature scheme with the help of $\mathcal{F}_{ms}$.

Based on the BLS instance $(g_1 \in \mathbb{G}_1, g_2 \in \mathbb{G}_2, pk = g_2^a)$, $\mathcal{F}_{bls}$ sets the system parameter as $par = (q, g_1, g_2, e, H_0, H_1)$ where H_0 is treated as a random oracle. $\mathcal{F}_{bls}$ initialises $\mathcal{F}_{ms}$ by giving it the tuple $(par, pk^* = pk)$ to implicitly set $sk^* = a$. $\mathcal{F}_{ms}$ can generate (pk, sk) of its favour, up to $N-1$ pairs, and issue sign queries (L, m) to $\mathcal{F}_{bls}$ where L is the list of public keys involved and $pk^* \in L$.

H_0 **Query.** Upon receiving a query on m, $\mathcal{F}_{bls}$ forwards the query to its hashing oracle and returns the corresponding answer as $H_0(m)$ to $\mathcal{F}_{ms}$.

$\mathcal{O}^{\mathsf{Sign}}$ **Query.** When $\mathcal{F}_{ms}$ queries for a signature on (L, m) where $pk^* \in L$, $\mathcal{F}_{bls}$ forwards the query as m to its signing oracle and receives the corresponding answer $s = H_0(m)^{sk^*}$. If $\mathcal{F}_{bls}$ is not the combiner, it returns s to $\mathcal{F}_{ms}$. Otherwise, it interacts with other signers and returns σ. $\mathcal{F}_{bls}$ updates the query (L, m, s) to the list of corrupted signatures SIG.

At some point, $\mathcal{F}_{ms}$ declares the challenge (L^*, m^*) such that $pk^* \in L^*$ and $(\cdot, m^*, \cdot) \notin SIG$. $\mathcal{F}_{ms}$ still can continue to interact with $\mathcal{F}_{bls}$ as before with the restriction of querying $(\cdot, m^*)$ to the signing oracle. Finally, $\mathcal{F}_{ms}$ outputs a

forgery $(L^* = \{pk_1^*, \ldots, pk_n^*\}, m^*, \sigma^* = (S_1^* = \prod_{i=1}^n s_i^{sk^*+a_i}, S_2^* = H_0(m)^{sk^*}))$
with $(\cdot, m^*, \cdot) \notin SIG$.

If $pk_1^* = pk^* = g_2^a$, $\mathcal{F}_{bls}$ outputs its forgery as $(m^*, S_2^* = H_0(m^*)^a)$ and wins
the game. In precise, the probability of $\mathcal{F}_{bls}$ winning the uf-cma game is:

$$\Pr[\mathbf{Game}_{\mathsf{BLS},\mathcal{F}_{bls}}^{\text{uf-cma}} = \mathsf{WIN}] = \Pr[\mathbf{Game}_{\mathsf{MS},\mathcal{F}_{ms}}^{\text{uf-cma}} = \mathsf{WIN}] \wedge \Pr[pk_1^* = g_2^a]$$

$$\varepsilon' = \frac{\varepsilon}{|L^*|}$$

where both run in time $t' = t + O(N)$ in which $O(N)$ is the network communi-
cation and $2 \le |L^*| \le N$.   □

Theorem 4. *The algorithms* (Sign, KAg, Vf) *are a batch verifier for the proposed
multi-signature scheme.*

Proof. The proof is similar to that in Theorem 2. The proposed multi-signature
$\sigma = (S_1, S_2)$ from Eq. (4) subsumes a MoniPoly multi-set commitment [16]:

$$S_1 = \prod_{i=1}^N s_i^{sk+a_i} = \prod_{i=1}^N H_0(m)^{sk_i(sk+a_i)} \iff \left(\prod_{i=1}^N g_{i,0}^{(x+a_i)}\right)^{o_i} = C$$

such that $\log_{h_{i,1}}(H_0(m)^{sk_i})$ is the (unknown) discrete logarithm of the public key
$g_{i,0} = H_0(m)^{sk_i}$ while the committed message is a_i and the commitment secret is
$x = sk$ with all opening values $o_1 = \ldots = o_N = 1$. Follows from the correctness
of set commitment S_1 and that of BLS signature S_2, when $\mathsf{BLS.Vf}(pk_i, m, s_i) = 1$
for all $(pk_i \in L, m, s_i \in \sigma)$, it is always the case $\mathsf{Vf}(par, \mathsf{KAg}(par, L), m, \sigma) = 1$
in the proposed multi-signature scheme.

Now we analyse the opposite direction. Without loss of generality, we con-
sider case of $\mathsf{BLS.Vf}(pk_N, m, s_N) = 0$ but $\mathsf{Vf}(par, \mathsf{KAg}(par, L), m, \sigma) = 1$. Let
$\log_{H_0(m)}(S_1) = \alpha_1$ and $\log_{H_0(m)}(S_2) = \alpha_2$. From Eq. (5), we have:

$$\alpha_1 + \alpha_2 \equiv \sum_{i=1}^N sk_i(sk_1 + a_i) + sk_1 \mod q$$

$$-x(sk_1 + a_N) \equiv \sum_{i=1}^{N-1} sk_i(sk_1 + a_i) + sk_1 - \alpha_1 - \alpha_2 \mod q$$

$$x \equiv \frac{\sum_{i=1}^{N-1} sk_i(sk_1 + a_i) + sk_1 - \alpha_1 - \alpha_2}{-(sk_1 + a_N)} \mod q. \qquad (6)$$

This indicates that for every set $X = (\alpha_1, \alpha_2, \beta_{i \ne N}, sk_{i \ne N}, \forall a_i : pk_i \in L) \in
\mathbb{Z}_q^{3N}$, there is exactly one $s_N = x \in \mathbb{Z}_q^*$ for Eq. (6) to hold. Therefore, if
$\mathsf{Vf}(par, \mathsf{KAg}(par, L), m, \sigma) = 1$ and every a_i is distinct, $\mathsf{BLS.Vf}(pk_N, m, s_N =
H(m)^x) = 0$ will not happen because it must be $x = sk_N$.

We also show that if a_i does not have an arithmetic sequence, the analysis
above remains valid. Essentially, given the same α_1, α_2 and m yet $s_N \ne x$ in

Eq. (6), there exists another valid set X' such that $L' \neq L$ for $L' \in X'$. This is analogy to breaking the binding property in the MoniPoly set commitment. That is, finding a tuple $(a_{i'}, o_{i'}) \in X' \neq (a_N, o_N = 1) \in X$ which leads to a success batch verification yet $s_{i'} = g_{i',0} = H(m)^{sk_{i'}} \neq g_{N,0}$ where $sk_{i'} = sk_N o_{i'}$. So, it is clear that even with this relaxation on a_i, we still have $\mathsf{BLS.Vf}(pk_{i'}, m, s_{i'}) = 1$. $\square$

4   Benchmarks

Table 3. Complexity comparison.

Scheme	Sign		KAg	Vf
	Signer	Combiner		
BDN [6]	$1H_1 + 1H_0 + 1m + 1M_1$	$(|L|-1)A_1$	$|L|(H_1 + M_2 + A_2) - 1A_2$	$2P + 1H_0$
Ours	$1H_0 + 1M_1$	$|L|(2a + M_1 + A_1) + 1H - 1A_1$	$|L|(M_2^* + 2A_2) - 1A_2$	$3P + 2A_1 + 1H_0 + 1H + M_T$

Note: H, H_x : hashing, (a, m) : addition and multiplication in $\mathbb{Z}_q$, L : list of pk, P : pairing,
(A_x, M_x) : point addition and scalar multiplication in $\mathbb{G}_x$, M_x^* : lightweight point multiplication in $\mathbb{G}_x$

We benchmark our proposed MS scheme to the BDN-MS scheme, which is also based on the BLS signature scheme, in Table 3. As our MS is a generalised version of the BDN-MS in addition to offering stronger security reduction, our Sign algorithm has a higher complexity than the latter as expected. However, the multi-signature verification ($\mathsf{KAg} + \mathsf{Vf}$) in our MS is faster than that of BDN-MS. In precise, instead of multiplying with $|\mathbb{Z}_q|$-bit scalars $a_1 = H_1(pk_1, L), \ldots, a_{|L|} = H_1(pk_{|L|}, L)$ in the public key aggregation (KAg) of BDN-MS, ours multiply with ℓ-bit scalars $a_1 = H(S_2)+1, \ldots, a_{|L|} = H(S_2)+|L|$ where $0 \leq \ell \leq 60$. As the extra 1 pairing, 2 addition in $\mathbb{G}_1$, 1 hashing and 1 multiplication in $\mathbb{G}_T$ in our Vf are of constant complexity regardless of the total signers $|L|$, our multi-signature verification ($\mathsf{KAg} + \mathsf{Vf}$) will be faster when the number of signatures is large.

To confirm this hypothesis, we implement the schemes in Table 3 using the MIRACL Core Rust library [1] on a laptop with Windows 10 Home that is equipped with AMD Ryzen 9 4900HS 3.0 Ghz CPU and 16 GB RAM. The curve is set to BLS12-381 and the message m is fixed as "testing message". We let H_0 be the library-provided hash-to-point function and both H_1, H be the SHA-256 algorithm. We use the entire 256-bit hash value as the output for H_1, and for H, we use the first ℓ bits only. To avoid bias from CPU caching, we run the algorithms[1] for 100 rounds before summarising the average running time of

---

[1] The time taken by signers is purposely left out to focus on the differences in the multi-signature generation and verification process. This actually creates a more advantageous environment for the BDN-MS scheme as their BLS signature generation is slower than ours.

1000 rounds in Table 4. Subsequently, we analyse the complexity in two different use cases:

1. (Combiner + KAg + Vf): the combiner completes the entire verification process itself, that is, from multi-signature generation to the subsequent verification; and
2. (KAg + Vf): the combiner computes the multi-signature σ only but the public key aggregation (KAg) and verification (Vf) are done by others.

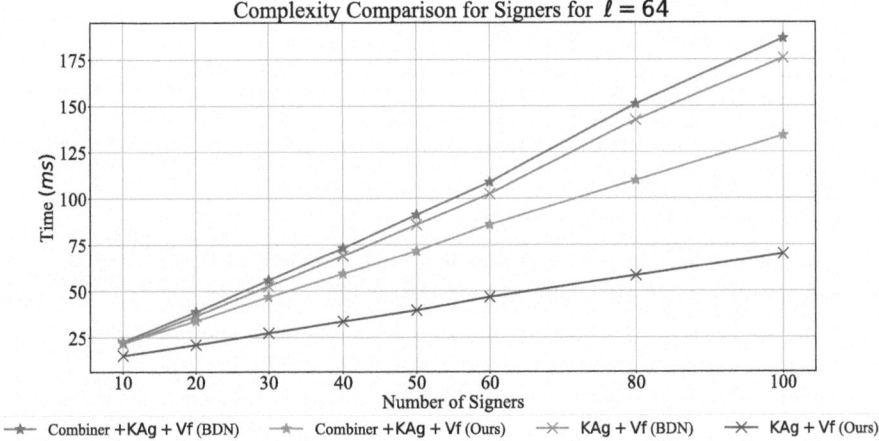

Fig. 1. Comparison of Complexity for (Combiner + KAg + Vf) and (KAg + Vf) between BDN-AMS and Ours with the Number of Signers, where $\ell = 64$.

In Fig. 1, we illustrate the performance comparison between BDN-MS and our proposed MS from multi-signature generation to verification (Combiner + KAg + Vf), and also the verification (KAg + Vf) process, from 10 to 100 signers. In the depicted figure[2], we demonstrate that with an increase in the number of signers, our proposed MS is deemed to be more efficient than BDN-MS. We attribute the efficiency of our proposed scheme to the public key aggregation operation, KAg, whereby we elicit a better performance efficiency of multi-signature generation to verification than the BDN-MS's sole verification operation as observed. In Table 4 whereby we tabulate the results for a total of 10,000 signers, our scheme maintains a much improved efficiency of approximately 42 times for KAg.

Table 4 shows that although our combiner is slower than that of BDN-MS, our public key aggregation is significantly faster, deeming our scheme to be suitable for multi-signature in large batches. As a result, at $\ell = 64$, the total

---

[2] We fix $\ell = 64$ in this figure, considering that the length ℓ does not heavily affect the performance much. We refer the reader to Appendix C for illustrations of performances as ℓ increases.

Table 4. Complexity difference for (Combiner, KAg, Vf) between BDN-AMS and our proposed AMS for $\ell = 64$ for 10,000 signers.

Scheme	Time Taken (ns)		
	Combiner	**KAg**	**Vf**
BDN [6]	1,054,011,560	283,856,451,130	6,942,090
Ours	6,378,739,140	6,678,836,280	9,332,200

time required from multi-signature generation to verification (Combiner + KAg + Vf) in our proposed scheme is only

$$\frac{6,378,739,140 + 6,678,836,280 + 9,332,200}{1,054,011,560 + 283,856,451,130 + 6,942,090} = \frac{13,066,907,620}{284,917,404,780} \approx 4.59\%$$

of the time taken by BDN-MS. If we consider the verification process (KAg + Vf) only, our scheme takes

$$\frac{6,678,836,280 + 9,332,200}{283,856,451,130 + 6,942,090} = \frac{6,688,168,480}{283,863,393,220} \approx 2.35\%$$

of the time taken by BDN-MS. We highlight that this complexity reduction comes at the price of only storing an extra $\mathbb{G}_1$ element in the multi-signature σ and having an extra $\mathbb{G}_2$ element in the aggregated public key apk.

Besides better efficiency, our proposed MS scheme offers additional features that are not presented in BDN-MS. Firstly, our proposed MS scheme is backward compatible with the BLS signature scheme as in Camenisch et al.'s batch signatures [9]. Subsequently, incremental signing is made possible as ours enables one to add new pk to the apk through the commitment approach but not through hashing.

5   Extension to Aggregate Multi-signature Scheme

Similar to the extension of the BDN-MS into BDN-AMS [6], assuming the signed messages are distinct, our proposed MS scheme can be extended to an AMS by further aggregating the multi-signatures. As MS and AMS share the same Pg, Kg and KAg algorithms, we describe only the Sign and Vf that include $K_1 = \prod_{i=1}^{N} pk_i$ in the signed message, and the extra SAg and AVf algorithms here.

Sign(par, L, sk, m): In this single round protocol, every i-th signer sends the signature $s_i = H_0(K_1||m)^{sk_i}$ to a designated combiner which is one of the signers in the list $L = \{pk_1, \ldots, pk_N\}$ whose key pair is (pk, sk). To simplify the notation, we assume it is always $pk = pk_1 \in L$. The combiner outputs the final signature as

$$\sigma = (S_1 = \prod_{i=1}^{N} s_i^{sk+a_i}, S_2 = H_0(K_1||m)^{sk}) \tag{7}$$

where $a_i = H(S_2) + i$.

$\mathsf{Vf}(par, apk, m, \sigma)$: Output 1 if the following holds:

$$e\,(S_1 S_2, g_2) = e\left(S_2 H_0(K_1 \| m)^{H(S_2)}, K_1\right) e\,(H_0(K_1 \| m), K_2) \qquad (8)$$

and output 0 otherwise.

$\mathsf{SAg}(par, \{apk_j, m_j, \sigma_j\}_{j=1}^k)$: Given a list of triples $\{apk_j, m_j, \sigma_j\}$, compute the aggregate multi-signature as $\Sigma = (\prod_{j=1}^k S_{j,1}, \{S_{j,2}\}_{j=1}^k)$.

$\mathsf{AVf}(par, \{m_j, apk_j\}_{j=1}^k, \Sigma)$: Let $\tilde{S}_1 = \prod_{j=1}^k S_{j,1}$ and $\tilde{S}_2 = \prod_{j=1}^k S_{j,2}$, output 1 if the following holds:

$$e\left(\tilde{S}_1 \tilde{S}_2, g_2\right) = \prod_{j=1}^k e\left(S_{j,2} H_0(K_{j,1} \| m_j)^{H(S_{j,2})}, K_{j,1}\right) e\,(H_0(K_{j,1} \| m_j), K_{j,2}) \quad (9)$$

and output 0 otherwise.

5.1   Security Analysis

Following Theorems 3, we claim the security for the proposed aggregate multi-signature as follows.

Theorem 5. *If BLS signature scheme is (ε', t')-uf-cma-secure, then our proposed AMS scheme is $(\varepsilon_{ams}, t_{ams})$-uf-cma-secure such that:*

$$\varepsilon' \geq \frac{\varepsilon_{ams}}{N}, t' = t_{ams}$$

where N is the total signers in the multi-signature scheme.

Proof. The proof is similar to that in Theorem 3 except now the forger $\mathcal{F}_{ams}$ outputs the forgery as an aggregate multi-signature $\Sigma^* = (\prod_{j=1}^k S_{j,1}^*, \{S_{j,2}^*\}_{j=1}^k)$ for the challenge (L^*, m^*) announced earlier, in addition to the tuple of sets $(\{apk_j\}_{j=1}^k, \{m_j\}_{j=1}^k)$. With that said, the BLS forger $\mathcal{F}_{bls}$ declares its challenge message as $K_1 \| m^*$.

If $\mathsf{AVf}(par, \{\mathsf{KAg}(par, L^*), m^*\} \cup \{apk_j, m_j\}_{j=2}^k, \Sigma^*) = 1$, $\mathcal{F}_{ams}$ wins the game. Subsequently, $\mathcal{F}_{bls}$ outputs its forgery as $(m^*, S_{1,2}^* = H_0(K_1 \| m^*)^{sk^*})$ to wins its game. The success probability is the same as that in Theorem 3 and this concludes the proof.   □

6   Conclusion

We introduced an efficient and uf-cma-secure multi-signature (MS) scheme that stems from the BLS signature without relying on forking lemma. The MS scheme is also secure against the rogue public key and splitting zero attacks without requiring proof of possession. Compared to the state-of-the-art, our scheme has a faster verification process besides supporting incremental signing and it is backward compatible with the original BLS signature. Lastly, we showed that our MS scheme is extendable into an aggregate multi-signature (AMS) scheme.

Acknowledgements. This work was supported by the Telekom Malaysia Research & Development Grant (RDTC/221045).

A   Multi-set Commitment Scheme Definition

We recall the definition of multi-set commitment scheme MSC [16] below:

1. Setup$(1^\kappa, N, n) \rightarrow (PK, SK)$. Generate a pair of public and secret keys (PK, SK) based on the security parameter 1^κ, the maximum number of sets supported N, and the maximal size n of each set.
2. Commit$(PK, A, O) \rightarrow (C)$. On the input of PK and a message multi-set $A = \{A_1, \ldots, A_N\}$, select a list of random opening values $O = \{o_1, \ldots, o_L\}$ to output the commitment C.
3. Open$(PK, C, A, O) \rightarrow (0 \text{ or } 1)$. Return 1 if C is a valid commitment for the multi-set A with the corresponding opening values O under PK. Return 0 otherwise.
4. OpenIntersection$(PK, C, A, O, (A', (\ell, \kappa))) \rightarrow (I, W)$ or $\perp$. Let $A' = \{A'_1, \ldots, A'_N\}, 1 \leq \ell \leq N, \kappa = \{k_1, \ldots, k_N\}$ and $I_{i,j} = A'_j \cap A_i$. If there are ℓ-many pair of indices (i, j) such that $|I_{i,j}| = k_j \leq |A'_j|$ holds where indices i and j are unique, respectively, return these intersecting sets $I_{i,j}$ as the multi-set I and the corresponding witnesses W, and return an error $\perp$ otherwise.
5. VerifyIntersection$(PK, C, (I, W), (A', (\ell, \kappa))) \rightarrow (0 \text{ or } 1)$. Return 1 if W is a witness for I being the intersecting multi-set of size ℓ for A' and the multi-set committed to in C. Return 0 otherwise.
6. OpenDifference$(PK, C, A, O, (A', (\bar{\ell}, \bar{\kappa}))) \rightarrow (D, W)$. Let $A' = \{A'_1, \ldots, A'_N\}, \bar{\kappa} = \{\bar{k}_1, \ldots, \bar{k}_N\}, 1 \leq \bar{\ell} \leq L$ and $D_{i,j} = A'_j \setminus A_i$. If there are $\bar{\ell}$-many A'_j such that $|D_{i,j}| = \bar{k}_i \leq |A'_j|$ holds for all $A_j \in A$, return these differing sets $D_{i,j}$ as the multi-set D and the corresponding witness W, and return an error $\perp$ otherwise.
7. VerifyDifference$(PK, C, (D, W), (A', (\bar{\ell}, \bar{\kappa}))) \rightarrow (0 \text{ or } 1)$. Return 1 if W is the witness for D being the differing multi-set of size $\bar{\ell}$ for A' and the multi-set committed to in C, and return 0 otherwise.

B   BDN Multi-signature Scheme

We briefly recall the BDN-MS [6] here for reference purposes.

Pg(1^k) : Choose two secure hash functions $H_0 : \{0, 1\}^* \rightarrow \mathbb{G}_1$ and $H_1 : \{0, 1\}^* \rightarrow \mathbb{Z}_q^*$. Generate a bilinear group parameter $(q, g_1 \in \mathbb{G}_1, g_2 \in \mathbb{G}_2, e : \mathbb{G}_1 \times \mathbb{G}_2 \rightarrow \mathbb{G}_T)$ and set the system parameter as $par = (q, g_1, g_2, e, H_0, H_1)$.

Kg(par) : Generate $pk = g_2^{sk}$ where $sk \in \mathbb{Z}_q^*$ is randomly selected and output the public and secret key pair as (pk, sk).

Sign(par, L, sk, m): In this single round protocol, every signer i computes and sends the signature $s_i = H_0(m)^{a_i \cdot sk_i}$ to a designated combiner where $a_i =$

$H_1(pk_i, L)$ and $L = \{pk_1, \ldots, pk_n\}$. The combiner outputs the final signature as $\sigma = \prod_{i=1}^{n} s_i$.

$\mathsf{KAg}(par, L)$: Given a list of public key $L = \{pk_1, \ldots, pk_n\}$, compute the aggregate public key as $apk = \prod_{i=1}^{n} pk_i^{a_i}$ where $a_i = H_1(pk_i, L)$.

$\mathsf{Vf}(par, apk, m, \sigma)$: Output 1 if $e(\sigma, g_2) = e(H_0(m), apk)$ holds and output 0 otherwise.

Theorem 6. *[6, Theorem 1] The MS scheme above is $(t, q_S, q_H, \varepsilon)$-unforgeable in the random oracle model if $q > 8q_H/\varepsilon$ and if co-CDH is $((t + q_H t_{exp_1} + q_S(t_{exp_2^1} + t_{exp_1}) + t_{exp_2^1}) \cdot 8q_H^2/\varepsilon \cdot \ln(8q_H/\varepsilon), \varepsilon/(8q_H))$-hard where t_{exp_1} and t_{exp_2} are the time required to compute exponentiation in $\mathbb{G}_1$ and $\mathbb{G}_2$ respectively, and $t_{exp_1^i}$ and $t_{exp_2^i}$ are the time required to compute i-multi-exponentiations in $\mathbb{G}_1$ and $\mathbb{G}_2$ respectively.*

C   Benchmark for Different Lengths of ℓ

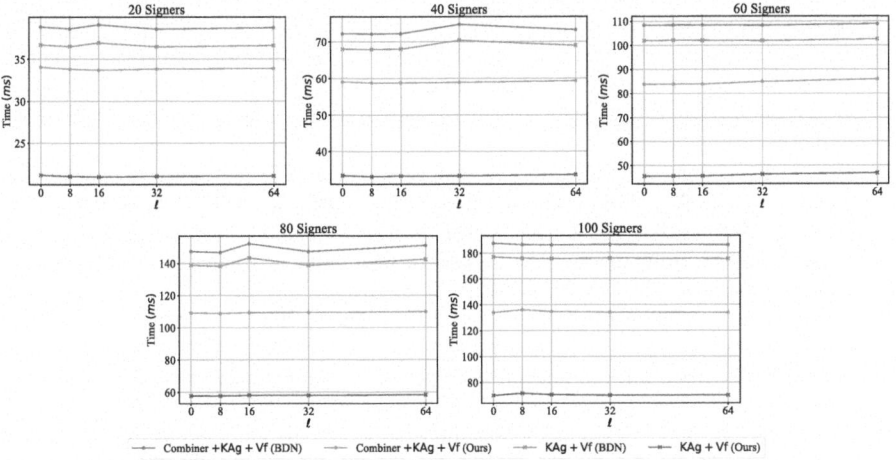

Fig. 2. Comparison of Complexity for (Combiner + KAg + Vf) and (KAg + Vf) between BDN-AMS and Ours with the Respective Number of Signers.

Figure 2 depicts the performance comparison between our proposed MS with the BDN-MS, as an extension of Fig. 1. Similarly, we compare the multi-signature generation to verification (Combiner + KAg + Vf) and the verification (KAg + Vf) for the different number of signers with an increasing length ℓ. It is noteworthy that regardless the number of signers involved, the length ℓ does not heavily impact the performance timing, as aforementioned.

References

1. The MIRACL Core Cryptographic Library (December 2023). https://github.com/miracl/core
2. Baldimtsi, F., et al.: Subset-optimized bls multi-signature with key aggregation. Cryptology ePrint Archive, Paper 2023/498 (2023). https://eprint.iacr.org/2023/498
3. Bellare, M., Garay, J.A., Rabin, T.: Fast batch verification for modular exponentiation and digital signatures. In: Nyberg, K. (ed.) EUROCRYPT 1998. LNCS, vol. 1403, pp. 236–250. Springer, Heidelberg (1998). https://doi.org/10.1007/BFb0054130
4. Bellare, M., Neven, G.: Multi-signatures in the plain public-key model and a general forking lemma. In: Proceedings of the 13th ACM Conference on Computer and Communications Security, pp. 390–399. CCS '06, Association for Computing Machinery, New York, NY, USA (2006). https://doi.org/10.1145/1180405.1180453
5. Boldyreva, A.: Threshold signatures, multisignatures and blind signatures based on the gap-diffie-hellman-group signature scheme. In: Desmedt, Y.G. (ed.) Public Key Cryptography – PKC 2003, pp. 31–46. Springer, Berlin, Heidelberg (2002)
6. Boneh, D., Drijvers, M., Neven, G.: Compact multi-signatures for smaller blockchains. In: Peyrin, T., Galbraith, S. (eds.) ASIACRYPT 2018. LNCS, vol. 11273, pp. 435–464. Springer, Cham (2018). https://doi.org/10.1007/978-3-030-03329-3_15
7. Boneh, D., Gentry, C., Lynn, B., Shacham, H.: Aggregate and verifiably encrypted signatures from bilinear maps. In: Biham, E. (ed.) EUROCRYPT 2003. LNCS, vol. 2656, pp. 416–432. Springer, Heidelberg (2003). https://doi.org/10.1007/3-540-39200-9_26
8. Boneh, D., Lynn, B., Shacham, H.: Short signatures from the Weil pairing. In: Boyd, C. (ed.) ASIACRYPT 2001. LNCS, vol. 2248, pp. 514–532. Springer, Heidelberg (2001). https://doi.org/10.1007/3-540-45682-1_30
9. Camenisch, J., Hohenberger, S., Pedersen, M.: Batch verification of short signatures. J. Cryptol. **25**, 723–747 (2012)
10. Chatterjee, S., Hankerson, D., Knapp, E., Menezes, A.: Comparing two pairing-based aggregate signature schemes. Des. Codes Crypt. **55**, 141–167 (2010)
11. Maxwell, G., Poelstra, A., Seurin, Y., Wuille, P.: Simple schnorr multi-signatures with applications to bitcoin. Des. Codes Crypt. **87**(9), 2139–2164 (2019)
12. Micali, S., Ohta, K., Reyzin, L.: Accountable-subgroup multisignatures: extended abstract. In: Proceedings of the 8th ACM Conference on Computer and Communications Security, pp. 245–254. CCS '01, Association for Computing Machinery, New York, NY, USA (2001). https://doi.org/10.1145/501983.502017
13. Quan, N.T.M.: 0. Cryptology ePrint Archive, Paper 2021/323 (2021). https://eprint.iacr.org/2021/323
14. Quan, N.T.M.: Attacks and weaknesses of bls aggregate signatures. Cryptology ePrint Archive, Paper 2021/377 (2021). https://eprint.iacr.org/2021/377
15. Tan, S.Y., Groß, T.: Monipoly–an expressive q-sdh-based anonymous attribute-based credential system. In: Moriai, S., Wang, H. (eds.) Advances in Cryptology - ASIACRYPT 2020, pp. 498–526. Springer International Publishing, Cham (2020)
16. Tan, S.Y., Sfyrakis, I., Gross, T.: A relational credential system from q-sdh-based graph signatures. Cryptology ePrint Archive, Paper 2023/1181 (2023). https://eprint.iacr.org/2023/1181

Threshold Ring Signatures: From DualRing to the $t + 1$ Rings

Tsz Hon Yuen[1($\boxtimes$)] and Shimin Pan[2]

[1] Department of Software Systems and Cybersecurity, Monash University,
Clayton 3168, Australia
john.tszhonyuen@monash.edu
[2] Department of Computer Science, University of Hong Kong, Hong Kong, China
smpan@connect.hku.hk

Abstract. A t-out-of-n threshold ring signature allows t signers to sign a message while anonymizing themselves within a set of n public keys. One of the key research directions is to build a practical threshold ring signature with a short signature size, which is logarithmic to the parameters (t, n).

In this paper, we extend the DualRing architecture (using one R-ring and one C-ring) for ring signatures (CRYPTO '21) to a new architecture for threshold ring signatures. We propose a generic construction of threshold ring signatures using one R-ring and t C-rings. We show that the t C-rings are constructed securely and efficiently.

In order to compress the n elements in the C-rings in the elliptic curve setting, we propose a new argument of knowledge for matrix multiplication. The proof size is $O(\log n)$. When combined with the generic threshold ring signature, we obtain the first practical threshold ring signature with size $O(\log n)$ only (independent to t).

Keywords: ring signature · threshold · anonymity

1 Introduction

Threshold ring signature, introduced by [6], offers anonymity to t signers who wants to hide their identities among a set of n public keys. The set of public keys are chosen arbitrarily by the signers and users do not need to join a group prior to the signing process.

One interesting application for t-out-of-n threshold ring signatures is *whistle-blowing* [22]. Although ring signatures (which can be viewed as 1-out-of-n threshold ring signature) can also allow a whistleblower to disclose some secret information of an organization anonymously [26], a single entity may not have enough credibility to persuade the public about the validity of the information. A threshold ring signature is more suitable in this case since multiple whistleblowers are needed to sign a message. Another practical application is to share cryptocurrency wallets that allow users to have a single key, even if they have multiple wallets [15]. Threshold ring signature is suitable for decentralized blockchain applications since it does not require trusted setup.

J. K. Liu et al. (Eds.): ProvSec 2024, LNCS 14903, pp. 269–288, 2025.
https://doi.org/10.1007/978-981-96-0954-3_14

In this paper, we focus on constructing a practical threshold ring signature scheme. Although the state-of-the-art ring signature schemes have a signature size of $O(\log n)$ [5,14,17–19,28,31], most threshold ring signature schemes have a signature size of $O(n)$ [4,8–10,13,16,20,21,24,27,29,32]. There are some recent threshold ring signature schemes that can achieve signature size of $O(t)$, but their concrete constructions require trusted setup for accumulator [22] or zk-SNARK [15]. It is an open problem to give a threshold ring signature with size logarithmic to the parameters (t, n).

1.1   From DualRing to $(t + 1)$ Rings

Yuen et al. proposed a generic construction of ring signature called *DualRing* [28]. DualRing uses a canonical identification scheme (with some special homomorphic properties) to build two rings: a ring of commitments (R-ring) and a ring of challenges (C-ring). Suppose that the set of public keys are $\{vk_1, \ldots vk_n\}$ and the signer is at index s with secret key sk_s. The signer firstly picks random challenges c_i for other $n - 1$ members of the set. The R-ring is formed by a randomness r_s and sk_s (running with the commit algorithm of the identification scheme), together with the random challenges c_i and the corresponding public keys vk_i for $i \neq s$. A commitment value R is the output of the R-ring. A challenge c is computed as the hash of the message, R and the set of public keys. The C-ring is formed by calculating the missing challenge c_s of the signer from c and all c_i. Finally, the signer runs the response algorithm of the identification scheme to obtain z from c_s, r_s and the secret key sk_s. The ring signature is $(z, c_1, \ldots, c_n)$.

In this paper, we propose how to use of the R-ring and C-ring architecture to construct a generic threshold ring signature. Suppose that the set of public keys are $\{vk_1, \ldots vk_n\}$ and the set of t signer indices is S. We propose the following modifications to achieve our goal.

1. In the formation of the R-ring, the input for the signers are (sk_j, r_j) for all $j \in$ S and the input for the non-signers are (vk_i, c_i) for $i \notin$ S.
2. The challenge $\mathbf{c} = (h_1, \ldots, h_t)$ is now a vector of t group elements. It is computed as the hash of the message, R, the set of public keys and also the threshold size t.
3. In order to calculate the t missing challenges c_j for all $j \in$ S, we form t different C-rings with $\mathbf{c}$. With these t C-rings, each signer can deterministically calculate his own c_j.
4. Each signer runs the response algorithm of the identification scheme to obtain z_j from c_j, r_j and the secret key sk_j.
5. All z_j are combined to form the final value z, and the threshold ring signature is $(z, c_1, \ldots, c_n)$.

Our high level construction is illustrated in Fig. 1. The main advantage of our construction is that the signature size is the same as DualRing. Since DualRing-EC and DualRing-LB in [28] are very efficient instantiations of ring signature in elliptic curve and lattice-based settings respectively, we can also construct highly efficient instantiations of threshold ring signature.

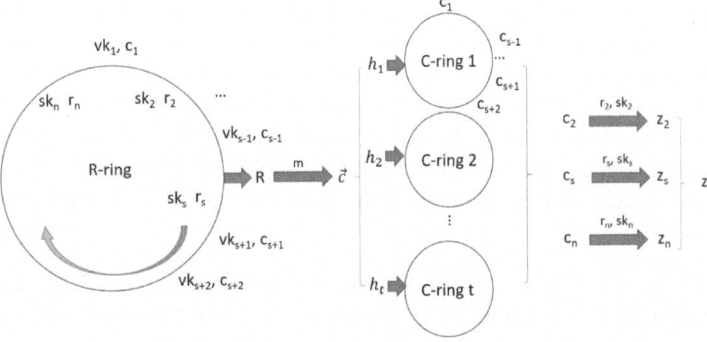

Fig. 1. High level construction of our threshold ring signature, assuming that the signer indices are 2, s and n.

Challenge 1: Construction of t Rings. In the above generic construction, the major difficulty is how to construct the t C-rings such that all missing challenges c_j can be computed deterministically (with overwhelming probability), without compromising privacy. Recall that in DualRing, there is only one C-ring with the relation:

$$c = c_1 \otimes c_2 \otimes \ldots \otimes c_n,$$

where $\otimes$ is instantiated as modular addition in DualRing-EC and as polynomial addition in DualRing-LB. Hence, c_s can be determined by this C-ring.

For threshold ring signatures, we now have t missing challenges c_j for $j \in \mathsf{S}$. Hence, we need t different relations to solve for these t unknowns. Here, we use a finite field $\mathbb{F}$ with additive and multiplicative operations. To construct a solvable system of equations in $\mathbb{F}$, we now define the challenge $\boldsymbol{c} = (h_1, \ldots, h_t) \in \mathbb{F}^t$. The t relations for the C-rings are defined as:

$$\begin{cases} 1 \cdot c_1 & +1 \cdot c_2 & +1 \cdot c_3 & +\ldots & +1 \cdot c_n & =h_1 \\ 1 \cdot c_1 & +2 \cdot c_2 & +3 \cdot c_3 & +\ldots & +n \cdot c_n & =h_2 \\ \ldots \\ 1^{t-1} \cdot c_1 & +2^{t-1} \cdot c_2 & +3^{t-1} \cdot c_3 & +\ldots & +n^{t-1} \cdot c_n & =h_t \end{cases} \tag{1}$$

Note that for $t = 1$, it is the same as the relation in DualRing.

When the signers in S want to jointly sign a message, they randomly pick $c_i \in \mathbb{F}$ for $i \in [n] \setminus \mathsf{S}$ and compute c_j for $j \in \mathsf{S}$ following the above relation. By writing $\mathsf{S} = (s_1, s_2, \ldots, s_t)^\top$, the solution $\boldsymbol{c}_\mathsf{S} = (c_{s_1}, c_{s_2}, \ldots, c_{s_t})^\top$ fulfills $\mathbf{A}_\mathsf{S}\boldsymbol{c}_\mathsf{S} = \mathbf{b}_\mathsf{S}$, where:

$$\mathbf{A}_\mathsf{S} = \begin{pmatrix} 1 & 1 & \cdots & 1 \\ s_1 & s_2 & \cdots & s_t \\ \vdots & \vdots & \ddots & \vdots \\ s_1^{t-1} & s_2^{t-1} & \cdots & s_t^{t-1} \end{pmatrix}, \quad \mathbf{b}_\mathsf{S} = \begin{pmatrix} h_1 - \sum_{i \in [n] \setminus \mathsf{S}} i^0 c_i \\ h_2 - \sum_{i \in [n] \setminus \mathsf{S}} i^1 c_i \\ \vdots \\ h_t - \sum_{i \in [n] \setminus \mathsf{S}} i^{t-1} c_i \end{pmatrix}.$$

Observe that $\mathbf{A_S}$ is a Vandermonde matrix and hence its determinant $\det(\mathbf{A_S}) \neq 0$ since all elements in S are distinct. Hence, all signers can deterministically calculate a unique $\mathbf{c_S} = \mathbf{A_S^{-1} b_S}$. In terms of correctness, we will show that all elements in $\mathbf{c_S}$ are non-zero with overwhelming probability.

Finally, we need to show that no adversary can distinguish whether any c_j is solved from the equations or not. Otherwise, it will break the anonymity of the threshold ring signature scheme. We achieve this by proving that $\mathbf{c_S}$ is uniformly distributed in $\mathbb{F}^t$.

Challenge 2: Argument of Knowledge for t Rings. In the elliptic curve setting, DualRing-EC is the shortest ring signature scheme because the challenges $(c_1, \ldots, c_n)$ can be replaced by an argument of knowledge for the sum relation:

$$c_1 + c_2 + \ldots + c_n = c.$$

Yuen *et al.* [28] proposed a non-interactive sum argument with size $O(\log n)$, which is the simplified Bulletproof [7] of the inner product relation.

In this paper, we would like to shorten the signature size of our threshold ring signature scheme by using an argument of knowledge for the relations of t C-rings, as shown in Eq. (1). We achieve our goal in two steps. Firstly, we give a one-sided inner product argument of for witness $\mathbf{a} \in \mathbb{Z}_p^n$ satisfying the relation:

$$P = \mathbf{g^a} \quad \wedge \quad h = \langle \mathbf{b}, \mathbf{a} \rangle,$$

where $\mathbf{g} \in \mathbb{G}^n, P \in \mathbb{G}, h \in \mathbb{Z}_p, \mathbf{b} \in \mathbb{Z}_p^n$ are public parameters. This argument of knowledge is in between Bulletproof [7] (in which $\mathbf{b}$ is also a witness for the relation) and the non-interactive sum argument [28] (in which $\mathbf{b}$ is a constant vector of 1). Secondly, we extend the one-sided inner product argument to matrix multiplication argument. It is an argument of knowledge for witness $\mathbf{a} \in \mathbb{Z}_p^n$ satisfying the relation:

$$V = \mathbf{v^a} \quad \wedge \quad \mathbf{c} = \mathbf{B} \cdot \mathbf{a},$$

where $\mathbf{v} \in \mathbb{G}^n, V \in \mathbb{G}, \mathbf{c} \in \mathbb{Z}_p^t, \mathbf{B} \in \mathbb{Z}_p^{t \times n}$ are public parameters. The size of the proof is $2 \log n$ elements in $\mathbb{G}$ and 2 elements in $\mathbb{Z}_p$, which is *independent* of t. Recently, Cong *et al.* [11] proposed an efficient zero-knowledge proof for matrix multiplication for committed $\mathbf{a}, \mathbf{B}$ and/or $\mathbf{c}$ and hence is not applicable here.

To combine the matrix multiplication argument with our threshold ring signature scheme in the elliptic curve setting, we can set $(c_1, \ldots, c_n)$ as the witness, $\mathbf{B}$ as the Vandermonde matrix, and $\mathbf{c}$ as $(h_1, \ldots, h_t)$ as in Eq.(1). As a result, we can obtain a threshold ring signature scheme of signature size $2 \log n + 1$ elements in $\mathbb{G}$ and 3 elements in $\mathbb{Z}_p$, which is *independent* of t.

1.2 Related Works

Existing research works on (threshold) ring signatures focus on different directions. Some papers focus on constructing a scheme with shorter signature size (less than $O(n)$); some focus on post-quantum security; some focus on security in a strong security model (standard model, plain model, with adversarial keys, anonymity between signers etc.). In this paper, we mainly focus on constructing an efficient scheme in elliptic curve.

Although there are a number of efficient ring signature schemes with $O(\log n)$ size [5,14,17–19,28,31], most threshold ring signature schemes have a large signature size of $O(n \log n)$ [6], $O(n)$ [4,8–10,13,16,20,21,24,27,29,32] or $O(tn)$ [23]. Yuen *et al.* [30] proposed a threshold ring signature with size $O(t\sqrt{n})$, which is sublinear to n. Beside, Munch-Hansen *et al.* [22] proposed a threshold ring signature with size $O(t)$, with anonymity between signers. It is based on RSA accumulator and requires a trusted setup for the RSA modulus. The concrete signature size is much larger than the ECC-based construction because of the use of RSA accumulator and the corresponding NIZK proofs. Haque *et al.* [15] proposed a threshold ring signature in the plain model with anonymity between signers. The signature size is $O(t \cdot \mathsf{polylog}(n))$ by using the general algebraic circuit for the NIWI proof. Pham *et al.* [25] proposed a threshold ring signature based on the OR proof of group action, and instantiated the protocols in both isogeny and lattice settings. Their signature size are both $O(n + t)$.

1.3 Our Contributions

We give a generic construction of threshold ring signature. In the ECC-based setting, it is the first threshold ring signature scheme which is logarithmic to the parameters (t, n). Our concrete construction is also very short in practice ($2 \log n + 1$ elements in $\mathbb{G}$ and 3 elements in $\mathbb{Z}_p$), and it is as short as the shortest ring signature scheme DualRing-EC.

2 Preliminaries

We denote all the available parties as $\mathsf{P} = \{1, 2, \dots\}$, which is scalable to cover all new verification keys. When any new generated key vk wants join P, we could just simply assign a new index $i = |\mathsf{P}| + 1$ for it, and append i to the P. For any $i \in \mathsf{P}$, we always assume that the verification key vk_i could be gotten by all signers and verifiers. Besides, we define the signer set S and the ring party set R, which fulfills the equation $\mathsf{S} \subseteq \mathsf{R} \subseteq \mathsf{P}$.

As the order of the indexes won't affect much, we could just simply assume the signer members $s_i < s_j$ for $i < j$. The same representation applies to the ring set R. Accordingly, we denote the secret keys as $\mathbf{sk_S} = (\mathsf{sk}_{s_1}, \mathsf{sk}_{s_2}, \dots)$, with the verification keys as $\mathbf{vk_R} = (\mathsf{vk}_{r_1}, \mathsf{vk}_{r_2}, \dots)$. To better demonstrate the knowledge argument, we define the Hadamard product $\mathbf{A} \circ \mathbf{B} = \mathbf{C}$ when $\mathbf{C}_{ij} = \mathbf{A}_{ij} * \mathbf{B}_{ij}$.

The space of variable z is written as Δ_z, and the distribution of variable z is written as $\mathcal{D}_z$. Sampling uniformly is denoted as $z \xleftarrow{} \Delta_z$, and sampling from special distribution is denoted as $z \xleftarrow{\$} \mathcal{D}_z$.

2.1 Type-T* Canonical Identification

Type-T canonical identification [28] is a tuple (Setup, KeyGen, Prove$_1$, Challenge, Prove$_2$, Verify). It uses an algorithm A to generate a commitment R, and uses an algorithm Z to generate a response z based on a random challenge c. The security of canonical identification is defined by the special impersonation attack.

Definition 1 (Special impersonation). *A canonical identification is secure against special impersonation under key only attack for any polynomial time adversary $\mathcal{A}$:*

$$\Pr\left[\begin{array}{c|c} \mathsf{Verify}(\mathsf{vk}, z, c) = 1 \wedge & \mathsf{params} \leftarrow \mathsf{Setup}(1^\lambda) \\ \mathsf{Verify}(\mathsf{vk}, z', c') = 1 \wedge & (\mathsf{sk}, \mathsf{vk}) \leftarrow \mathsf{KeyGen}(\mathsf{params}) \\ c, c' \in \Delta_c \wedge c \neq c' & (z, c, z', c') \leftarrow \mathcal{A}(\mathsf{params}, \mathsf{vk}) \end{array}\right] \leq \mathsf{negl}(\lambda)$$

2.2 Non-Malleable Commitment

Non-malleable commitment scheme is a commitment scheme containing the tuple of algorithms $(\mathsf{NCom}, \mathsf{NDecom})$, which requires *hiding* and *binding* properties as the normal commitment scheme plus *non-malleable* property additionally. Denote $\mathcal{D}_c$ as the message space. We use the definition from [12].

- $(C, D) \leftarrow \mathsf{NCom}(m)$ takes a message $m \in \mathcal{D}_c$ as input and outputs the commitment C and the decommitment D.
- $m/\bot \leftarrow \mathsf{NDecom}(C, D)$ outputs the message m if the decommitment D is correct with respect to C and outputs $\bot$ otherwise.

3 Threshold Ring Signature

In this paper, we use a security model that is extended from the ring signature [3]. In particular, we can consider the strong security model of *unforgeability with respect to insider corruption* and *anonymity against full key exposure*.

Definition 2 ((t, n)-Threshold ring signature). *A (t, n)-threshold ring signature scheme is the tuple of algorithms* $\mathsf{TRS} = (\mathsf{TRSetup}, \mathsf{TRKeyGen}, \mathsf{TRSign}, \mathsf{TRVerify})$.

- $\mathsf{params} \leftarrow \mathsf{TRSetup}(1^\lambda)$ *generates parameters as* params.
- $(\mathsf{vk}_i, \mathsf{sk}_i) \leftarrow \mathsf{TRKeyGen}(\mathsf{params})$ *generates key pair containing one verification key* vk_i *and its corresponding secret key* vk_i.
- $\sigma/\bot \leftarrow \mathsf{TRSign}(\mathsf{params}, m, \mathbf{vk_R}, \mathbf{sk_S})$ *let signers S use their secret key $\mathbf{sk_S}$ to jointly sign a message m, where the verification keys are inside $\mathbf{vk_R}$ of ring R (where $\mathsf{S} \subset \mathsf{R}$). It aborts if any dishonest behavior is found.*
- $1/0 \leftarrow \mathsf{TRVerify}(\mathsf{params}, m, \mathbf{vk_R}, t, \sigma)$ *verifies whether the σ is a correct signature on behalf of $\mathbf{vk_R}$ of message m. It outputs 1 if at least t signers are related with the verification keys inside $\mathbf{vk_R}$, and outputs 0 otherwise.*

Definition 3 (Correctness). *A (t, n)-threshold ring signature is correct if for all R of size $n' \leq n$, all S of size $t' \leq t$ with $\mathsf{S} \subset \mathsf{R}$, all messages m, $\mathbf{vk_R} = \{\mathsf{vk}_i\}_{i \in \mathsf{R}}$, $\mathbf{sk_S} = \{\mathsf{sk}_j\}_{j \in \mathsf{S}}$, it holds that:*

$$\Pr\left[\mathsf{TRVerify}(\mathsf{params}, m, \mathbf{vk_R}, t', \sigma) = 1 \,\middle|\, \begin{array}{c} \mathsf{params} \leftarrow \mathsf{TRSetup}(1^\lambda) \wedge \\ (\mathsf{vk}_i, \mathsf{sk}_i) \leftarrow \mathsf{TRKeyGen}(\mathsf{params}) \wedge \\ \sigma \leftarrow \mathsf{TRSign}(\mathsf{params}, m, \mathbf{vk_R}, \mathbf{sk_S}) \end{array}\right] = 1.$$

Similar to [16], we define S as the singer set, R as the current ring, C as the corrupted party set, and P for all available parties set. Sets are empty initially.

- OKGen(i) generates a key pair for party i if $i \notin$ P. Then it stores $(\mathsf{sk}_i, \mathsf{vk}_i) \leftarrow$ TRKeyGen(params), sends vk_i to $\mathcal{A}$, and extends P $\leftarrow$ P $\cup \{i\}$.
- OCorrupt(i) sets C $\leftarrow$ C $\cup \{i\}$ and returns sk_i if $i \notin$ C.
- ORegister(i, vk_i) adds auxiliary string vk_i as a verification key for party i, and puts i into C and P by C $\leftarrow$ C $\cup \{i\}$ and P $\leftarrow$ P $\cup \{i\}$.
- OSign(m, S, R) denotes an interactive signing oracle. It just ignore the query if S $\subseteq$ C. Then $\mathcal{A}$ engages the interactive signing on behalf of S $\cap$ C, and the oracle interacts of S $\setminus$ C and outputs whatever the TRSign required.

Definition 4 (Unforgeability). *The unforgeability with respect to insider corruption for a (t, n)-threshold ring signature is defined by the forge experiment* SigForge$_{\mathcal{A}}(\lambda)$.

- *Query Phase. The challenger runs* params $\leftarrow$ TRSetup(1^λ) *and sends* params *to $\mathcal{A}$.* P $\leftarrow \emptyset$ *and* C $\leftarrow \emptyset$. *$\mathcal{A}$ gets access to the oracles* OKGen, OCorrupt, ORegister, OSign.
- *Challenge Phase. It returns 1 if $\mathcal{A}$ successfully outputs $(m^*, R^*, t^*, \sigma^*)$ with the required conditions, and it returns 0 otherwise. The conditions are*
  1. $R^* \subseteq$ P *and* $t^* \le |R^*| \le n$,
  2. $|R^* \cap C| < t^* \le t$,
  3. (m^*, S', R^*) *is not queried to* OSign *for any set* S' *with size* t^*,
  4. TRVerify(params, $m^*, \mathbf{vk}_{R^*}, t^*, \sigma^*$) = 1.

It holds that $\Pr\left[\mathsf{SigForge}_{\mathcal{A}}^{\mathsf{TRS}}(\lambda) = 1 \right] \le \mathsf{negl}(\lambda)$, *for all probabilistic polynomial time adversary $\mathcal{A}$.*

Remark. Here we define a strong model of unforgeability against malicious parties, by including the ORegister oracle. We can also define the unforgeability against corrupted parties only, by removing the ORegister oracle. This model of unforgeability is used in [15].

Definition 5 (Anonymity). *The anonymity against full key exposure for a (t, n)-threshold ring signature is defined as the experiment* ExpAnon$_{\mathcal{A}}(\lambda)$.

- *Query Phase. The challenger runs* params $\leftarrow$ TRSetup(1^λ) *and sends to $\mathcal{A}$.* P $\leftarrow \emptyset$ *and* C $\leftarrow \emptyset$. *$\mathcal{A}$ get access to the oracles* OKGen, OCorrupt, ORegister, OSign, *where* OCorrupt(i) *additionally returns the randomness in* OKGen(i).
- *Challenge Phase*
  1. *$\mathcal{A}$ picks* S_0^* *and* S_1^* *with constraints* $|S_0^*| = |S_1^*| \le t$ *and* $S_0^* \ne S_1^*$. *$\mathcal{A}$ picks* R^* *with constraints* $|R^*| \le n$ *and* $S_i^* \subset R^*$ *for* $i \in \{0, 1\}$. *$\mathcal{A}$ picks a message* m^*. *Note that the set* R^* *can include adversarially generated public keys.*
  2. *The challenger returns* $\sigma^* \leftarrow$ TRSign(params, $m^*, \mathbf{vk}_{R^*}, \mathbf{sk}_{S_b^*}$) *for a random bit* $b \in \{0, 1\}$.
  3. *$\mathcal{A}$ returns the guess* b'. *It returns 1 when* $b' = b$ *and returns 0 otherwise.*

It holds that $\left| \Pr\left[\mathsf{ExpAnon}_{\mathcal{A}}^{\mathsf{TRS}}(\lambda) = 1 \right] - \frac{1}{2} \right| \le \mathsf{negl}(\lambda)$, *for all probabilistic polynomial time adversary $\mathcal{A}$.*

Evaluate($\mathbf{b}, \mathbf{c} = \{c_i\}_{i \in [n]}, S$)	Check($\mathbf{b}, \mathbf{c} = \{c_i\}_{i \in [n]}$)
1: Denote $\mathbf{b} = (h_1, \ldots, h_t)$	1: Denote $t = |\mathbf{b}|$
2: Solve $\{c_j\}_{j \in S}$ where	2: $h_j = \sum_{i=1}^{n}(c_i \cdot i^{j-1})$ for $j \in [t]$

$$\begin{pmatrix} h_1 \\ \vdots \\ h_t \end{pmatrix} = \begin{pmatrix} 1 & \cdots & 1 \\ 1 & \cdots & n \\ \vdots & \ddots & \vdots \\ 1^{t-1} & \cdots & n^{t-1} \end{pmatrix} \cdot \begin{pmatrix} c_1 \\ \vdots \\ c_n \end{pmatrix}$$

	3: if $\mathbf{b} \neq (h_1, \ldots, h_t)$ then
	4: return 0
	5: fi
3: return $\mathbf{c}' = (c_1, \ldots, c_n)$	6: return 1

Fig. 2. Challenge deriving scheme.

4 Building Block: Challenge Deriving Scheme

As discussed in Sect. 1, one of the key challenge in the paper is to define the relations between t C-rings. We formalize it as a *challenge deriving scheme* in this section. A challenge deriving scheme defined over a finite field $\mathbb{F}$ consists of two algorithms:

- Evaluate($\mathbf{b}, \mathbf{c}, S$): On input a vector $\mathbf{b} \in \mathbb{F}^t$, a vector $\mathbf{c} \in \mathbb{F}^n$ and a set S (where S is the set of t indices indicating all empty elements in $\mathbf{c}$), it returns a vector $\mathbf{c}' \in \mathbb{F}^n$ with no empty element.
- Check($\mathbf{b}, \mathbf{c}$): On input a vector $\mathbf{b} \in \mathbb{F}^t$, a vector $\mathbf{c} \in \mathbb{F}^n$, it returns 1 or 0.

For the challenge deriving scheme, we define *correctness* that for $t < n$, $\mathbf{b} \xleftarrow{\$} \mathbb{F}^t$, $S \subset [n]$, $\mathbf{c} = (c_1, \ldots, c_n)$ with $|S| = t$ and $c_i \xleftarrow{\$} \mathbb{F}$ for $i \in [n] \setminus S$ and $c_j = \emptyset$ for $j \in S$, it always holds Check($\mathbf{b}$, Evaluate($\mathbf{b}, \mathbf{c}, S$)) = 1.

We define *pseudorandomness* that a game such that the challenger picks $\mathbf{c} = (c_1, \ldots, c_n) \xleftarrow{\$} \mathbb{F}^n$, $\mathbf{b} \xleftarrow{\$} \mathbb{F}^t$ and a random set $S \subseteq [n]$ of size t. The challenger updates $c_i = \emptyset$ for all $i \in S$. The challenger returns $\mathbf{b}$ and $\mathbf{c}' \leftarrow$ Evaluate($\mathbf{b}, \mathbf{c}, S$). The adversary outputs a set S'. No polynomial time adversary can output $S = S'$ with non-negligible probability over $1/\binom{n}{t}$.

We define *threshold* that no polynomial time adversary can output $\mathbf{c}_S := \{c_i | i \in S\}$ when given $\mathbf{c}_{[n] \setminus S} := \{c_i | i \in [n] \setminus S\}$ and $\mathbf{b}$, where $|S| < |\mathbf{b}| \leq n$, with non-negligible probability over $1/\mathbb{F}$.

4.1 Our Construction

As introduced in Sect. 1, our construction of challenge deriving scheme is based on Vandermonde matrix. The algorithms are described in Fig. 2.

In order to solve $\{c_i\}_{i \in S}$ such that $\{c_i\}_{i \in S} \cup \{c_i\}_{i \in [n] \setminus S}$ fulfill Evaluate, we write $S = (s_1, s_2, \ldots, s_t)^\top$ where the number of undetermined challenges is t. The solution $\mathbf{c}_S = (c_{s_1}, c_{s_2}, \ldots, c_{s_t})^\top$ fulfills $\mathbf{A}_S \mathbf{c}_S = \mathbf{b}_S$, where

$$\mathbf{A_S} = \begin{pmatrix} 1 & 1 & \cdots & 1 \\ s_1 & s_2 & \cdots & s_t \\ \vdots & \vdots & \ddots & \vdots \\ s_1^{t-1} & s_2^{t-1} & \cdots & s_t^{t-1} \end{pmatrix}, \quad \mathbf{b_S} = \begin{pmatrix} h_1 - \sum_{i \in [n] \backslash \mathsf{S}} i^0 c_i \\ h_2 - \sum_{i \in [n] \backslash \mathsf{S}} i^1 c_i \\ \vdots \\ h_t - \sum_{i \in [n] \backslash \mathsf{S}} i^{t-1} c_i \end{pmatrix}.$$

$\mathbf{A_S}$ is a Vandermonde matrix. Hence we can obtain $\mathbf{c_S} = \mathbf{A_S}^{-1} \cdot \mathbf{b_S}$.

Lemma 1. *There is exactly one solution $\mathbf{c_S} = (c_{s_1}, c_{s_2}, \ldots, c_{s_t})$ of the equations for a fixed $\mathbf{b}$, and the solution is uniformly distributed over $\mathbb{F}^t$ when $\mathbf{b}$ is uniformly distributed.*

Apparently, $\mathbf{A_S}$ is a Vandermonde matrix with $\forall i \neq j, s_i \neq s_j$ and it is accordingly full-rank, which guarantees the equations have exactly one solution. Thus, it is easy to see the lemma holds. Furthermore, our challenge deriving scheme has correctness and pseudorandomness following the lemma above.

Lemma 2. *The Vandermonde supports threshold property computationally.*

Proof. When $|\mathsf{S}| = \hat{t}$ while there are t equations to fulfill, we show that it is negligible that there is a solution.

Without loss of generality, we can suppose $\hat{t} = t - 1$. Accordingly the formula turns to be $\mathbf{A} \in \mathbb{F}^{t \times (t-1)}$ and $b \in \mathbb{F}^t$ with $\mathbf{A}x = \mathbf{b}$. It has solution iff $\mathsf{Rank}(\mathbf{A}) = \mathsf{Rank}(\mathbf{A}|\mathbf{b})$ from Rouché-Capelli Theorem. And the probability that there is a solution, i.e. the random vector fall into the subspace, is $1/|\mathbb{F}|$. $\qquad \square$

5   General Construction of Threshold Ring Signature

Building on the top of Type-T^* canonical identification scheme T^*, we requires a zero-knowledge proof for the secret key sk in T^*. We denote the language

$$\mathcal{L}_{\mathsf{sk}} = \{\mathsf{sk} : (\mathsf{vk}, \mathsf{sk}) \in \mathsf{T}^*.\mathsf{KeyGen}(\mathsf{params})\}.$$

We denote $(\mathsf{ZKSetup}, \mathsf{ZKProof}, \mathsf{ZKVerify})$ as the non-interactive zero-knowledge proof for the language $\mathcal{L}_{\mathsf{sk}}$. We present the threshold ring signature scheme $\mathsf{TRS} = (\mathsf{TRSetup}, \mathsf{TRKeyGen}, \mathsf{TRSign}, \mathsf{TRVerify})$ in Fig. 3.

Theorem 1. *The threshold ring signature TRS is unforgeable with respect to insider corruption in the random oracle model if the Type-T^* canonical identification scheme T^* has special impersonation and the zero-knowledge proof has statistical witness-extended emulation.*

Proof. We now reduce the special impersonation of the underlying Type-T^* scheme to the unforgeability of TRS. For breaking the special impersonation of T^* with instance $(\mathsf{params}^*, \hat{\mathsf{vk}})$, the simulator $\mathcal{B}$ runs as follows.

– The simulator $\mathcal{B}$ runs $\mathsf{crs} \leftarrow \mathsf{ZKSetup}(1^\lambda)$ and returns $\mathsf{params} = (\mathsf{H}, \mathsf{params}^*, \mathsf{crs})$ to the adversary $\mathcal{A}$. $\mathcal{B}$ picks a random index $\tau \in [q_k]$, where q_k is the number of oracle queries to OKGen.

TRSetup(1^λ)

1 : pick $H : \{0,1\}^* \to \Delta_c$

2 : $\mathsf{params}^* \leftarrow T^*.\mathsf{Setup}(1^\lambda)$

3 : $\mathsf{crs} \leftarrow \mathsf{ZKSetup}(1^\lambda)$

4 : **return** $\mathsf{params} \leftarrow (H, \mathsf{params}^*, \mathsf{crs})$

TRSign($\mathsf{params}, m, \mathbf{vk_R}, S, \mathsf{sk_S}$)

1 : Denote $\mathbf{vk_R} = \{(\mathsf{vk}_i', \pi_i)\}_{i \in R}$

2 : $(r_s, R, \{R_i\}_{i \in S}, \mathbf{c}) \leftarrow$
   $\mathsf{TRChallenge}(\mathsf{params}, m, \mathbf{vk_R}, S, \mathsf{sk_S})$

3 : $z_s = Z(\mathsf{sk}_s, c_s, r_s)$

4 : broadcast z_s

5 : **for** $i \in S$

6 :   **if** $V_1(z_i) \odot V_2(\mathsf{vk}_i, c_i) \neq R_i$ **then**

7 :   **return** fail

8 :   **fi**

9 : **endfor**

10 : $z = \bigoplus_{i \in S} z_i$

11 : **return** $\sigma = (z, \mathbf{c})$.

TRVerify($\mathsf{params}, m, \mathbf{vk_R}, t, \sigma$)

1 : Denote $\mathbf{vk_R} = \{(\mathsf{vk}_i', \pi_i)\}_{i \in R}$

2 : $R' \leftarrow V_1(z) \odot \bigodot_{i \in R} V_2(\mathsf{vk}_i', c_i)$

3 : $b' = H(R', \mathbf{vk_R}, t, m)$

4 : **if** $\mathsf{ZKVerify}(\mathsf{crs}, \mathsf{vk}_i', \pi_i) \neq 1 \exists i \in R$ or
   $\mathsf{Check}(\mathbf{b}', \mathbf{c}) \neq 1$ **then**

5 :   **return** 0

6 : **fi**

7 : auxiliary check $(R', \mathbf{c}, z)$

8 : **return** 1

TRKeyGen(params)

1 : $(\mathsf{vk}', \mathsf{sk}) \leftarrow T^*.\mathsf{KeyGen}(\mathsf{params}^*)$

2 : $\pi \leftarrow \mathsf{ZKProof}(\mathsf{crs}, \mathsf{vk}, \mathsf{sk})$

3 : **return** $(\mathsf{vk} = (\mathsf{vk}', \pi), \mathsf{sk})$

TRChallenge($\mathsf{params}, m, \mathbf{vk_R}, S, \mathsf{sk_S}$)

1 : $r_s \xleftarrow{\$} \Delta_r, R_s \leftarrow A(\mathsf{sk}_s, r_s)$

2 : $(\Gamma_s, \gamma_s) \leftarrow \mathsf{NCom}(R_s)$

3 : $\alpha_s \xleftarrow{\$} \Delta_h, (\Theta_s, \theta_s) \leftarrow \mathsf{NCom}(\alpha_s)$

4 : broadcast commitments Γ_s, Θ_s to all S

5 : after receiving commitments from S,
   broadcast $R_s, \gamma_s, \alpha_s, \theta_s$ to all S

6 : **for** $i \in S$

7 :   **if** $\mathsf{NDecom}(\Gamma_j, R_j, \gamma_j) \neq 1$ or
     $\mathsf{NDecom}(\Theta_i, \alpha_i, \theta_i) \neq 1$ **then**

8 :   **return fail**

9 :   **fi**

10 : **endfor**

11 : $c_i \leftarrow H(\sum_{j \in S} \alpha_j, i)$ for $i \in R \setminus S$

12 : $c_j \leftarrow \emptyset$ for $j \in S$

13 : $\mathbf{c} = (c_1, \ldots, c_n)$

14 : $R \leftarrow \bigodot_{i \in S} R_i \odot \bigodot_{i \in R \setminus S} V_2(\mathsf{vk}_i', c_i)$

15 : $t = |S|, \mathbf{b} = H(R, \mathbf{vk_R}, t, m)$

16 : $\mathbf{c} \leftarrow \mathsf{Evaluate}(\mathbf{b}, \mathbf{c})$

17 : **if** $c_i = 0$ for some $i \in R$ **then**

18 :   **return**
     $\mathsf{TRChallenge}(\mathsf{params}, m, \mathbf{vk}, S, \mathsf{sk_S})$

19 : **fi**

20 : **return** $(r_s, R, \{R_i\}_{i \in S}, \mathbf{c})$

Fig. 3. Threshold DualRing scheme with real signers $S \subset R$.

– Oracle simulation.
  • $\mathsf{OKGen}(i)$ returns $\mathsf{vk}_i = (\mathsf{vk}_i', \pi_i)$, where $(\mathsf{vk}_i, \mathsf{sk}_i) \leftarrow \mathsf{KeyGen}(\mathsf{params})$ and
    $\pi_i \leftarrow \mathsf{ZKProof}(\mathsf{crs}, \mathsf{vk}_i', \mathsf{sk}_i)$. Except for $i = \tau$, $\mathcal{B}$ uses the simulator of the
    ZK proof for $\hat{\mathsf{vk}}$ to generate π_τ. $\mathcal{B}$ returns $(\hat{\mathsf{vk}}, \pi_\tau)$.
  • $\mathsf{OCorrupt}(i)$ returns sk_i if $i \neq \tau$, and declares failure otherwise.
  • $\mathsf{ORegister}(i, \mathsf{vk}_i)$ puts i into C and P with vk_i.
  • $\mathsf{OSign}(m, S, R)$ operates like a normal TRSign protocol if $\tau \notin S$. Otherwise,
    we denote $S = \{s_1, s_2, \ldots, s_{t'}\}$, $R = \{r_1, r_2, \ldots, r_{n'}\}$ and $S' = S \setminus C$ as the
    set of uncorrupted users in S. The simulator $\mathcal{B}$ only needs to run OSign
    for users in S'.

1. The simulator $\mathcal{B}$ picks $r_j \leftarrow \Delta_r$ and computes $R_j \leftarrow A(\mathsf{sk}_j, r_j)$ for $j \in \mathsf{S}' \wedge j \neq \tau$. For index τ, $\mathcal{B}$ samples a random value for $c_\tau \xleftarrow{\$} \Delta_c$ and $z_\tau \xleftarrow{\$} \mathcal{D}_z$. It then set $R_\tau \leftarrow \mathsf{V}_1(z_\tau) \odot \mathsf{V}_2(\mathsf{vk}'_\tau, c_\tau)$.

2. $\mathcal{B}$ picks $c_{i,j}$ for $j \in \mathsf{S}'$ and $i \in \mathsf{R} \setminus \mathsf{S}$. $\mathcal{B}$ runs $(\Gamma_j, \gamma_j) \leftarrow \mathsf{NCom}(R_j)$ and $(\Delta_{i,j}, \delta_{i,j}) \leftarrow \mathsf{NCom}(c_{i,j})$. $\mathcal{B}$ broadcasts Γ_j and $\Delta_{i,j}$.

3. All parties open the commitments by (γ_j, R_j) and $(\delta_{i,j}, c_{i,j})$. As the commitment scheme is non-malleable, we can argue that R and c_i where $i \in \mathsf{R} \setminus \mathsf{S}$ distribute uniformly.

4. $\mathcal{B}$ samples $c_i \xleftarrow{\$} \Delta_c$ for $i \in \mathsf{S}' \setminus \{\tau\}$ and calculates h_j by line 2 of Check. $\mathcal{B}$ sets the hash function $\{h_j\}_{j \in [t']} = \mathsf{H}(R, \mathsf{vk}_\mathsf{R}, t', m)$ such that the challenge for index τ is c_τ. $\mathcal{B}$ returns failure if such values have been assigned.

5. The remaining TRSign protocol keeps the same as the original one, except that $\mathcal{B}$ directly broadcasts z_τ for index τ.

– Challenge phase.

1. $\mathcal{A}$ returns a forgery $(\bar{m}, \bar{\mathsf{R}}, \bar{t}, \bar{\sigma} = (\bar{z}, \bar{\mathbf{c}}_{\bar{\mathsf{R}}}))$. If $\tau \notin \bar{\mathsf{R}}$, $\mathcal{B}$ returns failure. The signature tuple is expected to fulfill $R = \mathsf{V}_1(\bar{z}) \odot \bigodot_{r \in \bar{\mathsf{R}}} \mathsf{V}_2(\mathsf{vk}_r, \bar{c}_r)$, $\bar{\mathbf{b}} = \mathsf{H}(R, \mathsf{vk}_{\bar{\mathsf{R}}}, \bar{t}, \bar{m})$, $\mathsf{Check}(\bar{\mathbf{b}}, \bar{\mathbf{c}}_{\bar{\mathsf{R}}}) = 1$ and all verification keys in $\mathsf{vk}_{\bar{\mathsf{R}}}$ contains a valid ZK proof. From the ZK proofs in $\mathsf{vk}_{\bar{\mathsf{R}}}$, $\mathcal{B}$ can use the extractor to obtain all sk_i for $i \in \bar{\mathsf{R}} \setminus \{\tau\}$. By the property of the Type-T^* canonical identification, $\mathcal{B}$ could compute $\bar{z}_i = \mathcal{T}(\mathsf{sk}_i, \bar{c}_i)$ and $\bar{z}_\tau \leftarrow \bar{z} \oplus \bigoplus_{i \in \bar{\mathsf{R}} \setminus \{\tau\}} \bar{z}_i$. Note that:

$$
\begin{aligned}
R &= \mathsf{V}_1(\bar{z}) \odot \bigodot_{r \in \bar{\mathsf{R}}} \mathsf{V}_2(\mathsf{vk}_r, \bar{c}_r) \\
&= \mathsf{V}_1(\bar{z}) \odot \bigodot_{r \in \bar{\mathsf{R}} \setminus \{\tau\}} \mathsf{V}_1(\mathcal{T}(\mathsf{sk}_r, \bar{c}_r)) \odot \mathsf{V}_2(\mathsf{vk}_\tau, \bar{c}_\tau) \\
&= \mathsf{V}_1(\bar{z}) \odot \bigodot_{r \in \bar{\mathsf{R}} \setminus \{\tau\}} \mathsf{V}_1(\bar{z}_r) \odot \mathsf{V}_2(\mathsf{vk}_\tau, \bar{c}_\tau) \\
&= \mathsf{V}_1(\bar{z}_\tau) \odot \mathsf{V}_2(\mathsf{vk}_\tau, \bar{c}_\tau).
\end{aligned}
$$

2. $\mathcal{B}$ rewinds the $\mathcal{A}$ back to the point $\mathsf{H}(R, \mathsf{vk}_{\bar{\mathsf{R}}}, \bar{t}, \bar{m})$ was asked and returns a different $\bar{\mathbf{b}}^*$. We get another success forgery $\bar{\sigma}^* = (\bar{z}^*, \bar{\mathbf{c}}_{\bar{\mathsf{R}}}^*)$ with overwhelming probability. Similarly, we got another $(\bar{z}_\tau^*, \bar{c}_\tau^*)$ such that $R = \mathsf{V}_1(\bar{z}_\tau^*) \odot \mathsf{V}_2(\mathsf{vk}_\tau, \bar{c}_\tau^*)$.

3. If $\bar{c}_\tau^* \neq \bar{c}_\tau$, then $(\bar{z}_\tau, \bar{c}_\tau, \bar{z}_\tau^*, \bar{c}_\tau^*)$ is a valid attack to the special impersonation of T^*. If $\bar{c}_\tau^* = \bar{c}_\tau$, $\mathcal{B}$ returns failure.

Since the output of H are different after rewinding, there is at least one $h_j \in \bar{\mathbf{b}}$ is different after rewinding. We argue that at least one $\bar{c}_i$ is different from $\bar{c}_i^*$ for $i \in \bar{\mathsf{R}} \setminus \mathsf{C}$. As there are $\bar{t}$ equations and $|\bar{\mathsf{R}} \cap \mathsf{C}| \leq \bar{t} - 1$, $\mathcal{A}$ cannot simply use $\bar{t} - 1$ variables to satisfy $\bar{t}$ equations. Hence there is at least one unfixed variable $\bar{c}_i$ for some $i \in \bar{\mathsf{R}} \setminus \mathsf{C}$. If $i = \tau$, then $\mathcal{B}$ returns a valid attack to the special impersonation. It happens with probability at least $1/(|\bar{\mathsf{R}}| - (\bar{t} - 1)) \geq 1/n$, since $|\bar{\mathsf{R}}| \leq n$ and $\bar{t} \geq 1$.

Remark. We can also consider a weaker model of unforgeability with respect to insider corruption and *honest keys*, which is the common unforgeability model for ring signatures (i.e., all vks in the challenge set are honestly generated). If we adopt this model, we can remove all ZK proofs with respect to the secret keys.

Probability Analysis. By denoting the times of the OCorrupt being queried as q_c, the OKGen as q_k. The success probability for the corruption queries in the query phase is $(1 - \frac{1}{q_k})(1 - \frac{1}{q_k-1}) \dots (1 - \frac{1}{q_k-q_c+1}) = 1 - \frac{q_c}{q_k}$. Besides, the success probability of the signing oracle would be at least $(1 - \frac{q_H}{|\Delta_c|^t})(1 - \frac{q_H+1}{|\Delta_c|^t})(1 - \frac{q_H+2}{|\Delta_c|^t}) \dots \geq 1 - \frac{q_s(q_s+q_H-1)}{|\Delta_c|^t}$. By accumulating all the above probability together, we get a success probability before rewinding as

$$\epsilon = \epsilon_{\mathcal{A}}(1 - \frac{q_c}{q_k})(1 - \frac{q_s(q_s + q_H - 1)}{|\Delta_c|^t})(\frac{1}{q_k - q_c}) = \frac{\epsilon_{\mathcal{A}}}{q_k}(1 - \frac{q_s(q_s + q_H - 1)}{|\Delta_c|^t})$$

When we consider the generalized forking lemma in [1] and suppose $|\Delta_c|^t \geq 8q_h\epsilon$, the probability the rewinding would success in $\epsilon/8$. The final success probability would be at least $\frac{\epsilon_{\mathcal{A}}}{8nq_k}(1 - \frac{q_s(q_s+q_H-1)}{|\Delta_c|^t})$. □

Theorem 2. *The threshold ring signature* TRS *is anonymous in ROM.*

Proof. The query phase works indeed the same as the normal TRS protocol. For the challenge phase, the algorithm $\mathcal{B}$ picks random $c_i \xleftarrow{\$} \Delta_c$ for $i \in R$ and $z \xleftarrow{\$} \mathcal{D}_z$. Then $\mathcal{B}$ computes $R = V_1(z) \odot \bigodot_{i \in R} V_2(\text{vk}_i, c_i)$. The hash function outputs could be set accordingly as $\mathbf{A}_R c_R$. The simulation is correctly distributed by the pseudorandomness property of the challenge deriving scheme. Because the simulation uses no information about S, the $\mathcal{A}$ wins only at probability $\frac{1}{2}$. □

6   ECC-Based Construction

6.1   Matrix Multiplication Argument

To construct our logarithmic size threshold ring signature, we propose a new argument of knowledge named *Matrix Multiplication Argument.*

One-Sided Inner Product Argument. To construct a Matrix Multiplication Argument, we first give a simple protocol for *One-sided Inner Product Argument*, defined by the following relation:

$$\left\{ (\mathbf{g} \in \mathbb{G}^n, P \in \mathbb{G}, h \in \mathbb{Z}_p, \mathbf{b} \in \mathbb{Z}_p^n; \mathbf{a} \in \mathbb{Z}_p^n) : P = \mathbf{g}^{\mathbf{a}} \wedge h = \langle \mathbf{b}, \mathbf{a} \rangle \right\}. \tag{2}$$

Our NI-OIPA is given in Algorithm 4.

Theorem 3. *Our one-sided inner product argument fulfills statistical witness-extended emulation for DL relation among* $\mathbf{g}, u$ *or a valid witness* $\mathbf{a}$.

$\mathsf{NIOProve}(\{param, \mathbf{g}, P, h, \mathbf{b}\}, \mathbf{a})$

1 : **return** $\mathsf{NIOPf}(\mathbf{g}, u^{H'_Z(P,u,h,\mathbf{b})}, \mathbf{a}, \mathbf{b})$

$\mathsf{NIOPf}(\mathbf{g}, \hat{u}, \mathbf{a}, \mathbf{b})$

1 : **if** $n = 1$ **then**

2 :   **return** $(\mathbf{L}, \mathbf{R}, a, b)$

3 : **fi**

4 : $n' \leftarrow \dfrac{n}{2}$

5 : $c_L \leftarrow \langle \mathbf{a}_{[:n']}, \mathbf{b}_{[n':]} \rangle, c_R = \langle \mathbf{a}_{[n':]}, \mathbf{b}_{[:n']} \rangle$

6 : $L = \mathbf{g}_{[n':]}^{\mathbf{a}_{[:n']}} \hat{u}^{c_L} \in \mathbb{G}, R = \mathbf{g}_{[:n']}^{\mathbf{a}_{[n':]}} \hat{u}^{c_R} \in \mathbb{G}$

7 : $\mathbf{g}' = \mathbf{g}_{[:n']}^{x^{-1}} \circ \mathbf{g}_{[n':]}^{x} \in \mathbb{G}^{n'}$

8 : $\mathbf{b}' = x^{-1} \cdot \mathbf{b}_{[:n']} + x \cdot \mathbf{b}_{[n':]} \in \mathbb{Z}_p^{n'}$

9 : $(\mathbf{L}', \mathbf{R}', \tilde{a}, \tilde{b}) \leftarrow \mathsf{NIOPf}(\mathbf{g}', \hat{u}, \mathbf{a}', \mathbf{b}')$

10 : $\mathbf{L}' \leftarrow (\mathbf{L}, L), \mathbf{R}' \leftarrow (\mathbf{R}, R)$

11 : **return** $(\mathbf{L}', \mathbf{R}', \tilde{a}, \tilde{b})$

$\mathsf{NIOVerify}(param, \mathbf{g}, P, h, \mathbf{b}, \pi = (\mathbf{L}, \mathbf{R}, a, b))$

1 : $P' = P \cdot u^{h \cdot H'_Z(P,u,c,\mathbf{b})}$

2 : $x_j \leftarrow H_Z(L_j, R_j)$ for $j \in [\log_2 n]$

3 : $y_i \leftarrow \displaystyle\prod_{j \in [\log_2 n]} x_j^{f(i,j)}$ for $i \in [n]$

4 : $\mathbf{y} = (y_1, \ldots, y_n), \mathbf{x} = (x_1, \ldots, x_{\log_2 n})$

   where $f(i,j)$ is the j-th bit of $i - 1$

5 : **if** $\mathbf{L}^{\mathbf{x}^2} P' \mathbf{R}^{\mathbf{x}^{-2}} \neq \mathbf{g}^{a \cdot \mathbf{y}} u^{ab \cdot H'_Z(P,u,c)}$ **then**

6 :   **return** 0

7 : **fi**

8 : **if** $\langle \mathbf{b}, \mathbf{y} \rangle \neq b$

9 :   **return** 0

10 : **fi**

11 : **return** 1

Fig. 4. NI-OIPA protocol.

Proof. The proof consists of two parts: one for interactive NIOProve and one for interactive NIOPf and NIOVerify, of which the challenges are selected by the verifier instead of the random oracle.

For the second part, the proof is the same as the proof in [28] because we share the same algorithm. We repeat the proof here for completeness. We prove that there is an efficient extractor $\mathcal{X}$ which uses n^2 transcripts. The argument is trivially sound if $n = 1$ since the witness a is given to the verifier $\mathcal{V}$. Considering each iteration with input $(\mathbf{g}, u, P, \mathbf{b})$ there is an extractor that can easily extract a witness $\mathbf{a}$ or a non-trivial discrete logarithm relation between $\mathbf{g}, u$ from the prover. It has access to the prover to get L and R and can obtain four vectors $\mathbf{a}_i' \in \mathbb{Z}_p^{n'}$ after rewinding the prover three times with three challenges $\{x_i\}_{i \in [3]}$ such that $\{|x_i| \neq |x_j|\}_{1 \leq i < j \leq 3}$. Recall that

$$L^{x_i^2} P R^{x_i^{-2}} = \left(\mathbf{g}_{[:n']}^{x_i^{-1}} \circ \mathbf{g}_{[n':]}^{x_i} \right)^{\mathbf{a}_i'} u^{\langle \mathbf{a}_i', \mathbf{b}_i' \rangle}, i \in [3]. \tag{3}$$

Then we set $\{v_{j,i}\}_{j \in [3], i \in [3]}$ such that

$$
\begin{cases}
\sum_i v_{1,i} x_i^2 = 1 \\
\sum_i v_{1,i} = 0 \\
\sum_i v_{1,i} x_i^{-2} = 0
\end{cases}
\quad
\begin{cases}
\sum_i v_{2,i} x_i^2 = 0 \\
\sum_i v_{2,i} = 1 \\
\sum_i v_{2,i} x_i^{-2} = 0
\end{cases}
\quad
\begin{cases}
\sum_i v_{3,i} x_i^2 = 0 \\
\sum_i v_{3,i} = 0 \\
\sum_i v_{3,i} x_i^{-2} = 1
\end{cases}
$$

We raise the three equalities of (3) to powers $\{v_{1,i}\}_{i\in[3]}$ such that

$$\prod_i \left(L^{x_i^2} P R^{x_i^{-2}}\right)^{v_{1,i}} = \prod_i \left(\left(\mathbf{g}_{[:n']}^{x_i^{-1}} \circ \mathbf{g}_{[n':]}^{x_i}\right)^{\mathbf{a}'_i} u^{\langle \mathbf{a}'_i, \mathbf{b}'_i\rangle}\right)^{v_{1,i}}$$

$$L^{\sum_i v_{1,i} x_i^2} P^{\sum_i v_{1,i}} R^{\sum_i v_{1,i} x_i^{-2}} = \prod_i \left(\mathbf{g}_{[:n']}^{x_i^{-1}\mathbf{a}'_i} \mathbf{g}_{[n':]}^{x_i \mathbf{a}'_i} u^{\langle \mathbf{a}'_i, \mathbf{b}'_i\rangle}\right)^{v_{1,i}}$$

$$L = \mathbf{g}_{[:n']}^{\sum_i v_{1,i} x_i^{-1}\mathbf{a}'_i} \mathbf{g}_{[n':]}^{\sum_i v_{1,i} x_i \mathbf{a}'_i} u^{\sum_i v_{1,i}\langle \mathbf{a}'_i, \mathbf{b}'_i\rangle}.$$

We denote $L = \mathbf{g}^{\mathbf{a}_L} u^{c_L}$ for some $\mathbf{a}_L \in \mathbb{Z}_p^n, c_L \in \mathbb{Z}_p$, such that

$$\mathbf{a}_L = \left(\sum_i v_{1,i} x_i^{-1}\mathbf{a}'_i, \sum_i v_{1,i} x_i \mathbf{a}'_i\right), \quad c_L = \sum_i v_{1,i}\langle \mathbf{a}'_i, \mathbf{b}'_i\rangle.$$

Similarly, we can denote $P = \mathbf{g}^{\mathbf{a}_P} u^{c_P}$ and $R = \mathbf{g}^{\mathbf{a}_R} u^{c_R}$ for some $\mathbf{a}_P \in \mathbb{Z}_p^n, c_P \in \mathbb{Z}_p, \mathbf{a}_R \in \mathbb{Z}_p^n, c_R \in \mathbb{Z}_p$, such that

$$\mathbf{a}_P = \left(\sum_i v_{2,i} x_i^{-1}\mathbf{a}'_i, \sum_i v_{2,i} x_i \mathbf{a}'_i\right), \quad c_P = \sum_i v_{2,i}\langle \mathbf{a}'_i, \mathbf{b}'_i\rangle,$$

$$\mathbf{a}_R = \left(\sum_i v_{3,i} x_i^{-1}\mathbf{a}'_i, \sum_i v_{3,i} x_i \mathbf{a}'_i\right), \quad c_R = \sum_i v_{3,i}\langle \mathbf{a}'_i, \mathbf{b}'_i\rangle.$$

We note that (3) can be described as follows:

$$L^{x_i^2} P R^{x_i^{-2}} = \mathbf{g}_{[:n']}^{x_i^{-1}\mathbf{a}'_i} \mathbf{g}_{[n':]}^{x_i \mathbf{a}'_i} u^{\langle \mathbf{a}'_i, \mathbf{b}'_i\rangle}, i \in [3].$$

By putting back the definition of $L = \mathbf{g}^{\mathbf{a}_L} u^{c_L}$, $R = \mathbf{g}^{\mathbf{a}_R} u^{c_R}$ and $P = \mathbf{g}^{\mathbf{a}_P} u^{c_P}$, we also have:

$$L^{x_i^2} P R^{x_i^{-2}} = \mathbf{g}^{x_i^2 \mathbf{a}_L + \mathbf{a}_P + x_i^{-2}\mathbf{a}_R} u^{x_i^2 c_L + c_P + x_i^{-2} c_R}, i \in [3].$$

It implies for $i \in [3]$,

$$x_i^{-1}\mathbf{a}'_i = x_i^2 \mathbf{a}_{L,[:n']} + \mathbf{a}_{P,[:n']} + x_i^{-2}\mathbf{a}_{R,[:n']},$$
$$x_i \mathbf{a}'_i = x_i^2 \mathbf{a}_{L,[n':]} + \mathbf{a}_{P,[n':]} + x_i^{-2}\mathbf{a}_{R,[n':]},$$
$$\langle \mathbf{a}'_i, \mathbf{b}'_i\rangle = x_i^2 c_L + c_P + x_i^{-2} c_R. \tag{4}$$

Here we can get a non-trivial DL relation among $\mathbf{g}, u$ if any of these equations are not equal. Otherwise we have $\mathbf{a}'_i = x_i^3 \mathbf{a}_{L,[:n']} + x_i \mathbf{a}_{P,[:n']} + x_i^{-1}\mathbf{a}_{R,[:n']}$ and $\mathbf{a}'_i = x_i \mathbf{a}_{L,[n':]} + x_i^{-1}\mathbf{a}_{P,[n':]} + x_i^{-3}\mathbf{a}_{R,[n':]}$. Combining the two equations, we have

$$0 = x_i^3 \mathbf{a}_{L,[:n']} + x_i(\mathbf{a}_{P,[:n']} - \mathbf{a}_{L,[n':]}) + x_i^{-1}(\mathbf{a}_{R,[:n']} - \mathbf{a}_{P,[n':]}) - x_i^{-3}\mathbf{a}_{R,[n':]}, i \in [3].$$

Since the above holds for all x_i, it is easy to see $\mathbf{a}_{L,[:n']} = 0$, $\mathbf{a}_{R,[n':]} = 0$, $\mathbf{a}_{P,[:n']} = \mathbf{a}_{L,[n':]}$, and $\mathbf{a}_{R,[:n']} = \mathbf{a}_{P,[n':]}$. Subsequently, we have $\mathbf{a}'_i = x_i \mathbf{a}_{P,[:n']} + x_i^{-1}\mathbf{a}_{P,[n':]}, i \in [3]$. Then we compute an inner product

$$\langle \mathbf{a}'_i, \mathbf{b}'_i\rangle = \langle x_i \mathbf{a}_{P,[:n']} + x_i^{-1}\mathbf{a}_{P,[n':]}, x_i^{-1}\mathbf{b}_{[:n']} + x_i \mathbf{b}_{[n':]}\rangle$$
$$= \langle \mathbf{a}_P, \mathbf{b}\rangle + x_i^2\langle \mathbf{a}_{P,[:n']}, \mathbf{b}_{[n':]}\rangle + x_i^{-2}\langle \mathbf{a}_{P,[n':]}, \mathbf{b}_{[:n']}\rangle, \quad i \in [3]$$

where the vector $\mathbf{b}$ is public. Recall from Eq. (4) that

$$\langle \mathbf{a}'_i, \mathbf{b}'_i \rangle = x_i^2 c_L + c_P + x_i^{-2} c_R, \quad i \in [3].$$

The above holds for all x_i. Thus we can conclude that the extractor $\mathcal{X}$ extracts either a DL relation among $\mathbf{g}, u$ or a witness $\mathbf{a}_P$ such that $\langle \mathbf{a}_P, \mathbf{b} \rangle = c_P$.

For interactive NIOProve, we construct an extractor $\mathcal{X}_s$ which receives two witness $\mathbf{a}_1, \mathbf{a}_2$ using the extractor $\mathcal{X}$ twice with different challenges x_1, x_2. Thus we can compute:

$$u^{(x_1 - x_2)c} = \mathbf{g}^{\mathbf{a}_1 - \mathbf{a}_2} u^{x_1 \langle \mathbf{a}_1, \mathbf{b} \rangle - x_2 \langle \mathbf{a}_2, \mathbf{b} \rangle}.$$

Assuming we cannot find non-trivial DL relation among $\mathbf{g}, u$, we get $c = \langle \mathbf{a}_1, \mathbf{b} \rangle$ since $\mathbf{a}_1 = \mathbf{a}_2$. As a result, we conclude that our protocol has statistical witness-extended emulation. $\square$

Our protocol is as compact as the sum argument in [28]. In each iteration, we compute $(4n' + 2)$ exponentiations to generate a proof, then compute a multi-exponentiation of size $(1 + n + 2 \log_2(n))$ to verify. For an inner product argument [7], the corresponding computations are $(8n' + 8)$ exponentiations and a multi-exponentiation of size $(1 + 2n + 2 \log_2(n))$, respectively. The proof sizes are similar; however we omit almost half of exponentiations in [7].

Non-Interactive Matrix Multiplication Argument. Next, we extend the NI-OIPA into a Non-Interactive Matrix Multiplication Argument (NI-MMA) for the following relation.

$$(\mathbf{v} \in \mathbb{G}^n, V \in \mathbb{G}, \mathbf{c} \in \mathbb{Z}_p^t, \mathbf{B} \in \mathbb{Z}_p^{t \times n}; \mathbf{a} \in \mathbb{Z}_p^n) : V = \mathbf{v}^{\mathbf{a}} \wedge \mathbf{c}^\top = \mathbf{B} \cdot \mathbf{a}^\top \quad (5)$$

We first define $\mathbf{c} := [h_1, h_2, \ldots, h_t]$ and $\mathbf{B} := [\mathbf{b}_1, \mathbf{b}_2, \ldots, \mathbf{b}_t]^\top$. Then we can use multiple instance of NI-OIPA to show the relation $\mathbf{c}^\top = \mathbf{B} \cdot \mathbf{a}^\top$ since $h_i = \langle \mathbf{b}_i, \mathbf{a} \rangle$ for $i \in [t]$. Later, in order to combine these t equations by using a random challenge z, the prover shows that:

$$\langle \mathbf{a}, (\mathbf{b}_1 + z \cdot \mathbf{b}_2 + z^2 \cdot \mathbf{b}_3 + \ldots + z^{t-1} \cdot \mathbf{b}_t) \rangle = \sum_{i=1}^{t} z^{i-1} h_i.$$

We thus reduced the problem of proving that $\mathbf{c}^\top = \mathbf{B} \cdot \mathbf{a}^\top$ holds to proving a single NI-OIPA.

Next, we consider the relation $V = \mathbf{v}^{\mathbf{a}}$, where $\mathbf{v} = (v_1, \ldots, v_n)$. Here we do not assume the secrecy of the pairwise discrete logarithm between elements in $\mathbf{v}$. This requirement is needed for threshold ring signature but not needed for classical ring signature with $t = 1$ (to be discussed in Sect. 6.2). We solve this problem by converting the basis of the argument of knowledge.

Suppose that we have $\mathbf{f} = (f_1, \ldots, f_n)$ computed from the hash $\tilde{H}_0(\mathbf{v}, V)$, and define $F := \mathbf{f}^{\mathbf{a}}$. For a challenge $y = \tilde{H}_1(\mathbf{v}, V, F)$, we can set $g_i := v_i^y \cdot f_i$ and $\mathbf{g} = (g_1, \ldots, g_n)$. We define $P := V^y \cdot F = \mathbf{v}^{\mathbf{a}y} \cdot \mathbf{f}^{\mathbf{a}} = \mathbf{g}^{\mathbf{a}}$.

Lemma 3. *If there exists an adversary who can output the discrete logarithm between (g_1, g_2), then we can solve the discrete logarithm problem in $\mathbb{G}$ in the random oracle model.*

By the above lemma, we can see that the pairwise discrete logarithm between any two elements in $\mathbf{g}$ is not known. Hence, we can set $\mathbf{g}$ and P as the input to the NI-OIPA to show that relation Eq. 5 holds.

NI-MMA Protocol. Suppose that $\tilde{H}_0 : \mathbb{G} \to \mathbb{G}^n$, $\tilde{H}_1 : \{0,1\}^* \to \mathbb{Z}_p$ and $\tilde{H}_2 : \{0,1\}^* \to \mathbb{Z}_p$ are collision resistant hash function in param. The protocol is as follows.

- NI-MMA.PROVE($\{\text{param}, \mathbf{v}, V, \mathbf{c}, \mathbf{B}\}, \mathbf{a}$). The prover computes the points $\mathbf{f} = \tilde{H}_0(\mathbf{v}, V)$, $F = \mathbf{f}^{\mathbf{a}}$, $y = \tilde{H}_1(\mathbf{v}, V, F)$, $P = V^y F$, $\mathbf{g} = \mathbf{v}^y \circ \mathbf{f}$ and $z = \tilde{H}_2(\mathbf{g}, P, \mathbf{c}, \mathbf{B})$. Denote $\mathbf{c} := [h_1, h_2, \ldots, h_t]$ and $\mathbf{B} := [\mathbf{b}_1, \mathbf{b}_2, \ldots, \mathbf{b}_t]^\top$. The prover computes $\mathbf{d} = \mathbf{b}_1 + z \cdot \mathbf{b}_2 + z^2 \cdot \mathbf{b}_3 + \ldots + z^{t-1} \cdot \mathbf{b}_t \in \mathbb{Z}_p^n$ and $\zeta = \sum_{i=1}^t z^{i-1} h_i$. It computes $\pi' \leftarrow$ NI-OIPA.PROVE($\{\text{param}, \mathbf{g}, P, \zeta, \mathbf{d}\}, \mathbf{a}$) and returns $\pi = (F, \pi')$.
- NI-MMA.VERIFY($\{\text{param}, \mathbf{v}, V, \mathbf{c}, \mathbf{B}\}, \pi$). The verifier parses $\pi = (F, \pi')$ and computes $\mathbf{f} = \tilde{H}_0(\mathbf{v}, V)$, $y = \tilde{H}_1(\mathbf{v}, V, F)$, $P = V^y F$, $\mathbf{g} = \mathbf{v}^y \circ \mathbf{f}$ and $z = \tilde{H}_2(\mathbf{g}, P, \mathbf{c}, \mathbf{B})$. Denote $\mathbf{c} := [h_1, h_2, \ldots, h_t]$ and $\mathbf{B} := [\mathbf{b}_1, \mathbf{b}_2, \ldots, \mathbf{b}_t]^\top$. The verifier computes $\mathbf{d} = \mathbf{b}_1 + z \cdot \mathbf{b}_2 + z^2 \cdot \mathbf{b}_3 + \ldots + z^{t-1} \cdot \mathbf{b}_t \in \mathbb{Z}_p^n$ and $y = \sum_{i=1}^t z^{i-1} h_i$. It outputs $1/0 \leftarrow$ NI-OIPA.VERIFY($\text{param}, \mathbf{g}, P, y, \mathbf{d}, \pi'$).

Theorem 4. *The NI-MMA Protocol has statistical witness-extended-emulation for either extracting a valid witness $\mathbf{a}$.*

Proof. For witness extended emulation, we show that there exists an efficient extractor that uses $2t$ transcripts to obtain the witness $\mathbf{a}$. By rewinding the random oracle $\tilde{H}_2$ for $t-1$ times with the same input $(\mathbf{g}, P, \mathbf{c}, \mathbf{B})$, it returns distinct random challenges $z_1, z_2, \ldots, z_t$ such that:

$$\mathbf{d}_j = \mathbf{b}_1 + z_j \cdot \mathbf{b}_2 + z_j^2 \cdot \mathbf{b}_3 + \ldots + z_j^{t-1} \cdot \mathbf{b}_t \in \mathbb{Z}_p^n, \quad y_j = \sum_{i=1}^t z_j^{i-1} h_i.$$

for $j \in [t]$. By the extractor of NI-OIPA, we can obtain $\mathbf{a}_j$ such that $\langle \mathbf{d}_j, \mathbf{a}_j \rangle = y_j$ and $P = \mathbf{g}^{\mathbf{a}_j}$. With Lemma 3, we could assume all $\mathbf{a}_j$ is identical. And one could solve $\mathbf{E} = (\mathbf{e}_1, \mathbf{e}_2, \ldots, \mathbf{e}_t)$, with

$$\begin{pmatrix} 1 & 1 & \cdots & 1 \\ \vdots & \vdots & \ddots & \vdots \\ z_1^{t-1} & z_2^{t-1} & \cdots & z_t^{t-1} \end{pmatrix} \cdot \mathbf{E} = \mathbf{I}_t.$$

As $\mathbf{e}_i^\top (\mathbf{d}_1, \ldots, \mathbf{d}_t)^\top \mathbf{a} = \mathbf{e}_i^\top (y_1, y_2, \ldots, y_t)^\top = h_i$, one could get a valid $\mathbf{b}_i$.

And we consider rewinding the random oracle $\tilde{H}_1$ with the same input $(\mathbf{v}, V, F)$. With those outputs, it is also able to construct $V = \mathbf{v}^{\mathbf{a}}$. $\qquad \square$

Table 1. Comparison of t-out-of-n threshold ring signature with signature size less than $O(\sqrt{n})$. The proofs π and π' are the NIZK and NIWI proofs for [22] and [15] respectively. For $\lambda = 128$, $d = 0.08521 \log n$.

Scheme	Signature Size	No trusted setup
[22]	$t|\mathbb{G}| + t|\pi|$	$\times$
[15]	$2t|\mathbb{G}_T| + 4t(d^2 + d + 1)|\mathbb{G}_1| + t|\pi'|$	depends on π'
TRing	$(2\log n + 2)|\mathbb{G}| + 3|\mathbb{Z}_p|$	$\checkmark$

6.2 EC-Based TRS Construction

To give a concrete construction of our threshold ring signature in the elliptic curve, we instantiate the Type-T* identification with the Schnorr identification as in DualRing-EC [28].

Compared to [28], the TRS adversary knows $t - 1$ secret keys in the ring. When $t \geq 3$, the relative discrete logarithm between two public keys are known. Therefore, we cannot directly use **vk** as the set of generators in the argument of knowledge as [28]. Besides, compressing $(c_1, \ldots, c_n)$ is also a challenge. Therefore, we use two hash functions $\tilde{H}_0$ and $\tilde{H}_1$ to construct **g** and compress the challenges with the NI-MMA protocol, as shown in the previous section.

Our EC-based construction can be combined by the generic construction and the above building blocks. The security of the EC-based construction also follows from the generic construction. The signature size is $2 \log n + 2$ elements in $\mathbb{G}$ and 3 elements in $\mathbb{Z}_p$ (Table 1).

6.3 Comparison

[22] has the signature size of t elements in $\mathbb{G}$ and t ZK proofs π. Each ZK proof has size 4.4KB for using CP-SNARKs for set membership in [2]. Consider $\mathbb{G}$ as an ECC group using 32 bytes for each group element, the total signature size is $4432t$ bytes. The signature in [15] consists of t partial signatures using pairing groups $(\mathbb{G}_1, \mathbb{G}_2, \mathbb{G}_T)$. Considering the curve BLS12-381, the total threshold signature size is $t(1248 + 192(d^2 + d))$ bytes, where $d = 0.08521 \log n$ for $\lambda = 128$.

In our scheme, the signature size is $2 \log n + 1$ elements in $\mathbb{G}$ and 3 elements in $\mathbb{Z}_p$. We use 32 bytes for storing $\mathbb{G}$ and $\mathbb{Z}_p$ using ECC. The signature size is $64(\log n + 2)$ bytes.

Observe that the signature size of [22] and [15] are dominated by the large constant induced by the corresponding NIZK or NIWI proofs. Even when $t = 1$, their signature size are at least 4432 bytes and 1265 bytes respectively. In our TRing, even if the ring size is as large as $2^{16} = 65536$, our signature size is still 1152 bytes. Table 2 shows that TRing is at least 59% and 86% shorter than [15] and [22] respectively for the ring size of $n = 128$. For the ring size of $n = 8192$, TRing is at least 43% and 78% shorter than [15] and [22].

Table 2. Comparison of threshold ring signature with signature size less than $O(\sqrt{n})$ for different values of (t, n).

(t,n)	(t, n) Threshold Ring Signature Size (bytes)								
	(1,128)	(10,128)	(100,128)	(1,1024)	(10,1024)	(100,1024)	(1,8192)	(10,8192)	(100,8192)
[22]	4432	44320	443200	4432	44320	443200	4432	44320	443200
[15]	1431	14309	143084	1552	15511	155101	1697	16963	169629
TRing	576	576	576	768	768	768	960	960	960

Table 3. The running time (ms) for each party on singing and verification with using sk knowledge proof.

n	ECC-Plain		ECC	
(t = n/2)	Sign	Verify	Sign	Verify
8	2.82	1.37	8.34	7.63
16	5.72	2.60	16.79	14.33
32	13.70	19.04	40.01	27.17
64	43.37	40.50	99.04	54.91

6.4 Implementation

Our implementation is based on the Rust programming language, in which the ECC scenarios relies on the $curv^1$ library and the underlying Curve25519 curve. Basing on whether we treat the zero-knowledge proof of secret key as part of the public key or not, the implementation could be divided to two different scenarios. We implement the code for both scenarios and provide the benchmarks for them.

We use a laptop on Intel(R) Core(TM) i5-9300H CPU @ 2.40 GHz with 10 GB RAM to take the benchmark, of which the results are shown in Table 3.

7   Conclusion

In this paper, we give the first practical threshold ring signature with size $O(\log n)$ only (independent to t). We leave the lattice-based construction as an interesting future work.

Acknowledgments. The authors are supported by Hong Kong RGC GRF grant number 17207322.

References

1. Bagherzandi, A., Cheon, J.H., Jarecki, S.: Multisignatures secure under the discrete logarithm assumption and a generalized forking lemma. In: Ning, P., Syverson, P.F., Jha, S. (eds.) CCS 2008. pp. 449–458. ACM (2008)

---

[1] https://github.com/ZenGo-X/curv.

2. Benarroch, D., Campanelli, M., Fiore, D., Gurkan, K., Kolonelos, D.: Zero-knowledge proofs for set membership: Efficient, succinct, modular. In: Borisov, N., Díaz, C. (eds.) FC 2021. Lecture Notes in Computer Science, vol. 12674, pp. 393–414. Springer (2021). https://doi.org/10.1007/978-3-662-64322-8_19

3. Bender, A., Katz, J., Morselli, R.: Ring signatures: Stronger definitions, and constructions without random oracles. J. Cryptology **22**(1), 114–138 (2009)

4. Bettaieb, S., Schrek, J.: Improved Lattice-Based Threshold Ring Signature Scheme. In: Gaborit, P. (ed.) PQCrypto 2013. LNCS, vol. 7932, pp. 34–51. Springer, Heidelberg (2013). https://doi.org/10.1007/978-3-642-38616-9_3

5. Bootle, J., Cerulli, A., Chaidos, P., Ghadafi, E., Groth, J., Petit, C.: Short accountable ring signatures based on DDH. In: ESORICS 2015. Lecture Notes in Computer Science, vol. 9326, pp. 243–265. Springer (2015)

6. Bresson, E., Stern, J., Szydlo, M.: Threshold Ring Signatures and Applications to Ad-hoc Groups. In: Yung, M. (ed.) CRYPTO 2002. LNCS, vol. 2442, pp. 465–480. Springer, Heidelberg (2002). https://doi.org/10.1007/3-540-45708-9_30

7. Bünz, B., Bootle, J., Boneh, D., Poelstra, A., Wuille, P., Maxwell, G.: Bulletproofs: Short proofs for confidential transactions and more. In: SP 2018. pp. 315–334. IEEE Computer Society (2018)

8. Cayrel, P.-L., Lindner, R., Rückert, M., Silva, R.: A Lattice-Based Threshold Ring Signature Scheme. In: Abdalla, M., Barreto, P.S.L.M. (eds.) LATINCRYPT 2010. LNCS, vol. 6212, pp. 255–272. Springer, Heidelberg (2010). https://doi.org/10.1007/978-3-642-14712-8_16

9. Chang, Y., Chang, C., Lin, P.: A concealed t-out-of-n signer ambiguous signature scheme with variety of keys. Informatica **18**(4), 535–546 (2007)

10. Chen, J., Hu, Y., Gao, W., Li, H.: Lattice-based threshold ring signature with message block sharing. KSII Trans. Internet Inf. Syst. **13**(2), 1003–1019 (2019)

11. Cong, M., Yuen, T.H., Yiu, S.: zkmatrix: Batched short proof for committed matrix multiplication. In: Zhou, J., Quek, T.Q.S., Gao, D., Cardenas, A. (eds.) ASIA CCS 2024. ACM (2024). https://doi.org/10.1145/3634737.3645003

12. Di Crescenzo, G., Katz, J., Ostrovsky, R., Smith, A.: Efficient and Non-interactive Non-malleable Commitment. In: Pfitzmann, B. (ed.) EUROCRYPT 2001. LNCS, vol. 2045, pp. 40–59. Springer, Heidelberg (2001). https://doi.org/10.1007/3-540-44987-6_4

13. Dallot, L., Vergnaud, D.: Provably secure code-based threshold ring signatures. In: Parker, M.G. (ed.) 12th IMA International Conference, Cryptography and Coding 2009. Lecture Notes in Computer Science, vol. 5921, pp. 222–235. Springer (2009)

14. Groth, J., Kohlweiss, M.: One-Out-of-Many Proofs: Or How to Leak a Secret and Spend a Coin. In: Oswald, E., Fischlin, M. (eds.) EUROCRYPT 2015. LNCS, vol. 9057, pp. 253–280. Springer, Heidelberg (2015). https://doi.org/10.1007/978-3-662-46803-6_9

15. Haque, A., Krenn, S., Slamanig, D., Striecks, C.: Logarithmic-size (linkable) threshold ring signatures in the plain model. In: Hanaoka, G., Shikata, J., Watanabe, Y. (eds.) PKC 2022. vol. 13178, pp. 437–467. Springer (2022)

16. Haque, A., Scafuro, A.: Threshold Ring Signatures: New Definitions and Postquantum Security. In: Kiayias, A., Kohlweiss, M., Wallden, P., Zikas, V. (eds.) PKC 2020. LNCS, vol. 12111, pp. 423–452. Springer, Cham (2020). https://doi.org/10.1007/978-3-030-45388-6_15

17. Lai, R.W.F., Ronge, V., Ruffing, T., Schröder, D., Thyagarajan, S.A.K., Wang, J.: Omniring: Scaling private payments without trusted setup. In: CCS 2019. pp. 31–48. ACM (2019)

18. Libert, B., Nguyen, K., Peters, T., Yung, M.: One-shot fiat-shamir-based NIZK arguments of composite residuosity and logarithmic-size ring signatures in the standard model. In: Dunkelman, O., Dziembowski, S. (eds.) EUROCRYPT 2022. Lecture Notes in Computer Science, vol. 13276, pp. 488–519. Springer (2022)

19. Libert, B., Peters, T., Qian, C.: Logarithmic-Size Ring Signatures with Tight Security from the DDH Assumption. In: Lopez, J., Zhou, J., Soriano, M. (eds.) ESORICS 2018. LNCS, vol. 11099, pp. 288–308. Springer, Cham (2018). https://doi.org/10.1007/978-3-319-98989-1_15

20. Liu, J.K., Wong, D.S.: On the security models of (threshold) ring signature schemes. In: Park, C., Chee, S. (eds.) ICISC 2004. Lecture Notes in Computer Science, vol. 3506, pp. 204–217. Springer (2005)

21. Melchor, C.A., Cayrel, P., Gaborit, P., Laguillaumie, F.: A new efficient threshold ring signature scheme based on coding theory. IEEE Trans. Inf. Theory **57**(7), 4833–4842 (2011)

22. Munch-Hansen, A., Orlandi, C., Yakoubov, S.: Stronger Notions and a More Efficient Construction of Threshold Ring Signatures. In: Longa, P., Ràfols, C. (eds.) LATINCRYPT 2021. LNCS, vol. 12912, pp. 363–381. Springer, Cham (2021). https://doi.org/10.1007/978-3-030-88238-9_18

23. Okamoto, T., Tso, R., Yamaguchi, M., Okamoto, E.: A k-out-of-n ring signature with flexible participation for signers. IACR Cryptol. ePrint Arch. p. 728 (2018)

24. Petzoldt, A., Bulygin, S., Buchmann, J.: A multivariate based threshold ring signature scheme. Appl. Algebra Eng. Commun. Comput. **24**(3–4), 255–275 (2013)

25. Pham, M.T.T., Duong, D.H., Li, Y., Susilo, W.: Threshold ring signature scheme from cryptographic group action. In: Zhang, M., Au, M.H., Zhang, Y. (eds.) ProvSec 2023. Lecture Notes in Computer Science, vol. 14217, pp. 207–227. Springer (2023)

26. Rivest, R.L., Shamir, A., Tauman, Y.: How to Leak a Secret. In: Boyd, C. (ed.) ASIACRYPT 2001. LNCS, vol. 2248, pp. 552–565. Springer, Heidelberg (2001). https://doi.org/10.1007/3-540-45682-1_32

27. Tsang, P.P., Wei, V.K., Chan, T.K., Au, M.H., Liu, J.K., Wong, D.S.: Separable Linkable Threshold Ring Signatures. In: Canteaut, A., Viswanathan, K. (eds.) INDOCRYPT 2004. LNCS, vol. 3348, pp. 384–398. Springer, Heidelberg (2004). https://doi.org/10.1007/978-3-540-30556-9_30

28. Yuen, T.H., Esgin, M.F., Liu, J.K., Au, M.H., Ding, Z.: *DualRing*: Generic Construction of Ring Signatures with Efficient Instantiations. In: Malkin, T., Peikert, C. (eds.) CRYPTO 2021. LNCS, vol. 12825, pp. 251–281. Springer, Cham (2021). https://doi.org/10.1007/978-3-030-84242-0_10

29. Yuen, T.H., Liu, J.K., Au, M.H., Susilo, W., Zhou, J.: Threshold ring signature without random oracles. In: Cheung, B.S.N., Hui, L.C.K., Sandhu, R.S., Wong, D.S. (eds.) ASIACCS 2011. pp. 261–267. ACM (2011)

30. Yuen, T.H., Liu, J.K., Au, M.H., Susilo, W., Zhou, J.: Efficient linkable and/or threshold ring signature without random oracles. Comput. J. **56**(4), 407–421 (2013)

31. Yuen, T.H., Sun, S.-F., Liu, J.K., Au, M.H., Esgin, M.F., Zhang, Q., Gu, D.: RingCT 3.0 for Blockchain Confidential Transaction: Shorter Size and Stronger Security. In: Bonneau, J., Heninger, N. (eds.) FC 2020. LNCS, vol. 12059, pp. 464–483. Springer, Cham (2020). https://doi.org/10.1007/978-3-030-51280-4_25

32. Zhou, G., Zeng, P., Yuan, X., Chen, S., Choo, K.R.: An efficient code-based threshold ring signature scheme with a leader-participant model. Secur. Commun. Networks **2017**, 1915239:1–1915239:7 (2017)

Lattice-Based Non-interactive Blind Signature Schemes in the Random Oracle Model

Haoqi Zhang[1,2], Xinjian Chen[1,2], and Qiong Huang[1,2(✉)]

[1] College of Software Engineering, South China Agricultural University,
Guangzhou 510642, China
{haoqizhang,xchen}@stu.scau.edu.cn, qhuang@scau.edu.cn
[2] College of Mathematics and Informatics, South China Agricultural University,
Guangzhou 510642, China

Abstract. Blind signatures serve as a crucial cryptographic primitive within privacy-preserving protocols. Historically, the majority of blind signature schemes necessitated a minimum of two interactions (i.e., a two-move) involving the user and the signer. However, there exist certain applications, such as Privacy Pass or lottery systems where there is no requirement for the messages signed by the signer to adhere to a specific distribution. While a few non-interactive blind signature schemes based on integer factoring or discrete logarithms have been proposed, the situation is considerably less satisfactory when it comes to post-quantum assumptions. In this paper, we present a lattice-based non-interactive blind signature (LB-NIBS) and a lattice-based tagged non-interactive blind signature (LB-TNIBS) and prove their security under the random oracle model, based on lattice hardness problems M-SIS/M-LWE. Our schemes rely on the GPV signature and non-interactive zero-knowledge proof and can be easily implemented on module-lattice.

Keywords: Blind Signature · Non-Interactive Blind Signature · Lattice

1 Introduction

Blind signature is an important cryptographic primitive, first introduced by Chaum [13] and has a large number of applications in different areas, such as e-cash [13,32], e-voting [22], anonymous credentials [10,12] and many others. Informally, in blind signature, a user U, holding a public key and a message to be signed, may require a signature from a signer S, holding a secret key, such that the signer should not be able to see what the signed message is (blindness) and the user should not be able to forge signatures even after multiple interactions with the signer (one-more unforgeability). The system model is shown in Fig. 1.

Chaum's seminal work has shown how to construct an e-cash system using a blind signature scheme. The design of e-cash inspired many follow-up works

J. K. Liu et al. (Eds.): ProvSec 2024, LNCS 14903, pp. 289–308, 2025.
https://doi.org/10.1007/978-981-96-0954-3_15

[6,11,17]. The idea is natural. The bank issues a coin as the signature on random identifiers chosen by users. To spend, the user shows the identifier (i.e. message) and the corresponding signature to the merchant, who can withdraw the amount from the bank. The bank keeps a list of 'used' identifiers to prevent double-spending. To make transactions unlinkable, the bank uses a blind signature to create the signature together with the user.

However, in some applications, such as Privacy Pass [14], its main purpose is to reduce the repetitive verification process for users and improve user experience when preventing human-machine verification (e.g., solving CAPTCHA). In these applications, the signature message in the application is not an identifier but a random string. This means that users can randomly choose blind signature messages, and the selected message does not need to come from a specific distribution. Following the observation, Hanzlik et al. [23] considered a non-interactive blind signature and left an open problem: Can we design a non-interactive blind signature scheme that is resistant to quantum attacks? In this work, we give a positive answer and propose a lattice-based non-interactive blind signature scheme.

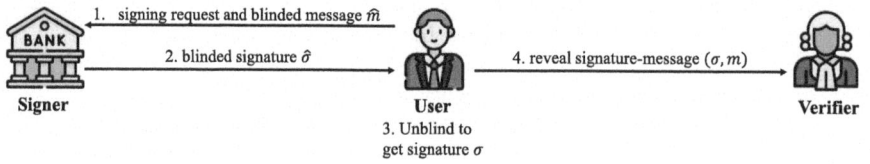

Fig. 1. Interactive Blind Signature System Model.

1.1 Prior Works on Lattice-Based Blind Signature

Lattice-based cryptography is widely believed to be resistant to quantum computing attacks. Since the seminal work of Ajtai [3], many lattice-based cryptographic constructions have been proposed such as digital signatures [21,28] and fully homomorphic encryptions(FHE) [20]. After Rückert first proposed lattice-based blind signatures, many lattice-based blind signatures had been proposed [4,5,18,26,27]. Unfortunately, these schemes all contain subtle flaws in the security proof or could be attacked [24]. In [24], Hauck et al. proposed a new three-round lattice-based blind signature scheme whose security can be proven from the standard SIS problem in the random oracle model. Recently, several schemes [2,29,33] that require only two interactions have been proposed based on the generic blind signature construction paradigm by Fischlin [16]. We call the above schemes the two-move blind signature with one message from the user and one from the signer. Table 1 shows the efficiency of these schemes. We note that interaction is inherent since the user must keep an internal state to de-blind the signer's response, even though in random oracle model or common reference string model. But in many scenarios, such as a lottery system, the user can randomly choose the message to design something new that was not considered in prior work. We can exploit this observation to design non-interactive blind signatures. Hanzlik et al. [23] proposed the first non-interactive blind signature scheme which is based on the discrete logarithm assumption. Very recently, independent of our work, Baldimtsi et al. [7] proposed a lattice-based non-interactive blind signature and a new generic paradigm for NIBS from circuit-private levelled homomorphic encryption.

Table 1. Comparison of transcript-size, signature-size and hardness problem for the line of work [2, 24, 29, 33].

Scheme	Transcript-size	Signature-size	Hardness Problem	Interactive
[24]	–	7.9 MB	R-SIS	Yes
[29]	16 MB	150 KB	M-SIS/M-LWE	Yes
[33]	100 KB	100 KB	SIS	Yes
[2]	1.5 KB	50 KB	One-More-SIS	Yes

Fig. 2. Non-Interactive Blind Signature.

1.2 Our Contribution

In this work, we present a lattice-based non-interactive blind signature (LB-NIBS). Specifically, we leverage the observation that users do not need to select messages from a specific distribution in certain scenarios, and combine it with other building blocks to construct our scheme. We employ the verifiable random function (VRF) and make slight modifications to certain parameters to enhance their suitability for our scheme. Furthermore, we employ the hash-and-sign paradigm instead of signatures on equivalence classes and incorporate zero-knowledge proofs into the construction of the resulting signature. This is done to bolster the security of our scheme and ensure that it satisfies the necessary security requirements. We show that the security of our scheme is based on the standard M-SIS/M-LWE assumptions in the random oracle model. M-SIS/M-LWE assumptions have proven to be at least as hard as standard lattice problems restricted to module lattices [25].

Moreover, we also propose a tagged lattice-based NIBS. Tagged-NIBS can be used to strengthen the supervision of signatures in certain scenarios or to provide additional information for signatures, such as the validity period of the signature. The system model of our scheme is shown in Fig. 2. Compared to the NIBS scheme in [23], our schemes are based on lattice hardness problems, which are widely believed to resist attacks from quantum computing. However, the scheme in [23] is based on the discrete logarithm problem, which is no longer secure in a quantum environment. Very recently, Baldimtsi et al. [7] proposed a NIBS scheme based on the randomized one-more ISIS assumption (rOM-ISIS), which is the randomized version of one-more ISIS assumption proposed by Agrawal et al. [2]. However, rOM-ISIS is not a standard lattice hardness problem and one does not succeed in obtaining a reduction from a well-studied problem (e.g. SIS or SIVP) to one-more-ISIS assumption [2]. Table 2 shows the comparison between our scheme and other schemes.

Table 2. Comparison with [7, 23].

Scheme	Hardness Problem	Interactive	Quantum resistant
[23]	CDH	No	No
[7]	rOM-ISIS	No	Yes
Our Schemes	Module-SIS	No	Yes

1.3   Our Technique

In this paper, we propose a lattice-based non-interactive blind signature(LB-NIBS) and a lattice-based tagged non-interactive blind signature(LB-TNIBS), respectively. The ideas of the two schemes are similar, except that LB-TNIBS has an additional tag. To this end, our scheme uses non-interactive zero knowledge proof [30, 34] and GPV signature [21] as a building block. In order to obtain the GPV signature for a certain message, the signer first hashes the message to obtain the hash value of the message and then performs the preimage sampling algorithm on the hash value, and the result is used as the signature. This is the standard hash-and-sign paradigm. Combining our previous observations, we obtain the idea of our scheme as follows. The signer first generates a GPV pre-signature on the user's public key pk_R. To ensure blindness, or more accurately recipient blindness, we require the signer to explicitly add a randomness **nonce** during the computation of the hash value $H(\textbf{nonce}\|pk_R)$, and return the randomness to the user together with the pre-signature of the user's public key. Upon receiving the pre-signature and randomness, the user executes the verification algorithm of the GPV signature. If the verification process fails, the protocol is aborted. If the verification succeeds, the user proceeds to generate a pseudorandom value, which will serve as the signed message. However, instead of generating the pseudorandom value through a conventional pseudorandom function, we employ a verifiable random function (VRF) to generate the message. This choice ensures the preservation of one-more unforgeability. Otherwise, users can use the same pre-signature to generate multiple valid signatures for different random messages, which violates the unforgeability of signature schemes. VRF can ensure that at most one of multiple different messages generated by the same pre-signature is valid. In the process of generating message m, VRF will generate a proof π_{VRF} along with m at the same time. Finally, we use a non-interactive zero-knowledge proof π to serve as the resulting signature, which proves the following relation holds:

$$VRF.V(pk_R, \pi_{VRF}, \mathbf{nonce}, m) = 1 \wedge ||\mathbf{x}|| \leq \beta \wedge \mathbf{A} \cdot \mathbf{x} = H(\mathbf{nonce}||pk_R).$$

1.4 Application

In addition to lottery systems and eliminating CAPTCHA, we think that NIBS can also be utilized for other functionalities, such as access control. Specifically, if we consider user identities as their public keys, signers can issue pre-signatures to designated public keys (user IDs). Users who do not possess a pre-signature will be unable to pass the verification process, thus achieving the goal of access control. This is particularly useful in various scenarios. Furthermore, by treating user attributes as their public keys, signers can issue pre-signatures to users with specific attributes, thereby further controlling user access privileges. Additionally, our scheme can be applied to whistle-blowing systems, for which the European Union has provided detailed regulations for [1]. The specific implementation of these concepts and the aforementioned ideas remains an open question. Furthermore, our scheme relies on a random oracle. Constructing a lattice-based non-interactive blind signature scheme that does not depend on a random oracle is also an unresolved issue.

2 Preliminaries

Notation. We denote the set of natural numbers, and integers by $\mathbb{N}, \mathbb{Z}$, respectively. For a set S, we write $x \xleftarrow{\$} S$ if x is sampled uniformly at random from S. For a (probabilistic) algorithm $\mathcal{A}$, we write $y \leftarrow \mathcal{A}(x)$, if y is the output $\mathcal{A}$ on input x. For any $n \in \mathbb{N}$, we denote $[n] := \{1, \cdots, n\}$. Moreover, We define the statistical distance between two distributions X and Y over a countable set D as $\Delta(X,Y) = \sum_{d \in D} |X(d) - Y(d)|$. A function f is negligible if $f < \frac{1}{poly(n)}$ for any polynomial $poly(n)$ in n. We write $negl(n)$ to denote an unspecified negligible function in n. We let $\mathcal{R}$ and $\mathcal{R}_q$ denote the polynomial rings $\mathbb{Z}[X]/\langle X^d + 1\rangle$ and $\mathbb{Z}_q[X]/\langle X^d + 1\rangle$ respectively, where q is an odd integer. For any x, y, we use $x||y$ to represent the concatenation of x and y. Bold lower-case letters denote vectors whose elements are composed of elements in $\mathcal{R}_q$ and bold upper-case denote matrices whose elements are also composed of elements in $\mathcal{R}_q$. We further define a set $\mathbb{S}_\beta = \{x \in \mathcal{R} : ||x||_\infty \leq \beta\}$.

2.1   Verifiable Random Function

Definition 1 (Verifiable Random Function [31]). *A verifiable random function consists of four polynomial-time algorithms* $ParamGen, PKeyGen, Eval,$ *and* $Verify,$ *where:*

- $ParamGen(1^\lambda)$: *On input a security parameter* 1^λ, *it outputs some global, public parameter* pp.
- $Gen(pp)$: *On input public parameter* pp *this probabilistic algorithm outputs two binary stings, a secret key* sk_{VRF} *and a public key* pk_{VRF}.
- $Eval(sk_{VRF}, x)$: *On input a secret key* sk_{VRF} *and an input* $x \in \{0,1\}^{\ell(\lambda)}$, *it outputs* (v, π) *for the VRF value* $v \in \{0,1\}^{m(\lambda)}$ *and the corresponding proof* π_{VRF} *proving the correctness of* v.
- $Verify(pk_{VRF}, v, x, \pi)$: *On input* $(pk_{VRF}, v, x, \pi_{VRF})$, *it outputs either* 1 *or* 0.

A VRF is required to have the following security properties [31].

- **Completness:** For every security parameter 1^λ and input $x \in \{0,1\}^{\ell(\lambda)}$,

$$Pr \begin{bmatrix} pp \leftarrow ParamGen(1^\lambda), \\ (sk_{VRF}, pk_{VRF}) \leftarrow Gen(pp), \\ (v, \pi_{VRF}) \leftarrow Eval(sk_{VRF}, x) \end{bmatrix} \leq negl(\lambda).$$

- **Uniqueness:** No values $(pk_{VRF}, v, v^*, x, \pi_{VRF}, \pi_{VRF}^*)$ can satisfy the following relation:

$$Verify(pk_{VRF}, v, x, \pi_{VRF}) = Verify(pk_{VRF}, v^*, x, \pi_{VRF}^*) = 1$$

when $v \neq v^*$.
- **Pseudorandomness:** Every PPT adversary $\mathcal{A}$ has at most negligible advantage in the following experiment:
  1. $b \leftarrow \{0,1\}$
  2. $pp \leftarrow ParamGen(1^\lambda)$
  3. $(pk_{VRF}, sk_{VRF}) \leftarrow Gen(pp)$
  4. $(x, st) \leftarrow \mathcal{A}^{\mathcal{O}(sk_{VRF}, \cdot)}(pk_{VRF})$
  5. $(v_0, \pi) \leftarrow Eval(sk_{VRF}, x)$
  6. $v_1 \leftarrow \{0,1\}^{m(\lambda)}$
  7. $b' = \mathcal{A}^{\mathcal{O}(sk_{VRF}, \cdot)}(st, v_b)$
  8. return $b = b'$

  The advantage of $\mathcal{A}$ is defined by $\mathbf{Adv}_{VRF}(\mathcal{A}) = |Pr[Exp_{\mathcal{A}, VRF}(1^\lambda) = 1] - 1/2|$.

2.2   Non-interactive Zero Knowledge Proof

Definition 2 (Non-interactive Zero Knowledge Proof [9]). *Let* λ *be the security parameter. A non-interactive zero-knowledge (NIZK) argument system* Π *for an NP-relation* R *consists of two polynomial-time probabilistic algorithms* $P(x, w), V(x, \pi)$. *The argument* π *of* V *represents the proof produced by* P.

We require the argument system Π should satisfy the following properties.

- **Completness:** *For any $(x, w) \in R$, we have*

$$Pr[\pi \leftarrow P(x, w) : V(x, \pi) = 1] = 1.$$

- **Soundness:** *Let L be the language corresponding to NP-relation R. For any statement $x \notin L$ and any adversary $\mathcal{A}$, we have*

$$Pr[\pi \leftarrow \mathcal{A}(x) : V(x, \pi) = 1] \leq negl(\lambda).$$

- **Honest Verifier Zero Knowledge:** *There is a PPT simulator Sim such that, for all statement x for which there exists w with $R(x, w) = 1$, for any probabilistic polynomial-time adversary $\mathcal{A}$, we have*

$$|Pr[1 \leftarrow \mathcal{A}((x, \pi) : \pi \leftarrow P(x, w))] - Pr[1 \leftarrow \mathcal{A}((x, \pi) : \pi \leftarrow Sim(1^\lambda, x))]| \leq negl(\lambda).$$

2.3 Lattice, Discrete Gaussians

Definition 3 (Lattice). *An n-dimensional lattice $\mathcal{L}$ is a discrete additive subgroup of $\mathbb{R}^n$. Let $\mathbf{B} = (\mathbf{b}_1, \mathbf{b}_2, \cdots, \mathbf{b}_n)$ consist of n linearly independent vectors. The n-dimensional lattice generated by $\mathbf{B}$ is defined as*

$$\Lambda = \mathcal{L}(\mathbf{B}) = \left\{ \sum_{i=1}^{n} x_i \mathbf{b}_i : x_i \in \mathbb{Z} \right\}.$$

We call $\mathbf{B}$ the basis of the lattice.

For a matrix $\mathbf{A} \in \mathbb{Z}_q^{n \times m}$, we define a q-ary lattice as:

$$\Lambda_q^\perp(\mathbf{A}) = \left\{ \mathbf{A} \cdot \mathbf{x} = \mathbf{0} \ mod \ q : \mathbf{x} \in \mathbb{Z}_q^m \right\}.$$

For a vector $\mathbf{u} \in \mathbb{Z}_q^n$, we define the following coset of $\Lambda_q^\perp(\mathbf{A})$:

$$\Lambda_q^\mathbf{u}(\mathbf{A}) = \left\{ \mathbf{A} \cdot \mathbf{x} = \mathbf{u} \ mod \ q : \mathbf{x} \in \mathbb{Z}_q^m \right\}.$$

We have $\Lambda_q^\mathbf{u}(\mathbf{A}) = \Lambda_q^\perp(\mathbf{A}) + \mathbf{t}$ for any $\mathbf{t}$ such that $\mathbf{A} \cdot \mathbf{t} = \mathbf{u} \ mod \ q$. Similarly, when $\mathbf{A} \in \mathcal{R}_q^{n \times m}$, then

$$\Lambda_{R_q}^\perp(\mathbf{A}) = \left\{ \mathbf{A} \cdot \mathbf{x} = \mathbf{0} \ over \ \mathcal{R}_q : \mathbf{x} \in \mathcal{R}_q^m \right\}.$$

Define the ℓ_∞ and ℓ_p norms for $w = w_0 + w_1 X \cdot + w_{d-1} X^{d-1} \in \mathcal{R}$ as follows:

$$||w||_\infty = \max_j ||w_j||_\infty, \ ||w||_p = \sqrt[p]{||w_0||_\infty^p + \cdots + ||w_0||_\infty^p}.$$

If $\mathbf{w} = (w_1, \cdots, w_m) \in \mathcal{R}^k$, then

$$||\mathbf{w}||_\infty = \max_j ||w_j||_\infty, \ ||\mathbf{w}||_p = \sqrt[p]{||w_0||_\infty^p + \cdots + ||w_0||_\infty^p}.$$

Unless otherwise stated, $||w|| = ||w||_2$ and $||\mathbf{w}|| = ||\mathbf{w}||_2$.

Definition 4 (Gaussians). *For any vector* $\mathbf{c} \in \mathbb{R}^n$, *any positive integer* n *and real* $\sigma > 0$, *we define the Gaussian function* $\rho_s : \mathbb{R}^n \to \mathbb{R}^+$ *of parameter* s *as:*

$$\forall \mathbf{x} \in \mathbb{R}^n, \rho_{s,\mathbf{x}}(\mathbf{x}) = \exp\left(-\frac{||\mathbf{x} - \mathbf{c}||^2}{2\sigma^2}\right),$$

where σ *is standard deviation,* $\mathbf{c}$ *is center parameter, if* $\mathbf{c} = \mathbf{0}$ *we omit it. The Gaussian distribution is* $\mathcal{D}_{\sigma,\mathbf{c}} = \rho_{\sigma,\mathbf{c}}(\mathbf{x})/\sigma^n$.

The discrete Gaussian distribution over a lattice Λ with standard deviation $\sigma > 0$ and center $\mathbf{c}$ parameter is defined as:

$$\forall \mathbf{x} \in \Lambda, \mathcal{D}_{\Lambda,\sigma,\mathbf{c}} = \frac{\rho_{\sigma,\mathbf{c}}(\mathbf{x})}{\rho_{\sigma,\mathbf{c}}(\Lambda)},$$

where $\rho_{\sigma,\mathbf{c}}(\Lambda) = \sum_{\mathbf{x} \in \Lambda} \rho_{\sigma,\mathbf{c}}(\mathbf{x})$. When $\mathbf{c} = 0$, we omit it.

2.4   Lattice Trapdoors

We use the following algorithms for generating a random lattice with a trapdoor, and for sampling short vectors in a lattice coset. The first algorithm is derived from [3, 8, 21, 35], whereas the second is derived from [8, 19, 21].

Lemma 1. *Let* q, n, m *be positive number with* $q \geq 2$ *and* $m \geq 6n\log^2 q$.
    There is a PPT algorithm $TrapGen(q, n, m)$ *that with probability* $1 - 2^{-\Omega(n)}$ *outputs a pair* $(\mathbf{A}, \mathbf{T_A}) \in \mathcal{R}^{n \times m} \times \mathcal{R}^{m \times m}$ *such that* $\mathbf{A}$ *is within* $2^{-\Omega(n)}$ *statistical distance to uniform in* $\mathcal{R}_q^{n \times m}$ *and* $\mathbf{T_A}$ *is a basis for* $\Lambda_q^{\perp}(\mathbf{A})$.
    There is a PPT algorithm $SamplePre(\mathbf{A}, \mathbf{T_A}, \mathbf{u}, \sigma)$, *which takes as input the above pair* $(\mathbf{A}, \mathbf{T_A})$, *a vector* $\mathbf{u} \in \mathcal{R}_q^n$ *and a sufficiently large* σ *and outputs a vector* $\mathbf{x}$ *from* $\mathcal{D}_{\Lambda_q^{\mathbf{u}}(\mathbf{A}),\sigma}$. *Further, with overwhelming probability* $2^{-\Omega(n)}$, *we have* $||\mathbf{x}|| \leq \gamma\sigma\sqrt{m}$ *and* $\mathbf{Ax} = \mathbf{u}$, *where* γ *is a factor number.*

2.5   Hardness Assumption

Definition 5 (MSIS$_{q,n,m,\beta}$[25]). *Let* $\mathcal{R}$ *be some polynomial ring and* $\mathcal{K}$ *a uniform distribution over* $\mathcal{R}_q^{n \times m}$. *Given a random matrix* $\mathbf{A} \in \mathcal{R}_q^{n \times m}$ *sampled from* $\mathcal{K}$, *find a non-zero vector* $\mathbf{v} \in \mathcal{R}_q^m$ *such that* $\mathbf{A} \cdot \mathbf{v} = \mathbf{0}$ *and* $||\mathbf{v}|| \leq \beta$.

Definition 6 (MLWE$_{q,n,m,\chi}$[25]). *Let* χ *be a distribution over* $\mathcal{R}_q$, $\mathbf{s} \xleftarrow{\$} \chi^m$ *be a secret key. The* **MLWE$_{q,\mathbf{s}}$** *distribution is obtained by sampling* $\mathbf{A} \xleftarrow{\$} \mathcal{R}_q^{n \times m}$ *and error* $\mathbf{e} \xleftarrow{\$} \chi^n$ *and outputting* $(\mathbf{A}, \mathbf{A} \cdot \mathbf{s} + \mathbf{e})$. *The goal is to distinguish the* **MLWE$_{q,\mathbf{s}}$** *output from the uniform distribution* $\mathcal{U}(\mathcal{R}_q^{n \times m}, \mathcal{R}_q^n)$.

$OM - UNF_{\mathcal{A},NIBS}$

$(sk, pk) \leftarrow KeyGen(1^\lambda)$

$((m_1, sig_1), \cdots, (m_\ell, sig_\ell)) \leftarrow \mathcal{A}^{\mathcal{O}_1(sk,\cdot,\cdot)}(pk)$

return $m_i \neq m_j$ for $1 \leq i < j \leq \ell \wedge Verify(pk, m_i, sig_i) = 1$ for $1 \leq i \leq \ell \wedge k < \ell$

2.6 Other Useful Theorems and Definitions

Definition 7 (Collision Resistance). *We say that a hash function H is collision resistant if for any PPT adversary $\mathcal{A}$, the following is negligible:*

$$Pr\left[H(x_1) = H(x_2) \wedge x_1 \neq x_2 \mid (x_1, x_2) \leftarrow \mathcal{A}(H)\right].$$

Definition 8 (Preimage Resistance). *A hash function H is preimage resistant if for any PPT adversary $\mathcal{A}$, the following is negligible:*

$$Pr[H(x) = H(x') \mid x' \leftarrow \mathcal{A}(H(x))].$$

3 Non-interactive Blind Signatures

Definition 9 (Non-Interactive Blind Signatures [23]). *A non-interactive blind signature scheme NIBS consists of four PPT algorithms and a deterministic algorithm:*

- *$KeyGen(1^\lambda)$: On input security parameter 1^λ, outputs a key pair (sk, pk).*
- *$Gen(\lambda)$: On input security parameter λ, outputs another key pair (sk_R, pk_R).*
- *$Issue(sk, pk_R, nonce)$: On input a secret key sk, a user public key pk_R and a randomness nonce $\in \mathcal{N}$, outputs a pre-signature psig.*
- *$Obtain(skR, pk, psig, nonce)$: On input a user secret key sk_R, a signer's public key pk, a pre-signature psig and a randomness nonce $\in \mathcal{N}$, outputs a message-signature pair (m, sig) or $\perp$.*
- *$Verify(pk, (m, sig))$: On input a public key pk, a message-signature pair (m, σ), deterministically outputs a bit $b \in \{0, 1\}$. If $b = 1$, accept the signature σ; otherwise, reject it.*

Definition 10 (Correctness [23]). *An NIBS scheme is correct if for all security parameters 1^λ, $(sk, pk) \leftarrow KeyGen(1^\lambda)$, $(sk_R, pk_R) \leftarrow RKeyGen(1^\lambda)$, nonce:*

$$Pr[Verify(pk, Obtain(sk_R, pk, Issue(sk, pk_R, nonce), nonce)) = 1] = 1.$$

Definition 11 (One-More Unforgeability [23]). *For scheme NIBS and adversary $\mathcal{A}$ we define the following experiment $OM - UNF_{\mathcal{A}, NIBS}$:*

$$
\begin{array}{l}
\mathcal{O}_1(sk, pk_R, nonce) \\
\hline
\textit{if } k \textit{ not initialized then} \\
\quad k = 0 \\
psig \leftarrow Issue(sk, pk_R, nonce) \\
k = k + 1 \\
\textit{return psig}
\end{array}
$$

An NIBS scheme satisfies one-more unforgeability if and only if for all PPT adversary $\mathcal{A}$, their advantage defined as $\mathbf{Adv}_{\mathcal{A}, NIBS}^{OM-UNF} = Pr[OM - UNF_{\mathcal{A}, NIBS}(\lambda) = 1]$ is negligible.

Definition 12 (Recipient Blindness [23]). *An NIBS scheme is recipient blind, if for all PPT adversaries $\mathcal{A}$, their advantage is negligible:*

$$\mathbf{Adv}_{\mathcal{A},NIBS}^{PBnd} = |Pr[RBnd_{\mathcal{A},NIBS}(\lambda) = 1] - 1/2|.$$

$RBnd_{\mathcal{A},NIBS}(\lambda)$

$(sk_{R_0}, pk_{R_0}) \leftarrow PKeyGen(1^\lambda)$
$(sk_{R_1}, pk_{R_1}) \leftarrow PKeyGen(1^\lambda)$
$(psig_0, nonce_0, psig_1, nonce_1, pk) \leftarrow \mathcal{A}(pk_{R_0}, pk_{R_1})$
$(m_0, sig_0) \leftarrow Obtain(sk_{R_0}, pk, psig_0, nonce_0)$
$(m_1, sig_1) \leftarrow Obtain(sk_{R_1}, pk, psig_1, nonce_1)$
if $sig_0 = \perp$ or $sig_1 = \perp$ then
$(m_0, sig_0) = \perp; (m_1, sig_1) = \perp;$
$b \xleftarrow{\$} (0, 1)$
$\hat{b} \leftarrow \mathcal{A}((m_b, sig_b), (m_{1-b}, sig_{1-b}))$
return $b = \hat{b}$

Definition 13 (Nonce Blindness [23]). *An NIBS scheme is nonce blind, if for all PPT adversaries $\mathcal{A}$, their advantage is negligible:*

$$\mathbf{Adv}_{\mathcal{A},NIBS}^{NBnd} = |Pr[NBnd_{\mathcal{A},NIBS}(\lambda) = 1] - 1/2|.$$

$NBnd_{\mathcal{A},NIBS}(\lambda)$

$(sk_R, pk_R) \leftarrow PKeyGen(1^\lambda)$
$(psig_0, nonce_0, psig_1, nonce_1, pk) \leftarrow \mathcal{A}(pk_{R_0}, pk_{R_1})$
$(m_0, sig_0) \leftarrow Obtain(sk_{R_0}, pk, psig_0, nonce_0)$
$(m_1, sig_1) \leftarrow Obtain(sk_{R_1}, pk, psig_1, nonce_1)$
if $sig_0 = \perp$ or $sig_1 = \perp$ then
$(m_0, sig_0) = \perp; (m_1, sig_1) = \perp;$
$b \xleftarrow{\$} (0, 1)$
$\hat{b} \leftarrow \mathcal{A}((m_b, sig_b), (m_{1-b}, sig_{1-b}))$
return $b = \hat{b}$

Definition 14 (Full Blindness [23]). *An NIBS scheme is fully blind if it is recipient and nonce blind.*

Definition 15 (Tagged Non-Interactive Blind Signatures [23]). *A tagged non-interactive blind signature scheme TNIBS consists of four PPT algorithms and a deterministic algorithm:*

- *$KeyGen(1^\lambda)$: On input security parameter 1^λ, outputs a key pair (sk, pk).*
- *$Gen(1^\lambda)$: On input security parameter 1^λ, outputs another key pair (sk_R, pk_R).*
- *$Issue(sk, pk_R, nonce, \tau)$: On input a secret key sk, a user public key pk_R, a randomness $nonce \in \mathcal{N}$ and the tag $\tau \in \mathcal{T}$, outputs a pre-signature $psig$.*
- *$Obtain(sk_R, pk, psig, nonce, \tau)$: On input a user secret key sk_R, a signer's public key pk, a pre-signature $psig$, a randomness $nonce \in \mathcal{N}$ and the $\tau \in \mathcal{T}$, outputs a message-signature pair (m, sig) or $\perp$.*

- $Verify(pk, (m, \tau, sig))$: On input a public key pk, a message-tag-signature pair (m, τ, σ) deterministically outputs a bit $b \in \{0, 1\}$. If $b = 1$, accept the signature σ; otherwise, reject it.

Definition 16 (Correctness [23]). A TNIBS scheme is correct if for all security parameters λ, $(sk, pk) \leftarrow KeyGen(1^\lambda)$, $(sk_R, pk_R) \leftarrow RKeyGen(1^\lambda)$, $nonce \in \mathcal{N}, \tau \in \mathcal{T}$:

$$Pr[Verify(pk, Obtain(sk_R, pk, Issue(sk, pk_R, nonce, \tau), nonce, \tau)) = 1] = 1.$$

The one-more unforgeability, recipient blindness and nonce blindness of TNIBS are similar to those of NIBS.

4 Our Construction

In this section, we propose our schemes, a lattice-based non-interactive blind signature scheme (LB-NIBS) and a tagged non-interactive blind signature scheme (LB-TNIBS). For the specific implementation of VRF and NIZK, readers can refer to [15] and [30], respectively. We will use several collision-resistant hash functions: $H : \mathcal{R}^m \to \mathcal{R}^n_q$, $G : \{0, 1\}^* \to \mathcal{R}^{n_1}$ and $H_{\mathcal{C}} : \{0, 1\}^* \to \mathcal{C}$, which will be modeled as random oracles in the security proofs. In addition, we define the following challenge set:

$$\mathcal{C} = \{c \in \mathcal{R} : ||c||_\infty \leq 1 \wedge ||c||_1 \leq \kappa\},$$

where κ is the VRF parameter.

4.1 Lattice-Based Non-interactive Blind Signature

- **Setup.** $KeyGen(1^\lambda)$: Upon input the security 1^λ, define n, m, q, σ, β as functions of λ such that q is odd prime and the MSIS problem is hard. Then do the following:
  - Compute $(\mathbf{A}, \mathbf{T_A}) \leftarrow TrapGen(n, m, q)$.
  - Output $BSig.vk = \mathbf{A} \in \mathcal{R}^{n \times m}_q$, $BSig.sk = \mathbf{T_A} \in \mathcal{R}^{m \times m}_q$.
- **Generate the user key pair.** $PKeyGen(1^\lambda)$: On input the security parameter 1^λ, do the following:
  - Sample a matrix $\mathbf{A'} \xleftarrow{\$} \mathcal{R}^{m \times n_1}$, where $n_1 > m$.
  - Randomly sample $\mathbf{s} \xleftarrow{\$} \mathbb{S}^{n_1}_1$ and compute $\mathbf{u} = \mathbf{A'} \cdot \mathbf{s} \in \mathcal{R}^n_q$.
  - Output $pk_R = \mathbf{u}$ and $sk_R = \mathbf{s}$.
- **Issue the pre-signature.** $Issue(BSig.sk, pk_R, \mathbf{nonce})$: Signer $\mathcal{S}$ does the following:
  - It first samples the randomness $\mathbf{nonce} \leftarrow \mathcal{D}^m_\sigma$ and computes $\mathbf{t} = H(\mathbf{nonce}||pk_R)$.
  - It samples a short vector $\mathbf{x} \leftarrow SamplePre(\mathbf{A}, \mathbf{T_A}, \mathbf{t}, \sigma)$ such that $\mathbf{Ax} = \mathbf{t}$ and $||\mathbf{x}|| \leq \beta$.
  - It sends $\mathbf{x}$ and $\mathbf{nonce}$ to $\mathcal{U}$.

- **Obtain the resulting signature.** $Obtain(sk_R, BSig.pk, \mathbf{x}, \mathbf{nonce})$: Upon receiving $\mathbf{x}$ and $\mathbf{nonce}$, $\mathcal{U}$ does the following:
  - It first verifies $||\mathbf{x}|| \leq \beta \wedge \mathbf{A} \cdot \mathbf{x} = H(\mathbf{nonce}||pk_R)$ and continues execution if the equation holds, otherwise outputs $\perp$ and aborts.
  - It computes the message and a VRF proof $(m, \pi_{VRF}) = VRF.Eval(\mathbf{A}, pk_R, sk_R, \mathbf{nonce})$.
  - It generates an NIZK π for the following relation: Given $x = (m, BSig.pk)$, there exists $w = (\mathbf{nonce}, \mathbf{x}, pk_R, \pi_{VRF})$ such that

    $$VRF.V(pk_R, \pi_{VRF}, \mathbf{nonce}, m) = 1 \wedge ||\mathbf{x}|| \leq \beta \wedge \mathbf{A} \cdot \mathbf{x} = H(\mathbf{nonce}||pk_R).$$

    holds.
  - The signature is π.
- **Verifying.** The verifier accepts if the proof π is valid; otherwise, reject it.

4.2   Lattice-Based Tagged Non-interactive Blind Signature

- **Setup.** $KeyGen(1^\lambda)$: Upon input the security 1^λ, define n, m, q, σ, β as functions of λ such that q is odd prime and the MSIS problem is hard. Then do the following:
  - Compute $(\mathbf{A}, \mathbf{T_A}) \leftarrow TrapGen(n, m, q)$.
  - Output $BSig.vk = \mathbf{A} \in \mathcal{R}_q^{n \times m}$, $BSig.sk = \mathbf{T_A} \in \mathcal{R}_q^{m \times m}$.
- **Generate the user key pair.** $PKeyGen(1^\lambda)$: On input the security parameter 1^λ, do the following:
  - Sample a matrix $\mathbf{A}' \xleftarrow{\$} \mathcal{R}^{m \times n_1}$, where $n_1 > m$.
  - Randomly sample $\mathbf{s} \xleftarrow{\$} \mathbb{S}_1^{n_1}$ and compute $\mathbf{u} = \mathbf{A}' \cdot \mathbf{s} \in \mathcal{R}_q^n$.
  - Output $pk_R = \mathbf{u}$ and $sk_R = \mathbf{s}$.
- **Issue the pre-signature.** $Issue(BSig.sk, pk_R, \mathbf{nonce}, \tau)$: Signer $\mathcal{S}$ does the following:
  - It first samples the randomness $\mathbf{nonce} \leftarrow \mathcal{D}_\sigma^m$ and computes $\mathbf{t} = H(\mathbf{nonce}||pk_R||\tau)$.
  - It samples a short vector $\mathbf{x} \leftarrow SamplePre(\mathbf{A}, \mathbf{T_A}, \mathbf{t}, \sigma)$ such that $\mathbf{Ax} = \mathbf{t}$ and $||\mathbf{x}|| \leq \beta$.
  - It sends $\mathbf{x}$ and $\mathbf{nonce}$ to $\mathcal{U}$.
- **Obtain the resulting signature.** $Obtain(sk_R, BSig.pk, \mathbf{x}, \mathbf{nonce}, \tau)$: Upon receiving $\mathbf{x}$ and $\mathbf{nonce}$, $\mathcal{U}$ does the following:
  - It first verifies $||\mathbf{x}|| \leq \beta \wedge \mathbf{A} \cdot \mathbf{x} = H(\mathbf{nonce}||pk_R||\tau)$ and continues execution if the equation holds, otherwise outputs $\perp$ and aborts.
  - It computes the message and a VRF proof $(m, \pi_{VRF}) = VRF.Eval(\mathbf{A}, pk_R, sk_R, \mathbf{nonce})$.
  - It generates an NIZK π for the following relation: Given $x = (m, BSig.pk, \tau)$, there exists $w = (\mathbf{nonce}, \mathbf{x}, pk_R, \pi_{VRF})$ such that

    $$VRF.V(pk_R, \pi_{VRF}, \mathbf{nonce}, m) = 1 \wedge ||\mathbf{x}|| \leq \beta \wedge \mathbf{A} \cdot \mathbf{x} = H(\mathbf{nonce}||pk_R||\tau).$$

    holds.
  - The signature is π.
- **Verifying.** The verifier accepts if the proof π is valid; otherwise, reject it.

4.3   Implementation

For VRF, we follow the protocol from [15]. Based on the VRF scheme, for the relation

$$VRF.V(pk_R, \pi_{VRF}, \mathbf{nonce}, m) = 1 \wedge ||\mathbf{x}|| \le \beta \wedge \mathbf{A} \cdot \mathbf{x} = H(\mathbf{nonce}||pk_R),$$

we actually aim to prove the following relationships:

- $||\mathbf{z}||_\infty \le \beta - \kappa,$
- $\mathbf{w}_1' = \mathbf{A}' \cdot \mathbf{z} - c \cdot \mathbf{t},$
- $w_2' = \langle \mathbf{b}, \mathbf{z} \rangle - c \cdot v,$
- $||\mathbf{x}|| \le \beta \wedge \mathbf{A} \cdot \mathbf{x} = H(\mathbf{nonce}||pk_R).$

For the above relationships, we can construct range proof, proof of linear relationships, and proof of knowledge of $\mathbf{A} \cdot \mathbf{t} = \mathbf{0}$ by following the protocols from [30].

5   Security Analysis

In this section, we only prove the security of LB-NIBS. The idea of proving LB-TNIBS is similar, except that an extra tag τ is needed.

5.1   One-More Unforgeability

Theorem 1. *Assume that NIZK is sound and that VRF is unique. H is modelled as a random oracle. Then if there exists a probabilistic polynomial-time $\mathcal{A}$ against LB-NIBS, that issues q_S signing queries and $q_H \ge q_S + 1$ hash queries and outputs at least $q_S + 1$ valid signatures with probability δ, then there exists a reduction $\mathcal{B}$ that runs in essentially the same time as $\mathcal{A}$ and requests q_H preimage queries and wins the $MSIS_{n,m,2\beta}$ game with probability at least ϵ_{MSIS} such that*

$$\delta \le \frac{q_H^2}{q^{nd}} + \epsilon_{VRF} + (q_S + 1) \cdot \epsilon_s + \epsilon_{MSIS},$$

where ϵ_s is the probability that the adversary succeeds against the soundness of NIZK, ϵ_{VRF} is the probability that the adversary succeeds against the uniqueness of VRF.

Proof. Let $\mathcal{A}$ be an adversary against the one-more unforgeability security NIBS. for simplicity, we require $\mathcal{A}$ outputs $q_S + 1$ signatures. We prove the theorem via a sequence of games.

Game $\mathbf{G}_0$: This is the original one-more unforgeability game $\mathbf{Adv}_{\mathcal{A},NIBS}^{OM-UNF}$.
Game $\mathbf{G}_1$: The game aborts if there is a collision in H i.e. there exist two queries $\mathbf{nonce} \ne \mathbf{nonce}'$ to H such that $H(\mathbf{nonce}, pk_R) = H(\mathbf{nonce}', pk_R)$. Clearly, the probability of the event happening is at most q_H^2/q^{nd}. So we have

$$|Pr[\mathbf{G}_0 \Rightarrow 1] - Pr[\mathbf{G}_1 \Rightarrow 1]| \le \frac{q_H^2}{q^{nd}}.$$

Game G_2: Here we introduce a new abort. Specifically, if for a certain valid pre-signature x, there exist two VRF message-proof pairs (m, π_{VRF}), (m', π'_{VRF}), where $m \neq m'$, such that the following equations

$$VRF.V(pk_R, \pi_{VRF}, \textbf{nonce}, m) = 1$$

and

$$VRF.V(pk_R, \pi'_{VRF}, \textbf{nonce}, m') = 1$$

simultaneously hold, the game is aborted. Based on the uniqueness of VRF, we know that the probability of this abort occurring is negligible. In other words, we have:

$$|Pr[\textbf{G}_1 \Rightarrow 1] - Pr[\textbf{G}_2 \Rightarrow 1]| \leq \epsilon_{VRF},$$

where ϵ_{VRF} is the probability that the adversary succeeds against the uniqueness of VRF.

Game G_3: In this game, we set a extractor $\mathcal{E}$ and introduce another abort. After $\mathcal{A}$ outputs signatures, $\mathcal{E}$ can extract the witness $w = (\textbf{nonce}, x, pk_R, \pi_{VRF})$ from these signatures. If at least one extraction was unsuccessful, then the game aborts. Because of the soundness of NIZK, the probability of the abort happening is at most

$$(q_S + 1) \cdot \epsilon_s,$$

where ϵ_s is the probability that the adversary succeeds against the soundness of NIZK. So we obtain

$$|Pr[\textbf{G}_2 \Rightarrow 1] - Pr[\textbf{G}_3 \Rightarrow 1]| \leq (q_S + 1) \cdot \epsilon_s.$$

Finally, we construct a reduction $\mathcal{B}$ that solves $MSIS_{n,m,2\beta}$ with advantage ϵ_{MSIS} such that

$$Pr[\textbf{G}_3 \Rightarrow 1] \leq \epsilon_{MSIS}.$$

The statement is followed by an easy calculation. Reduction $\mathcal{B}$ works as follows:

- $\mathcal{B}$ gets as input security parameter λ and n, m, q. The goal of $\mathcal{B}$ is to compute a short vector s such that $\mathbf{A} \cdot \mathbf{s} = \mathbf{0}$ and $||\mathbf{s}|| \leq 2\beta$. In this reduction, we require the adversary $\mathcal{A}$ to choose **nonce** instead of the signer.
- $\mathcal{B}$ calls the $PKeyGen(1^\lambda)$ to generate (sk_R, pk_R) and runs adversary $\mathcal{A}$ on input $BSig.vk = \mathbf{A}$, (sk_R, pk_R) and n, m, q with oracle access to a singer oracle and random oracles H, G and H_1. To do so, the oracles are provided as follows:
  - For a hash query of the form $H(\textbf{nonce}||pk_R)$, it samples a random short vector x, stores $((\textbf{nonce}, pk_R), x)$ (where $||x|| \leq \beta$) and compute $\mathbf{t} = \mathbf{A} \cdot \mathbf{x}$. It returns $\mathbf{t}$ to $\mathbf{A}$.
  - Whenever $\mathcal{A}$ makes a signing query on $(\textbf{nonce}, pk_R)$, $\mathcal{B}$ checks whether a hash query has been made for $(\textbf{nonce}, pk_R)$. If so, the corresponding x is returned. If not, $\mathcal{B}$ will first randomly samples a short vector x, stores $((\textbf{nonce}, pk_R), x)$ (where $||x|| \leq \beta$) and then returns the corresponding x to $\mathcal{A}$.
  - For other types of queries, the reduction honestly simulates the oracle.

We can see that $\mathcal{B}$ perfectly simulates $\mathbf{G}_2$. Assume now that $\mathcal{A}$ succeeds in $\mathbf{G}_2$. When it succeeds, it generates distinct messages $(m_i)_{i \in [q_S+1]}$ and corresponding signatures, i.e., proofs $(\pi_i)_{i \in [q_S+1]}$ such that all these proofs are accepted. As the adversary makes at most q_S signing queries, at least one of these m_i, i.e. $(\textbf{nonce}^*, pk_R^*)$ cannot be stored by $\mathcal{B}$. Let m_i, (correspondingly, $(\textbf{nonce}^*, pk_R^*)$) be an arbitrary such message and π^* be its associated signature.

Using the NIZK soundness, $\mathcal{B}$ can extract a witness $w = (\textbf{nonce}^*, \mathbf{x}^*, pk_R, \pi_{VRF}^*)$ from π^* such that $\|\mathbf{x}^*\| \leq \beta$ and $\mathbf{A} \cdot \mathbf{x}^* = H$ $(\textbf{nonce}^* \| pk_R)$. By definition, the message $(\textbf{nonce}^*, pk_R)$ cannot have been queried for a signature and must have been queried for a hash. This implies that $\mathcal{B}$ has previously sampled a short vector $\mathbf{x}$ such that $\mathbf{x} \leq \beta$ and $\mathbf{A} \cdot \mathbf{x} = H(\textbf{nonce}^* \| pk_R)$. So we obtain

$$\mathbf{A} \cdot \mathbf{x} = \mathbf{A} \cdot \mathbf{x}^*,$$

namely

$$\mathbf{A} \cdot (\mathbf{x} - \mathbf{x}^*) = \mathbf{0}.$$

Because $\|\mathbf{x}^*\| \leq \beta$ and $\|\mathbf{x}\| \leq \beta$ holds, so $\|\mathbf{x} - \mathbf{x}^*\| \leq 2\beta$. This is a solution to $MSIS_{n,m,q,2\beta}$.

5.2   Nonce Blindness

Theorem 2. *Assume that the NIZK proof system is honest verifier zero-knowledge and that VRF is pseudorandom, then our scheme is nonce blindness. Specifically, $\mathcal{A}$ breaks nonce blindness of against LB-NIBS with advantage at most*

$$\delta \leq \epsilon_z + 2 \cdot \mathbf{Adv}_{VRF}(\mathcal{A}'),$$

where $\mathcal{A}'$ is an adversary of the pseudorandomness of VRF, ϵ_z is the probability that the adversary succeeds against the honest-verifier zero knowledge of NIZK.

Proof. We prove the Theorem 2 via the following games.

Game $\mathbf{G}_0$: This is the original nonce blindness game $\mathbf{Adv}_{\mathcal{A},NIBS}^{NBnd}$.

Game $\mathbf{G}_1$: In this game, we set a simulator and introduce a new abort. In $\mathbf{G}_1$, instead of generating the resulting signature, i.e. an NIZK π from $w = (\textbf{nonce}, \mathbf{x}, pk_R, \pi_{VRF})$, we have the simulator generate a proof π^*. If there exists a distinguishing algorithm $\mathcal{D}$ that that can determine which proof was generated by the simulator and which was generated by recipient, the game aborts. So according to the honest verifier zero-knowledge property, we obtain

$$|Pr[\mathbf{G}_0 \Rightarrow 1] - Pr[\mathbf{G}_1 \Rightarrow 1]| \leq \epsilon_z,$$

where ϵ_z is the probability that the adversary succeeds against the honest-verifier zero knowledge of NIZK.

Game $\mathbf{G}_2$: Let $\{0,1\}^{m(\lambda)}$ be the output space of the VRF. $\mathbf{G}_2$ is similar to $\mathbf{G}_1$ but we replace m_0 with a random value for the space $\{0,1\}^{m(\lambda)}$. Notice that we do not use the secret VRF key and never call the $VRF.Eval$ algorithm. Thus, this claim follows directly using a straightforward reduction to the pseudorandomness of VRF. We claim that the adversary's $\mathcal{A}$ advantage in $\mathbf{G}_1$ and $\mathbf{G}_2$ only differs by a negligible factor, i.e. we have

$$|Pr[\mathbf{G}_1 \Rightarrow 1] - Pr[\mathbf{G}_2 \Rightarrow 1]| \leq \mathbf{Adv}_{VRF}(\mathcal{A}').$$

Game $\mathbf{G}_3$: Let $\{0,1\}^{m(\lambda)}$ be the output space of the VRF. $\mathbf{G}_3$ is similar to $\mathbf{G}_2$ but we replace m_1 with a random value for the space $\{0,1\}^{m(\lambda)}$. Similar to the previous change, from the pseudorandomness of VRF, we have

$$|Pr[\mathbf{G}_2 \Rightarrow 1] - Pr[\mathbf{G}_3 \Rightarrow 1]| \leq \mathbf{Adv}_{VRF}(\mathcal{A}').$$

Now we can obtain
$$Pr[\mathbf{G}_3 \Rightarrow 1] = 1/2.$$

This equation holds since the messages m_0 and m_1 are both random value, and independent of nonces $\mathbf{nonce}_1, \mathbf{nonce}_2$ and so $\mathbf{x}_1, \mathbf{x}_2$. Thus, the only thing adversary $\mathcal{A}$ can do is guess bit b.

5.3   Recipient Blindness

Theorem 3. *Assumeing that the NIZK proof system is honest verifier zero-knowledge and that VRF is pseudorandomness, then our scheme is recipient blindness. Specifically, $\mathcal{A}$ breaks recipient blindness of against LB-NIBS with probability at most*

$$\delta \leq \epsilon_z + 2 \cdot \mathbf{Adv}_{VRF}(\mathcal{A}'),$$

where $\mathcal{A}'$ is an adversary of the pseudorandomness of VRF, ϵ_z is the probability that the adversary succeeds against the honest-verifier zero knowledge of NIZK.

Proof. The idea of proving Theorem 3 is similar to the idea of proving Theorem 2. We prove the Theorem 3 via the following games.

Game $\mathbf{G}_0$: This is a original nonce blindness game $\mathbf{Adv}_{\mathcal{A},NIBS}^{RBnd}$.

Game $\mathbf{G}_1$: In this game, we set a simulator and introduce a new abort. In $\mathbf{G}_1$, instead of generating the resulting signature, i.e. an NIZK π from $w = (\mathbf{nonce}, \mathbf{x}, pk_R, \pi_{VRF})$, we have the simulator generate a proof π^*. If there exists a distinguishing algorithm $\mathcal{D}$ that can determine which proof was generated by the simulator and which was generated by the recipient, the game aborts. So according to the honest verifier zero-knowledge property, we obtain

$$|Pr[\mathbf{G}_0 \Rightarrow 1] - Pr[\mathbf{G}_1 \Rightarrow 1]| \leq \epsilon_z,$$

where ϵ_z is the probability that the adversary succeeds against the honest-verifier zero knowledge of NIZK.

Game $\mathbf{G}_2$: Let $\{0,1\}^{m(\lambda)}$ be the output space of the VRF. $\mathbf{G}_2$ is similar to $\mathbf{G}_1$ but we replace m_0 with a random value for the space $\{0,1\}^{m(\lambda)}$. Notice that we do not use the secret VRF key and never call the $VRF.Eval$ algorithm. Thus, this claim follows directly using a straightforward reduction to the pseudorandomness of VRF. We claim that the adversary's $\mathcal{A}$ advantage in $\mathbf{G}_1$ and $\mathbf{G}_2$ only differs by a negligible factor, i.e. we have

$$|Pr[\mathbf{G}_1 \Rightarrow 1] - Pr[\mathbf{G}_2 \Rightarrow 1]| \leq \mathbf{Adv}_{VRF}(\mathcal{A}').$$

Game $\mathbf{G}_3$: Let $\{0,1\}^{m(\lambda)}$ be the output space of the VRF. $\mathbf{G}_3$ is similar to $\mathbf{G}_2$ but we replace m_1 with a random value for the space $\{0,1\}^{m(\lambda)}$. Similar to the previous change, from the pseudorandomness of VRF, we have

$$|Pr[\mathbf{G}_2 \Rightarrow 1] - Pr[\mathbf{G}_3 \Rightarrow 1]| \leq \mathbf{Adv}_{VRF}(\mathcal{A}').$$

Now we can obtain

$$Pr[\mathbf{G}_3] = 1/2.$$

This equation holds since the messages m_0 and m_1 are both random values and independent of the recipient's public pk_R and so $\mathbf{x}_1$, $\mathbf{x}_2$. Thus, the only thing adversary $\mathcal{A}$ can do is guess bit b.

6   Conclusion

In this paper, we proposed a lattice-based non-interactive blind signature and a lattice-based tagged non-interactive blind signature and proved their security based on widely-used lattice hardness assumptions. Our schemes are efficient and easy to implement. Moreover, we believe that it is worth exploring the issue of constructing non-interactive blind signatures based on the standard model. Meanwhile, we also deem that more applications based on NIBS should be further investigated. Unfortunately, our security proof relies on the conventional Random Oracle Model (ROM) rather than the more rigorous Quantum Random Oracle Model (QROM), which inherently introduces potential vulnerabilities or limitations that may undermine the full quantum security claims of our schemes. In the future, we will further explore the possibilities of solving these open problems.

Acknowledgement. This work is supported by the Major Program of Guangdong Basic and Applied Research (2019B030302008), the National Natural Science Foundation of China (62272174), and the Science and Technology Program of Guangzhou (2024A04J6542).

References

1. Abazi, V.: The European Union whistleblower directive: a 'game changer' for whistleblowing protection? Ind. Law J. **49**(4), 640–656 (2020)
2. Agrawal, S., Kirshanova, E., Stehlé, D., Yadav, A.: Practical, round-optimal lattice-based blind signatures. In: Proceedings of the 2022 ACM SIGSAC Conference on Computer and Communications Security, pp. 39–53 (2022)
3. Ajtai, M.: Generating hard instances of lattice problems. In: Proceedings of the Twenty-Eighth Annual ACM Symposium on Theory of Computing, pp. 99–108 (1996)

4. Alkeilani Alkadri, N., El Bansarkhani, R., Buchmann, J.: BLAZE: practical lattice-based blind signatures for privacy-preserving applications. In: Bonneau, J., Heninger, N. (eds.) FC 2020. LNCS, vol. 12059, pp. 484–502. Springer, Cham (2020). https://doi.org/10.1007/978-3-030-51280-4_26
5. Alkeilani Alkadri, N., El Bansarkhani, R., Buchmann, J.: On lattice-based interactive protocols: an approach with less or no aborts. In: Liu, J.K., Cui, H. (eds.) ACISP 2020. LNCS, vol. 12248, pp. 41–61. Springer, Cham (2020). https://doi.org/10.1007/978-3-030-55304-3_3
6. Au, M.H., Susilo, W., Mu, Y.: Practical compact e-cash. In: Pieprzyk, J., Ghodosi, H., Dawson, E. (eds.) ACISP 2007. LNCS, vol. 4586, pp. 431–445. Springer, Heidelberg (2007). https://doi.org/10.1007/978-3-540-73458-1_31
7. Baldimtsi, F., Cheng, J., Goyal, R., Yadav, A.: Non-interactive blind signatures from lattices. Cryptology ePrint Archive (2024)
8. Bert, P., Eberhart, G., Prabel, L., Roux-Langlois, A., Sabt, M.: Implementation of lattice trapdoors on modules and applications. In: Cheon, J.H., Tillich, J.-P. (eds.) PQCrypto 2021 2021. LNCS, vol. 12841, pp. 195–214. Springer, Cham (2021). https://doi.org/10.1007/978-3-030-81293-5_11
9. Blum, M., Feldman, P., Micali, S.: Non-interactive zero-knowledge and its applications. In: Providing Sound Foundations for Cryptography: On the Work of Shafi Goldwasser and Silvio Micali, pp. 329–349 (2019)
10. Camenisch, J., Groß, T.: Efficient attributes for anonymous credentials. ACM Trans. Inf. Syst. Secur. (TISSEC) 15(1), 1–30 (2012)
11. Camenisch, J., Hohenberger, S., Lysyanskaya, A.: Compact E-Cash. In: Cramer, R. (ed.) EUROCRYPT 2005. LNCS, vol. 3494, pp. 302–321. Springer, Heidelberg (2005). https://doi.org/10.1007/11426639_18
12. Camenisch, J., Lysyanskaya, A.: An efficient system for non-transferable anonymous credentials with optional anonymity revocation. In: Pfitzmann, B. (ed.) EUROCRYPT 2001. LNCS, vol. 2045, pp. 93–118. Springer, Heidelberg (2001). https://doi.org/10.1007/3-540-44987-6_7
13. Chaum, D.: Blind signature system. In: Advances in Cryptology: Proceedings of Crypto 83, pp. 153–153. Springer, Heidelberg (1983). https://doi.org/10.1007/978-1-4684-4730-9_14
14. Davidson, A., Goldberg, I., Sullivan, N., Tankersley, G., Valsorda, F.: Privacy pass: bypassing internet challenges anonymously. In: Proceedings on Privacy Enhancing Technologies (2018)
15. Esgin, M.F., Kuchta, V., Sakzad, A., Steinfeld, R., Zhang, Z., Sun, S., Chu, S.: Practical post-quantum few-time verifiable random function with applications to algorand. In: Borisov, N., Diaz, C. (eds.) FC 2021. LNCS, vol. 12675, pp. 560–578. Springer, Heidelberg (2021). https://doi.org/10.1007/978-3-662-64331-0_29
16. Fischlin, M.: Round-optimal composable blind signatures in the common reference string model. In: Dwork, C. (ed.) CRYPTO 2006. LNCS, vol. 4117, pp. 60–77. Springer, Heidelberg (2006). https://doi.org/10.1007/11818175_4
17. Frankel, Y., Tsiounis, Y., Yung, M.: Fair off-line e-cash made easy. In: Ohta, K., Pei, D. (eds.) ASIACRYPT 1998. LNCS, vol. 1514, pp. 257–270. Springer, Heidelberg (1998). https://doi.org/10.1007/3-540-49649-1_21
18. Gao, W., Hu, Y., Wang, B., Xie, J.: Identity-based blind signature from lattices in standard model. In: Chen, K., Lin, D., Yung, M. (eds.) Inscrypt 2016. LNCS, vol. 10143, pp. 205–218. Springer, Cham (2017). https://doi.org/10.1007/978-3-319-54705-3_13

19. Genise, N., Micciancio, D.: Faster Gaussian sampling for trapdoor lattices with arbitrary modulus. In: Nielsen, J.B., Rijmen, V. (eds.) EUROCRYPT 2018. LNCS, vol. 10820, pp. 174–203. Springer, Cham (2018). https://doi.org/10.1007/978-3-319-78381-9_7

20. Gentry, C.: Fully homomorphic encryption using ideal lattices. In: Proceedings of the Forty-First Annual ACM Symposium on Theory of Computing, pp. 169–178 (2009)

21. Gentry, C., Peikert, C., Vaikuntanathan, V.: Trapdoors for hard lattices and new cryptographic constructions. In: Proceedings of the Fortieth Annual ACM Symposium on Theory of Computing, pp. 197–206 (2008)

22. Grontas, P., Pagourtzis, A., Zacharakis, A., Zhang, B.: Towards everlasting privacy and efficient coercion resistance in remote electronic voting. In: Zohar, A., et al. (eds.) FC 2018. LNCS, vol. 10958, pp. 210–231. Springer, Heidelberg (2019). https://doi.org/10.1007/978-3-662-58820-8_15

23. Hanzlik, L.: Non-interactive blind signatures for random messages. In: Annual International Conference on the Theory and Applications of Cryptographic Techniques, pp. 722–752. Springer, Heidelberg (2023). https://doi.org/10.1007/978-3-031-30589-4_25

24. Hauck, E., Kiltz, E., Loss, J., Nguyen, N.K.: Lattice-based blind signatures, revisited. In: Micciancio, D., Ristenpart, T. (eds.) CRYPTO 2020. LNCS, vol. 12171, pp. 500–529. Springer, Cham (2020). https://doi.org/10.1007/978-3-030-56880-1_18

25. Langlois, A., Stehlé, D.: Worst-case to average-case reductions for module lattices. Des. Codes Crypt. **75**(3), 565–599 (2015)

26. Le, H.Q., Susilo, W., Khuc, T.X., Bui, M.K., Duong, D.H.: A blind signature from module latices. In: 2019 IEEE Conference on Dependable and Secure Computing (DSC), pp. 1–8. IEEE (2019)

27. Liang, C., Yongquan, C., Xueming, T., Dongping, H., Xin, W.: Hierarchical id-based blind signature from lattices. In: 2011 Seventh International Conference on Computational Intelligence and Security, pp. 803–807. IEEE (2011)

28. Lyubashevsky, V.: Lattice signatures without trapdoors. In: Pointcheval, D., Johansson, T. (eds.) EUROCRYPT 2012. LNCS, vol. 7237, pp. 738–755. Springer, Heidelberg (2012). https://doi.org/10.1007/978-3-642-29011-4_43

29. Lyubashevsky, V., Nguyen, N.K., Plancon, M.: Efficient lattice-based blind signatures via gaussian one-time signatures. In: IACR International Conference on Public-Key Cryptography, pp. 498–527. Springer, Heidelberg (2022). https://doi.org/10.1007/978-3-030-97131-1_17

30. Lyubashevsky, V., Nguyen, N.K., Plançon, M.: Lattice-based zero-knowledge proofs and applications: shorter, simpler, and more general. In: Annual International Cryptology Conference, pp. 71–101. Springer, Heidelberg (2022). https://doi.org/10.1007/978-3-031-15979-4_3

31. Micali, S., Rabin, M., Vadhan, S.: Verifiable random functions. In: 40th annual Symposium on Foundations of Computer Science (cat. No. 99CB37039), pp. 120–130. IEEE (1999)

32. Okamoto, T., Ohta, K.: Universal electronic cash. In: Feigenbaum, J. (ed.) CRYPTO 1991. LNCS, vol. 576, pp. 324–337. Springer, Heidelberg (1992). https://doi.org/10.1007/3-540-46766-1_27

33. del Pino, R., Katsumata, S.: A new framework for more efficient round-optimal lattice-based (partially) blind signature via trapdoor sampling. In: Annual International Cryptology Conference, pp. 306–336. Springer, Heidelberg (2022). https://doi.org/10.1007/978-3-031-15979-4_11

34. Yang, R., Au, M.H., Zhang, Z., Xu, Q., Yu, Z., Whyte, W.: Efficient lattice-based zero-knowledge arguments with standard soundness: construction and applications. In: Boldyreva, A., Micciancio, D. (eds.) CRYPTO 2019. LNCS, vol. 11692, pp. 147–175. Springer, Cham (2019). https://doi.org/10.1007/978-3-030-26948-7_6
35. Yu, Y., Jia, H., Wang, X.: Compact lattice gadget and its applications to hash-and-sign signatures. In: Annual International Cryptology Conference, pp. 390–420. Springer, Heidelberg (2023). https://doi.org/10.1007/978-3-031-38554-4_13

Author Index